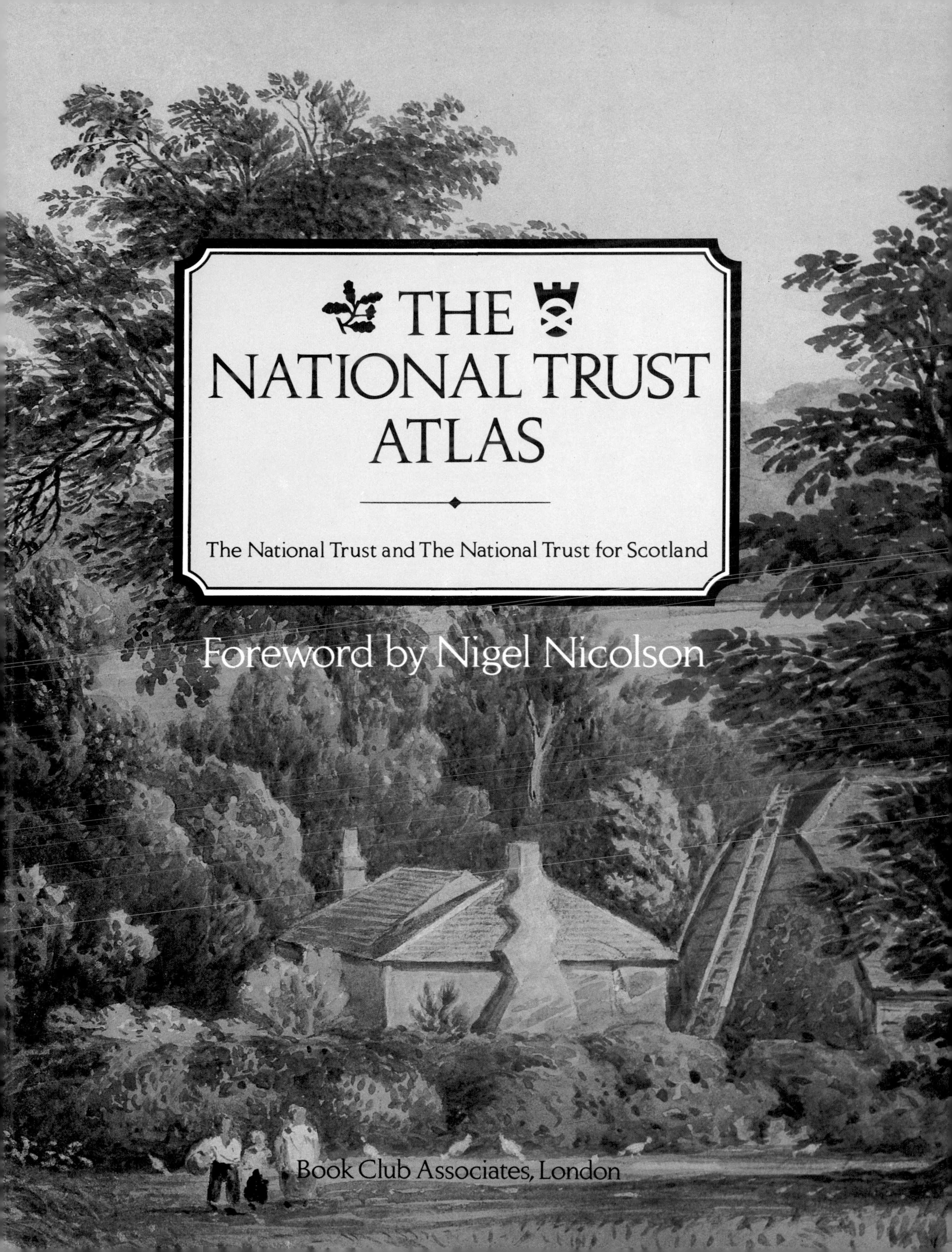

THE NATIONAL TRUST ATLAS

The National Trust and The National Trust for Scotland

Foreword by Nigel Nicolson

Book Club Associates, London

Illustrations

Half-title Detail of an early eighteenth-century view of Uppark, West Sussex, by Pieter Tillemans (1684–1734); *title page* Polesden Lacey, Surrey, from a watercolour (*c*.1825) by John Varley (1778–1842); *foreword* Hanbury Hall, Hereford and Worcester, in an engraving from Nash's *Worcestershire*, 1781; *contents page* Lindisfarne Castle in an oil painting by John Varley.

Acknowledgments

The watercolours at the beginning of each chapter (pp. 10, 20, 44, 62, 70, 78, 98, 104, 118, 153) are by Dorothy Tucker. All other illustrations of properties in England, Wales and Northern Ireland are the copyright of and have been supplied by The National Trust, with the exception of those of the Dunstable Downs and the Ashridge Estate on p. 62 which have been supplied by John Bethell. All other illustrations of properties in Scotland are the copyright of and have been supplied by The National Trust for Scotland. The marbled end paper was designed by Mitchell & Malik Ltd, © 1981.

Editor Lydia Greeves
Art Editor Frank Phillips

Maps and map index edited by R. W. Lidbetter, with research by H. Snape, and prepared by the cartographic staff of George Philip Cartographic Services Ltd under the direction of Alan Poynter MA, Director of Cartography.
Printed in Great Britain.

The representation in this atlas of a road or track is not evidence of the existence of a right of way.

This edition published 1981 by Book Club Associates by arrangement with George Philip & Son Ltd.

FOREWORD

This book can be read in three ways: it dangles before you a string of succulent baits enticing you to get into your car and go and see them; it is a useful and informative guidebook when you are on the spot; and it is an excellent gazetteer of many of the most pleasant places in the United Kingdom, all of them properties of the two National Trusts.

No other country possesses a richer variety of historic buildings, and none has taken more trouble to preserve the best. The best does not simply mean the biggest or most famous but includes, too, relatively obscure houses and gardens that are perfect of their type, prehistoric sites and medieval castles, and functional buildings such as chapels, windmills and market-halls. Together they provide the visual equivalent of our literature. The Trusts do not merely protect these buildings against decay. Most of them are not only in better condition than they ever were but are still inhabited and used. To have saved this legacy of our past is to hand over an irreplacable legacy to the future.

The two Trusts have also acquired land, for what are buildings divorced from their context? Throughout the United Kingdom they own large slices of wild and lonely places, Lakeland shores and Derbyshire moorland, rocky capes along the Cornish coast and the remote islands of Lundy and St Kilda. The Trusts also own important examples of the gentler landscapes of the British Isles, such as the meadows at Runnymede and East Anglian fen country. Wherever you live or travel, you will rarely be more than ten miles from a Trust property of some sort. This book will lead you to them, and compensate by its text and illustrations for those which the most ardent traveller will inevitably miss.

NIGEL NICOLSON

CONTENTS

KEY TO MAPS

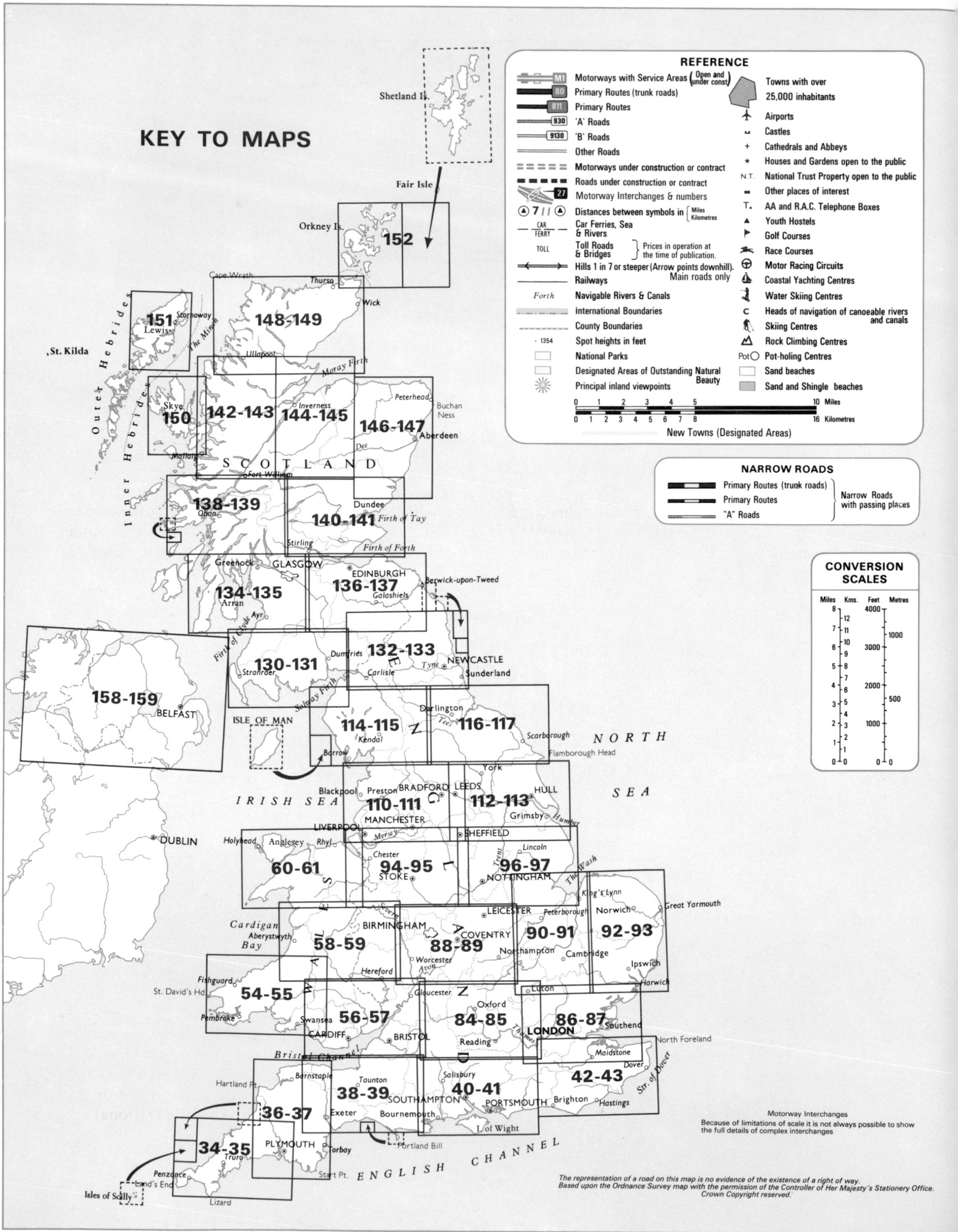
REFERENCE
M1 Motorways with Service Areas (Open and under const)
80 Primary Routes (trunk roads)
811 Primary Routes
930 'A' Roads
9130 'B' Roads
Other Roads
Motorways under construction or contract
Roads under construction or contract
27 Motorway Interchanges & numbers
7 Distances between symbols in Miles / Kilometres
CAR FERRY Car Ferries, Sea & Rivers
TOLL Toll Roads & Bridges } Prices in operation at the time of publication.
Hills 1 in 7 or steeper (Arrow points downhill). Main roads only
Railways
Forth Navigable Rivers & Canals
International Boundaries
County Boundaries
1354 Spot heights in feet
National Parks
Designated Areas of Outstanding Natural Beauty
Principal inland viewpoints
Towns with over 25,000 inhabitants
Airports
Castles
Cathedrals and Abbeys
Houses and Gardens open to the public
N.T. National Trust Property open to the public
Other places of interest
T. AA and R.A.C. Telephone Boxes
Youth Hostels
Golf Courses
Race Courses
Motor Racing Circuits
Coastal Yachting Centres
Water Skiing Centres
C Heads of navigation of canoeable rivers and canals
Skiing Centres
Rock Climbing Centres
Pot Pot-holing Centres
Sand beaches
Sand and Shingle beaches
0 1 2 3 4 5 10 Miles
0 1 2 3 4 5 6 7 8 16 Kilometres
New Towns (Designated Areas)
NARROW ROADS
Primary Routes (trunk roads)
Primary Routes
"A" Roads
Narrow Roads with passing places
CONVERSION SCALES
Miles Kms. Feet Metres
Shetland Is.
Fair Isle
Orkney Is.
152
Cape Wrath
Thurso
Wick
151
Stornoway
Lewis
148-149
St. Kilda
Outer Hebrides
The Minch
Ullapool
Moray Firth
150
Skye
142-143
144-145
Inverness
146-147
Peterhead
Buchan Ness
Aberdeen
Dee
Mallaig
SCOTLAND
Inner Hebrides
Fort William
138-139
Oban
Dundee
140-141
Firth of Tay
Stirling
Firth of Forth
Greenock
GLASGOW
EDINBURGH
136-137
Galashiels
Berwick-upon-Tweed
134-135
Arran
Ayr
Firth of Clyde
132-133
Dumfries
130-131
Stranraer
Carlisle
Tyne
NEWCASTLE
Sunderland
158-159
BELFAST
Solway Firth
ISLE OF MAN
Darlington
Tees
114-115
116-117
Kendal
Barrow
Scarborough
Flamborough Head
NORTH SEA
York
Blackpool
Preston
BRADFORD
LEEDS
HULL
IRISH SEA
110-111
112-113
MANCHESTER
Grimsby
Humber
LIVERPOOL
Mersey
SHEFFIELD
DUBLIN
Holyhead
Anglesey
Rhyl
Chester
Lincoln
60-61
94-95
96-97
STOKE
NOTTINGHAM
Trent
The Wash
King's Lynn
Great Yarmouth
Cardigan Bay
Aberystwyth
58-59
BIRMINGHAM
LEICESTER
Peterborough
Norwich
COVENTRY
90-91
92-93
88-89
Northampton
Cambridge
Worcester
Avon
Hereford
Ipswich
Harwich
Fishguard
St. David's Hd
54-55
WALES
ENGLAND
Gloucester
Luton
Oxford
Pembroke
Swansea
56-57
84-85
86-87
CARDIFF
LONDON
Southend
BRISTOL
Thames
Reading
North Foreland
Bristol Channel
Maidstone
Dover
Hartland Pt.
Barnstaple
Taunton
Salisbury
42-43
38-39
40-41
SOUTHAMPTON
PORTSMOUTH
Brighton
Hastings
Str. of Dover
36-37
Exeter
Bournemouth
I. of Wight
34-35
PLYMOUTH
Torbay
Portland Bill
Truro
Penzance
Land's End
Isles of Scilly
Start Pt.
Lizard
ENGLISH CHANNEL
Motorway Interchanges
Because of limitations of scale it is not always possible to show the full details of complex interchanges
The representation of a road on this map is no evidence of the existence of a right of way.
Based upon the Ordnance Survey map with the permission of the Controller of Her Majesty's Stationery Office.
Crown Copyright reserved.

INTRODUCTION

The properties in the care of The National Trust for Places of Historic Interest or Natural Beauty and The National Trust for Scotland are a priceless and unique heritage visited annually by millions of people. They include several hundred miles of unspoilt coastline, vast tracts of countryside, country houses on a majestic scale, and also many minor properties of architectural and historical importance.

This *Atlas* is a guide to properties of the Trusts throughout the United Kingdom, including Scotland and Northern Ireland as well as England and Wales. In each of the ten regional chapters, properties have been grouped in four sections. The first, *Coast and Countryside*, describes the open spaces in the Trusts' care and includes wildfowl refuges and nature reserves. The National Trust and The National Trust for Scotland are both major landowners and it has not been possible to describe every holding in detail. Sites of particular interest or beauty are covered individually in the text, general reference is made to many more and all are marked on the accompanying road maps.

The following three sections – *Houses, Gardens and Parks*; *Castles, Abbeys and other Buildings*; *Archaeological and Industrial Sites* – are alphabetical listings of all properties open to the public. Covenanted properties are excluded but important properties owned by the Trusts and managed by other bodies are included, and so are significant properties that can be viewed from the outside, such as Sailor's Walk (Fife) and Blaise Hamlet (Avon), but whose dwellings are privately tenanted. The majority of properties appear under *Houses, Gardens and Parks*. This section includes the many great houses in the Trusts' care, such as Petworth (West Sussex) and Saltram (Devon), and also buildings that have their origin in medieval castles but which have been much altered and improved over the centuries, such as Croft Castle (Hereford and Worcester). Lesser properties attached to great houses – churches, dovecotes, barns and villages – are also included.

Castles, Abbeys and other Buildings includes churches, chapels, villages, barns, follies, monuments, gatehouses, guildhalls and theatres. *Archaeological and Industrial Sites* includes prehistoric remains, Roman antiquities, windmills, water-mills and industrial monuments. Major prehistoric sites are described individually but in some parts of the country, such as the South-West, many of the open spaces in the Trust's care contain minor remains and not all these are listed. In the chapter on Scotland, this final section has been expanded to include historic sites, notably battlefields and their visitor centres.

Each property described in the text has been given a map reference. For example, the reference 35 G6 indicates that the site concerned is located on map page 35, in the square formed by the grid references G and 6. All properties are denoted on the maps by the symbols NT and the majority of the properties open to the public are also named. Anyone looking for properties to visit within a particular area should also consult the county index. Cross references to other properties within the text are italicized.

No information has been given on admission prices, availability of refreshments or facilities for the disabled. There is also no information on opening times, but where houses can only be viewed by appointment this is clearly stated. A complete register of the National Trust's holdings is given in *Properties of The National Trust**, reissued every five years. Both The National Trust and The National Trust for Scotland publish annual booklets on properties open to the public. These booklets give information on opening times, admission fees, shops, restaurants, facilities for the disabled, car parking, picnicking and new properties acquired.

Any enquiries about properties, publications or membership should be addressed to The National Trust, 42 Queen Anne's Gate, London SW1H 9AS, or to The National Trust for Scotland, 5 Charlotte Square, Edinburgh EH2 4DU.

**i.e. properties in England, Wales and Northern Ireland*

South-West England

HARDY'S COTTAGE

The south-west of England has a special character which sets it apart from the rest of the country. This is partly because of its geographical isolation, partly because of its Celtic affiliations, seen so clearly in the distinctive place names of Cornwall, and partly because of its associations with so many legends and tales of romance and adventure, from King Arthur and the knights of the Round Table to Daphne du Maurier's *Frenchman's Creek*. The south-west is also exceptionally beautiful, and despite the annual influx of tourists there are still many unspoilt stretches of coast and many wild and lonely places on the moors that fill the heart of the peninsula.

The National Trust plays a prominent part in helping to retain the area's uniquely unspoilt atmosphere. It cares for some of Britain's loveliest and most dramatic stretches of coastline from the craggy cliffs of the north Devon and Cornish coasts to the gentler chalk landscapes of the Dorset coastline. The Trust also controls key land along the shores of the characteristic 'drowned' valleys (rias) that are so much a feature of Devon and Cornwall.

The Trust's great houses in this part of the country range from Cotehele, centre of a self-contained community in Tudor times, through Saltram, a superb example of eighteenth-century gracious living, to Castle Drogo, probably one of the last houses to be built on the grand scale in this country. The many lesser properties include several with particular historical or literary connections, from T. E. Lawrence's Clouds Hill to the Wellington Monument in the Blackdown Hills which recalls the glories of Waterloo.

Coast & Countryside

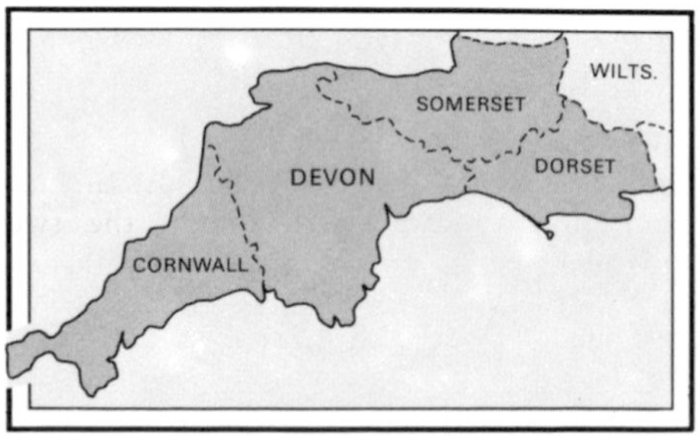

In the gap between Somerset's Mendip Hills and the North and South Dorset Downs, all the roads lead to the West Country. Yet Nature has still erected barriers along the way, as if to deter the traveller determined to reach the farthest south-western corner of England: the massive, granite bulk of Dartmoor, for example; or the rushing rivers of Exmoor; or even lonely Bodmin Moor, straddling the centre of Cornwall.

Yet it is on these inhospitable uplands that prehistoric man made his home and left behind many a reminder of his occupation. This corner of England is rich in Neolithic and Iron Age sites such as *Lanyon Quoit* (34 F1), north-west of Penzance. This massive granite slab balanced on three equally massive uprights is the remains of the tomb chamber of a Neolithic long barrow. Perhaps because of these visible remains of prehistoric man, the south-west has a feeling of mystery and timelessness, a primeval quality. The landscape – particularly between St Ives and Land's End – still has an oddly haunted atmosphere which is not wholly attributable to the unexpectedly wild scenery.

It is easy to believe the fairy stories in this part of the world: the stories of the 'little people' or Cornish 'piskies', and the tales of legendary giants. At **Bedruthan Steps** (34 C5), on the north Cornish coast near Padstow, the giant Bedruthan is said to have clambered from the sea by way of a 'staircase' of rocky islets just offshore – and the islets really do look like a giant's stepping stones. Although the Steps themselves do not belong to the Trust, the clifftop above Bedruthan Beach does, and the unspoilt view – north to Trevose Head and south towards Newquay – is rightly acclaimed as one of the most beautiful in Britain.

Besides fairy stories, there are legends such as the one attached to **Bodrugan's Leap** (35 E7), just south of Mevagissey on the coast of southern Cornwall. Sir Henry Trenowth is said to have leapt from this headland into the sea in a successful attempt to escape from Sir Richard Edgcumbe whose home, *Cotehele*, is one of the

Trust's prime properties in this part of the country. Realism returns with a look at some of the other magnificent scenery which is in the Trust's care. A big stretch of the **West Penwith** – or Land's End – peninsula (34 F1/2) belongs to the Trust and includes both cliff and inland scenery around Zennor, Porthmeor, Morvah and Pendeen. **Mayon and Trevescan Cliffs**, between Land's End and Sennen (34 G1), are a popular tourist attraction, while less well known are **St Levan Cliffs** (34 G1), on the southern side of the peninsula.

In Mount's Bay, separating the Land's End peninsula from the Lizard, and dominated by another Trust property, *St Michael's Mount*, the heather-covered **Rinsey Cliff** (34 G3) is noted for the dramatic ruins of *Wheal Prosper*, an abandoned tin and copper mine. On the **Lizard Peninsula** itself (34 H4/5), much of the coastline comes under the Trust's protection – from the odd but very attractive freshwater lake known as **The Loe**, two miles south of Helston, round to such famous beauty spots as **Mullion Cove and Island**; the cliffland above **Polurrian Cove**, one mile south-west of Mullion; **Kynance Cove**, with its richly-coloured serpentine cliffs and fantastic rock formations; and **Bass Point**, one mile east of Lizard Point. Prehistoric remains can be seen on the heath-covered **Lower Predannack Downs** (34 H4).

East of the Lizard, there are the great, flooded valleys of the Helford and Fal rivers. Much of the **Helford River** (34 G4/5) is owned by the Trust, including **Frenchman's Creek** on the south side, the peaceful, wooded creek from which Daphne du Maurier's novel took its name. In the larger Fal estuary the Trust owns **Turnaway Point** at the head of the Carrick Roads on the east bank of the Fal (34 F5) as well as cliffland near **St Mawes, St Anthony Head** at the eastern entrance to Falmouth Harbour (fortified in 1895, now much cleaned-up and restored), and a large stretch of coastal farmland and foreshore at **St Anthony-in-Roseland** and **St Just-in-Roseland**, south-east and north of St Mawes respectively. There are extensive holdings, too, on the coast north-east of the Fal: among them the land over-looking sandy **Pendower Beach** on Gerrans

above **Looking out to sea from Mullion Harbour. The quays are often damaged in stormy weather and need frequent repairs.**

below **The inlet of Crackington Haven, north of Boscastle, lies below some of the finest cliff-walking in England.**

Bay (34 F6), and land around **Dodman Point** (35 F7) and **Gorran Haven** (35 F7). Dodman Point is the *Dead Man's Rock* of Sir Arthur Quiller Couch's novel.

East of the china clay country behind St Austell, **Fowey** (35 E8) stands at the entrance to another of the drowned valleys and there is plenty of good walking on the unspoiled cliffs and countryside around the estuary and in the river valley itself, with **Hall Walk, Lanteglos**, opposite Fowey, and **St Catherine's Point** around Fowey Castle particularly noteworthy.

Then there are the famous ports and beauty spots of **Polperro** (35 E9) and **Looe** (35 E9/10). Besides cliffland on either side of Polperro harbour (Chapel Cliff, on the west of the village, is particularly good for walking), the Trust owns land close to East and West Looe.

Although Cornwall is only about twenty miles across in places, those twenty miles separate scenery that is worlds apart. The wooded river valleys and tiny, picturesque ports of the south give way to soaring cliffs and vast, sandy, dune-backed beaches in the north. They stretch from St Ives to Bude and beyond and include such beauty spots as the six-mile stretch of cliff and farmland from **Godrevy** to **Portreath** (34 E3/4), along which (from east to west) a footpath affords glimpses of Portreath harbour, the precipitous Ralph's Cupboard, the evocatively-named Hell's Mouth, Navax Point, the Godrevy peninsula, and coves and beaches where the only sign of life may be sea-birds or the inquisitive Atlantic seal.

North of Portreath, **St Agnes Beacon** (34 E4) soars to 628 feet to give views of no less than twenty-six miles of this coastline: a coastline which is often a wild, sandy wasteland pounded by the Atlantic rollers. Immediately to the north-east the Trust has holdings of cliffs, farmland, common land and dunes around **Cubert** (34 D5), including Cubert Common, one of the few enclosed commons in England, as well as Kelsey Head, Holywell Beach and West Pentire Head. Newquay, Cornwall's most famous holiday resort, shelters below West Pentire Head on the River Gannel, but it is worth noting that much of the south bank of the **Gannel Estuary** (34 D5) is protected from the encroachment of hotels and amusement arcades – and provides a haven for walkers and wildlife despite its proximity to the town.

The stretch of coastline to the north of Newquay, around Bedruthan Steps, has already been described. Farther north Padstow, on the south bank of the River Camel and nestling behind the protective arms of Trevose Head and Pentire Point, is a growing resort, but much of the farmland and coast around **Pentire Point** (34 A6), north of Padstow Bay, is Trust land. On Pentire Point itself there are the remains of an Iron Age Cornish cliff castle and there are also prehistoric remains on the beautiful headland known as the Rumps to the north. The same applies to the coastline round **Tintagel** (35 A7), reputedly the site of King Arthur's Castle. The Trust owns some dramatic cliffland here, with fine views. At neighbouring **Boscastle** (35 A8) the Trust owns the entire harbour as well as much of the nearby **Valency Valley**. The harbour, almost hidden behind a protective wall of cliffs, is one of the Trust's major success stories. Built partly by the famous mariner Sir Richard Grenville in the sixteenth century, and once used mainly for the shipping of slate, it fell into disuse after the outer jetty was blown up by a drifting mine in 1941. The Trust rebuilt the harbour in 1962, and has since acquired several harbourside buildings. It is now a pretty, as well as an historic, spot. Beyond Bude, where Cornwall gives way to Devon, there are more stretches of dramatic coastline on the west coast of the vast headland of **Hartland Point** (36 D/E1).

The splendours of the Cornish coast are most widely known but the Trust also owns many notable areas of countryside. These include the heath-covered moorland at **Chapel Porth** above St Agnes (34 E4), where a wild valley leads down to a tiny cove; and the typical moorland scenery of **Rough Tor** (35 B8), on Bodmin Moor. At 1,311 feet, Rough Tor is the second-highest point in Cornwall and contains a Bronze Age settlement as well as being at the heart of excellent walking country. Another noteworthy viewpoint is gorse-covered **Trencrom Hill** (34 F2), between St Ives and Penzance, where an Iron Age hill-fort overlooks stunning countryside and coastal scenery and at the same time acts as a memorial to the Cornishmen who died in the two World Wars. At the other end of the scenic scale, the Trust owns **Trelissick** (34 F5), just south of Truro, where parkland, farmland and woods, including the famous *Trelissick Garden*, overlook the Fal Estuary.

The Trust's holdings in Devon serve to emphasize the variety of the scenery. The accent is on the coast, particularly in the less well-known north, but properties also include land on Dartmoor and Exmoor, the two upland areas that provide a welcome contrast to the pastoral scenery of so much of Devon.

North of Bude is the promontory of Hartland Point, beyond which the coastline falls away to the east around Barnstaple – or

The view towards Ilfracombe from Bull Point encompasses a typically dramatic stretch of the north Cornish coast.

Bideford – Bay. Between **Hartland Point** (36 C1) and the very attractive hillside fishing village of **Clovelly** (36 C2), with its famous steep cobbled main street dropping precipitously down to the sea, much of the beautiful cliff scenery is protected by the Trust, and from the car park at Brownsham west of the village walkers can join the recently reopened coastal footpath. A good viewpoint over Bideford Bay is **Mount Pleasant**, just above Clovelly.

Offshore can be seen the granite cliffs of **Lundy Island**, eleven miles north of Hartland Point in the Bristol Channel. Bought by the Trust a decade ago, in conjunction with the Landmark Trust which administers the island, Lundy is, at 1,116 acres, far larger than it appears from the coast, and is now principally a bird sanctuary which can be visited from the ports of Bideford and Ilfracombe. Most of the buildings on the island, among them the ruins of the thirteenth-century Marisco Castle, and the late-Victorian church of St Helena, are now abandoned, but there are some interesting Neolithic and Bronze Age sites.

Farther along the mainland coast, at **Westward Ho!** (36 C3), Kipling Tors, eighteen acres of gorse-covered hillside to the west of the town, is famous as the setting for much of Rudyard Kipling's novel *Stalky & Co*. Farther east still, one comes to one of the Trust's finest stretches of coastline, running from **Croyde** (36 B3) up to **Woolacombe** (36 B3) and then in an uninterrupted five-mile expanse to the rocky bay below **Lee** (36 A3). The cliffland to the west of **Ilfracombe** (36 A4) also includes many stretches belonging to the Trust, and taken as a whole this is a spectacular and totally unspoiled piece of coast which includes many fine walks along well-defined footpaths and views of Lundy.

There is more fine coastal scenery to the east of Ilfracombe, where Exmoor reaches the sea. Trust holdings here are fragmented, but of note are cliffland at **Holdstone Down** (36 A5), between Coombe Martin and Heddon's Mouth, near Trentishoe; the **Heddon Valley** (36 A5), a large area of woodland and moorland leading down from Trentishoe Common to Heddon's Mouth, with good views of the Bristol Channel en route; and in particular the steep wooded valleys of the East Lyn above **Lynmouth** (36 A6) and at **Watersmeet**, between Lynmouth and Brendon, as well as land around **Foreland Point** – the eastern bastion of Lynmouth Bay – and **Countisbury Hill**. This very attractive area is again fine walking country (motorists can park at Barna Barrow, above Countisbury village), and there are many miles of signposted footpaths.

Like Cornwall, Devon's coasts present a contrast. From the cliffs in the north of the county it is a sharp change to the South Hams: farming country of steep-sided lanes which hide the view so that one seems always to come suddenly, and surprisingly, across the deeply-wooded valleys of the Salcombe and Dart estuaries or the beaches of Bigbury Bay, Start Bay and Torbay.

The sheer size of this area means that a car is needed to explore it properly, but the countryside is particularly lovely and repays exploration. Favourite viewpoints include **Clematon Hill, Bigbury-on-Sea** (37 L5), where there are panoramas over the Avon and Bolt Tail and to Burgh Island; the six-mile stretch of cliff between **Bolt Head** and **Bolt Tail** (37 M5/6); **Prawle Point** (37 M6/7), the most southerly point in Devon; and **Beesands Cliff** (37 L7), at the north end of Beesands Beach, half a mile south of Torcross. The Trust also has extensive holdings around the Salcombe estuary and, to the east, around the Dart Estuary, including cliffs and farmland forming the western approach to Dartmouth harbour at **Little Dartmouth** (37 L8). The Dart estuary itself, especially in early summer, is very attractive, with woodland stretching right down to the water's edge. With the Dart and Start Bay appeal, the Trust hopes to protect more of this coast. Much farther east, five miles from Sidmouth, the Trust owns much of the **Branscombe valley** (including the peaceful and attractive village), as well as part of the cliffs towards Beer Head on the east and Weston on the west (38 G5).

The lofty granite mass of Dartmoor, vast and inhospitable, has its status as a National Park, and its bleak character, to protect it. None the less, the Trust has representative holdings on the moor – among them a typical stretch of the south-west corner at **Goodameavy** (37 J4), which lies six miles north-east of Plymouth, near Clearbrook, and includes Dewerstone and Cadworthy Woods, the Dewerstone Rock (on which there are the remains of an Iron Age fort), and part of Wigford Down (on which there are Bronze Age hut circles); 3,333 acres of open moorland on the south-west flank of Dartmoor around **Hentor** and **Willings Walls Warrens** (37 J4), which rises to 1,550 feet and overlooks the head-waters of the River Plym; and **Holne Woods** (37 J6), an area of oak woodland on the upper reaches of the River Dart with fine views from the higher paths.

Also noteworthy in the Devon countryside are **Hembury** (37 J6), on the southern edge of Dartmoor, where there are woodland walks through the upper Dart Valley to a 500-foot summit with fine moorland views; **Lydford Gorge** (37 G4), on the far western side of Dartmoor between Okehampton and Tavistock, where the River Lyd has scooped out a deep ravine to form a series of potholes and is joined by a stream that falls over the dramatic 90-foot high White Lady Waterfall; and the **Plym Bridge Woods** (37 K4), a wooded river valley on the edge of the moor.

In Somerset, pride of place might be thought to go to the big Trust holdings on **Exmoor**. These include 12,500 acres between **Porlock** (36 A7/8) and Minehead, stretching from the coast to the south of Dunkery Beacon, and incorporate not only some very beautiful countryside but also the villages of Bossington, Luccombe and Selworthy; **South Hill, Dulverton** (36 C7); and the viewpoint of **Winsford Hill** just to the north (36 C7), between Exford and

In summer, the wooded lower reaches of Lydford Gorge are a patchwork of sunlight and shade.

Dulverton. But, in many visitors' minds, these landscapes cannot match the dramatic quality of the **Cheddar Gorge** (39 A8), where the Trust owns the north side of **Cheddar Cliffs**, including the Lion and Monkey Rocks. Sun Hole Cave, in the Gorge, is of great archaeological interest, and items dating back to the Palaeolithic Age have been found there. Mysterious **Glastonbury Tor** (39 B8), with its legends of Joseph of Arimathea and King Arthur and Queen Guinevere delving deep into England's religious and secular past, is another much-visited spot in the Trust's care.

In the Mendip Hills, north-west of Wells, the Trust owns **Ebbor Gorge** (39 B8), a wooded limestone gorge run by the Nature Conservancy as a nature reserve. Other beauty spots include the **Blackdown Hills** (38 E5), with their views across the Vale of Taunton and the Quantocks to the Bristol Channel and surmounted by the *Wellington Monument*; and the headland of **Brean Down** (56 H6) overlooking Weston-super-Mare from a 300-foot high vantage point. In the Quantocks the views from **Longstone Hill** should not be missed (38 B5); while on Sedgemoor there are good views from *Burrow Mump* (39 C7), a nine-acre hill just south of Othery near Burrow Bridge. At **Turn Hill** (39 C7), one mile west of High Ham, there is another good viewpoint, looking across the battlefield of Sedgemoor (the site of Monmouth's defeat in 1685) to the Quantocks; while in the Polden Hills, to the east of Sedgemoor, **Cock Hill** (39 C8) stands on the crest – again with good views – beside the course of a Roman road.

Dorset's countryside is perhaps best epitomized by the **Golden Cap Estate** (39 G7/8), the National Trust's large holding of hills, cliffs, farmland and beach between Charmouth (just east of Lyme Regis) and Eypemouth – including five miles of the coast itself. This south Dorset downland is particularly attractive, and with fifteen miles of footpaths the estate lends itself to walking.

One of its attractions is that it is still not very well known, and thus remains uncrowded. This cannot be said of the county's most famous landmark, the **Cerne Giant** (39 F10), a 180-foot high Romano-British figure cut into the chalk of the 600-foot high Giant Hill, eight miles north of Dorchester.

Dorset is a county that tourists often forget – visitors either head for the New Forest, to the east, or else drive on through Dorset towards Devon and Cornwall. But the countryside is very attractive, and the coastline – and in particular the vast shingle beach of **Chesil Bank** (39 H9) – is often totally unspoilt. Lovers of coastal scenery may especially enjoy **Burton Cliff** (39 G8), a high bluff running west from Burton Bradstock which rises to 100 feet sheer above the sea before dropping down to Freshwater Bay, and provides both riverside and cliff walks, and **Ballard Down** (40 H2), south-east of Studland, on the Isle of Purbeck. Inland, there is **Lambert's Castle Hill** (39 F7), near Marshwood, an 842-foot high wooded hilltop and escarpment with views across to Chesil Bank in the east and Dartmoor in the west; while three counties – Devon, Dorset and Somerset – can be seen from the top of **Lewesdon Hill** (39 F7/8), three miles west of Beaminster.

Finally, **Brownsea Island** (40 G2), in Poole Harbour. Famous as the site of Lord Baden-Powell's first Scout camp in 1907, the 500-acre island of heath and woodland, with magnificent views across Poole Harbour, was inaccessible for many years. It was transferred to the Trust in 1962, and although part of the island is a nature reserve its woodland walks and beach are now accessible to everyone. There is a famous heronry on the island, but wildfowl and holidaymakers both find room here, in tranquil and beautiful surroundings.

above **The heavily-wooded acres of Brownsea Island are a paradise for a rich variety of wildlife and are one of the last haunts of the red squirrel.**

below **Selworthy is contained within the Trust's holdings on Exmoor and lies at the heart of some exceptional countryside.**

Antony House overlooks a crossing-point of the River Tamar and must always have been of strategic importance.

Houses, Gardens & Parks

Antony House, Cornwall This fine, solid, rectangular house of silvery-grey Pentewan stone, with red-brick wings attached to it by colonnades, was built by an unknown architect for Sir William Carew in the early part of the eighteenth century. The Carew family – among them the seventeenth-century historian Richard Carew, author of *The Survey of Cornwall* – had lived on the site for nearly 300 years before the completion of Antony House in 1721, but the stable block and early seventeenth-century building beside it replace an earlier house on this site.

Most of the rooms in the house are panelled, and contain contemporary furniture and portraits of the Carew and Pole families, whose descendants have always lived there. The brilliantly-coloured tapestry coverings on the chairs outside the dining room, the Queen Anne pier-glass between the dining room windows, the three Reynolds in the saloon, and the Soho tapestries in the tapestry room are all worth noting. The library contains a copy of the original edition of Richard Carew's *Survey*, published in 1602. The cannon balls outside the house date from Charles I's unsuccessful siege of Plymouth in the seventeenth century.

The beautifully laid out gardens, much influenced by Repton, run down to the River Lynher. A splendid terrace, complementing the house, overlooks the lawns on the north front. Of special interest are the stone carvings and temple bell, brought back to Cornwall by Sir Reginald Pole-Carew after military expeditions in India and Burma, and the gingko – or maidenhair tree – in the yew alley leading to the terrace: one of the oldest and largest trees of its kind in Britain.

2M N of Torpoint, N of A374 (37 K3)

Arlington Court, Devon Designed for Colonel John Palmer Chichester by Thomas Lee of Barnstaple in 1820, Arlington Court contains a collection of model ships, shells, pewter, snuff boxes and small *objets d'art*. There is a good collection of horse-drawn vehicles in the stables. The grounds, with their wide lawns and clumps of rhododendrons, merge into the surrounding woods, where buzzards and ravens nest. The lake below the house is a wildfowl sanctuary, and the surrounding parkland contains flocks of Jacob sheep and a herd of Shetland ponies.

7M NE of Barnstaple, on E side of A39 (36 B5)

The south front of Barrington Court, crowned with finials and chimneystacks, with the red-brick stable block on the left.

Barrington Court, Somerset An imposing mid sixteenth-century house probably built by William Clifton, a Norfolk merchant, Barrington Court has changed little externally. The windows are late Gothic, and the red-brick stable block dates from 1670. The interior was restored this century. The garden is one of the best preserved of Gertrude Jekyll's schemes.

3M NE of Ilminster, at E end of Barrington, entrance on B3168 (39 D7)

Bradley Manor, Devon The Perpendicular chapel is the principal item of architectural interest at Bradley Manor, a small, roughcast, fifteenth-century manor house in the steep valley of the River Lemon.

On W edge of Newton Abbot, entrance on A381 (37 J7)

Buckland Abbey, Devon Associations with the Grenville and Drake families, of seafaring fame, have made this thirteenth-century Cistercian abbey one of Britain's best-known country houses. Sir Richard Grenville, captain of the *Revenge*, whose grandfather and namesake had been given the building by King Henry VIII in 1541, re-modelled the abbey and added the plaster ceiling in the hall. Sir Francis Drake bought the house from the Grenvilles in 1581, after completing his voyage around the world, and his arms are on the chimneypiece in the top storey. The house's contents include Grenville and Drake relics, and a naval and county folk museum, which among many exhibits contains Drake's Drum. There is a large medieval tithe barn in the grounds.

6M S of Tavistock, off A386 (37 J4)

above **Buckland Abbey is centred on the tower of the abbey church.**

right **The medieval dovecote and pond in the valley garden at Cotehele.**

Castle Drogo, Devon A romantically eccentric building, Castle Drogo is a cross between a medieval castle and an eighteenth-century country house. It is in fact entirely twentieth-century in origin, having been built between 1910 and 1930 by Sir Edwin Lutyens for Julian Drewe, the founder of a grocery chain. Constructed entirely of granite, Castle Drogo has a superb setting: it stands on a rocky outcrop 900 feet above the wooded gorge of the upper reaches of the River Teign. Below the castle windows on the far side of the river rise the steep slopes of Whiddon Deer Park, which dates from Elizabethan times and still has its original walls. The castle garden itself is formally terraced, and has an immense circular lawn hedged with yews.

The building's grey exterior is a profusion of castellations, turrets and mullioned windows – a mixture of architectural styles that is the result not of additions over the centuries but of frequent changes of plan during the actual building of Castle Drogo. The interior is equally haphazard: a jumble of styles and ideas that paid little heed to practicality. The kitchens, for example, are fifty yards from the dining room. With the notable exception of the drawing room, the interior is also stark and austere. With bare granite walls and timber, it is reminiscent of a medieval castle, an effect that is heightened by the tapestries that hang in the library and hall.

Already recognized as unique, Castle Drogo could find itself with a double place in English architectural history: as the last large building to be constructed of granite and as one of the last private houses to be built in Britain on the grand scale.

At Drewsteignton, off A382 (37 G6)

left **Castle Drogo is architecturally one of the Trust's most remarkable houses.**

Compton Castle, Devon The two portcullised entrances, handsome battlements and angular towers on the north front give Compton Castle an almost fairytale appearance. It is, in fact, one of the finest fortified manor houses in Britain, and is famous as the home of Sir Humphrey Gilbert, Sir Walter Raleigh's half-brother, who colonized Newfoundland. It was built in three distinct periods (the early fourteenth, fifteenth, and sixteenth centuries) and remained in the Gilbert family until 1800. The house is surrounded by a massive 24-foot high wall, and the towers have interior shafts which provided an early, if rudimentary, form of sanitation. The reconstructed hall is full of Gilbert mementoes and the old kitchen, probably built in about 1520, has an open fireplace which extends for its full width.

The house stands in 346 acres of land, and there is a beautifully built, eighteenth-century barn of limestone and thatch beside the house.

4M *NW of Torquay (37 J7)*

Cotehele, Cornwall This remarkable early Tudor manor house overlooking the Tamar, and fronted by a bright display of daffodils every spring, has hardly changed in the past 300 years. Built between 1485 and 1627 round three courts, on the foundations of an earlier house, it is a microcosm of an era – and a fine example of a self-contained community, with everything coming up by river from Plymouth to the picturesque Cotehele Quay, on a bend in the Tamar. It contains Cromwellian armour, and fine furniture and tapestries, which have always been there. Charles I is said to have slept in the Jacobean Tower in the north-west corner of the building; and in the South Room, one of the bedrooms, are peeps which enabled the occupants to see what was happening in the hall and chapel below. The medieval hall, 40 feet long, is one of the most impressive in the West Country. Another notable feature is the simple chapel, which has a barrel-vaulted ceiling with oak ribbing and a fine carved oak screen. The chapel contains a fifteenth-century clock which is one of the three oldest unaltered pre-pendulum clocks in Britain.

In the grounds there is a medieval barn and, alongside the path leading to Cotehele Quay, an old dovecote shaped like a giant beehive – both reminders of the house's ability to be self-supporting. The gardens have Victorian terraces, and there are several attractive eighteenth-century and nineteenth-century buildings, and a small shipping museum, at Cotehele Quay. Cotehele Mill, the manorial water-mill, lies on the Tamar half a mile up the valley from Cotehele Quay.

9M *SW of Tavistock, near Calstock (37 J3)*

Dunster Castle, Somerset The 600-year-old fortified home of the Luttrell family rises impressively above the village of Dunster, between the wooded hills of Exmoor and the sea. The castle – in fact a mansion, despite its name – was remodelled by Anthony Salvin in the nineteenth century, although the seventeenth-century staircase and plasterwork were retained. The stables date from Cromwellian times, and the castle stands in forty-nine acres of parkland which are sufficiently well protected from the elements for semi-tropical shrubs to flourish on the terraced walks.

3M *SE of Minehead, entrance on A39 (38 B3)*

Glendurgan, Cornwall The wooded valley garden of Glendurgan, running down to the estuary of the Helford River, contains many fine trees and shrubs, a walled garden, a water garden, and a maze.

½M *S of Mawnan Smith, on road to Helford Passage (34 G5)*

Killerton, Devon This fine eighteenth-century house was built to the design of John Johnson, and stands in a hillside garden with large, open lawns and a notable collection of rare trees and shrubs. Two nineteenth-century chapels, one with immense tulip trees outside, and an arboretum, are particularly worth seeing. One of the chapels stands beside the ruins of the Aclands' house at Culm John, which was destroyed during the Civil War. The house contains the Paulise de Bush collection of costumes, which is shown in a series of rooms furnished to 'match' the costumes in different periods. Killerton Park is 300 acres of park and woodland surrounding the isolated Dolbury Hill while the estate as a whole is over 6,300 acres of agricultural land and woodland.

7M *NE of Exeter, entrance off B3185 (38 F3)*

Knightshayes Court, Devon A sandstone house, built in idiosyncratic Gothic style by William Burges between 1869–74 and possessing a fine collection of pictures, Knightshayes Court is best-known for its garden. This was created by Sir John and Lady Heathcoat-Amory after World War II, and includes specimen trees,

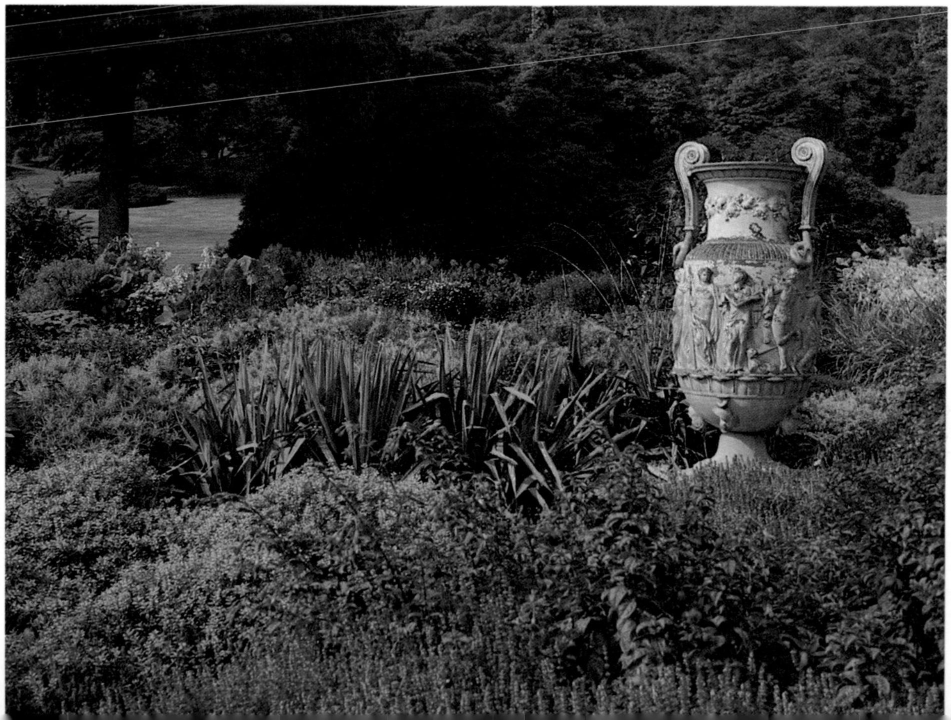

A Grecian urn in the terrace garden at Killerton.

formal terraces, rare shrubs, a collection of willows, and a fine display of spring bulbs. But not everything is new: the group of massive Douglas firs is over 100 years old.

2M *N of Tiverton, off B396 (38 E3)*

Lanhydrock, Cornwall One of the most beautiful houses in Cornwall, Lanhydrock is a seventeenth-century building which was severely damaged by fire and rebuilt in 1881, and it thus includes a variety of architectural styles. The gatehouse, and the north wing, are all that remain of the original building, completed in 1651, but the interior of the present house – which is on a larger scale than the original and epitomizes late Victorian splendour – is particularly interesting. Of special note are the English and Flemish tapestries on the walls of the morning room, and the panelled picture gallery with its 116-foot-long plaster barrel ceiling – a survivor of the fire – containing twenty-four panels depicting stories from the Old Testament starting with the Creation and ending with the burial of Isaac.

The 741 acres of park and woodland, falling away into the valley of the River Fowey, are particularly beautiful.

2½M *S of Bodmin, entrance on B3269 (35 C8)*

Lytes Cary, Somerset A typical Somerset manor house, and the home of the Lyte family for 500 years. It has been added to over the centuries, but the chapel, the oldest part of the present building, is fourteenth-century and the great hall fifteenth-century. The 365-acre grounds contain an ancient dovecote.

2½M *NE of Ilchester, on road to Charlton Adam off A372 (39 D8/9)*

Montacute, Somerset Built of Ham Hill stone from nearby Ham Hill to an H-shaped ground plan, Montacute is a magnificent Elizabethan mansion, glittering with glass and elaborate honey-coloured stonework. Inside there is some excellent heraldic glass, plasterwork, panelling and tapestries. There is an exhibition of sixteenth-century portraits, belonging to the National Portrait Gallery, in the Long Gallery. At 172 feet, this is the longest surviving sixteenth-century gallery. The house was completed in about 1600, and stands in contemporary gardens in which the two pavilions, which once flanked the entrance, are a feature.

4M *W of Yeovil, entrance off A3088 (39 E8)*

St Michael's Mount, Cornwall The magnificent, conical-shaped offshore island of St Michael's Mount rises 200 feet from the sea opposite Marazion, east of Penzance in Mount's Bay. It is crowned by a fourteenth-century castle. The island is reached by a causeway from Marazion at low tide, and by boat when the causeway is impassable.

The history of St Michael's Mount, which resembles the larger Mont St Michel in Brittany, goes back to Roman times, and it has been associated with Christianity since the fifth century. Edward the Confessor built a chapel on the Mount in 1047, then presented it to the Benedictine monks from the abbey on Mont St Michel. It later developed into a military stronghold, but in 1657 it became the property of the St Aubyn family and was converted into a private home.

There are remarkable views of Mount's Bay, and towards Land's End and the Lizard, from the terraces, and in the castle itself the drawing room (formed from the Lady Chapel), the refectory, the fifteenth-century chapel, and the armoury are all outstanding.

½M *S of Marazion, off A394 (34 G2)*

Saltram, Devon Standing in a landscaped park looking towards Plymouth Sound, Saltram was described by the eighteenth-century historian Polwhele as 'one of the most beautiful seats in the West of England' – a title to which it can still lay claim. The classical façade, built

above **The east front of Montacute seen across the late nineteenth-century balustraded pond.**

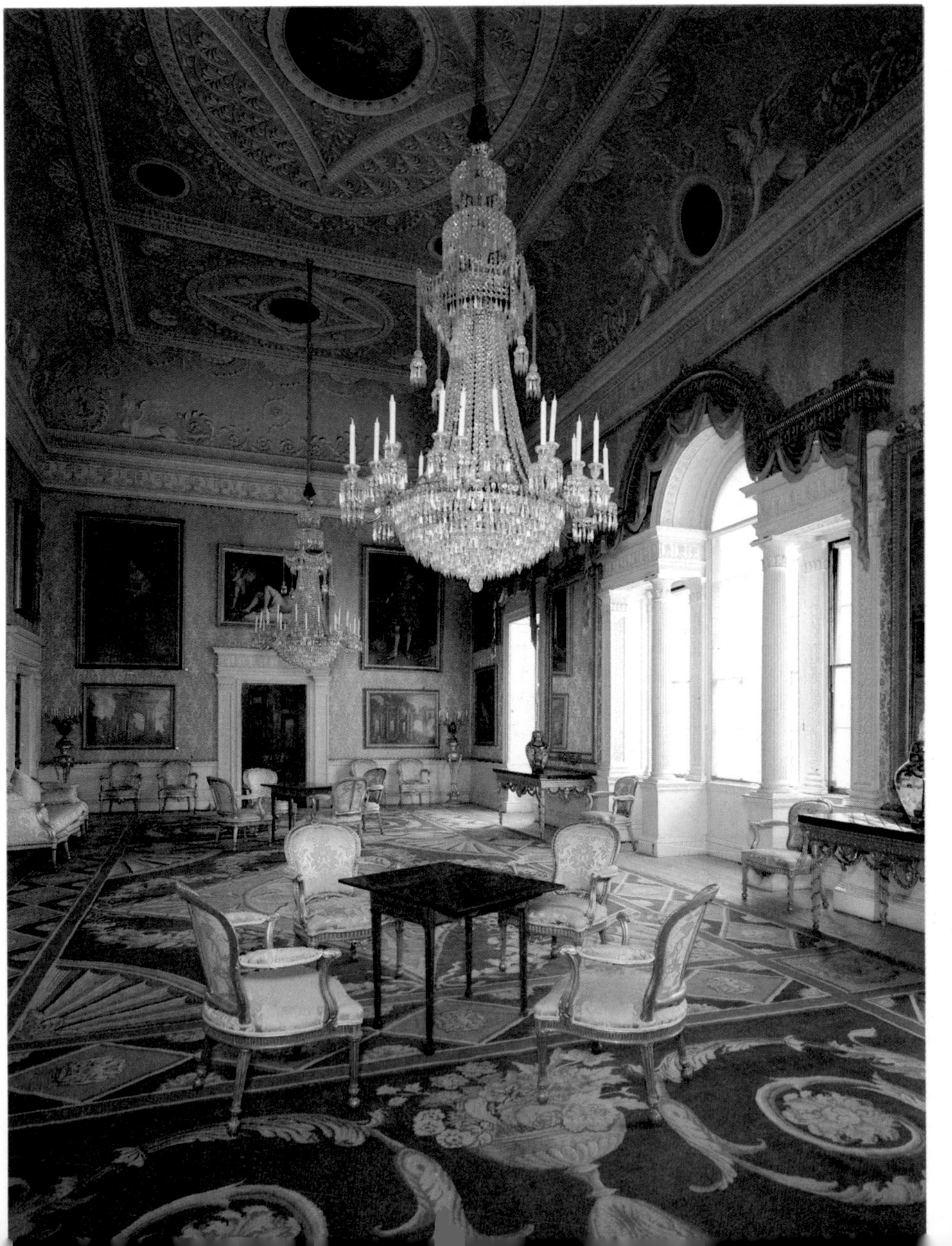

Every detail in the saloon at Saltram, including the gilt-brass door handles, was planned to contribute to the overall effect.

in the mid eighteenth century, masks the remains of a large Tudor house, and the house's history may go back even further than that, for there are references to a homestead on the site as long ago as 1218, when it may have been associated with the production of salt from the tidal estuary.

Today, the house is noteworthy as the finest complete and unspoiled example of the work of interior designer Robert Adam in the south-west – with the saloon and the dining room, completed in 1768, seen as his outstanding creations. Among the contents are fourteen portraits by Sir Joshua Reynolds, who lived nearby and had a lifelong association with Saltram, as well as fine period furniture and china. The great kitchen – which was still in use until 1962 – is of historic and social interest, and includes a Victorian range as well as a display of cooking utensils needed for catering on the grand scale.

The grounds include magnificent belts of timber on the higher points of the undulating parkland, which give Saltram a setting of considerable grandeur. There is also an orangery by the wood carver Henry Stockman, completed in 1775 and rebuilt by the Trust after a disastrous fire in 1932; the classical garden house or temple known as 'Fanny's Bower'; a chapel adjacent to the house which is thought to be a conversion of a medieval barn; and a pleasant little building known as The Castle, in the design of which Adam is thought to have had a hand.

3½M E of Plymouth city centre, between A38 and A379 (37 K4)

Sharpitor, Devon The six-acre garden of this early twentieth-century house affords beautiful views over Salcombe Bay and the entrance to Salcombe harbour to the east. The house contains a museum of local interest, with special appeal to children.

1½M SW of Salcombe (37 M6)

Tintinhull House, Somerset This is a fine seventeenth-century farmhouse with a classical façade. It is noted for its modern formal garden.

5M NW of Yeovil, in Tintinhull village, ½M S of A303 (39 D8)

Trelissick, Cornwall The grounds of Trelissick House, overlooking the Fal estuary and Falmouth harbour, include a very good collection of shrubs, and are interesting and attractive at all times of the year. In all, there are 376 acres of gardens and parkland, including farmland and some woodland, above the Fal estuary. There is a well-preserved Iron Age promontory fort at Round Wood, at the entrance to Cowlands Creek on the estate.

4M S of Truro, entrance on B3289 (34 F5)

Trengwainton, Cornwall The gardens of Trengwainton House contain a magnificent collection of shrubs, mainly magnolias and rhododendrons, including many half-hardy species. The theme of a place in which the climate permits the growth of many species not normally seen in England is continued in the walled garden, where there are many tender plants. The gardens and surrounding park total 98 acres.

2M W of Penzance (34 G2)

Trerice, Cornwall A fine Elizabethan manor house, Trerice contains notable plaster ceilings and fireplaces, oak and walnut furniture, portraits and tapestries. On the south side is a fine sixteenth-century two-storeyed bay, whose windows on the first floor light the solar (now the drawing room). The E-shaped east-facing frontage, with its splendid scrolled Dutch gables, betrays the house's Tudor origins – it was rebuilt in 1571. There are fourteen acres of delightful gardens.

3M SE of Newquay (34 D5)

Castles, Abbeys & other Buildings

Bruton Dovecote, Somerset This is a sixteenth-century, roofless tower used latterly as a dovecote, standing alone in the deer park of the abbey which once stood on the south side of the town.

½M S of Bruton, across railway, ½M W of B3081 (39 C10)

Burrow Mump, Somerset On the summit of isolated Burrow Mump, on Sedgemoor, is an unfinished late eighteenth-century chapel, built over the foundations of an earlier one. There was previously a small Norman castle on this site. Burrow Mump also serves as a World War II memorial.

2½M SW of Othery, just S of A361 (39 C7)

Clouds Hill, Dorset T. E. Lawrence – Lawrence of Arabia – retired to this cottage when he was discharged from the RAF. It contains some of Lawrence's furnishings.

9M E of Dorchester (39 G11)

Coleridge Cottage, Somerset The poet Samuel Taylor Coleridge lived in this cottage, at the west end of Nether Stowey, between 1797 and 1800, while he was writing *The Ancient Mariner* and the first part of *Christabel*. The parlour only is shown.

Nether Stowey, 8M W of Bridgwater, S side of A39 (38 B5)

Grange Arch, Creech, Dorset Commonly known as Bond's Folly, Grange Arch was built early in the eighteenth century by Denis Bond, of Creech Grange. It stands silhouetted against the sky to the south of Creech Grange, in the Purbeck Hills.

3M W of Corfe Castle (39 H12)

Hardy Monument, Dorset Erected in 1846, the monument commemorates Vice-Admiral Sir Thomas Masterman Hardy, flag-captain of the *Victory* at the Battle of Trafalgar (1805). The monument's site offers good views over Weymouth Bay.

6M SW of Dorchester (39 G9)

Hardy's Cottage, Dorset This small thatched house at Higher Bockhampton was the birthplace of Thomas Hardy in 1840 and was where he wrote *Under the Greenwood Tree* and *Far from the Madding Crowd*. It contains a small museum of items of Hardy memorabilia.

3M NE of Dorchester, S of A35 (39 G10)

King John's Hunting Lodge, Somerset Standing on a corner of the square in the centre of the ancient town of Axbridge, where Tudor-fronted houses line the High Street, King John's Hunting Lodge dates from about 1500 and is illustrative of the new prosperity enjoyed by the merchant class at that time. It contains a small museum.

Axbridge, at junction of A38 and A371 (39 A7)

Grange Arch, looking north over an unspoilt stretch of Dorset countryside. The sea can be seen in the view south.

Loughwood Meeting House is made of local sandstone and stands within a small burial ground.

Lawrence House, Cornwall This country town house, built in 1753, typifies the character of Castle Street, the attractive street in which it is situated. It contains a local museum.

Castle Street, Launceston (37 G2)

Loughwood Meeting House, Devon Built in the mid seventeenth century by Baptists from Kilmington, the Loughwood Meeting House stands in remote wooded countryside and is an unusual survival of an early Nonconformist chapel. The interior, which has a plastered barrel ceiling, contains simple, original eighteenth-century fittings.

1M S of Dalwood (38 F6)

Martock: The Treasurer's House, Somerset A small thirteenth- and fourteenth-century house, containing an interesting medieval hall and kitchen and a fine collar-braced timber roof. It was once the home of the Treasurer of Wells Cathedral. (Open by written appointment.)

1M NW of A303 between Ilminster and Ilchester, opposite Martock church (39 D8)

Muchelney Priest's House, Somerset This late medieval house with its large Gothic hall window was originally the residence of the secular priests serving the parish church. (Open by written appointment with the tenant.)

1½M S of Langport (39 D7/8)

Old Blundell's School, Devon This is the famous grammar school in Tiverton, Devon, which was built by a local clothier, Peter Blundell, in 1604. When a new school was built in 1882, the old building was converted into dwelling houses. Old Blundell's School is the setting for a dramatic fight in R. D. Blackmore's classic novel *Lorna Doone*.

Station Road, Tiverton (38 E3)

Old Post Office, Tintagel, Cornwall Used as Tintagel's Post Office (for incoming mail only) between 1844 and 1892, the Old Post Office is a very small, fourteenth-century stone manor house, with an ancient roof of uneven slates. The large hall is open to the roof.

In village centre, off B3263 (34 B/C1)

Shute Barton, Devon The remains of a fourteenth- to sixteenth-century manor house, whose battlemented tower and late Gothic windows still look attractive from the outside. Inside, a newel stair, a large open fireplace, a collar-beam hall roof and a late seventeenth-century panelled room survive. The detached gatehouse dates from the 1570s, but has nineteenth-century alterations.

3M SW of Axminster, entrance on B3161 (38 G6)

Stoke-sub-Hamdon Priory, Somerset Built of Ham Hill stone in the fourteenth and fifteenth centuries, Stoke-sub-Hamdon Priory formerly housed the priests of the chantry of St Nicholas in a nearby manor house, Beauchamp, which no longer exists. The great hall and screens passage of the chantry house remain, although only the former and the ruins are open.

2M W of Montacute, just N of A3088 (39 D/E8)

Watersmeet Cottage, Devon This nineteenth-century fishing lodge near Lynmouth serves as a National Trust Information Centre.

E of Lynmouth, close to A39 (36 A6)

Wellington Monument, Somerset A 175-foot-high obelisk designed by Thomas Lee (the architect of *Arlington Court*) and built 1817–18 to commemorate the military achievements of the Duke of Wellington. There are breath-taking views from the top.

2M S Wellington (38 E5)

West Pennard Court Barn, Somerset A fifteenth-century barn with five bays and an interesting roof. (Open on application.)

3M E of Glastonbury, S of West Pennard (39 C8/9)

Widecombe-in-the-Moor: Church House, Devon This fifteenth-century granite building near Widecombe-in-the-Moor church is used partly as a cottage with a National Trust Information Centre and shop, and partly as a village hall.

6M NW of Ashburton (37 H6)

Archaeological & Industrial Sites

Bolt Tail, Devon Bolt Tail Camp is an Iron Age promontory fort west of Salcombe, above the lovely beach of Hope Cove.

2½M W of Salcombe (37 L5/6)

Brean Down, Somerset There is a small Iron Age promontory fort on this 300-foot high headland, as well as field systems and evidence of occupation from Beaker times onwards.

2M SW of Weston-super-Mare (56 H6)

Cadsonbury, Cornwall This is an important hill-fort crowning a steep, isolated hill in the valley of the River Lynher. As yet unexcavated, it probably dates from the early Iron Age in the third to fifth centuries BC.

2M SW of Callington (35 C10)

Cerne Giant, Dorset Thought to date from Roman times, this 180-foot high figure is cut into the chalk of the hillside above the village of Cerne Abbas. The naked Giant brandishes a 120-foot-long club. He is thought to represent either a Celtic deity or the classical Hercules, but whichever, he must have been a local cult figure. (Best viewed from lay-by on A352.)

8M N of Dorchester (39 F10)

Chapel Carn Brea, Cornwall This 657-foot high hill, the most westerly on the British mainland, includes several Bronze Age barrows.

3M NE of Land's End (34 G1)

Coneys Castle, Dorset The defences on this hilltop belong to an Iron Age hill-fort.

6M E of Axminster, adjacent to Lambert's Castle Hill (39 F7)

Cornish Beam Engines, Cornwall Five Cornish beam engines, which were used to bring steam power to the Cornish mining industry, belong to the Trust, and are an interesting relic of the earliest stages of Britain's Industrial Revolution. The easiest to see are at **Holman's Museum,** Camborne (34 F3/4), and at the **East Pool and Agar Mine,** Camborne (34 F3/4), reached from an entrance on the A3047. The other engines are at the **Levant Mine,** St Just, which can be visited by arrangement (34 F1), and at the **South**

Crofty Mine, Camborne, which is not a working mine and therefore not open at present (34 F3/4). The tin mine pithead at Redruth (34 F4) is also open to the public. **Trevithick's Cottage**, the birthplace of the engineer Richard Trevithick (1771–1833), at Lower Penponds, Camborne, also belongs to the Trust and may be visited on application (34 F3/4).

The Dodman, Cornwall There are a well-preserved Iron Age promontory fort and the remains of a medieval field system on Dodman Point.

4M *S of Mevagissey (35 F7)*

Exmoor, Somerset Exmoor includes several interesting prehistoric sites: the Bronze Age barrow group known as the **Wambarrows**, and the **Caratacus Stone**, are on Winsford Hill, between Exford and Dulverton (38 C2); and the hill-fort of **Bury Castle** is on the Holnicote Estate, east and south of Porlock (38 B2). The Holnicote Estate also includes several groups of round barrows and a stone circle.

Goodameavy, Devon This south-west corner of Dartmoor is rich in prehistoric sites: the remains of an Iron Age promontory fort on the **Dewerstone Rock**, and Early to Middle Bronze Age hut circles on **Wigford Down**. An unusual pottery cup, probably dating from the Middle Bronze Age, was found at Dewerstone in 1960, and is now in Plymouth City Museum.

6M *NE of Plymouth, near Clearbrook (37 J4)*

Hembury, Devon Hembury Castle, on the 500-foot summit of Hembury, is an Iron Age hill-fort.

2M *N of Buckfastleigh (37 J6)*

Hentor, Devon The Trust's holdings at Hentor, Willings Walls and Trowlesworthy Warrens (see also entry under *Coast and Countryside*) were well populated in prehistoric times, and include a large number of ruined cists with partial covering cairns, more than a hundred hut circles, many enclosure walls, a standing stone, and possibly a stone circle, all of the Bronze Age.

On SW flank of Dartmoor (37 J4/5)

High Ham Mill, Somerset This is a thatched windmill, dating from 1820, which was in regular use until 1910. (Open by appointment.)

2M *N of Langport,* ½M *E High Ham (39 C7/8)*

Lambert's Castle Hill, Dorset This Iron Age hill-fort has more recently been the site of an annual pony fair. Wide views east and west.

5½M *E of Axminster (39 F7)*

Lanyon Quoit, Cornwall This huge granite capstone, on three upright stones, re-erected in 1824, is the remains of a megalithic chambered long barrow dating from 2000–1600 BC, and is one of the south-west's most famous prehistoric sites.

4M *NW of Penzance (34 F1/2)*

Maen Castle, Cornwall An Iron Age cliff castle on the Mayon and Trevescan cliffs between Sennen Cove and Land's End. *(34 G1)*

Old Mill, Wembury, Devon This medieval mill house stands on the shoreline of Wembury Bay, and is run as a shop.

5–6M *E of Plymouth (35 E12)*

Rough Tor, Cornwall There is a Bronze Age settlement site, preserving hut circles and enclosed fields, some with lynchets, on Rough Tor, the bleak moorland peak on Bodmin Moor.

3M *SE of Camelford (35 B8)*

Tolpuddle Martyrs' Monument, Dorset A seat commemorates the six Dorset farm labourers sentenced to transportation in 1834 for trying to form a trade union.

7M *NE of Dorchester, on S side of A35 (39 G11)*

Trencrom Hill, Cornwall A well-preserved Iron Age B hill-fort, stone-walled and enclosing hut circles, can be seen on this gorse-covered hill overlooking a wide panorama of countryside and the sea.

3M *S of St Ives (34 F2)*

Treryn Dinas (Treen Castle), Cornwall This is an Iron Age cliff castle of uncertain date consisting of a series of banks and ditches. Close by there is the famous, rocking Logan rock, a natural wonder.

4M *SE of Land's End (34 G1)*

Wind Hill, Lynmouth, Devon Countisbury Camp, an early Iron Age linear earthwork, is on Wind Hill, between Countisbury and the sea, while there are also two defensive earthworks on the spur of Myrtlebury Cleave.

E of Lynmouth, beside A39 (38 A1)

Wheal Betsy, Devon This is the roofless engine house and stack of an abandoned lead mine on Black Down, on the edge of Dartmoor. A romantic and picturesque industrial relic.

5M *N of Tavistock, just E of A386 (37 H4)*

Wheal Coates, Cornwall The ruined buildings and engine houses of the disused tin and copper mines of Wheal Coates, Towanwroath, Wheal Charlotte and Charlotte United stand on the cliff and heath-covered moorland of the Trust's holding at Chapel Porth, and can be reached on foot.

1½M *SW of St Agnes (34 E4)*

Wheal Prosper, Cornwall The dramatic ruin of the engine house and stack of the Wheal Prosper tin and copper mine, which was abandoned in about 1860, dominates Rinsey Cliff above sandy Porthcew Cove.

1½M *SW of Ashton (34 G3)*

The 1892 Harvey water pumping engine at Taylor's Shaft, East Pool mine.

The romantic ruin of Wheal Betsy stands on the western edge of Dartmoor.

Southern England

SCOTNEY CASTLE

The long, narrow strip that makes up this region – about 160 miles east to west but only forty miles north to south – is unified by the fact that chalk underlies most of it. The well-drained chalk lands gave early man access to the interior of the country, along downland routes like the Ridgeway and the Pilgrims' Way, and these prehistoric links are reflected in National Trust properties such as Cissbury Ring on the South Downs, the Coldrum Long Barrow on the North Downs, and above all in Avebury stone circle to the west.

This ancient region also contains the seed from which the whole wide-branching tree of the National Trust grew – the little Clergy House at Alfriston, on the South Downs behind Eastbourne, which was the first building ever bought by the Trust. Compared with the great mansions acquired since – Knole, Ham, The Vyne or Petworth – it is a pygmy among a group of giants; but it is linked to them by a host of intermediate-sized buildings, from small manor houses to water-mills, which cover the whole range of our ancestors' homes and places of work.

Leaving aside the Iron Age forts and the stronghold of Bodiam Castle, it is a region of peace rather than war; and the Trust's properties reflect this, in their emphasis on fine collections of paintings and furniture, in their gardens and arboreta, and in the domestication of their settings, which are lacking in any wildness or harshness.

Coast & Countryside

All the south coast resorts, from Ramsgate round almost to Bournemouth, come into this region; and the towns' insatiable appetite for building land has meant that the Trust's acquisitions have been of the greatest importance. The Trust has no properties at all on the north Kent coast. They begin south of the Kentish Stour, at **Sandwich Bay** (43 B12). Nearly 200 acres of estuary land are run as a nature reserve here by the Kent Trust for Nature Conservation. Heading south to Dover and beyond, the Trust has farmland above the White Cliffs to east and west of the port, with two-thirds of a mile of cliff-top walk above **St Margaret's Bay** (43 D12), and one mile or so westward from **Shakespeare Cliff**, above the old Channel Tunnel workings just west of Dover harbour (43 D11).

West of Romney Marsh towards Hastings there are two more fair-sized areas of farmland – nearly 400 acres in and around **Winchelsea** (43 F8), including the meadows that provide the background to Millais' painting of the *Blind Girl* (in the Birmingham Art Gallery); and more than 200 acres, including cliffland, at **Fairlight** (43 G7). Between Beachy Head and Seaford the Trust has a large holding of cliffland (42 H4). Central to this stretch are the spectacular **Seven Sisters**; the Trust has over 600 acres of farmland between the A259 and the cliffs, and further land on the Beachy Head side of Birling Gap. Along the rest of the South Downs coast its properties are mainly inland, like the lofty summits of **Ditchling Beacon** (42 G2) and **Cissbury Ring** (41 E12), and the 3,500 acres of the **Slindon Estate** (41 E11), inland from Bognor.

West of Chichester the Trust has fifty or so acres of dune and saltings at **East Head** (41 F9), which guards the entrance to Chichester Harbour opposite Hayling Island; while inside that sailor's paradise of small creeks and marinas it maintains **Quay Meadow** at Bosham (41 F9) – an acre of grass between the church and the water of the creek.

In contrast to the Trust's precarious grip on the south coast, it has so much property on the Isle of Wight – about 5,000 acres – that the island might almost be regarded as the Trust's private domain. The two main promontories, **St Catherine's Point** to the south (40 H6) and the **Needles Headland** at the westernmost extremity (40 G/H4/5), belong to the Trust, as does **Tennyson Down**, near Easton (40 G/H5), where the poet used to ramble when he lived at Farringford near by. The Needles Headland is a Site of Special Scientific Interest; rising to nearly 500 feet, it is a sanctuary for sea-birds. Apart from the downland areas, both on the coast and inland, the Trust owns the entire **Newtown River estuary** (40 G5/6) on the north side of the island, with footpaths giving views

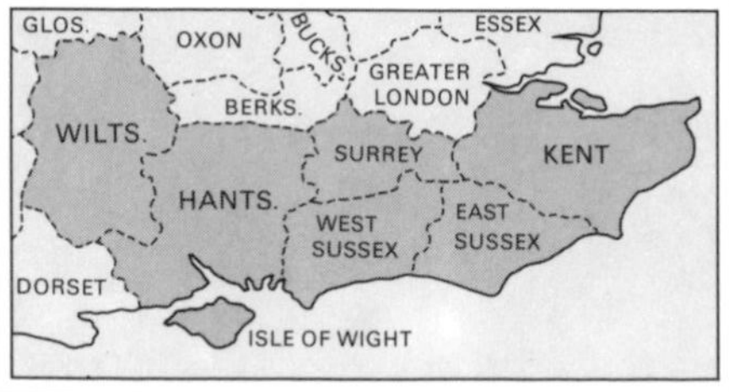

The Trust's meadow at Bosham. It may have been here that King Canute attempted to turn back the tide.

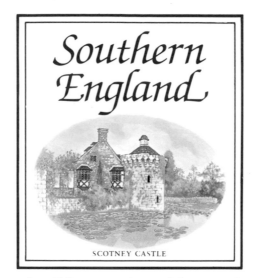

Box Hill rises to nearly 700 feet and is one of the best-known beauty-spots in south-east England.

over the Solent and plenty of sea-birds.

There is a cluster of important Trust properties in the Haslemere area on the border of West Sussex and Surrey: **Blackdown** (41 C10), 600 acres; **Woolbeding Common** (41 D10), more than 1,000 acres; **Frensham Common** (41 B9/10), 900 acres; and biggest of all **Hindhead Common** (41 C10), nearly 1,100 acres, with the great wooded valley of the Devil's Punch Bowl at its eastern edge.

Some twenty or so miles to the north-east another cluster of Trust-owned areas of countryside is dominated by the steep chalk bastion of **Box Hill** (42 C1). Like the Alfriston Clergy House, Box Hill was a key purchase for the Trust, as it was the first major piece of countryside it bought. The 230 acres of the Hill cost £16,000 in 1913, and now form the nucleus of the Trust's properties round Dorking, which total more than 6,500 acres. Box Hill is of major interest to naturalists, as it is one of the few areas on the North Downs without grazing animals or arable farming, and so the plant life grows unchecked, apart from the control exercised by forestry operations. The box trees from which it gets its name can still be found here and there; there are yew, ash and many other tree varieties; and the animals include roe and fallow deer, and colonies of badgers. Box Hill adjoins the bracken-covered expanses of **Headley Heath** (42 C1), on the summit of the Downs; while across on the west side of the valley of the River Mole (the route taken by the Dorking–Leatherhead road), **Ranmore** and **Bookham Commons** (41 A12) total up to a further 900 acres between them.

These naturalists' paradises would have delighted Gilbert White, the quiet eighteenth-century clergyman who lived at Selborne across the Hampshire border from Surrey. Here the Trust owns about 250 acres of **Selborne Hill** (41 C8/9), with its beech hangers and meadows, which White described meticulously in his *Natural History of Selborne*, jotting down his day-to-day observations in his ever-fresh *Naturalist's Journal*. Gilbert White fought against an enclosure scheme that threatened his beloved hangers. Had he lived a century longer, he might well have been a founder-member of the National Trust.

left **Gilbert White recorded many observations in the beech woods behind Selborne in his** *Natural History*.

above **Kipling's study at Bateman's. The walnut writing chair is fitted with blocks to raise it to the right height.**

right **Alfriston Clergy House was built in about 1350 and designed for a small community of parish priests.**

Houses, Gardens & Parks

Alfriston Clergy House, East Sussex One of the few pre-Reformation clergy houses remaining in England, it was the first building acquired by the National Trust, who bought it in 1896 for only £10. Built about 1350, it is a thatched and timbered building, with wattle and daub between the timbers, and a fine king-post roof in the hall. As late as the seventeenth century it was still lived in by the vicar, but it then became a farm labourer's cottage. By 1890 it was so dilapidated that it was proposed to pull it down. Fortunately it was saved by the combined protests of the vicar of the time and the Sussex Archaeological Society.

In Alfriston, 4M NE Seaford, E of B2108 (42 H4)

Bateman's, East Sussex Bateman's, where Rudyard Kipling lived from 1902 until his death in 1936, is a handsome stone-gabled building, with mullioned windows and brick chimneys. It was built by a local ironmaster about 1634, though parts of it are probably earlier; the stone comes from a quarry near by and has rusted in stripes where the iron ore runs through it. The rooms that are open form

a Kipling museum, with his upstairs study looking very much as he left it, the walls lined with novels, poetry and travel books, and the inkwell and pipe cleaners still lying on the desk.

Many of Kipling's best-known books were written at Bateman's, including *Puck of Pook's Hill* (1906), the hill of the title being visible from one of the bedrooms. *If*, the most famous of all his poems, was also written here.

The fine garden, largely planned by Kipling himself, leads down to the little River Dudwell. The water-mill that Kipling harnessed for electricity when he first came to Bateman's has been restored, and is now used for grinding flour sold in the Trust shop.

½M S Burwash, off A265 (42 F5)

Cedar House, Surrey Now an old people's home, this imposing red-brick house looks out across the River Mole. The river façade dates from the eighteenth century, but behind there is a far older building, basically of the fifteenth century, with a fine timbered dining-hall. This is lit by a large traceried Gothic window, which was removed from a Yorkshire church and

The design of Clandon Park betrays the origins of its Italian architect, Leoni.

An anonymous oil painting of Claremont (*c.*1740) showing Bridgeman's amphitheatre and Kent's lake with its island pavilion.

incorporated into Cedar House in the 1920s. The splendid wrought-iron gate comes from the house of the playwright Sheridan (*see also Polesden Lacey*) at Eltham, and incorporates his monogram. (House seen by appointment.)

On N side of A245, E side of old Cobham (85 H12)

Chartwell, Kent The home of Sir Winston Churchill from 1922 until his death in 1965, Chartwell evokes the spirit of one of the giants of the twentieth century. It stands in a south-facing combe with spectacular views across the Weald, and is basically a brick Victorian country house, remodelled by the architect Philip Tilden.

Chartwell embodies the private rather than the public face of Churchill, though there are plenty of mementoes of his long and active life, from the Boer War poster offering £25 for him 'dead or alive' to the assorted *objets d'art*, given to him by international statesmen and assembled in the Museum Room. There is a collection of his more exotic clothes, such as the full dress of Warden of the Cinque Ports, and a green velvet siren suit. The creative side of his nature is reflected both in the study where he wrote his *History of the English-Speaking Peoples* and other major works, and in his own paintings, which hang on the walls of Chartwell.

The garden reflects another side of Churchill's creativity, especially the famous wall round the kitchen garden, which he built as a hobby when he was in the political wilderness during the 1920s and 1930s. This part of the garden includes the 'Golden Rose Garden', planted in 1958 to mark the Churchills'

The study at Chartwell is as Churchill left it in 1964, with pictures and photographs of family and friends.

golden wedding with thirty-two yellow and gold species of rose.

(*Note:* Chartwell is liable to be extremely crowded, especially during the summer months. Visitors often have to wait a considerable time before entering the house, and there is a timed ticket system.)

2M S Westerham, off B2026 (42 C3)

Clandon Park, Surrey Designed by a Venetian architect, Giacomo Leoni, in the 1730s, Clandon is like an Italian villa set down in the Surrey countryside. It was built for Thomas Onslow (the 2nd Baron Onslow), whose family was unique in having provided three Speakers of the House of Commons.

Externally the house is remarkable for the contrast between the white stone of the central section and the red brick of the remainder. Internally the main feature is the Marble Hall, the first room the visitor enters, which runs the full height of both the ground and first floors. Painted white, it has superb plasterwork on the ceiling, representing subjects from classical mythology. The house is unusual in having one oak and one stone staircase of seemingly equal importance on either side of the hall.

The varied collection of furniture, porcelain and metalwork at Clandon came originally from Little Trent Park in Hertfordshire and was left to the National Trust by Mrs David Gubbay. Especially rare are the Chinese porcelain birds which stand on ledges and in niches round Clandon. In the basement is the restored old kitchen and the Museum of the Queen's Royal Surrey Regiment.

The main feature of the garden is a Maori house, brought home by the 4th Earl Onslow, who was Governor of New Zealand from 1888–92.

West Clandon, 3M E Guildford, on A247 (41 A11)

The entrance front of Ham House once had a pair of turrets and a central bay.

Great Chalfield Manor is today the centre of an agricultural estate, as it has been for 900 years.

Robert Adam had his first recorded commission as a decorator at Hatchlands and probably designed the ceiling in this hall.

Claremont Landscape Garden, Surrey Tucked away beside the old Portsmouth Road, Claremont is the epitome of the development of the eighteenth-century landscape garden, which became popular in reaction to the stiff formality of the seventeenth century. The greatest names in landscape design were associated with Claremont – Charles Bridgeman, who in about 1725 designed the huge grass amphitheatre, the only one of its kind to survive in Europe, setting off the round pond which forms the garden's main feature; William Kent, who in the 1730s enlarged the pond, altering its shape and giving it an island with a pavilion built on it; and Lancelot 'Capability' Brown, who planted trees on the amphitheatre, hiding it from view until it was cleared and restored by the Trust from 1975 to 1977.

Brown was working for Clive of India, who bought Claremont in 1768. One of his alterations was to move the Portsmouth Road a couple of hundred yards away from the lake – an improvement the visitor can appreciate today. Among other features of the garden are a long ha-ha, or sunken barrier, a grotto, a skittle alley and a bowling green.

1M S Esher, on A307 (formerly A3) (86 H1)

The Courts Garden, Wiltshire An interestingly varied garden, around a fine eighteenth-century stone house (house not open). The garden includes lawns with long herbaceous borders, a rectangular lily pond, and a small lake surrounded with gunnera and other water-loving plants.

3M N Trowbridge, S side of A3053 (57 H11)

Emmetts Garden, Kent A small, hilltop garden (4 acres) of fine trees and shrubs, with wide-ranging views south across the treetops towards the Bough Beech Reservoir. Some of the shrubs, which include pure white hydrangeas, were planted at the turn of the century. A good time to visit is May, when the bluebells and late daffodils are out.

½M N Ide Hill, near Sevenoaks, 2M S of A25 (42 C4)

Great Chalfield Manor, Wiltshire Great Chalfield was built by Thomas Tropnell, a successful politician and landowner, about 1470: the great hall, with first-floor solar on one side and dining room on the other, was built by Tropnell, though the wall beside the remains of the moat and the gatehouse is earlier, and there has been a good deal of reconstruction since. The house was originally much bigger, as is shown by the foundations that remain in the garden.

Though it is some way south of the Cotswolds, its gables, mullions and mellow stonework give it the look of a typical Cotswold manor. The gable ends are decorated with stone figures of soldiers in fifteenth-century armour, giving an almost playful appearance to the exterior. Inside there are fine beams and a reconstructed musicians' gallery in the main hall. The house's greatest curiosity is the three stone masks, of a bishop with mitre, a king with asses' ears, and a laughing face, which look down into the hall; the eyes are cut away so that the women of Tropnell's household could see what went on in the hall without being seen.

The house was restored in the early years of this century.

4M NE Bradford-on-Avon, off B3109 – there are two driveways, one NW of Broughton Gifford and one near Holt (57 H11)

Ham House, Surrey This grand and melancholy house looks north towards the Thames flowing by a couple of hundred yards away, and south beyond Ham Common to the Surrey hills. Little in it has changed since the period between about 1670 and 1730, when the main structural alterations were made, the furniture and pictures were collected, and the lawns and parterres were laid out.

It was built in 1610 in the reign of James I, but it owes its present appearance, both inside and out, to the Duke and Duchess of Lauderdale, two of the most ambitious and unpleasant characters of the late seventeenth century. A joint portrait of the Lauderdales by Lely hangs in the Round Gallery at Ham.

Externally, Ham is a sober red-brick house; the ground plan is in the form of a shallow U, with the projecting wings on the north or entrance front. Internally it is still largely as the Lauderdales left it, with much the same furniture and pictures. Their positions can be checked from the inventory of 1679 (in the Museum Room), and where the furniture is not original it has been possible to find near-equivalents. The layout of the rooms has the Duke and Duchess's living accommodation on the ground floor, with the state rooms, centring on the Queen's Bedchamber, on the first floor or *piano nobile*.

The most attractive rooms in Ham are not the great rooms so much as the little 'closets' leading off them, full of furniture and pictures, and with richly decorated walls. There are a good many portraits of the Dysart and Tollemache families, related to the Duchess, and some superb Elizabethan miniatures in the small room called the Cabinet of Miniatures.

The garden's formal lawns and parterres are at present being restored to their seventeenth-century appearance, following plans of the Lauderdales' time.

By the Thames, 1M SW Richmond, off the A307 (86 G2)

Hatchlands, Surrey Hatchlands is a four-square red-brick Georgian country house, only a couple of miles from *Clandon Park*, with which it makes a good contrast. It was built in 1757 for Admiral Boscawen, known as 'Old Dreadnought', who paid for it with prize money won from his victories over the French. The chief feature of the interior (not much of which is shown) is the decoration and plasterwork by Robert Adam. The most notable modern addition is a fine music room, designed by Sir Reginald Blomfield and built about 1903.

Externally there is one strange feature: the main south front has only two storeys, whereas part of the west front has three. This arrangement is due to the internal layout of the house, and six windows on the west front are in fact sham.

Just E of East Clandon, N of A246 (41 A12)

Knole, Kent Set in a magnificent park where deer browse among ancient gnarled trees, Knole must be high on the list for the National Trust's grandest house. It is popularly said to be linked to the days, weeks and months of the year by having 365 rooms, 7 courtyards, 52 staircases and 12 entrances; and its sheer size, best grasped by looking round the exterior before going in, makes it more like a village – or at least a large Oxford or Cambridge college – than a private house. The name comes from the low hill, or knoll, on which it stands.

Knole owes much of its dignified medieval appearance to Thomas Bourchier, Archbishop of Canterbury, who bought it for £266 in 1456 and transformed it into a palace fit for an archbishop. It passed from the Church to the Crown in the 1530s, when Henry VIII hinted to Archbishop Cranmer that he would like it and Cranmer naturally complied; then from the Crown into private ownership in 1566, when Queen Elizabeth I gave it to her cousin Thomas Sackville, whose descendants live in the private quarters of Knole to this day.

The interior of Knole combines the history of the Sackville family with the history of English furniture and design. This historical sense is at its strongest in the Brown Gallery, where rows of portraits gaze down upon seventeenth-century chairs which still keep their original upholstery. Among the furniture are the original drop-end Knole sofa or settee, dating from the time of James I (in the Leicester Gallery), and the silver-mounted table, mirror and candle-stands in the King's Bedroom. The paintings include a series of portraits by Sir Joshua Reynolds (in the Reynolds Room).

The 1,000-acre park is open to the public; it has plenty of hills and valleys, and is an ideal place for a walk on a fine day.

On S side of Sevenoaks, E of A225 (42 C4)

Lacock Abbey, Wiltshire Lacock is the goal of photographers from all over the world, since it was here, in 1835, that William Henry Fox Talbot made what is generally acknowledged as the world's first photographic negative. This was of the latticed oriel window in the South Gallery, where a print from that first negative, hardly bigger than a postage stamp, hangs near the window.

The Abbey is also of great architectural interest. A medieval nunnery was founded among the Lacock watermeadows in 1232 by Ela, Countess of Salisbury, who became the first abbess. Though it was dissolved by Henry VIII in 1539, fortunately the monastic buildings largely survived. In the mid eighteenth century, Lacock Abbey was in the forefront of the Gothic Revival, when the lofty Great Hall was rebuilt in Gothick style by John Ivory Talbot, Fox Talbot's great-grandfather. As it now stands, Lacock Abbey is a mixture of styles – medieval cloisters, Tudor stable court (shown in a number of Fox Talbot's early photographs), and the Gothick Hall.

A large barn outside the Abbey gates has been converted into an excellent small museum (the Fox Talbot Museum) tracing the history of photography.

Lacock village is now largely owned by the National Trust. It is a perfect, small, mainly stone-built village with a street plan in the form of a square, and with medieval timbered buildings here and there. There is a medieval packhorse bridge and a ford down a lane near the church.

3M S Chippenham, E of A350 (57 G12)

Lamb House, East Sussex A fine Georgian town house facing down a cobbled street in Rye, Lamb House is chiefly famous today for its connection with the American novelist Henry James, who lived in it from 1897 until shortly before his death in 1916. The house takes its name from James Lamb, the founder of a leading Rye family, who built it in 1723.

The small garden room where James wrote his novels was destroyed by a bomb in 1940. Mementoes of the author are kept in the Henry James Room.

West Street in the centre of Rye (43 F8)

Mompesson House, Wiltshire With its elegant stone façade looking across Choristers' Green to the soaring spire of Salisbury Cathedral, Mompesson House is the epitome of the Queen Anne town house. It was built about 1701 for Charles Mompesson, a Salisbury lawyer, and is chiefly remarkable for its superb interior

The famous silver furniture in the King's Bedroom at Knole, dating from the seventeenth century, is a rare survival.

The fine urban architecture of Mompesson House is shown here in a watercolour by George Henton (dated 1888).

moulded plasterwork, especially in the staircase hall, which dates from the 1740s, and includes flowers, fruit and even the head of King Midas with asses' ears. The comprehensive collection of over 370 English glasses assembled by Mr O. G. N. Turnbull is kept at Mompesson, and there are a number of pictures from *Stourhead*.

The brick-built back of the house is much less grand than the front, and looks out over a neat town garden.

In Salisbury Cathedral Close (40 C3)

Monks House, East Sussex A small weatherboarded house, down the lane in the centre of Rodmell village. Virginia Woolf lived here with her husband Leonard, from 1919 until her death in 1941. (Due to be opened in 1982.)

Rodmell, 3M S Lewes, on the A275 (42 G3)

Mottisfont Abbey, Hampshire Mottisfont is remarkable for the beauty of its setting, among lawns shadowed by vast cedar trees and a giant London plane, and with the Test flowing crystal-clear along the east side of the garden (since 1972 enhanced by an old-fashioned rose collection). It is also an extraordinary architectural blend of medieval, Tudor and Georgian elements. The original priory of Augustinian Canons was founded here in 1201. Dissolved at the Reformation in 1536, it was given by Henry VIII to his Lord Chamberlain, William Lord Sandys, whose main house was *The Vyne*. Instead of adapting the monk's living quarters, Sandys set about turning the priory church into a house, knocking down the north transept and choir, and keeping the nave, the base of the tower and the south transept, which he converted into a U-shaped Tudor mansion. The final adaptation came in the 1740s, when Sir Richard Mill turned it all into a Georgian country gentleman's home, reducing the projecting Tudor wings in size and building the elegant, red-brick south front, with its sash windows and pediment.

Mottisfont's elegant south front was the final stage in the transformation of the abbey into a country house.

Internally, the outstanding feature of the house is the Whistler Room, which takes its name from the wall and ceiling decoration by Rex Whistler, painted in 1938–9. The *trompe l'oeil* painting, done with amazing lightness and delicacy, gives the effect of moulded plasterwork, though it is all painted on the flat.

4M NW Romsey, W of A3057 (40 C5)

The Italian fountain in the centre of the walled garden at Nymans is guarded by four old topiary pieces.

Nymans Garden, West Sussex Nymans, conceived in 1885 by Ludwig Messel, is a garden that has something for all garden-lovers – huge red and white rhododendrons bursting into bloom in May, a heather garden with heather shoulder-high, formal topiary and carefully tended herbaceous borders, a gazebo crowned by a dovecote full of white doves. There is even a romantic ruin, in the form of the stone shell of the great house, much of which was gutted by fire in 1947 and now forms the background to the lawns and flowering shrubs. The sections of the garden form an attractive series of outdoor 'rooms', such as the Sunk Garden, which has a white Byzantine urn as its centrepiece.

4½M S Crawley, off M23/A23 (42 E2)

Old Soar Manor, Kent Originally a complete medieval manor stood on the site, but in the eighteenth century the main hall block was demolished and the present Georgian farmhouse built in its place. However, the original solar block remains; this was the lord of the manor's private quarters, and the solar, on the first floor, would have had a small viewing window through into the hall, as at *Great Chalfield*. Two small rooms lead out of the solar, a chapel in one corner and a *garderobe* or lavatory in the other. The ground floor consists of a vaulted undercroft and a *garderobe* pit that could be cleaned out.

1M E Plaxtol, off A227 (42 C5)

Owletts, Kent A handsome brick house of Charles II's time, built for a prosperous Kentish farmer, Bonham Hayes. Above the staircase well is a fine moulded plaster ceiling, dated 1684. Sir Herbert Baker, architect of the Bank of England and Lutyens' partner in New Delhi, was born and lived at Owletts until his death in 1946.

In Cobham village, off A2 (42 A5)

Petworth House and Park, West Sussex With its great main front, some 300 feet long, Petworth looks westwards across superb parkland, immortalized by Turner in a number of his finest landscapes. In many respects Petworth is as much an art gallery as it is a country house, since the ground-floor rooms are given over to paintings, from Italian primitives to the canvases of Turner himself. The present house is a virtually complete unity, as it was built almost entirely between 1688 and 1696 by Charles Seymour, the 6th Duke of Somerset, known as the 'Proud Duke' from his arrogant nature. There was a medieval manor house on the site, which belonged to the Percy family (the Earls of Northumberland) from the twelfth to the seventeenth century, but all that survives of this ancient building is the chapel and parts of the basement, embedded in the Proud Duke's mansion. Some alterations were made to the south and east fronts in the mid nineteenth century.

Apart from the Turners (all brought together

The delightful rococo decoration of the White and Gold Drawing Room at Petworth (*above*) was an eighteenth-century addition to the Proud Duke's house (*right*).

in the Turner Room), there are several portraits of the Northumberlands, including a sombre Van Dyck, some fine Dutch landscapes, and a whole room, somewhat flatteringly known as the 'Beauty Room', devoted to the ladies of Queen Anne's court. Turner's patron at Petworth, the 3rd Earl of Egremont, added the T-shaped North Gallery, which is filled with statues and busts and lined with pictures. The Proud Duke commissioned Grinling Gibbons to work at Petworth, and among Petworth's artistic triumphs are Gibbons' limewood carvings of dead game, fruit, flowers and musical instruments that riot over the wall surfaces of the Carved Room.

Petworth Park, visible to motorists over the wall as they approach Petworth along the A272, is still very much as Turner painted it, with deer browsing on the turf.

In Petworth, junction of A272/A283 (41 D11)

Philipps House, Dinton Park, Wiltshire An austere country house set in gently rolling parkland, Philipps House was built in 1814–17 for William Wyndham, whose family had lived in Dinton since the end of the seventeenth century. The architect was Jeffry Wyatt (later Sir Jeffry Wyatville), and the house has a neoclassical appearance, with an imposing south portico and symmetrical façade. It is built of Chilmark limestone, from a quarry whose stone had been used for Salisbury Cathedral 600 years previously. The main internal feature is the grand staircase, lit from above by a circular lantern window. Ducted air heating was installed as early as the 1820s.

Philipps House is let to the YWCA as a conference centre and subject to limited viewing.

9M W Salisbury, on N side of B3089 (40 C2)

Polesden Lacey, Surrey Polesden Lacey has a comfortably opulent appearance. Tucked away in glorious countryside on the fringes of the North Downs, it is a low sprawling house, yellow-stuccoed and white-painted, set above sloping lawns and looking across to the woodlands of *Ranmore Common.* A succession of houses has stood on the site since the Middle Ages; Polesden's most famous owner was the playwright Richard Brinsley Sheridan, who lived there from 1797 to 1818. The present house is basically a Regency country villa, built in the 1820s for Joseph Bonsor to designs by Thomas Cubitt. Bonsor took as much interest in the estate as in the house, planting no fewer than 20,000 trees which have grown into the fine specimens that now surround Polesden Lacey.

After various alterations and enlargements through the nineteenth century, the house was taken in hand in 1906 by the Hon. Mrs Greville. A leading society hostess in Edwardian times and later, she was also a great collector of paintings, porcelain and fine furniture. At her death in 1942, the house and its contents passed by bequest to the Trust. Her chief memorial is the sumptuously decorated drawing room, the walls glittering with mirrors and gilding, filled with the Louis XV and XVI furniture popular in the early years of this century.

The finest of the paintings are assembled in the corridor around the central courtyard; they include a delicate little Perugino, a number of sixteenth-century French court portraits, and some typical Dutch landscapes.

During the summer there is a short season of plays in the open-air theatre at the edge of a copse in the grounds.

3M NW Dorking, 1½M S Great Bookham, off the A246 (41 A12)

Quebec House, Kent Quebec House is a compact Tudor brick building, with a remarkable number of gables. It owes its fame to its connection with General Wolfe, the hero of the Heights of Abraham, who lived there for the first decade of his life (1727–38); Wolfe's statue is just up the hill, on the village green, as is that of Churchill, who lived at *Chartwell* nearby. The downstairs rooms are full of Wolfe possessions, such as his field canteen, and the dressing gown in which his body was brought back to England after he was killed at Quebec in 1759. A museum displays Wolfe relics.

At E end of Westerham, N side of A25 (42 C3)

St John's Jerusalem Garden, Kent The garden of St John's is an oasis of peace away from the main-road traffic and industry of Dartford. In the Middle Ages St John's was a 'commandery' (manor) of the Knights Hospitallers, a half-military, half-religious order. Henry VIII dissolved the Hospitallers in 1540, and their buildings were pulled down, apart from the former chapel which is open to the public. The brick house on the site was probably built about 1700 by Abraham Hill, who was one of the founders of the Royal Society and introduced cider-making from Devon to Kent; and from 1755 to 1776 Edward Hasted, the leading county historian of Kent, lived there. The moated garden has some splendid specimen trees, including the 'Napoleon willow', descended from the St Helena willows under which the Emperor was buried.

Sutton-at-Hone, 3M S Dartford, on E side of A225 (42 A4)

Polesden Lacey. The garden front on the left looks over a great lawn and is fronted by superb eighteenth-century urns.

The white garden at Sissinghurst is perhaps the most original of the outdoor 'rooms'.

Sheffield Park is magnificent in the autumnal colouring of its trees and shrubs.

Scotney Castle Garden, Kent A magnificently romantic landscape garden, Scotney is largely the creation of Edward Hussey, who from 1837 to 1843 built himself a new house (not open) designed by Anthony Salvin on top of the hill and turned old Scotney Castle into a picturesque centrepiece. The round stone tower of the medieval castle, reflected in the moat and backed by plantings of rhododendrons, azaleas and specimen trees, is a prospect that offers something new from all angles, and in all weathers and seasons. Apart from the tower, built about 1380, old Scotney is mainly seventeenth-century in date.

$1\frac{1}{2}$M S Lamberhurst, on the A21 (42 D/E5/6)

Sheffield Park Garden, East Sussex These famous gardens, covering some 100 acres and laid out round a series of lakes, were originally designed about 1775 by 'Capability' Brown for John Baker Holroyd, the 1st Earl of Sheffield. The five lakes stretch in the form of an inverted T below Holroyd's Gothic Revival house designed by James Wyatt in 1779 (not NT and not open). The gardens are a tree-lover's delight; many of the superb conifers were planted by the 3rd Earl towards the end of the nineteenth century, and have now reached full maturity, but the present appearance of the garden owes much to Arthur G. Soames, who acquired it in 1909.

The best time to see the gardens is in late October, when the leaves, especially those of the tupelo trees, are in their full autumn glory, but they are well worth a visit in late spring, when the rhododendrons and azaleas are in bloom.

5M NW Uckfield, E side of A275 (42 F3)

Sissinghurst Castle Garden, Kent All that survives of Sissinghurst Castle, a moated Tudor manor house built about 1550 by Sir John Baker, is a long low gatehouse, a tall red-brick tower and two isolated cottages beyond. These were the fragments round which Victoria Sackville-West and her husband Harold Nicolson built their famous garden, using the buildings and various brick walls to create a series of open-air 'rooms' – miniature gardens, each with a different theme, leading into one another.

When they came to Sissinghurst in 1930, the task must have seemed almost impossible; it took three years before the rubbish of generations of neglect had been cleared and they could embark on serious planting. Apart from individual beauties like the cottage garden where flowers of all sorts grow in jumbled profusion, the medieval-looking herb garden, and the white garden entirely planted with white or grey plants, Sissinghurst has an incomparably beautiful setting, in one of the lushest corners of Kent.

The tower rooms can be visited. The first floor was Victoria Sackville-West's writing room, and is as she left it; the second floor is a small museum devoted to the history of Sissinghurst; and the third floor houses an exhibition illustrating the work of the National Trust. The long library in the entrance block can also be seen.

2M NE Cranbrook, off the A262 (43 D7)

Smallhythe Place, Kent This timber-framed yeoman's house, built in the sixteenth century, was the home of the actress Ellen Terry from 1899 until her death in 1928, and now houses a theatrical museum illustrating her career as well as her interest in the theatre and its history. In the Middle Ages Smallhythe was the port of Tenterden for shipping coming up the Rother, and the house was built for the harbour-master; the rectangular pond below was once the repair dock.

Born in Coventry in 1847, Ellen Terry first appeared on the stage in 1856. Her last appearance was in 1926, only two years before her death. The exhibits at Smallhythe include costumes, many of them from her Shakespearean roles; portraits; and mementoes of some of the greatest names in acting.

2M S Tenterden, on the B2082 (43 E7)

Sprivers Garden, Kent A small garden, whose shrubs, herbaceous borders and spring and

The drawing room at Standen has a superb Morris carpet and original electric light brackets designed by Webb.

summer bedding form the background to a display of garden ornaments.

Horsmonden, 3M N Lamberhurst, on B2162 (42 D6)

Standen, West Sussex Standen was built in 1892–4 for James Beale, a prosperous solicitor, and his wife Margaret, by Philip Webb the friend and colleague of William Morris, and is the only one of Webb's major houses to remain intact. The interior was decorated with Morris and Co. textiles and wallpapers, and many of them survive. It stands on a terrace, half way down a steep hill with wide views southwards across Weir Wood Reservoir to the high ground of Ashdown Forest beyond.

Like Morris, Webb set great store by good materials and craftsmanship; and both can be found in abundance at Standen. The main front is on the garden side, facing the view, and is remarkable for its row of five weather-boarded gables. Webb cleverly linked the new house to the old farmyard at the back of the site; the stone he used comes from a quarry that now forms part of the garden.

1½M S East Grinstead (signposted from B2110) (42 D3)

Stoneacre, Kent A fine Kentish yeoman's house of about 1480, rescued from dereliction by Aymer Vallance in 1920 and restored and enlarged by the addition of two timber-framed houses from Faversham and Chiddingstone. Its most striking features are a twelve-light oriel window giving on to the great hall, an oak screen across the hall, and a rare king-post, made of four engaged shafts, supporting the roof.

Otham, 3M SE Maidstone, 1M N of A274 (43 C7)

Stourhead, Wiltshire The grounds of Stourhead are an idealized Italian landscape, like one of those painted by Claude, set down in the Wiltshire countryside. The dream was made reality by Henry Hoare II (a member of the famous banking family) from 1741, when he came to settle at Stourhead, until his death in 1785. All the elements of the dream landscape are there: the broad lake, reflecting the trees and shrubs that come down to the water's edge; the domed temples; the stone bridge that forms an attractive foreground to the picture; the grotto, complete with river god and nymph, built over the spring where the Stour rises.

The gardens are the part of Stourhead that most people visit, but it is well worth visiting the house as well; it lies on high ground above the lake, invisible both from the lakeside paths and from Stourton village. The Stourton estate was bought by Henry Hoare II's father, Henry Hoare I, in 1717. He commissioned Colen Campbell to build him a new villa in the Palladian style (the central block of Stourhead) – a severely classical stone building, with a grand porticoed entrance front on the east side. Henry II was more interested in the grounds than the house, and his excursions into architecture were limited to the temples and other buildings designed by Henry Flitcroft which are set round the lake. The main additions were made by Sir Richard Colt Hoare, 2nd Baronet, Henry II's grandson, in the 1790s; an antiquarian, scholar and amateur artist, he built the two projecting wings for his books and his picture collection. The library is a splendid room, with a barrel-vaulted ceiling. Its furniture, including a fine flight of library steps, was made by Thomas Chippendale the Younger in the early 1800s.

The little village of Stourton, down by the lake, enjoys an idyllic setting. The medieval church has several monuments to the Stourton family and the Hoares.

3M NW Mere (A303), off B3092 (39 C11)

An early nineteenth-century watercolour of Stourhead showing the lake, the Pantheon and the Temple of Apollo (*left*).

Tudor Yeoman's House, Kent A fourteenth-century hall house, bought and restored by Sir Herbert Baker (*see also Owletts*). The hall has a magnificent main beam and king-post. (Seen by appointment only.)

Sole Street, 1M SW Cobham, on B2009 (42 A5)

Uppark, West Sussex There can be few houses that owe their existence to a mechanical device, but Uppark is one of them. As its name suggests (it was originally split into Up Park), it stands very high up, on the summit of the South Downs; and it was not until Uppark's owner, Sir Edward Ford, invented a satisfactory water pump in about 1650 that it became possible to build a large house on the site. Uppark is a big square red-brick house, looking like a giant doll's house (suitably enough, as one of its prize exhibits is an eighteenth-century doll's house). It was built in the late 1680s for Sir Edward Ford's grandson, Lord Grey of Werke, later Lord Tankerville, a shady character who was one of the instigators of the Duke of Monmouth's rebellion of 1685, but got off by turning King's Evidence. The architect was William Talman, who gave his client a modern home in the latest Dutch style.

The rich interior of the house is mainly the work of Sir Matthew Fetherstonhaugh, who bought Uppark in 1747. Uppark's centrepiece is the magnificent saloon, decorated in greyish-white and gold and hung with large pictures such as the portraits of George III and Queen Charlotte by Nathaniel Dance. Sir Matthew left Uppark to his son Sir Harry, a rakish friend of the Prince Regent, with whom he drank, raced and gambled. When he was seventy, Sir Harry turned respectable by marrying Mary Ann, his head dairymaid; her tiled dairy along the terrace, probably designed for Sir Harry by Humphry Repton, is one of the minor delights of Uppark.

The open ground to the south has been left unplanted, and on a clear day there is a view across rolling farmland to the Solent and as far as the Isle of Wight.

1½M S of South Harting, 5M SE Petersfield, on B2146 (41 D9)

The Vyne, Hampshire The name of The Vyne harks back to medieval wine-producing days, if not earlier, as there may even have been a Roman villa called *Vindomis* (House of Wine) on the site. It lies within half a mile of the Roman roads to Winchester and Chichester, in a hollow beside a stream, now dammed and enlarged into a lake. The present house dates almost entirely from 1500–20. A long low comfortable building, made of glowing red brickwork laid in a diaper pattern, it typifies early Tudor domestic luxury.

The builder was William Lord Sandys, Lord Chamberlain to Henry VIII. The ground plan is in the form of a shallow U, with projecting wings on the south or entrance front; visitors now enter the house via a gallery on the west side, which takes them through a long series of interconnected rooms to Sandys' sumptuous private chapel, still with its original stained glass made about 1520. After Sandys acquired *Mottisfont Abbey* at the Dissolution in 1536, he seems to have lost interest in The Vyne, and about 1650 his descendants sold it and moved to Mottisfont.

The Vyne's most unexpected external feature – the classical portico on the north front – was added by the next owner during the 1650s. This was Chaloner Chute, Speaker of the House of Commons, who died in 1659; the portico is reputedly the oldest such embellishment on any

Uppark stands four-square on the crest of a steep hill looking southwards across the Sussex Downs to the Solent and the Isle of Wight.

English country house, and was probably designed by John Webb, pupil of Inigo Jones. The only other major alterations to the house were carried out by Chaloner's descendant John Chute about 1770. His main additions were the ingenious and graceful flight of stairs in the front hall, and the Tomb Chamber, with a splendid monument to Speaker Chute, opening off the chapel.

The Oak Gallery, which takes up the whole of the first floor of the west wing, has fine linenfold panelling covering the walls from floor to ceiling. Untouched since Tudor times, the panels are carved with the crests and devices of Lord Sandys and his contemporaries, together with purely imaginative decoration. Concerts are given in the gallery from time to time.

Before leaving The Vyne, it is well worth walking to the far side of the lake for the view of the house across the water.

4M N Basingstoke, just outside Sherborne St John, off A340 (41 A8)

Wakehurst Place Garden, West Sussex Conceived on an impressive scale, this garden is an offshoot of the Royal Botanic Gardens at Kew. The superb collection of trees and shrubs was largely built up during the first decades of this century by Gerald W. E. Loder, whose name lives on in the *loderi* group of rhododendrons. The garden is laid out in the form of a large horseshoe, and as there are several miles of pathway among the rocky outcrops and skirting the lake, it can take several hours to do justice to Wakehurst. Many of the trees are exotics, from places as far afield as Taiwan and Tibet; fortunately for the non-expert, they are all clearly labelled.

1½M NW Ardingly, on B2028 (42 E2)

Winkworth Arboretum, in one of the most beautiful parts of Surrey, was planted mainly for autumn colour. Bluebells and daffodils carpet the ground in spring.

West Green House, Hampshire A modest red-brick house, probably built about 1700, it was remodelled about 1750 by General Henry Hawley, nicknamed 'Hangman' Hawley because of his brutal treatment of the Scots after the Battle of Culloden in 1745. Unusually for a house of this size, a large panelled room (the saloon) takes up two storeys on the west front, filling almost a quarter of the entire house. There is a central staircase well, which is top-lit; the present stone staircase replaces the original oak one.

The attractive garden has been largely replanted. West Green has been let to a tenant who has introduced wildfowl and rare breeds of sheep and cattle.

1M W Hartley Wintney, off A30 (85 H8)

Westwood Manor, Wiltshire A small manor house in a fascinating amalgam of building styles. Now an L-shaped house, clearly showing the divisions of different phases of building, Westwood was originally U-shaped in plan, with a second wing across the courtyard corresponding to the existing west range. The great hall was probably built by Thomas Culverhouse, a prosperous Wiltshire farmer, about 1490. Some time early in the sixteenth century it was enlarged by Thomas Horton, one of the region's leading clothiers. It reached more or less its present appearance at the hands of John Farewell, early in the seventeenth century. He pulled down parts of the building, possibly the east wing, and decorated many of the rooms with fine moulded plasterwork and wooden panelling.

The topiary 'cottage' to the east of the house marks the end of the demolished east wing.

1½M SW Bradford-on-Avon, off Frome Road (B3109), beside Westwood Church (57 H11)

Winkworth Arboretum, Surrey Though it is small as arboreta go, Winkworth (started by Dr Wilfrid Fox in 1938) contains an amazing variety of trees and shrubs in a limited space. It is helped by its magnificent site, on a steep hillside falling away to two lakes in the valley, giving constantly changing vistas of landscape and foliage.

There are two useful leaflets, one for spring and one for autumn, for those exploring the arboretum.

3M S Godalming, on B2130 (41 B11)

Wool House, Kent A fifteenth-century timbered house, with very close-set vertical timbering. The stream that splashes down outside may well have been used for cleaning the wool that gave the house its name. Inside, the rooms (seen by appointment only) are long, low and heavily beamed.

Wells Street, Loose, 3M S Maidstone off A229 (42 C6)

Castles, Abbeys & other Buildings

Bodiam Castle, East Sussex Everyone's idea of the perfect medieval castle, Bodiam rises strong and sheer from a wide moat. It was built by Sir Edward Dalyngrygge in 1385, and formed part of the south coast defences against the French, guarding an important crossing of the River Rother, which in the Middle Ages was navigable right up to Bodiam. The castle was never attacked, and so the great gatehouse, round corner towers and curtain wall are still much as they would have been in Dalyngrygge's time. Inside, it is still possible to trace the medieval domestic arrangements, as a good deal of the inner walling still survives. The buildings – among them the great hall, ladies' bower, chapel and kitchen – were grouped round all four sides of a central courtyard; the castle's well can be seen in the south-west tower.

The castle was restored by Lord Curzon, who bought it in 1917 and left it to the Trust when he died nine years later.

A small museum in the curator's cottage contains relics found during the restoration, and also a fine model of the castle as it was in its prime.

3M S Hawkhurst, 1M E of A229 (42 F6)

Bramber Castle, West Sussex A tall stump of masonry is all that is left of what was one of the most powerful Norman castles in the south of England. It was built by William de Braose, who came over with the Conqueror, and it was probably complete by about 1090; it consisted of an outer and an inner bailey, each with a gatehouse or barbican, leading to the keep, of which the surviving stonework formed a part. The present parish church was originally the castle's chapel.

After surviving the Middle Ages largely unscathed, the Royalist castle was destroyed during the Civil War by the Parliamentarians.

In Bramber village, on A283 (42 G1)

Chiddingstone, Kent A perfectly preserved medieval and Tudor village. The oldest documentation of the houses goes back to 1453 (a deed of that year refers to what is now the village shop and post office); other houses carry the dates 1638 and 1645, though they are a good deal older.

The 'Chiding Stone', from which the village is said to get its name, lies behind the houses opposite the church. What kind of 'chiding' took place there has never been specified.

4M E Edenbridge, 1M S of B2027 (42 D4)

Eashing Bridges, Surrey The River Wey splits into two at Eashing, and so there are in effect two bridges, one across each arm of the river. The stonework of these picturesque medieval (probably thirteenth-century) bridges is built of local Bargate stone.

1½M W Godalming, off A3 (41 B10/11)

Joiners' Hall, Wiltshire A magnificent twin-gabled façade, dating from about 1550. Between the ground and first floors the ornate external beam is carved with dragon-like figures and roses, and the first-floor oriel windows are supported by carved corbels. (Let as an antique shop and not open.)

E end of St Ann's Street, Salisbury (40 C3)

Leith Hill Tower, Surrey A battlemented folly tower, built by Richard Hull in 1766, according to an inscription on it. Its top is 1,029 feet above sea-level. From the hilltop plateau there are magnificent views to the South and North Downs. The hill was the site of a battle in 851 between Danes and Saxons.

4M SW Dorking, reached from A25, A24 or A29 (41 B12)

Newtown, Isle of Wight Despite its name, Newtown is an ancient place, going back to the time of King Egbert in the ninth century. The borough got its present name in 1256, when Aymer de Valance, Bishop of Winchester elect, founded a 'new town' there. The estuary of the Newtown River provides an excellent harbour, and Newtown was prosperous throughout the Middle Ages, in spite of periodic raids by the French. But by Queen Elizabeth's time it was in decline.

Newtown's past glories are recalled by the Town Hall, built in 1699, with Gothic Revival windows inserted in the eighteenth century. After 1832 this neat little building was first a house, then a school, and finally became derelict. In 1933 it was restored by an anonymous band of conservationists, who called themselves 'Ferguson's Gang' (*see Shalford Mill*), and presented to the Trust; it now houses documents relating to Newtown's history, has a royal coat-of-arms (originally at Ryde), and has been refurnished.

The Trust owns a good deal of other property in Newtown, including the eighteenth-century building known as Noah's Ark. It has also acquired fourteen miles of bank on either side of the river, and four miles of foreshore along the Solent. The Isle of Wight Natural History and Archaeological Society runs a 300-acre nature reserve round Newtown, much of it on National Trust land.

Between Newport and Yarmouth, 1M N of A3054 (40 G5/6)

Bodiam Castle never had to withstand a serious siege and probably could not have done so as its defences are unimpressive for its time.

With its half-timbered houses, Chiddingstone is one of the most attractive villages in Kent. It was built at a time when the Wealden iron industry was thriving.

The Pepperbox may have been a viewpoint to enable ladies to follow the hunt.

The Pepperbox, Wiltshire Also called Eyre's Folly, an octagonal tower of 1606, of unknown purpose, standing on Brickworth Down. Fine viewpoint.

5M SE Salisbury, N of A36 (40 D4)

Avebury is perhaps the most important early Bronze Age monument in Europe. Dating from about 2000 BC, it is roughly contemporary with parts of Stonehenge.

Sandham Memorial Chapel, Hampshire A small red-brick chapel, built in 1923–6, and filled with Stanley Spencer's visionary paintings inspired by his experiences in World War I. The greatest of them is the *Resurrection of the Soldiers*, which covers the entire east wall; there are eighteen smaller paintings on the north and south walls, based on Spencer's war service in Macedonia. The chapel is named after Lieutenant H. W. Sandham, who died in 1919 from an illness contracted in Macedonia. The paintings took Spencer nine years to complete, from 1923–32.

In Burghclere village, 4M S Newbury, off A34 (84 H5/6)

Witley Common Information Centre, Surrey Witley Common is a small area of heathland, with a wide variety of animal and plant life. It centres on its Countryside Interpretation Centre, a modern chalet-like building. The Centre sets out the whole story of the Common on display panels, which describe, for example, the early enclosures, the soil types and the plants. There is also an audio-visual display programme. The Centre has a choice of leaflets for visitors wanting to explore the Common, with different walks covering every aspect of wildlife and countryside management.

1M SW Milford, between A3 and A286 (41 B10)

Archaeological & Industrial Sites

Avebury, Wiltshire The largest prehistoric stone circle in Europe, Avebury lacks the stark grandeur of Stonehenge, as it has been domesticated by the houses of Avebury village which cluster round it. Yet in some ways it is even more impressive than Stonehenge, because of its area (nearly thirty acres), the immense height of its outer bank and ditch, the number and size of its standing stones, and the complexity of its layout. It originally consisted of an outer circle with four main entrances, and two smaller inner circles; most of the surviving stones are on the west side of the circle, and especially in the south-west quadrant. Avebury was probably constructed about 2000 BC. One and a half miles to the north-west is the early Neolithic causewayed camp of Windmill Hill.

Near Marlborough, 1M N of A4, on A361 (84 G2)

Bembridge Windmill, Isle of Wight This fine example of an eighteenth-century tower mill is the last remaining windmill on the Isle of Wight. Built about 1700, it is of the type known as a 'cap' mill – that is, its stone tower is surmounted by a revolving wooden cap carrying the wind shaft, driving wheels and four 'sweeps' or sails. The windmill last functioned

above **For some two hundred years Bembridge windmill ground flour and meal for the village and surrounding countryside.**

Spencer's murals in Sandham Memorial Chapel illustrate the life of the British soldier, here shown washing and moving kit-bags.

The meadows at Runnymede have been enshrined in British history as the site of the signing of Magna Carta.

in 1913; after falling derelict, it was restored first in the 1930s, and then again about thirty years later, after being used as a look-out tower in World War II. It is now fully restored, and visitors can follow the whole process of milling from grain to flour, and admire the massive craftsmanship of the wooden shafts, cogwheels and other working parts.

½M S Bembridge (41 G8)

Cissbury Ring, West Sussex A magnificent Iron Age hill-fort, surrounded by a ditch and rampart, 600 feet above sea-level and covering about eighty acres. Hollows at the western end of the fort mark the positions of Neolithic flint mines, dug about 2000 BC.

Near Worthing, 1½M E Findon, off A24 (41 E12)

Coldrum Long Barrow, Kent Known also as Coldrum Stones, this Neolithic burial chamber consists of a chalk mound topped by a U-shaped group of standing stones and surrounded by a ditch. It stands beside the Pilgrims' Way, and was presumably the tomb of a local king or chieftain. There is a display cabinet with bones from Coldrum in Trottiscliffe church.

1M W Trottiscliffe, off A227 (42 B5)

Curbridge, Hampshire There are sites of Roman brick and tile kilns and other Roman buildings on the Curbridge Estate, beside a beautiful stretch of the Hamble.

On River Hamble, 1M S Botley via A3051 (40 E6)

Figsbury Ring, Wiltshire An impressive Iron Age hill-fort, covering about fifteen acres, with an outer ditch and rampart and a smaller inner ditch. There were probably gatehouses at the entrances to the fort.

4M NE Salisbury, just N of A30 (40 C3)

Highdown Hill, West Sussex A prehistoric site which combines an Iron Age hill-fort with a Bronze Age settlement. The Saxons later used it as a burial ground, and coins and spearheads have been found on the site.

Near Worthing, 1M N Ferring, S of A27 (41 F12)

Oldbury Hill, Kent A heavily wooded site, with a ditch and ramparts marking an Iron Age fort of about 100 BC.

Near Ightham, on N side of A25 (42 B/C4/5)

River Wey and Godalming Navigations, Surrey Twenty miles of waterway owned by the Trust, running from Godalming Wharf to the Thames at Weybridge. The Wey Navigation (15½ miles from Guildford to Weybridge) was made navigable for barge traffic in the reign of Charles II, while the remaining 4½ miles from Guildford upstream to Godalming was opened in 1760. In the early nineteenth century there were further canal links through to the south coast, but the coming of the railways killed this traffic. In the heyday of the Navigations timber and agricultural produce were taken by barge down to London, while corn and general merchandise was brought up to Guildford and Godalming. During the late nineteenth and twentieth centuries traffic dwindled, but with the rise in popularity of pleasure boating the Wey is crowded once again.

Good viewpoints are at Tilthams Bridge, Peasmarsh, half way between Guildford and Godalming; Guildford town bridges; and Pyrford Lock, upstream from Byfleet and not far from Wisley.

(41 B11, A11. 85 H11, G11)

Royal Military Canal, Kent The Royal Military Canal, which runs along the inner edge of Romney Marsh, linking the Rother near Rye with the sea at Hythe, was dug in 1804–07 as part of the defence system against invasion by Napoleon's forces. Now it is a tranquil waterway, lined in places by avenues of trees, and a delightful place for a peaceful stroll on a fine day.

3½M of canal, from Appledore (B2080) to Warehorne (43 E8)

Runnymede, Surrey It was in the Runnymede watermeadows – still surprisingly rural in spite of their nearness to London – that King John signed Magna Carta on 15 June 1215. The boundaries are marked by two pairs of pavilions, designed by Sir Edwin Lutyens, on either side of the road – tall-roofed bungalows at the upstream end, and small octagonal kiosks at the Egham end. On the south side of the A308 is a memorial to President Kennedy, erected in 1965.

On S side of Thames above Egham, off the A308 (85 G10/11)

Shalford Mill, Surrey A fine eighteenth-century water-mill on the Tillingbourne, a tributary of the Wey. Tile-hung and with a massive timber frame, it was still grinding corn until 1914. After World War I it fell into disrepair, and in 1932 it was given by its owner to the anonymous group of conservationists who called themselves 'Ferguson's Gang' (*see also Newtown, Isle of Wight*). They restored it and handed it over to the Trust. They held their secret meetings in the mill. The identity of 'Sister Agatha', the 'Bloody Bishop' and other members of the Gang, including Ferguson himself, has never been disclosed.

The mill still has much of the working machinery in place; one of the three sets of grinding-stones is complete. (Part open on application.)

1½M S Guildford, east side of A281 (41 A11)

Stonehenge Down, Wiltshire The monument is protected by the DOE, though Trust members have free entry to it; however, the Trust owns over 1,400 acres of farmland in the area, including some of the many Bronze Age barrows (burial mounds) that stand up above the fields.

2M W Amesbury, on A303 (40 B3)

Waggoners' Wells, Hampshire A string of three small lakes linked by sluices, they may have been the hammer ponds for an iron foundry known in the sixteenth century as Wakeners' Wells. Set in the valley below the 570-acre Ludshott Common (also National Trust), they are surrounded by beech trees, which make a magnificent sight in the autumn. The wishing well near by has links with Tennyson. The lakes are the starting-point for two nature trails.

1½M W Hindhead, S of B3002 (41 C10)

Winchester City Mill, Hampshire This attractive water-mill, brick below and tile-hung above, was built in 1743, on a site occupied by a succession of mills since Saxon times, and was working until 1928. It is powered by the fast-flowing Itchen, and the undershot water-wheels are still in place. Upstairs there are displays of milling and millwrighting. (Leased to the Youth Hostels Association.)

At foot of Winchester High Street (40 C6)

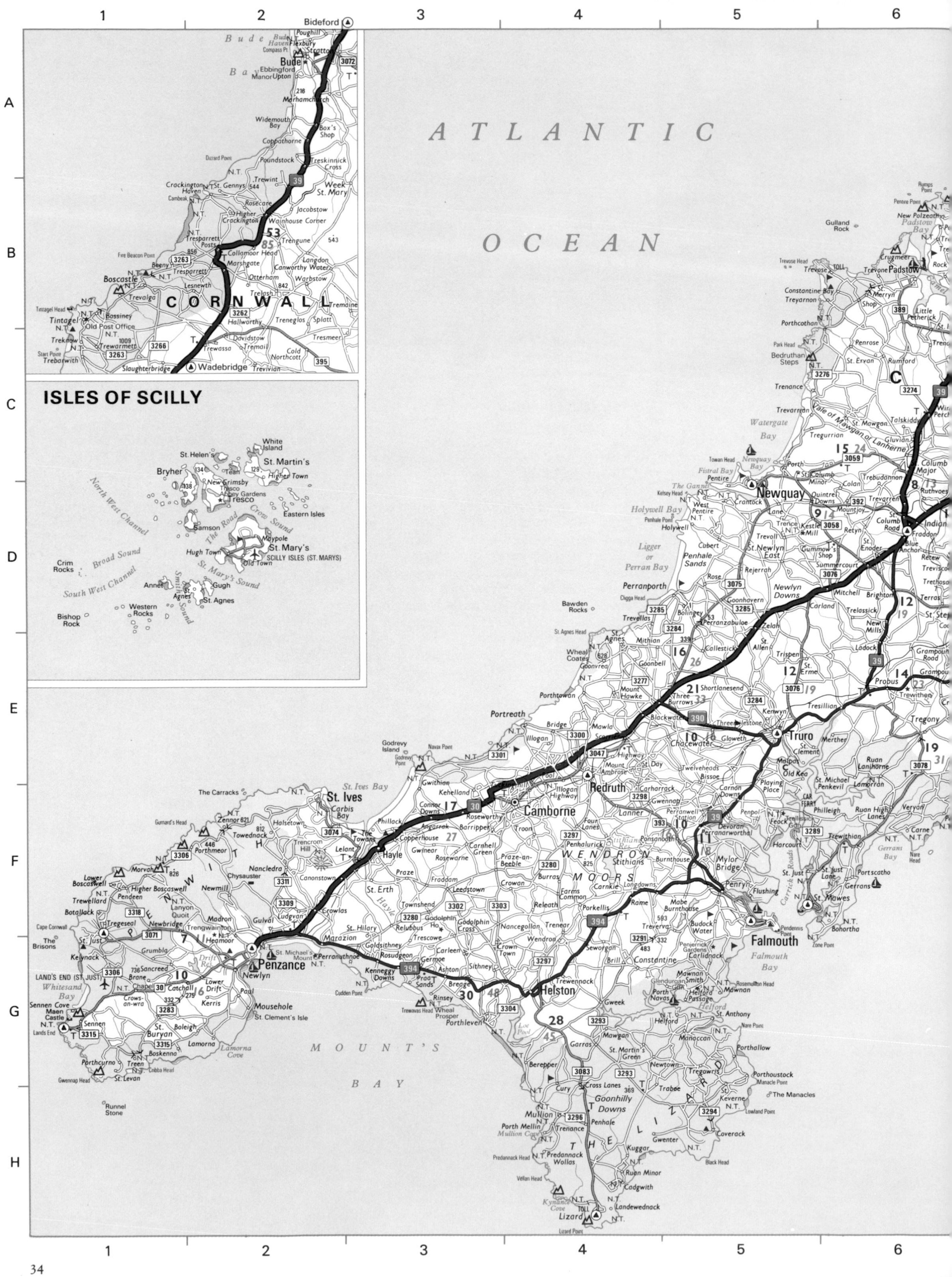
ATLANTIC
OCEAN
CORNWALL
ISLES OF SCILLY
MOUNT'S
BAY
THE LIZARD
WENDRON MOORS
Bideford
Bude
Bude Bay
Poughill
Flexbury
Stratton
Ebbingford Manor
Upton
Marhamchurch
Widemouth Bay
Box's Shop
Coppathorne
Poundstock
Treskinnick Cross
Dizzard Point
Trewint
Crackington Haven
St. Gennys
Week St. Mary
Cambeak
Rosecare
Jacobstow
Higher Crackington
Wainhouse Corner
Tresparrett Posts
Trengune
Collamoor Head
Fire Beacon Point
Beeny
Tresparrett
Marshgate
Langdon
Canworthy Water
Boscastle
Otterham
Warbstow
Lesnewth
Trevalga
Trelash
Tremaine
Tintagel Head
Tintagel
Bossiney
Old Post Office
Hallworthy
Treneglos
Splatt
Treknow
Trewarmett
Davidstow
Tresmeer
Start Point
Trebarwith
Trewassa
Tremail
Cold Northcott
Slaughterbridge
Wadebridge
Trevivian
White Island
St. Helen's
St. Martin's
Higher Town
Bryher
Tean
New Grimsby
Tresco
Abbey Gardens
North West Channel
Crow Sound
Eastern Isles
Samson
The Road
Maypole
St. Mary's
Hugh Town
Old Town
SCILLY ISLES (ST. MARYS)
Crim Rocks
Broad Sound
South West Channel
Annet
Gugh
St. Agnes
St. Mary's Sound
Smith Sound
Western Rocks
Bishop Rock
Rumps Point
Pentire Point
New Polzeath
Padstow Bay
Gulland Rock
Trevose Head
Trevose
Trevone
Padstow
Crugmeer
Constantine Bay
St. Merryn
Treyarnon
Porthcothan
Little Petherick
Park Head
Bedruthan Steps
Penrose
St. Ervan
Rumford
Trenance
Trevarrian
Vale of Mawgan or Lanherne
St. Mawgan
Talskiddy
Watergate Bay
Tregurrian
Gluvian
Towan Head
Newquay Bay
Fistral Bay
Pentire
Porth
St. Columb Minor
St. Columb Major
Trebudannon
The Gannel
Kelsey Head
Crantock
Newquay
Quintrell Downs
Colan
Trevarren
Ruthvoes
Holywell Bay
Penhale Point
Holywell
West Pentire
Lane
Trencreek
Kestle Mill
Mountjoy
Retyn
St. Columb Road
Fraddon
Indian Queens
Blue Anchor
Cubert
Trevoll
St. Newlyn East
Gummow's Shop
St. Enoder
Ligger or Perran Bay
Penhale Sands
Rejerrah
Summercourt
Retew
Perranporth
Droskyn Point
Rose
Goonhavern
Newlyn Downs
Mitchell
Brighton
Bawden Rocks
Trevellas
Bolingey
Perranzabuloe
Carland
Trelassick
St. Agnes Head
St. Agnes
Mithian
Zelah
New Mills
Wheal Coates
Goonvrea
Callestick
St. Allen
Ladock
Goonbell
Trispen
St. Erme
Grampound Road
Mount Hawke
Shortlanesend
Probus
Grampound
Porthtowan
Three Burrows
Kenwyn
Trewithen
Portreath
Bridge
Mawla
Blackwater
Threemilestone
Tresillian
Tregony
Illogan
Scorrier
Chacewater
Gloweth
Truro
Merther
Godrevy Island
Godrevy Point
Navax Point
Highway
St. Day
St. Clement
Mount Ambrose
Twelveheads
Malpas
Ruan Lanihorne
Gwithian
Redruth
Bissoe
Old Kea
St. Ives Bay
The Carracks
St. Ives
Carbis Bay
Kehelland
Illogan Highway
Carharrack
Carnon Downs
Playing Place
St. Michael Penkevil
Lamorran
Connor Downs
Camborne
Roseworthy
Gwennap
Lanner
Perranwell Station
Feock
Trelissick Gdn
Car Ferry
Philleigh
Ruan High Lanes
Veryan
Gurnard's Head
Zennor
Halsetown
Barripper
Troon
Four Lanes
Ponsanooth
Devoran
Perranarworthal
Penpol
Towednack
Phillack
Copperhouse
Angarrack
Carnhell Green
Trencrom Hill
The Towans
Lelant
Hayle
Gwinear
Rosewarne
Praze-an-Beeble
Stithians Res.
Stithians
Burnthouse
Mylor Bridge
Harcourt
Trewithian
Carne
Gerrans Bay
Nare Point
Nare Head
Porthmeor
Morvah
Nancledra
Praze
Fraddam
Leedstown
Crowan
Burras
Farms Common
Carnkie
Longdowns
Penryn
Flushing
Carrick Roads
St. Just Lane
Portscatho
Gerrans
Lower Boscaswell
Higher Boscaswell
Chysauster
Canonstown
St. Erth
Pendeen
Newmill
Trewellard
Lanyon Quoit
Townshend
Relubbus
Godolphin
Releath
Rame
Mabe Burnthouse
St. Mawes
Botallack
Tregeseal
Madron
Gulval
Ludgvan
Crowlas
Godolphin Cross
Nancegollan
Treneor
Treverva
Budock Water
Falmouth
Pendennis Point
Bohortha
Cape Cornwall
Trengwainton
Newbridge
Heamoor
Marazion
St. Hilary
Trescowe
Carleen
Wendron
Penjerrick Gardens
Zone Point
The Brisons
St. Just
Grumbla
Drift Res.
Penzance
St. Michael's Mount
Perranuthnoe
Goldsithney
Rosudgeon
Germoe
Crown Town
Sithney
Seworgan
Constantine
Carlidnack
Falmouth Bay
Kelynack
Sancreed
Brane
Newlyn
Kenneggy Downs
Ashton
Praa Sands
Breage
Trewennack
Helston
Brill
Glendurgan Gdn
Mawnan Smith
Mawnan
Rosemullion Head
LAND'S END (ST. JUST)
Whitesand Bay
Chapel
Crows-an-wra
Catchall
Lower Drift
Kerris
Paul
Cudden Point
Trewavas Head
Rinsey
Wheal Prosper
Porthleven
Loe Pool
Gweek
Porth Navas
Helford Passage
Helford
St. Anthony
Sennen Cove
Maen Castle
Mousehole
St. Clement's Isle
Lands End
Sennen
St. Buryan
Boleigh
Lamorna
Lamorna Cove
Mawgan
Garras
St. Martin's Green
Manaccan
Porthallow
Porthcurno
Treen
Boskenna
Gwennap Head
St. Levan
Cribba Head
Berepper
Cury
Cross Lanes
Newtown
Tregowris
Trabae
Porthoustock
Manacle Point
The Manacles
St. Keverne
Runnel Stone
Goonhilly Downs
Mullion
Mullion Cove
Porth Mellin
Trenance
Penhale
Lowland Point
Coverack
Predannack Head
Predannack Wollas
Kuggar
Gwenter
Black Head
Vellan Head
Ruan Minor
Cadgwith
Kynance Cove
Landewednack
Lizard
Lizard Point

7 8 9 10 11 12

Bideford · Holsworthy · Adjoining page 36 · Okehampton

D E V O N · C O R N W A L L · A B C D E F G H · Newton Abbot · Adjoining page 37 · Exeter · Kingsbridge

7 8 9 10 11 12

Bridgwater
Minehead
Adjoining page 38
Taunton
Taunton
Taunton
Honit
Wadebridge
BRISTOL CHANNEL
EXMOOR
SOMERSET
DEVON
BARNSTAPLE OR BIDEFORD BAY
Ilfracombe
Combe Martin
Lynton
Lynmouth
Porlock
Dulverton
Bampton
Tiverton
Barnstaple
Bideford
Northam
Appledore
Braunton
South Molton
Great Torrington
Chulmleigh
Crediton
Hatherleigh
Holsworthy
Bude
Kilkhampton
Hartland
Clovelly
Winkleigh
North Tawton
Morchard Bishop
Woolacombe

Adjoining page 38
Adjoining page 35
Exmouth
Bodmin
St. Austell
ENGLISH CHANNEL
DARTMOOR
CORNWALL
BODMIN MOOR
SOUTH HAMS
PLYMOUTH
Plymstock
Tavistock
Launceston
Liskeard
Saltash
Torpoint
Newton Abbot
Teignmouth
Dawlish
Torquay
Torbay
Paignton
Brixham
Dartmouth
Totnes
Kingsbridge
Salcombe
Ashburton
Buckfastleigh
Ivybridge
Moretonhampstead
Bovey Tracey
Princetown
Polperro
Start Bay
Bigbury Bay
Whitsand Bay
Eddystone Rocks

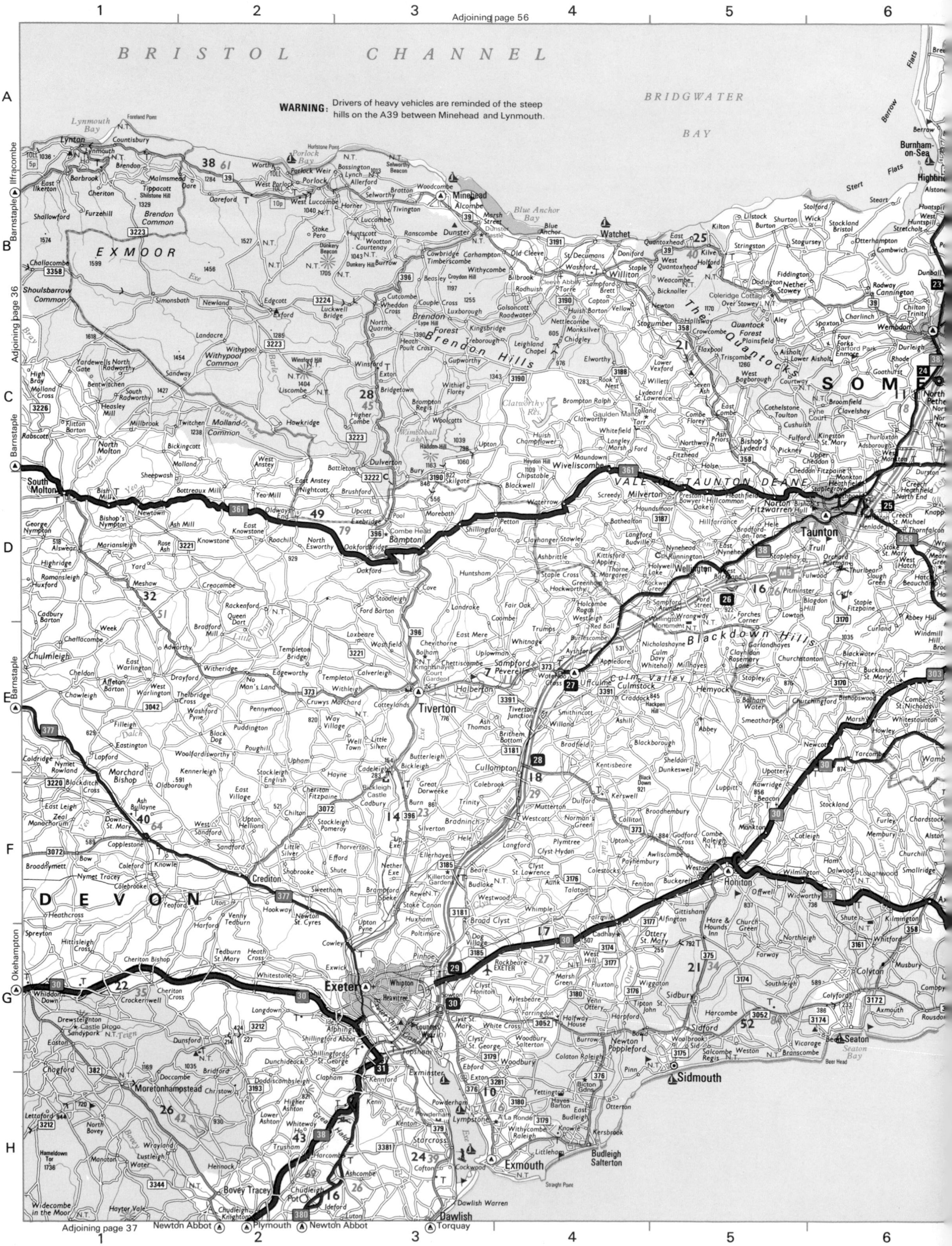

Adjoining page 56
Adjoining page 36
Adjoining page 37
BRISTOL CHANNEL
BRIDGWATER BAY
WARNING: Drivers of heavy vehicles are reminded of the steep hills on the A39 between Minehead and Lynmouth.
EXMOOR
Brendon Hills
The Quantocks
VALE OF TAUNTON DEANE
Blackdown Hills
Culm Valley
DEVON
SOMERSET
Lynton
Lynmouth
Porlock
Minehead
Dunster
Watchet
Williton
Burnham-on-Sea
Bridgwater
Barnstaple
Ilfracombe
South Molton
Dulverton
Bampton
Wiveliscombe
Taunton
Wellington
Tiverton
Cullompton
Crediton
Exeter
Honiton
Ottery St. Mary
Sidmouth
Budleigh Salterton
Exmouth
Dawlish
Teignmouth
Moretonhampstead
Chudleigh
Bovey Tracey
Okehampton
Newton Abbot
Plymouth
Torquay
Seaton
Colyton
Axminster

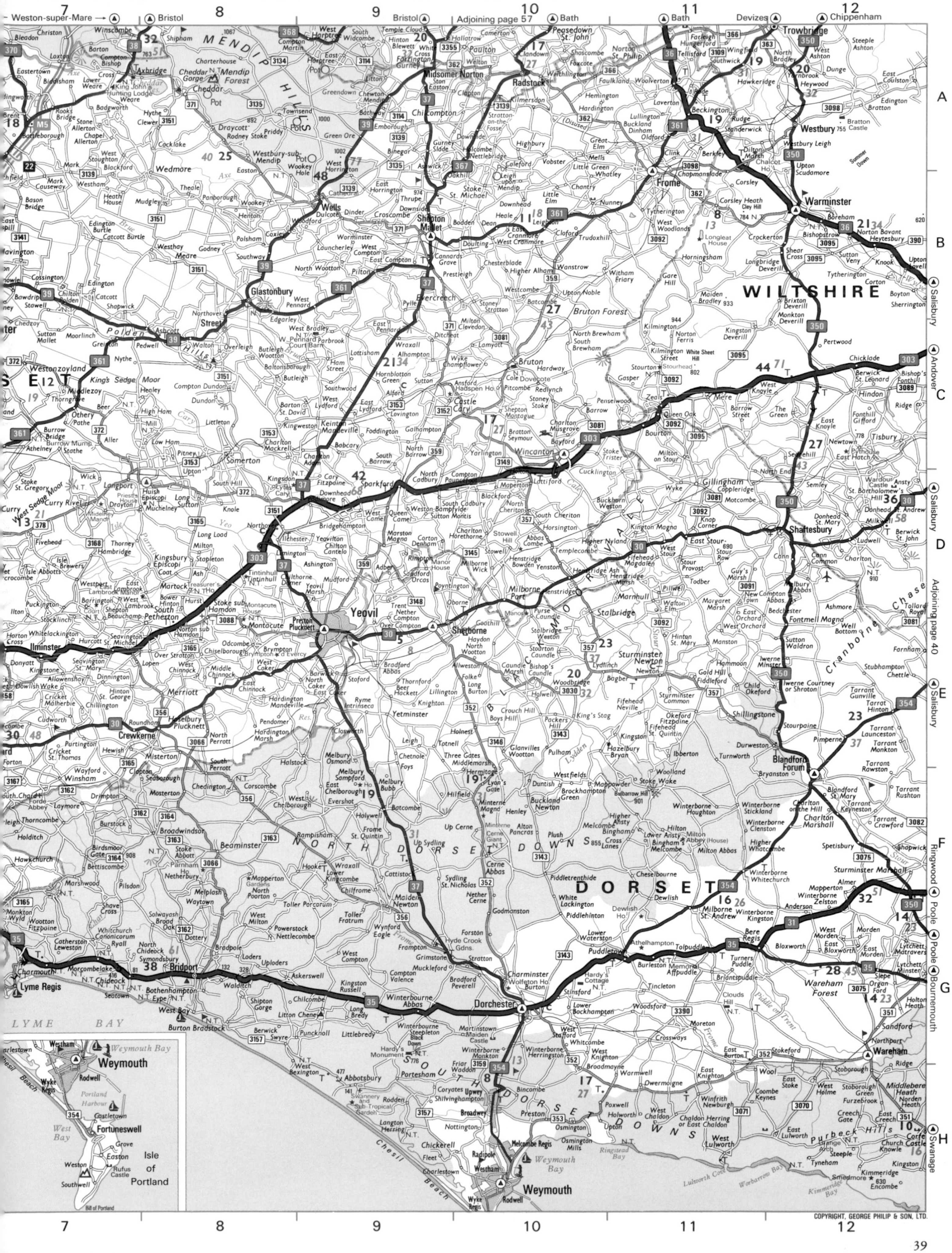
Weston-super-Mare
Bristol
Adjoining page 57
Bath
Devizes
Chippenham
Salisbury
Andover
Adjoining page 40
Ringwood
Poole
Bournemouth
Swanage
WILTSHIRE
DORSET
MENDIP HILLS
NORTH DORSET DOWNS
SOUTH DORSET DOWNS
BLACKMORE VALE
Cranborne Chase
Purbeck Hills
LYME BAY
Chesil Beach
Glastonbury
Wells
Shepton Mallet
Frome
Warminster
Westbury
Trowbridge
Radstock
Midsomer Norton
Wincanton
Yeovil
Sherborne
Shaftesbury
Gillingham
Blandford Forum
Dorchester
Weymouth
Bridport
Lyme Regis
Crewkerne
Ilminster
Wareham
Isle of Portland
Fortuneswell
7
8
9
10
11
12
A
B
C
D
E
F
G
H

1 | Devizes | 2 | Devizes | 3 | Marlborough Adjoining page 84 | 4 | Marlborough | 5 | Newbury | 6 | Newbury

1 | 2 | 3 | 4 | 5 | 6

Newbury 7 Reading 8 Reading Staines 9 Adjoining page 85 10 11 London 12

7 8 9 10 11 12

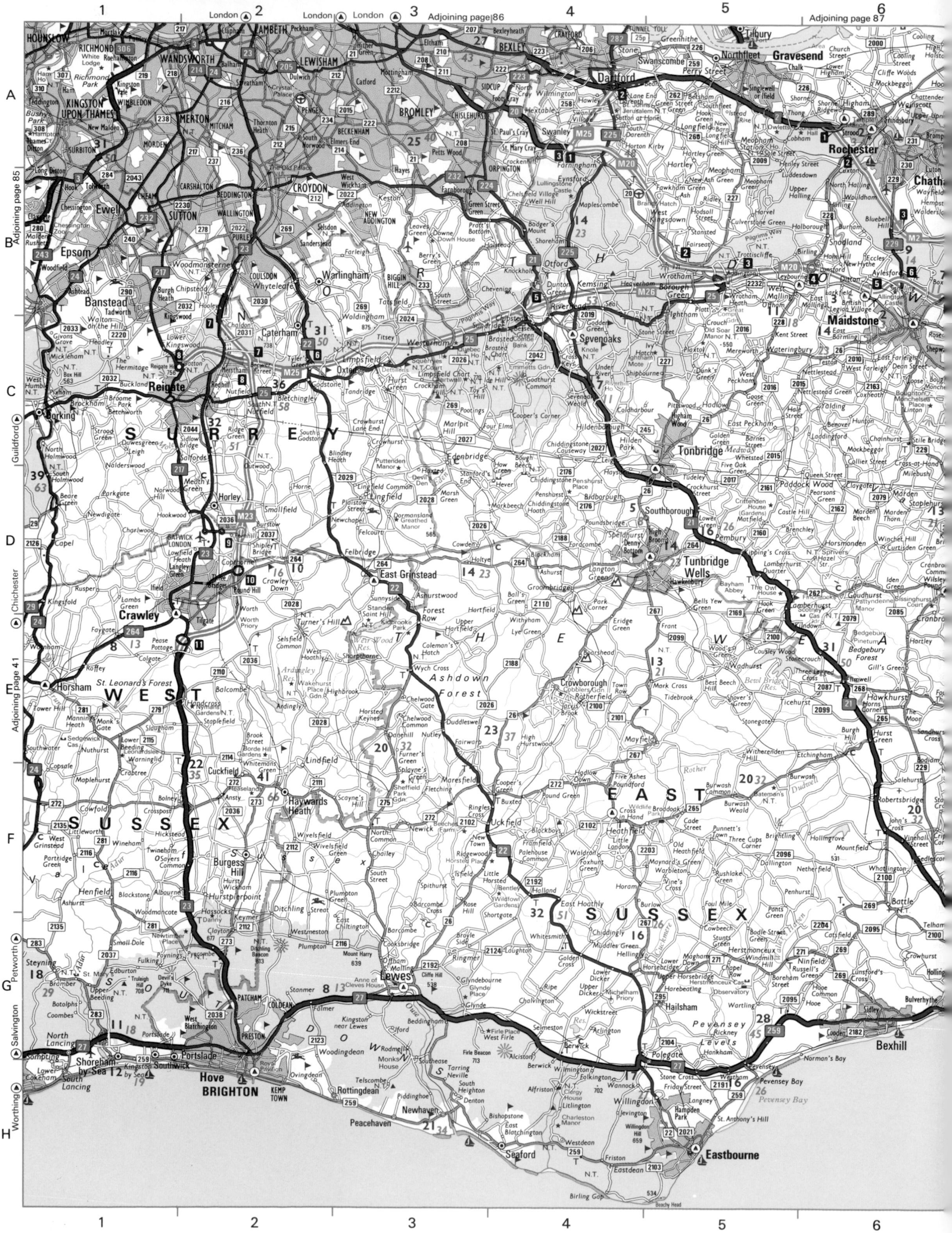

Adjoining page 86
Adjoining page 87
Adjoining page 85
Adjoining page 41
London
Guildford
Chichester
Petworth
Salvington
Worthing
HOUNSLOW
RICHMOND
WANDSWORTH
LAMBETH
LEWISHAM
BEXLEY
KINGSTON UPON THAMES
MERTON
BROMLEY
CROYDON
SUTTON
ORPINGTON
Tilbury
Gravesend
Northfleet
Dartford
Swanley
Rochester
Chatham
Epsom
Ewell
Banstead
Reigate
Redhill
Dorking
Caterham
Warlingham
Oxted
Westerham
Sevenoaks
Otford
Tonbridge
Maidstone
Horley
Crawley
Horsham
East Grinstead
Tunbridge Wells
Crowborough
Forest Row
Ashdown Forest
Haywards Heath
Burgess Hill
Cuckfield
Uckfield
Heathfield
Hailsham
Lewes
BRIGHTON
Hove
Shoreham by Sea
Portslade
Newhaven
Peacehaven
Seaford
Eastbourne
Bexhill
Battle
Hawkhurst
Mayfield
Wadhurst
S U R R E Y
W E S T
S U S S E X
E A S T
S U S S E X
Pevensey Bay
Beachy Head

Adjoining page 87

7
8
9
10
11
12
A
B
C
D
E
F
G
H
Sheerness
Queenborough
in-Sheppey
Minster-on-Sea
Queenborough
Eastchurch
Warden
Leysdown-on-Sea
ISLE OF SHEPPEY
Elmley Island
Isle of Harty
The Swale
Medway
Sittingbourne
Newington
Rainham
Teynham
Faversham
Whitstable
Seasalter
Herne Bay
Reculver
Margate
Westgate on Sea
Birchington
Isle of Thanet
Broadstairs
North Foreland
Ramsgate
Minster
Manston
Pegwell Bay
Sandwich
Sandwich Flats
Sandwich Bay
Canterbury
Sturry
Herne
Fordwich
Wickhambreaux
Littlebourne
Wingham
Bridge
Bekesbourne
Patrixbourne
Adisham
Aylesham
Barham
Eastry
Deal
Walmer
Kingsdown
St. Margaret's-at-Cliffe
St. Margaret's Bay
South Foreland
Dover
Buckland
Temple Ewell
Whitfield
Lydden
Capel le Ferne
Folkestone
Sandgate
Cheriton
Hythe
Saltwood
Newington
Lympne
Elham
Lyminge
Stelling Minnis
Rhodes Minnis
Lyminge Forest
Wye
Ashford
Willesborough
Kennington
Charing
Lenham
Harrietsham
Hollingbourne
Leeds
K E N T
Chilham
Godmersham
Boughton Street
Hernhill
Dunkirk
Selling
Challock Lees
Pluckley
Egerton
Headcorn
Smarden
Bethersden
Biddenden
Sissinghurst
Tenterden
Woodchurch
Appledore
Kenardington
Hamstreet
Orlestone
Warehorne
Bilsington
Royal Military Canal
Aldington
Mersham
Smeeth
Brabourne
Sellindge
Stanford
Newingreen
Burmarsh
Dymchurch
St. Mary's Bay
Romney Marsh
Snave
Brenzett
Ivychurch
St. Mary in the Marsh
Brookland
Old Romney
New Romney
Littlestone-on-Sea
Romney Sands
Greatstone-on-Sea
Lydd
Lydd-on-Sea
Denge Marsh
Denge Beach
Dungeness
East Road
Walland Marsh
Isle of Oxney
Wittersham
Rother Levels
Rother
Newenden
Northiam
Iden
Peasmarsh
Playden
Rye
Rye Foreign
East Guldeford
Camber
Camber Castle
Rye Harbour
Rye Bay
West Road
Winchelsea
Winchelsea Beach
Icklesham
Guestling Thorn
Three Oaks
Guestling Green
Pett
Cliff End
Fairlight
Fairlight Cove
Ore
Hastings
St. Leonards
Udimore
Brede
Broad Oak
Tillingham
STRAIT OF DOVER
East Wear Bay

Wales & the Welsh Borders

LOWER BROCKHAMPTON

National Trust holdings in Wales and the Border counties include some of the finest coast and countryside estates in Britain. These apart, the Trust's most notable properties are perhaps the dozen or so great houses, largely of the seventeenth and eighteenth centuries, which so splendidly illustrate contemporary spacious living and taste. Here leading architects and decorators rewarded their wealthy patrons with country mansions whose handsome exteriors were matched by similarly fine interiors. The delicate plasterwork and other interior decoration still delight and, as in the past, these houses are home to a wealth of exquisite furniture, *objets d'art* and pictures. National Trust gardens, too, are outstanding, some, such as Bodnant and Hidcote, enjoying an international reputation.

But splendid though the great houses are, there are also numerous more modest properties reflecting the life of their times. Bath's Assembly Rooms evoke Jane Austen, dovecotes are a reminder that pigeons were once valued as winter fresh meat, and massive tithe barns recall past imposts.

Medieval times are well and contrastingly represented by attractive manor houses such as Horton Court and Lower Brockhampton as also by the ruins of Skenfrith and Cilgerran castles and of the once prosperous abbey of Hailes. Farther back in time, Segontium with its museum tells of the Roman military presence, while something of Romano-British domestic life can be pictured at Chedworth Villa. National Trust lands are also rich in prehistoric sites. The most obvious are the many Iron Age defensive earthworks – Little Solsbury Hill and Croft Ambrey are outstanding – while the cultures of Bronze and Stone Age peoples survive in the scattered traces of their burials.

Coast & Countryside

The National Trust owns a total of over 80,000 acres in Wales and its border counties, made up of around 130 large and small individual properties. These include some 500 miles of Welsh coast, much of it of wild and rugged grandeur, and scenery as diverse as the high bare mountains of Snowdonia, glorious woodland threaded by impatient streams, the open rolling uplands of the Brecon Beacons and of Shropshire's Long Mynd, and the rich farming land to be found throughout the region.

Ignoring the north-east with its succession of popular resorts, caravan parks and holiday camps, as also the largely industrial Bristol

The spectacular Henrhyd Falls lie hidden in a deep ravine in Graigllech Woods, just north of Coelbren, Powys.

The Trust owns about half the great ridge of the Shropshire Long Mynd (Welsh mynydd = mountain). This is Carding Mill Valley.

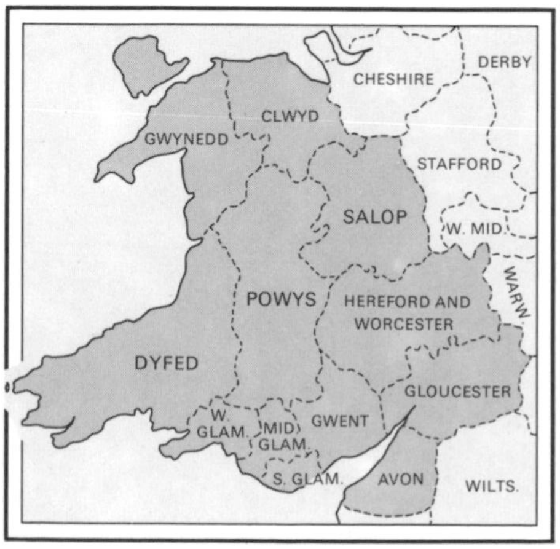

The impressive massif of the Brecon Beacons, Powys, is good walking country with spectacular views from the higher ground.

Channel east of Swansea, the Welsh coast divides into five regions, all scenic and all in part owned or otherwise protected by the National Trust. From north to south these regions are Anglesey, Lleyn, the great crescent of Cardigan Bay, south-western Dyfed, and Gower. Many areas are accessible only on foot.

The principal Anglesey properties, together providing some 375 acres of cliff, bay and agricultural land, form a group at the island's north-west corner, here being **Cemaes, Cemlyn** with a nature reserve and bird sanctuary, and **Dinas Gynfor**, this last the northernmost point of Wales and including part of an Iron Age promontory fort (60 A3).

The Lleyn peninsula, its coast officially designated an Area of Outstanding Natural Beauty, projects some thirty miles southwestward to separate Caernarfon Bay and Cardigan Bay. Here the Trust's properties form two groups, those close to Aberdaron near the tip of the peninsula (60 H1) and those of the Plas-yn-Rhiw estate (60 G2) a short distance to the east. Beyond Aberdaron will be found the open, green and steeply sloping cliffland of **Braich y Pwll**, below which from the fifth or sixth century onwards pilgrims embarked for Bardsey (not National Trust). Bardsey is an island of such sanctity that it is said that three pilgrimages here equated with one to Rome. On Braich y Pwll a holy well and the site of a chapel recall those times, while Bardsey is also well seen from the Trust's clifftop acres of **Pen y Cil** a short way to the south. To the east of Aberdaron Bay, along an outstandingly lovely stretch of coast, the **Plas-yn-Rhiw** estate provides seven National Trust properties in addition to the parent manor house. These include **Porth Ysgo**, with a sandy beach, cliffs and a waterfall; the rock, bracken and heather moor of **Mynydd-y-Graig**, site of a hill-fort and of megalithic remains and rising 800 feet above the west side of Porth Neigwl, a large arc of sand and cliffs known also as Hell's Mouth; the cliffs of **Mynydd Cilan** guarding the eastern arm of Porth Neigwl; and **Foel Felin Wynt** (Windmill Hill) to the north of Abersoch, a high point (700 feet) commanding long views seaward and towards Snowdonia (60 G2). Other properties on Lleyn, all along the south coast and very different from those just described, are **Tywyn-y-Fach**, nineteen acres of sandhills on the northern edge of Abersoch (60 G3); **Ynysgain** near Criccieth, an area of farmland and shore crossed by the railway (60 F4); the golf course and dunes of **Morfa Bychan** just south-west of Porthmadog (60 F5); and in Porthmadog itself **Ynys Towyn**, a modest small site where a rocky knoll provides a view across the Glaslyn estuary (60 F5).

Around Cardigan Bay, a crescent some eighty miles in length between Porthmadog and Cardigan, little is owned by the National Trust. However, one property, **Dinas Oleu** (58 A2), high above Barmouth and the Mawddach estuary (described by Wordsworth as 'sublime'), is of interest for being the first to come to the Trust, in 1895 the year of its founding, and an adjoining piece of land, **Cae Fadog**, was acquired in 1980. Farther south, there are five properties between New Quay and Cardigan, most of them farmland but with public access to quiet beaches (55 A7 to 54 B5).

From the mouth of the Teifi near Cardigan (54 B5) starts the Pembrokeshire Coast National Park's coastal path. This runs for 168 scenic miles, rounding the bold promontory of St David's Head, skirting St Bride's Bay and Milford Haven, and finally winding above the magnificent cliffs to the south-west of Pembroke to end at Amroth on Carmarthen Bay (54 F5). Along or close to this path there are three important groups of National Trust properties: those around St David's and along the north shore of St Bride's Bay; those on the peninsula forming the southern arm of the bay; and the clifftop sites to the south. Within the first group the Trust owns over fifteen miles of coast and protects another eight. Among the properties are **St David's Head** itself, mentioned by Ptolemy as *Octopitarum Promontarium* and with some prehistoric remains, and parts of **Whitesand Bay**, traditionally the site of St David's first monastery. **Marloes** and **Kete**, forming the second group, command striking views towards Skomer and Skokholm islands (not National Trust; nature reserves

The Llyn Ogwen valley lies in the heart of the wild, mountainous country of the Trust's great Carneddau estate in north Wales.

The red sandstone cliffs of Manorbier, Dyfed, typify the wild and rugged grandeur of the Pembrokeshire coast.

and bird sanctuaries). Finally, along the cliffs to the south of Pembroke, there are **Stackpole**, an estate of nearly 2,000 acres made up of woods, cliffs, beaches, farmland and lakes, the striated red sandstone cliffs of **Manorbier** (the name deriving from Maenor Pyr, the manor of Pyr, first abbot of Caldy), and **Lydstep Headland**, below which there are caves.

The long sweep of Carmarthen Bay is bounded on its southern side by the popular **Gower Peninsula** (55 H7/8/9) on which the National Trust owns sixteen scattered areas, all on or close to the coast and together embracing a remarkable variety of scenery – cliffs, sand burrows, salt marsh, commons, downland and rocky headland. There are caves below many of the cliffs, but access can be difficult. They are of interest only because the bones of animals such as lions and rhinoceros were found in them, while in 1823, in a cavern below **Paviland** (west of Port Eynon), were discovered the bones of a young man, subsequently radio-carbon dated to about the seventeenth millennium BC. Other Trust properties on Gower include earthworks, probably of the Iron Age, on **The Bulwark** and on **Thurba Head**; **Worm's Head**, with a cave and a blow hole, jutting seaward as the southern arm of the fine curve of the beach of Rhossili Bay; while above, on the grass and bracken covered hill of **Rhossili Down**, can be found burial chambers known as Sweyne's Houses (Howes), traditionally the resting place of the Viking who may have given his name to Swansea.

Of the National Trust's many inland countryside properties perhaps the most impressive is the **Carneddau** in Snowdonia (60 C/D6), a huge estate (15,860 acres) of breathtaking scenery which includes Carnedd Dafydd and much of Carnedd Llewelyn, mountains both well over 3,000 feet and named after the brother princes who stood against Edward I. Other features of this estate are the striking rocky pyramid of Tryfan, south of Llyn Ogwen, and, at the head of the steep Nant Ffrancon Pass, Cwm Idwal and the lake of the same name, a sombre place which is romantically associated with Prince Idwal who is said to have been drowned here, but more practically known as a nature reserve important for its Alpine flora. Other important properties in northern Wales are the precipitous wooded **Aberglaslyn Pass** to the south of Beddgelert (60 E5); the vast **Ysbyty Ifan** estate south of Betws-y-Coed (61 E/F7), with 25,820 acres of wooded hills and valleys, upland farming and moorland, and beautifully situated Llyn Conwy, source of the river of the same name; and farther south, but still in the county of Gwynedd, **Dolmelynllyn** (60 H6) where a short footpath ascends the Gamlan stream to Rhaiadr Ddu, one of the finest cascades in Wales, and **Cregennau**, near Arthog (58 A2), a fine open space of 705 acres embracing lakes, hill farms and mountain.

In the south of the principality there are important properties in Dyfed, Powys and Gwent. **Dolaucothi** at Pumpsaint (55 C10) includes ancient gold mines, principally exploited by the Romans but possibly in use even earlier and also worked intermittently through to modern times; nearby are an ancient standing stone and a mound of disputed origin. In the county of Powys the Trust owns much of the **Brecon Beacons** including the principal summits of Pen y Fan and Corn Dû (56 B3), both only a little under 3,000 feet in height. Open upland and crossed by many tracks, one of these a Roman road, the Brecon Beacons are one of the most visited walking districts in Wales. To the east, above Abergavenny in Gwent, roads and tracks ascend towards the two bare peaks of **Sugar Loaf** and **Skirrid Fawr** (56 B6) – alternatively Ysgyryd Fawr – both commanding views of the lovely Usk valley.

The National Trust has many countryside estates scattered throughout the border counties – farm, wood, moor and downland. Some properties are remote, but many are concentrated around urban centres, such as Bristol, Bath, Stroud, and Birmingham. The largest and most notable comprises nearly 5,000 acres of the high moor of the **Long Mynd** in Shropshire (59 C9/10). Crossed by a narrow road ascending sharply westward out of Church Stretton, and notable for its extensive views across Shropshire and Cheshire and towards the Black Mountains of Wales, Long Mynd is also known for its many prehistoric barrows, three lengths of defensive earthworks, and a section of the Port Way, a track used by Stone Age traders and in more modern times marking parish boundaries.

Houses, Gardens & Parks

Aberconwy House, Gwynedd Dating from the fourteenth century, Aberconwy House survives as an example of the better type of dwelling once common in Conwy. It now contains an exhibition illustrating life in Conwy from Roman to modern times.

Conwy, at the junction of Castle Street and High Street (61 B7)

Attingham Park, Shropshire The mansion was designed in 1782 by George Steuart for Noel Hill, later the 1st Lord Berwick. On Hill's instructions Steuart had to incorporate the earlier house, but this was almost wholly demolished in 1840 while an earlier and more significant alteration was that of 1805 when, to house the 2nd Lord Berwick's collection, largely the result of a visit to Italy in 1792, John Nash inserted the picture gallery and a new staircase. In 1827 Lord Berwick was forced to sell most of his collection, but his successor, who served as ambassador to Sardinia, Savoy and Naples, built up fresh collections of both pictures and Neapolitan furniture. Among the artists whose works hang today in the house are Angelica Kauffmann, Lawrence, Romney, Kneller and Sickert. The interior decoration of the mansion is notable, especially that of the boudoir, late eighteenth-century work attributed to the Frenchman Louis Delabrière and among the most delicate surviving examples of its period.

After much planting by Thomas Leggett between 1769–72, the park was greatly altered by Humphry Repton in 1797. The estate occupies part of the site of the Romano-British town of Viroconium and is crossed and bounded by Roman roads.

Atcham, 4M SE of Shrewsbury, on A5 (59 A11)

Benthall Hall, Shropshire On the site of a much earlier house, today's hall was probably built in the late sixteenth century, although tradition gives a date of 1535. As early as 1583 there seems to have been considerable alteration, and in the seventeenth century a wing was added on the north-east. But the estate and its family name are of far greater antiquity, traced by records back to 1100 and with indirect evidence suggesting a pre-Norman ownership. Except for the period 1844–1934, the estate was held by the same family until given to the National Trust in 1958. The carved stone decoration on the porch, possibly alluding to the five wounds of Christ, and the several hiding places within the house suggest that in Elizabethan times the family was Catholic in sympathy.

In local sandstone, with mullioned and transomed windows and moulded brick chimneys, Benthall is an attractive example of the domestic style of its period. The best feature of the interior is the carved main staircase, thought to date from 1618; also noteworthy are the late eighteenth-century Welsh pewter, the oak panelling of *c.*1610 in the dining room, the plasterwork of the drawing room ceiling (*c.*1630), and, in both the drawing and dining rooms, the mantelpieces designed in 1756 by T. F. Pritchard.

Broseley, 4M NE of Much Wenlock (59 B12)

Berrington Hall, Hereford and Worcester The present hall and park are the result of the association in the late eighteenth century between the then owner of the estate, Thomas Harley, 'Capability' Brown and the younger Henry Holland. Brown almost certainly advised on the commanding site of the house, enjoying a wide view and above a valley in which he fashioned a lake and island. Holland began work in 1778, achieving this imposing mansion – a rectangle with offices at the rear around a courtyard – the rather austere exterior of which contrasts with the rich internal decoration.

Beyond the marble hall, fairly typical of its period, the drawing room is the most splendid of the rooms, with a chimneypiece of Carrara marble and one of the most elaborate ceilings designed anywhere by Holland in which the central medallion and surrounding roundels are probably the work of Biagio Rebecca, who was also almost certainly responsible for work in the business room and the library. On Harley's death the estate passed to his daughter, wife of the eldest son of Admiral Rodney, a naval association recalled by the large battle paintings (three by Thomas Luny) in the dining room. Around the courtyard are the nineteenth-century laundry and the original dairy.

3M N of Leominster to W of A49 (59 F10)

Bodnant Garden, Gwynedd First laid out from 1875 onwards by Henry Pochin, Bodnant now ranks among the finest gardens in Britain. With backgrounds of large native trees and with views across the Conwy valley to Snowdonia, the garden is in two main sections. The upper, around the house, formed by lawns and a series of terrace gardens, is largely the achievement of the 2nd Lord Aberconway (grandson of Henry Pochin) between 1905 and 1914. The lower, known as the Dell and with a pinetum and wild garden, is along the valley of a stream.

8M S of Colwyn Bay on A470 (61 C7)

Chirk Castle, Clwyd This massive border fortress was completed in 1310 by Roger Mortimer to whom Edward I had given the estates of Chirk in 1282. Thereafter ownership changed frequently until 1595 when the estate was bought by the merchant adventurer Sir Thomas Myddelton (Lord Mayor of London in 1614), the property then belonging to this family until 1977 (the Myddeltons still live in the castle). The design is a square around a courtyard. The south wing had become a house by Tudor times and the outline of the many Tudor gables can still be traced on the filling-in carried out during the eighteenth century. The interior of the east wing, now a private house, was much altered during the nineteenth century by Augustus Welby Pugin. The west range, with its deep dungeon, survives largely untouched since 1300, while the state rooms occupy the north wing. Entered through a hall by Pugin, the rooms are notable for their elaborate decorative work of the sixteenth to the early nineteenth centuries and contain fine furniture, portraits and Mortlake tapestries. The park, which is crossed by Offa's Dyke (*c.*784), is entered from Chirk town through superb iron gates completed in 1721, the work of the Davies brothers.

1M W of Chirk off A5 (61 F12)

Clevedon Court, Avon A once partly fortified manor house, with a twelfth-century tower and a thirteenth-century hall. The interior houses collections of Nailsea glass and of Eltonware, the product of Sir Edmund Elton's Sunflower Pottery, established at Clevedon in 1880. The gardens are terraced, and planted with rare shrubs.

1½M E of Clevedon, on B3130 (57 G7)

Croft Castle, Hereford and Worcester Held by the Croft family from Norman times until 1745, again from 1923 until the 1950s, and today still occupied by them, Croft Castle has outer walls and corner towers of the fourteenth and fifteenth centuries but was later much modified, especially in about 1765 when it was given a new internal structure with Gothick features, notably the staircase and ceilings where much

The picture gallery at Attingham Park in a watercolour of 1810. The ceiling is notable for its early cast-iron window frames.

A flight of garden steps at Bodnant, showing some of the roses which are one of the garden's major summer attractions.

The Welsh name for Chirk Castle, Castell y Waun (Meadow Castle), aptly describes its beautiful setting in the Welsh borderlands.

The picturesque jumble of buildings that make up the Cotswold manor house of Horton Court betray its medieval origins.

of the decorative work is by T.F. Pritchard. Among the portrait painters whose works hang in the rooms are H. R. Morland, Gainsborough, Lawrence, Archer-Shee, Beetham and Phillip de Laszlo. Beside the castle stands a small fourteenth- and fifteenth-century church containing the impressive tomb of Sir Richard Croft (d.1509) and his wife (who was governess at Ludlow to the sons of Edward IV).

The grounds are known for their oak, beech, lime and Spanish chestnut avenues, the last perhaps dating back to 1588, and also for the large Iron Age fort of Croft Ambrey, occupied from the fourth century BC until the arrival of the Romans in AD 50. (*See also under Archaeological Sites.*)

5M NW of Leominster, approached from B4362 (59 F10)

Cwmmau Farmhouse, Hereford and Worcester A timber-framed and stone-tiled farmhouse of the early seventeenth century.

4M SW of Kington, to the W of A4111 (59 G8)

Dudmaston, Shropshire The estate probably existed as such as early as the twelfth century, but today's Dudmaston Hall, although incorporating Tudor fragments, dates from 1695 to 1701 and is attributed, though on circumstantial evidence, to the architect Francis Smith of Warwick; alterations, notably to the roof-line with the addition of pediments and a parapet, were made in the early nineteenth century and the south wing was heightened in the 1890s.

Dudmaston is visited principally for its varied collections of pictures, sculpture, furniture and applied art, much of the material having been assembled in recent years by Sir George and Lady Labouchere, who still live in the house. The collection of Dutch flower

The staircase in Croft Castle, with its delightful plasterwork, shows clearly the influence of the Gothick movement.

pictures in the library and dining room includes works by eighteenth-century artists such as Jan van Os, Jan van Huysum, Johannes Linthorst and Rachel Ruysch, while in the gallery devoted to botanical art there are examples of the skill of P. J. Redouté, P. Reinagle and, from our century, John Nash. Also to be seen are topographical watercolours, many of them Shropshire scenes, and an important collection of twentieth-century paintings and sculpture, including works by Barbara Hepworth, Henry Moore, Ben Nicholson, Sonia Delaunay, and Spanish painters such as A. Tàpies and L. Muñoz.

Quatt, 5M SE of Bridgnorth on A442 (88 C1)

Dyrham Park, Avon Dyrham is an ancient name (*deor-hamm*: deer enclosure), the site of the battle of 577 in which the Saxons defeated the early Welsh, thus cutting the latter off from their kinsmen in the West Country and confin-

The medieval church in the grounds of Dyrham Park is one of the few owned by the Trust. It contains Blathwayt monuments.

The stilt garden at Hidcote Manor (named after the hornbeam hedges on stems), looking down the red border to the old garden.

ing them within their present borders. The estate existed in pre-Norman times and from about 1100 onwards was owned by two family lines, the break coming in 1571 when George Wynter bought it. In 1686 Dyrham passed by marriage (with Mary Wynter) to William Blathwayt, a successful public servant who became Secretary of State to William III and between 1692–1704 so extensively remodelled the Tudor manor that effectively he built a new

left **The design of the dignified entrance front of Hanbury Hall reflects the influence of William Talman.**

below **This red japanned bureau-bookcase in the state bedroom at Erddig is described in the inventory of 1726.**

house. Two architects were concerned. The earlier was a Frenchman, S. Hauduroy, responsible for the west front, at that time with the entrance. The other, slightly later, was William Talman, who designed the east front. Sheltered below a steep escarpment, the house and its park command good views westward.

The interior well illustrates the Dutch influence on taste at the close of the seventeenth century, with tapestries, panelling, leather-hung walls, Delftware, and pictures by such masters as David Teniers the Younger, Melchior d'Hondecoeter, Abraham Storck and Samuel Hoogstraeten, two of whose perspective paintings are here.

8M N of Bath on A46, 2M S of M4, Tormarton (57 G10)

Erddig, Clwyd The house dates from two periods: the central portion of 1684–7 was built by a mason called Thomas Webb, and wings were added in 1724 by John Meller who bought the property in 1716. Later, in the 1770s, James Wyatt was associated with the stone facing of the west front, while in 1826 Thomas Hopper designed the neo-classical dining room. Meller, a successful lawyer of both means and taste, may well himself have designed his new wings and it was certainly he who enriched the house with the splendid furniture that is still Erddig's outstanding feature. The many paintings are also notable and include portraits by Gainsborough, Cotes and Kneller.

Erddig is also known for its range of outbuildings and domestic rooms complete with contemporary equipment. The various workshops (joiner's, blacksmith's), the stable, the bakehouse, servants' hall and kitchen, together with a remarkable series of portraits of estate and household staff, combine to give a perhaps unique picture of the domestic history of a great house of the period. The garden has been restored to its eighteenth-century formal design, and there is an agricultural museum in the park at Felin Puleston.

1M S of Wrexham, E of A483 (61 E12)

The Greyfriars, Hereford and Worcester is a timber-framed and tiled house, mainly of the late fifteenth century but with early seventeenth- and late eighteenth-century additions.

Friar Street, Worcester (88 G2)

Hanbury Hall, Hereford and Worcester Recorded in the Domesday survey, and belonging to the bishops of Worcester until seized by Queen Elizabeth, the Hanbury estate was purchased by the Vernon family in 1631, the present substantial brick house, by an unknown architect, being completed in 1701 for Thomas Vernon, a successful barrister. The formal gardens laid out at the same time by George London were broken up in the late eighteenth century as being no longer fashionable, their place being taken today by some splendid lawns. The orangery dates from soon after 1732.

The outstanding feature of the interior is James Thornhill's painted staircase with its great classical scenes (*c.*1710). Thornhill also carried out the ceiling paintings in the Long Room, today a gallery displaying the R.S. Watney collection of English porcelain figures and Flemish, Dutch and French flower paintings; the collection also includes eighteenth-century English furniture shown both here and in other rooms.

2½M E of Droitwich, N of B4090 (88 F3)

Hidcote Manor Garden, Gloucestershire An extensive series of small and mostly formal gardens, separated from one another by hedges of different species and containing many rare trees, shrubs, plants and bulbs. The garden was the creation between about 1908 and 1948 of the horticulturist Major Lawrence Johnston.

4M NE of Chipping Campden, E of A46 (88 H5)

Horton Court, Avon This Cotswold manor house, although restored and somewhat altered during the nineteenth century, preserves its mainly twelfth-century Norman hall (an interesting architectural link between the Saxon 'aula', known only from illuminated manuscripts, and the typical medieval manor hall), built by Robert Beaufeu, the first prebendary of the see of Salisbury. A later owner of the estate was William Knight (1476–1547), a diplomat serving Henry VIII, and it was he who built the house's porch with its early Renaissance carving and also the unique detached ambulatory in the style of the Italian loggia.

3M NE of Chipping Sodbury, W of A46 (57 F11)

Lower Brockhampton, Hereford and Worcester A secluded and pleasantly situated late fourteenth-century, half-timbered moated manor house, approached through an attractive and rare detached fifteenth-century gatehouse. Close by are the ruins of a twelfth-century chapel. The house lies deep in an estate of 1,895 acres of hilly farming land and woods.

2M E of Bromyard, off A44 (59 G12)

Morville Hall, Shropshire A modest Elizabethan house to which two wings were added during the eighteenth century. (Visits by appointment.)

3M W of Bridgnorth, off A458 (59 C12)

Penrhyn Castle, Gwynedd The Penrhyn estate, dating back to the thirteenth century, in 1765 came through marriage to Richard Pennant, the man who developed the slate quarries above Bethesda. His successor, through the female line, was G. H. Dawkins Pennant, who in 1827 commissioned Thomas Hopper to rebuild the Gothick house (by Samuel Wyatt, *c.*1800) which he had inherited. The result was this huge neo-Norman Penrhyn Castle which virtually obliterated Wyatt's house, although today's drawing room represents his great hall, itself modelled on a medieval predecessor. Hopper was allowed a free hand – his responsibility embraced the interior decoration and even the furniture – and with both the exterior and interior he achieved the spacious yet solidly massive effect that was his highly personal interpretation of Norman. At the same time, modern details included a hot air heating system and water closets.

Main features of the interior are the plasterwork and the elaborate stone and wood carving, and also the unusual craftsmanship in slate, the staircase being one of the most extraordinary features in any interior in Britain. The castle contains a collection of about 1,000 dolls and an industrial railway museum, with locomotives dating back to 1848, interesting pictures and examples of slate work.

2M E of Bangor, at junction of A5 and A55 (60 C5)

Plas Newydd, Gwynedd The seat beside the Menai Strait of the marquesses of Anglesey, Plas Newydd as seen today is the result of the work carried out between 1783 and 1809, principally by James Wyatt and Joseph Potter, which both externally and internally converted an early sixteenth-century manor into a stately mansion; at the same time Humphry Repton advised on the layout of the grounds. Some alteration, notably remodelling of the north wing, took place in the 1930s.

Of the house's many elegant rooms the largest and most splendid is the music room, occupying roughly the position of the hall of the earlier house and very possibly incorporating something of its structure. Plas Newydd is rich in furniture and pictures, much of both coming from Beaudesert, the family's Staffordshire home which was demolished in 1935. Among the artists whose works may be seen are Snyders, Hoppner, Romney, Lawrence, and Rex Whistler. Whistler was a close friend of the family and in addition to portraits and other works now collected here Plas Newydd houses one of his last and largest murals (1937). There is also a museum largely devoted to the 1st Marquess, who as Lord Uxbridge lost a leg while commanding the cavalry at Waterloo (1815). In the grounds, with views across the Menai Strait towards Snowdonia, large boulders mark the remains of a prehistoric burial chamber.

Anglesey, 3M SW of Menai Bridge on A4080 (60 C4)

Plas-yn-Rhiw, Gwynedd A small, part-medieval manor house with Tudor and Georgian additions; woodland and ornamental gardens. The estate includes several coastal and inland properties owned by the National Trust. (Visits by appointment.)

Lleyn peninsula, 3½M NE of Aberdaron on S coast road (60 G2)

Powis Castle, Powys Still inhabited after some 700 years, the present castle dates from the late thirteenth century when Edward I granted Gruffydd ap Gwenwynwyn the barony of De la Pole. In 1587 the castle was bought by Sir Edward Herbert who added the Long Gallery and did much internal remodelling; there was further reconstruction during the seventeenth to nineteenth centuries, the architects being William Winde, T. F. Pritchard and Robert Smirke, while the beginning of our century saw extensive remodelling of the interior and exterior by G. F. Bodley. Among features of the interior are the panelling and plasterwork; the carved late seventeenth-century staircase and the State Bedroom, probably by Winde; ceilings and murals by Lanscroon; Mortlake and Brussels tapestries; early Georgian furniture; many portraits by, amongst others, Romney, Reynolds and Gainsborough; a miniature by Isaac Oliver; a view of Verona by Bellotto; and Indian works of art collected by Clive of India and his son, who married the Powis heiress and was created Earl of Powis in 1804.

The late seventeenth-century formal garden, very likely the work of William Winde and a unique survival in original form, has four terraces nearly 200 yards in length; outstandingly developed since 1700, and especially in this century, it is now one of the finest gardens in Britain.

1M S Welshpool, on A483 (59 B7)

Snowshill Manor, Gloucestershire The Snowshill estate is an ancient one, owned by Hailes Abbey from 821 until 1539 when, at the

Plas Newydd (*above*) looks over the Menai Strait. The view from the house inspired Rex Whistler's *trompe l'oeil* mural in the dining room (*below*).

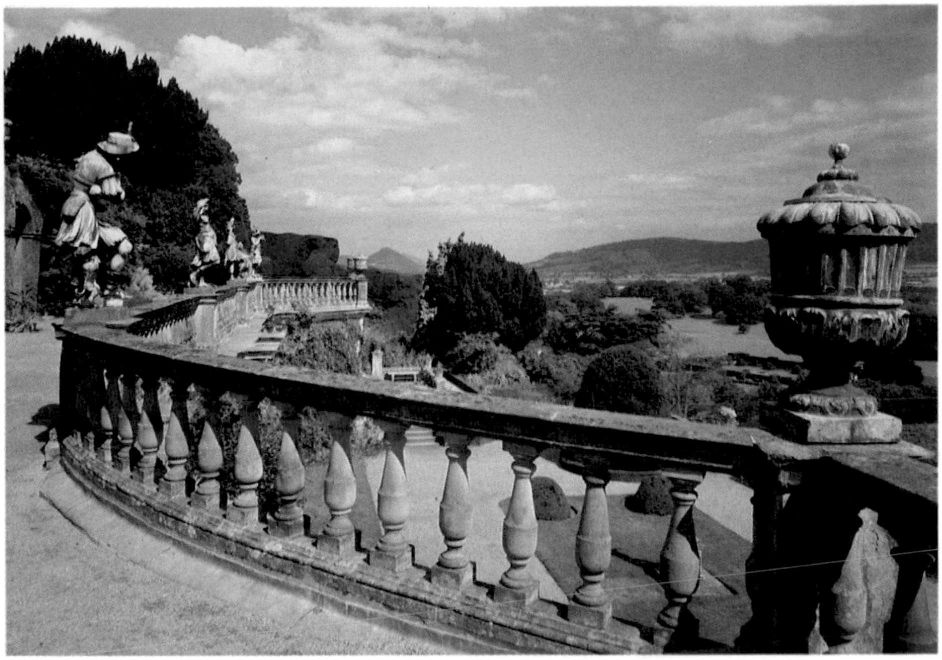

A view along one of the famous terraces at Powis Castle, showing the early eighteenth-century lead statues. The southerly aspect permits rare and tender shrubs to be grown.

Dissolution, it passed to the Crown. The rambling Cotswold manor house, dating mainly to *c.*1500, belongs only to the closing years of this long tenure; altered and enlarged in *c.*1600, the house was given a classical south front in about 1700. The last owner (1919–51) was Charles Wade, an eccentric whose hobby was to collect whatever took his fancy, and the astonishing results of this hobby – material as disparate as musical instruments, Japanese armour, clocks, toys, bicycles, oriental masks, spinners' and weavers' equipment and much else – cram the house.

3M *S of Broadway (84 A2)*

Tudor Merchant's House, Dyfed In part perhaps dating from the fourteenth century, but considerably rebuilt in the fifteenth, this house survives as a rare local example of a merchant's home. The interior frescoes, discovered only in the late 1960s under something like twenty-eight coats of lime wash, are contemporary with the rebuilding and typical of the interior decoration of the time.

Quay Hill, Tenby (54 G5)

Tŷ Mawr, Gwynedd A seventeenth-century farmhouse, successor to the one in which Bishop William Morgan, first translator of the Bible into Welsh, was born in 1541; his work, dedicated to Elizabeth I in 1588, became one of the foundations of Welsh literature and, as revised by Bishop Parry in 1620, remains in all essentials the Welsh Bible in use today.

3½M *SW of Betws-y-Coed, best approached from B4406 through Penmachno (61 E7)*

The Weir, Hereford and Worcester A garden with views of the river Wye and the Welsh mountains. The house (not open) dates from 1784.

Swainshill, 5M *W of Hereford on A438 (59 H10)*

Westbury Court Garden, Gloucestershire Laid out between 1696 and 1705, this formal water-garden with canals and yew hedges is an early example of its kind and something of a rarity because most such gardens were broken up when they became unfashionable in the eighteenth century.

Westbury-on-Severn on A48 (57 C10)

Wilderhope Manor, Shropshire Standing in a remote valley, Wilderhope is a late sixteenth-century house built of local limestone and little altered. The seventeenth-century decorated plasterwork ceilings are the principal attraction of the interior, that in the hall bearing the initials of Francis and Ellen Smallman who built the house.

7M *E of Church Stretton off B4371 (59 C11)*

Williamston Park, Dyfed In medieval times one of the deer parks of Carew Castle, and much quarried during the eighteenth and nineteenth centuries, the park is now a nature reserve. (Managed by the West Wales Naturalists' Trust. No parking; access only by footpath.)

The promontory between the Cresswell and Carew rivers, SE of Lawrenny (54 F4)

Castles, Abbeys & other Buildings

Arlington Row, Gloucestershire A row of early seventeenth-century stone cottages. (Cottages not open.) *Bibury, on S side of A433 (84 D2)*

Ashleworth Tithe Barn, Gloucestershire A barn of the fifteenth century, 120 feet long with a stone roof and two porch bays.

6M *N of Gloucester, E of A417 (57 B11)*

Assembly Rooms, Bath, Avon Built by the younger John Wood in 1771 when Bath was at its most fashionable, these elegant rooms are frequently mentioned by Jane Austen and also feature in Dickens's *Pickwick Papers*. The rooms as seen today were rebuilt after being gutted by a fire bomb in 1942, with redecoration (1979) in late eighteenth-century style. (The Rooms are leased to the City Council and used for public functions. The Museum of Costume is not National Trust.)

Alfred Street, Bath (57 H10)

Blaise Hamlet, Avon A group of ten cottages in differing styles around a green, built in 1809 by John Nash for John Harford to house his estate pensioners. (Cottages not open.)

4M *N of central Bristol, W of Henbury and just N of B4057 (57 F9)*

Bredon Tithe Barn, Hereford and Worcester A fourteenth-century barn 132 feet in length and unusual for having a stone chimney serving the bailiff's room over the easternmost porch. Seriously damaged by fire in 1980 and being restored, it will *not* be open until repairs are completed.

3M *NE of Tewkesbury, N of B4080 (57 A12)*

Chipping Campden Market Hall, Gloucestershire A Jacobean market hall of 1627 with pointed gables and an open arcade.

Chipping Campden, opposite the Police Station (88 H5)

Cilgerran Castle, Dyfed The ruins of a thirteenth-century castle, built on the site of an earlier one by William Marshall, son of the Earl of Pembroke. Marshall's work was short-lived and by 1326 the castle was recorded as a ruin, though later there was rebuilding from time to time and the Vaughan family lived here until the early seventeenth century.

Strikingly perched on rock above the Teifi, the ruins have inspired such artists as Turner and Richard Wilson. They comprise outer and inner wards, separated by a rock-cut ditch. Entered through a gatehouse which stood beyond a drawbridge over the ditch, the inner ward preserves lengths of curtain wall, round east and west towers and a very ruined rectangular north-west tower, this last a fourteenth-century addition. Only fragments recall the domestic buildings that would have leaned against the inner walls. Two short sections of wall – one just north-west of the gatehouse, the other on the cliff edge at the north-east – are remnants of the twelfth-century castle. (Under the guardianship of the Secretary of State for Wales.)

3M S of Cardigan, 1½M E of A478 (54 C5)

Clytha Park, Gwent The estate includes a hill-top mock castle of 1790 and a nineteenth-century house. (Picnic site. Castle not open. House open by appointment.)

4M SE of Abergavenny, on A40 (57 C7)

The Fleece Inn, Hereford and Worcester Dating in part from the fourteenth century, this half-timbered house was first licensed as an inn in 1848. It is still an inn today.

Bretforton, 4M E of Evesham on B4035 (88 H4)

Hailes Abbey, Gloucestershire The extensive excavated remains of a Cistercian abbey founded with great pomp in 1246 by Richard, Earl of Cornwall. Richard was buried here and the abbey was long famous for its relic of the Holy Blood, mentioned by Chaucer in his *Pardoner's Tale*. The seventeen cloister arches are the main surviving feature and the site includes a small museum. (Under the guardianship of the Department of the Environment.)

8M NE of Cheltenham, near Winchcombe, 1M E of A46 (84 A2)

Superbly positioned on a rocky promontory above the gorge of the Teifi River, Cilgerran Castle is almost unassailable on two sides.

Hawford Dovecote, Hereford and Worcester Sixteenth-century and half-timbered.

3M N of Worcester, ½M E of A449 (88 F2)

The Kymin, Gwent A hill over 800 feet high with a tower called the Round House, built by a dining club in 1794, and a 'naval temple' put up by the same club in 1800 in honour of the Royal Navy, commemorating sixteen admirals and crowned with a statue of Britannia. Nelson breakfasted here in 1802. (Buildings not open.)

1M E of Monmouth between A466 and A4136 (57 C8)

Little Fleece, Gloucestershire A modest Cotswold town house, probably seventeenth-century. (Let as a bookshop.)

Painswick, 4M N of Stroud, off A46 (57 C11)

Middle Littleton Tithe Barn, Hereford and Worcester A barn 140 feet in length and dating from the thirteenth or fourteenth century.

3M NE of Evesham, E of B4085 (88 G4)

Paxton's Tower, Dyfed A folly of 1811 built by Sir William Paxton as a memorial to Nelson. (Not open. Car park with view.)

7M E of Carmarthen, S of B4300 (55 E8)

Skenfrith Castle, Gwent An unusually small ruined castle with a raised round keep standing within a roughly square curtain wall. Although there was probably a primitive fortress here as early as 1071, what is seen today was largely built by Hubert de Burgh between 1201 and 1239, the design being interesting for the way in which the keep is deliberately set on a mound of spoil so that defenders could fire on targets beyond the curtain. The west range of buildings, contemporary with the rest of the castle, was discovered only in 1954. With White and Grosmont (neither National Trust), Skenfrith was one of three castles known as the 'Welsh Trilateral', granted by King John to Hubert de Burgh. (Under the guardianship of the Secretary of State for Wales.)

6M NW of Monmouth on B4521 (57 B8)

Town Walls Tower, Shrewsbury, Shropshire Built in the fourteenth century, this is Shrewsbury's only surviving watch-tower. (Not open.)

Shrewsbury, Town Walls on S of the inner town (59 A10)

Tu Hwnt i'r Bont, Gwynedd The 'House over the Bridge' is a fifteenth-century stone building which in turn served as a courthouse and two cottages. (Let as a tea-room.)

Llanrwst, at W end of the bridge of 1636 (61 D7)

Skenfrith Castle. With Grosmont and White Castle, it formed a line of defence for the Norman Lords Marcher (the 'Welsh Trilateral').

Westbury College Gatehouse, Avon The fifteenth-century gatehouse of a college of priests of which John Wiclif was a prebend. The college was founded in the thirteenth century on the site of an earlier Benedictine monastery.

Westbury-on-Trym, 3M N of central Bristol, key from 44 Eastfield Road (57 G9)

Wichenford Dovecote, Hereford and Worcester Seventeenth-century and half-timbered.

5½M NW of Worcester, N of B4204 (88 F1)

Archaeological & Industrial Sites

Breinton Springs, Hereford and Worcester Much of this farm and woodland is the site of a medieval village, the misnamed Breinton Camp in fact being a homestead enclosure. Footpath.

2M W of Hereford, left bank of the Wye (59 H10)

The Bulwark, West Glamorgan A complex Iron Age hill-fort.

Gower (55 H8)

Bushey Norwood, Avon Farmland with the

site of a field system and of a walled courtyard. The property is bounded on the north by part of a hill-fort. Footpath.

2M *SE of Bath (57 H11)*

Cadbury Camp, Avon An Iron Age hill-fort with a double rampart.

2½M *E of Clevedon (57 G8)*

Chedworth Roman Villa, Gloucestershire The extensive remains of a large Romano-British country house, occupied between about 180 to 350 and discovered and excavated in 1864. Some thirty-two rooms have been identified, including two sets of baths, one of these the damp heat type and the other the later dry system. There are some mosaic floors and the hypocaust system is well seen. Local material is shown in a site museum.

Near Yanworth, 8M SE of Cheltenham (84 C2)

Crickley Hill, Gloucestershire A Cotswold escarpment on which is part of an Iron Age fort.

6M *E of Gloucester, just N of A417 (57 C12)*

Croft Ambrey, Hereford and Worcester This large Iron Age fort above Croft Castle was first occupied in the fourth century BC, at that time being no more than a small defensive enclosure of some eight acres. When the Romans threatened in AD 43, the camp was much enlarged by second and third banks and outer defences, but was abandoned about seven years later after the defeat of Caractacus.

Croft Castle, 5M NW of Leominster, approached from B4362 (59 F10)

Dinas Gynfor, Gwynedd Part of an Iron Age fort on the northernmost point in Wales.

Cemaes, Anglesey, N of Llanbadrig (60 A3)

Dolaucothi, Dyfed A large property on which are the aqueducts, opencasts and shafts of gold mines, worked perhaps in prehistoric times but principally exploited by the Romans and also on and off since then. Close by (picnic site), the ancient Five Saints (Pumpsaint) Stone bears indentations, possibly the result of Roman rock-breaking but traditionally and more romantically left by five saints who used the stone as a pillow.

Pumpsaint on A482 (58 H2)

Haresfield Beacon and Standish Wood, Gloucestershire The Beacon (713 feet) may be the site of a hill-fort, and there is a Neolithic long barrow in Randwick Wood on the south.

2 to 3M NW of Stroud between A419 and A46 (57 C11)

Leigh Woods, Avon Woodland in which is the Iron Age hill-fort of Stokeleigh Camp.

Left bank of the Avon by Clifton suspension bridge (57 G9)

Little Solsbury Hill, Avon An Iron Age hill-fort with ramparts still faced with dry-stone walling.

2½M *NE of Bath between A46 and A4 (57 G11)*

Long Mynd, Shropshire On this large tract of upland moor there are some fifteen barrows, three stretches of defensive earthworks, and a length of the Port Way, a prehistoric track, later a drovers' road.

W of Church Stretton (A49) (59 C9)

Midsummer Hill, Hereford and Worcester An Iron Age hill-fort with hut sites.

Malvern Hills, N of A438 (88 H1)

Minchinhampton Commons, Gloucestershire Amberley Camp and Minchinhampton Bulwarks are Iron Age defences, and there are also remains of a long barrow.

N of Nailsworth and E of A46 (57 D11)

Mynydd-y-Graig, Gwynedd Iron Age hill-fort and megalithic remains.

Plas-yn-Rhiw, Lleyn (60 G2)

Pointz Castle, Dyfed A Norman motte.
5M *E of St David's, S of A487 (54 E2)*

Rainbow Wood Farm, Avon Iron Age field enclosures. Footpath.

Claverton Down, just SE of Bath (57 H11)

Rhossili Down, West Glamorgan The highest point in Gower, with the remains of two prehistoric burial chambers known as Sweyne's Houses (Howes), traditionally the grave of Sweyne Forkbeard, the Viking to whom Swansea is said to trace its name.

Gower, above Rhossili Bay (55 H7)

Rodborough Common, Gloucestershire Part of the site of an Iron Age enclosure.

1M *S of Stroud between A46 and A419 (57 D11)*

St David's Head, Dyfed The *Octopitarum* of Ptolemy. A stone rampart across the base may be Iron Age in origin. Near the headland there is a burial chamber, and there are remains of others in the area. *NW of St David's (54 D1)*

Sand Point, Kewstoke, Avon Here 'Castle Batch' is probably a Norman motte, while a mound to the east is the remains of a round barrow. (Leased to Axbridge Rural District Council.)

5M *N of Weston-super-Mare (56 H6)*

Segontium, Gwynedd A Roman fort probably built in AD 78 by Agricola for auxiliaries and occupied until about 380. What is seen is the ground plan, this including something of the defensive enceinte and gates, the barracks, and some administrative buildings, among them the commander's house. The excellent museum covers not only this site but also general aspects of Roman military life. Segontium is by tradition associated with Magnus Maximus (d.387), the Roman commander in Britain who was proclaimed emperor by disaffected troops and who lives in Welsh legend as Macsen Wledig. (Under the guardianship of the Secretary of State for Wales.)

SE outskirts of Caernarfon beside A487 (60 D4)

Telford Bridge, Gwynedd A suspension bridge across the Conwy completed by Thomas Telford in 1826 to replace the ferry. Telford exhibition in the Old Toll House.

Conwy (61 C7)

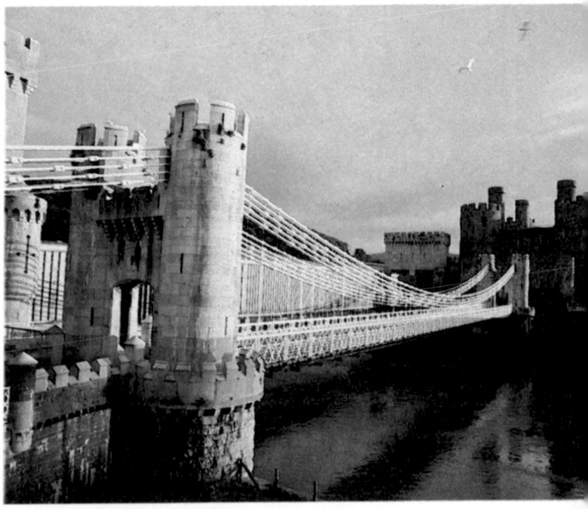

Telford's Conway Suspension Bridge was a major technical achievement of its time. Conwy Castle stands at the southern end.

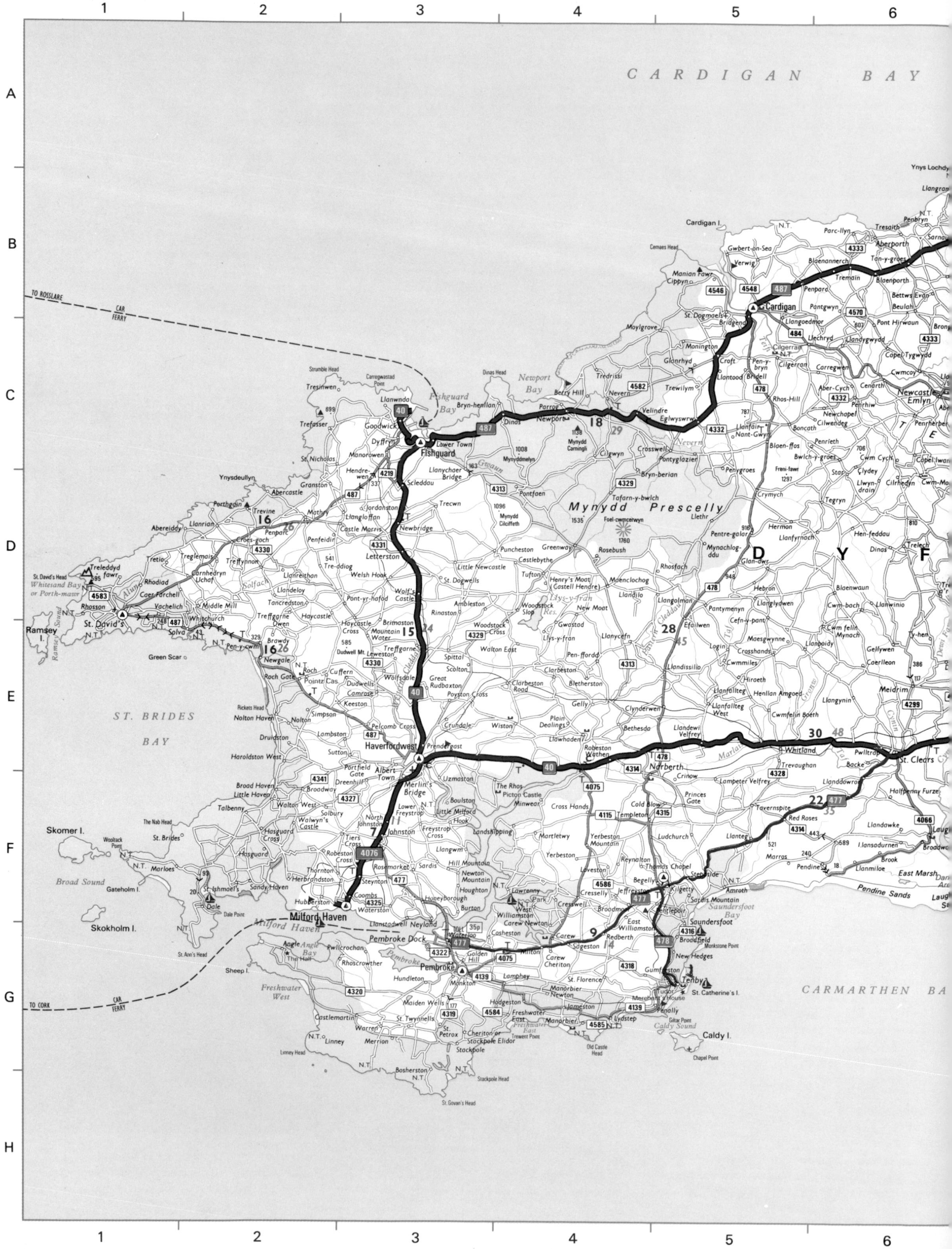
CARDIGAN BAY
ST. BRIDES BAY
CARMARTHEN BAY
Mynydd Prescelly
TO ROSSLARE CAR FERRY
TO CORK CAR FERRY
Fishguard
Cardigan
Newport
St. David's
Haverfordwest
Milford Haven
Pembroke
Pembroke Dock
Tenby
Narberth
Whitland
St. Clears
Saundersfoot
Newcastle Emlyn
Aberporth
Letterston
Solva
Ramsey I.
Skomer I.
Skokholm I.
Caldy I.
Cardigan I.
Dale
Angle
Neyland
Kilgetty
Amroth
Pendine
Laugharne
Crymych
Eglwyswrw
Dinas
Goodwick
Broad Haven
Little Haven
Manorbier
Lamphey
Castlemartin
Bosherston
Stackpole
Pendine Sands
Freshwater West
Broad Sound
Milford Haven
Newport Bay
Fishguard Bay
Whitesand Bay or Porth-mawr
St. David's Head
Strumble Head
Dinas Head
Cemaes Head
St. Ann's Head
St. Govan's Head
Linney Head
St. Catherine's I.

7 8 9 10 11 12

Aberystwyth — Aberystwyth — Adjoining page 58

A B C D E F G H

Adjoining page 58 — Builth Wells — Brecon — Adjoining page 56 — Brecon — Merthyr Tydfil

7 8 9 10 11 12

Cardiff — Adjoining page 56

1 Builth Wells 2 Adjoining page 58 3 4 Builth Wells 5 Willersley 6

Llandeilo Adjoining page 55 Swansea

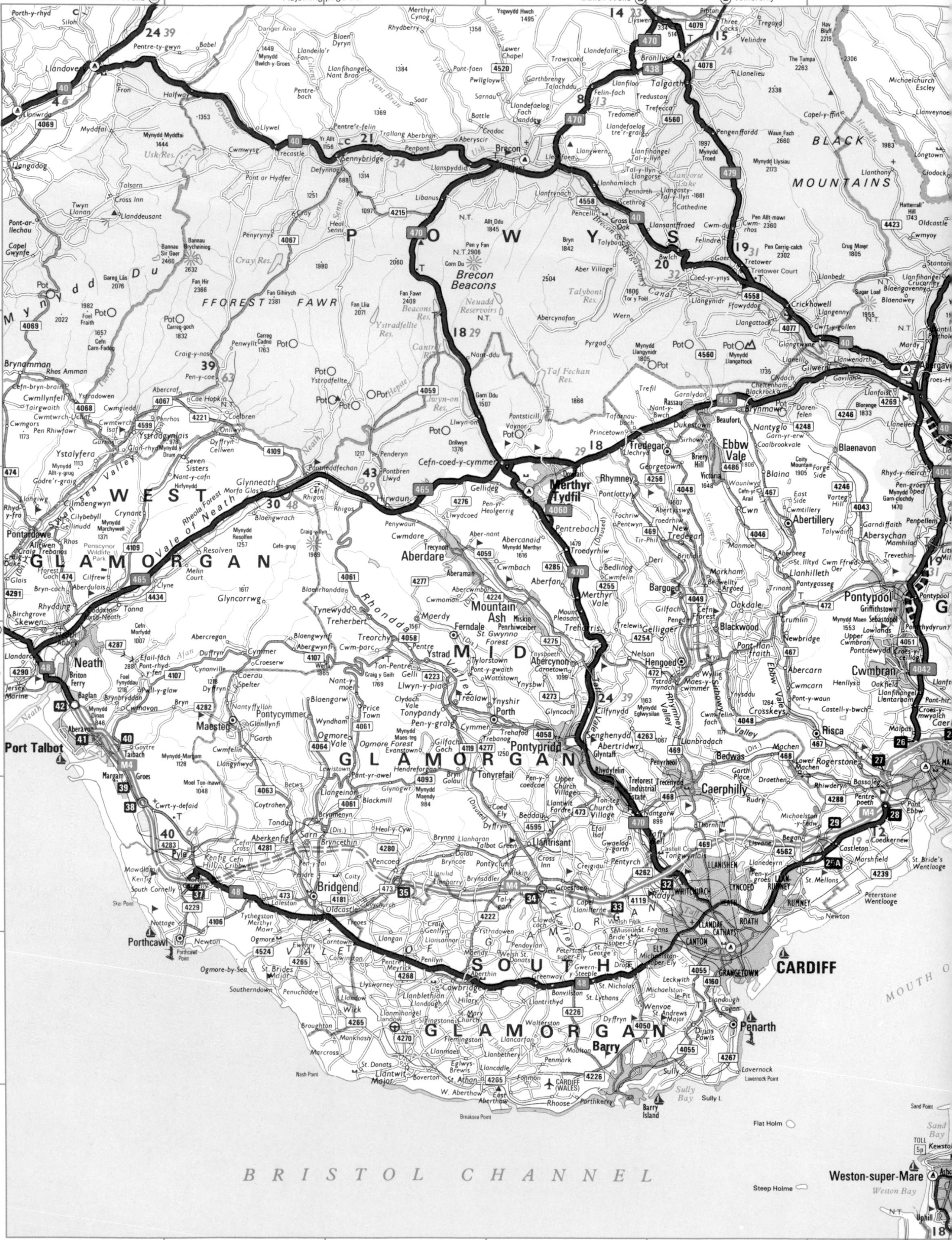

1 Adjoining page 38 2 3 4 5 6

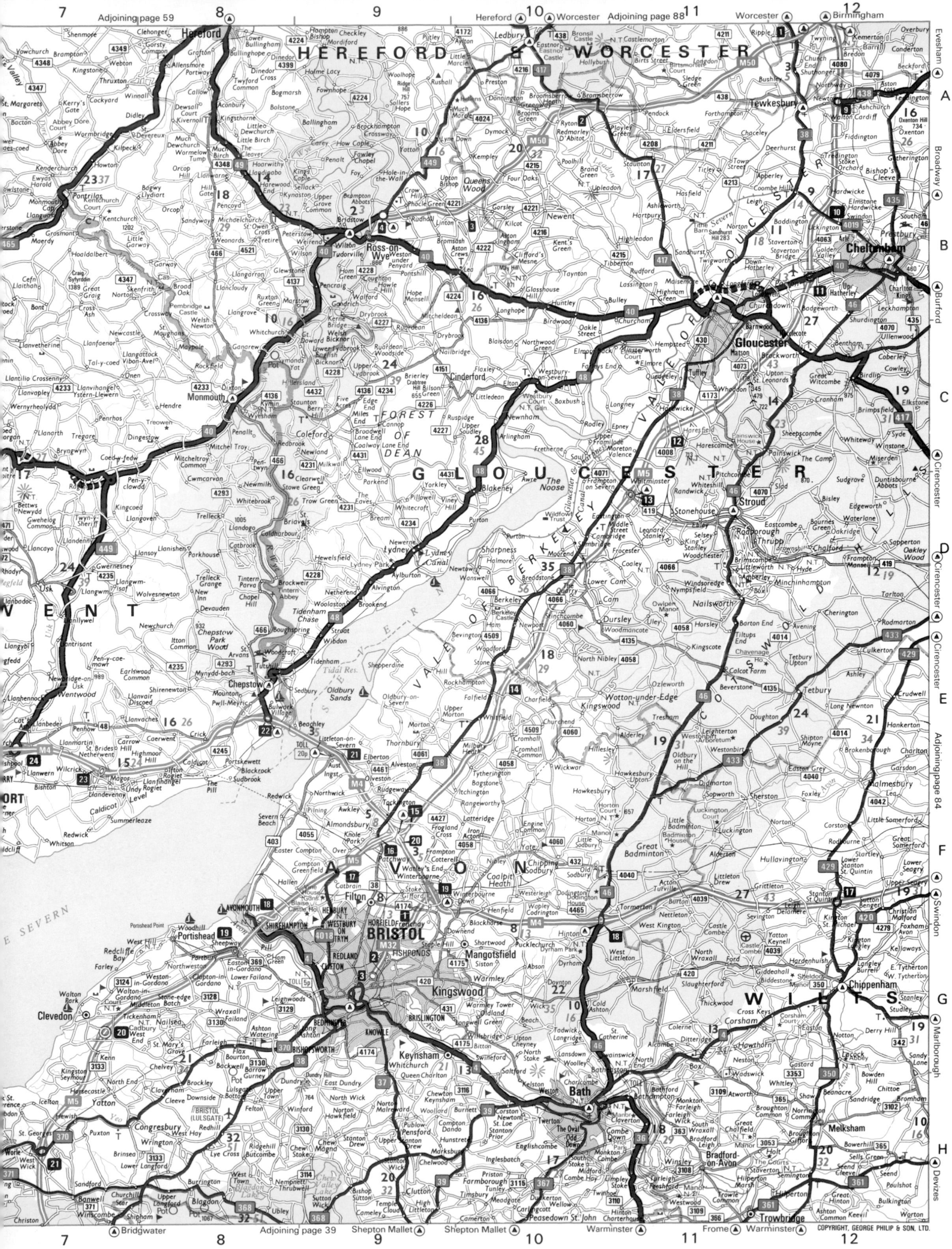
Adjoining page 59
Adjoining page 88
Adjoining page 39
Adjoining page 84
HEREFORD & WORCESTER
GLOUCESTER
AVON
WILTS.
FOREST OF DEAN
VALE OF GLOUCESTER
VALE OF BERKELEY
COTSWOLD HILLS
Hereford
Worcester
Birmingham
Evesham
Broadway
Burford
Cirencester
Swindon
Marlborough
Devizes
Bridgwater
Shepton Mallet
Warminster
Frome
Ross-on-Wye
Monmouth
Chepstow
Gloucester
Cheltenham
Tewkesbury
Stroud
Bristol
Bath
Chippenham
Trowbridge
Malmesbury
Tetbury
Clevedon
Portishead
Keynsham
Melksham
COPYRIGHT, GEORGE PHILIP & SON, LTD.

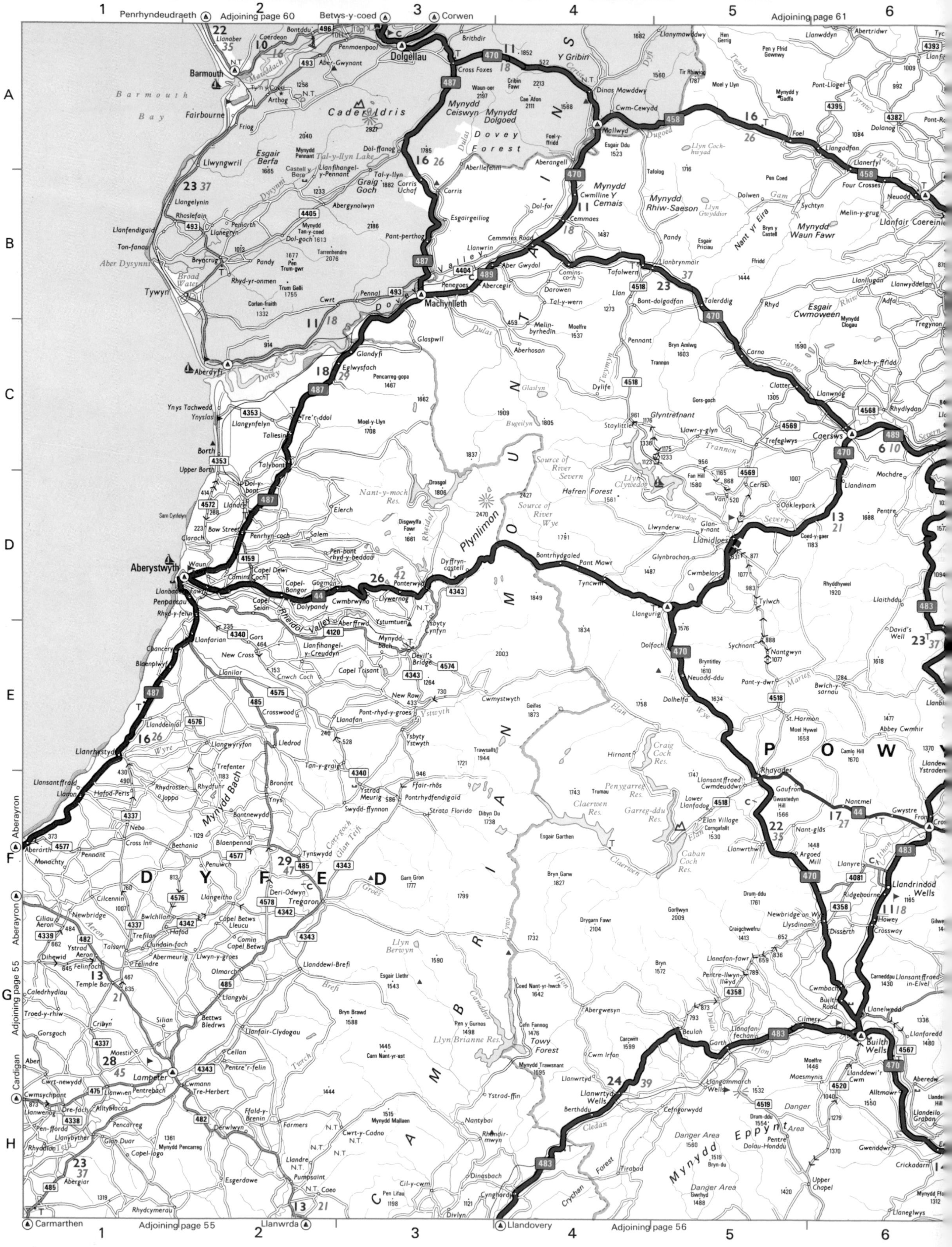

Penrhyndeudraeth
Adjoining page 60
Betws-y-coed
Corwen
Adjoining page 61
Adjoining page 55
Llanwrda
Llandovery
Adjoining page 56
Carmarthen
Aberayron
Cardigan
Barmouth
Barmouth Bay
Fairbourne
Dolgellau
Cader Idris
Mynydd Ceiswyn
Mynydd Dolgoed
Dovey Forest
Dinas Mawddwy
Mallwyd
Llwyngwril
Tal-y-llyn Lake
Corris
Abergynolwyn
Tywyn
Aberdyfi
Machynlleth
Dovey Valley
Cemmaes
Cemmaes Road
Llanbrynmair
Talerddig
Carno
Caersws
Llanidloes
Llangurig
Rhayader
Llandrindod Wells
Builth Wells
Llanwrtyd Wells
Borth
Talybont
Aberystwyth
Plynlimon
Ponterwyd
Devil's Bridge
Rheidol Valley
Nant-y-moch Res.
Hafren Forest
Source of River Severn
Source of River Wye
Llyn Clywedog
Llanrhystyd
Tregaron
Lampeter
Llandewi-Brefi
Strata Florida
Claerwen Res.
Craig Goch Res.
Penygarreg Res.
Garreg-ddu Res.
Caban Coch Res.
Elan Village
Llyn Brianne Res.
Towy Forest
Mynydd Eppynt
Danger Area
Llanfair Caereinion
Mynydd Waun Fawr
Mynydd Rhiw-Saeson
Esgair Cwmoween
Cambrian Mountains
Dyfed
Powys

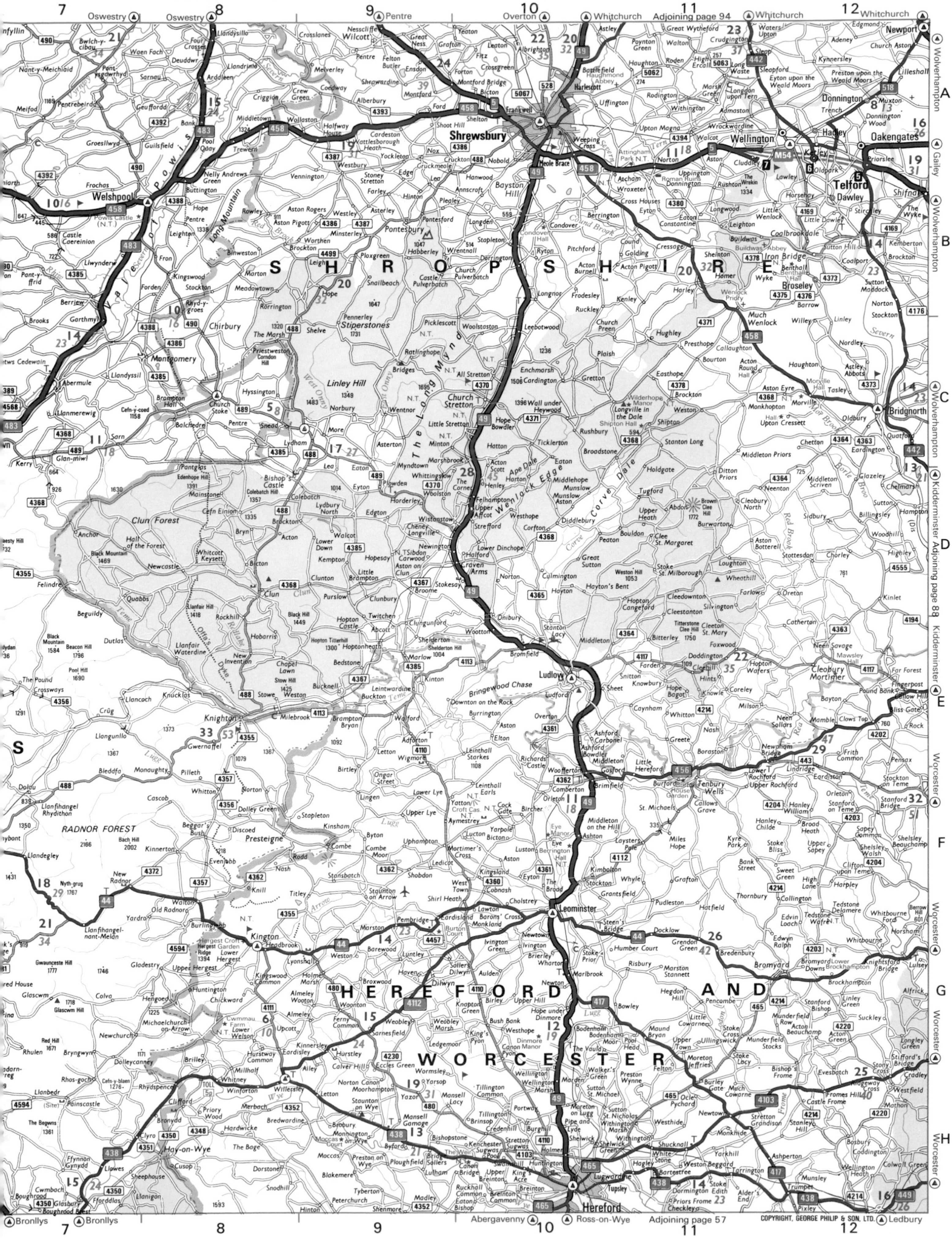
Adjoining page 94
Adjoining page 57
Adjoining page 88
Oswestry
Pentre
Overton
Whitchurch
Wolverhampton
Gailey
Kidderminster
Worcester
Bronllys
Abergavenny
Ross-on-Wye
Ledbury
S H R O P S H I R E
H E R E F O R D A N D W O R C E S T E R
RADNOR FOREST
Clun Forest
The Long Mynd
Wenlock Edge
Corve Dale
Ape Dale
Shrewsbury
Wellington
Telford
Oakengates
Newport
Welshpool
Montgomery
Bishop's Castle
Church Stretton
Craven Arms
Ludlow
Knighton
Presteigne
Kington
Leominster
Tenbury Wells
Bromyard
Bridgnorth
Much Wenlock
Iron Bridge
Cleobury Mortimer
Hay-on-Wye
Hereford
New Radnor
Clun
Weobley
Pontesbury
Stiperstones
Linley Hill
Bringewood Chase
COPYRIGHT, GEORGE PHILIP & SON, LTD.

1
2
3
4
5
6
A
B
C
D
E
F
G
H
The Skerries
Carmel Head
Cemlyn Bay
Cemaes Bay
Dinas Gynfor
Llanbadrig
Bull Bay
Amlwch Port
Point Lynas
Penrhyn
Tregele
Cemaes Bay
Burwen
Amlwch
Llaneilian
Llanfairynghornwy
Llanfechell
Bodewryd
Pentre-felin
Parys Mountain
Penysarn
Nebo
Dulas
Ynys Dulas
Church Bay
Llanrhyddlad
Rhosgoch
Carreglefn
Llanfflewyn
Rhydwyn
Holyhead
Bay
Llanbabo
Rhosybol
Tyn-y-pwll
City Dulas
Brynrefail
Dulas Bay
Din Lligwy
Ancient Village
Moelfre
Llanallgo
Marianglas
Benllech
Llanfaethlu
Llanddeusant
Llyn Alaw
Gwredog
Llandyfrydog
Maenaddwyn
TO DUN LAOGHAIRE
CAR FERRY
Elim
Llanerchymedd
Llanfwrog
Llantrisant
North Stack
Llaingoch
South Stack
Holyhead
Kingsland
Llanfachraeth
Llanfigael
Bachau
Coedana
Tyn-y-gongl
Brynteg
Pen-llyn
Llanynghenedl
Carmel
Capel-côch
Llyn Llywenan
Red Wharf Bay
Red Wharf
Mariandyrys
Puffin Island
Penmon
Penmon Priory
Porthdafarch
Penrhyn Mawr
Trearddur Bay
Valley
ANGLESEY
Bodedern
Trefor
Tregaian
Llanbedrgoch
Llanddona
Glan-yr-Afon
Llangoed
Caer-geiliog
Bryngwran
Llangwyllog
Llanddyfnan
Four Mile Bridge
Llanfihangel yn Nhowyn
Llynfaes
Rhos-meirch
Talwrn
Pentraeth
Llanfaes
Llanfair-yn-Neubwll
Rhoscolyn
Tywyn Trewan
Capel-gwyn
Gwalchmai
Bodffordd
Heneglwys
Llangefni
Ceint
Pen-y-garnedd
Llansadwrn
Beaumaris
Lavan Sands
Llanfairfechan
Penmaenmawr
Cymyran Bay
Pencarnisiog
Cerrigceinwen
Penmynydd
Llandegfan
Garizim
Nant-y-pandy
Gorddinog
Rhosneigr
Llanfaelog
Ty-croes
Llangristiolus
Gaerwen
Menai Bridge
Bangor
Aber
Penrhyn Castle
Pentre Berw
Malltraeth Marsh
Llanfairpwllgwyngyll
Llanddaniel Fab
Bryn-celli-ddu
Tal-y-bont
Llyn Coron
Bethel
Trefdraeth
Llangadwaladr
Llangwyfanisaf
Aberffraw
Hermon
Malltraeth
Plas Newydd
Llandegai
Moel Wnion
Aber Falls
Drum
Llanllechid
Rachub
Foel-fras
Llangaffo
Port Dinorwic
Bryn-Siencyn
Glasinfryn
Pentir
Tregarth
Bethesda
Gerlan
Bodorgan
Malltraeth Sands
Llangeinwen
Dwyran
Newborough
Llanddeiniolen
Sling
Rhiwlas
Douglas Hill
Bethel
Saron
Penisarwaun
Nant Ffrancon
Carnedd Llewelyn
Carnedd Dafydd
Pen Llithrig y-wrach
Malltraeth Bay
Newborough Warren
Caernarfon
Segontium
Llanrug
Pont-rug
Bryn Bras
Cwm-y-glo
Brynrefail
Clwyt-y-bont
Deiniolen
Dinorwic
Fachwen
Llyn Padarn
Mynydd Perfedd
Llyn Ogwen
Pont Rhyd-goch
Llugwy
The Bar
Fort Belan
Abermenai Point
CAERNARFON
Caeathraw
Ceunant
Llanberis
Llyn Peris
Pont Pen-y-benglog
Glyder Fach
Capel Curig
Llanfaglan
Bontnewydd
Gwyrfai
Waunfawr
Nant Peris
Glyder Fawr
Rhostryfan
Betws Garmon
Salem
Pass of Llanberis
Dinas Dinlle
Llandwrog
Llanwnda
Rhosgadfan
Moel Tryfan
Pen-y-Gwryd
Groeslon
Glynllifon Park
Carmel
Snowdon
Carnedd Moel-siabod
BAY
Fron
Nantlle
Llyn Cwellyn
Llyn Llydaw Res.
Penygroes
Talysarn
Rhyd-Ddu
Y Cribau
Pont-lyfni
Trwyn Maen Dylan
Llanllyfni
Yr Aran
Bethania
Llyn Gwynant
Blaenau-Dolwyddelan
Yr Arddu
Aberdesach
Tai'r-lon
Nebo
Nasareth
Clynnog-fawr
Capel-uchaf
Garnedd-goch
Nantgwynant
Glanaber
Pant-glas
GWYNEDD
Dwyfor
Trwyn y Tal
Bwlch Mawr
Gurn Ddu
Upper Clynnog
Beddgelert
Moel Hebog
Pass of Aberglaslyn
Nantmor
Cnicht
Rhiwbryfdir
Trwyn y Gorlech
Trevor
Yr Eifl
Dwyfach
Bryncir
Garn-Dolbenmaen
Llanfihangel-y-pennant
Moel-ddu
Tan-y-grisiau
Moelwyn Mawr
Llanaelhaearn
Glan-Dwyfach
Llyn Cwmystradllyn
Croesor
Glaslyn
Llithfaen
Carreg Ddu
Pistyll
Pencaenewydd
Llangybi
Dolbenmaen
Golan
Tan-lan
Rhyd-y-sarn
Tan-y-bwlch
Morfa-Nefyn
Nefyn
Rhos-lan
Penmorfa
Prenteg
Garreg
Rhyd
Llanfrothen
Maentwrog
Gellilydan
Groesffordd
Edern
Fron
Tan-y-graig
Yffor
Llanarmon
Wern
Tremadog
Penrhyndeudraeth
Rhos-y-llan
Bodfuan
Llannor
Chwilog
Llanystumdwy
Pentre'r-felin
Porthmadog
Minffordd
Tudweiliog
Efailnewydd
Abererch
Criccieth
Morfa Bychan
Borth-y-gest
Portmeirion
Harlech Point
Porth Colmon
Dinas
Garn
Rhydyclafdy
Pwllheli
Pen-ychain
Talsarnau
Trawsfynydd Res.
Moel Ysgyfarnogod
Trawsfynydd
LLEYN PENINSULA
Llangwnnadl
Llaniestyn
Penrhos
West End
South Beach
Carreg yr Imbill
Tremadog Bay
Llanfihangel-y-traethau
Glan-y-Wern
Morfa Harlech
Meillteyrn
Sarn
Bryncroes
Botwnnog
Windmill
Mynytho
Llanbedrog
Trwyn Llanbedrog
Harlech
Penrhyn Mawr
Ty-Hen
Pen-y-groeslon
Methlem
Rhydlios
Rhoshirwaun
Llangian
St. Tudwal's Road
Abersoch
Capel Carmel
Rhiw
Plas-yn-Rhiw
Porth Neigwl or Hell's Mouth
Llandanwg
Llanfair
Rhinog Fawr
Rhinog Fach
Braich Anelog
Aberdaron
Llanfaelrhys
Llanengan
Sarn-bach
Marchros
Pentre Gwynfryn
Y Llethr
Gamlan
Braich y Pwll
Pwlldefaid
Uwchmynydd
Trwyn Talfarach
Bwlchtocyn
St. Tudwal's Islands
Llanbedr
Aberdaron Bay
Ynys Gwylan-fawr
Pen y Cil
Trwyn yr Wylfa
Morfa Dyffryn
Coed Ystumgwern
Moelfre
Llyn Bodlyn
Diffwys
Bardsey Sound
Trwyn Cilan
Llanenddwyn
Dyffryn-Ardudwy
Y Garn
Bardsey Island
Ysgethin
Tal-y-bont
Llawlech
CARDIGAN BAY
Uwch-mynydd
Bontddu
Llanaber
Caerdeon
Penmaenpool
Aber-Gwynant
Barmouth
Aberdyfi

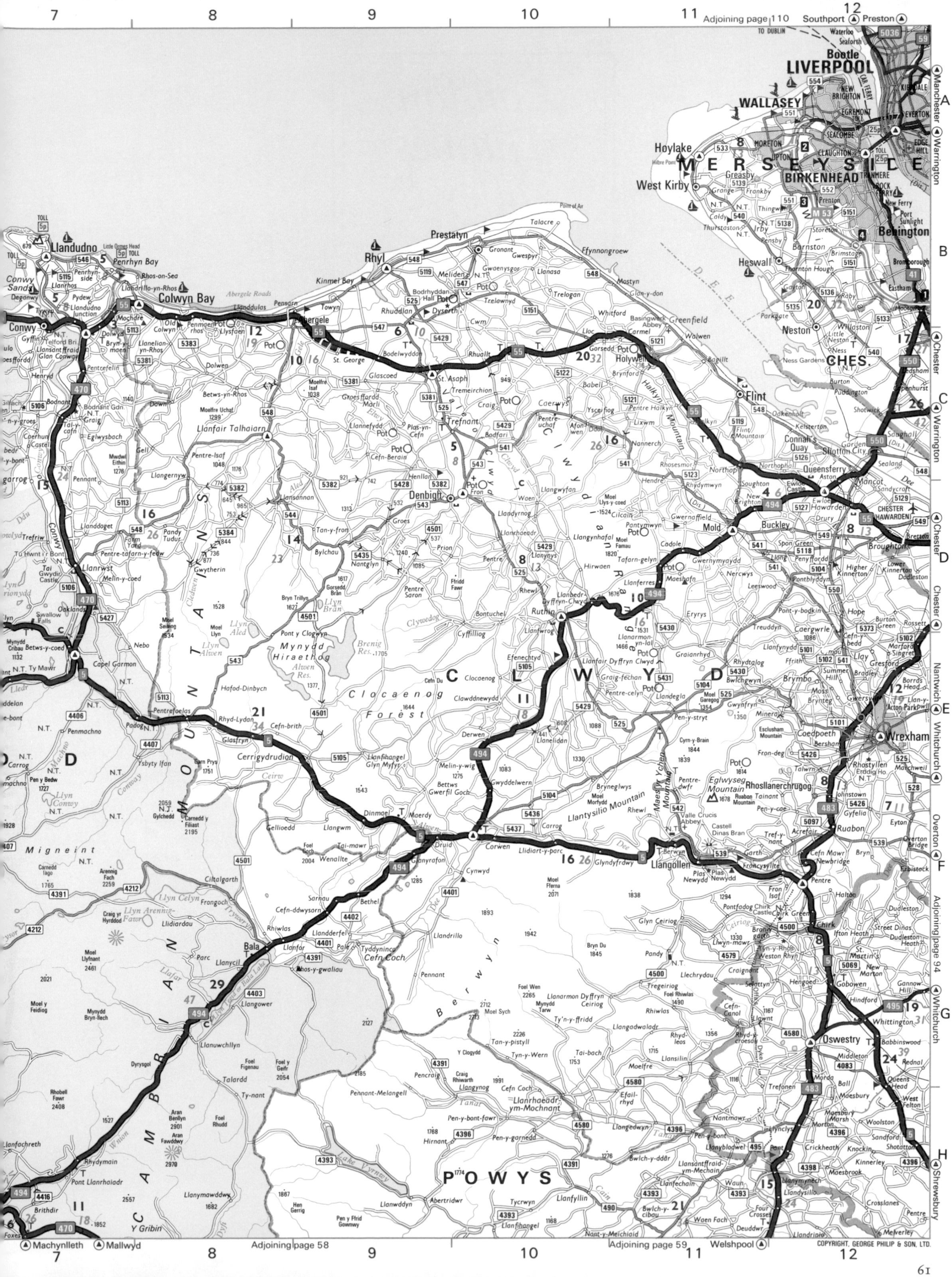

7
8
9
10
11
12
Adjoining page 110
Southport
Preston
LIVERPOOL
Bootle
WALLASEY
Hoylake
West Kirby
MERSEYSIDE
BIRKENHEAD
Bebington
Heswall
Neston
CHES.
Flint
Connah's Quay
Queensferry
Manchester
Warrington
Chester
Nantwich
Whitchurch
Shrewsbury
Adjoining page 94
A
B
C
D
E
F
G
H
Llandudno
Penrhyn Bay
Rhos-on-Sea
Colwyn Bay
Conwy
Conwy Sands
Deganwy
Abergele
Pensarn
Towyn
Kinmel Bay
Rhyl
Prestatyn
Meliden
Dyserth
Rhuddlan
Talacre
Point of Air
Gronant
Mostyn
Holywell
Greenfield
St. Asaph
Bodelwyddan
St. George
Trefnant
Denbigh
Llanfair Talhaiarn
Llangernyw
Llansannan
Llanrwst
Betws-y-coed
Capel Garmon
Pentrefoelas
Mold
Buckley
Hawarden
CHESTER (HAWARDEN)
Broughton
Ruthin
Llanbedr-Dyffryn-Clwyd
Llanfwrog
Clwydian Range
Moel Famau
Clocaenog Forest
Mynydd Hiraethog
Brenig Res.
Alwen Res.
Llyn Aled
Llyn Alwen
CLWYD
Cerrigydrudion
Derwen
Bettws Gwerfil Goch
Corwen
Llangollen
Wrexham
Ruabon
Chirk
Oswestry
Bala
Llyn Tegid or Bala Lake
Llanuwchllyn
Cefn Coch
Llandrillo
Berwyn
Llanrhaeadr-ym-Mochnant
Lake Vyrnwy
POWYS
Llanfyllin
Llansantffraid-ym-Mechain
Welshpool
CAMBRIAN MOUNTAINS
Migneint
Llyn Celyn
Machynlleth
Mallwyd
Adjoining page 58
Adjoining page 59

London, Thames Valley & Chilterns

PITSTONE WINDMILL

Here lovers both of open country and of elegant houses are well served by the Trust. It owns considerable areas on the breezy chalk hills, with their exhilarating views along the ridges and over the extensive plains, and others in the gentler Thames valley (a number of them, surprisingly unspoilt, in the northward loop of the river around Cookham). At the same time it owns some great houses – houses which seem largely to match the calm landscape and to reflect the spirit of their former occupants: urbane, civilized, and confident. Only the earthworks of ancient hill-forts recall times of constant fear and strife; the Trust owns no later castles here – indeed with the notable exception of Windsor there are very few in the whole region.

Some who enjoy visiting houses are more interested in the personalities that pervade them than in their architecture, decoration, or contents for their intrinsic worth. For them Carlyle's House (Thomas Carlyle), Hughenden Manor (Benjamin Disraeli), and Shaw's Corner (Bernard Shaw) will hold a special appeal, although on all the important houses the previous owners have left their mark.

Variety is a characteristic of the Trust's properties everywhere. Those in this region include four villages, two inns, a moated gate-house, a huge and remarkable dovecote, a seventeenth-century windmill, a duck decoy, a 'Roman bath', and a monastic barn considered by William Morris to be 'as noble as a cathedral'.

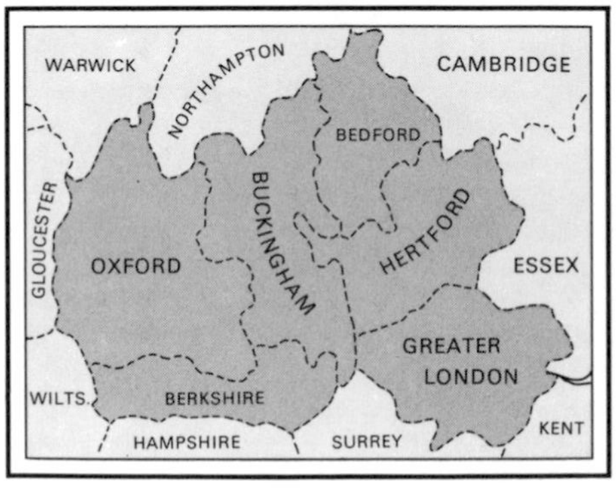

Countryside

The dominant features of this part of Britain are the ring of chalk hills – the Berkshire Downs and the Chilterns – to the west and north of London, and the River Thames, which breaks through the chalk at Goring Gap. The hills bear numerous signs of early human habitation, and of having provided in prehistoric times the chief highway across this part of the country.

The Trust cares for some of the most spectacular heights and viewpoints on these chalk uplands. **The Clappers, Sharpenhoe** (85 A11), is a dense beech clump at the northern end of the Chilterns; the steep flanks of the hill-side are clothed in trees and scrub covered with Traveller's Joy, or Old Man's Beard. There is an easy approach to it on foot (half a mile) from the car park to the south. **Dunstable Downs**

left **The Ashridge Estate (north of Berkhamsted) includes much fine woodland.**

below **The view to the west from Dunstable Downs, a 285-acre property on the Chilterns. Ivinghoe Beacon, also National Trust, is in the left background.**

(85 B10/11), partly Trust property, is another steep ridge commanding long views over the Midland Plain. **Ivinghoe Beacon** (85 B/C10) is perhaps the best-known viewpoint, while **Coombe Hill**, further west (85 C9), is, at 852 feet, the highest; from here one looks north-east back to Ivinghoe, north to Mentmore Towers, north-west to Aylesbury, and west to the distant line of the Cotswolds beyond Oxford, while at the head of a valley a mile or so to the south stands Chequers, the Prime Minister's country residence. Beyond the chalk ridge of the Chilterns, the beech wood known as **Badbury Hill** (84 E4), above the village of *Coleshill*, covers an Iron Age fort, from the edge of which is a good and very distant view across the Upper Thames valley. These view-points are exhilarating; but seekers after solitude should turn elsewhere, even, surprisingly, to **Cock Marsh** (85 E9), on the south bank of the Thames facing Bourne End, one of the Trust's many properties in the Cookham and Maidenhead area. Here from a chalk ridge affording a superb view over the Thames and the town of Marlow a footpath descends to an enormous flat green expanse stretching to the river.

A countryside property of a different kind is to be found at Whipsnade (85 B11), where from the edge of the village green a footpath leads to the **Tree Cathedral**, with deciduous trees and conifers enclosing glades of quiet and mystery. Another is at **Finchampstead Ridges** (85 H9), a steep ridge of sand and heath covered with birch and sweet-smelling pine, with long southward views through the gaps in the trees.

Prehistoric sites abound in these counties. **Uffington White Horse** (84 E/F4) is an ancient landmark (*see below under Archaeological and Industrial Sites*); there are many Iron Age forts on the hills, notably on Ivinghoe Beacon, while in **Maidenhead Thicket** between the A4 and the A423 (85 F9) are the remains of an ancient British settlement.

An interesting survival is the **Boarstall Duck Decoy**, a stretch of water, acquired by the Trust in 1980, near *Boarstall Tower* (85 C7). Decoys were introduced into England from Holland by Charles II. Ducks are decoyed into netted-over funnels of water, called 'pipes', by a dog controlled by a decoyman. Nowadays they are, once caught, ringed for purposes of scientific study; in former times, however, they were killed and sent to market. At Boarstall there are also woodland walks in the vicinity of the lake; notes are supplied to help visitors interested in studying the local flora and fauna.

The traveller in these regions who likes gardens and parks will be well rewarded. Former landowners cherished their grounds as much as their houses, from Sir Francis Dashwood at *West Wycombe*, Ferdinand de Rothschild at *Waddesdon*, and the various owners of *Cliveden*, to Carlyle in his 'poor sooty patch' in Chelsea. The Trust, in the far from easy circumstances of today, strives to maintain the tradition.

Houses, Gardens & Parks

Ascott, Buckinghamshire People come here to see a lovely garden and an important collection of pictures, furniture, and Chinese porcelain. The house itself is a half-timbered building of the 1870s incorporating a farmhouse dating from the early seventeenth century.

Ascott was bought in 1873 by Baron Mayer de Rothschild of nearby Mentmore, and taken over as a hunting-lodge by Leopold de Rothschild, who employed the architect George Devey to transform and enlarge the old house. In 1937 Ascott passed to his son, the late Anthony de Rothschild, who with his wife was responsible for the present interior, and who gave Ascott and its great collection to the Trust in 1949.

The thirty-acre garden, laid out by Leopold de Rothschild, is remarkable for its specimen trees and shrubs. There are also fountains, sculptures, a sunken flower garden, a lily pond and an evergreen sundial – not to mention the cricket ground, still very much in use.

Indoors, the Ascott collection includes excellent examples of French and English furniture, of English, Dutch, French and Italian paintings, and of Chinese porcelain, particularly of the Ming dynasty (1368–1644) and of the K'ang Hsi period (1662–1722) collected by Anthony de Rothschild.

2M SW Leighton Buzzard, entrance on A418 (85 B9)

Ashdown House, Oxfordshire The fascination of this house lies in its lonely situation, its unusual – even bizarre – appearance, and the story of the man who built it, William, 1st Earl of Craven (1608–97), and his single-minded devotion to Elizabeth ('The Winter Queen'), sister of Charles I.

The house, built about 1663, probably by William Winde, is without any external ornamentation, and looks, even with its flanking pavilions, somewhat too tall and narrow. Inside, however, the rooms are light and well-proportioned, while from beside the cupola above there is a splendid view of the rolling chalk downs among which the house stands.

Although the 1st Earl of Craven died a bachelor, Ashdown House remained in the Craven family until 1956, when, little altered structurally but virtually empty and almost derelict, it was given with an endowment to the Trust. It was fortunate indeed when in 1968 twenty-three portraits from the large Craven collection of pictures were presented to the Trust by the Treasury to be hung here – portraits of the first owner, of the lady whose cause he championed and her large family, and of some of the people with whom they were both acquainted during the turbulent years of the seventeenth century.

2½M S Ashbury on B4000 (84 F4)

Basildon Park, Berkshire Basildon was built between 1776 and 1783 by the Yorkshire architect, John Carr, for Sir Francis Sykes, also a Yorkshireman, who had made his fortune in India. It has had a chequered history: from 1910 until the outbreak of World War II it stood empty, and was then requisitioned; in 1952 it was bought by Lord and Lady Iliffe, who restored and furnished it with great skill, using items acquired from another Carr house which was being demolished.

Notable features are the recessed portico of the west front, with its four tall Ionic columns, and the Octagon Drawing Room, whose three great windows look out across the Thames valley to the beechwoods beyond; but it was not until about 1840 that the interior decoration of this room was completed by J. B. Papworth during the ownership of James Morrison, a haberdasher who built up his large

Ashdown House, set off by a restored seventeenth-century formal garden, looks like an enormous doll's house.

fortune on the principle of 'small profits and quick returns', but who was also a man of taste and discernment.

The house contains much good plasterwork, and a splendid collection of pictures, particularly Italian pictures of the eighteenth century, acquired by Lord Iliffe. The spacious park and gardens set off the house to perfection.

7M NW Reading, on A329 (85 F7)

The Blewcoat School, London was founded in 1688, and moved here in 1709, when the house was built. The statue of a boy in a blue tunic stands in a niche above the front door. The handsome schoolroom is shown to visitors. (Open by prior arrangement.)

In Caxton Street, near St James's Park Underground station (see map below)

Buscot, Oxfordshire This property includes the village of Buscot and part of the surrounding countryside; Buscot Park, housing the Faringdon Collection of works of art; and Buscot Old Parsonage, an early eighteenth-century house of Cotswold stone.

Buscot Park was built shortly before 1780 by the then owner of the manor, Edward Loveden Townsend, probably acting as his own architect. The main façade was considerably altered in the nineteenth century by a later owner, Alexander Henderson, 1st Baron Faringdon, a renowned connoisseur and collector. In the 1930s it was restored to its original appearance by the 2nd Lord Faringdon, advised by the architect Geddes Hyslop, who also designed the two pavilions that now stand east and west of the house.

Within, there is an outstanding collection of paintings of the Italian, Dutch, Flemish, Spanish, and English Schools, and of English and French furniture. There are also some excellent examples of Chinese porcelain.

The formal water-garden, which blends so well with the house and park, was laid out early in the twentieth century by Harold Peto for the 1st Lord Faringdon.

(Buscot Old Parsonage open by appointment with the tenant.)

Between Faringdon and Lechlade, on A417 (84 D/E3)

Carlyle's House, London This modest eighteenth-century house, where Thomas Carlyle (1795–1881), writer and philosopher, lived from 1834 onwards, has about it the aura of this great man and of his lively and intelligent wife.

The kitchen in the basement and the sitting room on the ground floor – 'unfashionable in the highest degree', wrote Carlyle, 'but in the highest degree comfortable and serviceable' – look much as they did in the Carlyles' time. Most of the furniture now in the library or drawing room was theirs too.

Upstairs in what for a time was Mrs Carlyle's bedroom is her famous 'red bed', its red hangings long since decayed. In the dressing room stands a mahogany washstand, given by Carlyle to 'the neatest of all Women'. And at the top of the house is the Attic Study, which was intended to be sound-proof but turned out not to be. The 'poor sooty patch of garden', on the other hand, where Carlyle cut the grass with a sickle, provided some solace.

Note: Certain rooms have no electric light. Visitors wishing to make a close study of the interior should avoid dull days early and late in the season.

24 Cheyne Row, Chelsea (see map below)

97–100 Cheyne Walk, London Comprises most of Lindsey House, built in 1674 on the site of Sir Thomas More's garden, and much altered in the mid eighteenth century. (Not open.)

Just W of the N end of Battersea Bridge (86 F3)

Claydon House, Buckinghamshire From 1620 Claydon was the seat of the Verney family, of violently fluctuating fortunes. The present house dates almost wholly from the mid eighteenth century, the creation of the improvident 2nd Earl Verney, and is decorated in flamboyant rococo style. The Earl built a huge rotunda attached to the north side of the surviving west wing, with another identical wing beyond, but both proved to have inadequate foundations and had to be demolished shortly after the Earl's death.

What remains, however, is quite enough to satisfy the most demanding student of architecture and interior design. The North Hall, with swirling designs on walls and ceiling; the saloon, equally magnificent but more restrained; the library, with its superb ceiling and frieze; above all the Chinese Room and the great staircase – these are some of the delights of Claydon.

In Victorian times Florence Nightingale (whose sister was the wife of Sir Harry Verney, the 2nd Baronet) was a frequent visitor here; the bedroom she always occupied is shown, as are a number of letters and relics.

In the grounds are three lakes, and, less than fifty yards from the house, the church of Middle Claydon.

3½M SW Winslow, near the village of Middle Claydon (85 B8)

Cliveden, Buckinghamshire This great house, standing above a beautiful reach of the Thames, was built in the Italianate style in 1851 by Sir Charles Barry, chief architect of the (quite different) Houses of Parliament. But there had been a house on the site from soon after 1666, when the 2nd Duke of Buckingham commissioned William Winde to design the terrace and on it to build a four-storeyed brick house.

Carr's great staircase at Basildon Park is unusually lit by giant semi-circular windows. The delicate plasterwork repeats neo-classical themes established in the hall.

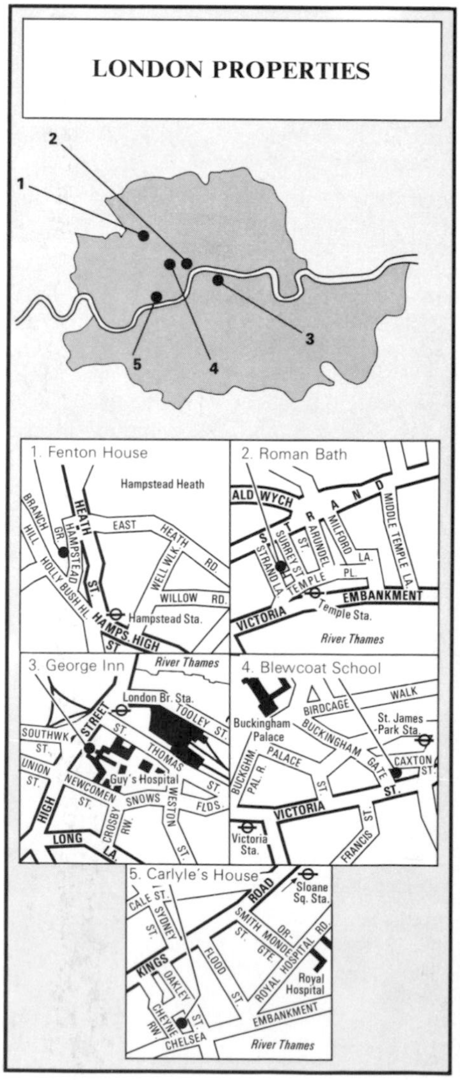

above **The Chinese Room, Claydon House, decorated by Luke Lightfoot, reflects the eighteenth-century fashion for chinoiserie.**

below left **The formal water garden at Buscot Park was laid out by Harold Peto early in this century.**

below **The beds of the magnificent parterre at Cliveden are now bordered with box and planted with lavender and *Senecio*.**

It is fascinating to follow the development of the buildings and grounds through various changes of ownership and of fortune, including two disastrous fires. Now Cliveden is let to Stanford University of California for overseas courses; but although only two rooms of the house are shown to visitors for a limited season, the extensive grounds are open daily throughout the year.

The grounds are formal in character, and contain two eighteenth-century buildings by Giacomo Leoni (the architect of *Clandon Park* in Surrey and *Lyme Park* in Cheshire) as well as

above The garden at Greys Court makes no attempt to be grand or impressive – its informal charm reflects years of slow growth and change.

left Fenton House is noted for its collection of keyboard instruments and for Lady Binning's porcelain collection. Both are represented here – the harpsichord is by Jacob and Abraham Kirckman, 1777.

below The interior of Osterley Park is almost wholly the creation of Robert Adam. His decoration of the Etruscan Room was inspired by the ornamentation on Greek vases found at Pompeii in the mid eighteenth century.

some good examples of classical Roman sarcophagi and of Italian Renaissance statuary collected by the 1st Viscount Astor, a former owner.

On N bank of the Thames 2M N *Taplow, off B476 (85 F10)*

Dorneywood Garden, Buckinghamshire A garden with pleasant lawns and many flowering shrubs. The house (not open) is the residence of a Secretary of State or a Minister of the Crown. (Garden open at certain times in August and September on written application.)

2M N *Burnham (85 F10)*

Eastbury House, London Typical Elizabethan brick manor house in the middle of a twentieth-century housing estate. (Not open.)

In Eastbury Square, Barking, ¼M W *of junction of A123 and A13 (86 F4/5)*

Fenton House, London Probably built in 1693, when Hampstead was still a country village, Fenton House is a large William and Mary house, much altered in Regency times. It is not known by whom or for whom it was built, but we know that in 1707 it was bought by Joshua Gee, friend of William Penn and champion of protectionism, whose writings had considerable influence in their time.

In 1793 the property was acquired by Philip Fenton; it was his son, James, who after 1807 carried out Regency-style alterations inside and out, moving the main entrance from the south side to the east, and perhaps giving the house its present name. Despite (or possibly because of) many later changes of ownership, it has hardly been touched since.

The last owner, Lady Binning, left to the Trust not only the house but also the collection of pictures, furniture, and outstanding English, Continental and Chinese porcelain that graces its elegant rooms. Here too is the beautiful Benton Fletcher Collection of early keyboard instruments, formerly kept at Old Devonshire House, which was destroyed by bombs in World War II.

300 yards N of Hampstead Underground Station, on W side of Hampstead Grove *(see map p. 64)*

Greys Court, Oxfordshire From the 1080s to the 1930s, with only two short breaks, Greys Court belonged to but three families: de Grey, Knollys, Stapleton. Today, the Tudor house of the Knollyses, with eighteenth-century improvements by the Stapletons, stands within the medieval courtyard of the de Greys. Visitors to Greys Court who enjoy architectural detective work will not find it hard to fill in the main details.

Merely to list some of the features of the place gives a hint of its flavour: the great medieval tower of the de Greys; the Dower House; the Cromwellian stables; the early-Tudor wheelhouse, containing the largest surviving example of a donkey wheel; the even older well, 200 feet deep. In the gardens is a stupendous tulip tree and a weeping ash, and one of the oldest larch trees in England; a rose garden, a wistaria garden, a nut avenue and an avenue of cherries, and a Chinese bridge leading over a ha-ha to irises and shrubs.

In the house itself, modest and unassuming, are some delightful examples of late seventeenth- and eighteenth-century furniture, mainly English, and a drawing room with beautiful eighteenth-century plasterwork on ceiling and walls.

3M NW Henley-on-Thames (85 F8)

Hughenden Manor, Buckinghamshire Hughenden was the country home of the Conservative leader Benjamin Disraeli from 1847 to his death in 1881. The plain eighteenth-century brick house was drastically Gothicized for the Disraelis in the fashion of the time by the architect E. B. Lamb in 1863. The gardens and grounds were also much altered.

The main interest of the house derives from its connection with the great statesman, who was Prime Minister in 1868 and from 1874 to 1880. It contains many portraits and busts of Disraeli, of members of his family, and of his distinguished contemporaries (his 'Gallery of Friendship'). The library (the only room to retain its eighteenth-century fireplace and plaster ceiling) reflects the literary tastes of a man who was both politician and novelist. 'I have a passion', he wrote, 'for books and trees . . . When I come down to Hughenden I pass the first week in sauntering about my park and examining all the trees, and then I saunter in the library and survey the books.' The drawing room, with its Gothic architectural features, is typically Victorian, as is the rather sombre dining room. The study remains much as Disraeli left it.

1½M N High Wycombe on A4128 (85 E9)

---

33 Kensington Square, London Built in 1695, this narrow but attractive brick house was the home of the actress Mrs Patrick Campbell (1865–1940). (Not open.)

At NW corner of the square (86 F2/3)

Osterley Park, London An Elizabethan house transformed by Robert Adam in 1761–80 (after a start had been made by Sir William Chambers). The design, decoration, and furnishing of the state rooms remain almost entirely as originally carried out by Adam, or by John Linnell under Adam's general supervision.

The architecture throughout is characteristically cool, dignified, meticulous. The rooms were designed for show rather than for comfort, with the furniture standing against the wall in the eighteenth-century manner, and at Osterley each piece is placed, so far as possible, where Adam intended. The result is superb, and we are surely more likely to agree with Horace Walpole's opinion of the drawing room, for instance – 'worthy of Eve before the Fall' – than of the Etruscan Dressing Room – 'a profound tumble into the Bathos'.

Shaw's Corner is full of Shaw relics. The desk in his study (shown here) remains exactly as he left it.

After Adam's almost overwhelming perfection the comparatively rustic stable block, perhaps the original Tudor manor house, comes as something of a relief. To north-west of it is Adam's semi-circular garden house; facing this across the lawn is the Doric Temple, possibly by Sir William Chambers. In the park are three lakes and some huge cedar trees.

Just N of Osterley Station (London Transport) on A4, access from Syon Lane or from Thornbury Road (85 F12)

Princes Risborough Manor House, Buckinghamshire Elegant red-brick house of about 1670 with spectacular oak staircase rising by an open stair-well from the hall. Good seventeenth-century panelling. (Hall and drawing room shown by appointment only.)

Opposite the church near town centre (85 D9)

40, 42, 44 Queen Anne's Gate, London Part of a row of Queen Anne houses, and the headquarters of The National Trust. No 42 is of stone and stuccoed, while nos 40 and 44 are of brick. (Not open.)

On S side of St James's Park (86 F3)

Rainham Hall, London Brick house of 1729 with stone dressings, a typical example of the period. It has a beautiful porch, concealed cupboards under an archway in the hall, and a large garden. (Open on written application to the tenant.)

Rainham, just S of the church (86 F5)

Shaw's Corner, Hertfordshire This unpretentious house at the south-west end of Ayot St Lawrence was for forty-four years (1906–50) the home of the great Irish writer and dramatist, George Bernard Shaw. All the rooms shown are full of Shaw relics and are arranged very much as they were during his lifetime. His famous hats hang in the hall, above his glove box and walking-sticks; the desk he worked at is in the study, with filing cabinets alongside – one of the drawers labelled 'Keys and Contraptions'. The drawing room next door was almost entirely Mrs Shaw's room. In the dining room Shaw would read during his vegetarian lunch (which consequently might last for as long as two hours); here too, after his wife's death in 1943, he was wont to sit in the evenings. From the dining room, which contains many personal relics, the visitor passes into the garden, with its revolving summer-house in which Shaw did much of his work. After his death at the age of ninety-four his ashes were scattered in this garden.

Like *Bateman's* in East Sussex, this place breathes the very spirit of a famous and most individual writer.

Ayot St Lawrence, 3½M W Welwyn (86 B2)

Waddesdon Manor, Buckinghamshire This house is a huge mansion of Bath stone built for Baron Ferdinand de Rothschild in the French Renaissance style between 1874 and 1889, by the French architect Destailleur. The grounds were laid out by the French landscape gardener Lainé. The hilltop on which the house stands had first to be levelled. The Bath stone and other materials were brought halfway up by special steam tramway, and hauled the rest of the way by teams of horses. The bare hillside was planted with hundreds of fully grown trees, the largest requiring as many as sixteen horses to shift.

The house contains much of Baron Ferdinand's collection of eighteenth-century French pictures and English portraits, and paintings by earlier Dutch and Flemish masters; of Miss Alice de Rothschild's collection of Sèvres china and of arms and armour, and Baron Edmund de Rothschild's equally important collection of pictures, furniture, carpets, and china.

The grounds of 160 acres include a large aviary in the eighteenth-century style and a

top **The centrepiece of this fountain pool is part of a fine collection of garden sculpture at Waddesdon Manor.**

above **West Wycombe Park reflects Sir Francis Dashwood's personal genius. The tapestry room shown here is hung with Flemish arras.**

herd of Sika deer. There is also a play area for young children. A huge Italian fountain dominates the approach from the south.

Children under 12 not admitted to house.

6M NW Aylesbury, entrance in Waddesdon village, on A41 (85 B8)

West Wycombe Park, Buckinghamshire This eighteenth-century house owes its character to that of its presiding genius, Sir Francis Dashwood, the 2nd Baronet.

The Dashwoods acquired the estate in 1698. (Most of the 4,000-acre estate, together with the contents of the house, still remains in the family today.) From 1739 onwards Sir Francis transformed the Queen Anne house built by his father into one which, although it may broadly be described as Palladian, cannot be placed in any neat architectural pigeon-hole. Fortunately it has hardly been altered since. 'If the total effect . . . is one of a series of stage sets rather than an entity that is perhaps part of the secret of its charm.'

As interesting as the house, with its pictures, furniture and sculpture, and its impressive façades, are the grounds, with which Sir Francis was equally concerned. On an island in the lake, from which issues a cascade flanked by reclining nymphs, stands the Temple of Music. Three more temples are disposed around, while from the side of the lake opposite the cascade a broad walk passes through woods where serpentine streams run, crossed by footbridges.

The Trust also owns most of West Wycombe village, which extends east from the gates of West Wycombe Park and contains many old cottages. On Church Hill to the north is an Iron Age fort. The mausoleum and caves are not Trust property.

2M W High Wycombe on A40 (85 E9)

Castles, Abbeys & other Buildings

Boarstall Tower, Buckinghamshire Intriguing fourteenth-century moated gatehouse, with later alterations, of a manor house demolished in the eighteenth century (open by prior appointment with the tenant). *Boarstall Decoy (see Countryside section)* lies a few fields away to the north.

Midway between Thame and Bicester, 2M NW Oakley, off B4011 (85 C7)

Bradenham Village, Buckinghamshire A huge green slopes down from the church and the seventeenth-century brick manor house, where Disraeli's father once lived. The village is set amongst rolling hills, woods and cornfields.

4M NW High Wycombe on E side of A4010 (85 D9)

Chantry Chapel, Buckinghamshire Fifteenth-century building incorporating a good Norman

The Norman doorway is the most interesting feature of Buckingham Chantry Chapel and probably predates the building itself.

south doorway. Much restored in 1875. Key obtainable in accordance with notice at the site.

In the narrow part of Market Hill, Buckingham, near its junction with West Street (85 A8)

Coleshill Village, Oxfordshire Handsome village of Cotswold stone houses and farm buildings running down to the River Cole, where Wiltshire begins. *Badbury Hill* (*see Countryside section*) is just up the road towards Faringdon.

On B4019 3M SW Faringdon (84 E3)

Falkland Memorial, Berkshire Nineteenth-century obelisk commemorating Royalists killed in the 1st Battle of Newbury (1643), especially Lord Falkland. Wordy inscription, supplemented by quotations from Thucydides, Livy, and Burke.

Beside A343 1M SW Newbury (84 H5)

Gray's Monument, Buckinghamshire Massive monument commemorating the writer of the famous *Elegy*. Erected in 1799, it stands on the edge of a field east of the churchyard.

Stoke Poges, 1½M N Slough on B473 (85 F10)

Great Coxwell Barn dates from the mid thirteenth century and belonged to the Cistercian monks of Beaulieu Abbey.

Willington Dovecote was built in the sixteenth century and is lined with nesting boxes for 15,000 pigeons.

The George Inn, London This is the only galleried inn left in London. It was built soon after the Southwark fire of 1676, replacing a former inn, burnt in the fire, which had stood there at least since the middle of the previous century. The George became a well-known coaching terminus during the eighteenth and early nineteenth centuries. Sadly in 1889 much of the galleried part was demolished. Since 1937 the inn has been cared for by the Trust; it is still very much an inn, providing food and drink – but not accommodation – for weary travellers. Shakespeare's plays are occasionally performed in the courtyard.

The George is referred to more than once in literature, notably by Dickens in *Little Dorrit*, but also in the works of E. V. Lucas, H. V. Morton, and the American writer F. Hopkinson Smith. The old, pre-fire, inn features in a poem published in 1655, unkindly entitled 'Upon a Surfeit caught by drinking evill Sack at the George Tavern at Southwark'.

Southwark, on E side of Borough High Street, near London Bridge station (see map p. 64)

Great Coxwell, Oxfordshire: The Great Barn Immense thirteenth-century monastic barn of stone, roofed with Cotswold stone tiles. The main oak timbers have lasted with only minor renewal for over 700 years.

2M SW Faringdon (84 E4)

The King's Head, Aylesbury, Buckinghamshire Lovely old hostelry, partly fifteenth-century, with cobbled courtyard. In a lounge of the hotel is a specially interesting fifteenth-century window with stained-glass armorials.

Off NW corner of Market Square (85 C9)

Long Crendon Courthouse, Buckinghamshire Fourteenth-century staple hall at the end of the picturesque High Street. Only the large upper room is open. It has remarkable roof timbers and a most uneven floor.

2M N Thame, via B4011 (85 C8)

Priory Cottages, Oxfordshire Range of fourteenth-century houses, formerly monastic buildings. South Cottage only is shown; it includes the great hall of the priory, and a small inner courtyard.

On corner of The Causeway and Mill Street, Steventon, 4M S Abingdon (84 E5/6)

Willington Dovecote and Stables, Bedfordshire Large sixteenth-century stone dovecote with curious stepped gables, and, across a farm lane, the stables, with rooms above for the men. (Open by written appointment only.)
7M E Bedford, N of A603 (91 K2)

Archaeological & Industrial Sites

Maidenhead Thicket, Berkshire Wooded area between two main roads, containing **Robin Hood's Arbour**, an ancient British enclosure of roughly one acre probably dating from about the time of Christ. Re-inhabited in World War II by the bodyguard of Queen Wilhelmina of the Netherlands.

Between A4 and A423, 2M W Maidenhead (85 F9)

Pitstone Windmill, Buckinghamshire One of Britain's oldest post mills, bearing the date 1627. In working order, except that it cannot be revolved to face the wind.

In a large field just S of Ivinghoe (85 C10)

'Roman' Bath, London An archaeological puzzle, although almost certainly not Roman, and probably not a bath. The most likely date is thought to be the seventeenth century, but evidence is scanty. Viewable from the pavement. (The 'bathroom' interior can be visited by arrangement.)

5 Strand Lane, accessible from The Strand via Surrey Street and Surrey Steps, or from The Embankment via Temple Place (see map p. 64)

White Horse Hill, Oxfordshire This property includes the White Horse hill figure, an ancient barrow or burial mound just above it, and Uffington Castle, a large hill-fort probably of the Iron Age. It can be reached by car from the B4507, or on foot from the Ridgeway to the south.

The Uffington White Horse, 360 feet long and 130 feet high, is one of the most ancient landmarks in England, although its origin is unknown. It is a lively representation of a horse cut in the chalk of the Downs, over 800 feet up. From the seventeenth century or earlier 'The Scouring of the White Horse' became an occasion for merrymaking by the people of the Vale, when a fair was held within the earthen ramparts of Uffington Castle. The last such ceremonial cleaning was in 1857.

On the knob below, known as Dragon Hill (also Trust property), St George is supposed to have slain the Dragon, the bare patch being caused by the spilling of the Dragon's blood.

(Under the guardianship of the Department of the Environment.)

S Uffington, 6M W Wantage, on S side of B4507 (84 E/F4)

The Heart of England

KINWARTON DOVECOTE

The heart of England has an irregular beat. There could hardly be a greater contrast than that between the ruggedness of the Derbyshire Peak and the gentle meadowland of Northamptonshire, or between the bustling streets of Birmingham and the leafy lanes linking Preston Bagot with Wootton Wawen where a youthful Shakespeare may have roamed.

National Trust properties in the heart of England reflect this almost infinite variety. Ten minutes driving separates the Tudor charm of Little Moreton Hall on the Cheshire Plain from the starkness of Mow Cop Castle, an eighteenth-century folly high up on the western edge of the Pennines looking out across wild moorland to the pastoral plain beyond.

These two properties exemplify not only the variety but also the two main strengths of the Trust in the region: houses and scenic viewpoints. The houses provide a lesson in the development of large-scale domestic buildings. Baddesley Clinton, a recent acquisition, is a splendid example of a late medieval moated manor house. The simplicity of Little Moreton and the opulence of Hardwick tell us much about contrasting Tudor building styles and Tudor attitudes. Sudbury and Shugborough display the increasing elegance of seventeenth- and eighteenth-century interiors; Wightwick Manor the lavishness of late Victorian times. Dunham Massey, another newly-acquired property, is a mixture of sixteenth- and early eighteenth-century styles. Like its comparatively close neighbour Lyme, it stands on the edge of the Peak, an area where the Trust owns a sizable slice (nearly ten per cent of the Peak Park) of some of the finest, most varied scenery in the region.

Countryside

The heart of England has no coastline, but it can offer almost every other kind of scenery. Some of the finest (and some of the best viewpoints) lies within the Peak District National

The dramatically beautiful gorge of Dovedale is one of the most popular spots in the Peak District.

The wild moors of the Longshaw estate, only eight miles from Sheffield, typify the upland landscapes of Derbyshire.

Bare grit and shale on Mam Tor, the 'shivering mountain', fringes the view towards Lose Hill Ridge.

Park at the southern end of the Pennines in Derbyshire and the adjoining counties of Staffordshire, Cheshire and South Yorkshire. The National Trust acquired its first purely scenic property in Derbyshire in 1930. This was **Alport Height** (95 E11), 1,032 feet above sea-level, from which it is possible to see across half Derbyshire and the width of Staffordshire to the Wrekin in Shropshire. Fifty years later the Trust held well over 20,000 acres, with a further 3,000 acres protected under covenant.

More than half of this total is contained in one vast parcel of land listed under the generic title of **Hope Woodlands**. Most of this is not woodland at all but wild peat moorland which includes parts of the plateaux of Kinder Scout and Bleaklow (both reaching 2,000 feet) and a short section of the Pennine Way (95 A/B9). Close by lie nearly 2,000 acres of **Edale**, including Mam Tor, the Shivering Mountain, so called because of its sliding strata of grit and shale, and the Winnats Pass, a steep and narrow defile between towering limestone sides which is now a Site of Special Scientific Interest. Just to the east, a further stretch of heather-covered moors and woodland around **Longshaw** (95 B/C11) runs almost up to the Sheffield boundary.

South of these gritstone moorlands of the Dark Peak, the Trust now owns virtually all **Dovedale** (95 D/E9/10), arguably the most beautiful, and certainly the most popular, of the limestone dales of the White Peak, as well as the greater part of the connecting valleys of the **Manifold** and **Hamps** across the county boundary in Staffordshire. For all but short sections of the Manifold and Hamps, the delights of these valleys are denied to motorists, and therefore are all the more loved by walkers.

Motorists, however, can enjoy the views from **Alderley Edge** (95 B7), just west of the Peak, or from **Mow Cop** on its western fringe (95 D7), without moving far from their cars. This higher northern portion of the region naturally possesses most of the more spectacular viewpoints, but by no means all. From **Kinver Edge** (88 D2), in that unexpectedly attractive salient of south-west Staffordshire that pushes down from the Black Country with the borders of Worcestershire and Shropshire close on either flank, one looks out across the Severn Valley to the Shropshire hills to enjoy a view of 'coloured counties' to challenge those that Housman enjoyed from Wenlock Edge or Bredon. Below the wooded escarpment a cave-dwelling known as Holy Austin Rock – possibly once a hermitage – has been hewn out of the sandstone. Other 'rock cottages' were occupied well into the nineteenth century. They are some of the most bizarre dwellings in National Trust ownership.

The attractive pink brick gatehouse of Charlecote Park on whose walls Shakespeare is said to have written ribald verses.

Staffordshire, indeed, is a much maligned county containing fine stretches of country off the usual tourist routes. One of these is **Downs Banks** (95 G7), north of Stone, where the National Trust owns 166 acres of undulating moorland with a stream running through its centre. Another is **Hawksmoor** (95 F9), a larger stretch of woodland with open spaces on the edge of the delightful Churnet Valley. Much of this is a nature reserve founded by Mr J. R. B. Masefield, a cousin of the poet John Masefield, and there are interesting relics of its industrial past as well as glimpses through the trees of modern industry in an unusually attractive setting.

Houses, Gardens & Parks

Baddesley Clinton, Warwickshire 'The perfect medieval manor house' is Sir Nikolaus Pevsner's opinion of this recently-acquired property in a secluded setting in a remnant of Shakespeare's Forest of Arden. The present house dates predominantly from the mid fifteenth century, but the wide moat surrounding it may have encircled the earlier fortified manor house of the Clintons. The grey stone entrance front, approached across the moat by a Queen Anne brick bridge, was erected by the Bromes, who inherited the estate about 1438, but the entrance tower with its tall porch and fine Elizabethan window to light the banqueting hall were alterations made by the Ferrers family who owned the house from 1509. The Elizabethan fireplaces were theirs, as presumably were the numerous hiding places, including one by Nicholas Owen, the leading hide-builder, below the level of the lake. Panelled rooms, tapestries and heraldic glass add to the medieval atmosphere of a house which Pevsner says 'could not be better'.

5M SE Knowle, off A41 (88 E6)

Charlecote Park, Warwickshire Queen Elizabeth I slept here for two nights on her way to Kenilworth in 1572, but there is no evidence for the tradition that young William Shakespeare was caught poaching deer in Charlecote Park by Sir Thomas Lucy and took revenge by portraying Sir Thomas as Justice Shallow in *The Merry Wives of Windsor*.

Sir Thomas Lucy built the present house on the site of an earlier one in 1558, and it retains its basic plan though much altered and enlarged in the nineteenth century. The gatehouse in mellow red brick with polygonal angle-turrets, stone balustrade and oriel window was built slightly earlier than the house and remains unaltered, as do the stables, and brewhouse and the two-storied Renaissance porch of the house. Much of the collection of furniture, ceramics and lacquer came from the sale of William Beckford's Fonthill collection. (William Beckford (1760–1844) was a wealthy eccentric who built himself an extravagant Gothic revival

top **The avenue of elms which once framed the front of Coughton Court are now no longer.**

above **The beautifully-proportioned north front of Dunham Massey is seen here reflected in the waters of the moat.**

Wood was still plentiful when Little Moreton Hall was built in the sixteenth century. This fantastic house is perhaps the most famous example of half-timbering.

mansion, Fonthill Abbey in Wiltshire, now demolished.) The principal rooms are decorated in the Elizabethan Gothic revival style by Warwickshire craftsmen, and there are good collections of books and pictures.

The Lucy deer still roam the park, laid out in its present form by 'Capability' Brown. There is also a flock of Jacob sheep.

4M *E Stratford-upon-Avon, on B4086 (88 F6)*

Clumber Park, Nottinghamshire Early in the eighteenth century the Duke of Newcastle created the largest estate in the Dukeries, ten miles in circumference. Clumber Park was described as 'a black heath full of rabbits . . . with a small boggy close or two' within Sherwood Forest. Of its 3,800 acres, about 2,000 are woodland and over 600 acres heathland. The ducal mansion of 1770, designed by Stephen Wright, was demolished in 1938, except for the Smoke Room, or Duke's Study, now housing an exhibition, and the stable block (which probably pre-dates the house), but Wright's fine bridge, Doric temples and lodges remain, as does the eighty-acre lake. The two-mile double lime avenue was planted in the nineteenth century.

Near the lake is G. F. Bodley's ornate Victorian Gothic church, in the style of fourteenth-century Decorated and built for the 7th Duke between 1886 and 1889. It contains exquisite limewood carvings to the designs of the Rev. Ernest Geldhart, stained-glass windows by C. E. Kempe and some first-class metalwork, much of it wrought by estate blacksmiths.

2½M *SE Worksop, via A57 or A614 (96 C3)*

Coughton Court, Warwickshire Throckmortons have remained at Coughton since 1409, despite suffering the penalties imposed on Roman Catholic families after the Reformation. They were closely involved in the Throckmorton Plot of 1583 but not directly in the Gunpowder Plot of 1605, though it was at Coughton that Lady Digby and her companions awaited news from London on the night of 5 November, the house having been lent to Sir Everard Digby while Throckmorton was abroad.

The splendid early Tudor gatehouse is the most substantial portion of the fabric to have survived from that time. It is now flanked by battlemented Gothic wings of 1780. A wide archway in the gatehouse leads through what is now an entrance hall into a courtyard flanked by half-timbered north and south wings, the east wing having been destroyed by Protestant rioters in 1688. A secret hiding place reached from the tower room is a reminder of those stormy times. There is a fine collection of family portraits, particularly outstanding being that of Sir Robert Throckmorton, 4th Baronet, by Nicolas de Largillière. This hangs above a Tudor fireplace in the drawing room where tradition says Lady Digby and her ladies waited for Catesby's servant to bring her news from Westminster.

2M *N Alcester on E side of A435 (88 F4)*

Dunham Massey, Cheshire In the reign of Elizabeth I, Sir George Booth built himself a moated courtyard house close to the site of a Norman castle of which only the motte remains. A later George Booth, 2nd Earl of Warrington, whose daughter and heiress married the 4th Earl of Stamford, rebuilt it in the first half of the eighteenth century. It is basically this house which stands today, though it was altered and redecorated by J. C. Hall for the 9th Earl between 1905 and 1909. It was acquired by the Trust under the will of the 10th and last Earl in 1976.

The house contains a series of portraits of the Grey family, Earls of Stamford, kinsfolk of Lady Jane Grey, as well as some outstanding early eighteenth-century furniture and Huguenot silver.

Within the deer park stands an Elizabethan mill in working order, two ranges of handsome early Georgian stables and a deer house bearing the date 1740. A row of dogs' tombs north of

Sixteenth-century tapestries hang below a painted frieze in Hardwick Hall.

the house have dates of death ranging between 1702 and 1836.

3M SW Altrincham off A56 (94 B6)

Farnborough Hall, Warwickshire This honey-coloured, classical stone house on a 'little hill of ferns' looking out to Edge Hill three miles away was acquired in 1684 by the Holbech family (who still live here). William and Francis Smith of Warwick probably built the early eighteenth-century west front, but the rest of the house was reconstructed around 1750, almost certainly to the design of the skilful amateur architect Sanderson Miller, who lived close by at Radway.

The interior of the house is notable for the exuberant rococo plasterwork by William Perritt. The splendid dining room was planned to house large views of Rome and Venice by Panini and Canaletto (now replaced by copies).

A most attractive feature of Farnborough is the gently curving terrace walk along the ridge to the south-east. This leads to an obelisk three-quarters of a mile from the house where there is a magnificent view across to Edge Hill. The obelisk, and a temple and oval pavilion along the walk, are again probably by Sanderson Miller.

6M N of Banbury, ½M W of A423 (89 G8)

Hardwick Hall, Derbyshire A complete late Elizabethan mansion built by Bess of Hardwick shortly after the death of her fourth and most influential husband, the Earl of Shrewsbury, as her initials and coronets on the six towers remind us. The house is important architecturally for the innovations introduced by Bess and her locally-born architect Robert Smythson. These include the ground plan H-shape instead of the conventional arrangement round a courtyard; a great hall at right angles to the façade instead of running parallel to it; windows becoming progressively taller to suit the interior arrangement of servants' quarters on the ground floor, family apartments on the first floor and state rooms on the second floor reached by a magnificent stone staircase soaring up through the house.

The High Great Chamber, described by Sir Sacheverell Sitwell as 'the finest room not only in England but in all Europe', was evidently built to take eight pieces of Brussels tapestry depicting a hunting scene bought by Bess in 1587. These fit perfectly between dado and painted plasterwork frieze. Similarly, the long gallery must have been planned to take a set of thirteen pieces of Flemish tapestry telling the story of Gideon. On them hang an interesting series of early family portraits.

Most of the excellent craftsmanship was the work of local men using local materials mainly from the Hardwick estate, from which also came the fabric of the house, though the marble comes from elsewhere in Derbyshire. The ruins of Bess's earlier house stand close by.

6½M NW Mansfield, 9½M SE Chesterfield, approach from M1 (junction 29) (96 D2)

Ilam Park, Staffordshire Eighty-four acres of thick woodland and park on both sides of the River Manifold adjacent to the National Trust's Dovedale and Manifold valley properties. Within the park the Manifold emerges from a subterranean course before passing below St Bertram's Bridge to join the Dove. Paradise Walk (twelve acres of woodland alongside the Manifold) contains the remains of a Saxon cross. Dr Johnson, who refused to believe that the river ran underground, used this area as the setting for *Rasselas*.

The surviving portion of Ilam Hall, a battlemented, turreted sham-Gothic mansion rebuilt 1821–6 and partly-demolished 1935, is a youth hostel and not normally open to the public.

4½M NW Ashbourne (95 E9)

Little Moreton Hall, Cheshire An idyllic, much loved, moated, half-timbered manor house. Ralph Moreton, whose family held the land for over six centuries, began building the house about 1480, and John Moreton virtually completed it about 1580. Apart from minor additions and modifications it has remained untouched since, mainly because the Royalist Moretons had little money after the Civil War for more than careful maintenance. They let the house to farmers for two centuries before it passed to a cousin, Bishop Abraham, who with his son gave it to the National Trust in 1937.

A bridge over the moat leads to the gatehouse, built around 1580, beyond which the original H-shaped house of 1480 forms the north side of an irregular quadrangle open to the west. The Great Hall, entered through an ornate porch, remains the focal point of the house. Much of the sixteenth-century character of Little Moreton comes from the patterned glazing of the windows and from the elaborate joiner's and carpenter's work. The painted panelling in the parlour was discovered during alterations in 1977–9.

4M SW Congleton, on E side of A34 (95 D7)

Lyme Park, Cheshire For 600 years until 1946, Lyme was the home of the Leghs, eleven of whom were christened Peter (or Piers). Sir Peter Legh VII greatly enlarged an existing house about 1560, but his sizable Elizabethan house is now partly hidden behind Giacomo Leoni's vast Palladian mansion of around 1725 with early nineteenth-century additions by Lewis Wyatt. The north (entrance) front is Elizabethan, though partly disguised by later sash windows and end bays, but the more imposing south front, with its three-storey Ionic portico, is by Leoni.

One of the most remarkable rooms in the

A detail of Gibbons' carvings in the saloon at Lyme Park.

house is the oak wainscoted Elizabethan drawing room, darkened in Victorian times by stained glass from Disley Church and heavy varnishing. The fine Baroque ceiling over the grand staircase was carved by a local craftsman, and another local man, an estate carpenter, made the present ceiling to the Elizabethan long gallery. Family tradition attributes the magnificent limewood carvings in the saloon to Grinling Gibbons.

Beyond the formal gardens, the deer park stretches on to the wild Peakland moors. Lyme Cage, a stone building on a ridge in the park, is probably an Elizabethan hunting tower rebuilt by Leoni, but its name suggests that it may also have been used as a poachers' prison.

(The whole estate is managed for the National Trust by the Metropolitan Borough of Stockport and Greater Manchester Council.)

6½M SE Stockport, entrance on S side of A6 on W edge of Disley (95 B8)

Lyveden New Bield, Northamptonshire This extraordinary atmospheric shell of a stone-built house is set in a rolling, empty landscape of cornfields and woodlands half a mile from the nearest minor road. Started in 1594 as a lodge to Lyveden Manor House – the 'Old Bield' – it was probably incomplete when its owner, Sir Thomas Tresham, died in September 1605 shortly before his son's arrest for complicity in the Gunpowder Plot, and it may never have been intended to be finished.

The cruciform shape of the house and the inscriptions and symbols on the frieze of the upper entablature illustrate the twin themes of the Passion of Christ and the Mother of Christ, recalling the symbolism of Tresham's better-known Triangular Lodge at Rushton, also in Northamptonshire.

To reach the house, two fields (half a mile) have to be crossed. The National Trust guide book, obtainable from the nearby cottage, is fairly essential reading for an understanding of Sir Thomas Tresham and his house.

4M SW Oundle via A427 (1½M from Oundle, bear left), 3M E of Brigstock (A6116) by road from its S end. (There is a small lay-by for cars.) (91 G1)

Moseley Old Hall, Staffordshire Charles II slept here for three nights after the Battle of Worcester in 1651. They must have been uncomfortable nights as the secret hiding place below what is now the King's Room is only five feet long and Charles was a tall man. He stayed here after his two days at Boscobel, nine miles away, and before his five weeks' circuitous journey to safety in France.

Victorian brick has unfortunately encased the original late-Elizabethan half-timbering, but the shape and the chimneys are unmistakably Elizabethan. Some early seventeenth-century panelling in the parlour has survived mining subsidence and a long period of neglect.

The house contains contemporary portraits of Charles and some of those who aided his escape, including his host Thomas Whitgreave and Whitgreave's chaplain Father John Huddlestone, who thirty-four years later administered the last rites to Charles.

The reconstruction of a seventeenth-century garden includes the then popular quince, mulberry and medlar trees, as well as knot and herb gardens.

4M N Wolverhampton, ¾M W of A460 (88 B3)

Packwood House, Warwickshire Charmingly situated in a clearing in the Forest of Arden, Packwood is famous for its gardens, particularly for its yew topiary work said to represent The Sermon on the Mount. A raised walk is flanked by twelve yews known as The Apostles, with four larger ones, The Evangelists, in the centre. A spiral walk leads to The Mount, crowned by a single yew, The Master. The layout probably dates from 1650–70, but the

Sir Thomas Tresham's Lyveden New Bield, representing the Passion, illustrates the Elizabethan love of symbolism and stands as a monument to the Catholic faith.

Packwood House (*centre above*) is a fine example of domestic Tudor architecture but is best known for its topiary garden (*above*) representing The Sermon on the Mount.

clipped yews representing The Multitude lower down the garden may be a nineteenth-century addition.

The house and red-brick stable block form a delightful group. The main block of the house dates from the mid sixteenth century, but its original timber frame has been rendered over. Its preservation owes much to Alfred Ash, who bought it in 1905, and his son Graham Baron Ash, who carefully restored it before giving it to the National Trust in 1941. Graham Baron Ash created a new great hall, which had been used as a cow-byre and barn, and linked it to the house by a new long gallery. Queen Mary's Room commemorates the Queen's visit in 1927. Ireton's Room is the one occupied by General Henry Ireton on the eve of the Battle of Edge Hill in 1642.

1½M E Hockley Heath, off A34 (88 E5)

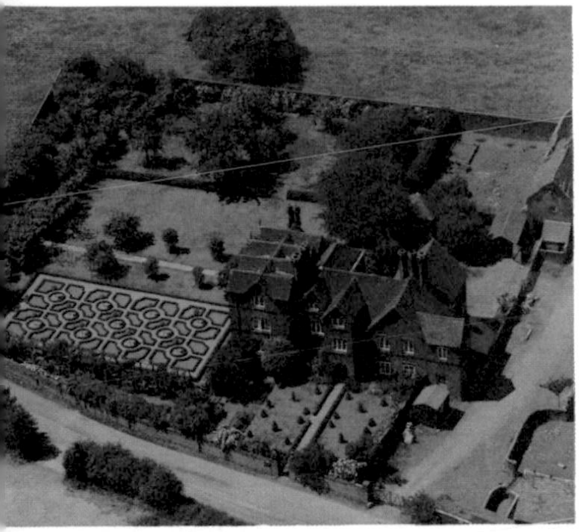

The principal feature of the garden at Moseley Old Hall is a copy of a seventeenth-century knot garden, using coloured gravels and beds edged with dwarf box.

Shugborough, Staffordshire This imposing, white-fronted country house stands in a large park owned by the Anson family from 1624 to 1960, and the 5th Earl of Lichfield (Patrick Lichfield) still occupies part of the house. The present house was started in 1693, enlarged around the mid eighteenth century and further enlarged by Samuel Wyatt from 1794 to 1806. Its contents include much that was brought back by Admiral Sir George Anson (later Lord Anson) from his circumnavigation of the world and other voyages, as well as a great amount of French furniture. The extensive picture collection includes two portraits by Reynolds.

The gardens and park are famous for their monuments, mainly by James (Athenian) Stuart in the neo-Greek style which he made fashionable. The Doric Temple, Lanthorn of Demosthenes and Triumphal Arch are outstanding. The Arch is a copy of Hadrian's Arch in Athens and honours the memory of Lord and Lady Anson.

Staffordshire County Council, who administers and maintains the property, has a folk museum in the stable block and a farming museum, with rare livestock breeds, around the Georgian farmstead in the park.

5½M SE Stafford on A513, entrance at Milford (95 H8)

Sudbury Hall, Derbyshire The extravagance of Charles II's reign is exemplified at Sudbury, the most richly decorated surviving house of the period. George Vernon spent most of the second half of the seventeenth century in building and decorating it. At first he employed mainly local craftsmen, like William (later Sir William) Wilson of Leicester who was responsible for the frontispieces on the two main fronts, the outstanding features of the exterior.

The eighteenth-century porcelain at Upton House includes this rare Chelsea yellow ground tea service with panels of chinoiserie figures dating from *c.* 1760.

Later he turned to London men: Grinling Gibbons and Edward Pierce as carvers, Robert Bradbury and James Pettifer as plasterers, and the Frenchman Louis Laguerre for the decorative paintings in the dome and over the Great Staircase, which is considered the finest staircase of its period *in situ* in any English country house. The fine long gallery is a surprising feature in a house built as late as Charles II's reign.

Sudbury continued in Vernon ownership until acquired by the Trust in 1967, but in 1840 it was leased for three years to Queen Adelaide, William IV's widow, and her instructions for her own funeral are framed beside the bed in the Queen's Room.

Sudbury also houses a museum of childhood exhibits in the Victorian servants' wing.

6M E Uttoxeter, off A50 (95 G10)

Tatton Park, Cheshire Tatton is an ideal centre for family parties because of the variety of attractions within its 2,000-acre park. The colourful sixty-acre garden contains a small beech maze, one of only two on National Trust properties; a large mere is a haunt of wildfowl and of sailing enthusiasts, and nearby a former manor house is being restored by Cheshire County Council – who finance and manage the property in close consultation with the National Trust – and is open to the public along with a tithe barn and the site of the deserted village of Tatton.

At the heart of the park stands the stone-built mansion of the Egertons, who owned the estate from 1598 to 1958. The house is largely the work of the Wyatts, Samuel and his nephews Jeffry and Lewis, who worked here between 1774 and 1825. Most of the exterior, and the interior decoration, were designed by Lewis Wyatt between 1808 and 1813. Gillow of Lancaster, the cabinet makers, were responsible for the execution of much of his interior decorations and for most of the exquisite furniture and fittings.

The Egertons built up interesting collections of pictures, silver and books as well as furniture, but the 4th and last Lord Egerton had even wider tastes. Beyond the kitchens and servants' quarters, which are of great interest to students of social history, he built in 1935 the Tenants' Hall to house a remarkable collection of souvenirs of his astonishingly full life and extensive travels.

3½M NW Knutsford, entrance on A5034 just N of junction of A5034 and A50 (94 B6)

Upton House, Warwickshire Standing slightly back from the edge of the ridge less than a mile south of the battlefield of Edge Hill, Upton was bought by the 2nd Viscount Bearsted in 1927 to house his magnificent collection of works of art, which is particularly outstanding in the fields of ceramics and paintings. The ceramics collection is especially strong in the eighteenth-century soft-paste porcelains of Sèvres and

These William de Morgan tiles illustrate the Pre-Raphaelite influence at Wightwick Manor.

Chelsea. More than 250 paintings cover a wide range of artists and subjects, with English sporting and country scenes of the eighteenth and early nineteenth centuries particularly well represented.

The house dates from the late seventeenth century, but was extensively remodelled by Percy Morley Horder in 1927 to provide a suitable setting for the collection.

The garden makes charming use of the natural landscape. One notably felicitous feature is a lake formed in the mid eighteenth century more than a mile from the house. This has a small classical temple in the style of Robert Adam on its eastern bank.

1M S Edge Hill, 7M NW Banbury, on W side of A422 (89 G7)

Wightwick Manor, West Midlands Here is Victorian splendour on the edge of Wolverhampton. The house was built in two portions in 1887 and 1893 by Liverpool architect Edward Ould for Theodore Mander, paint and varnish manufacturer, and its furnishings have been heavily influenced by Ruskin and the Pre-Raphaelites. It has William Morris wallpaper, tapestries and tiles, Kempe glass and Pre-Raphaelite pictures, though some things were brought in after 1935 when Sir Geoffrey and Lady Mander decided to make it a treasure house of the period.

The earlier, western, range has a black-and-white timber upper storey over a ground floor of Ruabon red brick. The eastern half, inspired by the Tudor houses of the Welsh marcher country, is predominately timber resting on a low plinth of local stone. The Great Parlour rises impressively through two storeys in the Tudor fashion. The drawing room has a superb Italian Renaissance fireplace and one of the several imitation Jacobean plaster ceilings by L. A. Shuffrey.

A charming, secluded garden, with yew hedges and topiary work, slopes down to a lake.

3M W Wolverhampton, on A454 (88 B2)

Castles, Abbeys & other Buildings

Colston Bassett Market Cross, Nottinghamshire The National Trust's earliest property in Nottinghamshire, the Cross was given by the Society for the Protection of Ancient Buildings in 1933. The Doric shaft on a medieval moulded base was put up to commemorate William IV's coronation in 1831, but its square head surmounted by a ball dates from the eighteenth century.

10M SE Nottingham, 5M S Bingham, 2½M E of Fosse Way (96 G4)

Duffield Castle, Derbyshire Only the foundations of the keep on a mound remain of the Norman castle of the powerful Ferrers family. The rest was destroyed in 1266 by Prince Henry, nephew of Henry III, in the Barons' War. The keep, commanding the Derwent Valley, measured 95 feet by 93 feet and had walls 15 feet thick, figures comparable with those of Colchester, Dover and the White Tower of London.

The site was given to the National Trust in 1899 and it is thus the oldest of the Trust's properties in Derbyshire. (It is managed for the National Trust by Duffield Parish Council.)

½M N Duffield station, 2½M S Belper on W side of A6 (95 F11)

Easton-on-the-Hill: Priest's House, Northamptonshire Pre-Reformation priest's lodge in village street of originally stone-built village. (Open only by appointment.)

3M SW Stamford, off A43 (90 E1)

Kinwarton Dovecote, Warwickshire This fourteenth-century circular stone dovecote stands in a field at the end of a lane beyond a charming group of buildings – church, rectory and farm – that make up the hamlet of Kinwarton. Its interior retains its *potence* (French for gallows), a rare feature nowadays. This is a vertical beam in the centre of the building to which are attached several horizontal beams at varying heights. The vertical beam pivots so that all the 500 nesting boxes can be reached from ladders fixed to the end of each horizontal beam. The birds nesting there were probably pigeons rather than doves. In the Middle Ages pigeons could be kept only by the lord of the manor, here probably the Abbot of Evesham.

1½M NE Alcester, just S of B4089 (88 F4)

Staunton Harold Church, Leicestershire 'In the yeare: 1653 When all thinges sacred were throughout ye nation Either demollisht or profaned Sr Robert Shirley Barronet Founded this Church Whose singular praise it is to haue done the best thinges in ye worst times And hoped them in the most callamitous The righteous shall be had in everlasting remembrance'.

So runs the inscription over the west doorway of Staunton Harold Church. Sir Robert Shirley went to the Tower of London for his act of defiance in illegally building this church – one of very few erected during the Commonwealth period – and died there aged 29.

The exterior is in the then outmoded Gothic style, but the interior is pure seventeenth-century and has changed little since. A painted ceiling signed 'Samuell Kyrk 1655' depicts the Creation. The wrought-iron altar rail and grille over the chancel screen are by the local craftsman Robert Bakewell. There is rich panelling on walls and piers, a Father Schmidt organ – older than the church – box pews, a sumptuous altar cloth and other draperies on the altar and in the pulpit in velvet. The seventeenth-century separation of the sexes in church is maintained at Staunton Harold, where the men sit on the south side of the aisle and the women on the north.

The church forms part of a charming group with lake and hall. The hall is now a Cheshire Home, but Group Captain Leonard Cheshire VC gave covenants over it to the Trust in 1956.

5M NE Ashby de la Zouch, just W of B587 (95 H12)

Winster Market House, Derbyshire This charming old building stands at the centre of a long main street in a ruggedly attractive ancient lead-mining village. Its stone-built ground floor with pointed arches was originally open but is now filled in, supporting an upper floor of brick with gable ends, and windows with single mullions and transoms. It dates from the late seventeenth or early eighteenth century, and was bought by the National Trust in 1906 after repairs from funds raised locally by Mrs Childers Thompson.

4M W Matlock, on S side of B5057 (95 D11)

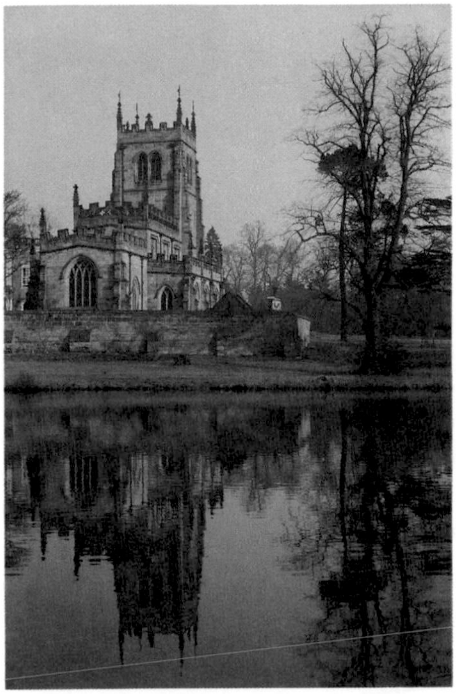

Staunton Harold Church is one of the few built between the outbreak of Civil War and the Restoration.

Archaeological & Industrial Sites

Letocetum, Wall, Staffordshire The excavated bath-house of a Roman posting station on Watling Street close to its intersection with Ryknild Street. The bath-house is attached to a dwelling which may have been a resting place for official travellers. A small museum contains finds from the site as well as some from another Roman site (at Shenstone, one and a half miles south-east). (The property is under the guardianship of the Department of the Environment.)

2M SW Lichfield, on N side of A5 (88 A4)

Nether Alderley Mill, Cheshire This sixteenth-century corn mill is built of warm red local sandstone and set into a picturesque wooded bank. Water from a small stream was reinforced from reservoirs behind the mill to drive the two wheels.

Lath and plaster have replaced the original wattle and daub in the half-timbered gables, but the original mullion remains in a blocked-up window. The framed woodwork – all of oak – inside the building is as old as the mill, but the machinery was renewed about a century ago.

left **Nether Alderley Mill is built right up against the dam of its reservoir; hence the unusual sweep of the roof.**

below **The cotton industry was the first in which rural cottage production was replaced by a factory system. Quarry Bank Mill, Styal, was built in 1784.**

The mill continued to work until 1939. The fabric was restored about 1950, and the machinery repaired and put back into working order in 1967. It is now grinding corn again.

1½M S Alderley Edge, on E side of A34 (95 C7)

Stratford-upon-Avon Canal, Warwickshire The property comprises the southern section of the canal from Kingswood Junction, Lapworth, to the Royal Shakespeare Theatre gardens in Stratford-upon-Avon. It includes thirty-six locks, twenty-one cast-iron split bridges and impressive cast-iron aqueducts at Wootton Wawen (built 1813 on tapering brick piers) and Edstone. Construction of the canal began in 1793, but it did not reach Stratford until 1816. It passed into railway ownership in 1856 and eventually became completely derelict. It was the object of a pioneer restoration by volunteers and prison labour after being leased by the National Trust in 1960, and was reopened by Queen Elizabeth the Queen Mother in July 1964.

There is access to the River Avon by a wide-beam lock, with an attractive steel bridge made in Wormwood Scrubs gaol, and to the Grand Union Canal at Kingswood Junction. Throughout the thirteen miles in National Trust ownership, the canal passes through pleasant countryside.

(88 E5 to F5)

Styal, Cheshire A complete Industrial Revolution colony in 252 acres of well-wooded parkland in the Bollin valley. Samuel Greg built his Quarry Bank cotton mill in this narrow, isolated valley in 1784, attracted by the power of the stream. To this handsome Georgian mill, surmounted by a cupola, he, and later his son Robert Hyde Greg, added further buildings, including a warehouse and weaving sheds in the 1820s and 1830s. Before that – in 1790 – he had built an apprentice house near the mill to house the pauper children who formed the bulk of the labour force, for Styal was a small scattered place where little labour was available. Later it became necessary to recruit workers from farther afield, and to provide houses for them.

These houses form the major portion of the village of Styal, along with a shop, a school and the Norcliffe Unitarian Chapel (built in 1822). The chapel was given to the National Trust in 1979 by the chapel trustees to whom it has been leased back, but most of the rest of the estate has been National Trust property since 1939.

Much of the mill is now open to the public and is being developed as a charitable trust museum by Quarry Bank Mill Trust to illustrate the role of the textile industry in the north-west by means of many galleries and working exhibits. Part of the estate is now designated a country park.

1½M N Wilmslow (95 B7)

Eastern Counties

LAVENHAM GUILDHALL

Until quite recent times East Anglia was very remote. Even in the last century the fens, on the westernmost edge of the region, were not completely drained, and river crossings in the fens are still comparatively few. The coast, hospitable enough on a windless summer day, can be virtually unapproachable in winter, and those famous East Anglian skies tend to dwarf even grand country houses that in softer, more cosy countryside would dominate their setting.

Of all the Trust's properties in these Eastern Counties it is, coincidentally, probably the most recent major acquisition of real note that is outwardly most impressive. Wimpole Hall, near Royston, commands a low hill and, being seen to best advantage from the south, enjoys correspondingly superb views from its south-facing rooms. Such houses are comparatively few in this part of Britain, and their distance from each other and from main centres of population lends enchantment.

Appropriately, the National Trust owns examples of two types of property that sum up some essential characteristics of the region's history. One reflects the importance of the wool trade in the fifteenth and sixteenth centuries and includes the Guildhall at Lavenham and Paycocke's, in Coggeshall, the other the region's importance as a grain producer, with no fewer than three preserved mills among the properties owned.

There are also a number of properties that are built over or incorporate remains of abbeys or monasteries. These too are evidence of the isolation that the region has long enjoyed.

Coast & Countryside

The north Norfolk coast, part of which is officially an Area of Outstanding Natural Beauty, belies its comparatively easy access to London. British Rail trains run as far as Sheringham and the North Norfolk Railway, operated privately by steam enthusiasts, runs between Sheringham and Weybourne. That railhead roughly marks the western boundary of that part of the Norfolk coast that has been colonized by caravanners and the beginning of a wilder terrain where wildfowl are more numerous than holidaymakers.

On the south side of The Wash the coast is exposed and, in winter, exceptionally bleak, though in the height of summer it throngs with holidaymakers who know something of the underrated charms of one of the country's most remarkable sandy coastlines. The Trust is responsible for two of the best parts of the Norfolk coast – Blakeney Point and Scolt Head. **Scolt Head** (92 A1), the most northerly point of the Norfolk coast, is an island, and though it is ostensibly accessible across the marshes at low tide, these are dangerous, and the only safe access is by boat. Owned by the Trust since 1923, Scolt Head is rich in rare bird life – oystercatchers, gannets, kittiwakes, Arctic skuas, among others – a distinction matched only by the varieties of rare freshwater and saltwater plant species.

Blakeney Point (92 A3), Wells-next-the-Sea, was acquired by the Trust in 1912. The sand dunes and mud flats here, which are accessible on foot from Cley (pronounced Cly) at low tide or by boat at high tide, make a natural bird sanctuary: the long shingle beach is a barrier, and behind it are high dunes out of the reach of anything but exceptional tides. Many rare birds are regularly seen here, including Lapland buntings and long-tailed duck, and as many as 263 different species have been recorded, thirty-three breeding.

More easily accessible is the beach at **Brancaster**, a little over 2,000 acres of tidal foreshore, sand dunes, marsh and saltings (92 A1). The beach, while submerged at high tide, is one of the widest, most sandy and unspoilt on the Norfolk coast. The Trust also owns land on the **Stiffkey Saltmarshes**, between Wells and Blakeney (92 A3), with access off the A149 at both ends of Stiffkey village, and about two miles of the south shoreline of Blakeney harbour between Stiffkey and Blakeney. Ten miles west of Blakeney, the Trust owns just over 100 acres of heathland south of West Runton (92 A5). This includes the highest point in Norfolk and **Beeston Regis Heath**, a ridge of wooded and open heathland with good views of the coast. About twenty miles to the south-east, only a barrage of sand dunes divides **Horsey Mere** (92 C7), the most salt of all the Norfolk Broads, from the North Sea. Because

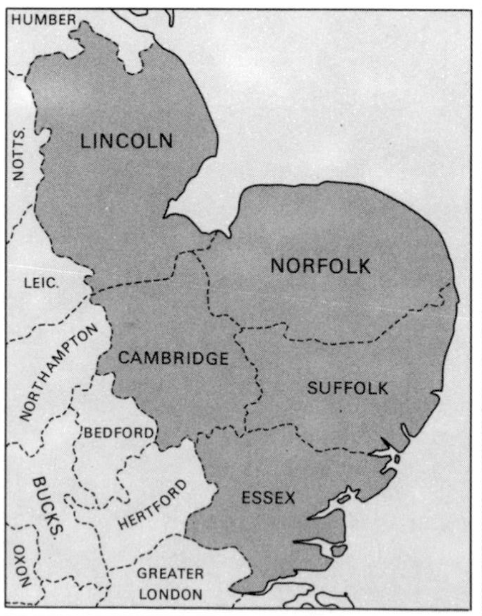

Wicken Fen is noted for its insect, plant and bird life and is visited by ecologists from all over the world.

of its brackishness, the plant and marine life is unusual and rare birds, including bitterns, can be seen. The 120-acre mere is part of a total holding of 1,734 acres.

The fen country that makes up a large part of Cambridgeshire is often dismissed as dull and uninspiring. **Wicken Fen**, near Soham (91 H7), however, is an exceptional and haunting place. The last substantial remnant of the Great Fen of East Anglia, this is one of Europe's most important 'wet' nature reserves. Surrounded by drained fenland, composed mainly of peat which contracts as it dries, Wicken is undrained and is therefore more prominent, a kind of island in an inland sea. The property consists of about 730 acres of exceptional sanctuary for rare insects, spiders, birds and plants, with, for example, 700 kinds of butterflies and moths alone. There is an imaginative display in the Thorpe Building at the access point to the Fen.

The wild and lonely stretches of Scolt Head are rich in marine flora and contain large nesting colonies of sea-birds.

In Essex the National Trust owns two properties in the remnants of Epping Forest, which once covered almost the whole country. **Blakes Wood** (87 C7), between Danbury and Little Baddow, is one of the few areas of true woodland left. It is best known for hornbeams, chestnuts and wild flowers and is well served by public footpaths. More usually, the Forest is represented by little pockets of heath and scrub, like the 200 or so acres that make up **Danbury and Lingwood commons** (87 C/D7/8) situated on a ridge between Chelmsford and Maldon. Danbury is more open, more typical of the common land on which 'commoners' could graze their cattle and sheep, while Lingwood is more forested, with open glades and clearings. Both are rich in unusual flora.

Similar to Epping Forest, though consisting only of about a thousand acres, **Hatfield Forest** (86 B5) was a Royal hunting ground even before the Norman Conquest. Here there are still fallow deer, foxes, badgers and, among the bird population, woodpeckers, hawfinches and grasshopper warblers. On the lake and the adjoining marsh are snipe, grebe and water-hen, among other wildfowl. There are hornbeams among the trees, but the most famous tree of all is the Old Doodle Oak, which 'died' over a hundred years ago.

Only six miles north-west of what is now Southend, a fortress was created almost a thousand years ago by cutting off access to a spur of land jutting out from the **Rayleigh Hills** (87 E8), and though nothing except impressive earthworks remains of what was a primitive motte-and-bailey castle, further defended by ditches and stockades, this is an imposing site. The Domesday Book of 1086 mentions the castle.

The Trust's most important properties in rural or coastal Suffolk are at **Dunwich Heath** (93 H/J7/8), just over 200 acres of sandy cliff and heathland forming a coastal beauty spot, and **Flatford Mill** (93 M4). Though neither the mill, which belonged to John Constable's father, and where John himself worked for a time, nor the nearby Willie Lott's Cottage, are open, they are worth visiting for their setting.

Houses, Gardens & Parks

Angel Corner, Suffolk In a Queen Anne house acquired by the Trust in 1943 is the John Gershom Parkington Memorial Collection of Time Measurement Instruments. Housed in the principal rooms in the building, the collection is perhaps best known for the 'Atmos' clock, which operates by changes in temperature. A change of only 2°F provides enough energy to run the clock for forty-eight hours.

Angel Hill, Bury St Edmunds (93 J2)

Anglesey Abbey, Cambridgeshire Little remains of the Augustinian priory that was founded here in 1135 except for a crypt under the present house that dates from about 1235, parts of the chapter house – much altered before 1600 and embedded in the core of the present building – and the vaulted Canon's Parlour, now the dining room. Outwardly Anglesey Abbey looks like a typical Elizabethan manor house of local greyish stone, with bay windows, mullions, dormer windows and a steep tiled roof, partly covered by creeper.

The house is best known for being surrounded by one of the most remarkable gardens in East Anglia, with a layout dating roughly from 1926, when Lord Fairhaven bought the abbey. He planted herbaceous borders, rare flowers and trees and planned woodland walks that still have not reached full

The lake in Hatfield Forest was created in the eighteenth century; it is now a favourite haunt of water-birds.

Oxburgh Hall, rising sheer from its formal moat, was built at a time when protection was needed against widespread unrest.

maturity – all of them part of a grand and intricate geometric pattern rarely seen since Elizabethan times.

Inside the house there is a cornucopia of treasures, an Aladdin's cave of priceless furniture, silver, paintings, porcelain, from Ming Dynasty lacquered effects to Egyptian *objets d'art*. The statuary in the garden includes busts of Roman emperors and lions couchant.

The house that Lord Fairhaven saved and recreated was once owned by Thomas Hobson, the carter from whose name the phrase 'Hobson's Choice' derives, and Sir George Downing, whose name lives on in Cambridge University's Downing College, which he founded.

6M NE of Cambridge on B1102 Cambridge to Mildenhall Road (*91 J6*)

Blickling Hall, Norfolk This exceptional house, both beautiful and historic, is enhanced by the spacious hamlet in which it is situated. Set well back from the road, its red-brick Jacobean façade contrasts with the dark, high yew hedges that border the wide approach drive. Between these hedges and the house itself are harmonious and elegant outbuildings, partly creeper-clad, with ornate Dutch-style gables and 'Elizabethan' chimneys.

Blickling Hall was built between 1616 and 1625 by the Hobart family, who became the Earls of Buckinghamshire. It then passed to the Marquesses of Lothian, and was bequeathed to the Trust by the 11th Marquess, who died in 1940, along with 4,500 acres.

Though much of the exterior is original the interior has been radically changed, and the best of it owes much to the eighteenth century, when the Hall was owned by the 2nd Earl of Buckinghamshire. He was ambassador to St Petersburg in the 1760s, and had one room redesigned in the classical style to accommodate a tapestry given to him by Catherine the Great. Other remarkable rooms include the Chinese Bedroom and the long gallery, with an exquisitely plastered ceiling.

The garden, though partly reorganized in modern times, is largely Georgian in layout: a rare survival, with wooded walks, an orangery, a pre-1730 'temple', topiary and now-mature rare trees.

1½M NW of Aylsham, off B1354 (*92 C5*)

Felbrigg Hall, Norfolk Felbrigg combines an almost perfect, unaltered Jacobean exterior (built in the 1620s, at roughly the same time as *Blickling Hall*) with a sumptuous and beautiful eighteenth-century interior: the best of two elegant worlds. The house was built by the Windham family and is the result of 300 years' growth and change. William Windham I added

This exquisite bureau by Roentgen at Anglesey Abbey was made for Tsar Paul I. The Regency clock is by James McCabe.

Blickling Hall is a splendid Jacobean house, seen here across the formal garden.

Gunby Hall, built of beautiful rose-red brick, is a good example of a country house in William III's reign.

With its chimneys and turrets, Melford Hall is a typical mid sixteenth-century building.

The rotunda at Ickworth is the centrepiece of an extraordinary building.

a new wing in 1670 in symmetrical Reformation style and is also responsible for the fine plaster ceilings that can be seen in the drawing room and cabinet. He was a forester and it was he who planted the great chestnuts that today shield the house from winds off the North Sea, and many other trees in the great park.

His son, William Windham II, was largely responsible for the decoration and contents of the Georgian rooms. After his return from the Grand Tour in 1741, he began to refurbish the house in contemporary style and created a new dining room, staircase and Gothick library. The Georgian rooms remain largely unaltered today and are the most notable aspect of the house. Among later changes was the addition in about 1825 of battlemented stables in the revived Gothic style.

3M Cromer, W B1436 (92 B5)

Grantham House, Lincolnshire This is a mainly seventeenth- and eighteenth-century house, which does however retain some traces of its fifteenth-century origins. With quiet gardens that border the River Witham, Grantham House is a pleasant, comfortable-seeming marriage of different styles both internally and externally.

Opposite the parish church, in Castlegate, Grantham (96 G6)

Gunby Hall, Lincolnshire Gunby was one of the country houses acquired by the Trust during World War II. At first sight it could be a town house built by Wren, and it was probably designed by a master builder with knowledge of London. It was commissioned in 1700 by Sir William Massingberd, whose family had already been associated with Lincolnshire for 300 years. Built of a distinctive dark red brick fired from clay actually dug from the estate, the house is set off by formal gardens that do not follow the original design but do contain, within the walled garden, rare original fruit trees. Among the comparatively small rooms inside the house, several of them oak panelled, is a dining room added in 1873 that has the elegant Queen Anne ambience of the house as a whole.

The half-timbered front of Paycocke's, showing the richly-carved bressummer and the oriel windows on the upper storey.

Gunby has some associations with Dr Johnson: the dining room has a portrait of Bennet Langton, a friend of Johnson, who brought to Gunby a drawing of Boswell and one of only six autographed copies of Boswell's *Life of Johnson.*

7M W of Skegness, on S side of A158, the Lincoln/Skegness road (97 D11)

Ickworth, Suffolk Remarkable both for its unusual shape and for the fact that today, almost 200 years since it was built, it is not quite finished, Ickworth was conceived by the immensely wealthy Frederick Hervey, 4th Earl of Bristol and Bishop of Derry, as a storehouse for treasures collected during his continental tours. The two wings on either side of the massive, three-storeyed and domed rotunda which makes Ickworth so unusual were intended to house Hervey's paintings, silver, furniture and sculpture, most of which he acquired in Italy. But before many of these could reach Ickworth they were impounded by French armies invading Italy. The present collection is nevertheless impressive, comprising Hogarth, Gainsborough and Velasquez paintings in the library and drawing room, and silver (mainly in the West Corridor) collected by the 1st and 2nd Earls and including priceless pieces made by early eighteenth-century Huguenot refugees.

The Rotunda was completed in the 1820s. Intended as a grand reception, entertainment and exhibition room, it is linked to the two rectangular pavilions by the semi-elliptical wings. After the death of the Bishop, his son, the 5th Earl and later 1st Marquess, considered demolishing Ickworth, but did in fact virtually complete it, and adapted the East Pavilion for living quarters.

The 2,000-acre park was laid out by 'Capability' Brown. The grounds are particularly distinguished by massive oak and cedar trees.

3M SW of Bury St Edmunds, off A143 (93 J1)

Melford Hall, Suffolk This is an outstandingly well-preserved warm red-brick house, more typical of the Tudor era than the more flamboyant Elizabethan one. It was probably complete by 1578, when Queen Elizabeth was royally entertained by Sir William Cordell who had built the house after acquiring the land around 1550 after the Dissolution of the Monasteries. Sir William's family retained Melford Hall, except for a period in the mid seventeenth century, until the last quarter of the eighteenth century, when it was sold to the Parker family. Parker and Cordell family portraits are displayed in the two-storeyed banqueting hall. This and the library contain many treasures of historical as well as aesthetic interest: Restoration furniture, oriental ceramics, paintings of naval actions in which the 5th Baronet and his second son, Sir Hyde Parker (one of Nelson's admirals), took part. There is a portrait of Nelson himself. In the Blue Drawing Room are Sèvres china, and rare seventeenth- and eighteenth-century furniture, among other treasures.

Beatrix Potter was related to the 11th Baronet, and there are displays in the Hall of some of her paintings, drawings and other mementoes.

Long Melford, 3M N of Sudbury on A134 (93 K2)

Oxburgh Hall, Norfolk From the top of Oxburgh Hall's great and distinctive gatehouse – a rare, virtually untouched example of fifteenth-century architecture and brickwork – it is possible on a clear day to see the outline of Ely Cathedral, eighteen miles away. Not only has the gatehouse escaped the modernization and remodelling suffered by most of the building, but the superb King's Room inside the gatehouse, which gets its name from Henry VII's stay here in 1487, is also intact. In a room nearby are wall hangings with sections worked by Mary, Queen of Scots, and Bess of Hardwick (whose own *Hardwick Hall* is remarkable for its tapestries). There are also letters from Tudor kings to the family living in Oxburgh Hall, and wood carvings by Grinling Gibbons.

Oxburgh Hall was threatened with demolition just after World War II, but survived and was presented to the Trust in 1952. Apart from the gatehouse, much of the best of the interior was created in the 1830s, notably the library, dining room and drawing room. These rooms also contain mementoes of the family that has been associated with Oxburgh Hall for most of the house's existence – the Bedingfelds, who in 1661 were granted a Baronetcy by Charles II.

7M SW of Swaffham, on Stoke Ferry road (90 E8)

Paycocke's, Essex Paycocke's is an outstanding example of the fine, half-timbered houses that were built by successful tradesmen and merchants in the Middle Ages, often from fortunes made in the wool trade. Originally the fabric between the timber frames would have been of wattle and daub, slats of wood woven basket-style and filled in with dung, clay and horsehair, but it is now of brick. The house, which has been much restored, is named after Thomas Paycocke, whose family is represented by four tombs in Coggeshall's parish church.

Upstairs there are five identical gables, each with an oriel window, above an intricately carved 'bressummer', a horizontal wooden beam, and this first floor juts out slightly above the ground floor.

West Street, on W side of Coggeshall (87 B8)

Peckover House is the most imposing of the merchant's houses along the River Nene.

Peckover House, Cambridgeshire Peckover House, built in 1722, is just one of several imposing town mansions in Wisbech along the north bank of the River Nene. When Wisbech was a port there was much trade with Holland, and the Dutch influence on the Georgian architects of Peckover House and its neighbours is easy to see. The house was built by Jonathan Peckover, a banker from a prominent Quaker family. Though the hallway and the main reception rooms at the front of the older part of the house are not large, the way the house opens out on to magnificent mature gardens gives a sense of spaciousness. The garden was laid out in Victorian times and retains its original plan, enhanced by summer houses, hothouses and serpentine, wooded paths.

Wisbech, N bank of River Nene (90 D6)

4, South Quay, Great Yarmouth, Norfolk The elegant, early nineteenth-century exterior of this house actually masks a much older building – an Elizabethan house believed to date from 1596. Much of the interior is original, particularly the chimneypieces and some of the oak panelling. It is now a local museum.

(92 E8)

Wimpole Hall, Cambridgeshire The biggest house in Cambridgeshire and a very recent acquisition (bequeathed in 1976 and opened to the public in 1979), its position on a low hill in fairly flat countryside emphasizes its grandeur.

The original house, of which some internal walls are incorporated in the present mansion, was built in the mid seventeenth century, and for the next 200 years the house and the grounds were frequently and radically altered. 'Capability' Brown extended the Park in about 1767 and in the last decade of the century Sir John Soane designed the domed Yellow Drawing Room.

Between 1740 and 1894 Wimpole was owned by the Earls of Hardwicke, and it was the 4th Earl who, in the 1840s, made the last large-scale additions to the house. It was his son, known as 'Champagne Charlie', who sold Wimpole Hall which in due course was bought, in 1938, by Captain George Bambridge, whose wife Elsie was Rudyard Kipling's daughter. She, after demolishing some of the later and less harmonious additions to the house, bequeathed it, along with 3,000 acres, to the Trust.

Though from the south especially Wimpole Hall seems immense and palatial, several of the elegant rooms are surprisingly intimate – especially the Book Room which leads into the great library of 1719, planned by James Gibbs and containing over 50,000 volumes. The same atmosphere is sensed in the ante-room, between the entrance hall (exceptional partly because of its remarkable views over the Park) and the South Drawing Room. Soane's Yellow Drawing Room and Gibbs's Chapel decorated by James Thornhill are just two more of the many jewels in this country treasure-house.

1M E of A14 Royston to Huntingdon road, 6M N of Royston (91 K4)

Woolsthorpe Manor, Lincolnshire Tucked unobtrusively behind rows of twentieth-century houses, in a low-lying situation overlooking farmland, Sir Isaac Newton's former home gives few outward clues to its famous associations: it is small for a 'manor house', and might pass for a rather charming seventeenth-century farmhouse.

Woolsthorpe was a fairly new house when Isaac, son of Isaac and Hannah, was born there on Christmas Day 1642. The record of his baptism is still in the parish church of St John the Baptist, which also contains a sundial made by Newton at the age of nine. Visitors can see the room in which the great scientist and mathematician was born, and, in the garden at the front of the house, what is said to be a direct descendant of the apple tree from which Newton saw an apple fall when he 'discovered' gravity. Newton left Woolsthorpe for Cambridge as a teenager but returned for about a year and a half when the Great Plague of 1665 reached the city, and the study in which he did much of his creative work during that stay is on view. New evidence concludes that his spectrum experiments were carried out there during his 'evacuation' from the Plague.

½M NW of Colsterworth and 7M S of Grantham on B6403 (96 H6)

Castles, Abbeys & other Buildings

The Guildhall, Lavenham, Suffolk Dominating the market place in this remarkably well-preserved medieval 'wool town', the Guildhall is an exceptional timber-framed building.

It was built in the 1520s by the Guild of Corpus Christi, one of three guilds that locally controlled the all-important wool industry. The Guild was dissolved soon after Henry VIII's Dissolution of the Monasteries. Over the centuries the building has been a proxy-church, a magistrates' court, a priory, a Town Hall, a workhouse, an almshouse, a restaurant, a home for wartime evacuees and a nursery school. During its period as a prison, in the seventeenth century, it was the main place of confinement in Suffolk, and a pillory, whipping post and stocks were set up in the market square immediately outside. It now contains a collection of local bygones and archaeology.

The building has some interesting examples of wood carvers' skill, particularly on the doorposts of the porch and on the carved corner post. It has been heavily restored, but is still one of the most remarkable buildings in a remarkable small town.

Market Place, Lavenham (93 K2)

Ramsey Abbey Gatehouse, Cambridgeshire The Benedictine monastery of Ramsey was founded in the Saxon period, in the year 974. It was founded by St Oswald, Archbishop of York, with the help of Eolwin, foster brother of the Saxon King Eadgar. (Eolwin's remains lie here in a marble tomb of about 1230.) Little remains of the abbey, which, like Ely, once stood on an island in undrained and virtually impenetrable fen country. But the gatehouse, which was built around 1500, still stands. Even this is incomplete, because after the Dissolution of the Monasteries by Henry VIII in about 1538 it was partly dismantled and used as building stone. Enough still stands of the gatehouse, however, to indicate how richly carved and ornate the abbey buildings must have been, with panelled buttresses and decorative friezes carved in the stone around the doorway and the oriel window. There are some remains, too, of the Lady Chapel.

Ramsey, 10M SE of Peterborough (91 G4)

St George's Guildhall, King's Lynn, Norfolk The largest surviving medieval Guildhall in England, now used as a theatre, but retaining many of its original fifteenth-century features. Open for performances etc, particularly during the King's Lynn Festival.

On W side of King Street (90 C/D7)

Sun Inn, Essex An antique shop, formerly an inn, that dates from the fifteenth century but has seventeenth-century pargetting, an exterior plaster decoration commonly found in Essex and other East Anglian counties. (Not open.)

At the junction of Church Street and Market Hill, Saffron Walden (91 L6)

Tattershall Castle, Lincolnshire The impressive red-brick tower that is all that remains of Tattershall Castle is the highest point for many miles around: from it there are lovely views across the fen country and to the Lincolnshire Wolds to the north-east. On a clear day, both Lincoln Cathedral and the Boston 'Stump' can be seen.

Tattershall Castle is an outstandingly good example of the fortified house which appeared during the Wars of the Roses that dominated the early and mid fifteenth century. In contrast to the great spartan castles of the Normans, these were comparatively comfortable to live in. Many of the architectural details, such as the machicolated gallery, suggest Continental influence of the late fourteenth and fifteenth centuries.

The original Castle was built by Robert de Tatershale in 1231, but only vestiges remain. The red-brick keep, built by Ralph Cromwell, Henry VI's Lord Treasurer, between 1434 and 1445, now stands alone, but it was once inside the castle's enclosed inner ward. Although Tattershall's plan followed that of castles built in the twelfth century, architectural and domestic details still intact show that it was really much more of a country house than a castle proper: there is a decorative roof-gallery unlike anything found in more purely functional buildings; there are unusually large and therefore vulnerable windows, deep window recesses, cosy turret rooms.

The carved stone chimney-pieces in the empty and echoing rooms that the visitor enters as he climbs up to Tattershall's highest levels are original, but were reinstated after being retrieved on their way to the United States in the nineteenth century. They were traced by Lord Curzon, who bought Tattershall in 1911 after it had stood in ruins since about 1695. He bequeathed Tattershall to the Trust in 1926.

3½M SE of Woodhall Spa, off the A153 Sleaford to Louth Road (97 D9)

Theatre Royal, Bury St Edmunds, Suffolk Built in 1819, restored 1962–63, and an outstanding example of the Regency period. Leased from Greene King, the nearby brewers. Open for performances etc.

In Westgate Street (93 J2)

Tattershall Castle is a country mansion masquerading as a medieval defensive keep.

Dutch influence on the design of Bourne Mill shows clearly in the gables.

Archaeological & Industrial Sites

Bourne Mill, Essex Bourne Mill was built as a fishing lodge by Sir Thomas Lucas in about 1590, using materials from the ruined Abbey of St John, which had been razed by Henry VIII half a century earlier. The design shows considerable Dutch influence and it is thought Sir Thomas may have employed Dutch Protestant refugees. It is also believed that the pond might originally have been a stockpond for the monks.

The Lucas family paid during the Civil War for their Royalist sympathies. The property was confiscated and passed to Dutch refugees (an interesting twist of fate) who used it for weaving. By 1860 it had become a flour mill, and the machinery, recently restored, can still be seen.

1M S of Colchester, just east of the B1025 Mersea road (87 B10)

Burnham Overy Mill, Norfolk This is unusual in that a complete complex of late eighteenth-century mill buildings and outbuildings has survived intact: the three-storeyed mill itself, the barn, maltings, miller's house and mill-hands' cottages. It is a pretty setting, where warm red brick is well set off by white paintwork. Many of the original features of the mill survive, including the windows (louvred to aid ventilation) on the maltings, and cantilevered 'lucams', which project from either side of the roof and which housed the lifting gear that enabled grain to be raised to storage areas high in the driest and best ventilated part of the building. A wooden windmill stands nearby.

½M SW of Overy Staithe, on SE side of A149 Hunstanton to Wells road (92 A1)

Houghton Mill, Cambridgeshire It is said that a mill has existed here, on an artificial island in the River Ouse, for over a thousand years. When Eolwin built Ramsey Abbey in 974 he presented the mill and an adjacent meadow to the monks; the miller retained water rights over the local inhabitants, and tenants of the abbey had to have their corn ground at the mill.

After the dissolution of the abbey the mill became Crown property. The present building dates from the seventeenth, eighteenth and nineteenth centuries, and, having ceased to operate as a mill in 1930, is used as a Youth Hostel. Originally thatched, it now has a slate roof. *2½M from St Ives, S of A1123 (91 H4)*

The wooden tower of Burnham Overy windmill set against a dramatic East Anglian sky.

Evesham 1 Stratford-upon-Avon 2 Evesham Adjoining page 88 3 Warwick Stratford-upon-Avon 4 Adjoining page 89 5 Banbury 6

A B C D E F G H

Stroud · Gloucester · Adjoining page 57 · Stroud · Bath · Chippenham · Severn Bridge · Chippenham · Frome

1 Salisbury 2 Andover Salisbury 3 Salisbury 4 Adjoining page 40 5 Andover Winchester 6

Towcester
7
Towcester
8
Adjoining page 89
9 Towcester
10 Northampton
11 Bedford
Adjoining page 91
12
Adjoining page 91
A
Baldock
B
C
Hertford
London
D
Adjoining page 86
E
London
London
F
London
G
London
Adjoining page 42
H
Basingstoke
7
Basingstoke
8
Alton
Basingstoke
9
Adjoining page 41
10
Guildford
11
12
Milton Keynes
Buckingham
Bletchley
Leighton Buzzard
Dunstable
Luton
Letchworth
Hitchin
Harpenden
Aylesbury
Tring
Berkhamsted
Hemel Hempstead
St. Albans
Chesham
Amersham
Watford
Rickmansworth
Borehamwood
High Wycombe
Beaconsfield
Marlow
Henley-on-Thames
Maidenhead
Slough
Windsor
Reading
Wokingham
Bracknell
Staines
Camberley
Woking
Weybridge
Walton-on-Thames
Esher
Epsom
Leatherhead
Harrow
Ealing
Hounslow
Hillingdon
Uxbridge
Richmond
Kingston upon Thames
Princes Risborough
Thame
Winslow
B U C K S
B E D F O R D
H E R T F O R D
S U R R E Y
K S H I R E
C H I L T E R N
COPYRIGHT, GEORGE PHILIP & SON, LTD.

Bedford
St. Neots
Adjoining page 91
Royston
Stump Cross
Stump Cross
Northampton
Towcester
Aylesbury
Adjoining page 85
High Wycombe
Slough
Guildford
Adjoining page 41
Horsham
Crawley
East Grinstead
Guildford
Adjoining page 42
Tonbridge
Tonbridge
H E R T F O R D
S U R R E Y
E
Letchworth
Baldock
Hitchin
Stevenage
Luton
Harpenden
Welwyn Garden City
Hertford
Ware
St. Albans
Hatfield
Hemel Hempstead
Harlow
Bishop's Stortford
Stansted Mountfitchet
Great Dunmow
Thaxted
Hoddesdon
Cheshunt
Potters Bar
Watford
Borehamwood
Rickmansworth
Epping
Chigwell
Brentwood
Enfield
Barnet
Harrow
Haringey
Waltham Forest
Redbridge
Havering
Romford
Barking
Ilford
Newham
Hackney
Islington
Camden
Brent
Ealing
Hillingdon
Uxbridge
London
Westminster
Kensington
Hammersmith
Southwark
Lambeth
Wandsworth
Lewisham
Greenwich
Bexley
Bromley
Croydon
Sutton
Merton
Kingston upon Thames
Richmond
Hounslow
Tower Hamlets
Dartford
Grays
Tilbury
Gravesend
Northfleet
Swanley
Orpington
Sevenoaks
Caterham
Epsom
Leatherhead
Esher
Weybridge
Walton-on-Thames
Chertsey
Staines
Sunbury on Thames
Shepperton
Thames
M1
M4
M10
M11
M20
M23
M25
M26

Adjoining page 91
Haverhill
Sudbury
Ipswich
Adjoining page 93
Felixstowe
Harwich
Dovercourt
Manningtree
Mistley
Halstead
Colchester
Wivenhoe
Alresford
Brightlingsea
Great Bentley
Weeley
Thorpe-le-Soken
Walton on the Naze
Frinton-on-Sea
Little Clacton
St. Osyth
Clacton on Sea
Holland-on-Sea
Jaywick
Braintree
Coggeshall
Kelvedon
Witham
Tiptree
Mersea Island
West Mersea
Tolleshunt D'Arcy
Tollesbury
Heybridge
Maldon
Blackwater
Osea I.
Bradwell-on-Sea
St. Peter's Flat
Dengie Flat
Buxey Sand
Tillingham
Dengie Marshes
Ray Sand
Southminster
Burnham-on-Crouch
Crouch
Foulness Sands
Foulness Island
Maplin Sands
Chelmsford
Great Baddow
Danbury
South Woodham Ferrers
Wickford
Rayleigh
Hockley
Hawkwell
Rochford
Basildon
South Benfleet
Thundersley
Hadleigh
Leigh-on-Sea
Prittlewell
Westcliff on Sea
SOUTHEND-ON-SEA
Thorpe Bay
Shoeburyness
Canvey Island
Corringham
Stanford le Hope
Thames
Blyth Sands
Cliffe
Isle of Grain
Sheerness
Queenborough-in-Sheppey
Minster-on-Sea
Eastchurch
Leysdown-on-Sea
ISLE OF SHEPPEY
Medway
Rochester
Strood
Chatham
Gillingham
Rainham
Sittingbourne
Faversham
Whitstable
Herne Bay
Birchington
Margate
Ramsgate
Adjoining page 43
Canterbury
Maidstone
Ashford
Dover
KENT
ESSEX
A
B
C
D
E
F
G
H
7
8
9
10
11
12
COPYRIGHT, GEORGE PHILIP & SON, LTD.

Newport 1 Newport 2 Stafford 3 Stafford Stone 4 Adjoining page 95 5 ← Burton-on-Trent 6 →

Wellington A Wellington B Shrewsbury C Adjoining page 59 D Ludlow Leominster E Ludlow F Leominster G Hereford H Ross-on-Wye

Adjoining page 57 1 Ross-on-Wye 2 Tewkesbury 3 Cheltenham Cheltenham 4 Adjoining page 84 5 ← Stow-on-the-Wold → Oxford 6

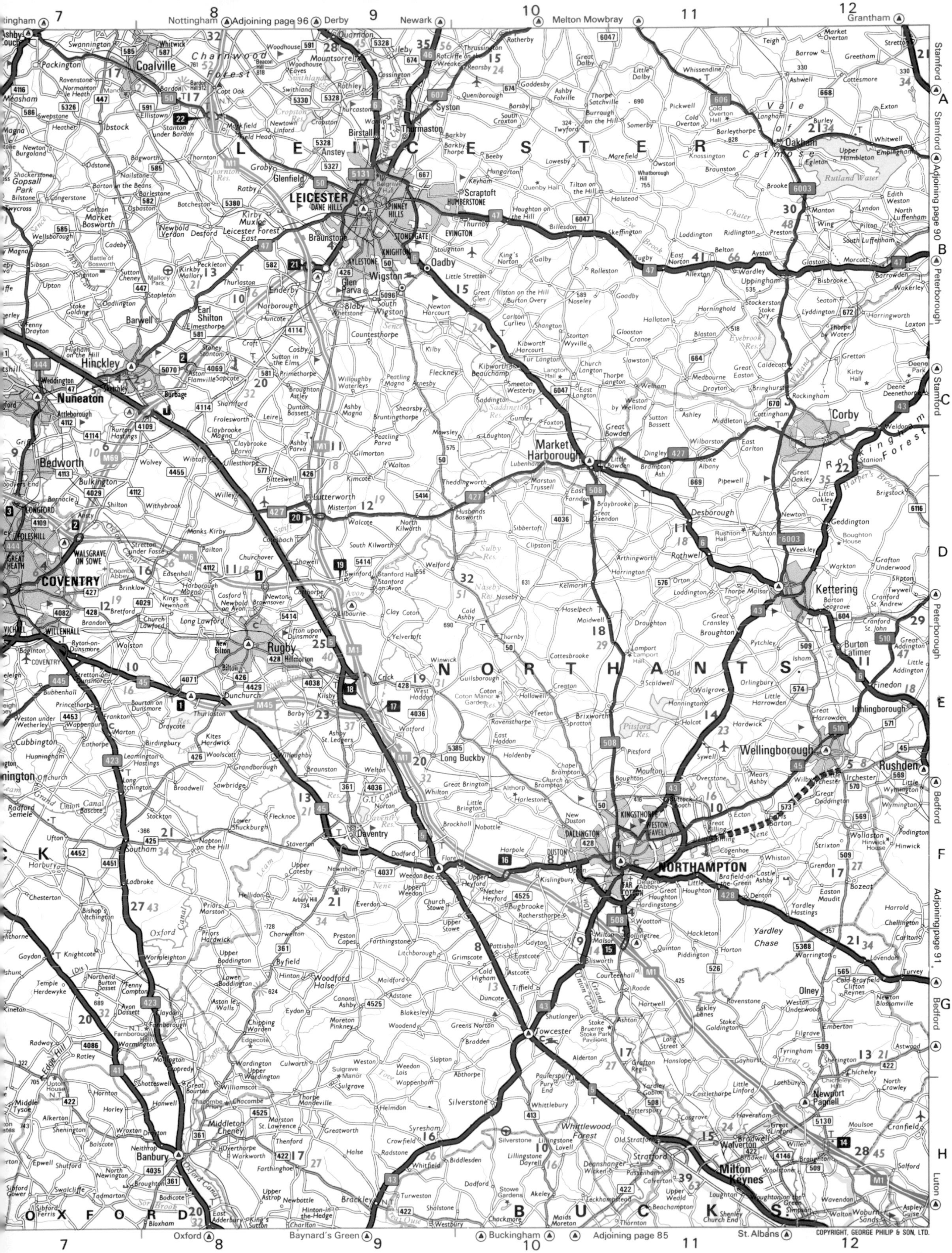
Nottingham
Adjoining page 96
Derby
Newark
Melton Mowbray
Grantham
Stamford
Adjoining page 90
Peterborough
Adjoining page 91
Bedford
Luton
Oxford
Baynard's Green
Buckingham
Adjoining page 85
St. Albans
L E I C E S T E R
N O R T H A N T S.
O X F O R D
B U C K S.
Vale of Catmose
Charnwood Forest
Rockingham Forest
Whittlewood Forest
LEICESTER
COVENTRY
NORTHAMPTON
Coalville
Hinckley
Nuneaton
Bedworth
Rugby
Lutterworth
Oadby
Wigston
Market Harborough
Corby
Kettering
Wellingborough
Rushden
Daventry
Towcester
Banbury
Oakham
Uppingham
Milton Keynes
Newport Pagnell
Olney
Brackley
Rothwell
Desborough

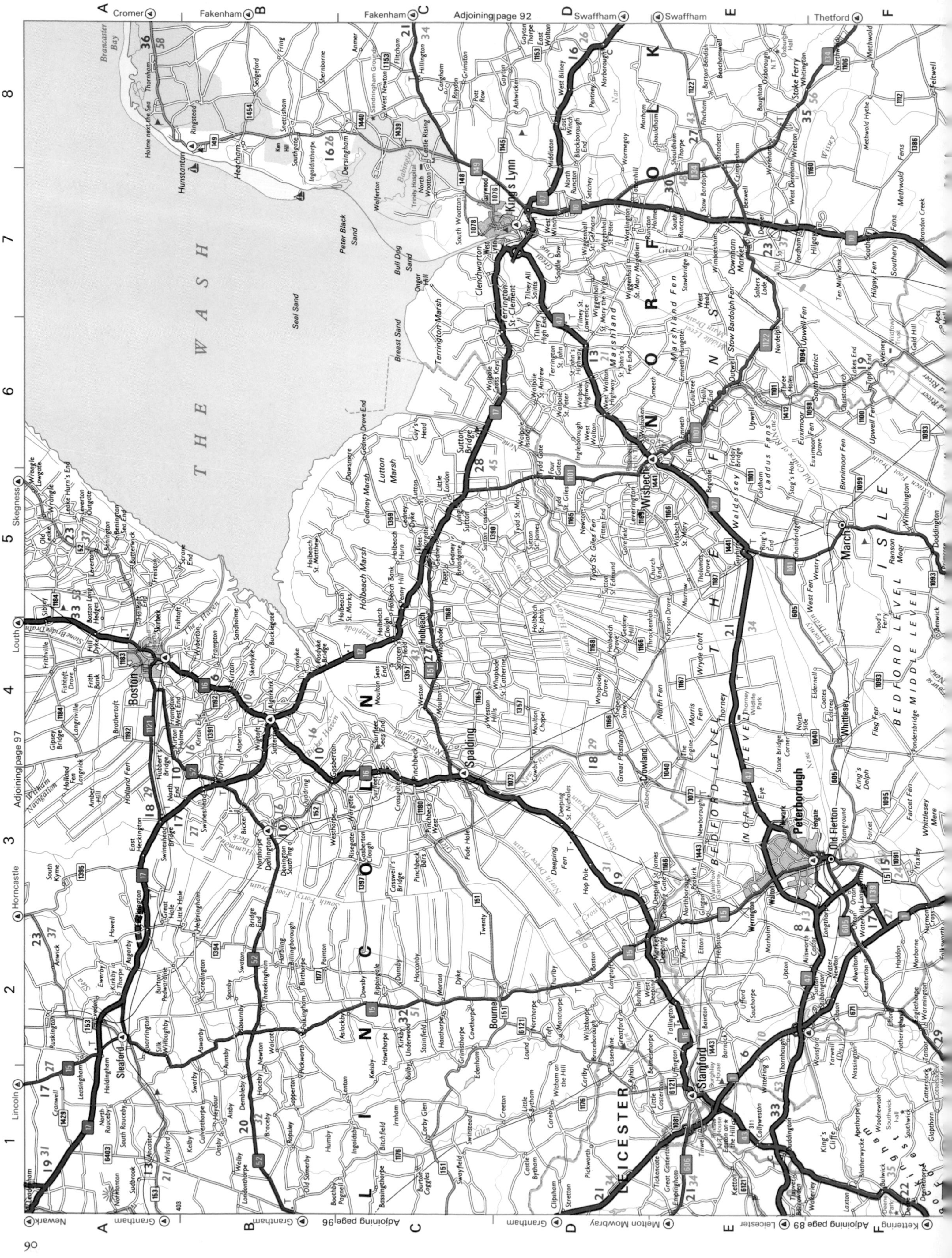
Cromer
Fakenham
Adjoining page 92
Swaffham
Thetford
Skegness
Louth
Adjoining page 97
Horncastle
Lincoln
Newark
Grantham
Adjoining page 96
Melton Mowbray
Leicester
Adjoining page 89
Kettering
THE WASH
Hunstanton
King's Lynn
Downham Market
Wisbech
March
Whittlesey
Peterborough
Stamford
Market Deeping
Crowland
Spalding
Holbeach
Boston
Sleaford
Bourne
Brancaster Bay
Peter Black Sand
Bull Dog Sand
Seal Sand
Breast Sand
Terrington Marsh
Gedney Marsh
Holbeach Marsh
Lutton Marsh
Sutton Bridge
Long Sutton
Deeping Fen
Morris Fen
Flag Fen
LEICESTER

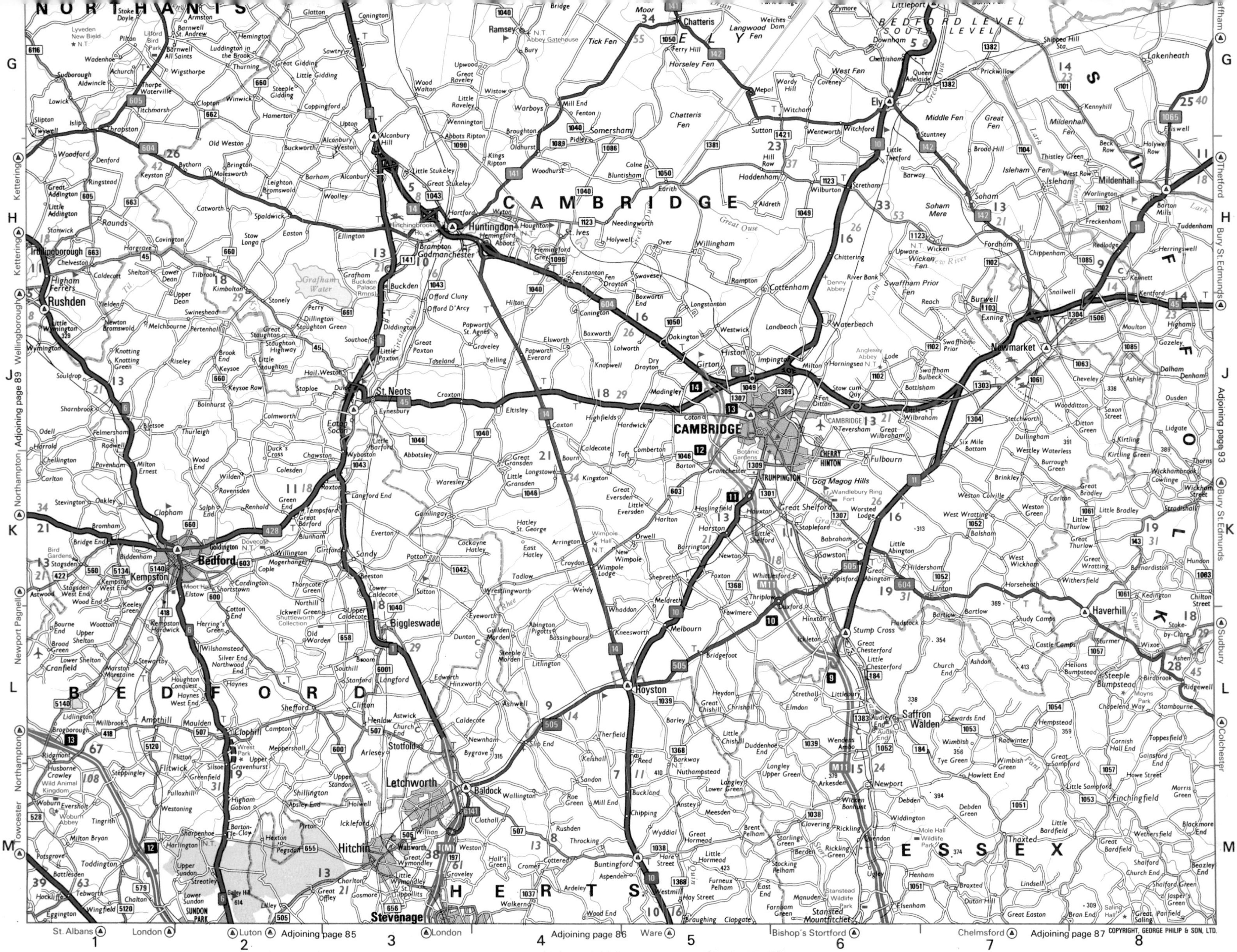

NORTHANTS
CAMBRIDGE
BEDFORD
HERTS
ESSEX
SUFFOLK
ELY
BEDFORD LEVEL SOUTH LEVEL
CAMBRIDGE
Huntingdon
St. Neots
Bedford
Kempston
Rushden
Biggleswade
Letchworth
Hitchin
Stevenage
Baldock
Royston
Saffron Walden
Haverhill
Newmarket
Ely
Mildenhall
Chatteris
Ramsey
Adjoining page 93
Adjoining page 89
Adjoining page 85
Adjoining page 86
Adjoining page 87
Thetford
Bury St. Edmunds
Sudbury
Colchester
Kettering
Wellingborough
Northampton
Newport Pagnell
Towcester
St. Albans
London
Luton
Ware
Bishop's Stortford
Chelmsford
COPYRIGHT, GEORGE PHILIP & SON, LTD.

NORTH
SEA
N O R F O L K
THE BROADS
B R E C K L A N D
NORWICH
Great Yarmouth
Lowestoft
Cromer
Sheringham
Wells-next-the-Sea
Blakeney
Holt
Fakenham
North Walsham
Aylsham
Reepham
Foulsham
East Dereham
Swaffham
Wymondham
Attleborough
Watton
Shipdham
Mundesley
Happisburgh
Stalham
Hoveton
Horning
Wroxham
Acle
Reedham
Loddon
Beccles
Gorleston on Sea
Caister-on-Sea
Hunstanton
King's Lynn
Wisbech
Adjoining page 90
Holkham Bay
Brancaster Bay
Blakeney Point
Salt Marshes

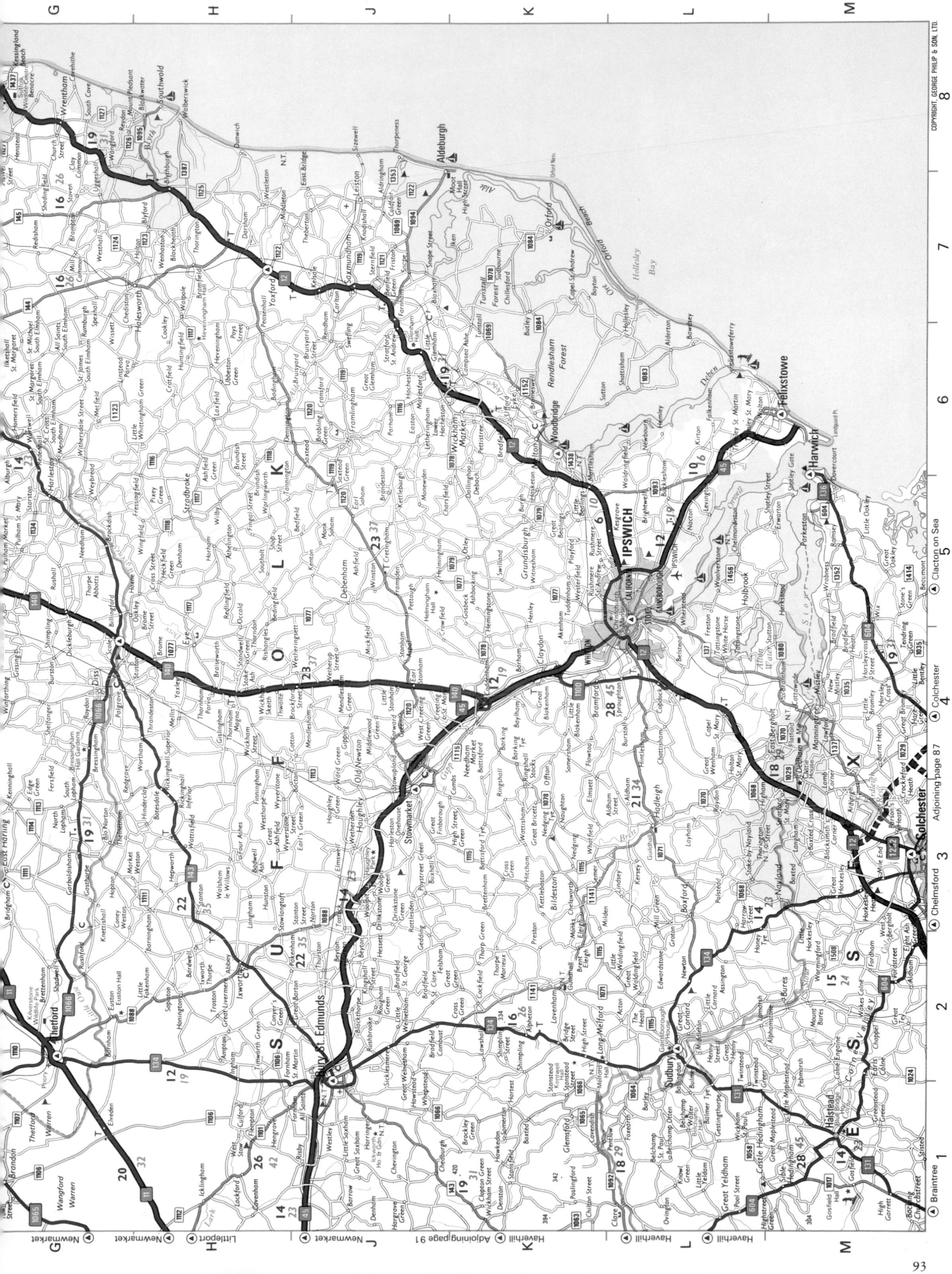

IPSWICH
Felixstowe
Harwich
Aldeburgh
Southwold
Woodbridge
Stowmarket
Bury St. Edmunds
Thetford
Sudbury
Halstead
Colchester
Hadleigh
Framlingham
Saxmundham
Halesworth
Diss
Eye
Debenham
Needham Market
Lavenham
Long Melford
Orford
Wrentham
Yoxford
Leiston
Rendlesham Forest
Hollesley Bay
S U F F O L K
E S S E X
Adjoining page 87
Adjoining page 91
Newmarket
Littleport
Haverhill
Braintree
Chelmsford
Colchester
Clacton on Sea
COPYRIGHT, GEORGE PHILIP & SON, LTD.

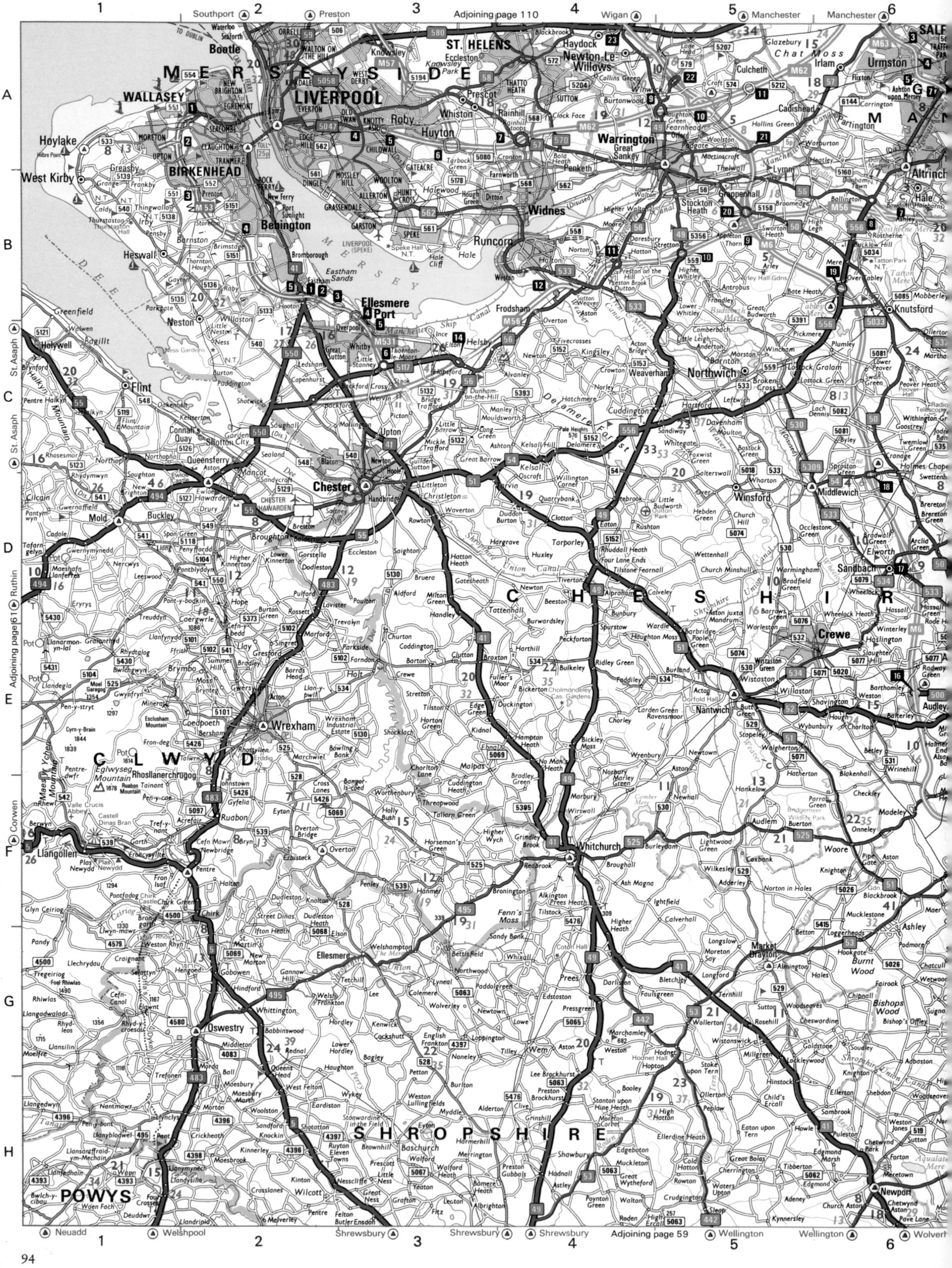

Adjoining page 110
Southport
Preston
Wigan
Manchester
Adjoining page 59
Neuadd
Welshpool
Shrewsbury
Wellington
Wolverh
St. Asaph
Ruthin
Adjoining page 61
Corwen
MERSEYSIDE
LIVERPOOL
WALLASEY
BIRKENHEAD
Bootle
Bebington
ST. HELENS
Newton-Le-Willows
Warrington
Widnes
Runcorn
Ellesmere Port
Chester
Northwich
Winsford
Middlewich
Crewe
Nantwich
Knutsford
Altrincham
Sandbach
Wrexham
Whitchurch
Market Drayton
Oswestry
Ellesmere
Llangollen
Mold
Flint
Holywell
Hoylake
West Kirby
Heswall
Neston
Frodsham
Tarporley
Malpas
Newport
CHESHIRE
CLWYD
SHROPSHIRE
POWYS
MERSEY
DEE

7 Manchester 8 Flouch Inn 9 Adjoining page 111 10 Flouch Inn 11 Barnsley Leeds 12

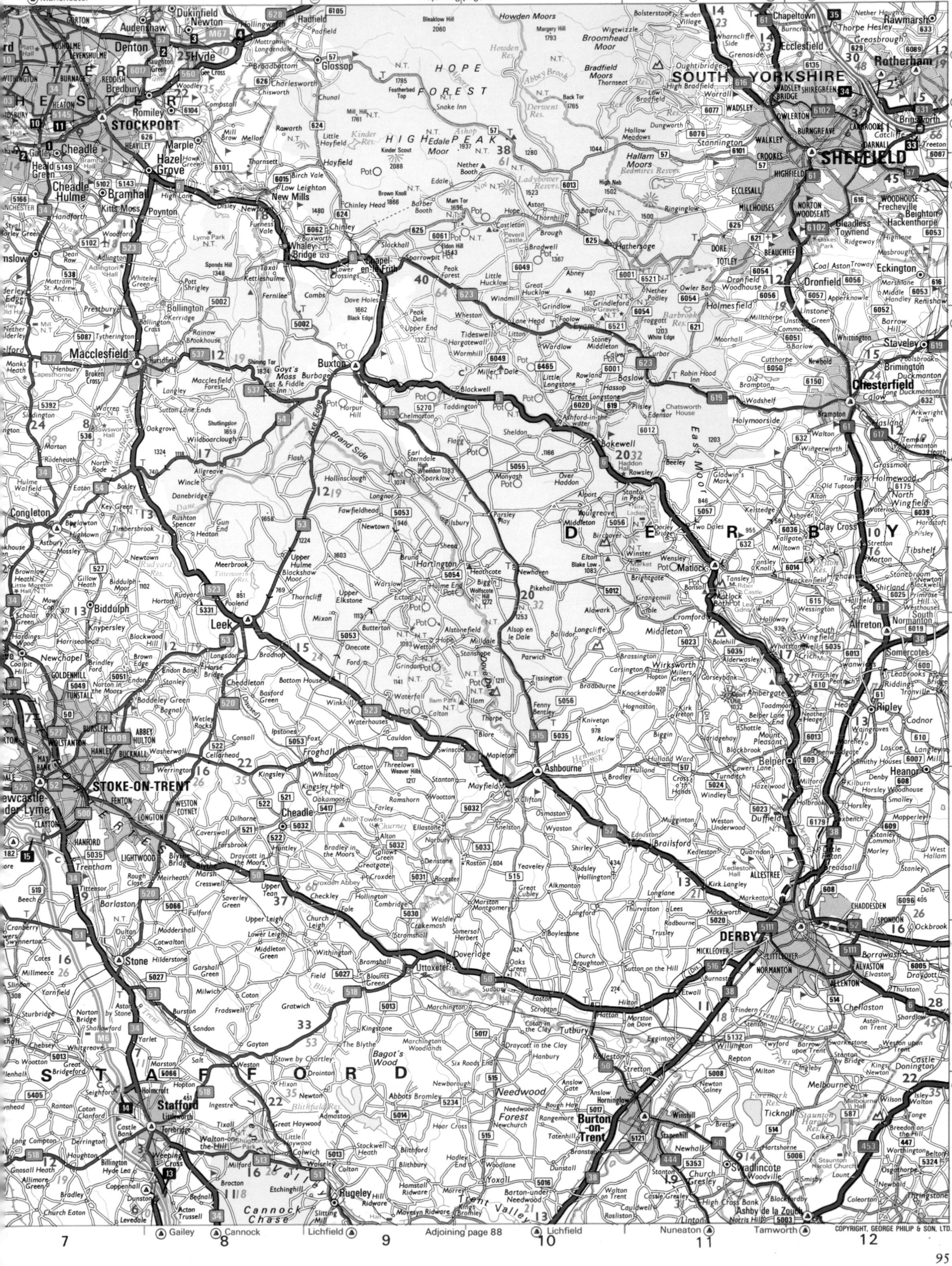

Doncaster Bawtry Nottingham Lincoln Worksop Mansfield Adjoining page 96 Nottingham Leicester Nottingham

A B C D E F G H

Gailey Cannock Lichfield Adjoining page 88 Lichfield Nuneaton Tamworth

7 8 9 10 11 12

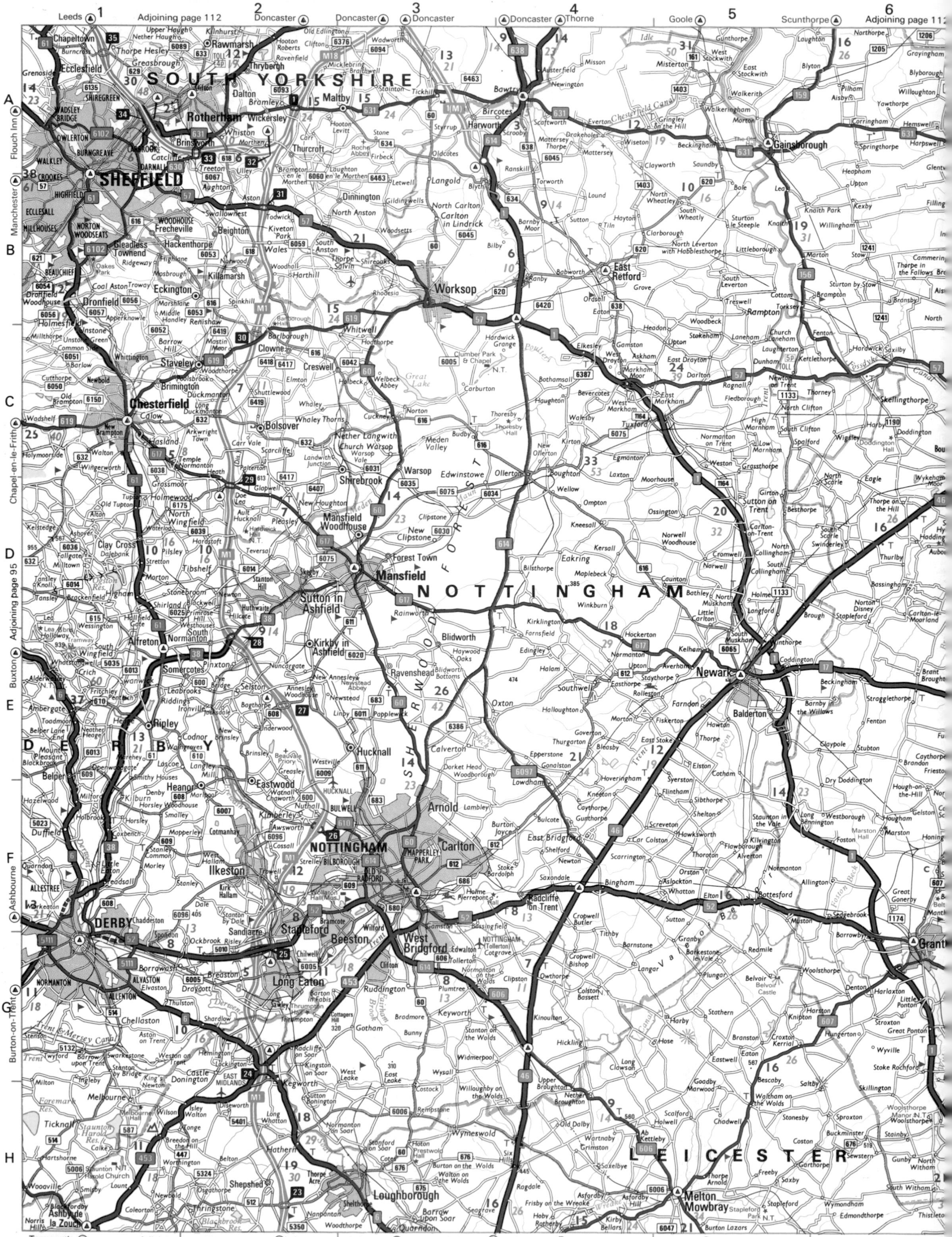

Leeds
Adjoining page 112
Doncaster
Thorne
Goole
Scunthorpe
Flouch Inn
Manchester
Chapel-en-le-Frith
Adjoining page 95
Buxton
Ashbourne
Burton-on-Trent
Tamworth
Adjoining page 89
Leicester
Stamford
SOUTH YORKSHIRE
NOTTINGHAM
DERBY
LEICESTER
SHERWOOD FOREST
Sheffield
Rotherham
Chesterfield
Worksop
Gainsborough
East Retford
Mansfield
Sutton in Ashfield
Kirkby in Ashfield
Newark
Nottingham
Derby
Ilkeston
Long Eaton
Beeston
West Bridgford
Loughborough
Melton Mowbray
Grantham
Alfreton
Ripley
Heanor
Eastwood
Hucknall
Arnold
Carlton
Southwell
Bawtry
Bolsover
Dronfield
Eckington
Staveley
Clay Cross
Belper
Duffield
Stapleford
Shepshed
Ashby de la Zouch
Bingham
Tuxford
Ollerton
Dinnington
Maltby

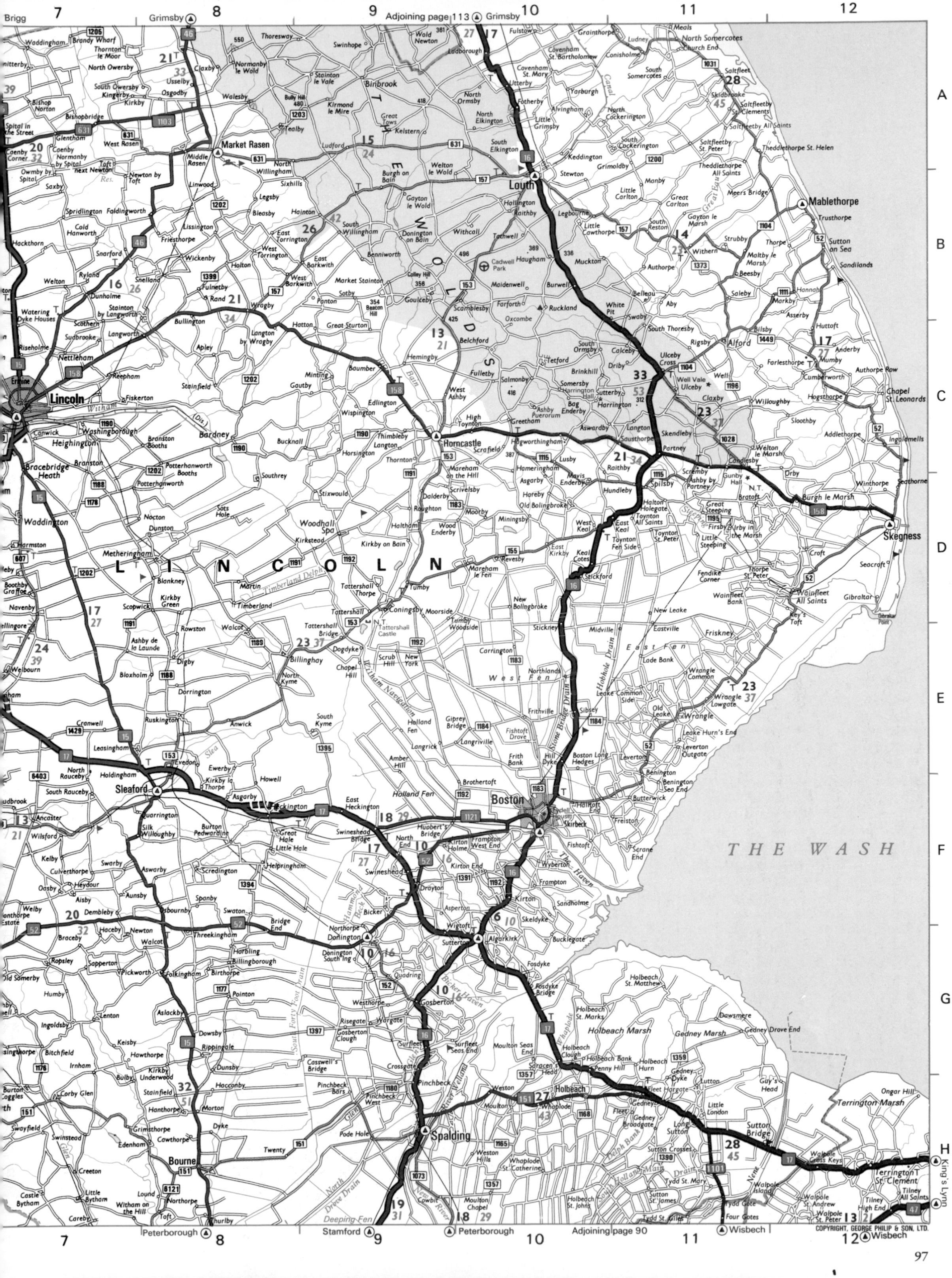

Adjoining page 113
Adjoining page 90
Brigg
Grimsby
Peterborough
Stamford
Wisbech
King's Lynn
7
8
9
10
11
12
A
B
C
D
E
F
G
H
L I N C O L N
T H E   W O L D S
THE WASH
Lincoln
Market Rasen
Louth
Mablethorpe
Sutton on Sea
Alford
Skegness
Horncastle
Woodhall Spa
Coningsby
Spilsby
Wainfleet All Saints
Boston
Sleaford
Donington
Spalding
Holbeach
Sutton Bridge
Bourne
Wragby
Binbrook
North Somercotes
Saltfleet
Theddlethorpe St. Helen
Trusthorpe
Sandilands
Anderby
Chapel St. Leonards
Ingoldmells
Burgh le Marsh
Wrangle
Kirton
Algarkirk
Sutterton
Gosberton
Pinchbeck
Long Sutton
Gedney
Fleet
Whaplode
Moulton
Weston
Terrington St. Clement
Walpole St. Andrew
Walpole St. Peter
Tydd St. Mary
Deeping Fen
Cowbit
Crowland
Folkingham
Billingborough
Heckington
Swineshead
Billinghay
Tattershall
Metheringham
Navenby
Waddington
Bracebridge Heath
Washingborough
Heighington
Bardney
Nettleham
Welton
Faldingworth
Holton
Saxby
Glentham
Middle Rasen
Tealby
Ludford
Kelstern
Burgh on Bain
Donington on Bain
Cadwell Park
Tetford
Ulceby Cross
Partney
Candlesby
Gunby Hall
Firsby
Stickford
Stickney
Sibsey
Frithville
Old Leake
Leverton
Benington
Butterwick
Freiston
Fishtoft
Skirbeck
Frampton
Wyberton
Fosdyke
Holbeach Marsh
Gedney Marsh
Gedney Drove End
Terrington Marsh
Guy's Head
Timberland Delph
Witham Navigation
Hobhole Drain
Stone Bridge Drain
The Haven
Bicker Haven
South Forty Foot Drain
River Welland
North Drove Drain
Great Eau
Canal

North-West England

GAWTHORPE HALL

Extending from the Dee estuary to the Solway Firth, from the Pennines to the Irish Sea, north-west England presents landscapes and seascapes of immense variety. With modern industry and urban growth concentrated in the southern half of the region the Trust's properties there, though few, assume a greater significance. Pockets of attractive countryside such as commons and woodlands in the Wirral, and dunes on the Lancashire holiday coast, are safeguarded. So, too, are two of England's finest half-timbered houses, Speke Hall and Rufford Old Hall.

But it is in Cumbria that the National Trust plays its most powerful preservationist role, owning or protecting about a quarter of the Lake District National Park. From its first purchase in 1902 of Brandelhow on the western shore of Derwentwater, to its largest, recent acquisition of the Leconfield Commons – 32,000 acres of magnificent fell country in the west of the Lake District – the Trust has, over seventy-five years, fulfilled many of the hopes expressed by one of its founding fathers, Canon Rawnsley. The unmatched beauty of many lakes and shores, of valley-heads with their farms, fields and surrounding fells, as well as all the highest land in the centre of the Lake District, is now safeguarded for the nation.

The Trust's Cumbrian properties reflect Lakeland history. Fourteenth-century pele towers contrast with the comfortable functionalism of seventeenth-century 'statesmen's' farmhouses, while the modestly elegant birthplace of the Lake District's greatest publicist, Wordsworth, provides an interesting comparison with Hill Top, Sawrey, home of Beatrix Potter, one of the most generous of the Trust's many Lake District benefactors.

Coast & Countryside

With fine views across the estuary of the Dee to the Clwydian Hills, **Thurstaston Common** (94 B1) is the largest and best-known of Trust properties in the Wirral peninsula, with pleasant paths and picnic places among sandstone outcrops and gorse. Woodland and watermeadows at **Harrock Wood**, east of Irby (94 B1), and Scots pine at **Burton Wood** (94 C2) farther south are welcome scenic contrasts. If these are important open spaces on Merseyside's doorstep, even more critical is **Medlock Vale** (111 G8), Greater Manchester, now part of the Daisy Nook Country Park, a refreshing ribbon of rural peace among quiet pastures within a few hundred yards of the suburbs of Oldham and Ashton under Lyne.

On the Lancashire coast, midway between Liverpool and Southport, is a different kind of oasis. **Formby Dunes** (110 F2), an Enterprise Neptune acquisition in 1967, comprises 472 acres of splendid sand-dunes, inhabited by shelduck, oystercatchers and species of wading birds. Rare plants among the brushwood and pines may have originated from grain swept off merchant ships berthing in Liverpool that was gradually washed northwards on the tides.

Seventy-five miles away across the sea the Trust safeguards the **Calf of Man** (114 H1). This is an important nature reserve, where Atlantic seals breed, together with large colonies of sea-birds including guillemots, kittiwakes, puffins and razorbills. Bona-fide naturalists and day visitors are welcome at the farmhouse that now serves as a bird-observatory, wardened during the summer months.

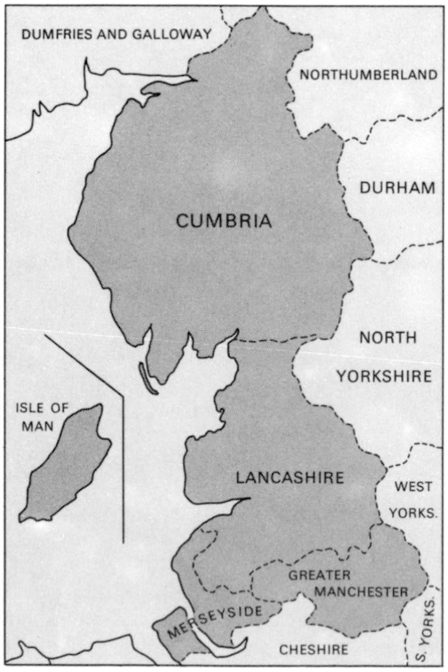

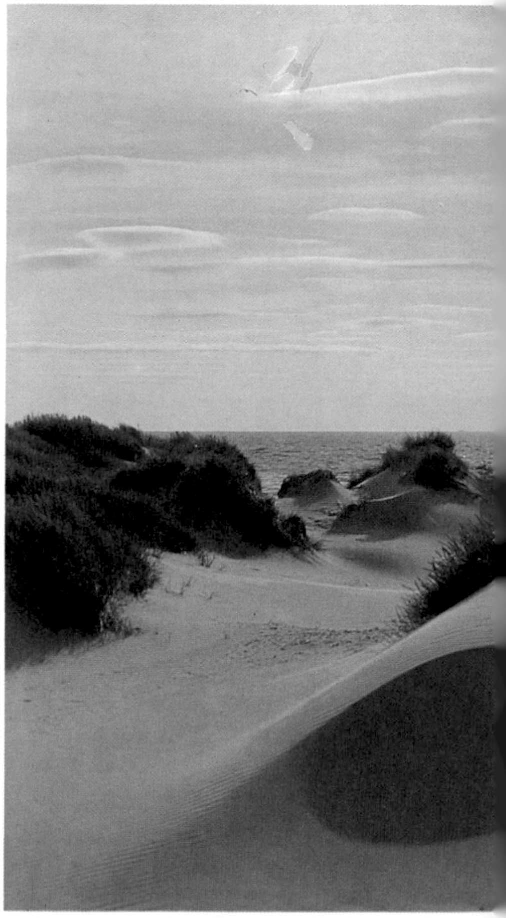

Formby dunes is a unique stretch of unspoilt coastline between Liverpool and Southport. Red squirrels can still be seen here.

Lancashire's long coastline ends at Morecambe Bay, by the mudflats, marshes and sheltered woods of Silverdale. Here, the Trust owns **Eaves Wood** (115 H7), where venerable oaks and yews mingle with beech, hornbeam, and larch planted last century. Hazel is still coppiced, spring flowers add their carpet of colour, and in association with Lancashire Naturalists' Trust a rewarding two-mile nature trail has been established, which includes a section of limestone pavement and culminates on **Castlebarrow**, a rocky outcrop with extensive views. Even wider views are enjoyed from **Arnside Knott** (115 G7), two miles to the north, in Cumbria. Inviting tracks through bracken, gorse, and silver birch lead easily to the wooded 500-feet high summit, with a superb panorama, particularly northwards across the Kent estuary to the mountains of the Lake District.

About a quarter of all the land owned by the National Trust is in the Lake District, where it is now one of the largest landowners. Canon Rawnsley, Vicar of Crosthwaite (Keswick), one of the three co-founders of the Trust, and

Derwentwater, looking towards Skiddaw. Derwent Isle, off this shore, was Beatrix Potter's 'Owl Island' in *The Tale of Squirrel Nutkin.*

for twenty-five years its first Honorary Secretary, was the dynamic driving force who ensured that the Lake District became so closely associated with the aims and ideals of the National Trust. Initially, the greatest concern was for the lake shores, and in 1902 the Trust bought its first Lake District property, **Brandelhow** (114 C5), 100 acres of woodland and rocky bays on the west side of Derwentwater. Over the next quarter century a further 100 acres at **Manesty** at the south end of the lake (114 C5) were added. Today a delightful woodland track links these two pioneer properties, with glorious views across the lake to Skiddaw and Blencathra, and motor launches call regularly at the landing-stages on the shore of the lake.

The Trust now owns the western half of Derwentwater, much of the western shore, and the wooded part of the eastern shore and islands near Keswick, from **Calf Close Bay** to **Friar's Crag** (114 C5), that rocky headland yielding a memorable view towards Borrowdale, always associated with the early conservationist John Ruskin. If Derwentwater was for early tourists to Lakeland the quintessential aesthetic experience, only marginally less so was the charm of Ullswater, long, sinuous, and naturally divided into three distinctive reaches. **Gowbarrow Park** (114 C6), above the western shore, with **Aira Force** and **Aira Crag**, was the Trust's foothold here, quickly followed by **Glencoyne Wood** and **Stybarrow Crag** (114 C6) nearer to Glenridding, thus ensuring for public enjoyment an important three-mile stretch of the lake's western shore and adjoining woodlands by the main Penrith road. It was by the lakeside, near Lyulph's Tower, a neat Gothick folly, that Wordsworth saw the field of daffodils which inspired one of his best-known poems.

Windermere is the largest of the lakes, the first one seen by Victorian travellers arriving at Windermere station after the railway came in 1847, and the first seen by today's motorist a few miles after leaving the A6 at Kendal. As long ago as 1900 Canon Rawnsley and the Trust successfully opposed the idea of a tramway along the eastern shore of Windermere between Bowness and Ambleside. At the head of the lake, **Borrans Field** (114 E6), adjoining the Brathay outlet, with the remains of a Roman fort, Galava, was an early Trust acquisition. Round on the western shore beyond **Wray Castle**, Low Wray (114 F6), whose landscaped grounds are freely open, the Trust owns three miles of **Claife's** (114 E6) ancient woodlands where oak, ash, alder and hazel were cultivated centuries ago by Furness Abbey monks. Now, as far as Ferry Nab they offer quiet walks and good access to the lake shore.

At the opposite end of the lake, the Trust's land at **Fell Foot** (114 F6) has become a very popular country park, with extensive car-parking, launching facilities for boats, picnic and bathing facilities, an information centre and café, and the riot of colour of rhododendrons in late spring. The latest Trust attraction at nearby Coniston Water is the restored Victorian steam-yacht *Gondola*, operating from **Monk Coniston** (114 E5) at the lake's northern end, and the Trust safeguards extensive areas of wooded shore on both eastern and western sides.

No powered boats are allowed to disturb the tranquillity of **Buttermere** (114 D4), **Crummock Water** (114 C4) and **Loweswater** (114 C4), in the west of the Lake District. These three lakes occupy a long, glacial valley, enclosed by steep-sided, craggy mountains so darkly dominant in the view from Honister Pass, Fleetwith Pike, or Haystacks, but, towards Loweswater, more pastoral and wooded. Lakeside paths encourage exploration away from the road that threads their eastern margins, and for many lovers of the Lake District the Buttermere valley is a special paradise. The appeal of **Wastwater** (114 D/E4) is different: an incomparable amalgam of mystery and majesty, where screes 2,000 feet high tumble dramatically into the lake's eastern side, and the road opposite yields increasingly impressive views as it winds tortuously towards the Lake District's grandest valley head, at **Wasdale Head** (114 D4). There, towering mountains overlook the tiny, wall-enclosed fields first farmed by Norse settlers a thousand years ago; and now by tenant farmers of the Trust.

The Trust has been concerned for many years with the upper reaches of vulnerable valleys, and, through gift and purchase, now owns many dalehead farms. Thus, the Trust has assumed the landowning role of the Lake District's 'statesmen' of three or four generations ago, in a hill-farming economy, based on sheep, where the tradition is continued of 'heafed' flocks, which are let to tenants of the farms. The Trust owns nearly 30,000 sheep in the Lake District, mainly the local Herdwicks,

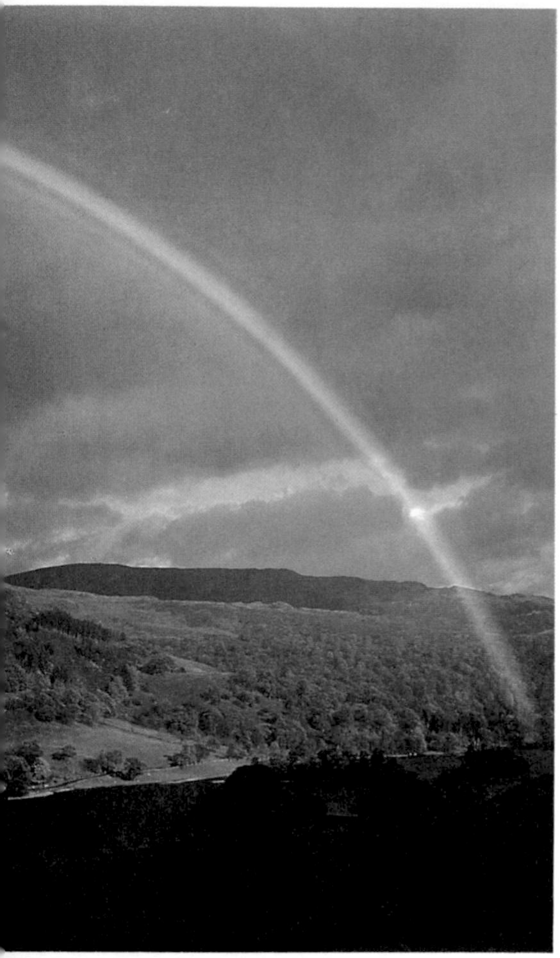

above **The wooded northern shore of Rydal Water, in the view from Loughrigg looking towards Rydal Fell.**

below **There are glorious views over Derwentwater from the ridge of Catbells to the west of the lake.**

so familiar in the scene of fells and farms. Typical of dalehead farms and their walled intakes are those at the head of **Great Langdale** (114 E5), running up to Langdale Fell, whose mountain backcloth of the Langdale Pikes, Bowfell and Crinkle Crags is one of the best-loved and most majestic scenes in Britain. Much of **Little Langdale** (114 E5), too, is safe in Trust hands, while across the hills to the west, over the exciting passes of Wrynose (half National Trust) and Hardknott (entirely National Trust), Trust ownership of many farms in **Eskdale** ensures that the rare beauty of that exquisite valley will remain sacrosanct.

The neighbouring **Duddon Valley** (114 E4), beloved by Wordsworth and now heavily afforested, retains a sylvan character, with river scenery unequalled in the Lake District. This makes it a particular favourite for discerning visitors who appreciate the quiet miles of excellent walking, rather than climbing, which it offers. Many of the farms in the head of the valley are owned by the Trust.

But it is Borrowdale (114 D5) which probably claims first place in the affections of many walkers and climbers, for generations of whom **Stonethwaite** and **Seathwaite** (114 D5) have seen the beginning and the end of memorable days among the noblest mountains in England. Above the valley farms and intake pastures are the great upland commons of the central Lake District, thousands of acres of tawny hillsides, frowning crags, proud peaks, chuckling becks and lonely tarns that mirror the changing sky. All the central mountain summits belong or are on lease to the Trust – **Scafell Pike, Lingmell, Kirkfell, Great End** and **Great Gable** (114 D4/5). In addition, the **Lonsdale** and **Leconfield Commons** (114 D/E5 and 114 C/D4) bring under Trust protection further huge areas of wild mountainous country in a broad swathe from Seat Sandal at the southern end of the Helvellyn range to Bowfell, and westwards from Derwentwater to Wastwater.

Lesser hills should not be forgotten. Here, youngsters experience the joys of discovery that only the Lake District can give. Their more modest slopes can still challenge older limbs, and a summit at 1,000 feet can be as exciting and rewarding as one three times higher. Lakes and hills are still in perfect proportion, as **Loughrigg's** (114 E6) broad, knobbly summit reveals, west of the road between Ambleside and Grasmere. Above Borrowdale, and forming its eastern wall, **Grange Fell**'s (114 D5) rocky outcrops among grass, heather and bracken afford a sense of achievement with the rewards of glorious views of Derwentwater, matched, perhaps, by the irresistible challenge of **Catbells'** (114 C5) friendly slopes to the west of the lake. Overlooking Grasmere from the north, **Helm Crag** (114 D6) has the most famous profile in the Lake District, a rocky crest whose pinnacles can be reached only by a careful scramble, yet its summit is under 1,300 feet.

Among the lesser hills quiet tarns abound. Some, like **Burnmoor** (114 E4) above Eskdale, are forever lonely mirrors of the hills; others, like **Tarn Hows** (114 E6), north-west of Hawkshead, have become justifiably popular beauty spots, where the Trust provides well-screened carparks. Yet not far away, two miles north of Coniston, above the unique enchantment of **Tilberthwaite** (114 E5), are little-known jewels on **Holme Fell** (114 E5), capturing in miniature those magic elements that make the Lake District, for many people, beloved over all – water, rock, grass, trees, bracken, and the everlasting hills.

Nearer to the northern Pennines than to the Lake District hills, **Wetheral Woods** (132 H3), in the lower Eden valley, is one of the Trust's lesser-known Cumbrian properties.

In marked contrast, the Trust also protects 1,800 acres of commonland along a dozen miles of the **Solway shore** (132 G1/2), mainly at Burgh Marsh and farther west between Bowness-on-Solway and Anthorn. Across the mudflats and shining sands, where the tide comes in, as Scott described, like a galloping horse, are the hills of Galloway and Scotland.

Houses, Gardens & Parks

Acorn Bank, (Temple Sowerby Manor), Cumbria Dorothy Una Ratcliffe, the Yorkshire dialect poet and travel writer, lived in this beautifully-situated house built of local red sandstone. Used now as a Sue Ryder home, the house can be visited only on application. The garden, however, is open, and is renowned for its spring bulbs, herbaceous border and herb garden.

6M E Penrith, off A66 (115 B8)

Gawthorpe Hall, Lancashire An unusual house built 1600–05 for the Rev. Lawrence Shuttleworth, possibly by Robert Smythson. Rare for a Jacobean house in having neither wings nor courtyard, its compact plan is emphasized by its three storeys. The original medieval fortified tower round which the later building was designed was heightened in the middle of the last century by Sir Charles Barry, who made other elaborate changes at the same time.

Gawthorpe's essential Jacobean character survives, as incidentally do its complete building accounts. The ground floor drawing room and top floor gallery are outstanding for their rich panelling and stucco ceilings, and contain many rare pieces of furniture. In former Victorian nurseries are displayed selected exhibits from Rachel Kay-Shuttleworth's remarkable collection of treasures and textiles from all over the world, including embroideries, laces, costumes and ceramics.

(The house is let to Lancashire County Council and forms part of the Nelson and Colne College of Further Education, with the Jacobean dining hall now a lecture room, and basement serving as kitchen and refectory.)

3M W Burnley, on N of A671 (111 D7)

An eighteenth-century painting of Gawthorpe Hall shows what may be the remnants of a formal seventeenth-century garden.

The drawing room at Rufford Old Hall has an apparently sixteenth-century roof and yellow wallpaper made specially for it.

Hill Top, Cumbria From 1905 to 1913 the home of Beatrix Potter. It is a typical, modest seventeenth-century Lake District farmhouse. It is heavily over-visited, to the detriment of the house and the peace of the village. The National Trust would be grateful to all those who can bear to forgo a visit.

Near Sawrey, 2M S Hawkshead, on B5285 (114 F6)

Rufford Old Hall, Lancashire This home of the Hesketh shows three phases of building spanning 350 years. Originally a typical H-shaped house of Tudor times, only the central part of this survives – the magnificent timbered old hall of the fifteenth century facing down the approach drive. Studding, quatrefoils and wood-mullioned windows are the impressive outer display of an interior whose exuberance is unmatched in England. A noble hammer-beam roof spans a room whose rich decorative detail is emphasized by its being above window level and thus well illuminated. Unique among the furniture is an enormous, finely carved contemporary, movable screen.

The Carolean wing of 1662 was added at right-angles to the medieval hall, its brick contrasting with the older timberwork, and in 1821 an ingenious architectural addition in place of the old office wing linked the two, and provided more comfortable living accommodation for the family. This part also contains the main staircase, giving access to a large, elegant drawing room on the first floor.

A feature of the house is the fine collection of seventeenth- and eighteenth-century furniture of the Hesketh family. This is displayed throughout and includes many superb court-cupboards, chests, tables and chairs, mainly in oak, several dated and crested. Also shown is the Hesketh armour, while part of the 1821 and Carolean wings house the Philip Ashcroft Museum of local life.

7M N Ormskirk, on A59 (110 F3)

Sizergh Castle, Cumbria This home of the Strickland family for 700 years looks impressive from any angle. Glimpsed first at a distance across its mature parkland, a closer view of its north-western front reveals the various additions made through the centuries to the fortress at its heart. This large, three-storey, massive pele tower of 1350 is characteristic of Border refuges built to withstand Scottish raids. Adjoining it is a Tudor great hall, re-modelled during Elizabethan times and again in the eighteenth century, an Elizabethan gabled corner block next to it, with two long sixteenth-century wings projecting so that a three-sided courtyard results.

Apart from the persona which continued occupation by one family imparts to a house, Sizergh is outstanding in having a wealth of fine quality early Elizabethan woodwork, including benches, chairs and panelling, with the oak linenfold work in a passage room upstairs dating from Henry VIII's time. Five exceptional chimney-pieces from 1563–75 are carved with a remarkable delicacy. A collection of the more interesting Strickland family treasures, including a number of Stuart relics, is housed in the top floor of the pele tower.

3½M S Kendal, close to A6/A591 interchange (115 F7)

Speke Hall, Merseyside Sandwiched between industrial buildings and a runway of Speke Airport is this astonishing survival – one of the finest English half-timbered houses. Although started by Sir William Norris in 1490, the present quadrangular form of Speke Hall, surrounding a flagged, yew-gloomy courtyard, is largely the work of Sir Edward Norris between 1598 and 1606 and the outside appearance has scarcely changed since then. Structurally one of the least altered of Tudor houses, with contemporary panelling and elaborate plasterwork in a series of quite small rooms, it is also unusually well supplied with secret hiding places and observation holes associated with the recusant activities of the Norris family in the early seventeenth century.

The great hall, with its marvellously incongruous chimney-piece and fine Flemish wainscoting, and the great parlour with its sumptuous stucco ceiling, are perhaps the most memorable rooms in this remarkable house.

Richard Watt, a wealthy Liverpool merchant, acquired Speke in 1795, and he and his family restored it, most of the furniture and fittings introduced in mid Victorian times being a revival of styles which prevailed during the sixteenth and seventeenth centuries. Thus Speke successfully juxtaposes Tudor and nineteenth-century influences, each complementing the other.

(The house is let to Liverpool Corporation.)

8M SE Liverpool, S of A561 (94 B3)

Stagshaw Garden, Cumbria Overlooking the northern end of Windermere lake, this steeply-sloping woodland garden is renowned for its unique collection of rhododendrons, azaleas, camellias and spring bulbs.

½M S Ambleside, on A591 (114 E6)

Townend, Cumbria The Brownes lived at Townend from the reign of Henry VIII until 1944, and their house, built in 1623, is a remarkably intact, unchanged survival of the home of successive generations of Lake District 'statesmen'. These were yeoman-farmers who emerged as a rural middle-class in Tudor times, enjoying the right at death to hand on their estates to their next-of-kin, even though they may have been tenants of a lord. Having customary tenure of land more akin to freehold than copyhold, they eventually became freeholders.

Townend's roughcast, white-washed walls, slate roof, round chimneys and mullioned windows typify Lake District vernacular building. The Brownes had a passion for carving and, inside, panelled walls and carved oak furniture, much of it with family initials, and canopied bedsteads, combine into a homely record of a yeoman family. The library reflects the tastes of literate people, with books accumulated and used over many generations. Locally-woven fabrics provide evidence of a cottage industry of the seventeenth-century and there are old household utensils, now obsolete. Across the road is a magnificent ramp-entrance barn, with wooden galleries, of the same date as the house.

Troutbeck, 3M SE Ambleside, off A592 (114 E6)

Wordsworth House, Cumbria In 1766 John Wordsworth, agent to Sir James Lowther, moved into this modest, rather austere house which had been completed about twenty years earlier. His second son, William, was born here in April 1770, and his daughter, Dorothy, the following year. In the secure atmosphere of a happy family home the children grew up, loving the house and its garden which fringed the River Derwent. There, Dorothy first influenced her brother, nurturing a relationship which became one of the most creative in English literature, a fact recognized in the poet's own words:

'She gave me eyes; she gave me ears;
And humble cares, and delicate fears;
A heart, the fountain of sweet tears;
And love, and thought, and joy.'

above Sizergh Castle, seen across the lake and the eighteenth-century terraces. The pele tower is on the right.

right With its slate roof, roughcast walls and mullioned windows, Townend typifies traditional Lake District architecture.

The stone, many-windowed house retains original fireplaces, brass door fittings, a handsome staircase with elegant balusters and softwood panelling in a number of rooms. Among the poet's own pieces are a Crown Derby dinner service, a bureau bookcase with some first editions, a late Georgian longcase clock, and a set of Georgian chairs which belonged to Wordsworth's friend Robert Southey.

Main Street, Cockermouth, off A66 (114 B4)

Castles, Abbeys & other Buildings

Bridge House, Cumbria One of the smallest but best-known of all National Trust buildings, this whimsical little early sixteenth-century garden house on a stone bridge over Stock Beck in the middle of Ambleside is now used as a Trust Information Centre.

In Ambleside (A591) (114 E6)

Cartmel Priory Gatehouse, Cumbria Apart from the fine monastic church, this is the only surviving building of the Augustinian Priory. Built 1130–40, with the character and appearance of a fortified tower, after the Reformation it became a courthouse and then a grammar school. It is now used as a shop.

4M S Newby Bridge (114 G6)

Cautley: Cross Keys Inn, Cumbria A white-washed, stone-built Temperance Hotel at the foot of the steep eastern slopes of the Howgill Fells, dating from about 1600, but extensively altered in the eighteenth and nineteenth centuries. A carved inscription above one of its inside doorways quotes William Blake's lines:

'Great things are done when men and
mountains meet:
These are not done by jostling in
the street.'

5M NE Sedbergh, on A683 (115 F9)

Dalton Castle, Cumbria A fourteenth-century pele tower in the former regional capital of Low Furness, dating from about 1350, and formerly the Court House of Furness Abbey. Upper floors are reached by a spiral staircase within the thickness of the walls, and retain some original Gothic windows. Others are nineteenth-century insertions. Inside is a collection of armour, old documents, and items of local historical interest.

In Dalton-in-Furness, on A590 (114 H5)

Hawkshead Courthouse, Cumbria A fifteenth-century building surviving from the days when the manor of Hawkshead was owned by Furness Abbey. Manorial courts were traditionally held in the upper room which now houses a museum of local rural life, jointly managed with the Abbot Hall Art Gallery, Kendal.

In Hawkshead, on B5285 (114 E6)

Keld Chapel, Cumbria This modest, rubble-built chapel, probably of the early sixteenth century, may have been a chantry chapel, or erected by the abbot of nearby Shap Abbey for his tenants in Keld village. Services are occasionally held in the chapel.

1M W Shap (A6) (115 D8)

above **Bridge House, the smallest dwelling owned by the Trust, has been a teahouse, a weaving shop and a cobbler's shop.**

below **Hawkshead Courthouse is one of the few secular buildings of the medieval period to have survived in the Lake District.**

Tower Bank Arms, Cumbria Next door to Beatrix Potter's home, Hill Top, and formerly called 'The Blue Pig', this inn is illustrated in *The Tale of Jemima Puddle-Duck*. Keeping its 'real ale' cool in old cellars, and containing oak furnishings in 'Lakeland vernacular', it is one of three inns not only owned but managed by the Trust, and provides accommodation and refreshments in a comfortable, homely atmosphere.

At Near Sawrey, 2M S Hawkshead, on B5285 (114 F6)

Archaeological & Industrial Sites

Castlerigg Stone Circle, Cumbria An almost complete stone circle, about one hundred feet across, of thirty-eight stones of various shapes and textures, dating from the Bronze Age. Apart from its prehistoric significance, the circle is dramatically and beautifully situated on a plateau, with surrounding hills forming an impressive amphitheatre.

2M E Keswick, off A591 (114 C5)

Castlerigg stone circle is at its most dramatic in stormy or wintry weather, when curtains of rain or snow sweep the fells.

Steam Yacht 'Gondola', Cumbria After lying derelict for many years at the southern end of Coniston Water, this 85-feet long steam yacht has been renovated and is in full working condition, operating a passenger service from the pier at Monk Coniston at the northern end of the lake. Commissioned originally by the Furness Railway Company in 1860, her two ornate saloons carried thousands of passengers during her eighty years of service, an enterprise now happily revitalized, so that once more a beautiful steam yacht adds its own unique distinction to Coniston Water.

1½M NE Coniston, on B5285 (114 E5)

North-East England

RIEVAULX TEMPLE

The landscape of the north-east is one of great beauty and variety. It is a land of farms and mineral exploitation, of castles and monasteries, of industry and fine houses and parks. It sweeps down from the tops of the bleak Pennines to the wild coasts of Northumberland, and from the Cheviots on the Scottish border to the flats of Humberside.

Well-dispersed through the area, National Trust properties epitomize many aspects of the life and history of the region.

Hadrian's Wall and Housesteads Fort recall the might of Rome, while castles are later reminders of Northumberland's frontier position. Mount Grace Priory, the finest Carthusian ruin in England, is in striking contrast to the great eighteenth-century houses of Wallington and Nostell Priory, with their collections of furniture and china; and Beningbrough Hall makes a perfect setting for the eighteenth-century portraits loaned by the National Portrait Gallery.

York is a handy centre for exploring the grotesque shapes of Brimham Rocks and the classical landscapes of Rievaulx Terrace and Temples, and The Treasurer's House in the city itself is a fine repository of seventeenth- and eighteenth-century furniture.

Three buildings neatly point the area's links with industry: George Stephenson's Cottage at Wylam; James Paine's coolly elegant Gibside Chapel – built on and from the wealth of coal – and Cragside, one of the architectural peaks of Victorian imagination and self-confidence, home of the industrialist and inventor William Armstrong.

Coast & Countryside

Three National Parks, together with part of a fourth, display the varied scenery of this part of Britain. Rivers flow eastwards from the Pennines; austere gritstone moors give way to lush upland pastures on the limestone of the Yorkshire Dales. East of the Vale of York chalk wolds and heather moorland reach towards an exciting coastline. Beyond the Tyne, Northumberland's spacious uplands with their castles and pele towers recall a troubled past, and on the coast a Christian culture flowered thirteen centuries ago.

In the northern part of the Peak District National Park the undulating moorlands of the **Derwent Estate** (111 G/H10) overlook the Ladybower, Derwent and Howden reservoirs, while to the north-west, within easy reach of Huddersfield, the peat hags and heather of **Marsden Moor** (111 F9), crossed by the Pennine Way, typify the sombre solitudes of gritstone uplands.

In sharp contrast, near the southern edge of the Yorkshire Dales National Park, are the finest limestone landscapes in Britain, around Malham, where stone walls, fissured 'pavements', and great natural cliffs gleam white in sunlight. North of the horseshoe-shaped Malham Cove is **Malham Tarn** (111 A7), one of the few natural lakes in the Dales and a Site of Special Scientific Interest. The nature reserve is leased to the Field Studies Council, but on the 4,000-acre estate there is access to the southern shore. Also, there are many public footpaths and tracks in the surrounding countryside, where monastic flocks of Fountains Abbey grazed in medieval times, their fleeces the foundation of the Yorkshire wool trade.

In later centuries the wool trade was centred on Halifax, and near Hebden Bridge to the west are many survivals of the domestic industry of the seventeenth and eighteenth centuries, including farms, cottages and a mill in **Hebden Dale** (111 D8), a steep-sided oak-wood valley with miles of fine walks, gay with bluebells in spring.

Wind and weather carve gritstone outcrops into strange shapes, none more fantastic than those among the heather and silver birches at **Brimham Rocks** (111 A10), on the eastern margin of the Dales, where giant rock towers form one of the most remarkable natural scenic wonders in England. **The Bridestones**, (117 F9), on the North Yorkshire Moors to the east (two miles off the A169), are similar, though smaller and less spectacular. At the western edge of the moorland plateau **Scarth Wood Moor** (116 E5), north of Osmotherley,

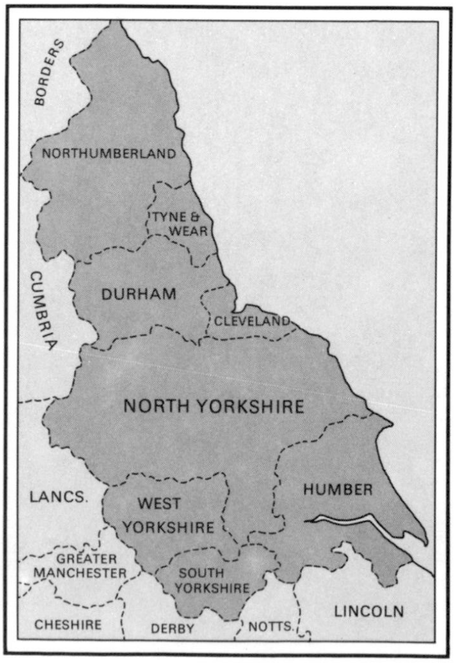

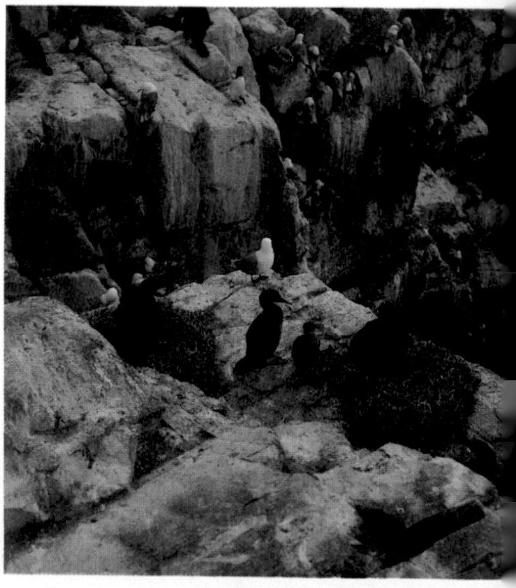

Shags (nesting) and kittiwakes are among the sea-birds that frequent the Farne Islands.

provides a superb viewpoint, with the Cleveland Way passing through its bracken and heather.

A spectacular stretch of coastline at **Ravenscar** (117 E9/10) on the southern end of Robin Hood's Bay is now safeguarded by the Trust, with steep access to a rocky shore. A few miles to the south, **Hayburn Wyke** (117 E10), recently acquired, incorporates woodland walks, access to the shore and a nature reserve.

From the north of the Coquet to the estuary of the Tweed the Northumberland coast is one of outstanding beauty, where sandy, dune-backed bays alternate with rocky outcrops and headlands. The four-mile stretch between **Craster** and **Low Newton by-the-Sea** (133 A10) is characteristic, and is owned or protected by the Trust. Car-parking facilities at each end encourage access to one of the most enjoyable coastal walks in the north-east. The Trust's observation hide at Newton Pool provides good opportunities for watching the wide range of breeding birds which use it during the year.

The Farne Islands (133 D12), known to St Aidan and St Cuthbert, are an important nature reserve, breeding-place for grey seals and huge colonies of many species of sea-birds. Best visited in late spring they are reached by boat from Seahouses, landing being restricted to Inner Farne and Staple Island. Prominent in the seaward view from **St Aidan's Dunes** (133 D12), two miles south-east of Bamburgh, the Farne cliffs are a distant highlight when seen from **Ross Castle** (133 A9), a heathery hill-top forming part of an Iron Age fort above Chillingham, many miles inland, and one of the finest viewpoints in Northumberland.

Malham Tarn is a natural lake formed by a dam of glacial moraine. The bare limestone landscapes of the North Yorkshire moors stretch away on every side.

Houses, Gardens & Parks

Bellister Castle and Pele Tower, Northumberland A large, seventeenth-century farmhouse adjoins the grey stone ruins of an older pele tower, all on a semi-artificial mound. Three farms, cottages in nearby Park village, and parts of the South Tyne river also belong to the estate. (Not open.)

1M SW Haltwhistle, off A69 (132 G5)

Beningbrough Hall, North Yorkshire Beningbrough's welcoming façade of fine rubbed red brick with stone quoins is little changed from 1716, when it was completed for John Bourchier. A York carpenter-architect, William Thornton, supervised the building of this outstanding house, probably with some advice from the better-known Thomas Archer.

Its cool, dignified architecture is enriched by decorative detail of superb quality, exemplified by Thornton's elaborate wood-carving. The central Great Hall, rising through two storeys, is one of the most beautiful of English Baroque interiors, with restrained plasterwork, elegant arches, and fluted pilasters.

Though it came to the Trust with few contents, Beningbrough has been enriched with generous loans and gifts, especially of furniture and oriental porcelain, and it provides an ideal setting for about a hundred paintings from the National Portrait Gallery. The state rooms of the ground and first floors display famous contemporaries of the Bourchiers between 1688 and 1760, including Kneller's noted portraits of members of the Kit-cat Club.

The top floor has been skilfully adapted to display, using modern exhibition techniques, various aspects of English society in the eighteenth century as revealed by portraits and architectural styles, and examples of owner's collections. An audio-visual presentation in the stable block sets the scene for a tour of the house; another one in the Bell Tower of the laundry courtyard supplements it. Beningbrough is not just a superbly restored mansion, it is an experience.

8M NW York, off A19 (112 A3)

Braithwaite Hall, North Yorkshire This late seventeenth-century farmhouse, containing some Jacobean furnishings, is open on prior application to the tenant at Braithwaite Hall.

2M W East Witton, off the A6108 (116 G1)

Hebden Dale includes survivals of the domestic wool industry, such as this mill.

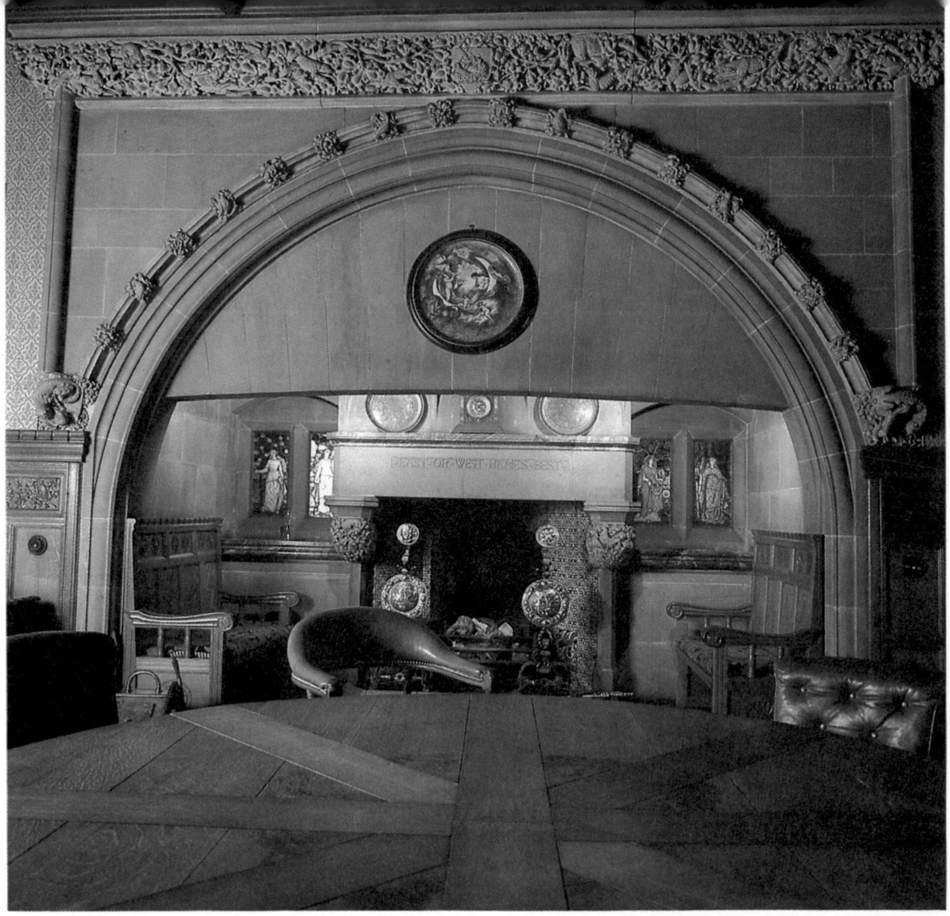

Cragside (*above*), set against a sea of sombre conifers, is dramatically Victorian. The inglenook fireplace in the dining room (*right*) has Pre-Raphaelite stained glass by Morris & Co.

Cragside, Northumberland This dramatic Victorian country mansion was built between 1864 and 1895 for the Newcastle industrialist Sir William (later the first Lord) Armstrong. At first an unexciting stone villa, it was continually added to by Richard Norman Shaw from 1870 to 1884 to create a building large enough to be a family home and showy enough to impress visiting clients.

A contrived approach through the now heavily wooded estate suddenly reveals Shaw's 'Old English' style in a bewildering array of timber-framed gables and tall chimney stacks and towers. Most of the living rooms are sited to enjoy superb views to the west.

This remarkable house has retained most of its original fittings. Shaw himself designed some of the furniture, and the remainder represents a mixture of eighteenth-century revival and the Arts and Crafts Movement. The library survives as one of the best Victorian interiors still intact, with furniture by Gillow and stained-glass made by William Morris & Co. from a design by Rossetti. In 1880 this room became the first in the world to be lit by electricity powered by a hydro-electric generator. This was in the grounds and invented by Sir William.

The drawing room – Shaw's last great addition to the house – shows Victorian opulence at its most magnificent. The room is dominated by a massive carved marble chimney-piece and inglenook, designed by Lethaby and made by the firm of Farmer and Brindley.

The grounds of Cragside form a 900-acre country park, with steep, rocky hillsides, artificial lakes, several million trees, and a single-track driveway of five miles, best seen in June when it is ablaze with rhododendrons and azaleas.

15M NW Morpeth, entrance on B6344 (133 C9)

Wheeling gulls recall Lindisfarne Castle's links with the sea and its past importance in coastal defence.

The Chinese wallpaper in the state bedroom at Nostell Priory is decorated with every sort of bird, from peacocks to pheasants.

East Riddlesden Hall, West Yorkshire Most of this impressive house was built about 1648 for James Murgatroyd, a Halifax clothier. Although the masonry is sadly darkened, both main façades are remarkably impressive, with mullioned windows, gables, finials, and great porches with circular windows. The main part of the house lies to the left of the north entrance, with the banqueting hall to the right. Beyond that, to the west, only the façade of the Starkie wing of 1692 remains, its classical appearance a contrasting foil to the rest of the house.

The stone-flagged kitchen contains furniture and domestic items from the seventeenth and eighteenth centuries. In the dining room and drawing room, oak panelling and moulded plaster friezes and ceilings are contemporary with the house, with seventeenth-century furniture, portraits and Delftware contributing to the fine period flavour.

Adjoining the visitors' car park is the timbered barn. Stone built, of eight bays, with two cart entrances, this is contemporary with the house, and is outstanding for its oak pillars and tie-beam roof with king-posts. It now houses a collection of agricultural bygones.

1M NE Keighley, on A650 (111 C9)

Lindisfarne Castle, Northumberland Clinging to a crest of hard dolerite rock, the castle was completed by 1550 as a fort to protect English merchantmen and naval vessels using Holy Island's sheltered anchorage. It was garrisoned until the end of the Napoleonic Wars, then used by coastguards, and finally fell into disuse. Edward Hudson, founder and editor of *Country Life*, bought it in 1902, and engaged Edwin Lutyens to restore and convert it into a private house.

Imaginatively exploiting the unusual site,

The entrance front of East Riddlesden Hall, with the façade of the Starkie wing on the right.

Perseus and Andromeda, one of the mythological frescoes painted by Borgnis in the Ionic Temple at Rievaulx (exterior p. 104).

Lutyens transformed the derelict shell into a comfortable country home. Inside the lower part of the building he created a modern entrance hall of low arches on strong round piers, and passages, hewn from the rock, leading to two beautiful vaulted chambers, formerly the castle's magazines, their masonry very little changed from the original. Upstairs, a timbered and brick-floored long gallery, of typical Lutyens design, links a series of bedrooms with beamed ceilings and windows looking out to the sea and along Northumberland's coast.

English and Flemish oak furniture, together with a good collection of prints, are in complete harmony with this delightful miniature castle.

5M E Beal across causeway, off A1 (133 B12)

Maister House, Humberside Built by a Hull merchant, Henry Maister, in 1744 to replace a house destroyed by fire the previous year. Behind its plain brick façade, the hall and staircase are open to visitors. A wrought-iron balustraded stone staircase rises round three sides of the richly-ornamented hall lit from above by a glazed octagonal lantern. The coved and plastered ceiling completes a picture of Palladian perfection.

160 High Street, Hull (113 D8)

Moulton Hall, North Yorkshire A compact stone house of 1650, with large Dutch gables and a very fine carved wood staircase. (Open only by prior arrangement with the tenant.)

5M E Richmond, off A1 (116 E3)

Nostell Priory, West Yorkshire People visit Nostell to see an almost unchanged example of eighteenth-century architecture, with superb decoration and furniture reflecting contemporary tastes of successive generations of the Winn family. The young James Paine designed the main block from about 1736, and Robert Adam, called in thirty years later to complete work on the interior, also added the north wing.

Paine's two noble staircases, dining room and state bedchamber all show rococo exuberance, with magnificent plasterwork by Joseph Rose the elder. Furniture by Chippendale, who served part of his apprenticeship here, is one of Nostell's greatest glories, the house being one of only three where his complete accounts survive. There is also a superb Palladian doll's house standing in the hall which may be the earliest surviving example of Chippendale's work.

Adam's contribution is cool, meticulous, and elegantly neo-classical. The saloon, top hall, library and tapestry room all contain fine plasterwork by the younger Rose, with decorative painting by Zucchi. An overall sumptuousness of quality characterizes the rooms of Nostell, from the grandest items such as Chippendale's library table down to the smallest details like door handles and escutcheons, all made to Adam's design. He was also responsible for two wings of the elegant stable-block.

6M SE Wakefield, on A638 (111 E12)

Nunnington Hall, North Yorkshire This large stone manor house in the gentle Ryedale countryside is essentially of two dates and styles. The Tudor west range is now the entrance front with a modern porch, while the main south front shows a characteristic late seventeenth-century façade to the neat lawns and gardens. Robert Huickes, who leased Nunnington from the Crown in the mid sixteenth century, was physician to Henry VIII, Edward VI and Elizabeth I. A century later the house was commandeered for Parliamentary troops, who left it in a sorry state.

Inheriting the house in 1685, Richard Graham, first Viscount Preston, removed the old north wing and remodelled the south front, giving it a classical entrance. He was also responsible for much of the fine panelling throughout the house.

Contemporary furniture, tapestries and porcelain include items probably presented to Lord Preston when he was Charles II's ambassador to Louis XIV. The Carlisle Collection of miniature rooms fully furnished in different period styles is in the attics.

4½M SE Helmsley, off B1257 (117 G7)

Ormesby Hall, Cleveland The architect of this modest house, built for Dorothy Pennyman about 1750, is not known. Its plain façade suggests an earlier date, and probably reflects provincial conservatism in style. Inside, there is an unexpected opulence of design and decoration indicative of high-quality craftsmanship.

Ionic columns in the entrance hall, together with Palladian motifs there and in the library, are clearly of the middle of the century. The drawing room and dining room, decorated in the 1770s, reveal in the classical delicacy of their stuccowork an Adamesque influence. Carr of York is said to have designed the plasterwork of the ceilings. The most remarkable feature of the house is a first-floor gallery across the middle, with rooms along each side, with elaborately pedimented doorcases.

To the north of the house, a handsome stable-block with cupola tower and open courtyard is attributed to Carr, and is leased to the Mounted Police.

3M SE Middlesbrough, W of A171, but access only from A174 (116 C5)

Rievaulx Terrace and Temples, North Yorkshire Above the wooded valley of Ryedale, a level grass terrace follows a gently serpentine course for half a mile, with a classical temple at each end, both of dressed sandstone, and dating from about 1760. The whole concept is one of Britain's most imaginative pieces of eighteenth-century landscaping, the work of Thomas Duncombe.

A woodland walk parallel to the terrace leads visitors to the southern Rotunda encircled by its Doric colonnade. The return by the terrace reveals a succession of planned views of the ruins of Rievaulx Abbey far below, each framed by hanging woodlands, with moorland beyond.

The Ionic temple, pedimented and with a portico of six columns, contains elaborate plasterwork and a superb painted ceiling by Giovanni Borgnis. Enhancing this elegance, furniture on loan from the Treasury includes William Kent settees, George II tables, and a magnificent Worcester dinner service. In the basement a display illustrates the significance of the terrace in English landscape design.

2½M NW Helmsley, on B1257 (116 G6)

The Treasurer's House, York Bases of Roman columns in the cellars suggest that a house has occupied this site for almost 2,000 years. Successive Treasurers of York Minster lived here from 1100 to 1547, but the present building is mainly of the seventeenth and eighteenth centuries. The garden front and centre range are Thomas Young's work of 1630, while the Venetian windows and Dutch gables were added a century later when the house was subdivided. When Frank Green bought it in 1897 it was three dwellings, and today's structure owes much to his restoration work.

Apart from the medieval character of the great hall and its staircase leading to a half-timbered gallery, the flavour of the house is essentially Palladian and early Georgian. Throughout there is a rare quality of decorative detail, with outstanding examples of plasterwork and panelling, and elaborate chimney-pieces.

The quality of furniture matches its elegant setting. Two centuries of craftsmanship are represented, covering a remarkable range of items augmented by collections of early English china, pottery and glass, while the paintings include a number of English and Flemish portraits from the sixteenth to eighteenth centuries.

Chapter House Street, behind York Minster (112 B4)

Wallington, Northumberland Set in remote Northumberland countryside this square, dignified and elegant house of local sandstone dates from 1688. Sir Walter Calverley Blackett extensively re-modelled it in the 1740s, and it was his artistic taste and creative talents which resulted in the superb quality of decoration in the main rooms. Plasterwork, panelling, furniture, portraits and collections, especially of fine porcelain, all reveal eighteenth-century craftsmanship at its best.

If the Blacketts gave Wallington its architectural flavour, successive generations of Trevelyans made no less distinguished a contribution. Sir John Trevelyan, nephew of Sir Walter Blackett, inherited the estate in 1777, and it remained in the family until Sir Charles transferred it to the National Trust in 1941.

Sir Walter Trevelyan, a man of wide knowledge and interests, who inherited in 1846, and his artistically talented wife Pauline, enclosed the central hall in 1853. To Wallington came poets and painters, including Millais, Ruskin, Swinburne and Augustus Hare. Lady Trevelyan actively supported the Pre-Raphaelites, and engaged young William Bell Scott to paint eight canvases for the hall depicting episodes of Northumbrian history. Her parlour contains Ruskin drawings and Turner watercolours. The working collection of Lord Macaulay, the historian, is housed in the library, a comfortable, homely, well-used room.

Other attractions at Wallington include a famous collection of dolls' houses, a handsome stable-block, and extensive gardens, grounds and woodlands.

12M W Morpeth, on B6342 (133 E8)

Wallington's sober exterior gives no hint of the elaborate decoration within, as seen here in the staircase hall.

Washington Old Hall, Tyne and Wear Saved from demolition in 1936, this small manor house is an object lesson in Anglo-American cooperation. Washingtons had lived at the Old Hall from 1183, finally selling the manor to the Bishop of Durham in 1613. The present house, of local sandstone, dates from this sale, though parts of the earlier house are incorporated.

At the west end of the stone-flagged great hall, two arched doorways of the original house lead into the kitchen. In the east wing is some excellent Jacobean panelling. Most of the furniture is seventeenth-century, much of it and other items being bought by the Trust with money given by Americans.

Genuine George Washington relics include a bust by Houdon, who visited Mount Vernon in 1785, and the fan given to Martha Washington by General Lafayette.

On the second floor, one room is furnished as a bedroom, with an interesting seventeenth-century bed and other furniture of the same date. A picture presented by President Carter on his visit to the Hall in 1977 hangs here.

Two other rooms on this floor are in daily use as a community centre, and the property is leased to, and maintained by, Sunderland Borough Council.

5M W Sunderland in the old village of Washington New Town (signposted District 4). The Old Hall is on the E side of The Avenue, which runs through the village (133 G11)

Castles, Abbeys & other Buildings

Dunstanburgh Castle, Northumberland Approached only by a mile's walk, from Craster to the south or Embleton to the north, Dunstanburgh's gaunt ruins crown a rocky headland on a hauntingly beautiful coast. Built about 1314 by the Earl of Lancaster, and extending over eleven acres, the castle was largely destroyed during the Wars of the Roses. Only its gentler southern slopes made a curtain wall necessary; this survives, together with two towers and the massive, unusual gatehouse-keep which completely dominates the coastal scene. (Under the guardianship of the Department of the Environment.)

9M NE Alnwick, off B1339 (133 A10)

Gibside Chapel, Tyne and Wear Gibside Chapel is the main building to have survived on the large Gibside estate of a wealthy eighteenth-century landowner, Sir George Bowes. He planned it as the family mausoleum to face along an avenue of trees to the British Liberty statue on its tall column. Designed by James Paine, work started on Gibside Chapel in 1760 but money shortages delayed its completion until 1812.

James Paine's chapel, in the form of a Greek cross, is very much influenced by Palladio's Villa Rotonda at Vicenza, and only internally is its ecclesiastical character revealed.

The outside is beautifully proportioned, with a classical portico of Ionic columns supporting a pediment, and a central dome behind. Fine-quality sandstone is tooled and carved with superb craftsmanship.

Inside, the central altar is surrounded by communion rails. A three-decker pulpit, and box-pews curved to fit the semi-circular apses, are of mahogany and cherrywood. Together with excellent plasterwork they create an impression of exquisite, restrained dignity.

6M SW Gateshead, A694, then B6314 (133 G10)

left **The interior of Gibside Chapel, showing the central altar, the rare mahogany three-tier pulpit and the cherrywood box pews.**

right **Hadrian's Wall runs across northern England for 73 miles. Housesteads, shown here, is the best preserved of its forts.**

below **The special nature of the Carthusian rule is particularly well seen in the layout of Mount Grace Priory.**

Lady's Well, Northumberland This large trough in a tree-shaded grove was probably used by nuns of the twelfth-century Augustinian priory. Walled-in during medieval days, repaired in 1780, with a wheel-head cross added last century, it continues to supply Holystone village with clear, fresh water.

Holystone, 7M W Rothbury, off B6341 (133 C8)

Mount Grace Priory, North Yorkshire Beneath the wooded western edge of the Cleveland Hills are the most important Carthusian ruins in England. Founded in 1398 and quietly surrendered in 1539, the priory passed into lay hands, part of it becoming a country house.

Monks' individual two-storey cells, each twenty-seven feet square with walled garden behind, were spaced round the Great Cloister, an irregular quadrangle with a longest side of 272 feet. Ruins survive of the simple, narrow priory church, with its later tower and side-chapels. Monks met here for services, but most of their life was spent in seclusion. Tranquillity pervades this rare Carthusian priory in its enchanting setting. (Under the guardianship of the Department of the Environment.)

6M NE Northallerton, off A19 (116 E5)

Penshaw Monument, Tyne and Wear Splendidly incongruous, a roofless Doric temple crowns a windy hill, visible for miles across industrial landscapes. Built in 1844 as a memorial to the first Earl of Durham, its honeyed sandstone, now darkened and sombre, adds a touch of magic to the skyline.

5M SW Sunderland, E of A183 (133 G11)

Ripon: Sanctuary Cross, North Yorkshire The stump remains of the only surviving cross which marked the limits of sanctuary associated with St Wilfrid's Abbey.

Sharow, ¾M NE Ripon, off A61 (116 H3)

George Stephenson's Cottage, Northumberland A stone cottage, built about 1750, and the birthplace in 1781 of George Stephenson, the 'Father of Railways'. Appropriately it adjoins the track of the old Wylam colliery wagonway, now a riverside walkway. (The room in which Stephenson was born is open at any reasonable time, April–September, by appointment with the lessee.)

½M E Wylam village, 8M W Newcastle-upon-Tyne, off B6528 (133 F9)

Archaeological & Industrial Sites

Beadnell Limekilns, Northumberland An imposing group of late eighteenth-century limekilns overlooking the tiny, west-facing harbour of Beadnell.

½M SE Beadnell, off B1340 (133 E12)

Hadrian's Wall Estate and Housesteads Fort, Northumberland Striding confidently over the hackled crests of lonely hills, this defensive structure is Britain's most impressive Roman monument, begun by Emperor Hadrian in AD 122, subsequently strengthened with forts, milecastles and turrets, and flanked by a ditch and vallum. The Trust owns about four miles of the most spectacular section, from east of Housesteads Fort westwards to Winshields Crag, including milecastles and turret sites, and Housesteads itself, best-preserved of all the forts. (Housesteads, and its associated museum of Roman finds, is in the guardianship of the Department of the Environment.)

Plainly visible at Housesteads (*Vercovicium*) are the remains of ramparts and gateways, barracks and headquarters blocks, granaries and latrines, and a nearby milecastle is well-preserved. A walk along the Wall westwards from Housesteads follows the route of part of the Pennine Way, over Cuddy's Crags, Hotbank Crags, Milking Gap, and high above the reed-fringed waters of Crag Lough to Peel Crags and Winshields. Wide views extend northwards to Northumberland's forests, southwards to the gentler landscape of the South Tyne valley, while to east and west the Wall's own sinuous, surging course leads the eye to far horizons.

4M NE Haltwhistle, off B6318 (132 F6)

Stainforth Bridge, North Yorkshire This graceful, single-arch, seventeenth-century packhorse bridge spans the river Ribble in a beautiful wooded valley.

2½M N Settle, off B6479 (115 H10)

Adjoining page 114
Adjoining page 115
Adjoining page 94
Kendal
Settle
Chester
Stoke-on-Trent
Isle of Walney
Walney Channel
Barrow
Rampside
Roa Island
Piel Castle
Piel Island
Foulney Island
Sheep Island
South End
TO DOUGLAS
Morecambe
Heysham
Lancaster
Halton
Caton
Caton Moor
Littledale
Clougha
Ward's Stone 1836
Tatham Fells
Burn Moor
Goodber Common
White Hill 1784
Croasdale Fell
FOREST OF BOWLAND
Gisburn Forest
Hawthornthwaite Fell
Sykes Fell
Slaidburn
Newton
Easington Fell
Dunsop Bridge
Shoulder of Lune
Cockerham Sands
Cockerham
Pilling
Knott End-on-Sea
Fleetwood
Rossall Point
Preesall
Stalmine
Garstang
Bleasdale Moors
Calder Vale
Oakenclough
Chipping
Longridge Fell
Waddington
Clitheroe
Whalley
Cleveleys
Thornton
Poulton-Le-Fylde
BISPHAM
BLACKPOOL
NORTH SHORE
SOUTH SHORE
Kirkham
Wesham
Lytham St. Anne's
Lytham
Warton
Freckleton
PRESTON
Fulwood
Higher Penwortham
Walton Le Dale
Longridge
Ribchester
Samlesbury
BLACKBURN
Great Harwood
Oswaldtwistle
Rishton
Darwen
LANCASHIRE
Hesketh Bank
Tarleton
Leyland
Chorley
Anglezarke Moor
Southport
Birkdale Sands
Rufford
Ormskirk
Burscough Bridge
Standish
Wigan
Coppull
Horwich
BOLTON
Westhoughton
Hindley
Farnworth
Formby
Formby Hills
Freshfield
Ainsdale
Woodvale
Maghull
Skelmersdale
Up Holland
Orrell
Ince-in Makerfield
Atherton
Tyldesley
Walkden
Leigh
Astley
Eccles
Worsley
LIVERPOOL BAY
TO DUBLIN CAR FERRY
TO BELFAST
TO DOUGLAS (I.O.M.) CAR FERRY
Crosby
Bootle
Litherland
Kirkby
Rainford
St. HELENS
Haydock
Newton-Le-Willows
Ashton-in-Makerfield
Golborne
Lowton Common
Chat Moss
Irlam
Urmston
Culcheth
MERSEYSIDE
WALLASEY
BIRKENHEAD
LIVERPOOL
Hoylake
West Kirby
Huyton
Roby
Prescot
Whiston
Rainhill
Widnes
Warrington
Great Sankey
Partington
Cadishead
Lymm
Thelwall
Grappenhall
Stockton Heath
Halewood
Woolton
Penketh
Farnworth
GREATER MANCHESTER
M6
M55
M61
M58
M57
M62
M63
M53
M56

7 Adjoining page 115 8 9 10 Adjoining page 116 11 Ripon 12 Scotch Corner

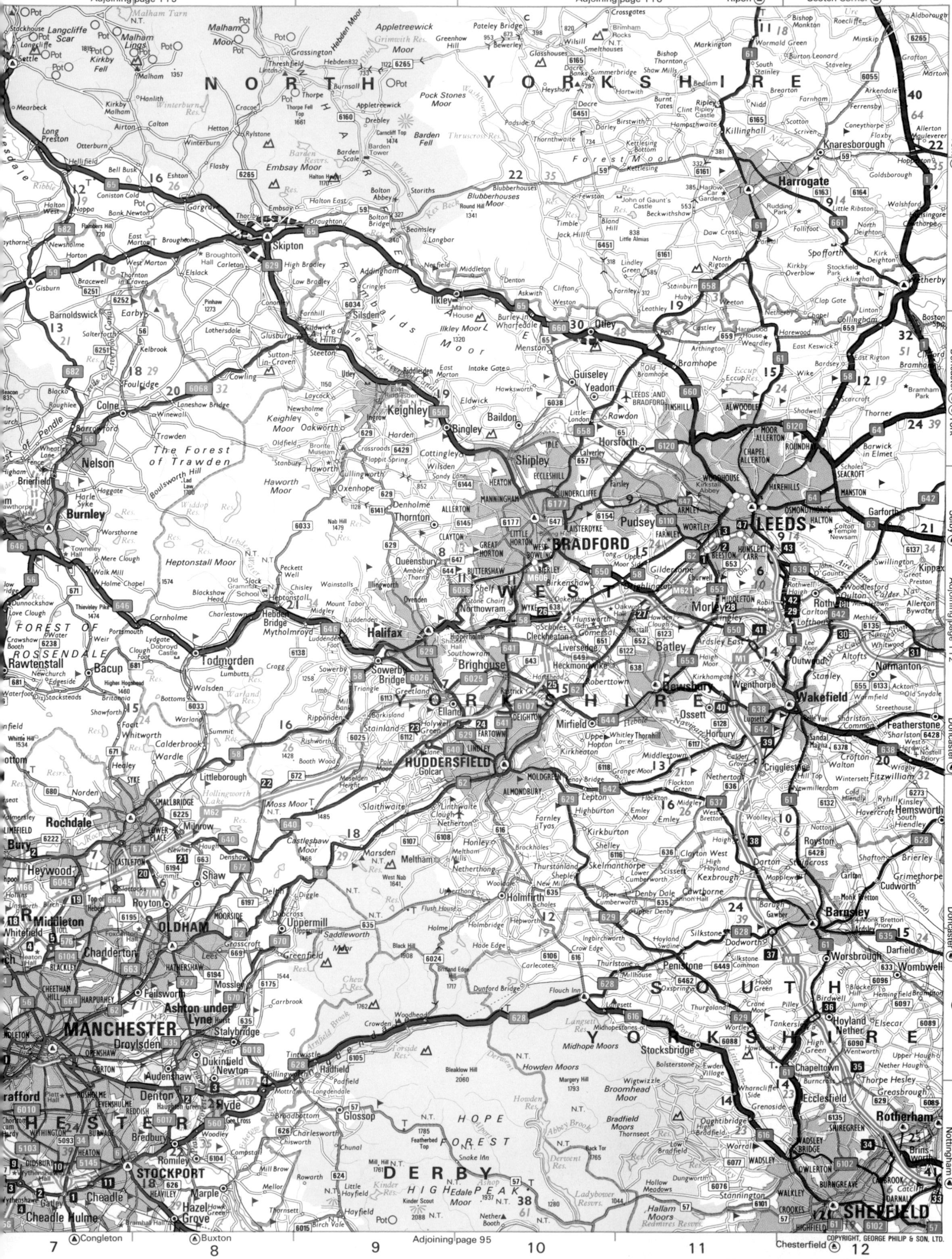

A
B
C
D
E
F
G
H

York
Doncaster
York
Selby
Adjoining page 112
Doncaster
Doncaster
Nottingham
7 Congleton 8 Buxton 9 Adjoining page 95 10 11 Chesterfield 12

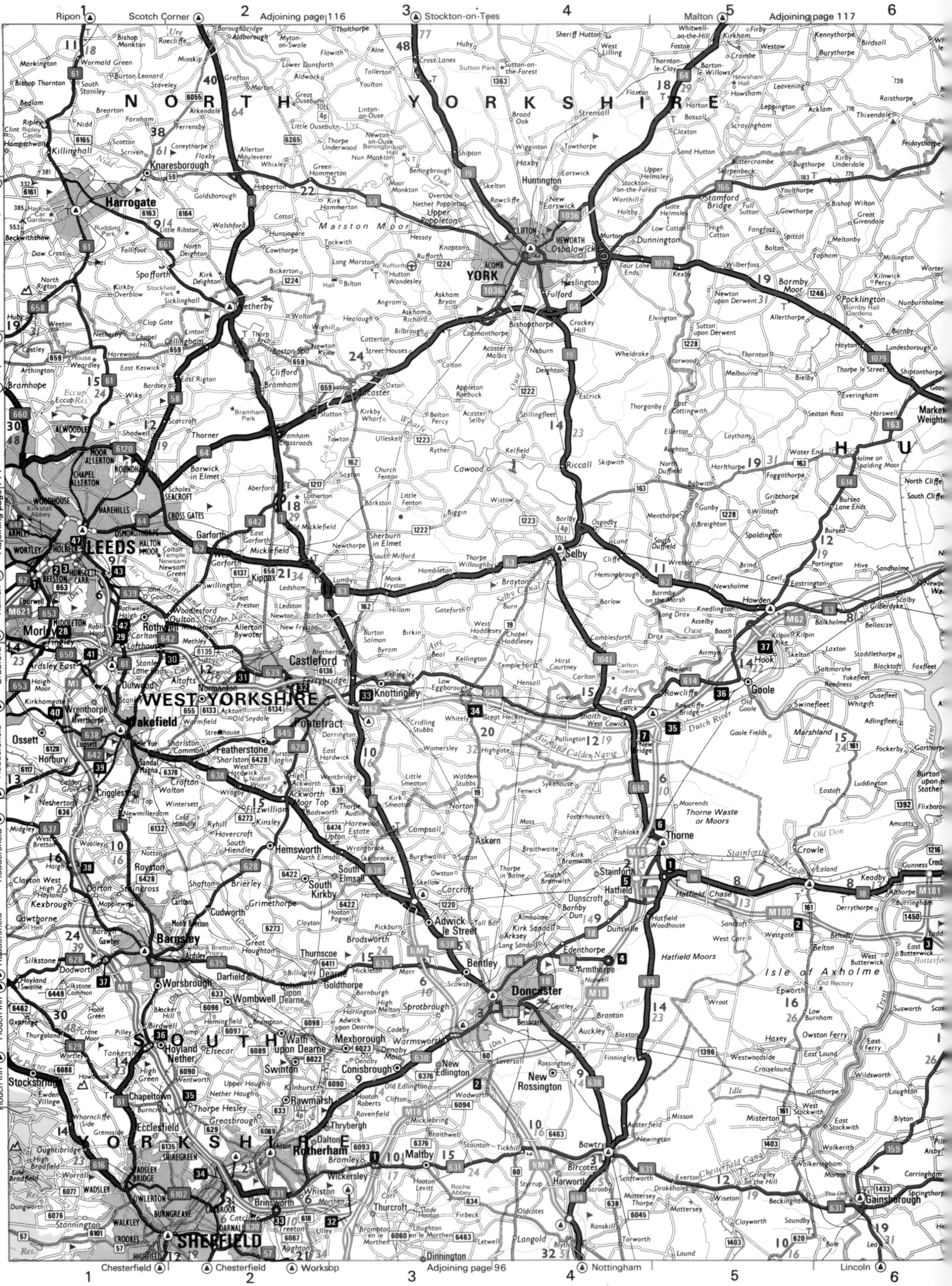

1 2 3 4 5 6
A B C D E F G H
Ripon
Scotch Corner
Adjoining page 116
Stockton-on-Tees
Malton
Adjoining page 117
Skipton
Bradford
Adjoining page 111
Halifax
Huddersfield
Flouch Inn
Chesterfield
Worksop
Adjoining page 96
Nottingham
Lincoln
NORTH YORKSHIRE
WEST YORKSHIRE
SOUTH YORKSHIRE
HUMBERSIDE
Harrogate
Knaresborough
Wetherby
Marston Moor
YORK
Huntington
Stamford Bridge
Pocklington
Tadcaster
Selby
Howden
Goole
LEEDS
Garforth
Castleford
Pontefract
Knottingley
Wakefield
Ossett
Morley
Barnsley
Hemsworth
Thorne
Doncaster
Rotherham
SHEFFIELD
Mexborough
Conisbrough
Maltby
Bawtry
Gainsborough
Isle of Axholme
Hatfield Moors
Thorne Waste or Moors

Adjoining page 117
Scarborough
Adjoining page 97
Lincoln
Lincoln
Boston
7
8
9
10
11
12
A
B
C
D
E
F
G
H
NORTH SEA
Bridlington Bay
Bridlington
Hilderthorpe
Langtoft
Bessingby
Carnaby
Haisthorpe
Kilham
Burton Agnes Hall
Thornholme
Burton Agnes
Sledmere
Sledmere House
Ruston Parva
Harpham
Fraisthorpe
Garton-on-the-Wolds
Lowthorpe
Little Kelk
Nafferton
Gransmoor
Wetwang
Elmswell
Little Driffield
Driffield
Great Kelk
Lisset
Barmston
Gembling
Foston on the Wolds
Ulrome
Tibthorpe
Kirkburn
Eastburn
Wansford
Skipsea Castle
Skipsea
Southburn
Skerne
North Frodingham
Skipsea Brough
Beeford
North Dalton
Cranswick
Hutton
Brigham
Dunnington
Bainton
Rotsea
Atwick
Middleton-on-the-Wolds
Watton
Hempholme
Kilnwick
Bewholme
Lund
Beswick
Burshill
Hornsea
Lockington
Thorpe
Brandesburton
Seaton
Hornsea Bridge
Hornsea Mere
Holme on the Wolds
Aike
Catwick
Sigglesthorne
Rolston
South Dalton
Scorborough
Leven
Goxhill
Leven Canal
Arram
Little Hatfield
Mappleton
Etton
Leconfield
Routh
Great Hatfield
Great Cowden
Gardham
Cherry Burton
Long Riston
Rise
Tickton
Bishop Burton
Molescroft
Beverley
Arnold
Withernwick
New Ellerby
Weel
South Skirlaugh
Marton
Aldbrough
West Newton
Woodmansey
Old Ellerby
North Newbald
Walkington
Bentley
Thearne
Wawne
Burton Constable
South Newbald
High Hunsley
Swine
Coniston
Flinton
Garton
Grimston
Skidby
Dunswell
Ganstead
Sproatley
Fitling
Humbleton
Hilston
Cottingham
Bilton
Lelley
Rowley
Little Weighton
Elstronwick
Owstwick
Tunstall
Newland
Sculcoates
Stoneferry
Sutton-on-Hull
Riplingham
Preston
North End
Roos
South Cave
Wauldby
Willerby
Burton Pidsea
Waxholme
Ellerker
Brantingham
Kirk Ella
Marfleet
West Ella
Hedon
Rimswell
Elloughton
Swanland
Anlaby
Wilberforce House
Kingston upon Hull
Burstwick
Halsham
Withernsea
Welton
East End
Brough
Melton
Camerton
Thorngumbald
Hessle
North Ferriby
Paull
Ryhill
Keyingham
Hollym
Hull (Brough)
Goxhill Haven
New Holland
Ottringham
Winestead
Humber
Car Ferry
Barrow Haven
East Halton Skitter
Thorney Crofts
Holmpton
Read's I.
Barton-upon-Humber
Patrington
Goxhill
Foulholme Sands
Out Newton
Barrow upon Humber
South End
Partington Haven
Welwick
Skeffling
Easington
South Ferriby
East Halton
Winterton
Horkstow
Thornton Curtis
North Killingholme
Sunk Island
Mouth of the Humber
Old Hall
Burnham
Sunk Island Sands
Saxby All Saints
Wootton
Immingham Dock
South Killingholme
Kilnsea
Roxby
Bonby
Ulceby
Risby
Appleby
Ulceby Skitter
Immingham
Habrough
Worlaby
Low Santon
Land Drain
Croxton
Stallingborough
Brocklesby
Elsham
Elsham Hall
New Ancholme
Weir Dyke
Kirmington
Great Coates
Grimsby
Healing
Spurn Head
Scunthorpe
Melton Ross
Keelby
West Marsh
Old Clee
Barnetby le Wold
Great Limber
Cleethorpes
Broughton
Riby Cross Roads
Aylesby
Wrawby
Freshney
Thrunscoe
Brigg
Riby
Laceby
Bigby
Nunsthorpe
Holme
Scawby Brook
Bradley
Somerby
Scawby
Manton Warren
Searby
Scartho
Humberston
Sturton
Owmby
Grasby
Irby upon Humber
Barnoldby le Beck
Waltham
New Waltham
Howsham
Clixby
Cadney
Swallow
Holton le Clay
Manton
Hibaldstow
North Kelsey Beck
Brigsley
Tetney Lock
Cabourne
Caistor
North Kelsey
Cuxwold
Beelsby
Ashby cum Fenby
Tetney
North Coates
Nettleton
Hatcliffe
Marsh Chapel
Danger Area
Moortown
East Ravendale
Grainsby
North Thoresby
Eskham
Kirton in Lindsey
Redbourne
Rothwell
West End
Wragholme
South Kelsey
Holton le Moor
Croxby
Thorganby
Fulstow
Grainthorpe
Meals
Brandy Wharf
Thoresway
North Somercotes
Church End
Waddingham
Swinhope
Wold Newton
Ludney
Grayingham
Thornton le Moor
Ludborough
Covenham St. Bartholomew
Conisholme
Blyborough
Snitterby
North Owersby
Normanby le Wold
Claxby
Covenham St. Mary
Austen Fen
South Somercotes
Saltfleet
South Owersby
Kingerby
Usselby
Stainton le Vale
Binbrook
Utterby
Yarburgh
Canal
Skidbrooke
Willoughton
Bishop Norton
Osgodby
Kirkby
Walesby
Bully Hill
Kirmond le Mire
North Ormsby
Fotherby
Alvingham
North Cockerington
Saltfleetby St. Clements
Hemswell
Spital in the Street
Bishopbridge
Great Tows
North Elkington
Little Grimsby
Saltfleetby All Saints
Harpswell
Glentham
Tealby
Kelstern
Caenby Corner
Normanby by Spital
West Rasen
Market Rasen
Ludford
South Elkington
South Cockerington
Saltfleetby St. Peter
Theddlethorpe St. Helen
Glentworth
Owmby by Spital
Toft next Newton
Newton by Toft
Middle Rasen
North Willingham
Keddington
Grimoldby
Theddlethorpe All Saints
Saxby
Res.
Linwood
Sixhills
Burgh on Bain
Welton le Wold
Stewton
Manby
Fillingham
Legsby
Gayton le Wold
Louth
Meers Bridge
Y O R K S H I R E W O L D S
H O L D E R N E S S
B E R S I D E
L I N C O L N
COPYRIGHT, GEORGE PHILIP & SON, LTD.

Adjoining page 131
Carlisle
Carlisle Adjoining page 132

1 2 3 4 5 6

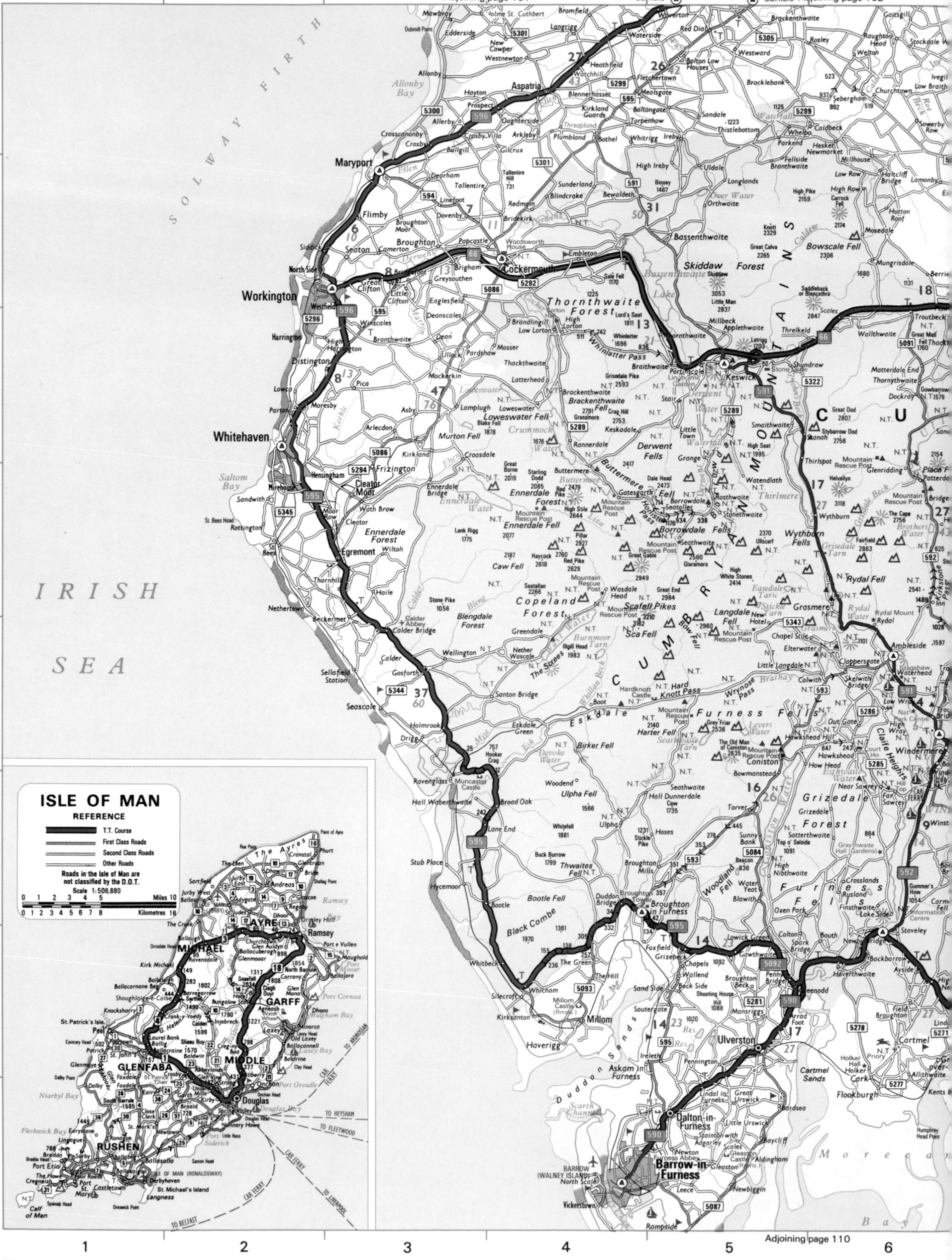

A B C D E F G H

Adjoining page 110

7 8 Adjoining page 132 9 Haydon Bridge 10 11 Adjoining page 133 12

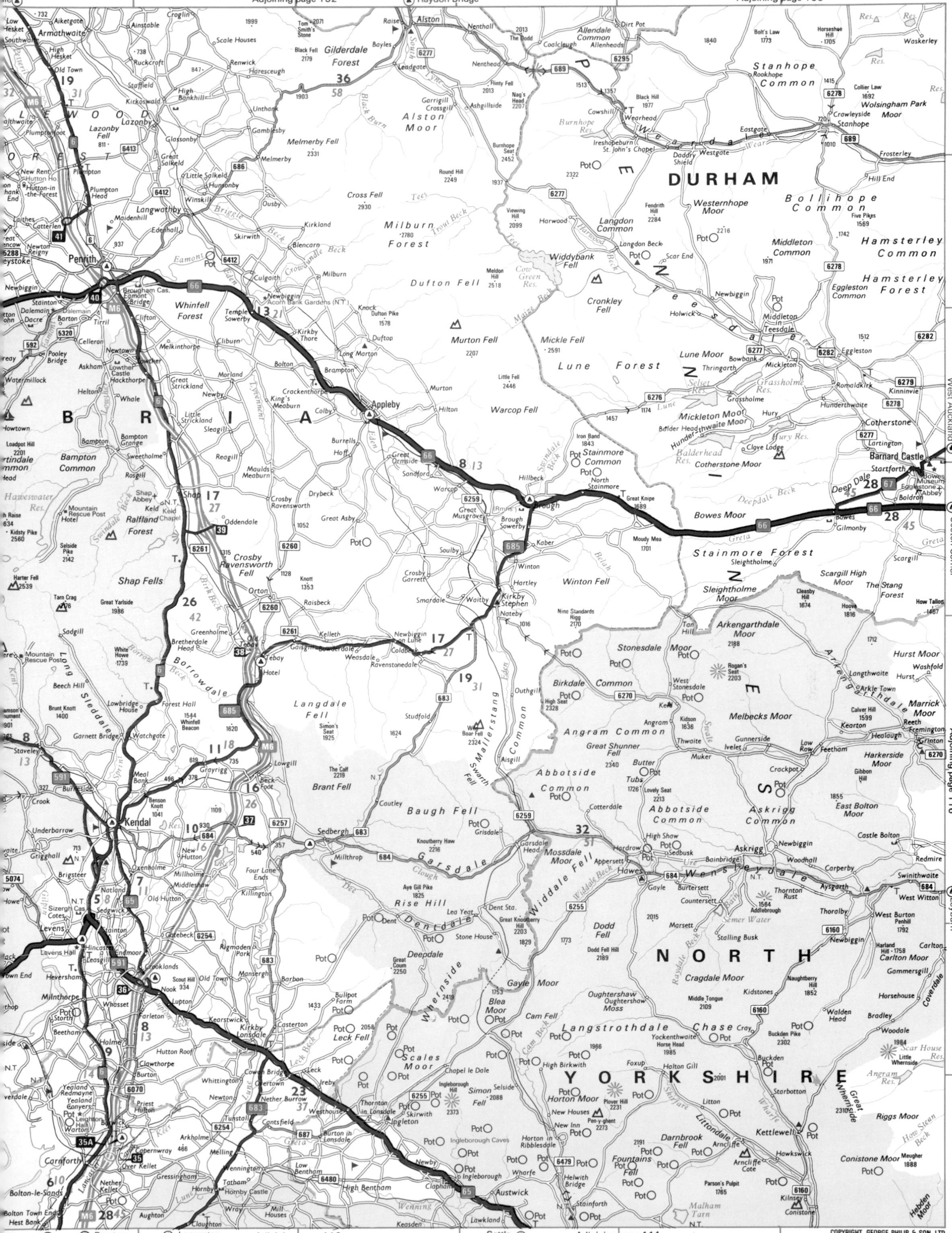

A B C D E F G H
West Auckland
Scotch Corner
Adjoining page 116
Leyburn

Lancaster 7 Preston Lancaster 8 Adjoining page 110 9 Settle 10 Adjoining page 111 11 12

Castleside | Castleside | Adjoining page 133 | Newcastle upon Tyne | Sunderland | Sunderland

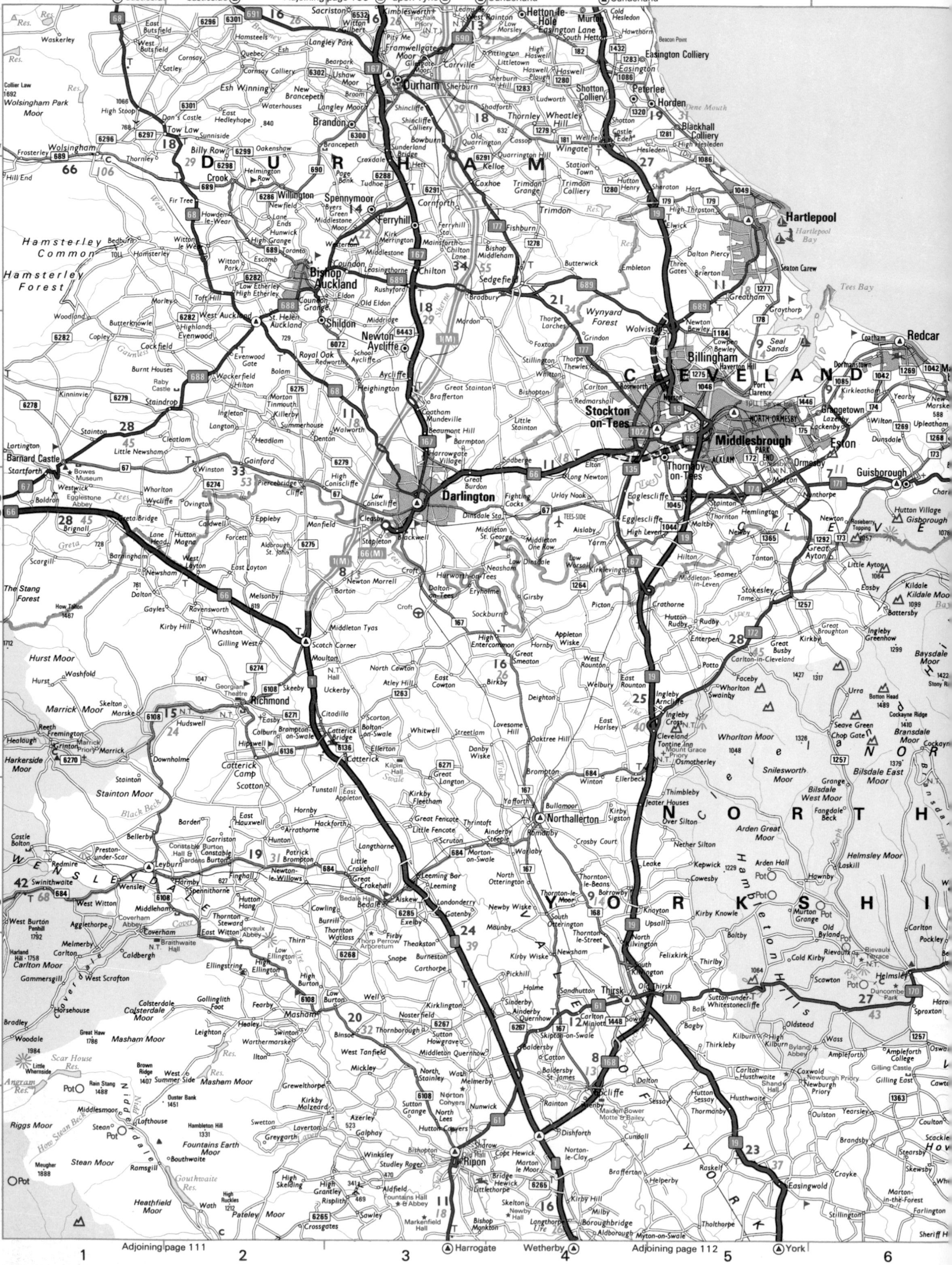

1 | 2 | 3 | 4 | 5 | 6
A | B | C | D | E | F | G | H
Adjoining page 115
Carlisle | Brough | Brough | Kendal
Adjoining page 111 | Harrogate | Wetherby | Adjoining page 112 | York

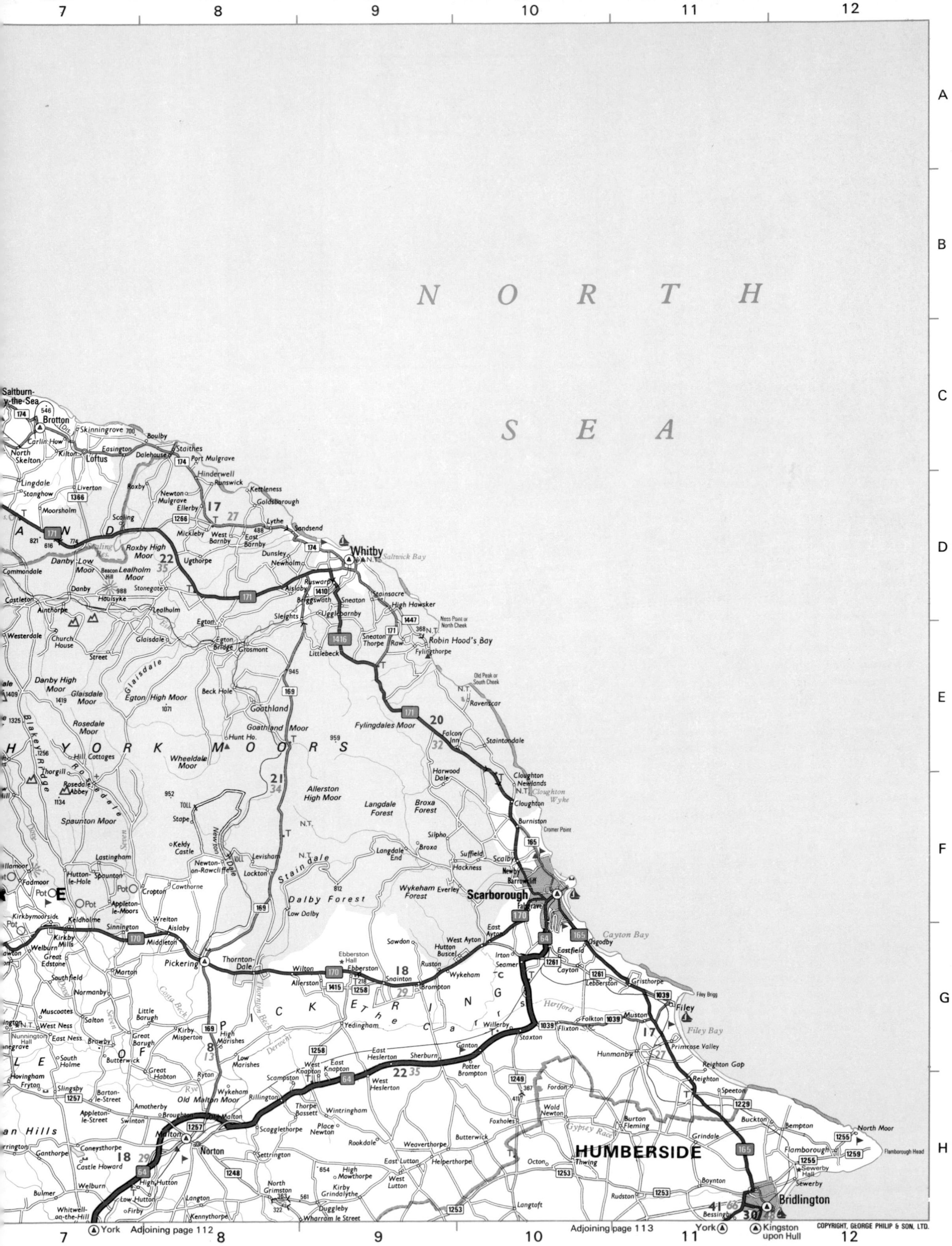

7
8
9
10
11
12
A
B
C
D
E
F
G
H
NORTH
SEA
Saltburn-by-the-Sea
Brotton
Skinningrove
Boulby
Staithes
Carlin How
Kilton
Loftus
Easington
Dalehouse
Port Mulgrave
North Skelton
Hinderwell
Runswick
Lingdale
Stanghow
Liverton
Roxby
Kettleness
Newton Mulgrave
Goldsborough
Moorsholm
Ellerby
Scaling
Lythe
Sandsend
Mickleby
West Barnby
East Barnby
Whitby
Saltwick Bay
Roxby High Moor
Danby Low Moor
Lealholm Moor
Ugthorpe
Dunsley
Newholm
Commondale
Beacon Hill
Danby
Stonegate
Aislaby
Ruswarp
Houlsyke
Castleton
Ainthorpe
Lealholm
Briggswath
Sneaton
Stainsacre
High Hawsker
Egton
Sleights
Ugglebarnby
Westerdale
Church House
Glaisdale
Egton Bridge
Grosmont
Littlebeck
Sneaton Thorpe
Raw
Ness Point or North Cheek
Robin Hood's Bay
Fylingthorpe
Street
Glaisdale
Old Peak or South Cheek
Danby High Moor
Glaisdale Moor
Egton High Moor
Beck Hole
Goathland
Ravenscar
Rosedale Moor
Goathland Moor
Fylingdales Moor
Falcon Inn
Staintondale
Hunt Ho.
YORK MOORS
Blakey Ridge
Hill Cottages
Wheeldale Moor
Harwood Dale
Cloughton Newlands
Thorgill
Rosedale Abbey
Rosedale
Cloughton
Cloughton Wyke
Allerston High Moor
Langdale Forest
Broxa Forest
Spaunton Moor
TOLL
Stape
Burniston
Cromer Point
Silpho
Broxa
Kelday Castle
Newton Dale
Newton-on-Rawcliffe
Levisham
Lockton
Staindale
Langdale End
Suffield
Hackness
Scalby
Newby
Barrowcliff
Lastingham
Hutton-le-Hole
Spaunton
Fadmoor
Cropton
Cawthorne
Dalby Forest
Wykeham Forest
Everley
Scarborough
Falsgrave
Appleton-le-Moors
Low Dalby
Kirkbymoorside
Keldholme
Wrelton
Kirkby Mills
Sinnington
Aislaby
Middleton
Welburn
Great Edstone
Pickering
Thornton-Dale
Wilton
Allerston
Ebberston Hall
Ebberston
Snainton
Sawdon
Hutton Buscel
West Ayton
East Ayton
Irton
Seamer
Cayton
Eastfield
Osgodby
Cayton Bay
Lebberston
Gristhorpe
Filey Brigg
Filey
Filey Bay
Southfield
Marton
Normanby
Little Barugh
Ruston
Wykeham
Brompton
Hertford
Folkton
Flixton
Muston
Muscoates
Salton
West Ness
East Ness
Nunnington Hall
Great Barugh
Kirby Misperton
High Marishes
Brawby
Yedingham
Willerby
Staxton
Hunmanby
Primrose Valley
South Holme
Butterwick
Low Marishes
Derwent
East Heslerton
Sherburn
Ganton
Reighton Gap
Hovingham
Fryton
Great Habton
Ryton
Scampston
West Knapton
East Knapton
West Heslerton
Potter Brompton
Reighton
Slingsby
Barton-le-Street
Wykeham
Old Malton Moor
Rillington
Fordon
Speeton
Appleton-le-Street
Amotherby
Broughton
Old Malton
Thorpe Bassett
Wintringham
Wold Newton
Burton Fleming
Buckton
Bempton
Swinton
Malton
Norton
Scagglethorpe
Place Newton
Foxholes
Gypsey Race
Grindale
North Moor
Coneysthorpe
Rookdale
Weaverthorpe
Butterwick
HUMBERSIDE
Flamborough
Flamborough Head
Ganthorpe
Castle Howard
Settrington
East Lutton
Helperthorpe
Octon
Thwing
Sewerby Hall
Sewerby
High Hutton
High Mowthorpe
West Lutton
Boynton
Welburn
North Grimston
Kirby Grindalythe
Langtoft
Rudston
Bridlington
Bulmer
Low Hutton
Langton
Duggleby
Bessingby
Whitwell-on-the-Hill
Firby
Kennythorpe
Wharram le Street
York
Adjoining page 112
Adjoining page 113
York
Kingston upon Hull

Scotland

PRESTON MILL

The rich variety of properties now in the care of the National Trust for Scotland not only embraces much of the country's grandest scenery (Glen Coe, Torridon and Kintail are but three examples) but also provides an insight into a colourful past.

Pride of place must go to that synthesis of comfortable home and minor castle, the tower-house. The Trust owns several of these ranging from twelfth-century Drum through simple Scotstarvit to the sixteenth- and seventeenth-century castles of Mar (Castle Fraser, Craigievar and Crathes). All are splendid examples of a local style which crowned otherwise stern keeps with elaborate yet purely decorative defensive features. The following century was that of the Adams, Scotland's most distinguished family of architects. Of their achievements the Trust owns the houses of Haddo and Dun by William the father, while the more renowned Robert is represented by Culzean and Edinburgh's Charlotte Square. More modest properties include the Bachelors' Club and Souter Johnnie's Cottage, both associated with Robert Burns; 'doocots', those providers of winter meat; the birthplaces of Carlyle, Barrie and the geologist Hugh Miller; the small houses of Dunkeld and Culross; and the weaver's cottage at Kilbarchan.

The Trust's many gardens include Inverewe, Threave and Pitmedden, all widely known, while for the lover of more intimate places there is a fine choice scattered throughout much of the country.

Lastly there are the many visitor centres, some introducing the great mountain estates, some describing towns where the Trust has been active with restoration, some associated with great houses or gardens, while Bannockburn, Culloden, Glenfinnan and Killiecrankie tell their own dramatic stories.

Coast & Countryside

The National Trust for Scotland owns many coast and countryside properties together amounting to some 85,000 acres and descending in size from the great tracts of mountain which make up estates such as Glen Coe and Dalness, Kintail and Morvich, and Torridon down through a rich choice of other places which, though smaller, are almost all of scenic worth. Among these smaller properties there are a number of islands, including **Iona**, landing place of Columba in 563 and hallowed in the story of Scotland's early Christianity (the Trust does not own the abbey and other sacred and historic buildings); **Fair Isle**, Britain's most isolated inhabited island and of international renown in the study of migrating birds; and remote **St Kilda**, a group of islands and rocks some fifty miles west of the Outer Hebrides, uninhabited since 1930 when the thirty-five people still there were evacuated at their own request (leased to the Nature Conservancy Council).

Much of Scotland's grandest scenery lies along or behind the country's north-western coast and here too will be found many of the Trust's most splendid coast and countryside estates, the most northern (apart from

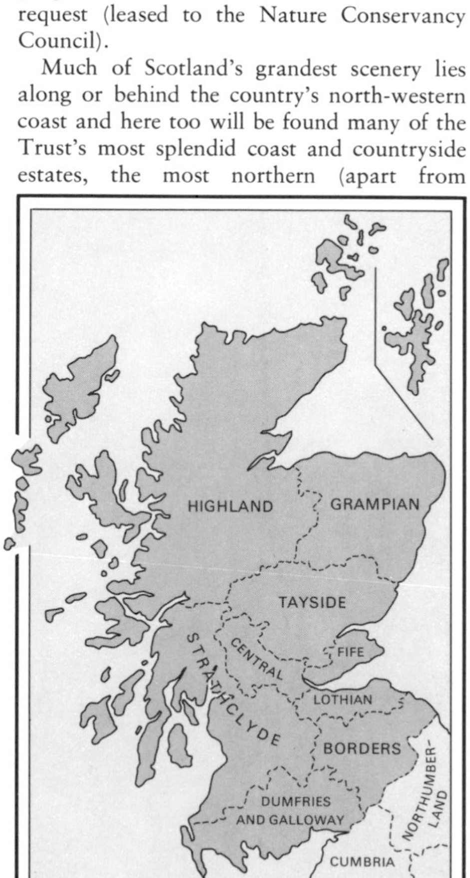

Inverewe), beside the A835 to the south of Ullapool, being **Corrieshalloch Gorge** (148 H3). A mile long and 200 feet deep, this steep and narrow cleft is known for the Falls of Measach which plunge 150 feet into its depths. Some twenty-five miles to the south-west the great mass of **Torridon** towers high above the glen and sea loch of the same name; in the loch lies the Trust's island of **Shieldaig** whose thirty-two acres are almost entirely covered in Scots pine (142 D2). A tract of over 14,000 acres of some of the best mountain scenery in Scotland, and with several heights of over 3,000 feet, Torridon is a magnet as much for walkers and climbers, and naturalists and geologists, as for those content simply to enjoy the place's scenic grandeur. The principal heights are Liathach (a string of summits extending over some five miles) and Beinn Eighe which forms the Trust's boundary. Both are made up of crags, corries and high ridges and both also illustrate the estate's best-known geological feature of white quartzite summits, some 500 million years old, crowning a mass of rather older red sandstone. Wildlife, though sparse and not easily seen, includes red and other deer, wildcat, pinemarten, buzzards and the golden eagle. There is a visitor centre, with a deer museum, at the junction of the A896 and the road to Diabaig (142 D3).

A total contrast is provided by the **Balmacara Estate** filling most of the promontory between lochs Carron and Alsh opposite Skye (143 G2). Here the countryside is one of winding roads, villages, woodland and constantly changing glimpses of sea, loch and islands. Not far inland, though, the road running east (A87) forms the southern boundary of the Trust's huge **Kintail and Morvich** estate. Together with the land around the **Falls of Glomach** to the north this provides some 15,000 acres of remote and magnificent Highland scenery. The chain of abrupt, sharp peaks known as the Five Sisters hangs an almost sheer 3,000 feet above the road (143 H3), a barrier behind which extends first the lonely country of Kintail, home of red deer and feral goats, and then, as a narrow finger of Trust land, the southern approach to the Falls of Glomach, one of the highest and wildest waterfalls in Britain (143

above **Fair Isle, where the summer sun never sets, is Britain's most isolated inhabited island.**

right **The houses in the village street of Hirta, St Kilda, are being gradually restored by volunteer work parties.**

G4). The best access to the mountains is from Morvich (visitor centre) off the A87 at the eastern end of Loch Duich. There is also a Trust information board farther east beside the road below the Five Sisters, maps and plans here describing the estate and also explaining a skirmish fought nearby in 1719 as part of an attempt to put the Old Pretender on the throne.

Glen Coe, a name with infamous historical associations but today almost synonymous with awesome mountain grandeur, ascends some twelve miles from sea-level at Loch Leven to a watershed at just over 1,000 feet (139 B8); it is a place which will probably never wholly lose its reputation for sombre gloom, earned partly because this can indeed be its effect, especially when descended in lowering weather, but also perhaps because of its ever-present association with the treachery and massacre of February 1692 as also through the influence of the paintings and writings of romantically imaginative travellers of the eighteenth and nineteenth centuries. But whatever its reputation and whatever its mood, Glen Coe is a splendid mountain wilderness towering above the rushing River Coe, a glen moreover which can readily be enjoyed by all (because a road runs its length) yet which at the same time offers walks and challenging climbs to the more ambitious.

As to the massacre – the worst of which occurred in the lower glen, outside the boundary of the Trust lands – it is the smell of treachery both here in Glen Coe and in London that lingers. Very briefly what happened was that the government set the last day of 1691 as

The Five Sisters of Kintail from a viewpoint high above the north side of Loch Duich. The highest peak is 3,505 feet.

the final date for submission by the Highlanders to William and Mary. Glencoe delayed but recorded his oath on 2 January. Meanwhile in London the Master of Stair, William's ruthless Scottish minister who was determined to inflict an example on the Highlands, wrote to the Commander-in-Chief in Scotland that he was glad that Glencoe did not 'come in within the time prescribed' and that it would be a great advantage to the nation if 'that thieving tribe were rooted out and cut off'. On 1 February a company under the command of Campbell of Glenlyon moved into the glen and was warmly received by the unsuspecting Macdonalds; on 12 February the order was received that all under the age of seventy should be put to the sword, and early the next morning Glenlyon and his men turned on their hosts, shooting the elderly chief in the back and butchering some thirty-eight people while as many more died of exposure and starvation on the mountains.

The Trust's Glen Coe lands of over 14,000 acres were acquired between 1935 and 1937 and are thus one of its earliest properties. Embracing the scenic best of the glen, the estate is also of considerable and varied geological interest (an aspect well explained and illustrated in the Trust's booklet) although, largely because it is so bare, it is not rich in either fauna or flora. Nevertheless there are attractions for the specialist, and the ordinary visitor may with luck see a soaring eagle or a herd of red deer, while wildcat have their home on the heights. The road ascends the left bank of the Coe, soon reaching the beautifully situated visitor centre, built by the Countryside Commission for Scotland but operated by the Trust; from here easy paths lead to Signal Rock, traditionally the place from which the signal was given to start the massacre, and to An Tor, a hill commanding a good view up the glen. Ascending, the road crosses the river just below Loch Achtriochtan to reach its grandest stretch, to the north being the rock-face of jagged Aonach Eagach and to the south Aonach Dubh on which is Ossian's Cave, legendary birthplace and home of that shadowy early bard. Some four miles above the visitor centre the Study (*studdie*: anvil) is reached, a terrace offering a view down the glen and also marking the limit of Trust property on the north. On the other side, though, the Trust cares for a huge tract of mountain, the limits being roughly marked by this road (A82), Glen Etive on the south as far as Dalness, and a line running north-west across Bidean nam Bian (3,766 feet) back to the visitor centre. A road descends the right bank of the Etive below the mass of Buachaille Etive Mór, known for its rock climbs.

At Scotland's centre **Ben Lawers** (140 C1), rising to nearly 4,000 feet above the north shore of Loch Tay and commanding views of both coasts, is another mountain range of geological interest, in this case because an overfold has brought the oldest rocks to the surface. The Trust owns 8,000 acres of the summits and southern slopes, the property, famed for its Alpine flora, being a national nature reserve under the joint control of the Trust and the Nature Conservancy Council. A road climbs from the loch shore to a visitor centre at 1,400 feet from where start a nature trail and a path to the summit.

above **The Grey Mare's Tail waterfall cascades down a rugged gorge. The area around is rich in wild flowers.**

right **The spectacular promontory of St Abb's Head is an important locality for cliff-breeding sea-birds.**

Three other sizable countryside properties merit mention, the first two being on islands. On Mull, **The Burg** (138 E2) embraces 1,525 acres of the Ardmeanach promontory (five miles rough walk) and includes a petrified tree set in the basalt cliffs and perhaps fifty million years old, while on Arran the Trust owns **Goatfell** (134 F5), 2,866 feet and the highest point on the island, Cir Mhor, adjacent and only slightly lower, and part of Glen Rosa which provides an approach towards the mountains from the south. The third large property, in Scotland's south-west off the A708 near Moffat, is **Grey Mare's Tail** (136 H4), a site of nearly 2,400 acres named after the 200-foot waterfall which is the principal feature.

Among more modest coast and countryside properties are **Linn of Tummel**, fifty acres with a nature trail along the rivers Tummel and Garry below the Killiecrankie visitor centre (140 A4); **Craigower**, a beacon-hill 1,300 feet high above Pitlochry (140 A4); **Bucinch** and **Ceardoch**, two small islands in Loch Lomond (139 H11); **Dollar Glen**, a wooded walk which offers an attractive approach to Castle Campbell (140 G4); **Blackhill**, three miles west of Lanark, a viewpoint over the valley of the Clyde (136 E1); **Threave Wildfowl Refuge**, on the Dee near Castle Douglas and known for its many species of wild geese and duck (131 E8); and, by the Solway shore near Dalbeattie, the bird sanctuary of **Rough Island** and the fifty acres of coastline known as **Muckle Lands and Jubilee Path** (131 F9). Finally, and acquired only in 1980, there is **St Abb's Head** on Scotland's south-east coast not far above the border (137 B11), a grand headland named after Ebba, a seventh-century Northumbrian princess who founded a nunnery here, reputedly in gratitude for surviving shipwreck. It was destroyed by Vikings two centuries later. The cliffs rise to 300 feet and the headland is of considerable botanical and ornithological importance.

Houses, Gardens & Parks

Abertarff House, Highland Long a town residence of the Lovats, Abertarff dates from 1593 and is one of the oldest houses in Inverness. (Let to the Highland Association – An Comunn Gaidhealach.)

Church Street, Inverness (144 E2)

Bachelors' Club, Strathclyde A seventeenth-century house in which Robert Burns and some friends formed a club in 1780 and where in the following year he became a Freemason. Period furnishings.

In Tarbolton (on B744 off A758), $7\frac{1}{2}$M NE of Ayr (135 G9)

The drawing room at Brodie Castle is part of the extension begun in the 1820s.

Barrie's Birthplace, Tayside The modest home in Kirriemuir, the 'Thrums' of his books, in which J. M. Barrie (1860–1937) was born, the son of a handloom weaver who at the time of his son's birth still worked on the premises. Personal and literary material is shown.

9 Brechin Road, Kirriemuir (141 B8)

Branklyn Garden, Tayside A garden of two acres, the personal achievement from 1922 onwards of the late Mr and Mrs J. T. Renton. The outstanding collection of plants includes alpines and also many of specialist interest.

Dundee Road, Perth (140 E6)

Brodick Castle and Country Park, Strathclyde In 1503 James IV appointed the 2nd Baron Hamilton royal justiciary in Arran (with the title Earl of Arran). Brodick then remained a seat of the Hamiltons until 1895 when it passed to the Duchess of Montrose, only child of the 12th Duke. The castle is of several periods, the oldest masonry being the remnants of a round tower of the later thirteenth century. These remains are within the tower-house built by the 2nd Earl of Arran in about 1558 and now forming the eastern end. In 1653, when in English hands after the defeat of Charles II at Worcester, the castle was enlarged by a western block, and finally, in 1844, the architect Gillespie Graham was commissioned to add a major extension to the west, the western terminal becoming a tower of four storeys.

The beautifully decorated interior houses notable collections of furniture, silver (including specially-commissioned items by great craftsmen), porcelain and paintings. Many of these treasures derive from the wealthy connoisseur William Beckford (*see Charlecote Park*) who, on his death in 1844, bequeathed them to his daughter Susan Euphemia, who married the 10th Duke of Hamilton. Among the artists whose works hang here are Van Dyck, Fragonard, Watteau, Gainsborough, Kneller, Winterhalter, Pollard and Turner.

The country park was formed in 1980 and is managed by the Trust in conjunction with Cunninghame District Council. It includes the gardens and grounds of the castle, while Goatfell and its neighbouring hills, although not a part of the park, will be managed in association with it.

The gardens of about sixty-five acres comprise two principal areas, a walled formal garden dating from 1710 and a large woodland garden which was started by the Duchess of Montrose in 1923 and is internationally famous, especially for its rhododendrons.

Brodick, Isle of Arran (134 F5)

Brodie Castle, Grampian Malcolm IV gave these lands to the Brodies in 1160, but although the present house may well incorporate something of an earlier building it is basically of 1567, much modified and extended in later centuries and especially after 1824 when the architect William Burn was involved in extensive rebuilding. Features of the interior are the rich seventeenth-century plasterwork ceilings, the drawing room designed by Burn, the Victorian kitchen, and an important collection of paintings which includes Dutch works (Van Dyck, Jacob Cuyp and others), English and French Impressionists and early English watercolours. There are also important collections of French furniture and Chinese export porcelain. In the grounds are a woodland walk, a wildlife observation hide, an adventure playground and a picnic area.

Between Nairn and Forres, off A96 (144 D5)

Carlyle's Birthplace, Dumfries and Galloway The house in which Thomas Carlyle (1795–1881) was born. It was built by his father and uncle, both master masons. Letters and other personal articles are shown in a contemporary setting. (*See also Carlyle's House, London.*)

Ecclefechan, on A74 (131 D12)

Castle Fraser, Grampian Castle Fraser is one of the most splendid of the great houses in this district, historically the lands of Mar. Built between 1575 and 1636, the castle is the work of two well-known local families of master masons, Bel and Leiper. Among noteworthy features of the granite exterior are the corner turrets reaching through two floors, the blind machicolation, the rope design of the mouldings, and the magnificent heraldic panel (signed I. Bel) on the north side. In the grounds a formal garden occupies what was the old walled garden.

16M W of Aberdeen, 3M S of Kemnay, off B993 (146 F5)

Charlotte Square and Georgian House, Edinburgh Charlotte Square was designed by Robert Adam in 1791 and its superb north side is widely accepted as one of his most distin-

The north side of Charlotte Square, Edinburgh, is Robert Adam's urban masterpiece.

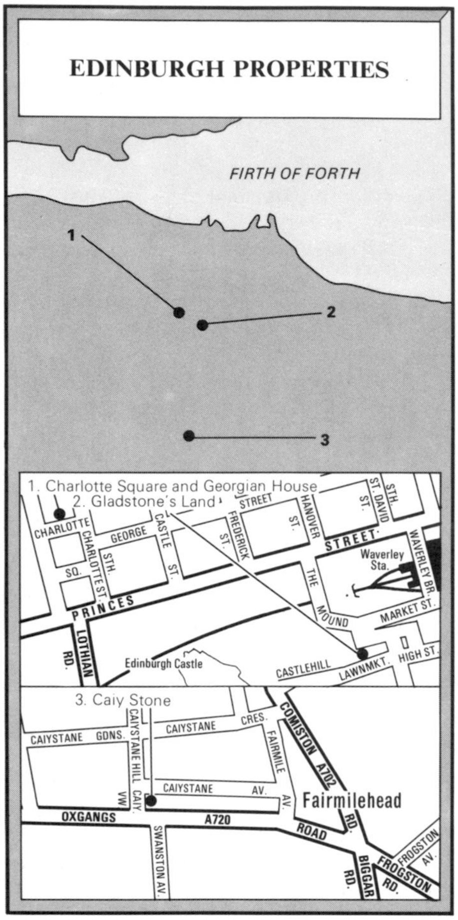

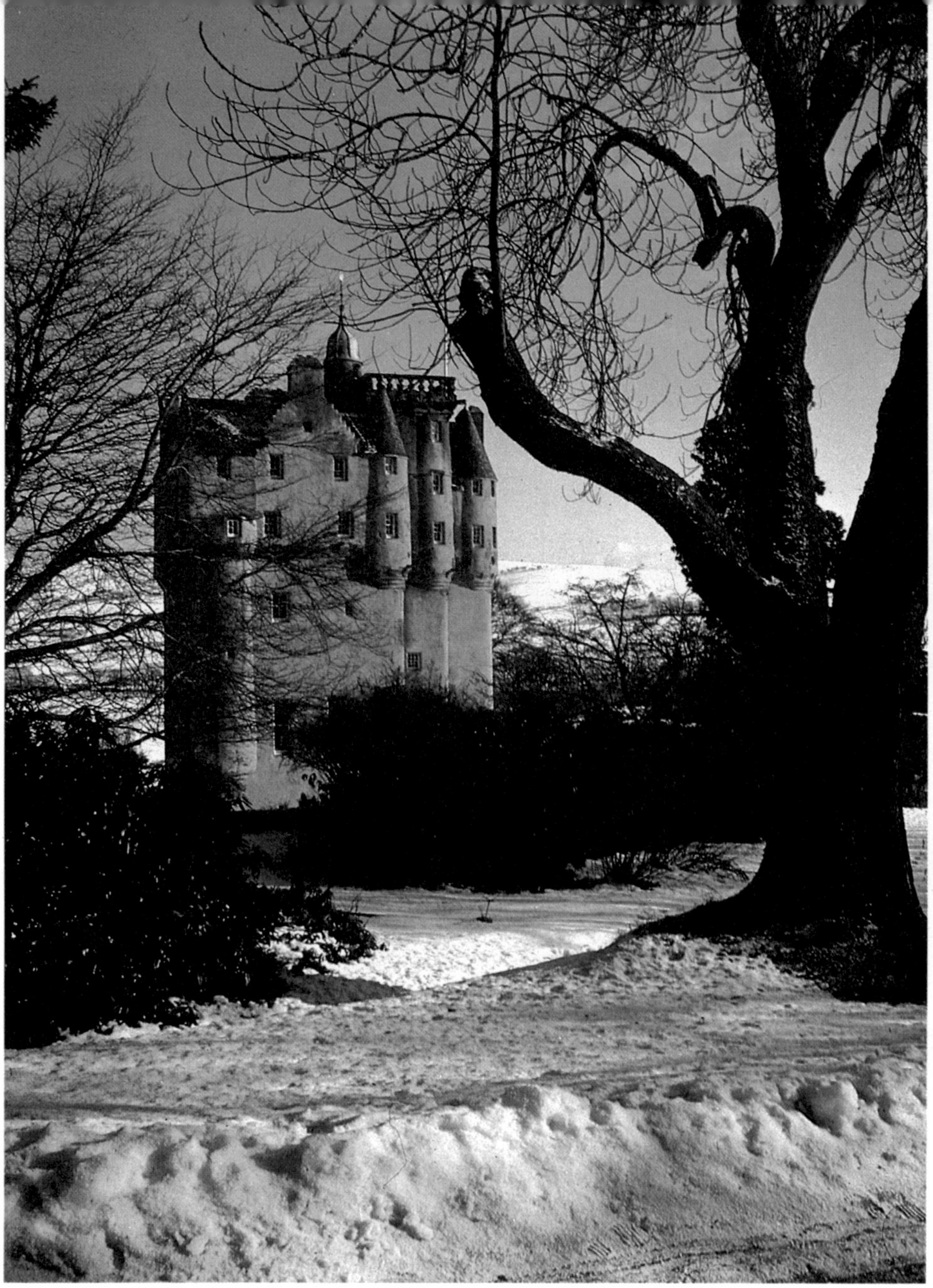

Craigievar Castle, crowned with a profusion of corbels, turrets and cupolas, is an outstanding example of the contemporary Scottish Baronial style.

guished urban achievements. Later much altered to meet Victorian tastes, the north side was largely restored to its original form during the 1920s and 1930s, one feature of the restoration being the return of the first-floor window levels to their correct eighteenth-century height. Eleven houses are contained within a single façade; No 5 is the headquarters of the National Trust for Scotland, No 6 the official residence of the Secretary of State for Scotland, and No 7 what is now known as the Georgian House. The upper floors of No 7 are the residence of the Moderator of the General Assembly of the Church of Scotland, while the lower ones have been furnished to illustrate the interior, family and domestic, as it may have been during the period *c.*1790 to 1820. During this period the house was owned by John Lamont of Lamont, eighteenth chief of the clan of that name.

Central Edinburgh (see map above)

Craigievar Castle, Grampian It is recorded that men of Craigievar fought for the Earl of Mar at Harlaw in 1411, and known too that by 1457 these lands belonged to the Mortimers who are thought to have started to build the castle around the end of the sixteenth century. However, by 1610 financial difficulties forced the family to sell, the purchaser being an Aberdeen merchant called William Forbes. By the time his home was finished in 1626 it stood as an outstanding example of the contemporary local Scottish Baronial style, a tall tower-house, plain below but on top crowded with turrets, corbelling, cupolas and other decorative features. With the great hall typically occupying the main part of the first floor, the castle's interior is notable for the plasterwork of the ceilings, a choice which at this period was superseding painted decoration in popularity, and also for the magnificent carved Royal Arms of the United Kingdom over the hall's fireplace, a decoration to which William Forbes was entitled as a tenant-in-chief holding his lands direct from the Crown. The architect of Craigievar may well have been that same I. Bel whose name appears on the heraldic panel at *Castle Fraser.*

On A980, 6M S of Alford (146 F3)

Crathes Castle, Grampian Crathes seems to have been started in about 1553 by Alexander Burnett of Leys, the head of a family granted lands here by Bruce in 1323. Progress was slow, partly because of frequent deaths in the succession, and it was not until the last decade of the century that the house was occupied. A typical Scottish Baronial tower-house of the district and time, plain below but turreted in its upper part, Crathes is best known for the decorative work of its interior and especially for its splendid painted ceilings with their allegorical figures, among the last of their kind before plasterwork became popular, and for the ribbed and carved ceiling of the long gallery, unique in Scotland for being of oak. The grounds of nearly 600 acres are made up of woodland, fields and a garden area of about six acres in which there are several individual gardens, each on a particular theme. The yew hedges dating from 1702 may be survivals of a formal garden, and there are four nature trails.

3M E of Banchory on A93 (147 H5)

Crathes Castle is best known for its painted ceilings, illustrating an art of which few examples have survived.

The Study in Culross is so called because of the small withdrawing room at the top of the tower.

Culross, Fife Ever since its formation the Trust has been active here and Culross is now preserved as an unspoilt example of a small Royal Burgh of the sixteenth and seventeenth centuries, at which time it thrived through its trade in salt and coal fostered by its enterprising laird Sir George Bruce.

The principal building owned by the Trust here is Culross Palace, which stands virtually unaltered since it was built by Sir George Bruce between 1597 and 1611. The earlier date with the simple initials GB appears on the building on the west of the courtyard, while SGB (Sir George Bruce) and the date 1611 on a pediment on the building on the north side of the courtyard indicate that this newer part of the house was completed after its owner had been knighted. The most important feature of the interior is the painted woodwork of the walls, ceilings and beams, much of this found dismantled and scattered when the house was taken over by the Office of Works in 1932 but since carefully reassembled. (The Palace is under the guardianship of the Scottish Development Department, Ancient Monuments.)

Two other houses in Culross can also be visited: the Town House of 1626, with a clock tower and façade of 1783 (visitor centre); and the Study, built for a merchant in 1633 and with a small room used as a study by Bishop Leighton of Dunblane (1611–84). Several other Trust buildings can be viewed from the outside.

12M W of N side of Forth road bridge, off A985 (136 A3)

Culzean Castle and Country Park, Strathclyde This estate was owned by the Kennedy family (earls of Cassillis) from the fourteenth century, but Culzean Castle as seen today, apart from some alterations of the nineteenth century, is the achievement of Robert Adam working for the 10th Earl between 1777 and 1792. Adam designed and built the castle in three stages. The first was the conversion of the existing sixteenth-century tower-house into an elegant and comfortable mansion facing southward; the second involved the replacement of the old domestic buildings on the north by a wing of rooms along the rim of the cliff, including the unique round drawing room with windows sheer above the sea; and in the third stage the old courtyard which still survived between the new mansion and the cliff-top wing became the site of the Oval Staircase, generally accepted as one of Adam's most ingenious creations. Completed, Culzean successfully combined Georgian symmetry, romantic mock fortification and also Italianate elements. Since the castle's acquisition by the Trust in 1945, the interior decoration has been the subject of much carefully researched restoration and, since 1972, nearly all the original eighteenth-century colour schemes have been restored.

The country park of 560 acres, run by the Trust on behalf of local authorities, includes the walled garden, swan pond, deer park, woodland walks and picnic places, and also a Park Centre (restaurant, shop, exhibition) occupying the restored and adapted Adam home farm.

On A719, 12M S of Ayr (130 A3)

Drum Castle, Grampian The castle was built in three separate stages. The tower-house is believed to have been built in 1286 by Richard Cementarius, the royal mason; a brewhouse was added to the tower's north wall during the fifteenth century, and a Jacobean mansion built on by the ninth laird in 1619. Later changes included the addition of a central door and steps to the south front of the mansion in about 1800 and the construction in 1875 (to the design of David Bryce) of a hall and door on the north front within the courtyard. The tower-house is notable for being one of the oldest in Scotland, but Drum is also interesting for having been in the possession of the same family for 653 years, from 1323 when Robert Bruce gave these lands to his armour-bearer William de Irwin until 1976 when the estate came to the National Trust for Scotland.

The tower, its early origin suggested by the unusually high battlements, is a square keep with three vaulted storeys, the first of which, once the great hall, was converted into a library in about 1845, the large arched window on the east being thrown out at the same time. Above is a large upper hall, from which a modern wooden stair allows access to the battlements. In the mansion the rooms contain family portraits, porcelain, *objets d'art* and furniture mainly of the eighteenth and nineteenth centuries. The grounds of 400 acres include mixed woodland, an attractive picnic area and a chapel roughly contemporary with the mansion.

10M W of Aberdeen, off A93 (147 G5)

Dunkeld, Tayside Here the Trust owns twenty little houses along Cathedral and High streets. Most of these date from the rebuilding of the town after its destruction in 1689 during the battle in which the Covenanter Cameronians beat off the attacking Highlanders, thus reversing the decision of Killiecrankie and finally assuring the cause of William and Mary. From 1954 to 1965 the houses were restored by the Trust and now provide modern homes behind modest late seventeenth-century exteriors. The restoration is explained in photographs at a visitor centre. Nearby Stanley Hill is a mock fortification raised by the Duke of Atholl in 1730. (Houses not open. Visitor Centre run in conjunction with Dunkeld and Birnam Mercantile and Tourist Association.)

On A9 15M N of Perth (140 C5)

Falkland Palace and Garden, Fife There was a castle here as early as the twelfth century and by the fifteenth Falkland had become a favoured hunting-palace of the Stuarts. It was so popular

The garden at the Royal Palace of Falkland showing planting against the long retaining wall under the ruined East Range.

Gladstone's Land is the most important example of seventeenth-century high-tenement housing to survive in Edinburgh.

that James IV began a new palace sometime before 1500, this being completed and much embellished by James V who died here in 1542. Still technically the property of the sovereign, Falkland has for centuries been held in the care of a hereditary Keeper, the position of the Trust today being that of Deputy Keeper.

Most of the palace is in ruin but the South Range was restored by the 3rd Marquess of Bute who became Keeper in 1887. Built by James IV, this range's street façade, with long, narrow windows, buttresses and battlement, and twin-towered gatehouse, stands as an attractive example of Scottish Gothic. In contrast the early Renaissance courtyard façade, added by James V, is distinctive for the influence of French craftsmen, recalling that James married two French wives and that his reign marked the high point of the Scottish–French alliance. The range includes the Chapel Royal, with Falkland's only surviving original interior. The East Range housed the royal apartments and here the Trust has restored the King's Bedchamber.

In the grounds a rose garden occupies the site of the North Range, burnt down in 1654, while just to the north of this something of the outline of the early castle survives. The royal tennis court of 1539 is attached to the stables, and there is a visitor centre at the East Port.

11M N of Kirkcaldy on the A912 (141 F7)

Gladstone's Land, Edinburgh This tall, narrow building, completed by Thomas Gledstanes in 1620, is typical of those that once crowded old Edinburgh. The interior, with characteristic wall and ceiling paintings, has been in part refurbished to seventeenth-century domestic style.

Lawnmarket, Edinburgh (see map p. 122)

Greenbank Garden, Strathclyde The garden and grounds of a Georgian house of 1763. The Advice Centre is likely to be of particular interest to owners of small gardens. (House not open.)

Clarkston, on B761 on S edge of Glasgow (135 D10)

Haddo House, Grampian This great house was designed for the 2nd Earl of Aberdeen in 1731 by William Adam, father of Robert, as successor to the House of Kellie, the mansion of the Gordons of Methlick until burnt down by Covenanters in 1644. With its simple and well-proportioned symmetry the house stands virtually unchanged apart from the front porch which was remodelled by the 7th Earl in 1880 to lower the entrance from the balcony to ground level. The 7th Earl was also largely responsible for the elegant 'Adam Revival' of much of the interior. The house is notable too for its portraits, outstanding among which is one by Lawrence of the 4th Earl (Prime Minister 1852–5), whose care and energy transformed a neglected inheritance into a thriving estate. The chapel of 1880, the last achievement of G. E. Street, contains a window by Burne-Jones.

The Trust owns the house and gardens, while about 180 acres of park are owned and managed by Grampian Regional Council as a country park. The Haddo Choral and Operatic Society ranks as one of Scotland's leading musical societies.

On A9005 near Methlick (146 D6)

Hamilton House, Lothian A house of 1628 built by John Hamilton, a wealthy citizen of Edinburgh. (Open only by prior arrangement.)

Prestonpans (136 B6)

Hill of Tarvit, Fife A seventeenth-century country house remodelled in 1906 by Sir Robert Lorimer and containing Chippendale, Jacobean and eighteenth-century French furniture, Flemish tapestries, Chinese porcelain and bronzes, Dutch paintings and portraits by, amongst others, Raeburn and Ramsay.

2½M S of Cupar, off A916 (141 F8)

House of The Binns, Lothian The site is thought to have been occupied in prehistoric times and it is known that there was a house here during the fifteenth century. In 1612 the estate was bought by Thomas Dalyell who had accompanied James VI/I to London and made money there, and between that date and 1630 he enlarged and decorated the house converting it to a comfortable mansion. Thomas's son, the colourful General Tam (who, amongst other exploits, escaped from the Tower of London, campaigned in Russia for the Tsar and on his return raised the Scots Greys), added a west wing. During the eighteenth and nineteenth centuries there were further modifications such as the addition of the morning and dining rooms, the reversal of the house (the front moving from the south to the north side) and the enlargement of the east and west ranges.

The interior is known for its moulded plaster ceilings, the best being those in the High Hall

The elegant rooms of Haddo House contain fine antique furniture and a notable collection of portraits.

The House of The Binns was built at a time when fortified houses were no longer essential in Scotland.

and the King's Room, both put up in 1630. The house also contains good Regency furniture, porcelain, and souvenirs of General Tam, while the artists represented include Jamesone, Wilkie and Kneller. The grounds include a nineteenth-century folly and a woodland walk to a view over the Forth.

15M W of Edinburgh, off A904 (136 A3)

House of Dun, Tayside This modest country house dates from 1730 and stands on the site of two earlier houses. It was designed by William Adam for David Erskine, Lord Dun, twelfth laird in a succession reaching back to 1375. The interior is notable for its plasterwork, chimney-pieces and panelling. The estate, which came to the Trust in 1980, includes some 800 acres of farm and woodland. (Not open until 1982–3.)

4M W of Montrose, off A935 (141 A11)

Inveresk Lodge Garden, Lothian The garden of a seventeenth-century house specializing in plants suitable for the small garden. (House not open.)

Just S of Musselburgh, 7M E of Edinburgh, on A6124 (136 B6)

Inverewe Garden, Highland Pleasantly situated on a small headland into a sea loch, this famous garden was the creation from 1862 on of Osgood Mackenzie. After his death in 1922 his work was continued by his daughter, Mrs Sawyer. Despite the northern latitude, many subtropical species are able to flourish on this secluded site washed by the warm North Atlantic Drift and there is normally colour throughout the year.

On A832, 6M NE of Gairloch (148 H1)

Kellie Castle and Garden, Fife Although called 'castle', Kellie is in fact a noteworthy example of Lowland Scottish domestic architecture. The house seen today was completed in about 1606, the last stage in development from a single tower of *c.*1360. Owned first by the Siwards, then by the Oliphants, Kellie was bought in 1613 by Thomas Erskine, later 1st Earl of Kellie. In 1876, by which date the place had long been virtually abandoned, Kellie passed first by lease and then by purchase to the Lorimers who over three generations restored and cared for it. The interior is particularly noteworthy for the painted panelling and the sixteenth-century tapestry in the dining room (formerly the drawing room), and, in the Vine Room, for a ceiling painting (*c.*1685) of Mount Olympus by Jacob de Wet the Younger. Additionally there are displays on the Lorimer family, notably Professor James, the jurist, who first leased Kellie in 1876, and his son Robert, the architect.

3M NNW of Pittenweem, off B9171 (141 G10)

Lamb's House, Edinburgh The combined home and warehouse of a wealthy merchant of the

late sixteenth or early seventeenth century. (Leased as an old people's day centre. Visits by appointment only.)

Water Street, Leith, Edinburgh (136 B5)

Leith Hall and Garden, Grampian The hall was started in 1649 by James Leith, the head of a family first recorded as landowners near Leith (Edinburgh) but who moved northwards in perhaps the thirteenth century and appear as Aberdeen shipowners by the fourteenth. The original design of the hall – a rectangle around a courtyard – has survived, although modifications and enlargements, notably the addition of further storeys, were made during the eighteenth and nineteenth centuries. The house contains portraits and personal souvenirs of the successive lairds, most of whom followed military careers in many parts of the world. The grounds of 236 acres include a bird observation hide, a picnic area and two country walks.

On B9002, 34M NW of Aberdeen (146 E3)

Linlithgow Houses, Lothian Two locally typical late sixteenth- or early seventeenth-century small town houses. (Not open.)

Nos 44 and 48 High Street, Linlithgow (136 B3)

Lochalsh Woodland Garden, Highland A system of footpaths covers most of the garden and woodland around Lochalsh House on the Balmacara Estate, and there is a small countryside interpretation centre in the coach house. (House not open.)

2M E of Kyle of Lochalsh (143 G2)

Leith Hall contains collections recording the family's political and military achievements.

Malleny Garden, Lothian The garden of a house of about 1635, last in a succession of houses on an estate dating back, though with many changes in ownership, to the fifteenth century. The house was probably built by Sir James Murray, Master of the King's Works. The shrub roses are a feature of the garden. Also, four magnificent yew trees survive from a planting of twelve to commemorate the Union of Crowns in 1603. (House not open.)

Balerno, off A70 (136 C4)

Pitmedden Garden, Grampian The main feature here is the interesting formal Great Garden, laid out in the second half of the seventeenth century by Sir Alexander Seton and recreated by the Trust. Terraces, formed when Seton had to level off a slope, allow a raised view of the four parterres (patterned beds). Three of these are to designs thought to have been used in 1647 for the gardens of Holyroodhouse in Edinburgh and the fourth has a heraldic theme derived from Sir Alexander's coat-of-arms.

A museum of farming life has recently been formed in the outbuildings at Pitmedden, based largely on the collection of Mr William Cook. A fascinating assortment of old farm imple-

right **Threave Garden is particularly known for its daffodils, as featured in this magnificent display near the house.**

below **The four parterres in the Great Garden at Pitmedden contain some 40,000 bedding plants, best seen in summer.**

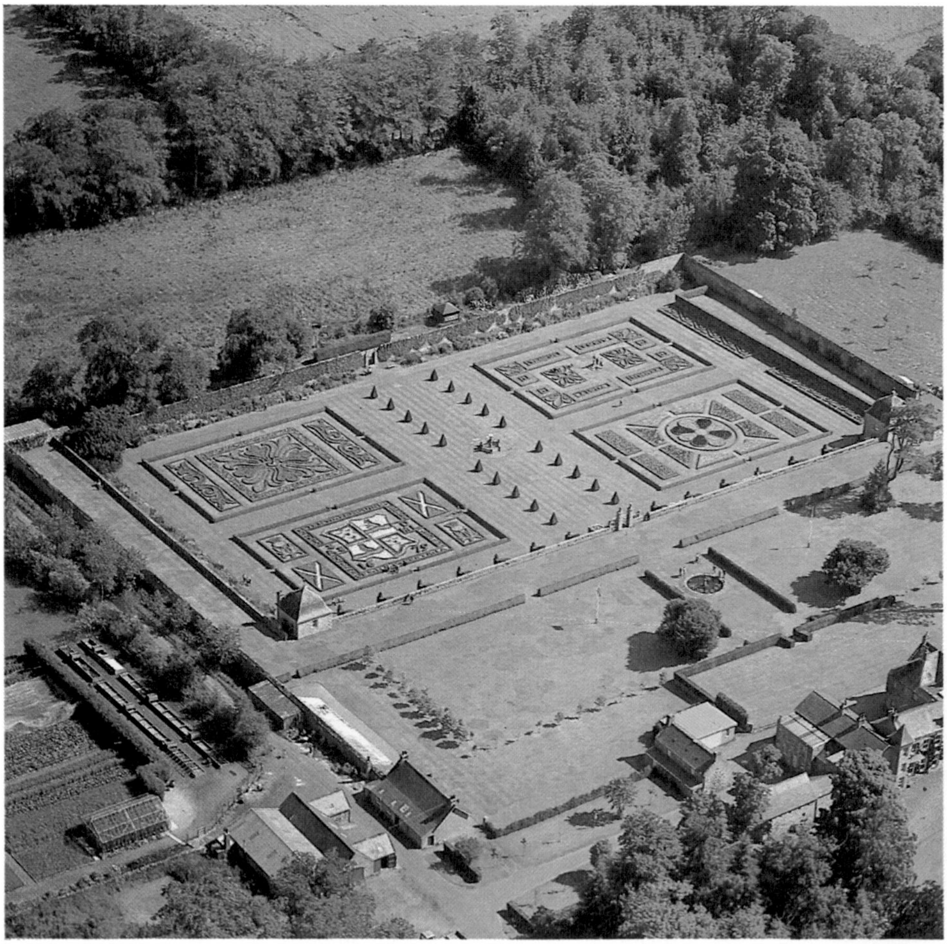

ments and domestic artefacts is on display. Other local attractions are an exhibition on the development of the formal garden, woodland and farmland walks, rare breeds of cattle and a picnic area.

14M N of Aberdeen on A920 (146 E6)

Plewlands House, Lothian A small town house of 1643. (Not open.)

South Queensferry (136 B4)

Priorwood Garden, Borders A garden specializing in flowers for drying. Visitor centre and picnic area.

Melrose, adjacent to the Abbey (137 F8)

Provan Hall, Strathclyde A well-restored, fifteenth-century mansion (1450–71), considered to be the most perfect survival of its kind in Scotland. There are two buildings

either side of a courtyard, the original hall on the north and, on the south, an addition of the seventeenth and eighteenth centuries. (Let to Glasgow District Council.)

Auchinlea Road, eastern Glasgow (135 C11)

Provost Ross's House, Grampian A town house of 1593, now converted into a maritime museum run by Aberdeen District Council.

Shiprow, central Aberdeen (147 G7)

Sailor's Walk, Fife A group of seventeenth-century merchants' houses by the harbour. (Not open.)

Kirkcaldy (141 H7)

Stenhouse Mansion, Edinburgh A town house built by a prosperous Edinburgh merchant in the early seventeenth century. (Not open.)

Gorgie Road, south-west Edinburgh (136 B5)

Suntrap, Lothian A gardening advice centre at which instructional courses are available. (Administered in cooperation with Lothian Regional Council.)

Gogarbank, W of Edinburgh, between A8 and A71 (136 B4)

Threave Garden, Dumfries and Galloway An estate of some 1,500 acres made up of farms, woodland and a nineteenth-century house and garden of sixty-five acres. The house (not open) is the Trust's School of Gardening. Although especially known for its daffodils, the garden is of wide interest and includes separate rose, woodland, walled, nursery, peat, rock, vegetable, herbaceous and heather areas, while there is also a way-marked woodland walk.

1M W of Castle Douglas, S of A75 (131 E8)

below **The domestic, agricultural and social history of Angus over more than two centuries is illustrated in the folk museum.**

Castles, Abbeys & other Buildings

Angus Folk Museum, Tayside Housed in a row of restored and adapted nineteenth-century cottages, the Angus Folk Collection (the achievement of Jean, Lady Maitland) is one of the most important of its kind in Scotland. Considerable expansion of the agricultural side was made possible by the construction of a new building in 1976.

Glamis, off A94 (141 C8)

Balmerino Abbey, Fife The ruins of a monastery founded in 1229 by Alexander II and his mother for Cistercians from Melrose and largely destroyed by the English in 1547. (Not open, but seen from outside.)

Balmerino, on the Firth of Tay, 5M SW of Newport-on-Tay (141 E8)

Boath Doocot, Highland A seventeenth-century dovecote standing on the motte of a twelfth-century castle. There was a battle here in 1645 in which Montrose defeated a numerically greatly superior army of Covenanters under General Urry and this is well explained.

Auldearn, 2M E of Nairn (144 D5)

Castle Campbell, Central Strikingly perched on a steep hillside and on a mound which may represent a Norman motte, Castle Campbell grew between the fifteenth to the late sixteenth or early seventeenth centuries. The oldest part is the north-east tower, almost certainly built by Colin Campbell, 1st Earl of Argyll, soon after 1481, and known to have been successor to an earlier structure. John Knox is believed to have preached here in 1556, and on the evidence of a letter from Monk to Cromwell it seems that the castle was burnt in 1654. The tower is the most complete and most interesting part. It contains a pit prison within the wall, the vaulted great hall on the first floor, and on the underside of the vaulting of the top floor two unusual late sixteenth- or early seventeenth-century grotesque masks from the mouths of which may have hung lamps. The attractive open loggia between the tower and the south range is also noteworthy. The castle may be approached on foot by way of the Trust's wooded Dollar Glen. (Under the guardianship of the Scottish Development Department, Ancient Monuments.)

Dollar, off A91 (140 G4)

Crookston Castle, Strathclyde The early fifteenth-century tower-house of a branch of the Stewarts (from about 1473 lords Darnley) standing on the site of a twelfth-century castle probably built by Sir Robert Croc. Mary, Queen of Scots, and Darnley stayed here after their marriage in 1565. In the basement there is a large room with a vaulted roof, and the great hall, also vaulted, is on the first floor. (Under the guardianship of the Scottish Development Department, Ancient Monuments.)

Crookston, SE of Paisley and SW of Glasgow, off A736 (135 C10)

The Hermitage, Tayside A minor folly built in 1758 by the future 3rd Duke of Atholl as a summer retreat in the wooded cut of the small river Braan. The site includes thirty-seven acres of woodland, mostly Douglas fir and Scots pine.

2M *W of Dunkeld, off A9 (140 C5)*

Hugh Miller's Cottage, Highland Built in about 1711 this cottage was the birthplace in 1802 of Hugh Miller, the stonemason who achieved fame as a geologist and writer. Material on both these activities is exhibited together with a period cottage kitchen and bedroom.

Church Street, Cromarty (144 C3)

Phantassie Doocot This dovecote, once with over 500 nests and probably of the seventeenth century, is of the round domed or 'beehive' type introduced by the Normans. It is unusual in Scotland for the way in which the top is sliced to form a south-facing slope, although this design is common in southern France as a means of giving weather protection. *Preston Mill* stands nearby.

East Linton, off A1 (137 B8)

The Pineapple, Central A strange garden retreat of 1761 built in the shape of a pineapple forty-five feet high. The sixteen acres of grounds include a walled garden, woodland and picnic area. (Leased to the Landmark Trust and let as a holiday home.)

Near Airth, 7M *E of Stirling off A905, then B9124 (140 H4)*

St Mungo's Chapel, Fife This ruined chapel of 1503 was built by Glasgow's Bishop Blacader on the traditional birthplace in 514 of St Mungo (or Kentigern), said to have been founder of the church which eventually became Glasgow cathedral. The story goes that the saint's mother, a Christian convert fleeing across the Forth from her pagan father, was driven ashore here.

On A985, just E of Culross (136 A3)

Scotstarvit Tower, Fife Probably built between 1550 and 1579, and in about 1611 the home of Sir John Scot, a distinguished lawyer and writer, Scotstarvit survives as one of Scotland's most complete and unspoilt examples of a simple tower-house. Designed for both residential and minor defensive purposes, the tower is a free-standing rectangular keep, its lines broken by a small side wing for the spiral stairway. The interior is of several levels, from the ground floor, used for storage, up to the parapet. The first floor was the most important, here being the hall with its three windows and their flanking stone seats and also a garderobe. Above was the laird's private room. The parapet, still with gun-loops at its angles, was at one time battlemented, and above the door to the cap-house (the superstructure roofing the stair) can be seen the initials of Sir John Scot and his wife Dame Anne Drummond. (Under the guardianship of the Scottish Development Department, Ancient Monuments.)

Dovecotes, such as Phantassie Doocot here, were the prime source of winter meat before the advent of winter feed for cattle.

The Pineapple was built as a garden retreat in 1761 by an unknown architect.

S of Cupar, off A916 (141 F8)

Souter Johnnie's Cottage, Strathclyde Robert Burns (1759–96) spent the summer of 1775 in Kirkoswald, and it was here that he met the people from whom he drew the now famous characters of his poem *Tam o' Shanter*, notably Douglas Graham of Shanter and John Davidson, respectively the prototypes for Tam and Souter (cobbler) Johnnie. At this time, though, Davidson lived elsewhere, only building this cottage in 1785. The interior contains souvenirs of Burns, contemporary cobbler's tools, and also what is probably the actual cobbling chair used by Davidson. In the garden there are life-sized stone figures, carved in 1802 by James Thom, of Tam, Souter Johnnie, the innkeeper and his wife.

Kirkoswald, on A77 4M *W of Maybole (130 A3)*

Strome Castle, Highland This small ruin by the shore of Loch Carron, now little more than a confusion of stones, was long an outpost stronghold of the MacDonalds of Glengarry. It was also a constant challenge to the nearby Mackenzies of Kintail who finally blew it up in 1602. The story goes that some MacDonald women who had just fetched water from the well inadvertently emptied their buckets into the gunpowder vat; a Mackenzie prisoner overheard the women being upbraided, made his escape and told his chief, who was on the point of giving up the siege, that the defenders were now helpless.

N shore of Loch Carron (142 F2)

Threave Castle, Dumfries and Galloway This ancient and massive tower-house standing stark on a low island in the river Dee has played its part in the wars of Scotland and England. The castle was probably started soon after 1369 by Black Archibald the Grim, Lord of Galloway and later 3rd Earl of Douglas. When the Black Douglases rebelled in 1455 Threave was taken by James II in person, though only after a siege and artillery bombardment; in 1545, now owned by Lord

Maxwell who had sided with the Tudors, Threave was subdued by the Regent Arran; in 1588 the place was surrendered to James VI who had hastened to south-western Scotland when it seemed that the Catholic 8th Lord Maxwell was planning to aid a Spanish landing; and finally, in 1640 when held for Charles I by the Earl of Nithsdale, Threave was taken by the Covenanters and dismantled.

The keep is of several levels rising above a cellar area in which are the well and a dungeon. On the next two floors are the kitchen and then the hall, both with their garderobes and the latter with stone benches in the window bays. Above again would have been the lord's private rooms, while the garrison was quartered at the top. (Under the guardianship of the Scottish Development Department, Ancient Monuments.)

2½M W of Castle Douglas, N of A75 (131 E8)

Archaeological, Industrial & Historical Sites

Antonine Wall, Central and Strathclyde The Trust owns sections of this Roman wall built between the Forth and the Clyde in *c.*140 but abandoned by the end of the century. The wall is of turf on a stone base, with an outer mound and ditch on the north, a road along the south, and forts at intervals. The best preserved fort is Rough Castle which is Trust property. Here the above features are well seen, the road running through the fort while a confusion of earthworks marks the sites of the barracks (to the north of the road), the commander's house, granary and headquarters (to the south), and a bath house just east of the fort wall and south of the road. (Under the guardianship of the Scottish Development Department, Ancient Monuments.)

A803 and B816 from Bonnybridge (136 A1)

Bannockburn Monument, Central It was near here in June 1314 that Robert Bruce routed England's Edward II and thus assured Scotland's independence. The Trust area includes an equestrian statue of Bruce (Pilkington Jackson, 1964), the Rotunda enclosing the Borestone site, traditionally Bruce's command post, and a visitor centre in which are displayed fragments of the Borestone in which Bruce is said to have planted his standard and where the wars of independence and the tactical details of the battle are explained.

2M S of Stirling, off M80 (140 H3)

The battlefield of Bannockburn, where the seal was set on Scotland's independence, is surveyed by a statue of Robert the Bruce.

Bruce's Stone, Dumfries and Galloway A boulder on Raploch Moss where Bruce won a skirmish with the English in 1307.

6M W of New Galloway by A712 (130 D6)

Caiy Stone, Edinburgh A prehistoric standing stone, probably on its original site and bearing traces of cup markings.

Oxgangs Road, southern Edinburgh (see map p. 122)

Culloden, Highland The site of the battle of April 1746 in which Prince Charles Edward, the Young Pretender, was defeated by the Duke of Cumberland. This battle, with Bannockburn, was one of the two most important in Scottish history; it not only destroyed the Stuart cause but, more important for Scotland, sounded the knell for a Highland clan way of life that had changed little over twelve or more centuries. The site embraces a memorial cairn; scattered stones marking the graves of the clans; the Well of the Dead where wounded Highlanders are said to have been killed while trying to drink; the Cumberland Stone where the duke may for a while have taken up position; Leanach farmhouse, now a museum; and a visitor centre.

5M E of Inverness, on B9006 (144 E3)

Glenfinnan Monument, Highland This tower topped by the figure of a Highlander stands at the head of Loch Shiel on the site where Prince Charles Edward, the Young Pretender, raised his standard on 19 August 1745. Put up in 1815 by MacDonald of Glenaladale, descendant of the man at whose house the prince had rested the previous night, the tower was given its Highlander, the work of John Greenshields, in 1834. A visitor centre describes the whole course of the campaign from the raising of the standard to the tragedy of Culloden and the prince's later wanderings.

On A830, 18M W of Fort William (143 L3)

Mote of Mark, Dumfries and Galloway An Iron Age hill-fort.

7M S of Dalbeattie, off A710 (131 F9)

Pass of Killiecrankie, Tayside It was down this wooded gorge in July 1689 that the troops of William III fled in panic after their defeat about a mile to the north by Jacobite Highlanders under Claverhouse, Viscount Dundee. However, this Jacobite victory was both tragic and short-lived since Dundee was killed and twenty-five days later the Highlanders were in their turn defeated at Dunkeld.

Its historic interest apart, Killiecrankie is a renowned beauty spot and the visitor centre exhibitions feature not only the battle but also local natural history.

A9, 2½M N of Pitlochry (140 A4)

Preston Mill, Lothian Dating from the sixteenth century and the oldest mechanically working water-driven meal mill in Scotland, Preston Mill's buildings form a picturesque group beside a stream. They occupy a site believed to have been home to a mill in medieval times, and the adjacent kiln may well belong to that period. Last used commercially in 1957, the mill's machinery has since been renovated by Messrs Rank Hovis McDougall Ltd. *Phantassie Doocot* stands nearby.

East Linton, off A1 (137 B8)

Stones of Clava, Highland An important prehistoric site of perhaps 2000–1500 BC made up of a small stone circle and three large burial cairns, two of the passage type and the third a ring cairn. All the cairns are surrounded by standing stones and the site is known for its many examples of cup and other markings. (Under the guardianship of the Scottish Development Department, Ancient Monuments.)

6M E of Inverness, off B851 (144 E3)

Weaver's Cottage, Strathclyde This cottage, built in 1723 and typical of those occupied by the handloom weavers of the eighteenth and nineteenth centuries, now serves as a memorial museum of this local industry. When it was at its peak in the 1830s Kilbarchan boasted some 800 looms. The industry survived until the 1950s, though by then the number of looms had dropped to four. In addition to looms and other weaving equipment, the museum shows local fabrics, shawls and domestic utensils and bygones of many kinds. The cruck construction of a part of the cottage is unusual for this part of Scotland.

Kilbarchan, 8M SW of Glasgow, off A737 (135 C9)

Adjoining page 135

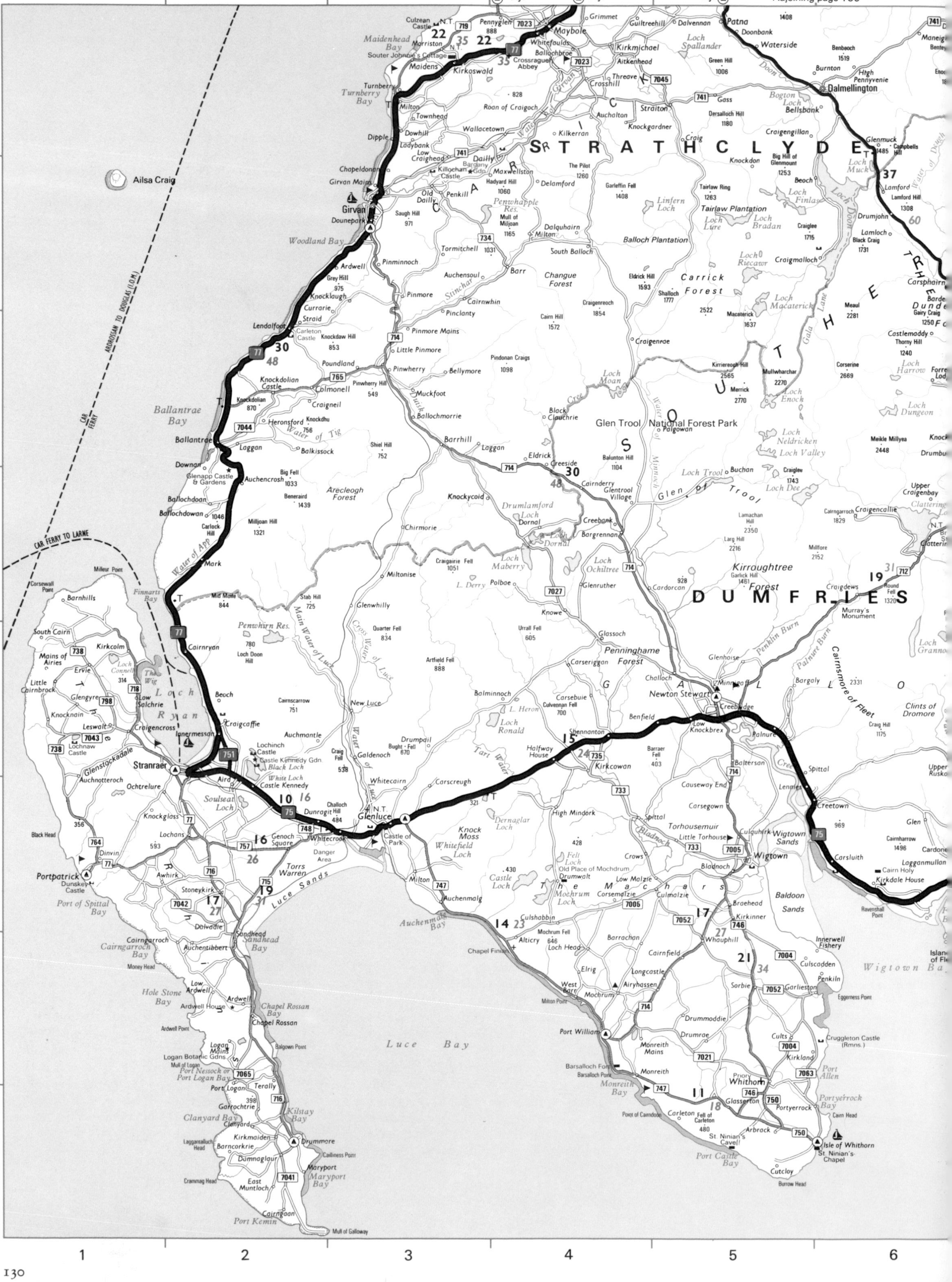

1
2
3
4
5
6
A
B
C
D
E
F
G
H
Ayr
Ayr
Ayr
STRATHCLYDE
CARRICK
DUMFRIES
GALLOWAY
THE RHINNS
THE MACHARS
SOUTH
Culzean Castle
N.T.
Maidenhead Bay
Morriston
Souter Johnnie's Cottage
Maidens
Kirkoswald
Pennyglen
888
Maybole
Whitefoulds
Ballochbroe
Crossraguel Abbey
Grimmet
Guiltreehill
Dalvennan
Kirkmichael
Aitkenhead
Loch Spallander
Patna
Doonbank
Waterside
1408
Benbeoch
1519
Burnton
High Pennyvenie
Dalmellington
Green Hill
1006
Turnberry
Turnberry Bay
Milton
Townhead
Roon of Craigoch
Threave
Crosshill
Straiton
Gass
Dersalloch Hill
1180
Bogton Loch
Bellsbank
Dowhill
Ladybank
Low Craighead
Wallacetown
Auchalton
Kilkerran
Knockgardner
Craig
Craigengillan
Glenmuck
Campbells Hill
1485
Dipple
Dailly
Bargany Gdn
Killochan Castle
Old Dailly
Maxwellston
Penkill
Hadyard Hill
1060
The Pilot
1260
Delamford
Knockdon
Big Hill of Glenmount
1253
Beoch
Loch Muck
Lamford
Lamford Hill
1308
Ailsa Craig
Chapeldonan
Girvan Mains
Girvan
Dounepark
Saugh Hill
971
Penwhapple Res.
Mull of Miljoan
1165
Dalquhairn
Milton
Garleffin Fell
1408
Linfern Loch
Tairlaw Ring
1263
Tairlaw Plantation
Loch Finlas
Loch Doon
Drumjohn
Woodland Bay
Tormitchell
1031
South Balloch
Balloch Plantation
Loch Lure
Loch Bradan
Craiglee
1715
Lamloch
Black Craig
1731
Ardwell
Grey Hill
975
Pinminnoch
Auchensoul
Barr
Changue Forest
Eldrick Hill
1593
Carrick Forest
Loch Riecawr
Craigmalloch
Carsphairn
Knocklaugh
Currarie
Straid
Pinmore
Stinchar
Cairnwhin
Pinclanty
Shalloch
1777
2522
Loch Macaterick
Macaterick
1637
Meaul
2281
Gala Lane
Lendalfoot
Carleton Castle
Knockdaw Hill
853
Pinmore Mains
Little Pinmore
Cairn Hill
1572
Craigenreoch
1854
Craigenrae
Castlemaddy
Thorny Hill
1240
Poundland
Pinwherry
Bellymore
Pindonan Craigs
1098
Loch Moan
Kirriereoch Hill
2565
Mullwharchar
2270
Corserine
2669
Loch Harrow
Knockdolian Castle
Colmonell
Pinwherry Hill
549
Muckfoot
Merrick
2770
Loch Enoch
Loch Dungeon
Knockdolian
870
Craigneil
Ballochmorrie
Black Clauchrie
Glen Trool National Forest Park
Palgowan
Ballantrae Bay
Heronsford
Knockdhu
756
Water of Tig
Loch Neldricken
Loch Valley
Meikle Millyea
2448
Ballantrae
Laggan
Balkissock
Shiel Hill
752
Barrhill
Laggan
Balunton Hill
1104
Water of Minnoch
Eldrick
Creeside
Loch Trool
Buchan
Craiglee
1743
Loch Dee
Glenapp Castle & Gardens
Downan
Auchencrosh
Big Fell
1033
Arecleoch Forest
Cairnderry
Glentrool Village
Glen of Trool
Upper Craigenbay
Ballochdoan
Beneraird
1439
Knockycoid
Drumlamford Loch
Ballochdowan
1046
Carlock Hill
Milljoan Hill
1321
Chirmorie
Dornal
Creebank
Loch Dornal
Bargrennan
Lamachan Hill
2350
Cairngarroch
1829
Craigencallie
Larg Hill
2216
Millfore
2152
CAR FERRY
CAR FERRY TO LARNE
ARDROSSAN TO DOUGLAS (I.O.M.)
Milleur Point
Corsewall Point
Barnhills
Water of App
Mark
Finnarts Bay
Miltonise
Craigairie Fell
1051
L. Derry
Loch Maberry
Polbae
Loch Ochiltree
Glenruther
928
Cardorcan
Kirroughtree Forest
Garlick Hill
1461
Craigdews
Round Fell
1320
Mid Moile
844
Stab Hill
725
Glenwhilly
Knowe
Murray's Monument
Penkiln Burn
South Cairn
Penwhirn Res.
Quarter Fell
834
Urrall Fell
605
Glassoch
Cairnryan
780
Loch Doon Hill
Main Water of Luce
Cross Water of Luce
Artfield Fell
888
Penninghame Forest
Palnure Burn
Cairnsmore of Fleet
Loch Grannoch
Mains of Airies
Kirkcolm
Loch Connell
Ervie
314
The Wig
Carseriggan
Glenhoise
Little Cairnbrock
Glengyre
Low Salchrie
Loch Ryan
Beoch
Cairnscarrow
751
New Luce
Balminnoch
Carsebuie
Colvennan Fell
700
Challoch
Minnigaff
Newton Stewart
Bargaly
2331
Clints of Dromore
Knocknain
Leswalt
Craigencross
Innermessan
Craigcaffie
L. Heron
Loch Ronald
Benfield
Shennanton
Low Knockbrex
Creebridge
Palnure
Craig Hill
1175
Lochnaw Castle
Glenstockadale
Stranraer
Lochinch Castle
Auchmantle
Castle Kennedy Gdn.
Craig Fell
538
Galdenoch
Drumpail
Bught Fell
670
Tart Water
Halfway House
Kirkcowan
Barraer Fell
403
Baltersan
Spittal
Auchnotteroch
Ochtrelure
Aird
Black Loch
White Loch
Castle Kennedy
Whitecairn
Carscreugh
321
Causeway End
Lennies
Carsegown
Creetown
Knockglass
Soulseat Loch
Challoch Hill
484
Dunragit
Glenluce
Knock Moss
Dernaglar Loch
High Mindork
Spittal
Torhousemuir
Little Torhouse
Culquhirk
Wigtown Sands
969
Glen
Black Head
Lochans
593
Genoch Square
Whitecrook
Castle of Park
Whitefield Loch
428
Bladnoch
Carsluith
Cairnharrow
1496
Cardoness
Dinvin
Danger Area
Crows
Wigtown
Logganmullan
Portpatrick
Dunskey Castle
Awhirk
Torrs Warren
Milton
430
Castle Loch
Fell Loch
Old Place of Mochdrum
Drumwalt
Low Malzie
Mochrum Loch
Corsemalzie
Culmalzie
Baldoon Sands
Cairn Holy
Kirkdale House
Ravenshall Point
Port of Spittal Bay
Stoneykirk
Luce Sands
Auchenmalg
Braehead
Kirkinner
Dalvadie
Auchenmalg Bay
Culshabbin
Mochrum Fell
646
Alticry
Loch Head
Innerwell Fishery
Cairngarroch
Cairngarroch Bay
Sandhead
Sandhead Bay
Chapel Finian
Barrachan
Whauphill
Auchentibbert
Cairnfield
Culscadden
Money Head
Elrig
Longcastle
Wigtown Bay
Hole Stone Bay
Low Ardwell
Ardwell
West Barr
Airyhassen
Sorbie
Garlieston
Penkiln
Ardwell House
Chapel Rossan Bay
Chapel Rossan
Mochrum
Milton Point
Eggerness Point
Ardwell Point
Drummoddie
Balgown Point
Luce Bay
Port William
Drumrae
Cults
Cruggleton Castle (Rmns.)
Logan Mains
Logan Botanic Gdns
Mull of Logan
Port Nessock or Port Logan Bay
Monreith Mains
Kirkland
Port Allen
Barsalloch Fort
Barsalloch Point
Monreith
Priory
Whithorn
Port Logan
Terally
Monreith Bay
Portyerrock Bay
398
Garrochtrie
Kilstay Bay
Point of Cairndoon
Carleton
Fell of Carleton
480
Glasserton
Portyerrock
Cairn Head
Clanyard Bay
Clanyard
Arbrack
Logganalloch Head
Kirkmaiden
Drummore
St. Ninian's Cave
Isle of Whithorn
St. Ninian's Chapel
Barncorkrie
Damnaglaur
Cailliness Point
Port Castle Bay
Crammag Head
Maryport
Maryport Bay
Cutcloy
East Muntloch
Burrow Head
Cairngaan
Port Kemin
Mull of Galloway

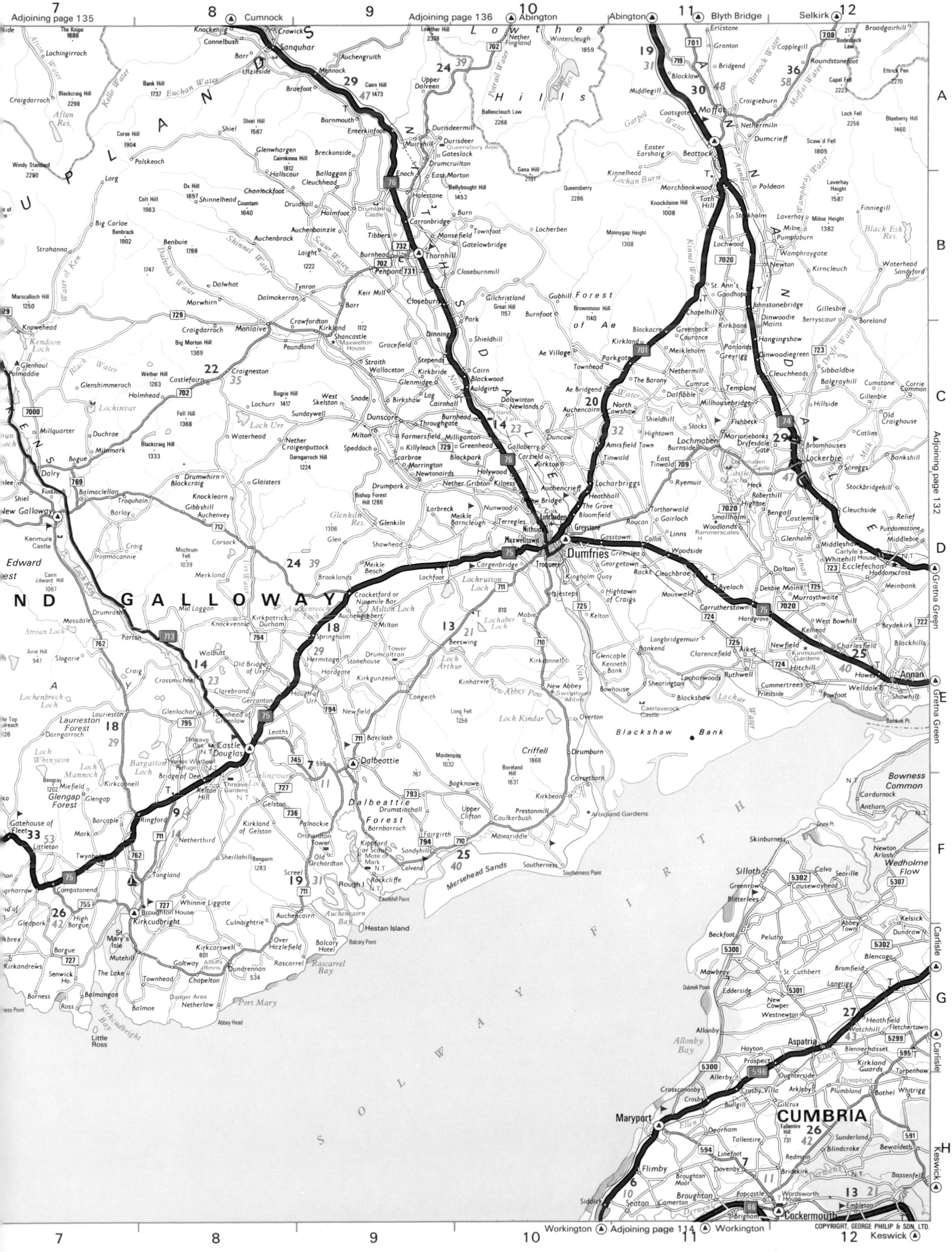
Adjoining page 135
Adjoining page 136
Adjoining page 132
Adjoining page 114
Cumnock
Abington
Blyth Bridge
Selkirk
Gretna Green
Carlisle
Keswick
Workington
U P L A N D S
L o w t h e r   H i l l s
N I T H S D A L E
A N N A N D A L E
N D   G A L L O W A Y
S O L W A Y   F I R T H
CUMBRIA
Sanquhar
Moffat
Beattock
Thornhill
Penpont
Moniaive
Dumfries
Maxwelltown
Lochmaben
Lockerbie
Ecclefechan
Annan
Castle Douglas
Dalbeattie
Kirkcudbright
Gatehouse of Fleet
New Galloway
Dalry
Silloth
Aspatria
Maryport
Cockermouth
Criffell
Hestan Island
Little Ross
Blackshaw Bank
Mersehead Sands
Allonby Bay
Rascarrel Bay
Kirkcudbright Bay
Auchencairn Bay
Port Mary
Loch Ken
Loch Urr
Loch Arthur
Loch Kindar
Afton Res.
Kendoon Loch
Lochinvar
Glenkiln Res.
Dalbeattie Forest
Forest of Ae
Laurieston Forest
Glengap Forest
Wedholme Flow
Bowness Common
COPYRIGHT, GEORGE PHILIP & SON, LTD.

1 Adjoining page 136 Selkirk 2 3 Selkirk 4 Adjoining page 137 Lauder 5 Kelso 6

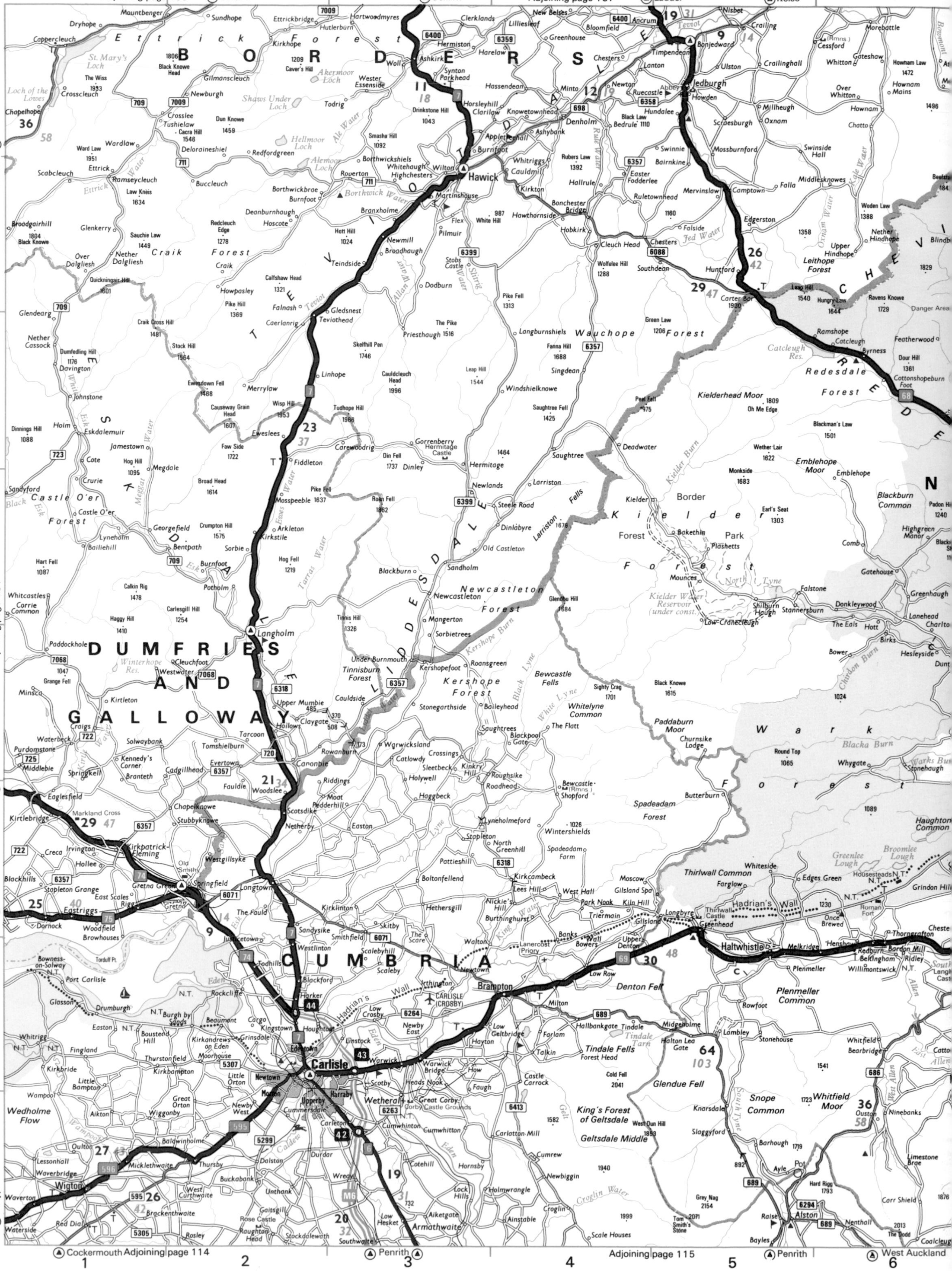

Beattock
Adjoining page 131
Beattock
Dumfries
Maryport

A B C D E F G H

Cockermouth Adjoining page 114 Penrith Adjoining page 115 Penrith West Auckland

Adjoining page 137

7 8 9 10 11 12

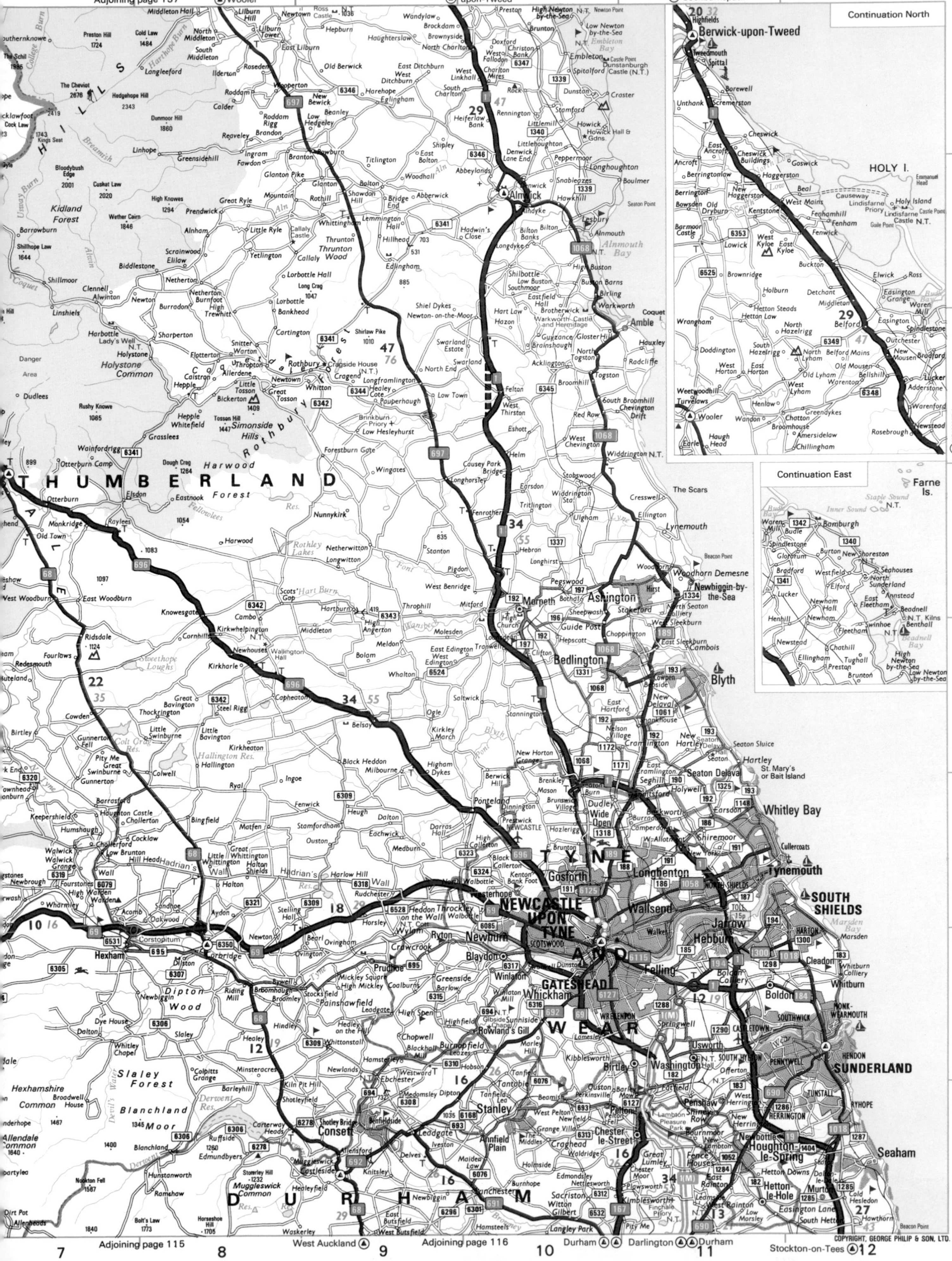

Adjoining page 115 Adjoining page 116

7 8 9 10 11 12

Adjoining page 138
Oban
Inveraray
Strachur
Adjoining page 139
JURA
Killchianaig
Ardlussa
Tarbert
Lagg
Knockrome
Leargybreck
Feolin Ferry
SOUND OF JURA
Carsaig
Tayvallich
Achanamara
Kilmichael of Inverlussa
Lochgilphead
Ardrishaig
Achnaba
Castleton
Keillmore
I. of Danna
Loch Sween
Achahoish
Ormsary Ho.
Kilmory
Brenfield
Auchbraad
Creagan Beag
Erines
Stonefield Castle Hotel
Barmore Island
Barfad
Tarbert
West Tarbert
Escart
Corranbuie
Rhu
Kilberry
Dunmore
Ardpatrick
Ardpatrick Ho.
Kennacraig
Redhouse
Whitehouse
Garthagrenach
Portachoillan
Eilean Traighe
Clachan
Achaglachgach Forest
Glenrisdell
Skipness
Skipness Castle
Claonaig
KNAPDALE
LOCH FYNE
Otter Ferry
Auchnaha
Kilfinan
Kilfinan Bay
Acharosson
Drum
Melldalloch
Auchalick Bay
Tighnabruaich
Kames
Millhouse
Portavadie
Blair's Ferry
Ardlamont House
Kildavanan
Eilean Aoidhe
Glendaruel
Clachan of Glendaruel
Ardachearanbeg
Conchra
Glendaruel Forest
Largiemore
The Highland Hotel
Auchenbreck
Ardachuple
Port an Eilein
Ardentraive
Colintraive
Altgaltraig
Rhubodach
South Hall
Kyles of Bute
Glen Massan
Glenmassan
Younger Botanic Garden
Invechaolain
Rashfield
Dalinlongart
Sandbank
Clachaig
BUTE
Ardmaleish
Port Bannatyne
Ardbeg
Rothesay
Rothesay Bay
Craigmore
Ascog
Ballochgoy
Ballianlay
Straad
Meikle Grenach
Upper Scoulag
Kerrylamont
Kingarth
Kerrytonlia
Kilchattan
South Garrochty
Inchmarnock
STRAIT
GREAT CUMBRAE ISLAND
Little Cumbrae I.
Sound of Bute
Toward
Toward Quay
Port Lamont
Innellan
Dunan
CAR FERRY
TO PORT ASKAIG
GIGHA
Kinerarach
Ardminish
Achamore Farm
Achamore Gardens
South Druimachro
Gigalum I.
Cara I.
West Tarbert Bay
East Tarbert Bay
Sound of Gigha
Ballochroy
Auchinadrian
Loch Garasdale
Rhunahaorine
Largie Castle
Tayinloan
Killean
A' Chleit
Muasdale
Belloch
Glenbarr
Bellochantuy
Bellochantuy Bay
Westport
Kilchenzie
Crossaig
Crossaig Glen
Cour
Grogport
Brackley
Carradale Forest
Carradale
Dippen
Torris Dale
Carradale House and Garden
Saddell
Saddell Bay
Saddell Glen
Ugadale
Skeroblingarry
Peninver
Milton of Smerby
Kilmichael
E. Darlochan
W. Darlochan
CAMPBELTOWN (MACHRIHANISH)
Machrihanish
Machrihanish Bay
Campbeltown
Campbeltown Loch
Island Davaar
Stewarton
Drumlemble
Kildalloig
Killellan
Feochaig
Kilkerran
Culinlongart
Kepprigan
Benton Polliwilline
Polliwilline Bay
North Carrine
South Carrine
Carskiey
Southend
Glemanuilt
Brunerican Bay
KINTYRE
KILBRANNAN SOUND
ARRAN
Lochranza
Catacol
Catacol Bay
Mid Thundergay
Pirnmill
Whitefarland
Imachar
Dougarie
Auchagallon
Machrie Bay
Tormore
Torbeg
Blackwaterfoot
Drumadoon Bay
South Feorline
North Feorline
Kilpatrick
Shiskine
Corriecravie
Sliddery
Lagg
Kilmory
Bennecarrigan
Shannochie
Levencorroch
Kildonan
Pladda
Sound of Pladda
Dippin
Largymore
Whiting Bay
Knockenkelly
Kingscross
Monamore Br.
Lamlash
Lamlash Bay
Holy Island
Margnaheglish
Corrygills
Brodick
Brodick Bay
Glencloy
Brodick Castle N.T.
Glenloig
Corrie
Mid Sannox
Sannox Bay
Glen Sannox
Goat Fell 2866
Glen Rosa
Glen Iorsa
Loch Tanna
ARDROSSAN TO DOUGLAS (I.O.M.)
FIRTH OF CLYDE

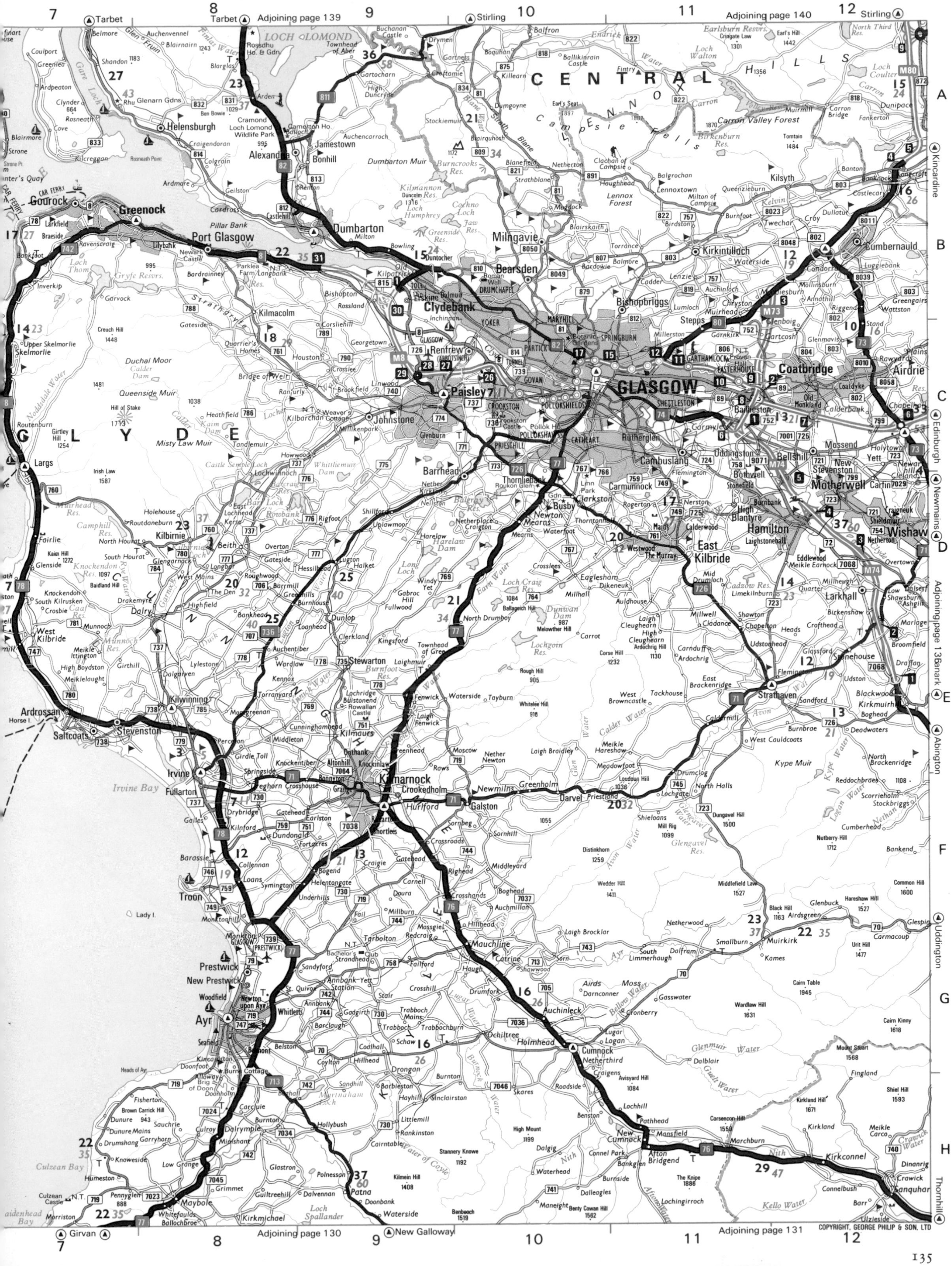

Adjoining page 139
Adjoining page 140
Adjoining page 130
Adjoining page 131
Adjoining page 136
Tarbet
Stirling
Kincardine
Edinburgh
Newmains
Lanark
Abington
Uddington
Thornhill
New Galloway
Girvan
7
8
9
10
11
12
A
B
C
D
E
F
G
H
CENTRAL
HILLS
LENNOX
Campsie Fells
CLYDE
CUNNINGHAME
LOCH LOMOND
GLASGOW
Paisley
Clydebank
Greenock
Gourock
Port Glasgow
Dumbarton
Helensburgh
Alexandria
Jamestown
Bonhill
Milngavie
Bearsden
Bishopbriggs
Kirkintilloch
Kilsyth
Cumbernauld
Coatbridge
Airdrie
Motherwell
Wishaw
Hamilton
East Kilbride
Rutherglen
Cambuslang
Uddingston
Bellshill
Barrhead
Johnstone
Renfrew
Erskine
Kilmacolm
Bridge of Weir
Largs
Skelmorlie
Fairlie
West Kilbride
Ardrossan
Saltcoats
Stevenston
Kilwinning
Irvine
Kilbirnie
Beith
Dalry
Stewarton
Kilmarnock
Kilmaurs
Galston
Newmilns
Darvel
Hurlford
Troon
Prestwick
New Prestwick
Ayr
Mauchline
Catrine
Auchinleck
Cumnock
New Cumnock
Strathaven
Larkhall
Stonehouse
Kirkmuirhill
Muirkirk
Sanquhar
Kirkconnel
Maybole
Dalrymple
Patna
Drongan
Kirkmichael
Culzean Bay
Irvine Bay
Lady I.
Horse I.
Kype Muir
Misty Law Muir
Duchal Moor
Dumbarton Muir
Carron Valley Forest
Lennox Forest
COPYRIGHT, GEORGE PHILIP & SON, LTD

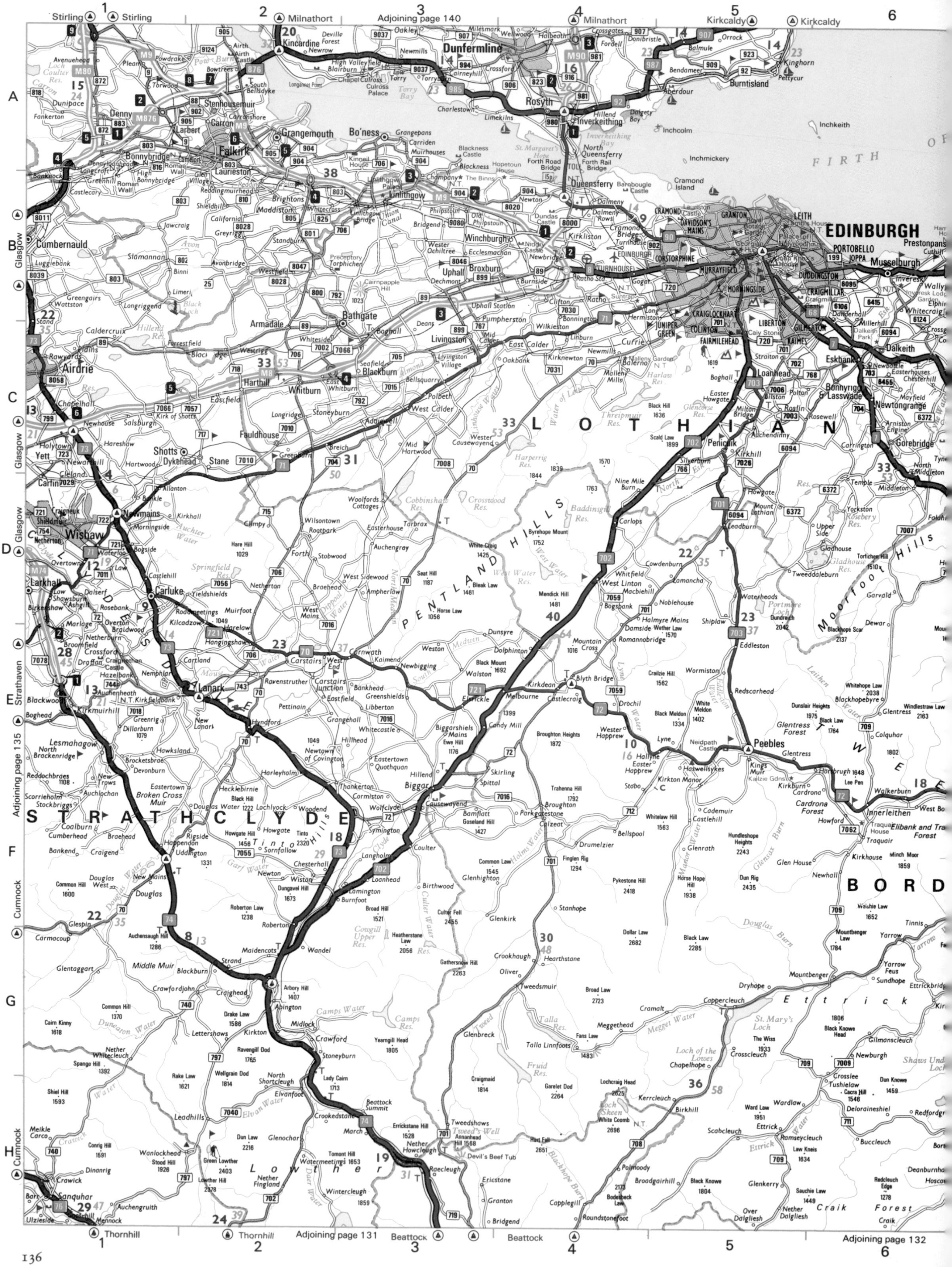
Adjoining page 140
Adjoining page 131
Adjoining page 132
Adjoining page 135
Stirling
Milnathort
Kirkcaldy
Glasgow
Strathaven
Cumnock
Thornhill
Beattock
FIRTH OF
EDINBURGH
Dunfermline
Falkirk
Grangemouth
Bo'ness
Linlithgow
Queensferry
Livingston
Bathgate
Airdrie
Wishaw
Lanark
Biggar
Peebles
Dalkeith
Penicuik
Musselburgh
L O T H I A N
S T R A T H C L Y D E
B O R D
PENTLAND HILLS
Moorfoot Hills
Tinto Hills
Lowther
Ettrick
Craik Forest
T W E E D

7 8 9 10 11 12

Adjoining page 141

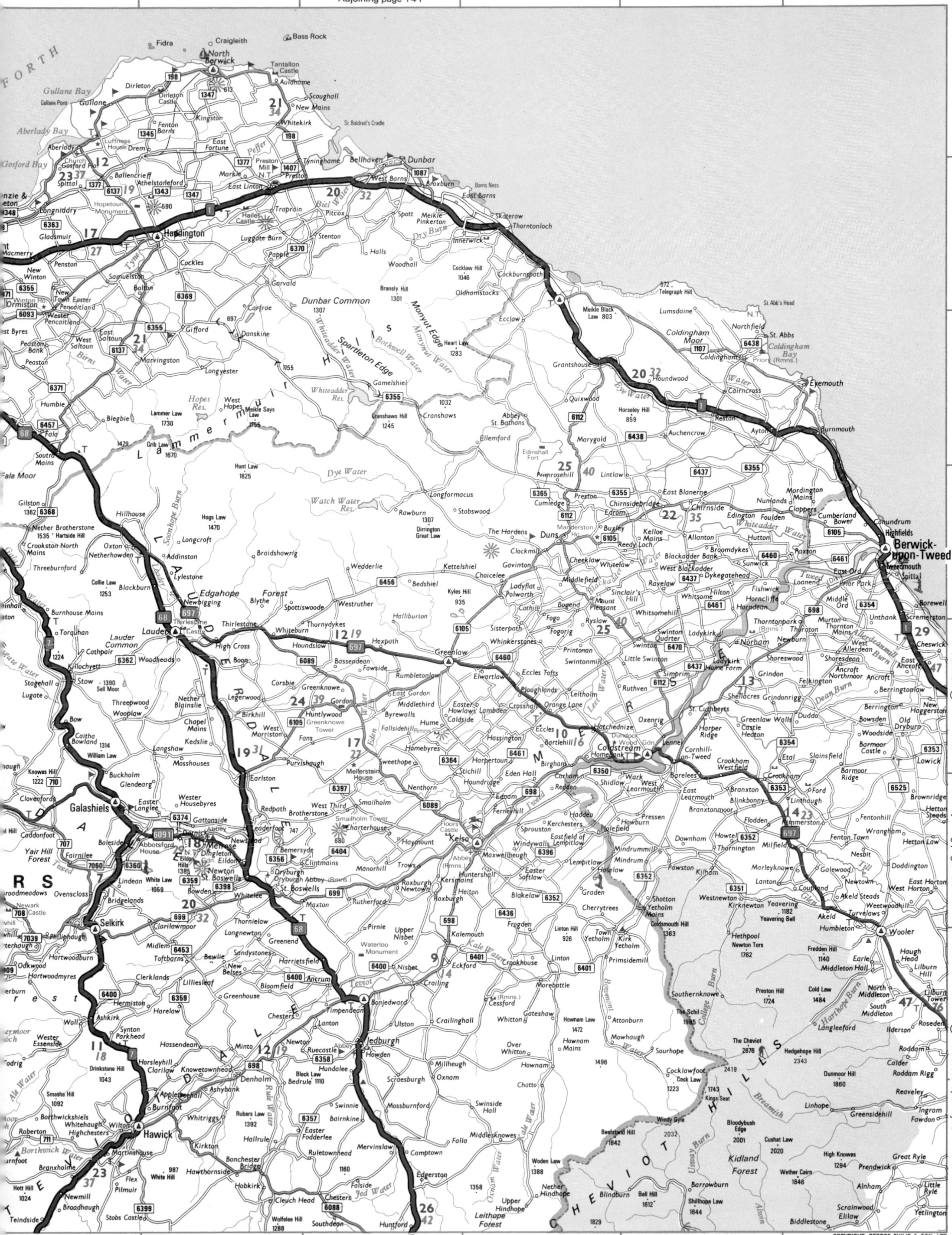

Adjoining page 132
Adjoining page 133
Adjoining page 133

7 8 9 10 11 12

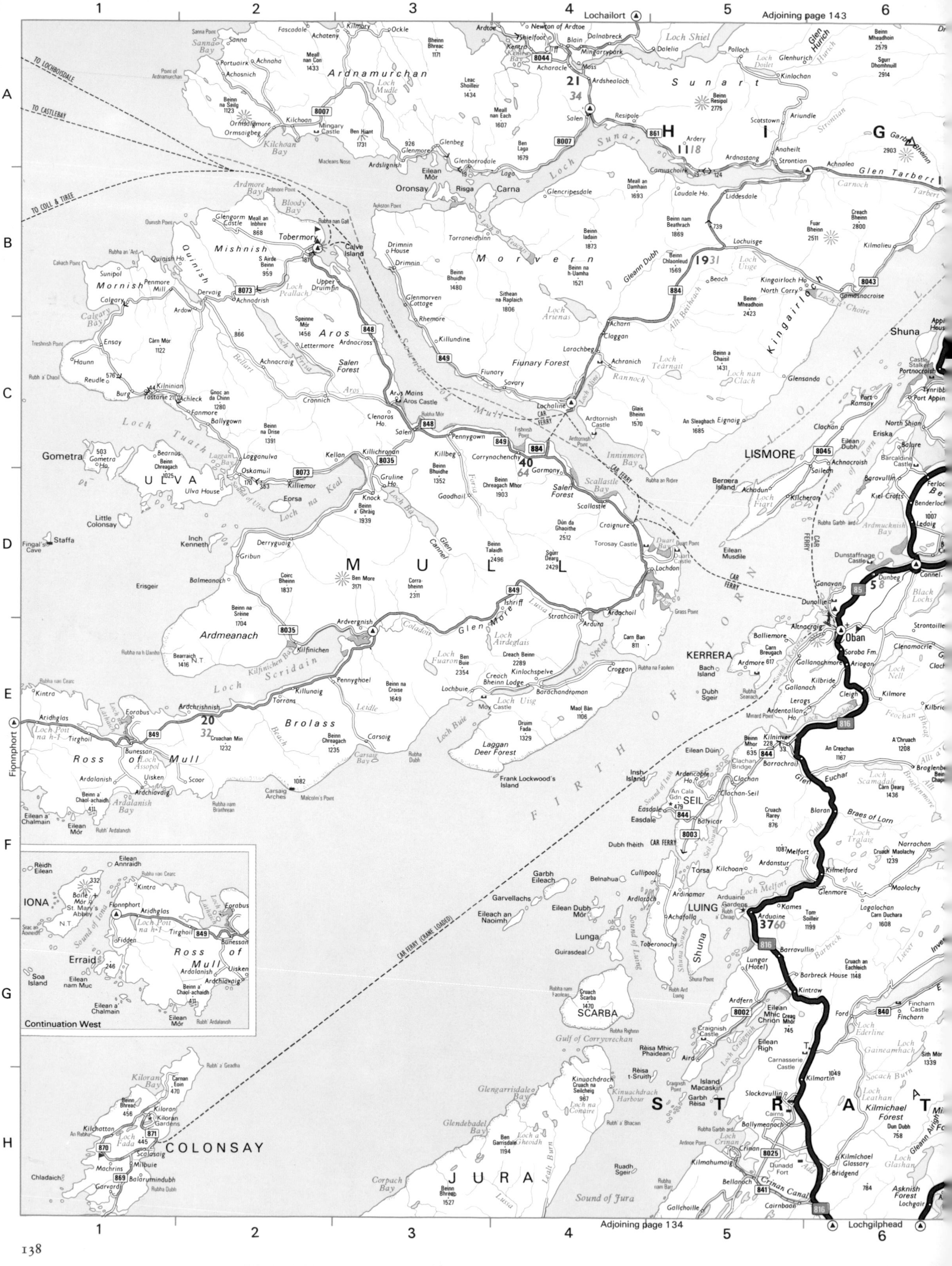

Lochailort
Adjoining page 143
Ardnamurchan
Sanna Point
Sanna
Sanna Bay
Fascadale
Achateny
Kilmory
Ockle
Portuairk
Achnaha
Achosnich
Beinn na Seilg 1123
Ormsaigmore
Ormsaigbeg
Kilchoan
Kilchoan Bay
Mingary Castle
Ben Hiant 1731
Meall nan Con 1433
Bheinn Bhreac 1171
Loch Mudle
Leac Shoilleir 1434
Meall nan Each 1607
Ben Laga 1679
Glenbeg
Glenmore
Glenborrodale
Macleans Nose
Ardslignish
Eilean Mòr
Oronsay
Risga
Carna
Laga
Ardtoe
Newton of Ardtoe
Shielfoot
Kentra
Kentra Bay
Blain
Dalnabreck
Mingarrypark
Acharacle
Moss
Ardshealach
Salen
Resipole
Loch Sunart
Loch Shiel
Dalelia
Polloch
Loch Doilet
Glenhurich
Glen Hurich
Kinlochan
Sunart
Beinn Resipol 2775
Ardery
Scotstown
Ariundle
Strontian
Anaheilt
Ardnastang
Camuschoirk
Glencripesdale
Meall an Damhain 1693
Laudale Ho.
Liddesdale
Beinn Mheadhoin 2579
Sgurr Dhomhnuill 2914
Garbh Bheinn 2903
Achnalea
Glen Tarbert
Carnoch
Tarbert
TO LOCHBOISDALE
TO CASTLEBAY
TO COLL & TIREE
Ardmore Bay
Ardmore Point
Bloody Bay
Auliston Point
Quinish Point
Glengorm Castle
Meall an Inbhire 868
Tobermory
Rubha nan Gall
Calve Island
Mishnish
Quinish
Quinish Ho.
S Airde Beinn 959
Rubha an 'Ard
Caliach Point
Sunipol
Mornish
Penmore Mill
Dervaig
Achnadrish
Loch Peallach
Upper Druimfin
Calgary
Calgary Bay
Ardow
Speinne Mòr 1456
Aros
Ardnacross
Lettermore
Loch Frisa
Salen Forest
Treshnish Point
Ensay
Càrn Mòr 1122
Haunn
Reudle
Burg
Kilninian
Tostarie
Achleck
Gnoc an da Chinn 1280
Fanmore
Ballygown
Achnacraig
Bellart
Cronnich
Aros Mains
Aros Castle
Clenaros Ho.
Salen
Drimnin House
Drimnin
Torraneidhinn
Morvern
Beinn Bhuidhe 1480
Glenmorven Cottage
Rhemore
Killundine
Sithean na Raplaich 1806
Loch Arienas
Beinn Iadain 1873
Beinn na h-Uamha 1521
Fiunary
Fiunary Forest
Savary
Lochaline
Larachbeg
Achranich
Loch Tearnait
Rannoch
Beinn Chlaonleud 1569
Loch Uisge
Gleann Dubh
Beinn nam Beathrach 1869
Fuar Bheinn 2511
Creach Bheinn 2800
Lochuisge
Kilmalieu
Beach
Kingairloch Ho.
North Corry
Camasnacroise
Loch a' Choire
Beinn Mheadhoin 2423
Kingairloch
Beinn a Chaisil 1431
Loch nan Clach
Glensanda
Shuna
Castle Stalker
Portnacroish
Port Ramsay
Tynribbie
Port Appin
Loch Linnhe
Glais Bheinn 1570
Ardtornish Castle
Ardtornish Point
An Sleaghach 1685
Eignaig
Inninmore Bay
Rubha an Ridire
Clachan
North Shian
Eriska
Eilean Dubh
Balure
Barcaldine Castle
LISMORE
Achnacroish
Saileán
Baravullin
Bernera Island
Achadun
Loch Fiart
Kilcheran
Lynn of Lorn
Kiel Crofts
Benderloch
Ledaig
Rubha Garbh-àird
Ardmucknish Bay
Gometra
Gometra Ho.
Beinn nà Drise 1391
Loch Tuath
Beàrnus
Beinn Chreagach 1025
Laggan Bay
Lagganulva
Oskamuil
Killiemor
ULVA
Ulva House
Sound of Ulva
Kellan
Killichronan
Gruline Ho.
Killbeg
Pennygown
Fishnish Point
Corrynachenchy
Garmony
Beinn Bhuidhe 1352
Beinn Chreagach Mhor 1903
Gaodhail
Forsa
Salen Forest
Scallastle Bay
Scallastle
Sound of Mull
Loch na Keal
Eorsa
Knock
Beinn a' Ghràig 1939
Little Colonsay
Staffa
Fingal's Cave
Inch Kenneth
Derryguaig
Gribun
Glen Cannel
Dùn da Ghaoithe 2512
Craignure
Torosay Castle
Duart Bay
Duart Castle
Duart Point
Beinn Talaidh 2496
Sgùrr Dearg 2429
MULL
Coirc Bheinn 1837
Ben More 3171
Corra-bheinn 2311
Erisgeir
Balmeanach
Beinn na Srèine 1704
Ardmeanach
Ardvergnish
Ishriff
Lussa
Glen More
Strathcoil
Ardura
Ardachoil
Lochdon
Grass Point
Eilean Musdile
Dunstaffnage Castle
Dunbeg
Connel
Black Lochs
Ganavan
Dunollie
Oban
Altnacraig
Soroba Fm.
Strontoille
Balliemore
Carn Breugach 617
KERRERA
Ardmore
Bach Island
Gallanachmore
Gallanach
Ariogan
Clenamacrie
Loch Nell
Kilbride
Cleigh
Kilmore
Coladoir
Loch Airdeglais
Rubha na h-Uamha
Bearraich 1416
Kilfinichen
Kilfinichen Bay
Loch Scridain
Loch Fuaron
Ben Buie 2354
Creach Beinn 2289
Kinlochspelve
Loch Spelve
Croggan
Rubha na Faoilinn
Carn Ban 811
Creach Bheinn Lodge
Lochbuie
Loch Uisg
Barachandroman
Moy Castle
Maol Bàn 1106
Dubh Sgeir
Rubha Seanach
Lerags
Ardentallan Ho.
Minard Point
Feochan Bhag
Rubha nan Cearc
Kintra
Aridhglas
Eorabus
Loch Lathaich
Ardchrishnish
Torrans
Killunaig
Pennyghael
Beinn na Croise 1649
Leidle
Fionnphort
Loch Poit na h-I
Tirghoil
Bunessan
Loch Assopol
Uisken
Ross of Mull
Cruachan Min 1232
Brolass
Beach
Beinn Chreagach 1235
Carsaig
Carsaig Bay
Rubha Dubh
Loch Buie
Druim Fada 1329
Laggan Deer Forest
Scoor
Ardalanish
Ardchiavaig
Beinn a' Chaol-achaidh 411
Ardalanish Bay
Eilean a' Chalmain
Eilean Mòr
Rubh' Ardalanish
Rubha nam Bràithrean
Carsaig Arches
Malcolm's Point
Frank Lockwood's Island
Firth of Lorn
Eilean Dùin
Insh Island
Beinn Mhor 635
Kilninver
Clachan Bridge
Clachan
Barrachrail
Glen Euchar
An Creachan 1167
A' Chruach 1208
Loch Scamadale
Carn Dearg 1436
Braes of Lorn
Ardencaple Ho.
An Cala Gdn
SEIL
Clachan-Seil
Easdale
Balvicar
Sound of Insh
Cruach Rarey 876
Blaran
Loch Tralaig
Narrachan
Cruach Maolachy 1239
Dubh fhèith
CAR FERRY
Melfort
Ardanstur
Kilmelford
Glenmore
Maolachy
Garbh Eileach
Belnahua
Cullipool
Torsa
Kilchoan
Loch Melfort
Garvellachs
Eileach an Naoimh
Eilean Dubh Mòr
Ardlarach
Ardinamar
LUING
Arduaine Gardens
Kames
Tom Soilleir 1199
Arduaine
Lagalochan
Carn Duchara 1608
Achafolla
Lunga
Sound of Luing
Toberonochy
Shuna
Shuna Sound
Guirasdeal
Barravullin
Barbreck
Lungar (Hotel)
Barbreck House
Cruach an Eachlaich 1148
Shuna Point
Rubha nam Faoileag
Cruach Scarba 1470
SCARBA
Kintraw
Ardfern
Eilean Mhic Chrion
Creag Mhor 745
Ford
Fincharn Castle
Fincharn
Loch Ederline
Craignish Castle
Loch Craignish
Gulf of Corryvreckan
Rèisa Mhic Phaidean
Eilean Righ
Aird
Carnasserie Castle
Kilmartin
Loch Gaineamhach
Sith Mòr 1339
Rèisa t-Sruith
Kinuachdrach
Cruach na Seilcheig 967
Kinuachdrach Harbour
Island Macaskin
Garbh Rèisa
Slockavullin
Socach Burn
Loch Leathan
Kilmichael Forest
Dun Dubh 758
STRATHCLYDE
Glengarrisdale Bay
Loch na Conaire
Rubh' a' Bhacain
Cairns
Ballymeanoch
Ardnoe Point
Loch Crinan
Crinan
Dunadd Fort
Kilmichael Glassary
Bridgend
Loch Glashan
Kilmahumaig
Bellanoch
Crinan Canal
Cairnbaan
Gallchoille
Asknish Forest
Lochgair
Glendebadel Bay
Ben Garrisdale 1194
Loch a Gheoidh
Lealt Burn
Ruadh Sgeir
Rubha nam Bart
Sound of Jura
Corpach Bay
Beinn Bhreac 1527
JURA
Lussa
Adjoining page 134
Lochgilphead
Kiloran Bay
Carnan Eoin 470
Beinn Bhreac 456
Kiloran
Kiloran Gardens
Kilchattan
Loch Fada
Scalasaig
COLONSAY
Machrins
Milbuie
Balarumindubh
Garvard
Chladaich
Rubha Dubh
Rubh' a Geodha
CAR FERRY (CRANE LOADED)
CAR FERRY
Continuation West
IONA
Rèidh Eilean
Eilean Annraidh
Baile Mòr
St. Mary's Abbey
Sound of Iona
Erraid
Soa Island
Eilean nam Muc
Eilean a' Chalmain
Eilean Mòr
Rubh' Ardalanish

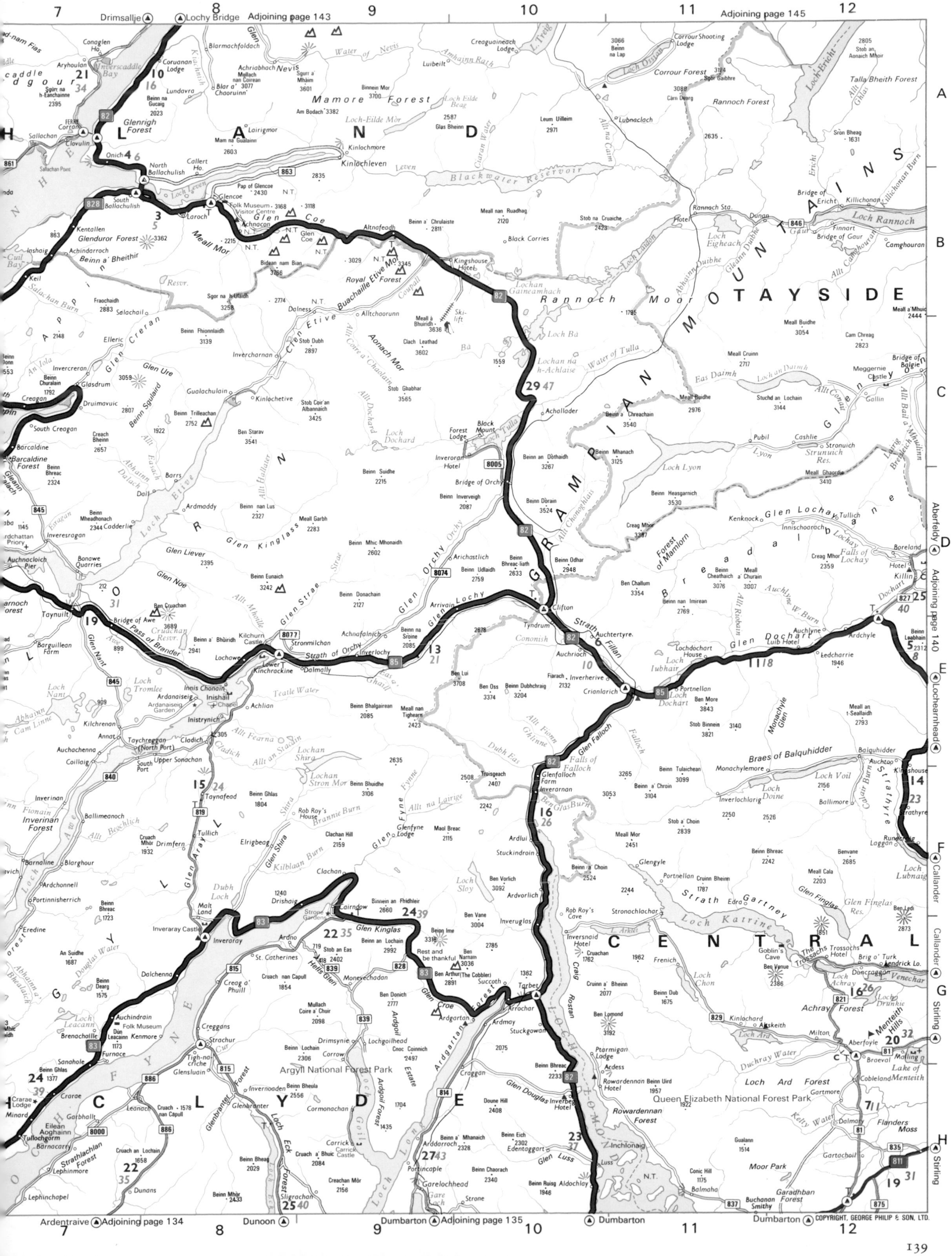

Drimsallie
Lochy Bridge
Adjoining page 143
Adjoining page 145
Adjoining page 134
Adjoining page 135
Adjoining page 140
Ardentraive
Dunoon
Dumbarton
Aberfeldy
Lochearnhead
Callander
Stirling
COPYRIGHT, GEORGE PHILIP & SON, LTD.
HIGHLAND
GRAMPIAN MOUNTAINS
TAYSIDE
CENTRAL
CLYDE
ARGYLL
Mamore Forest
Glen Nevis
Water of Nevis
Kinlochleven
Loch Leven
Blackwater Reservoir
Glencoe
Glen Coe
Rannoch Moor
Loch Rannoch
Rannoch Forest
Corrour Forest
Loch Ossian
Loch Ericht
Talla Bheith Forest
Rannoch Sta.
Bridge of Gaur
Kinlochmore
North Ballachulish
South Ballachulish
Onich
Glenrigh Forest
Kentallen
Glenduror Forest
Kingshouse Hotel
Buachaille Etive Mor
Royal Forest
Glen Etive
Loch Etive
Loch Creran
Glen Creran
Glen Ure
Glen Kinglass
Glen Strae
Glen Orchy
Glen Lochy
Strath of Orchy
Bridge of Orchy
Inveroran Hotel
Loch Tulla
Black Mount
Loch Ba
Forest Lodge
Loch Lyon
Glen Lochay
Glen Lyon
Breadalbane
Forest of Mamlorn
Tyndrum
Clifton
Strath Fillan
Crianlarich
Glen Dochart
Loch Dochart
Killin
Ben Lui
Ben More
Braes of Balquhidder
Balquhidder
Loch Voil
Loch Doine
Strathyre
Dalmally
Loch Awe
Pass of Brander
Ben Cruachan
Taynuilt
Bonawe Quarries
Kilchurn Castle
Inveraray
Inveraray Castle
Loch Fyne
Glen Shira
Glen Aray
Glen Fyne
Glen Kinglas
Cairndow
Rest and be thankful
Ben Arthur (The Cobbler)
Glen Croe
Arrochar
Tarbet
Loch Lomond
Ben Lomond
Loch Katrine
Loch Arklet
Inversnaid Hotel
Stronachlachar
The Trossachs
Ben Venue
Loch Achray
Loch Venachar
Ben Ledi
Loch Lubnaig
Glen Finglas
Strath Gartney
Loch Chon
Loch Ard
Loch Ard Forest
Aberfoyle
Menteith Hills
Lake of Menteith
Queen Elizabeth National Forest Park
Rowardennan Forest
Inverbeg Hotel
Glen Douglas
Glen Luss
Luss
Inchlonaig
Balmaha
Drymen
Gartmore
Flanders Moss
Moor Park
Garadhban Forest
Argyll National Forest Park
Ardgoil Estate
Lochgoilhead
Loch Goil
Loch Long
Loch Eck
Garelochhead
Gare Loch
Strachur
Furnace
Auchindrain
Crarae
Minard
Strathlachlan Forest
Inverinan Forest
Kilchrenan
Portsonachan
Cladich
Lochawe
Loch Awe
Ardanaiseig

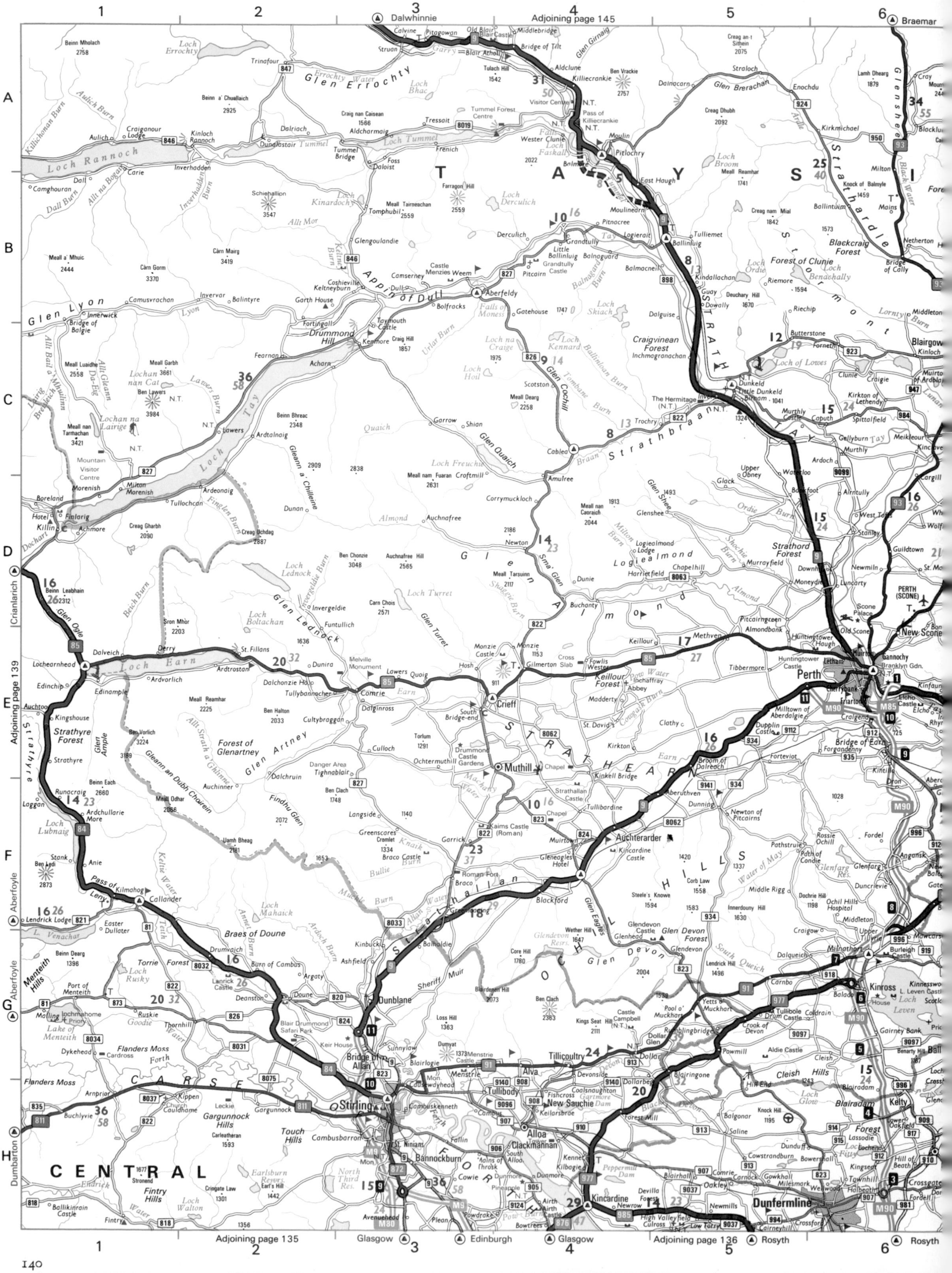

Dalwhinnie
Adjoining page 145
Braemar
Adjoining page 139
Adjoining page 135
Adjoining page 136
Glasgow
Edinburgh
Rosyth
Crianlarich
Aberfoyle
Dumbarton
T A Y S I D E
CENTRAL
Loch Rannoch
Loch Errochty
Glen Errochty
Loch Tummel
Loch Bhac
Trinafour
Struan
Calvine
Pitagowan
Old Blair
Blair Castle
Blair Atholl
Middlebridge
Bridge of Tilt
Glen Girnaig
Tulach Hill 1542
Aldclune
Killiecrankie
Pass of Killiecrankie
Visitor Centre
Ben Vrackie 2757
Moulin
Pitlochry
Loch Faskally
Wester Clunie
Tummel Forest Centre
Tressait
Aldchamaig
Dalriach
Dunalastair
Tummel Bridge
Foss
Daloist
Frenich
Kinloch Rannoch
Craiganour Lodge
Aulich
Aulich Burn
Killichonan Burn
Carie
Inverhadden
Camghouran
Dall
Dall Burn
Allt na Bogair
Beinn Mholach 2758
Beinn a' Chuallaich 2925
Craig nan Caisean 1566
Schiehallion 3547
Loch Kinardochy
Tomphubil
Meall Tairneachan 2559
Farragon Hill 2559
Loch Derculich
Derculich
Allt Mor
Glengoulandie
Keltney Burn
Coshieville
Keltneyburn
Dull
Appin of Dull
Camserney
Castle Menzies
Weem
Aberfeldy
Bolfracks
Falls of Moness
Garth House
Fortingall
Taymouth Castle
Drummond Hill
Kenmore
Craig Hill 1857
Glen Lyon
Camusvrachan
Invervar
Balintyre
Innerwick
Bridge of Balgie
Càrn Mairg 3419
Càrn Gorm 3370
Meall a' Mhuic 2444
Meall Luaidhe 2558
Meall Garbh 3661
Lochan nan Cat
Ben Lawers 3984
Lochan na Lairige
Meall nan Tarmachan 3421
Mountain Visitor Centre
Lawers
Ardtalnaig
Loch Tay
Fearnan
Acharn
Milton Morenish
Morenish
Ardeonaig
Tullochcan
Finglen Burn
Boreland
Hotel
Killin
Finlarig
Achmore
Dochart
Creag Gharbh 2090
Creag Uchdag 2887
Beinn Bhreac 2348
Gleann a' Chilleine
Quaich
Garrow
Shian
Glen Quaich
Loch Freuchie
Croftmill
Meall nam Fuaran 2631
Amulree
Corrymuckloch
Dunan
Almond
Auchnafree
Newton
Glen Almond
Sma' Glen
Meall Tarsuinn 2117
Ben Chonzie 3048
Auchnafree Hill 2565
Loch Lednock
Invergeldie
Glen Lednock
Funtullich
Carn Chois 2571
Loch Turret
Glen Turret
Loch Boltachan
Sron Mhòr 2203
Derry
St. Fillans
Loch Earn
Ardtrostan
Dalveich
Lochearnhead
Ardvorlich
Edinample
Edinchip
Glen Ogle
Beinn Leabhain 2312
Dunira
Melville Monument
Lawers
Quoig
Comrie
Dalchonzie
Tullybannocher
Dalginross
Cultybraggan
Ben Halton 2033
Meall Reamhar 2225
Forest of Glenartney
Glen Artney
Ben Vorlich 3224
Glen Ampil
Strathyre Forest
Kingshouse
Strathyre
Auchtoo
Gleann an Dubh Choirein
Auchinner
Dalchruin
Danger Area
Tighnablair
Beinn Each 2660
Runacraig
Laggan
Loch Lubnaig
Ardchullarie More
Meall Odhar 2066
Findhu Glen
Stank
Ben Ledi 2873
Anie
Pass of Leny
Kilmahog
Callander
Uamh Bheag 2181
Culloch
Torlum 1291
Ochtermuthill
Drummond Castle Gardens
Muthill
Chapel
Strathallan Castle
Tullibardine
Langside
Greenscares
Cromlet 1334
Braco Castle
Braco
Roman Fort
Kaims Castle (Roman)
Garrick
Bullie
Knaik
Machany Water
Crieff
South Bridge-end
Hosh
Monzie Castle
Monzie
Gilmerton
Cross Slab
Fowlis Wester
Keillour Forest
Inchaffray Abbey
Madderty
St. David's
Clathy
Kirkton
Kinkell Bridge
Strathearn
Earn
Broom of Dalreoch
Aberuthven
Dunning
Auchterarder
Kincardine Castle
Gleneagles Hotel
Muirtown
Blackford
Glen Eagles
Glendevon Castle
Glen Devon Forest
Glenhead
Glendevon
Glen Devon
Ochil Hills
Wether Hill 1647
Core Hill 1780
Sheriff Muir
Blairdenon Hill 2073
Ben Cleuch 2363
Kings Seat Hill 2111
Castle Campbell (N.T.)
Dollar
Dollar Glen
Tillicoultry
Alva
Menstrie
Dumyat 1373
Menstrie Castle
Blairlogie
Bridge of Allan
Dunblane
Keir House
Sunnylaw
Loss Hill 1363
Doune
Argaty
Burn of Cambus
Kinbuck
Ashfield
Greenloaning
Balhaldie
Strathallan
Allan Water
Braes of Doune
Drumvaich
Lanrick Castle
Deanston
Blair Drummond Safari Park
Loch Mahaick
Torrie Forest
Loch Rusky
Menteith Hills
Port of Menteith
Inchmahome Priory
Malling
Lake of Menteith
Ruskie
Goodie
Thornhill
Flanders Moss
Cardross
Dykehead
Forth
Carse of Forth
Arnprior
Kippen
Buchlyvie
Cauldhame
Leckie
Gargunnock
Gargunnock Hills
Carleatheran 1593
Touch Hills
Stirling
Cambuskenneth
Causewayhead
Cambusbarron
St. Ninians
Bannockburn
Fallin
Cowie
Stronend 1677
Fintry Hills
Fintry
Endrick
Loch Walton
Cringate Law 1301
Earlsburn Resrs.
Earl's Hill 1442
North Third Res.
Avenuehead
Ballikinrain Castle
Tullibody
Cambus
Alloa
Clackmannan
Sauchie
New Sauchie
Fishcross
Coalsnaughton
Devonside
Dollarbeg
Forest Mill
Kennet
Kilbagie
Kincardine
Airth
Airth Castle
Dunmore
Pineapple
Powdrake
Bowtrees
Plean
Throsk
Alloa Castle
Devilla Forest
High Valleyfield
Culross
Low Torry
Newmills
Dunfermline
Crossford
Cairneyhill
Oakley
Comrie
Carnock
Gowkhall
Blairhall
Saline
Balgonar
Knock Hill 1195
Powmill
Crook of Devon
Rumbling Bridge
Yetts o' Muckhart
Pool o' Muckhart
Aldie Castle
Cleish Hills
Cleish
Hill End
Loch Glow
Blairadam
Blairadam Forest
Kelty
Lassodie
Lochend
Kingseat
Townhill
Halbeath
Crossgates
Lumphinnans
Dunduff
Bowershall
Cowstrandburn
Carnbo
Balado
Kinross
Loch Leven
Tullibole Castle
Coldrain
Gairney Bank
Benarty Hill
Milnathort
Burleigh Castle
Dalqueich
Craigow
Upper Tillyrie
Middleton
Ochil Hills Hospital
Dochrie Hill 1198
Innerdouny Hill 1630
Steele's Knowe 1594
Corb Law 1558
Lendrick Hill 1496
South Queich
Middle Rigg
Glenfarg
Glenfarg Res.
Path of Condie
Pathstruie
Rossie Ochill
Fordel
Duncrievie
Newton of Pitcairns
Forteviot
Forgandenny
Bridge of Earn
Kintillo
Dron
Dupplin Castle
Milltown of Aberdalgie
Cragend
Craigend
Friarton
Cherrybank
Perth
Huntingtower Castle
Tibbermore
Methven
Keillour
Almondbank
Pitcairngreen
Huntingtower Haugh
Letham
Muirton
Gannochy
Branklyn Gdn.
Kinfauns
Elcho Castle
Scone Palace
Old Scone
New Scone
Perth (Scone)
Luncarty
Moneydie
Redgorton
Murrayfield
Strathord Forest
Stanley
Newmiln
Guildtown
Wolfhill
Whitefield
West Tofts
Airntully
Bankfoot
Waterloo
Glack
Upper Obney
Logiealmond Lodge
Logiealmond
Chapelhill
Harrietfield
Dunie
Buchanty
Glenshee
Milton Burn
Shochie Burn
Ordie
Meall nan Caoraich 2044
Trochry
Strathbraan
Braan
Cablea
The Hermitage (N.T.)
Inver
Dunkeld
Little Dunkeld
Birnam
Glen Cochill
Scotston
Meall Dearg 2258
Tombane Burn
Ballinloan Burn
Loch Kennard
Loch na Craige
Loch Hoil
Gatehouse
Loch Skiach
Craigvinean Forest
Inchmagranachan
Dalguise
Strath Tay
Balnaguard
Little Ballinluig
Grandtully
Grandtully Castle
Pitcairn
Balnaguard Burn
Pitnacree
Logierait
Ballinluig
Tulliemet
Balmacneil
Kindallachan
Guay
Dowally
Moulinearn
East Haugh
Balmore
Dalnacarn
Straloch
Glen Brerachan
Enochdu
Creag Dhubh 2092
Creag an-t Sithein 2075
Kirkmichael
Loch Broom
Meall Reamhar 1741
Creag nam Mial 1842
Strathardle
Stormont
Forest of Clunie
Loch Benachally
Blackcraig Forest
Riemore
Deuchary Hill 1670
Riechip
Butterstone
Forneth
Loch of Lowes
Clunie
Craigie
Kirkton of Lethendy
Murthly Castle
Caputh
Spittalfield
Gellyburn
Murthly
Meikleour
Ardoch
Blairgowrie
Kinloch
Lornty Burn
Middleton
Lamh Dhearg 1879
Glenshee
Black Water
Knock of Balmyle 1459
Ballintuim
Mains
Netherton
Bridge of Cally
Cray
Blacklunans
Forest
Lendrick Lodge
Loch Venachar
Easter Dullater
Glen Ogle

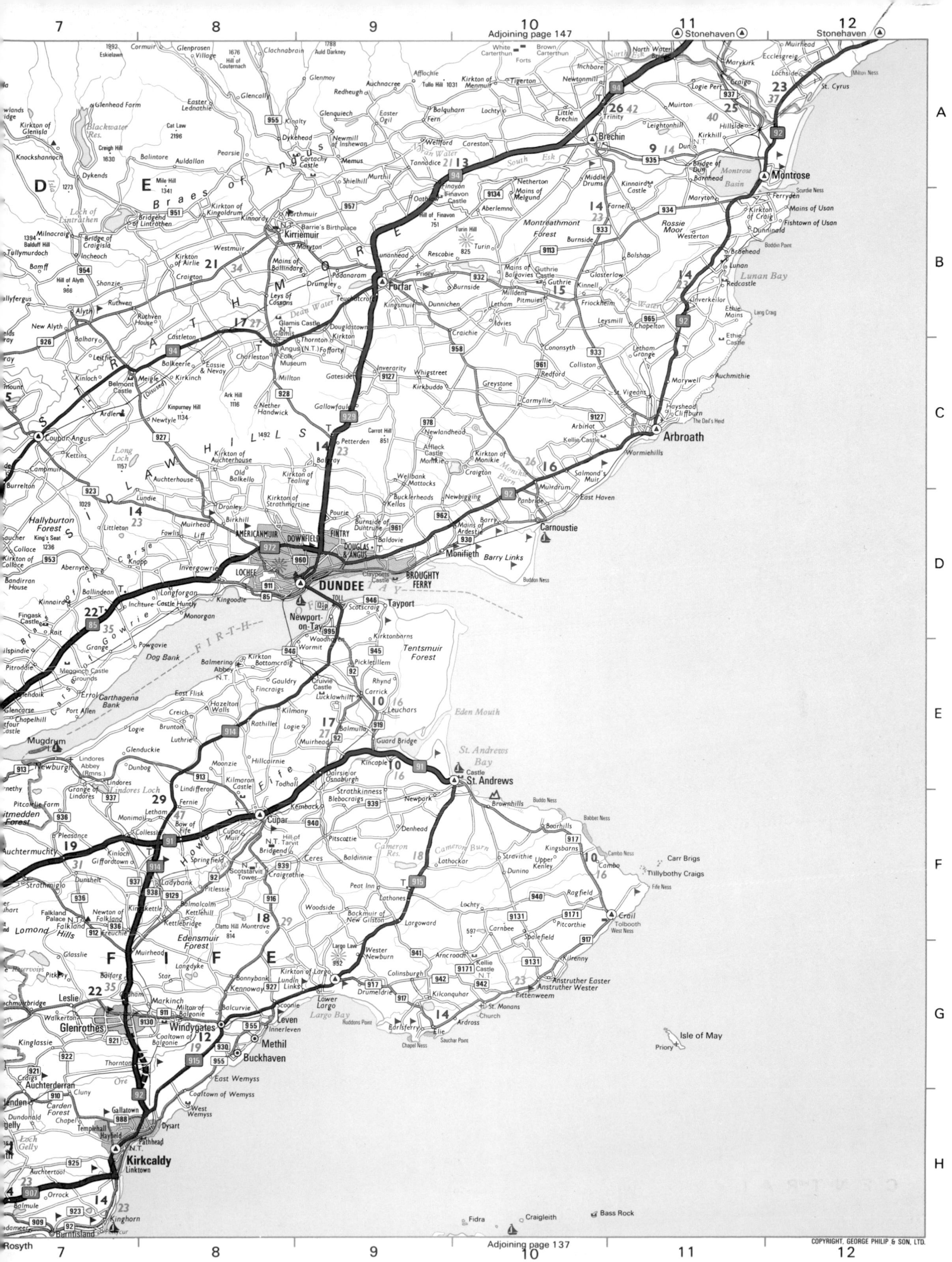
Adjoining page 147
Stonehaven
Adjoining page 137
7
8
9
10
11
12
A
B
C
D
E
F
G
H
Braes of Angus
STRATHMORE
SIDLAW HILLS
Carse of Gowrie
FIRTH OF TAY
FIFE
Howe of Fife
DUNDEE
BROUGHTY FERRY
Arbroath
Montrose
Brechin
Forfar
Kirriemuir
Carnoustie
Monifieth
Coupar Angus
Alyth
Newport-on-Tay
Tayport
St. Andrews
Cupar
Glenrothes
Kirkcaldy
Leven
Methil
Buckhaven
Crail
Anstruther Easter
Anstruther Wester
Pittenweem
Newburgh
Auchtermuchty
Kinghorn
Burntisland
Rosyth
Tentsmuir Forest
Lunan Bay
Montrose Basin
St. Andrews Bay
Largo Bay
Isle of May
Bass Rock
Fidra
Craigleith
Carr Brigs
Fife Ness
Glamis Castle
Barry Links
Edensmuir Forest
Lomond Hills

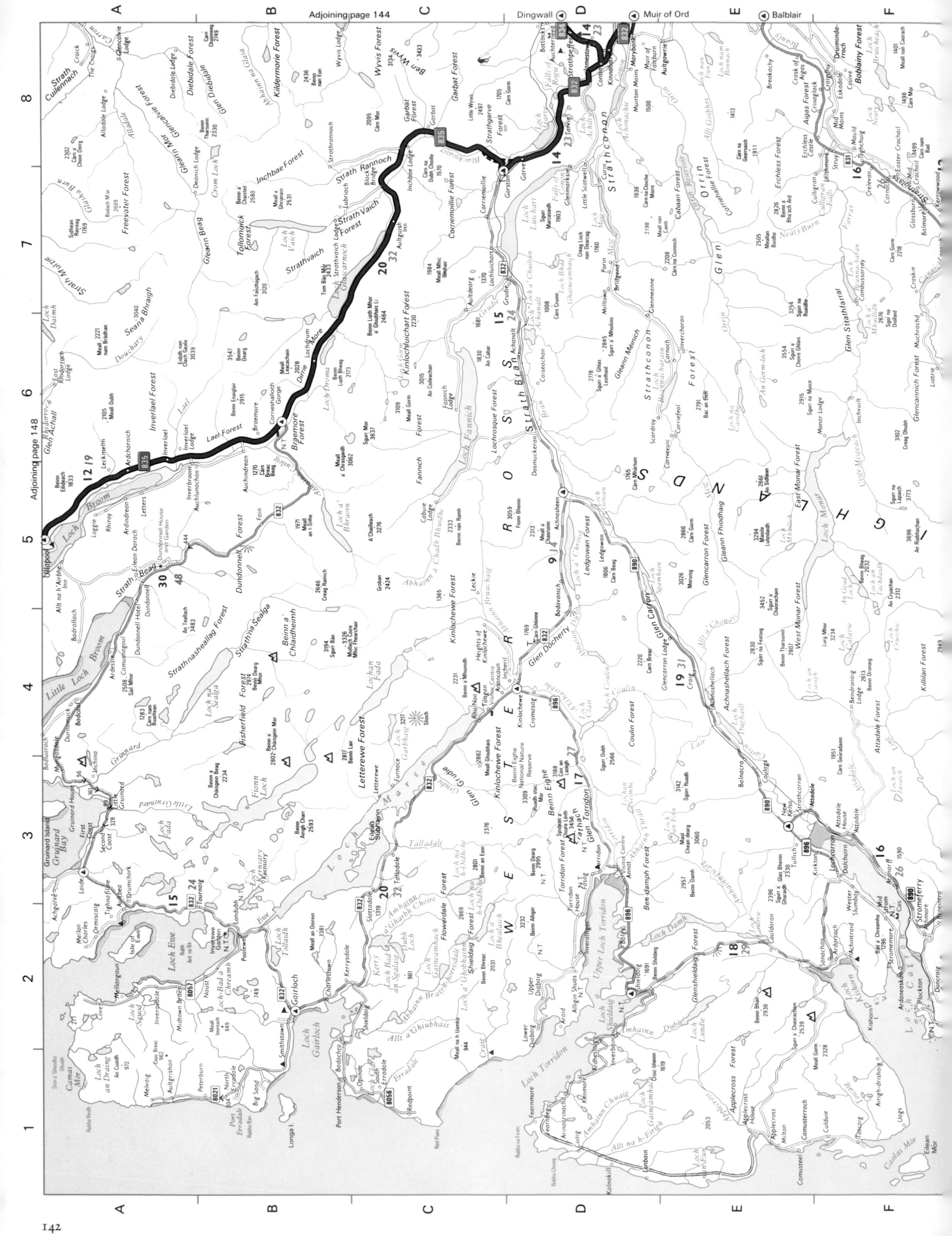

Adjoining page 144
Adjoining page 148
Dingwall
Muir of Ord
Balblair
Ullapool
Loch Broom
Little Loch Broom
Gruinard Bay
Gruinard Island
Loch Ewe
Poolewe
Gairloch
Loch Gairloch
Loch Maree
Kinlochewe
Glen Docherty
Achnasheen
Strath Bran
Loch Fannich
Garve
Gorstan
Strathpeffer
Contin
Glen Carron
Achnashellach
Lochcarron
Strathcarron
Kishorn
Plockton
Stromeferry
Shieldaig
Torridon
Glen Torridon
Upper Loch Torridon
Loch Torridon
Applecross
Applecross Forest
Beinn Eighe
Beinn Eighe National Nature Reserve
Letterewe Forest
Fisherfield Forest
Strathnasheallag Forest
Dundonnell
Braemore Forest
Inverlael Forest
Freevater Forest
Wyvis Forest
Ben Wyvis
Garbat Forest
Strathgarve Forest
Strathconon
Glen Orrin
Orrin Forest
Strathconon Forest
East Monar Forest
West Monar Forest
Loch Monar
Glen Strathfarrar
Aigas Forest
Erchless Forest
Boblainy Forest
Attadale Forest
Achnashellach Forest
Coulin Forest
Ben-damph Forest
Flowerdale Forest
Kinlochewe Forest
Lochrosque Forest
Fannich Forest
Kinlochluichart Forest
Corriemoillie Forest
Inchbae Forest
Strath Vaich
Strath Rannoch
Gleann Mor
Glencalvie Forest
Diebidale Forest
Kildermorie Forest
Loch Kishorn
Loch Carron
Loch Luichart
Glen Achall
WESTER ROSS
STRATHCONON

Adjoining page 145
Adjoining page 139
Adjoining page 138
Drumnadrochit
Newtonmore
Broadford
Ardvasar
Salen
North Ballachulish
COPYRIGHT, GEORGE PHILIP & SON LTD.
H I G H L A N D
Kyle of Lochalsh
Dornie
Eilean Donan Castle
Loch Duich
Five Sisters
Kintail Forest
Glen Shiel
Cluanie Inn
Loch Cluanie
Glen Moriston
Invermoriston
Fort Augustus
Loch Ness
Invergarry
Loch Lochy
Spean Bridge
Glen Spean
Roybridge
Glen Roy
Fort William
Ben Nevis
Loch Linnhe
Corpach
Loch Eil
Glenfinnan
Loch Shiel
Lochailort
Arisaig
Mallaig
Morar
Loch Morar
Knoydart
Loch Hourn
Loch Nevis
Glenelg
Loch Quoich
Glen Garry
Loch Arkaig
Loch Treig
Sound of Sleat
Moidart
Ardgour
CAR FERRY

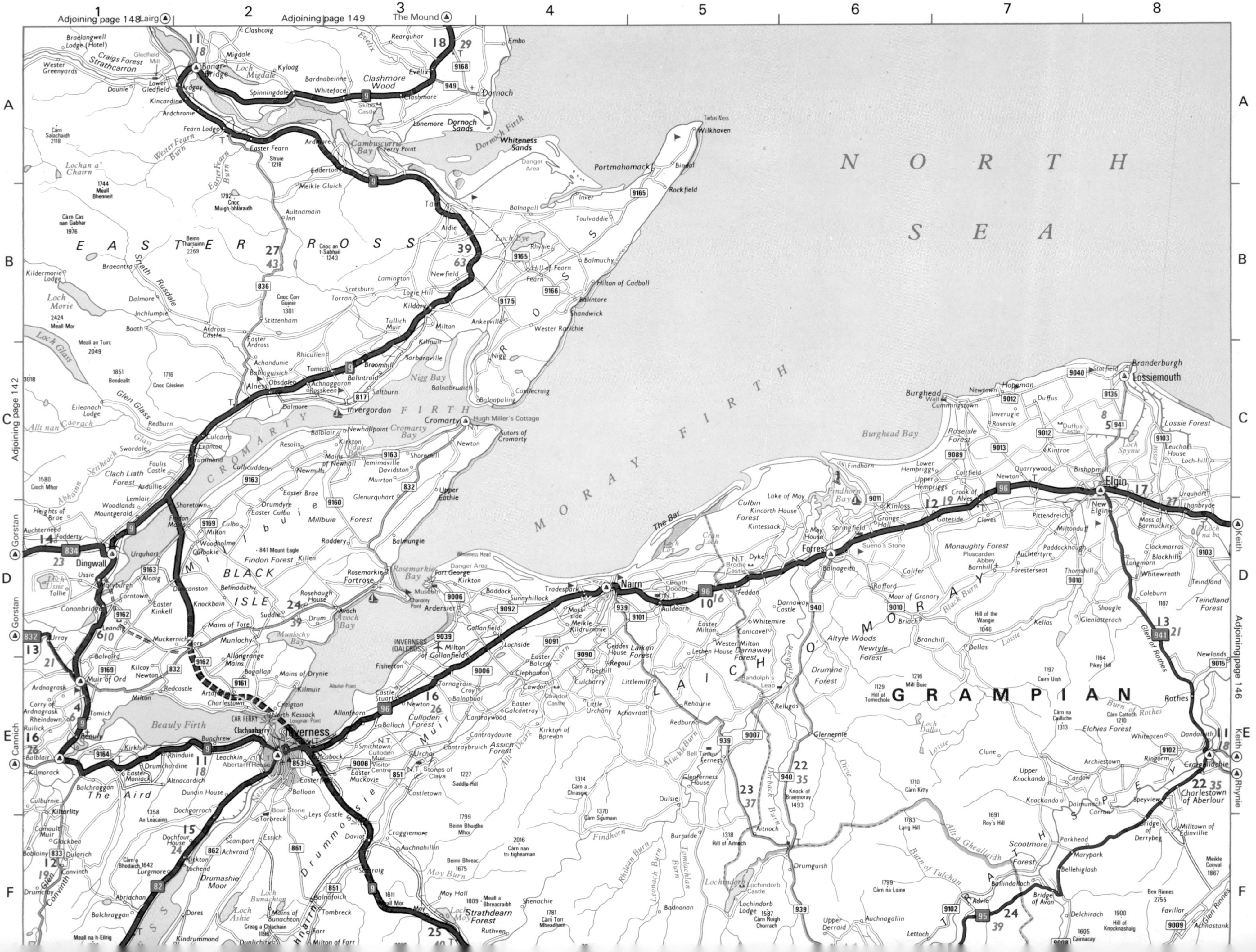
Adjoining page 148
Lairg
Adjoining page 149
The Mound
Adjoining page 142
Adjoining page 146
Gorstan
Cannich
Keith
Rhynie
NORTH SEA
MORAY FIRTH
CROMARTY FIRTH
EASTER ROSS
BLACK ISLE
GRAMPIAN
MORAY
LAICH O' MORAY
Dornoch Firth
Beauly Firth
Burghead Bay
Nigg Bay
Dornoch
Bonar Bridge
Tain
Invergordon
Alness
Cromarty
Dingwall
Fortrose
Rosemarkie
Inverness
Beauly
Nairn
Forres
Elgin
Lossiemouth
Burghead
Portmahomack
Tarbat Ness
Rothes
Craigellachie
Charlestown of Aberlour
Culloden Muir
Drumossie Muir
The Aird
Strathdearn Forest
Monaughty Forest
Millbuie Forest
Clashmore Wood
Strathcarron
Strath Rusdale
Glen Glass
Glen of Rothes
Elchies Forest
Inverness (Dalcross)
Car Ferry
Hugh Miller's Cottage

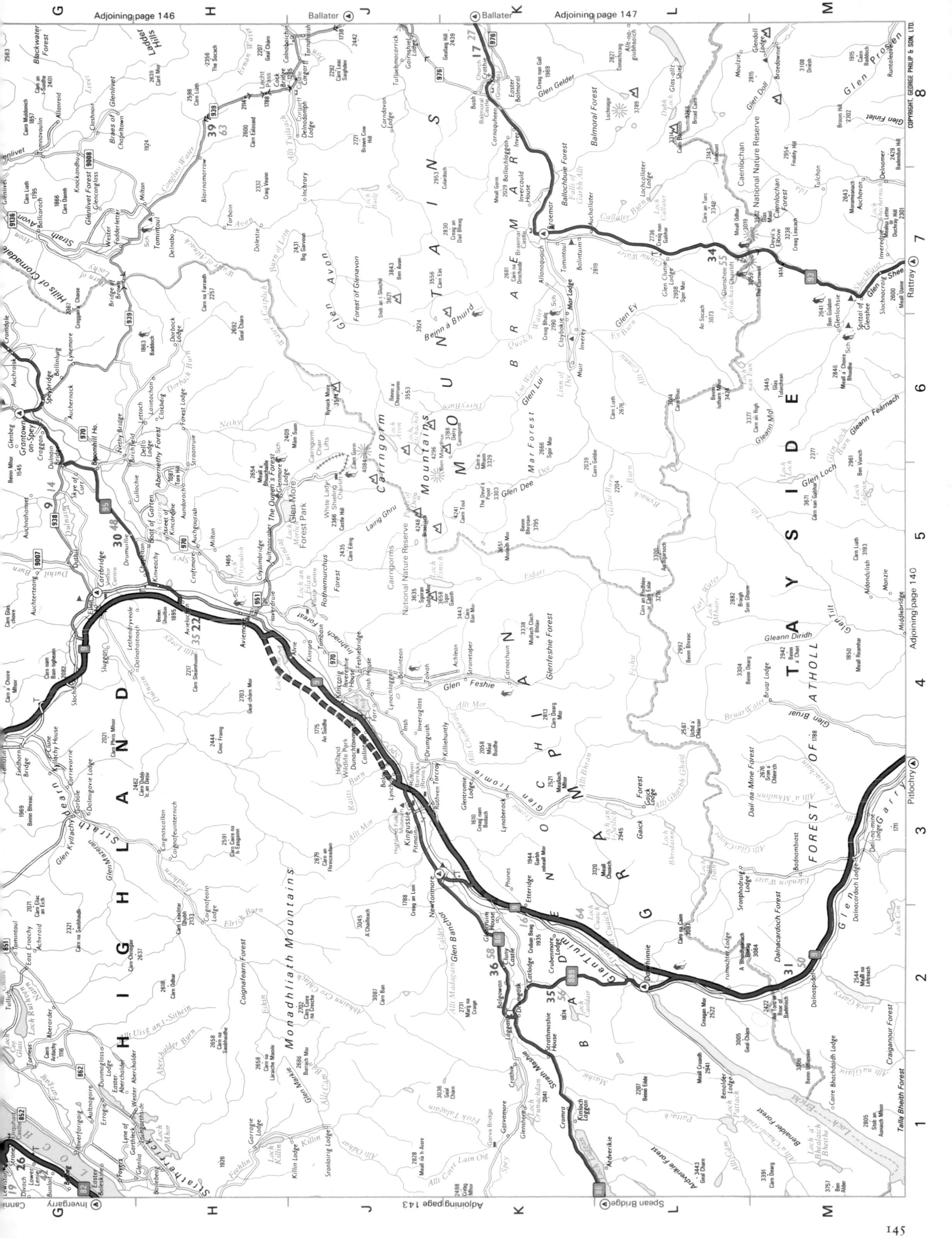

Adjoining page 146
Adjoining page 147
Adjoining page 140
Adjoining page 143
Ballater
Rattray
Pitlochry
Spean Bridge
Invergarry
H I G H L A N D
G R A M P I A N   M O U N T A I N S
T A Y S I D E
Monadhliath Mountains
Cairngorm Mountains
FOREST OF ATHOLL
Cairngorms National Nature Reserve
Caenlochan National Nature Reserve
Glen More Forest Park
Balmoral Forest
Mar Forest
Glenfeshie Forest
Abernethy Forest
Rothiemurchus Forest
Coignafearn Forest
Dalnacardoch Forest
Ben Alder Forest
Ardverikie Forest
Talla Bheith Forest
Craiganour Forest
Glenlivet Forest
Braemar
Tomintoul
Grantown-on-Spey
Carrbridge
Aviemore
Kingussie
Newtonmore
Dalwhinnie
Laggan
Kinloch Laggan
Glen Feshie
Glen Dee
Glen Shee
Glen Ey
Glen Tilt
Glen Garry
Strathspey
Strath Avon
Strathdearn
Glen Truim
Strath Mashie
COPYRIGHT, GEORGE PHILIP & SON, LTD.

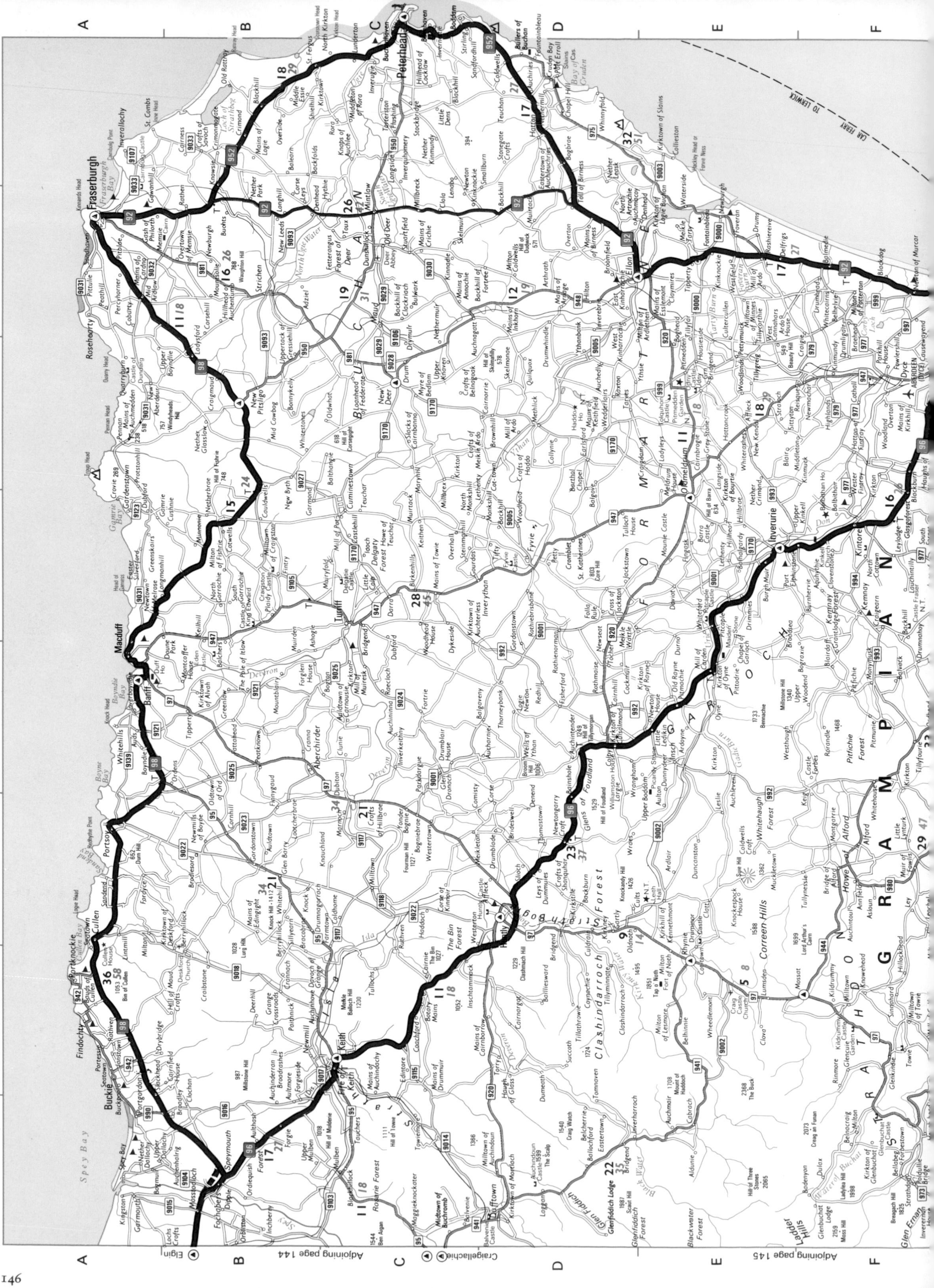
Fraserburgh
Peterhead
Macduff
Banff
Portsoy
Cullen
Buckie
Keith
Huntly
Turriff
Inverurie
Ellon
Oldmeldrum
Kintore
Dufftown
Rhynie
Alford
Newburgh
New Pitsligo
Strichen
Mintlaw
Maud
New Deer
Fochabers
Aberchirder
Insch
Aberdeen (Dyce)
Spey Bay
Bay of Cruden
Correen Hills
Clashindarroch Forest
The Bin Forest
Bin of Cullen
Buchan
Formartine
Garioch
Grampian
To Lerwick
Car Ferry
Adjoining page 144
Adjoining page 145
Elgin
Craigellachie

ABERDEEN
Stonehaven
Montrose
Brechin
Forfar
Kirriemuir
Laurencekirk
Inverbervie
Banchory
Aboyne
Ballater
Tarland
Torphins
Edzell
Johnshaven
St. Cyrus
DEESIDE
MAR
TAYSIDE
Braes of Angus
MOUNTH
Glen Esk
Forest of Glentanar
Forest of Birse
Howe of the Mearns
Fetteresso Forest
Durris Forest
Midmar Forest
Blackhall Forest
Drumtochty Forest
Montreathmont Forest
Inglismaldie Forest
Lunan Bay
Montrose Basin
Bervie Bay
Thornyhive Bay
Cammachmore Bay
Nigg Bay
Cove Bay
Loch Lee
Glen Clova
Glen Tanar
Glen Muick
Glen Mark
Glen Lee
Mount Keen 3077
Mount Battock 2555
Coupar Angus
Dundee
Arbroath
Rattray
Crathie
Grantown on-Spey
Adjoining page 141
Adjoining page 145
COPYRIGHT, GEORGE PHILIP & SON, LTD.
G
H
J
K
L
M
1
2
3
4
5
6
7
8

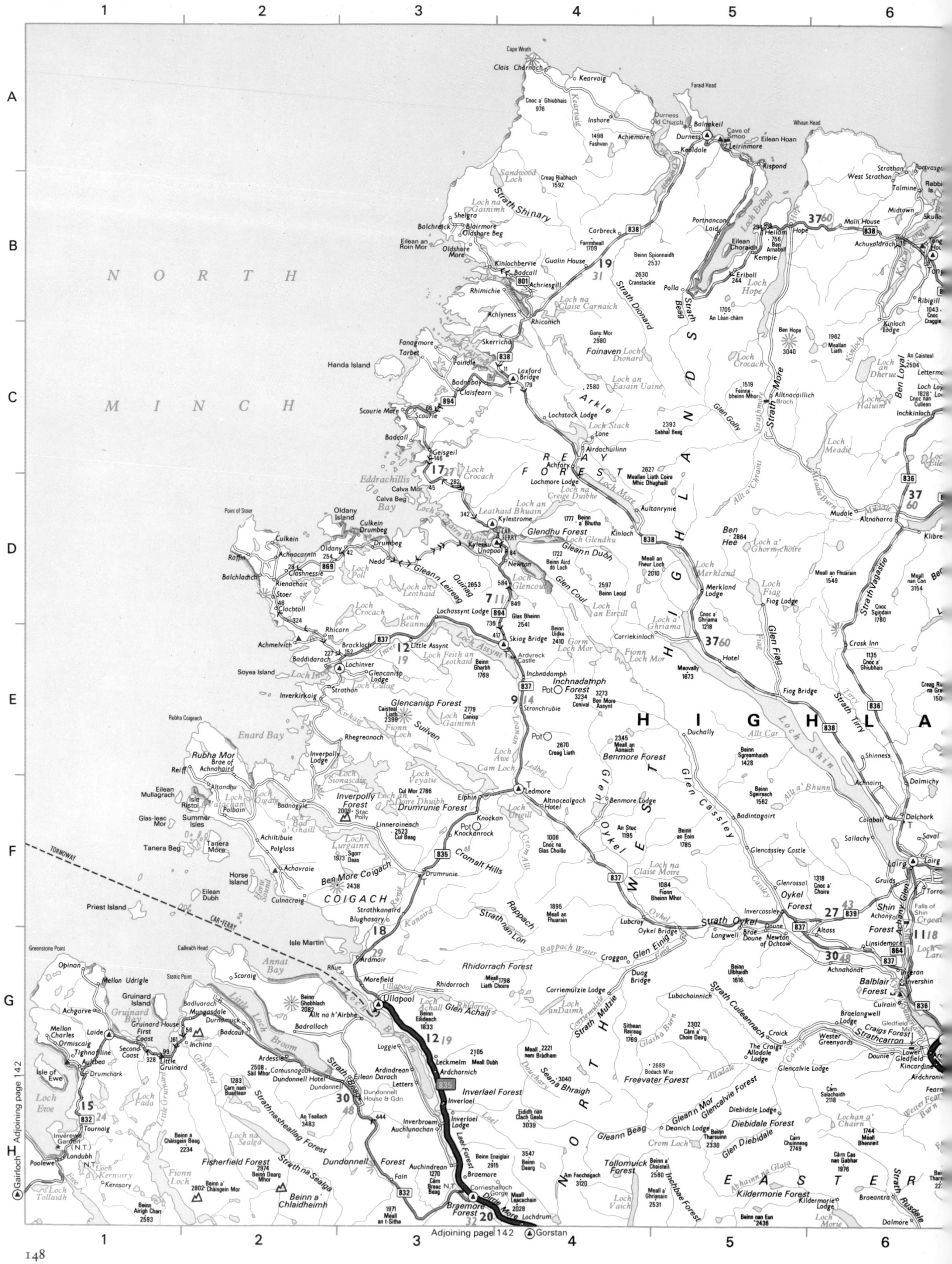
NORTH MINCH
HIGHLAND
NORTH WEST HIGHLANDS
EASTER ROSS
REAY FOREST
Cape Wrath
Clais Charnach
Kearvaig
Faraid Head
Cnoc a' Ghiubhais 976
Inshore
Durness Old Church
Balnakeil
Cave of Smoo
Durness
Leirinmore
Eilean Hoan
Whiten Head
1498 Fashven
Achiemore
Keoldale
Rispond
Sandwood Loch
Creag Riabhach 1592
Strath Shinary
Loch na Gainimh
Sheigra
Balchrick
Blairmore
Oldshore Beg
Oldshore More
Eilean an Roin Mor
Kinlochbervie
Badcall
Achriesgill
Rhimichie
Gualin House
Carbreck
Farrmheall 1709
Beinn Spionnaidh 2537
2630 Cranstackie
Portnancon
Laid
Loch Eriboll
Eilean Choraidh
Heilam
Ben Arnaboll
Kempie
Eriboll
Polla
Strath Beag
Loch Hope
Hope
Moin House
Strathan
West Strathan
Portvasgo
Talmine
Midtown
Achuvoldrach
Ribigill
Kinloch Lodge
Strath Dionard
Loch na Claise Carnaich
Achlyness
Rhiconich
1705 An Lean-charn
Ganu Mor 2980
Foinaven
Loch Dionard
Ben Hope 3040
1962 Meallan Liath
Fanagmore
Tarbet
Loch Laxford
Skerricha
Handa Island
Foindle
Laxford Bridge
Badnabay
Claisfearn
Scourie More
Scourie
Badcall
Loch an Easain Uaine
Arkle
Lochstock Lodge
Loch Stack
Lone
Airdachuilinn
2393 Sabhal Beag
Glen Golly
1519 Feinne-bheinn Mhor
Loch Crocach
Strath More
Alltnacaillich Broch
Loch Meadie
Ben Loyal
Loch an Dherue
Loch Haluim
Inchkinloch
Geisgeil
Eddrachillis Bay
Calva Mor
Calva Beg
Loch Crocach
Achfary
Lochmore Lodge
Loch More
2627 Meallan Liath Coire Mhic Dhughaill
Loch na Creige Duibhe
Aultanrynie
Allt a' Chraois
Mudale
Altnaharra
Point of Stoer
Oldany Island
Culkein Drumbeg
Culkein
Achnacarnin
Raffin
Balchladich
Clashnessie
Oldany
Drumbeg
Nedd
Loch Poll
Gleann Leireag
Quinag
Loch an Leothaid
Kylestrome
Leathaid Bhuain
Loch an Leathaid Bhuain
Kylesku
Unapool
Newton
Glendhu Forest
Loch Glendhu
Gleann Dubh
1777 Beinn a' Bhutha
Kinloch
1722 Beinn Aird da Loch
Glen Coul
Loch Glencoul
Meall an Fheur Loch 2010
Ben Hee 2864
Loch a' Ghorm-choire
Loch Merkland
Merkland Lodge
Loch Fiag
Fiag Lodge
Meall an Fhuarain 1549
Strath Vagastie
Meall nan Con 3154
Rienachait
Stoer
Clachtoll
Loch Crocach
Loch Beannach
Lochassynt Lodge
Glas Bheinn 2541
Beinn Uidhe 2410
2597 Beinn Leoid
Loch an Eircill
Loch a' Ghriama
Cnoc a' Ghriama 1218
Cnoc Sgiodain 1780
Crask Inn
Achmelvich
Rhicarn
Brackloch
Little Assynt
Loch Assynt
Skiag Bridge
Loch Feith an Leothaid
Ardvreck Castle
Gorm Loch Mor
Fionn Loch Mor
Corriekinloch
Glen Fiag
Hotel
Baddidarach
Lochinver
Soyea Island
Glencanisp Lodge
Loch Culag
Beinn Gharbh 1769
Inchnadamph
Inchnadamph Forest
3234 Conival
3273 Ben More Assynt
Maovally 1673
Fiag Bridge
1135 Cnoc a' Ghiubhais
Strathan
Inverkirkaig
Glencanisp Forest
Caisteal Liath 2399
2779 Canisp
Suilven
Fionn Loch
Loch Gainimh
Stronchrubie
Loch Shin
Strath Tirry
Rubha Coigeach
Enard Bay
Rhegreanoch
Pot
2670 Creag Liath
2345 Meall an Aonaich
Benmore Forest
Duchally
Allt Car
Shinness
Rubha Mor
Brae of Achnahaird
Reiff
Inverpolly Lodge
Loch Sionascaig
Loch Veyatie
Cam Loch
Loch Awe
Ledbeg
Glen Oykel
Glen Cassley
Beinn Sgreamhaidh 1428
Eilean Mullagrach
Altandhu
Loch Osgaig
Isle Ristol
Polbain
Badnagyle
Inverpolly Forest
Cul Mor 2786
Loch an Doire Dhuibh
Elphin
Ledmore
Altnacealgach Hotel
Benmore Lodge
Beinn Sgeireach 1562
Allt a' Bhunn
Achnairn
Dalmichy
Glas-leac Mor
Summer Isles
Stac Polly 2009
Drumrunie Forest
Knockan
Knockanrock
Loch Urigill
Badintagairt
Colaboll
Dalchork
Tanera Beg
Tanera Mor
Achiltibuie
Polglass
Loch Bad a' Ghaill
Loch Lurgainn
Linneraineach
2523 Cul Beag
Cromalt Hills
Crom Allt
1006 Cnoc na Glas Choille
An Stuc 1195
Beinn an Eoin 1785
Sallachy
Glencassley Castle
TORNOWAY
Horse Island
Horse Sound
Achavraie
1973 Sgorr Deas
Ben More Coigach 2438
Drumrunie
Rappach
Loch na Claise Moire
1084 Fionn Bheinn Mhor
Glenrossal
1318 Cnoc a' Choire
Lairg
Eilean Dubh
COIGACH
Culnacraig
Priest Island
CAR FERRY
Strathkanaird
Blughasary
Strath nan Lon
1895 Meall an Fhuarain
Lubcroy
Oykel Bridge
Strath Oykel
Invercassley
Oykel Forest
Shin Forest
Achany
Falls of Shin
Achany Glen
Isle Martin
Kanaird
Rappach Water
Craggan
Glen Einig
Langwell
Brae
Doune
Newton of Ochtow
Altass
Linsidemore
Greenstone Point
Cailleach Head
Annat Bay
Ardmair
Rhidorroch Forest
Achnahanat
Gledfield
Opinan
Mellon Udrigle
Static Point
Scoraig
Rhue
Morefield
Rhidorroch
Meall Liath Choire 1798
Corriemulzie Lodge
Dubh Bridge
Beinn Ulbhaidh 1616
Lubachoinnich
Strath Cuileannach
Inveran
Invershin
Balblair Forest
Gruinard Island
Gruinard Bay
Badluarach
Mungasdale
Dundonnell
Little Loch Broom
Beinn Ghobhlach 2082
Allt na h'Airbhe
Ullapool
Loch Achall
Glen Achall
Loch an Daimh
Strath Mulzie
Culrain
Braelangwell Lodge
Achgarve
Mellon Charles
Ormiscaig
Laide
Gruinard House
First Coast
Second Coast
Inchina
Badcaul
Badrallach
Loch Broom
Beinn Eilideach 1833
Sithean Rairéag 1769
Glasha Burn
2302 Càrn a' Choin Deirg
Croick
Wester Greenyards
Craigs Forest
Strathcarron
Tighnafiline
Aultbea
Little Gruinard
Ardessie
Strath Beag
Loggie
Leckmelm
2105 Meall Dubh
Meall nam Bràdham 2221
The Craigs
Alladale Lodge
Isle of Ewe
Drumchork
2508 Sàil Mhor
Camusnagoul
Dundonnell Hotel
Eilean Darach
Ardindrean
Ardcharnich
Letters
2689 Bodach Mòr
Freevater Forest
Alladale
Glencalvie Lodge
Lower Gledfield
Kincardine
Ardchronie
Dounie
Loch Ewe
1283 Càrn nam Buaitean
Loch Fada
Little Gruinard
Dundonnell House & Gdn
Strathnasheallag Forest
Inverlael
Inverlael Forest
Seana Bhraigh 3040
Douchary
Gleann Mor
Glencalvie Forest
Diebidale Lodge
Diebidale Forest
Càrn Salachaidh 2118
Lochan a' Chairn
Fearn
Tournaig
Inverewe Garden (N.T.)
Londubh
Poolewe
An Teallach 3483
Beinn a' Chàisgein Beag 2234
Loch na Sealga
Inverbroom
Auchlunachan
Inverlael Lodge
Lael Forest
Eididh nan Clach Geala 3039
Gleann Beag
Deanich Lodge
Beinn Tharsuinn 2330
Crom Loch
Gleann Diebidale
Càrn Chuinneag 2749
1744 Meall Bhenneit
Càrn Cas nan Gabhar 1976
Loch Kernsary
Kernsary
Fionn Loch
Beinn a' Chàisgein Mor 2802
Fisherfield Forest
2974 Beinn Dearg Mhor
Strath na Sealga
Dundonnell Forest
Beinn a' Chlaidheimh
Fain
Auchindrean
1270 Càrn Breac Beag
Braemore
Beinn Enaiglair 2915
3547 Beinn Dearg
Am Faochagach 3120
Tollomuick Forest
Beinn a' Chaisteil 2580
Inchbae Forest
Abhainn na Glasa
Kildermorie Forest
Kildermorie Lodge
Braeantra
Strath Rusdale
Loch Tollaidh
Beinn Airigh Charr 2593
1971 Meall an t-Sitha
Braemore Forest
Corrieshalloch Gorge
Meall Leacachain 2028
Dirrie More
Lochdrum
Loch Vaich
Meall a' Ghrianain 2531
Beinn nan Eun 2438
Loch Morie
Dalmore
Adjoining page 142
Gorstan
Gairloch

Adjoining page 152

Dingwall Adjoining page 144 Dingwall

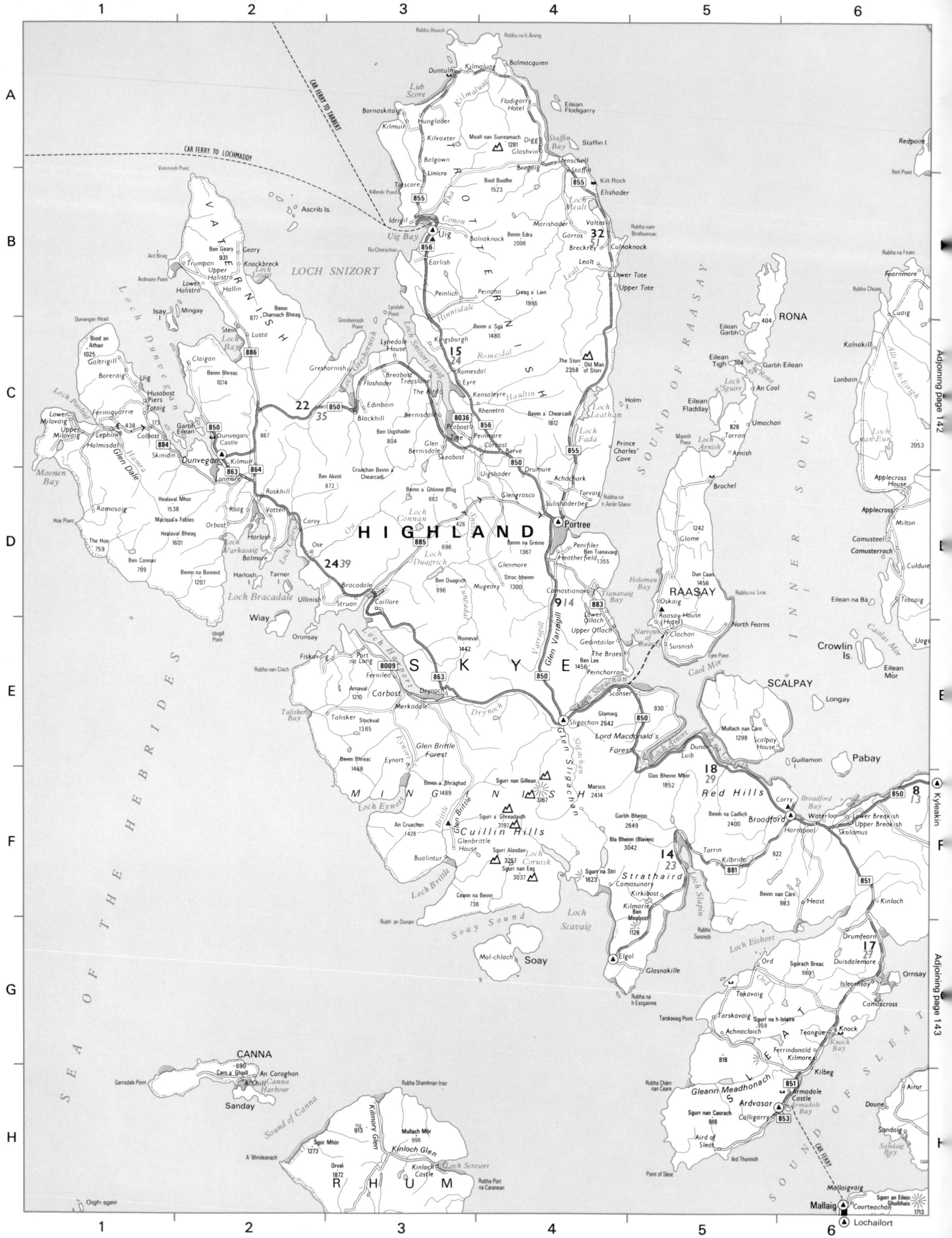

HIGHLAND
SKYE
TROTTERNISH
VATERNISH
MINGINISH
SLEAT
RAASAY
RONA
SCALPAY
CANNA
RHUM
Sanday
Soay
Pabay
LOCH SNIZORT
SOUND OF RAASAY
INNER SOUND
SEA OF THE HEBRIDES
SOUND OF SLEAT
Soay Sound
Sound of Canna
Loch Scavaig
Loch Bracadale
Loch Harport
Loch Eynort
Loch Brittle
Loch Slapin
Loch Eishort
Loch Sligachan
Loch Dunvegan
Loch Pooltiel
Loch Greshornish
Loch Snizort Beag
Uig Bay
Staffin Bay
Moonen Bay
Talisker Bay
Caol Mor
Caolas Mor
Broadford Bay
Knock Bay
Armadale Bay
Canna Harbour
Holoman Bay
Tianavaig Bay
Cuillin Hills
Red Hills
Strathaird
Glen Brittle Forest
Lord Macdonald's Forest
CAR FERRY TO TARBERT
CAR FERRY TO LOCHMADDY
CAR FERRY
Adjoining page 142
Adjoining page 143
Duntulm
Kilmaluag
Balmacquien
Flodigarry Hotel
Eilean Flodigarry
Digg
Staffin I.
Stenscholl
Staffin
Kilt Rock
Elishader
Valtos
Culnaknock
Lealt
Lower Tote
Upper Tote
Bornaskitaig
Kilmuir
Hungladder
Kilvaxter
Balgown
Linicro
Totscore
Idrigil
Uig
Earlish
Balnaknock
Peinlich
Kingsburgh
Romesdal
Eyre
Kensaleyre
Rhenetra
Prabost
Peinmore
Carbost
Borve
Drumuie
Achachork
Torvaig
Sulishaderbeg
Portree
Penifiler
Heatherfield
Camastianavaig
Lower Ollach
Upper Ollach
Gedintailor
The Braes
Peinchorran
Sconser
Sligachan
Glamaig 2542
Marsco 2414
Sgurr nan Gillean 3167
Sgurr a' Ghreadaidh 3197
Sgurr Alasdair 3257
Sgurr nan Eag 3037
Glenbrittle House
Bualintur
Ceann na Beinn 736
Bla Bheinn (Blaven) 3042
Garbh-Bheinn 2649
Glas Bheinn Mhor 1852
Camasunary
Kirkibost
Kilmarie
Elgol
Glasnakille
Torrin
Kilbride
Broadford
Harrapool
Waterloo
Corry
Lower Breakish
Upper Breakish
Skulamus
Kyleakin
Dunan
Luib
Heast
Kinloch
Drumfearn
Duisdalemore
Isleornsay
Ornsay
Camuscross
Ord
Tokavaig
Tarskavaig
Achnacloich
Teangue
Knock
Ferrindonald
Kilmore
Kilbeg
Armadale Castle
Ardvasar
Calligarry
Aird of Sleat
Point of Sleat
Mallaig
Mollaigvaig
Lochailort
Dunvegan
Dunvegan Castle
Kilmuir
Lonmore
Roskhill
Vatten
Roag
Orbost
Harlosh
Balmore
Caroy
Ose
Bracadale
Struan
Caillore
Ullinish
Wiay
Oronsay
Fiskavaig
Portnalong
Fernilea
Carbost
Drynoch
Merkadale
Talisker
Eynort
Glendale
Holmisdal
Lephin
Colbost
Skinidin
Husabost
Borreraig
Galtrigill
Milovaig
Ramasaig
Stein
Lusta
Hallin
Geary
Trumpan
Isay I.
Mingay
Ascrib Is.
Greshornish
Edinbain
Flashader
Lynedale House
Breabost
Treaslane
Bernisdale
Skeabost
Uigshader
Glengrasco
Glenmore
Mugeary
Raasay House (Hotel)
Oskaig
Clachan
Suisnish
North Fearns
Brochel
Eilean Fladday
Crowlin Is.
Applecross
Milton
Camusteel
Camusterrach
Toscaig
Kalnakill
Cuaig
Fearnmore
An Coroghon
A' Chill
Carn a' Ghaill 690
Kinloch Castle
Kinloch Glen
Orval 1872
Sgor Mhor 1273
Mullach Mor 996

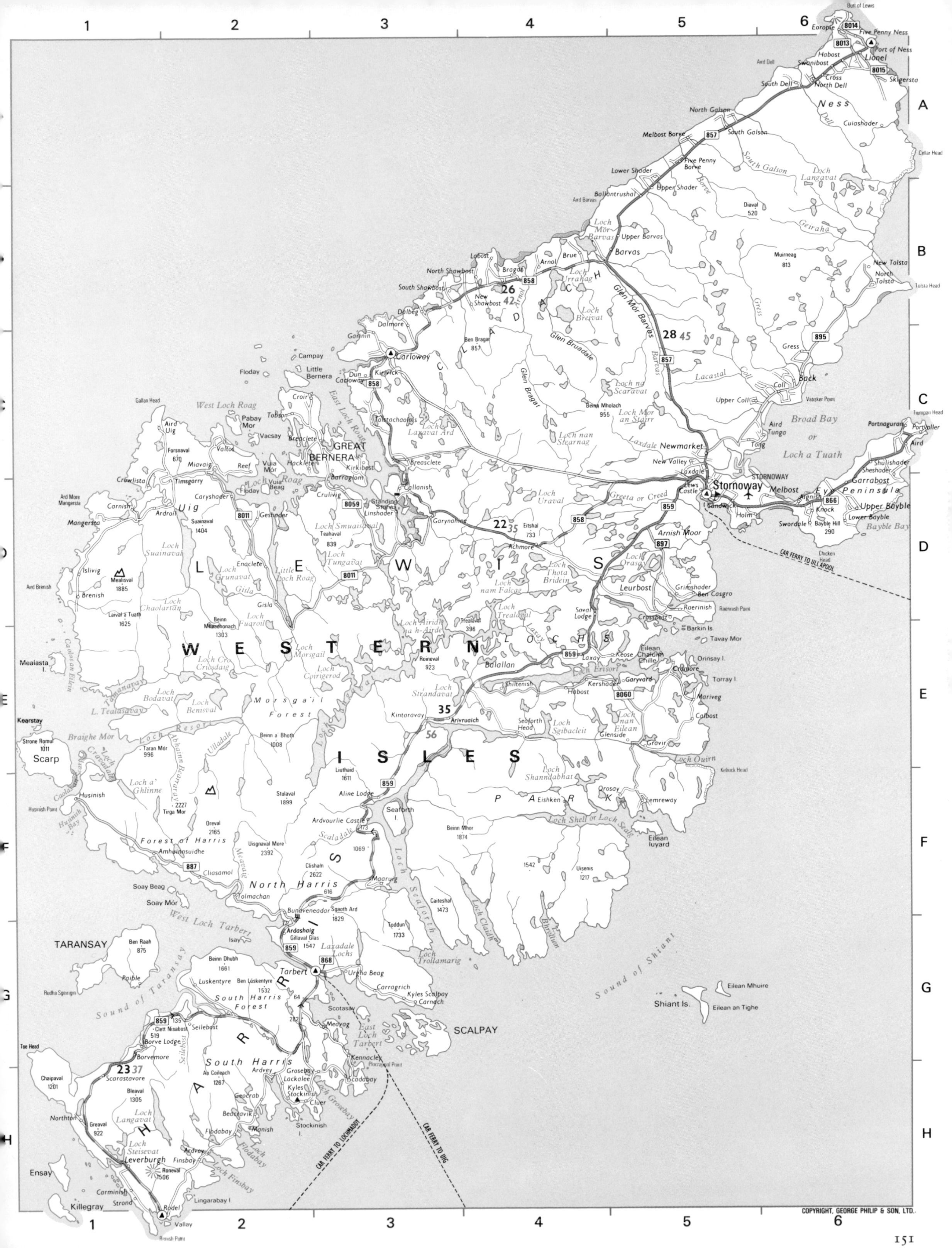
WESTERN ISLES
LEWIS
HARRIS
Butt of Lewis
Europie
Five Penny Ness
Port of Ness
Lionel
Habost
Swainbost
Aird Dell
Cross
North Dell
South Dell
Skigersta
Ness
North Galson
South Galson
Melbost Borve
Cuiashader
Cellar Head
Five Penny Borve
Lower Shader
Upper Shader
Ballantrushal
Ard Barvas
Loch Langavat
Diaval 520
Loch Mor Barvas
Upper Barvas
Barvas
Geiraha
Muirneag 813
New Tolsta
North Tolsta
Tolsta Head
Labost
Bragar
Arnol
Brue
Loch Urrahag
North Shawbost
South Shawbost
New Shawbost
Dalbeg
Dalmore
Garenin
Carloway
Ben Bragar 857
Loch Breivat
Glen Bruadale
Glen Mor Barvas
Gress
Back
Coll
Upper Coll
Lacastal
Campay
Little Bernera
Floday
Dun Carloway
Kirivick
Croir
West Loch Roag
East Loch Roag
Gallan Head
Aird Uig
Pabay Mor
Tobson
Vacsay
Valtos
Forsnaval 670
Miavaig
Reef
Vuia Mor
Vuia Beag
Breaclete
GREAT BERNERA
Hacklete
Kirkibost
Barraglom
Loch Roag
Floday
Crowlista
Timsgarry
Caryshader
Uig
Ard More Mangersta
Carnish
Ardroil
Mangersta
Gisla
Tolstachaolais
Loch Laxavat Ard
Breasclete
Callanish
Cruliviig
Standing Stones
Linshader
Garynahine
Beinn Mholach 955
Loch Mor an Stairr
Loch na Scaravat
Glen Bragar
Loch nan Stearnag
Laxdale
Newmarket
New Valley
Tong
Aird Tunga
Broad Bay or Loch a Tuath
Vatisker Point
Tiumpan Head
Portnaguran
Portvoller
Aird
Shulishader
Sheshader
Garrabost
Eye Peninsula
Melbost
Aignish
Knock
Upper Bayble
Lower Bayble
Bayble Hill 290
Swordale
Bayble Bay
Chicken Head
STORNOWAY
Stornoway
Lews Castle
Sandwick
Holm
Loch Urabal
Greeta or Creed
Eitshal 733
Achmore
Arnish Moor
Loch Smuaisaval
Teahaval 839
Loch Tungavat
Suainaval 1404
Loch Suainaval
Enaclete
Loch Grunavat
Little Loch Roag
Islivig
Mealisval 1885
Aird Brenish
Brenish
Loch Chaolartan
Lavval a Tuath 1625
Beinn Mheadhonach 1303
Loch Fuaroil
Loch Thota Bridein
Loch nam Falcag
Loch Orasay
Leurbost
Grimshader
Ben Casgro
Raerinish
Raerinish Point
Soval Lodge
Crossbost
Barkin Is.
Tavay Mor
Loch Trealaval
Trealaval 396
Loch Airidh na h-Airde
LOCHS
Laxay
Keose
Eilean Chaluim Chille
Orinsay I.
Cromore
Torray I.
Mealasta I.
Caolas an Eilein
Loch Cro Criosdaig
Loch Morsgail
Loch Coirigerod
Roineval 923
Balallan
Loch Erisort
Shiltenish
Kershader
Garyvard
Habost
Marvig
Calbost
Loch Bodavat
Loch Benisval
Morsgail Forest
L. Tealasavay
Loch Langavat
Loch Strandavat
Kintaravay
Arivruaich
Seaforth Head
Loch Sgibacleit
Glenside
Loch nan Eilean
Gravir
Kearstay
Braighe Mor
Loch Resort
Strone Romul 1011
Scarp
Taran Mor 996
Ulladale
Abhainn Bearnaraig
Beinn a' Bhoth 1008
Liuthaid 1611
Loch Ouirn
Kebock Head
Loch Shanndabhat
Loch a' Ghlinne
PARK
Eishken
Orosay
Lemreway
Husinish
Husinish Point
Husinish Bay
Tirga Mor
Stulaval 1899
Aline Lodge
Seaforth I.
Ardvourlie Castle
Loch Shell or Loch Sealg
Eilean Iuvard
Oreval 2165
Beinn Mhor 1874
Forest of Harris
Amhuinnsuidhe
Uisgnaval More 2392
Scaladale
Loch Seaforth
Cliasamol
Clisham 2622
Uisenis 1217
Soay Beag
Soay Mor
Tolmachan
North Harris
Maaruig
Caiteshal 1473
Loch Claidh
West Loch Tarbert
Bunaveneadar
Sgaoth Ard 1829
Ardashaig
Gillaval Glas 1547
Toddun 1733
Loch Bhrollum
Isay
TARANSAY
Ben Raah 875
Paible
Laxadale Lochs
Loch Trollamarig
Sound of Shiant
Beinn Dhubh 1661
Tarbert
Urgha Beag
Carragrich
Kyles Scalpay
Carnach
Eilean Mhuire
Shiant Is.
Eilean an Tighe
Rudha Sgeirigin
Luskentyre
Ben Luskentyre 1532
South Harris Forest
Sound of Taransay
Scotasay
Meavag
SCALPAY
East Loch Tarbert
Seilebost
Clett Nisabost
Borve Lodge
Toe Head
Borvemore
Kennacley
Rhenigidale Point
Chaipaval 1201
Scarastavore
South Harris
Ardvey
Ab Coileach 1267
Grosebay
Scadabay
Lackalee
Kyles Stockinish
Cluer
Loch Grosebay
Bleaval 1305
Loch Langavat
Geocrab
Beacravik
Manish
Northton
Greaval 922
Flodabay
Stockinish I.
Loch Steiseval
Ardvey
Loch Flodabay
Leverburgh
Finsbay
Loch Finsbay
Roneval 1506
Ensay
Carminish
Strond
Lingarabay I.
Killegray
Rodel
Vallay
Renish Point
CAR FERRY TO ULLAPOOL
CAR FERRY TO LOCHMADDY
CAR FERRY TO UIG
1 2 3 4 5 6
A B C D E F G H

ORKNEY ISLANDS
SHETLAND ISLANDS
0 1 2 3 4 5 10 15 Miles
0 1 2 3 4 5 6 7 8 16 24 Kilometres
North Ronaldsay
Papa Westray
WESTRAY
SANDAY
Calf of Eday
Eday
ROUSAY
Egilsay
Papa Stronsay
STRONSAY
SHAPINSAY
Kirkwall
Stromness
HOY
Flotta
Burray
SOUTH RONALDSAY
South Walls
Island of Stroma
Pentland Skerries
PENTLAND FIRTH
SCAPA FLOW
Copinsay
Auskerry
John o' Groats
Castletown
Dunnet Bay
CAR FERRY TO SCRABSTER
TO LERWICK
UNST
FETLAR
YELL
Uyea
Out Skerries
WHALSAY
Papa Stour
Muckle Roe
Vementry
Vaila
ST. MAGNUS BAY
Lerwick
BRESSAY
Isle of Noss
West Burra
Mousa
Sumburgh Head
Horse Island
CAR FERRY TO ABERDEEN
TO KIRKWALL
Adjoining p.149
COPYRIGHT, GEORGE PHILIP & SON, LTD.

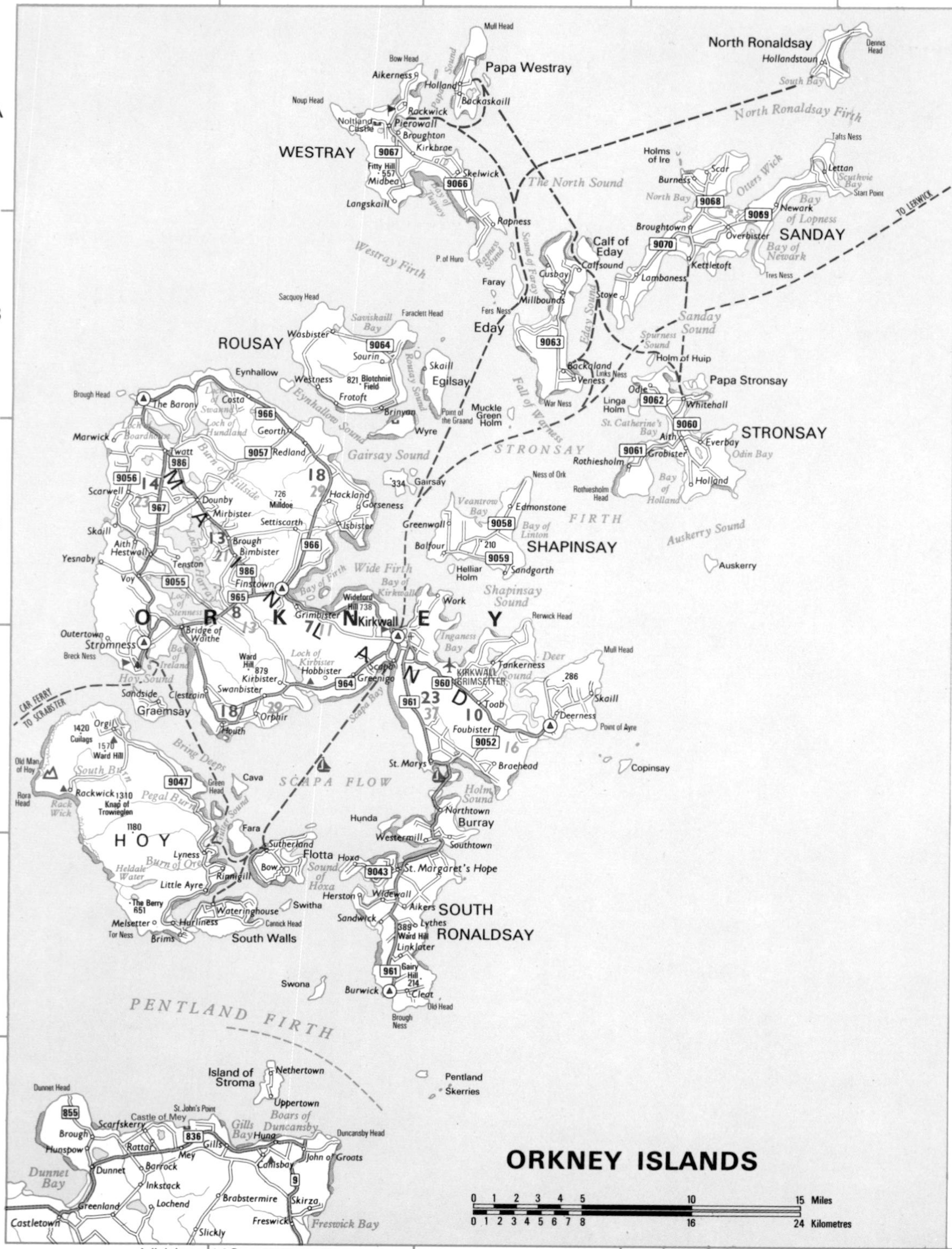

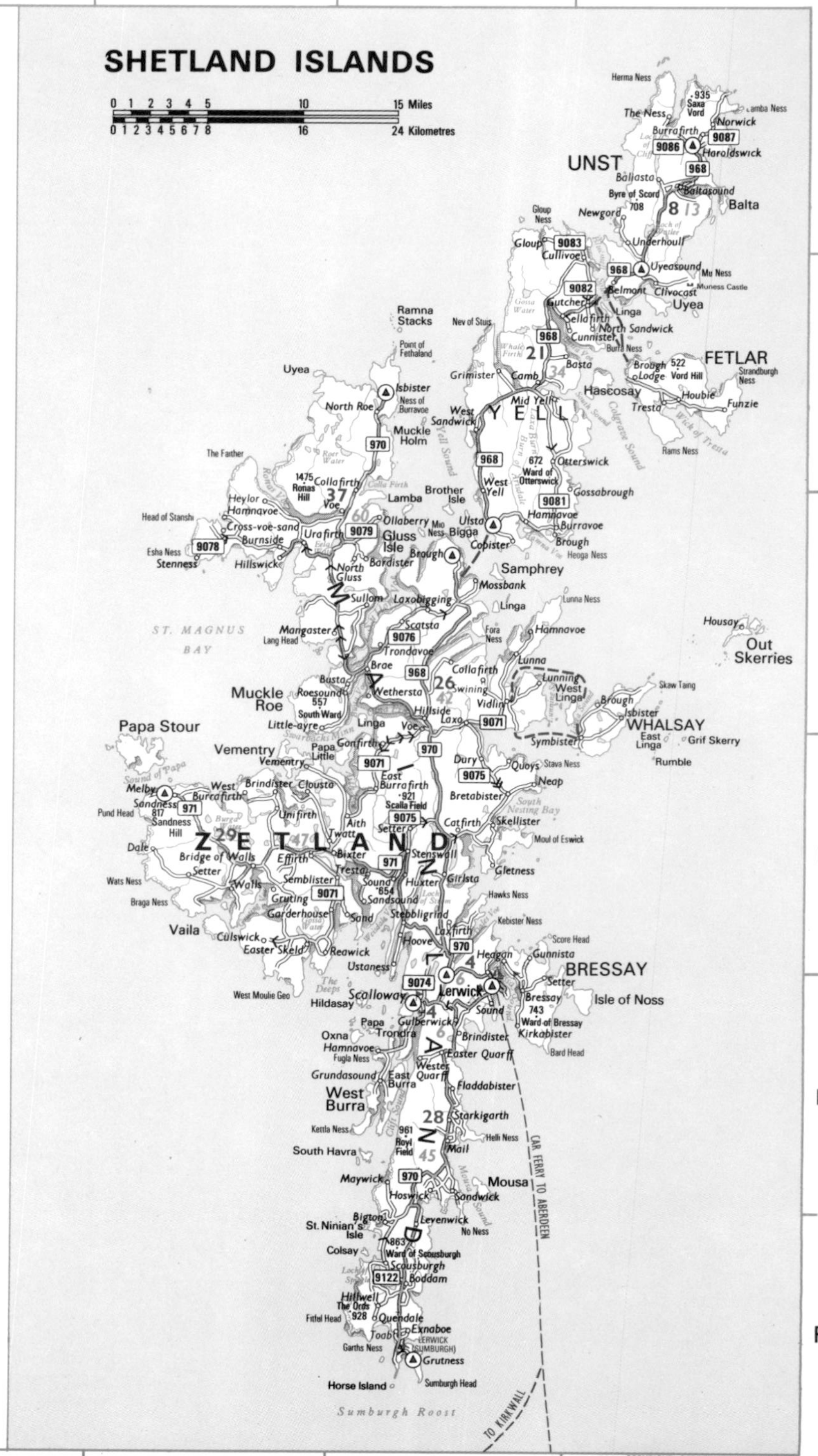

Northern Ireland

THE GIANT'S CAUSEWAY

Outside the conurbations of Belfast and Derry, Northern Ireland largely consists of unspoilt countryside, of a quiet and haunting beauty. Water, and the sea, are never far away however, and it is the sea which has shaped the history and the appearance of the province today, bringing invaders and taking emigrants away on its tides.

From the architectural point of view, the sixteenth- and seventeenth-century 'plantations' of Ulster with settlers from the north of England and Scottish Lowlands were decisive. Scottish town-houses, and later settlers' houses in the Anglo-Dutch style, like Springhill, replaced the medieval churches and abbeys whose remains are still to be seen in the south. Palladianism and neo-classicism became the accepted norms in the eighteenth century, culminating in masterpieces by English architects such as Wyatt's Castle Coole. But there is a streak of wholly Irish eccentricity to be found in the long-drawn-out entrance front of Florence Court,. the mixture of Gothic and classical at Castle Ward, or the 1830s Greek Revival interiors of The Argory – recently acquired by the Trust. Apart from country houses the Trust has a wide variety of other holdings in Northern Ireland, ranging from important gardens like those at Mount Stewart and Rowallane, and ruined castles like Dunseverick, to an early printing press and linen mill, an Adam mausoleum and a High Victorian pub. Had it not been for their rescue, most would not exist today, and Ulster's historic heritage would have been much the poorer.

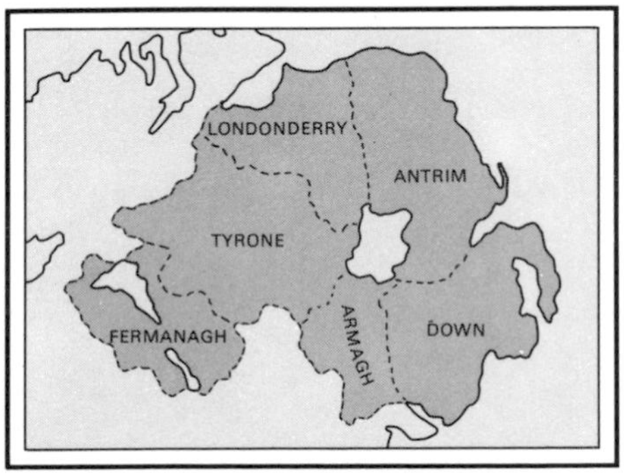

Island-studded Strangford Lough is best known for its wildfowl but is also important in the study of marine biology.

Murlough Bay, Co. Antrim, with its woodlands, is one of the most beautiful stretches of coast in Northern Ireland.

Coast & Countryside

Some of the finest and most varied natural scenery in the British Isles is to be found in Northern Ireland, from the soft green hedgerowed landscape of County Down to the dramatic cliffs of the north coast swept by Atlantic gales – from the lonely marshes and rush-beds which border the vast expanse of Lough Neagh, to the myriad islands, creeks and inlets of Upper Lough Erne.

Most of the 'places of natural beauty' held by the Trust in this region are coastal. Undoubtedly the best-known is the **Giant's Causeway** (159 A7), one of the most extraordinary natural phenomena in the world with its peninsula of basalt rock in the shape of faceted columns marching out into the sea – the result of volcanic activity some sixty million years ago. Enterprise Neptune has had some of its greatest successes in saving the coastline of north Antrim eastwards from the Giant's Causeway, including the ten-mile cliff-path from here to **Dunseverick** and **White Park Bay**, **Carrick-a-rede** with its famous rope bridge and salmon fisheries near Ballintoy, and **Fair Head** and **Murlough Bay** at the north-eastern extremity of Ulster, with views on a clear day as far as Islay and the Paps of Jura (159 A7/8/9).

Further south in County Down, the **Strangford Lough** Wildlife Scheme, established in 1966, has safeguarded the many species of wildfowl which frequent the broad mudflats of this inland sea from the combined effects of poaching and pollution (159 E/F10/11). Other stretches of coast here include two miles of foreshore at **Kearney** and **Knockinelder** (159 F11) east of Portaferry, the **Mourne coastal path** (159 G10), and Ulster's first national nature reserve at **Murlough Bay** (159 G10), near Dundrum. **Blockhouse** and **Green Islands** (159 H9) at the mouth of Carlingford Lough provide some important nesting sites for Arctic and Roseate terns.

Among the inland properties, the glen and waterfall at **Lisnabreeny**, near Newtownbreda, and **Minnowburn Beeches**, with its walks along the Lagan and Minnowburn river banks, are remarkable in being only two or three miles south of the centre of Belfast (159 E9/10).

Houses, Gardens & Parks

Ardress House, Co. Armagh A typical seventeenth-century manor house of the 'plantation' period, Ardress was completely transformed in 1770 by the Dublin architect George Ensor, who had married the heiress to the estate, Sarah Clarke, ten years earlier. On the garden side he added curving screen walls with niches in the Palladian manner, and on the entrance front a bay at each end with urns set on the parapets, and a classical porch. Both façades are washed in a distinctive pale pink colour, which Ensor may also have introduced, and overlook an unspoilt 'natural landscape' framed by great beech trees on one side, and a terraced garden on the other, equally little changed since the eighteenth century.

The finest interior is the drawing room, with delicate plasterwork in the Adam style by the Dublin stuccadore Michael Stapleton. The other rooms, simpler in treatment, contain good Irish furniture of the eighteenth century, and the picture gallery in the centre of the garden front has an interesting collection of paintings on loan from the Earl of Castle Stewart.

7M W Portadown, on B28 (159 F7)

The Argory, Co. Armagh The Argory is an unusually complete and evocative example of the way of life of the Irish gentry in the early nineteenth century. Built about 1820 by a barrister, Walter MacGeough Bond, it was designed by a firm of Dublin architects, A. and J. Williamson, in the newly-fashionable Greek Revival style, and retains most of its original contents. Out in the stable yard is the last surviving example in Northern Ireland of a working acetylene gas plant, and this still provides the house with lighting, by means of a series of bronze gasoliers throughout the main rooms. A magnificent cast-iron stove still exists in the central staircase hall.

The house stands on a hill overlooking a bend in the River Blackwater, with a walled

Castle Coole, perhaps the finest neo-classical house in Ireland, is set in a magnificent landscaped park.

Florence Court is known for its rococo plasterwork, shown here in the staircase hall. The staircase handrail is of tulipwood.

The battlemented Gothick façade of Castle Ward (*above*). **The domestic offices of the house, such as the laundry** (*left*), **are concealed in a sunken courtyard.**

pleasure ground to the north, a charming Victorian rose garden, and heavily-wooded parkland around it, adding to its sense of remoteness and isolation.

4M *SE Moy, on Derrycaw road* (*159 F7*)

Castle Coole, Co. Fermanagh As the acknowledged masterpiece of James Wyatt, Castle Coole ranks as one of the finest neo-classical houses not just in Northern Ireland but in the British Isles. The Corry family settled here in 1656, later building a house near the lough with its famous colony of greylag geese. But it was Armar Lowry-Corry, 1st Earl of Belmore, who in 1788 decided to rebuild on a new site high above the lake.

The house was begun to designs by the Irish architect, Richard Johnston, who was only later superseded by Wyatt, and this explains the still Palladian layout of the main block and end pavilions linked by colonnades. But the scale and assurance of Wyatt's façades give an effect of austere magnificence that makes it a palace rather than a villa. The superb masonry and carving of the exterior is in Portland stone, brought from a specially-constructed quay on the coast, while inside the joinery and plasterwork are also of the highest quality. Wyatt's interiors, with ceilings by Joseph Rose (the elder) and chimneypieces by Richard Westmacott, are now filled with elaborate Regency furniture bought by the 2nd Earl from the Dublin upholsterer John Preston. Castle Coole has been remarkably little changed since that date, and remains the home of the present Earl of Belmore.

1M *SE Enniskillen, on A4* (*158 F4*)

Castle Ward, Co. Down Even for Ireland, Castle Ward is an eccentric house. Though built at one period, between 1762 and 1770, it has two strongly contrasted fronts: a classical entrance façade on the west, and a battlemented Gothick composition on the east. This curious arrangement is said to have come about because the builder, Bernard Ward (later 1st Viscount Bangor) and his wife, Lady Anne Magill, each favoured a different style of architecture. Nor was this the end of their differences for they were formally separated soon after the house was completed. The division between Gothick and classical goes right through the centre of the building – the saloon, the morning room, and Lady Anne's boudoir on the west are all decorated in a charming rococo Gothick style, while the hall, the dining room and Lord Bangor's library on the east are in a more conventional Palladian vein.

The house stands on an eminence with marvellous views over Strangford Lough, and with its domestic offices, including a fully-equipped laundry, carefully concealed in a sunken courtyard to the north. Near the shores of the lough are the old pele tower, built by Nicholas Ward in 1610, the formal canal called the Temple Water (now a wildfowl reserve) and above it a little classical temple, again dating from about 1762.

7M *NE of Downpatrick, on A25* (*159 F11*)

Derrymore House, Co. Armagh A late eighteenth-century *cottage ornée*, Derrymore was built for Isaac Corry, an MP and Chancellor of the Irish Exchequer, as an occasional summer lodge. The 'natural landscape' around it, with carefully-placed clumps of trees, undulating lawns and drives intended to give a variety of viewpoints, was laid out by John Sutherland, the most distinguished Irish landscape gardener of his day – and Sutherland may also have designed the house, which was apparently built in 1776. The thatched roof and rendered walls, Gothic quatrefoils and hood-moulded windows, show that it was conceived more as a picturesque incident in the tour of the grounds than as a full-blown country house.

The central pavilion, linked to two slightly smaller wings (all of one storey), contains the Treaty Room, so called because the Treaty of Union between England and Ireland is said to have been drafted here in 1801 by Isaac Corry, Lord Castlereagh and others.

1½M *NW Newry, off A25* (*159 G8*)

Florence Court, Co. Fermanagh The first house on this wild and romantic site, looking west to the mountains of Cuilcagh, was built about 1710 by Sir John Cole, and named after his wife Florence, daughter and heiress of Sir Bourchier Wrey. Their son John, created Lord Mount Florence, built the present main block with its elaborate, and somewhat archaic, Baroque entrance front about 1750, traditionally to the designs of Richard Castle, though a master-mason using the pattern-books of Serlio, Palladio and Gibbs could equally have been responsible. The riotous rococo plasterwork of the staircase, the dining room ceiling and the Venetian Room on the first floor have been attributed to the Dublin stuccadore, Robert West.

In 1771, the 2nd Lord Mount Florence (later 1st Viscount Enniskillen) employed the Sardinian-born architect, Davis Ducart, to add the long colonnades and wings flanking the original entrance front, making a façade 350 feet in length. Much of the planting of the demesne was carried out at the same date, and in the early nineteenth century under the guidance of John Sutherland. It was here too that the celebrated Florence Court yew (*Taxus baccata* 'Fastigiata'), now generally known as the Irish Yew, was first discovered in 1767.

7M *SW Enniskillen, off A32* (*158 G3*)

Hezlett House, Co. Londonderry A thatched cottage or 'long-house' probably built as a parsonage in 1691, the Hezlett House is of particular importance for the cruck-truss construction of its roof, fairly common at this date in Westmorland and Cumberland but rare in Northern Ireland. The house was acquired in 1761 by a family of well-to-do farmers, the Hezletts, who continued to live there for more than two hundred years and who made only minor additions and alterations to it. Some of the rooms contain simple eighteenth-century oak furniture, and there is a small display of early building and joinery techniques.

4M W Coleraine, on A2 (158 A6/7)

Mount Stewart, Co. Down The demesne was acquired by Alexander Stewart in 1744, but his original house was rebuilt by his son and grandson, the 1st and 3rd Marquesses of Londonderry, in the early nineteenth century. The 1st Marquess employed James 'Athenian' Stuart to design the octagonal Temple of the Winds on a promontory overlooking Strangford Lough in 1782–3, one of the architect's finest buildings and his only one in Ireland. But plans for James Wyatt to remodel the main house at this time came to nothing, and it was not till 1804–5 that the present west wing was built, using drawings sent from London by George Dance. The Music Room and the domed staircase behind it, with Stubbs' famous picture of the racehorse *Hambletonian* on the half-landing, both date from this period.

The rest of the house, including the entrance portico and two-storey hall, were added in the late 1830s by William Vitruvius Morrison, working for the 3rd Marquess, Castlereagh's half-brother. Much of the interior was redecorated and furnished a century later by Edith, Lady Londonderry, wife of the 7th Marquess. She also laid out the celebrated gardens which surround the house, filled with rare (many of them subtropical) trees and plants benefiting from the 'island' climate of the Ards peninsula.

5M SE Newtownards, on A20 (159 E11)

Rowallane, Co. Down The garden at Rowallane is largely the creation of Hugh Armytage Moore, who inherited the house in 1903 and devoted most of his life to its development, planting acres of large-leafed rhododendrons among the whinstone rock outcrops of the drive, converting the walled kitchen garden into a sheltered nursery for rare bulbs, plants, shrubs and trees, and creating a unique spring garden in an area of rocky pastures intersected by dry stone walls. The original chaenomeles, viburnum, hypericum, and the primula named after Rowallane, grow in the walled garden, and maples and dogwoods, birches, nothofagus, magnolia and hydrangea in the spring garden. It is at its best in March, April and May, and again in autumn when the colours are especially brilliant.

1M S Saintfield, on A7 (159 F10)

Springhill, Co. Londonderry Springhill is a simple 'planter's' manor-house, built by the Conyngham family who came from Scotland in the reign of James I and bought the estate in 1658. The house itself dates from the last quarter of the seventeenth century, but represents one of the earliest purely domestic buildings in Ulster, its original defensive barrier and fencework having disappeared. Roughcast and white-washed, it stands among old yew trees, the last trace of an ancient forest which once stretched to Lough Neagh. The lower wings with bay-windows flanking the entrance front are additions of 1765, but most of the original outbuildings – laundry, brewhouse, slaughterhouse, dovecote and stables – still survive. The interior of the house contains much original panelling, an early eighteenth-century balustered staircase, a good library, and furniture of many different dates collected by the Conyngham family, while one of the outbuildings houses a wide-ranging collection of costumes.

Near Moneymore, on the B18 (159 D7)

Rowallane has superb displays of azaleas and rhododendrons.

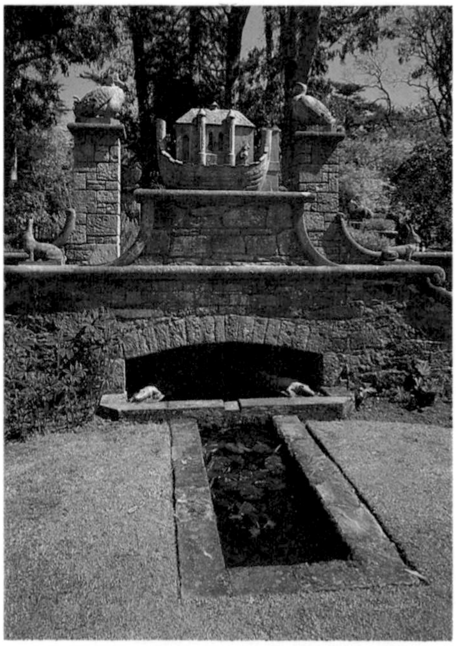

Stone dodos flank the ark on the dodo terrace in the gardens at Mount Stewart; many rare plants are grown here.

Castles, Abbeys & other Buildings

Clough Castle, Co. Down The remains of a Norman castle consisting of a motte and bailey on the Inner Harbour above Dundrum, then an important strategic position, is leased by the Trust to the Historic Monuments Department of the Northern Ireland Government.

5M NE Dundrum, on A24 (159 G10)

The Crown Liquor Saloon, Belfast Perhaps the finest surviving example of a Victorian 'gin palace' anywhere in Britain stands on the corner of Great Victoria Street and Amelia Street in the centre of Belfast. The ground-floor façades are covered in brightly-coloured glazed tiles, with columns and pilasters, but it is the interior that takes the breath away: a riot of engraved and painted glass and mirrors, plasterwork garlands and festoons, tiles and mosaics. The 'snugs' or boxes have tall red oak partitions, elaborately carved and inlaid, to give complete privacy to their occupants. The designer of this Baroque fantasy is said to have been a Mr Flanagan, the son of the proprietor, who in the 1870s and 1880s obtained from Dublin and from London a vast array of manufacturers' stock items, which he then proceeded to put together with remarkable skill and bravura.

A great number of Belfast's splendid nineteenth-century public houses have been demolished or stripped of their original decoration in recent years, but it is some consolation that the Crown – acquired by the Trust in 1978 – has been saved for future generations.

Centre of Belfast, opposite the Europa Hotel (159 E9)

Cushendun, Co. Antrim The village of Cushendun lies at the mouth of a salmon river, the Dun, in the loveliest of the nine Glens of Antrim. With the old stone bridge spanning the estuary, the wide sandy bay beyond the green, the whitewashed and tile-hung cottages (some of them designed by Clough Williams-Ellis, the creator of Portmeirion, Gwynedd), it is picturesque without being self-conscious – like the poetry of its own bard, Moira O'Neill. Behind her house, Rockport, lies the ruined Keep of Castle Carra, where in 1567 the

MacDonnells fêted Shane O'Neill before striking him down and sending his head to Dublin. A cairn further up the hillside on the road to Torr Head marks his grave.

4M N Cushendall, on B92 (159 A9)

Dunseverick Castle, Co. Antrim Part of a ruined watch-tower and curtain wall poised dramatically on a rocky peninsula of the north Antrim coast is all that now remains of one of the oldest and strongest fortified places in Ireland. Said to be the spot where Deirdre of the Sorrows landed on her return from Scotland two thousand years ago, it was stormed by the Vikings in the ninth and tenth centuries, and later became a stronghold of the MacDonnells and the O'Cahans. The remaining fragments are part of the sixteenth-century castle, burnt out by Cromwellian troops in 1642, when the last O'Cahan owner lost both his life and lands.

3M E Giant's Causeway, off B146 (159 A7)

Mussenden Temple, Bishop's Gate and Black Glen, Downhill, Co. Londonderry Downhill was the creation of that colourful character, Frederick Hervey, Bishop of Derry, and 4th Earl of Bristol, known as the Earl-Bishop. The great house, now a ruin, was begun in about 1772 on a bleak and treeless headland overlooking the mouth of Lough Foyle and with superb views along the Donegal and Antrim coasts. Behind it, on the very edge of the cliff, is the Mussenden Temple, a domed rotunda based on the Temple of Vesta at Tivoli, and called after his cousin, Mrs Mussenden, who died shortly before its completion in 1785. The interior was originally furnished as a library, where the Bishop could study with only the roar of the wind and the crash of the waves below as accompaniment. The temple, executed by the Irish architect Michael Shanahan (though originally proposed by James Wyatt) also illustrates the Bishop's obsession with circular buildings – to blossom fully in his two other main houses, Ballyscullion on Lough Beg, and *Ickworth* in Suffolk.

The Bishop's Gate, once the main entrance to the demesne, is in the form of a triumphal arch, again strictly neo-classical in style, with Coade stone ornaments. It leads into Portvantage (otherwise called the Black) Glen, a steep wooded valley leading northwards to the house and temple.

1M W of Castlerock, on A2 (158 A6)

Templetown Mausoleum, Co. Antrim The quiet graveyard at Castle Upton, next to the home farm buildings, and not far from Robert Adam's castellated stables, contains one of the finest monuments the architect ever designed: a perfect little neo-classical temple decorated with Coade stone plaques. The mausoleum was built in 1789 in memory of the Hon. Arthur Upton, who had died over twenty years previously, but it also contains plaques to later members of the Upton family, holders of the title of Lord Templeton.

At Templepatrick on A6, the Belfast–Antrim road (159 D9)

Archaeological & Industrial Sites

Coney Island, Lough Neagh, Co. Armagh Traces of Neolithic settlements have recently been found on this thickly wooded island of about eight acres, once joined to the mainland by a causeway. Later, St Patrick is thought to have used it as a retreat, while a ruined tower remains from the sixteenth-century stronghold of the O'Neills of Tyrone. The island is also an important nesting place for wildfowl.

Mussenden Temple, where the Earl-Bishop studied to the accompaniment of waves breaking on the rocks below.

Wellbrook beetling mill is a reminder of the days when linen manufacture was the most important industry in Ulster.

Reached by boat from Maghery on B196 (159 E7)

Gray's Printing Press, Co. Tyrone In the late eighteenth century Strabane was an important publishing centre with two newspapers and at least ten printing concerns. John Dunlap, printer of the American Declaration of Independence in 1776, and founder of the first daily newspaper in the United States, is said to have learned his trade at Gray's Press before emigrating – like many other Strabane publishers and printers who set up in America and the Colonies. The works were housed in the upper storey of the long whitewashed buildings, now arranged as a museum with various early nineteenth-century presses, while the old bow-fronted shopfront still survives below.

In High Street, Strabane (158 C4)

Rough Fort, Co. Londonderry An impressive rath or Celtic ring fort, surrounded by Scots pines, oaks and beeches, this has as yet remained unexcavated, but may date from the first or second centuries BC.

1M W Limavady, on A2 (158 B6)

Wellbrook Beetling Mill, Co. Tyrone 'Beetling' is the last stage in the manufacture of linen, traditionally Northern Ireland's most famous industry, and involves the pounding of the cloth with heavy timbers to give it its final sheen. The process was originally carried on by hand but in the eighteenth century water-mills were built to make it quicker and more efficient. That on the little trout stream known as the Wellbrook was built in 1765, and continued in operation until 1965, three years before it came to the Trust. In collaboration with the Landmark Trust, it has now been put back into working order, retaining all its original mechanism. The upper floor with its louvred windows still has the airing racks where the pounded cloth was hung to dry.

3M W Cookstown, A505 (158 D6)

White Park Bay, Co. Antrim As well as being one of the most beautiful stretches of coastland on the north Antrim coast, this is one of the most important Neolithic sites in Ulster. Excavations have yielded large amounts of flints and pottery, five or six thousand years old, including a clay figurine of a 'Mother Goddess', the only one of its kind ever found in Ireland. The floors of round huts, kitchen middens, and a burial cairn are all clearly visible.

1½M W Ballintoy (159 A8)

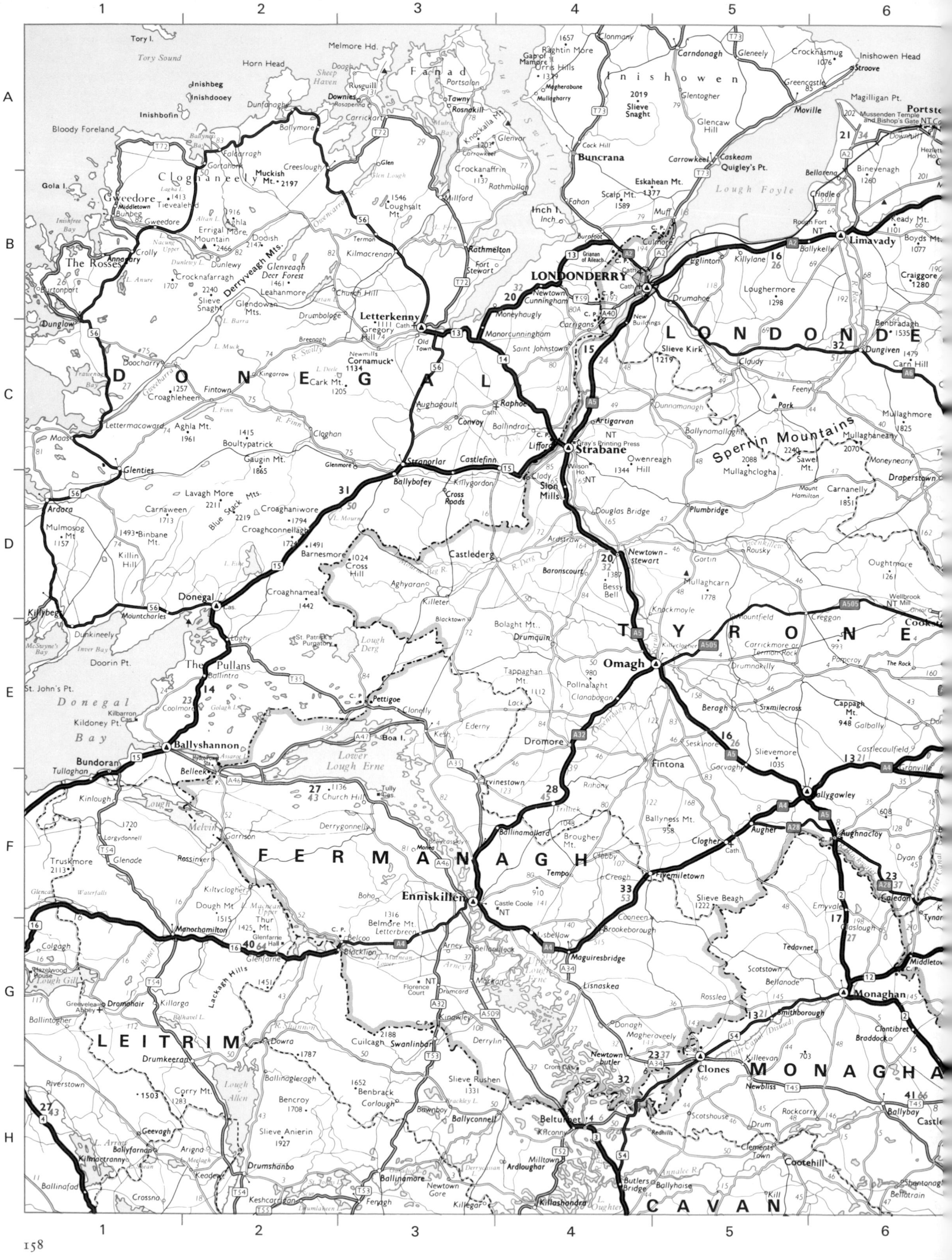

Tory I.
Tory Sound
Melmore Hd.
Horn Head
Fanad
Inishbeg
Inishdooey
Inishbofin
Bloody Foreland
Gola I.
Cloghaneely
Muckish Mt. 2197
Gweedore
The Rosses
Burtonport
Dungloe
Derryveagh Mts.
Errigal Mountain 2466
Glenveagh Deer Forest
Letterkenny
Inishowen
Slieve Snaght
Carndonagh
Inishowen Head
Moville
Greencastle
Magilligan Pt.
Mussenden Temple and Bishop's Gate NT
Buncrana
Lough Swilly
Lough Foyle
Rathmullan
Rathmelton
Milford
Limavady
LONDONDERRY
Newtown Cunningham
Manorcunningham
Saint Johnstown
Slieve Kirk
Dungiven
LONDONDERRY
DONEGAL
Raphoe
Lifford
Strabane
Gray's Printing Press
Sperrin Mountains
Owenreagh Hill
Mullaghclogha
Sawel Mt.
Draperstown
Glenties
Stranorlar
Ballybofey
Castlefinn
Killygordon
Sion Mills
Blue Stack Mts.
Barnesmore
Donegal
Mountcharles
Killybegs
Ardara
Douglas Bridge
Newtown-stewart
Castlederg
Baronscourt
Bessy Bell
Gortin
Mullaghcarn
Plumbridge
TYRONE
Omagh
Cookstown
Lough Derg
St. Patrick's Purgatory
Pettigoe
The Pullans
Ballintra
Donegal Bay
Ballyshannon
Bundoran
Belleek
Lower Lough Erne
Boa I.
Kesh
Irvinestown
Dromore
Fintona
Beragh
Sixmilecross
Ballygawley
Aughnacloy
Clogher
Fivemiletown
FERMANAGH
Enniskillen
Castle Coole NT
Lough Melvin
Garrison
Kinlough
Belcoo
Florence Court NT
Lisbellaw
Maguiresbridge
Lisnaskea
Upper Lough Erne
Manorhamilton
Lough Gill
Dromahair
LEITRIM
Lough Allen
Drumkeeran
Drumshanbo
Ballinamore
Swanlinbar
Cuilcagh 2188
Slieve Rushen
Ballyconnell
Belturbet
Newtownbutler
Clones
Monaghan
MONAGHAN
Emyvale
Glaslough
Smithborough
Ballybay
Castleblayney
Cootehill
Redhills
Killashandra
Butlers Bridge
CAVAN
Arigna
Ballyfarnan
Ballinafad
Crossna
Keshcarrigan
Fenagh

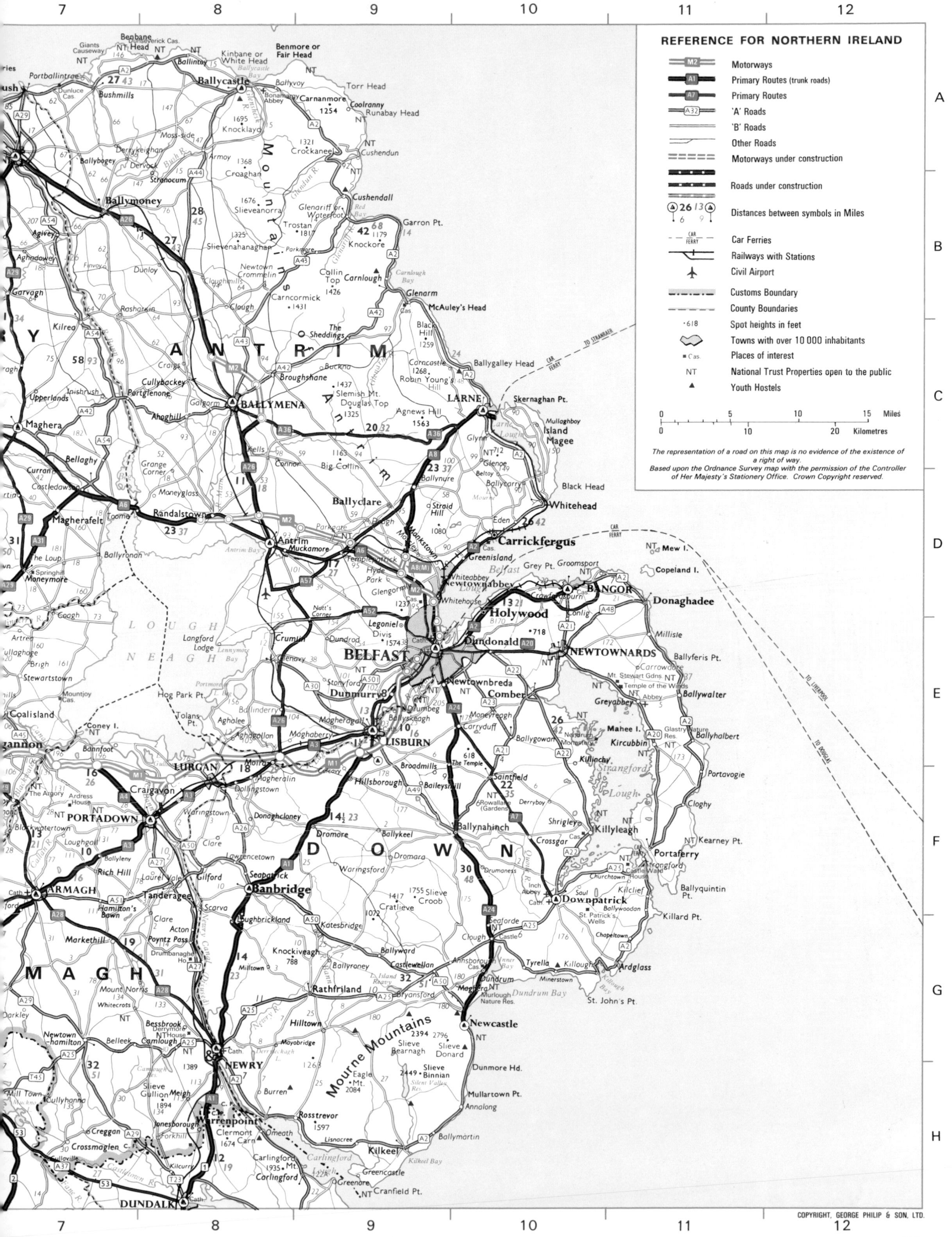

REFERENCE FOR NORTHERN IRELAND
Motorways
Primary Routes (trunk roads)
Primary Routes
'A' Roads
'B' Roads
Other Roads
Motorways under construction
Roads under construction
Distances between symbols in Miles
Car Ferries
Railways with Stations
Civil Airport
Customs Boundary
County Boundaries
Spot heights in feet
Towns with over 10 000 inhabitants
Places of interest
National Trust Properties open to the public
Youth Hostels
Miles
Kilometres
The representation of a road on this map is no evidence of the existence of a right of way.
Based upon the Ordnance Survey map with the permission of the Controller of Her Majesty's Stationery Office. Crown Copyright reserved.
ANTRIM
DOWN
LOUGH NEAGH
Mourne Mountains
BELFAST
Ballymena
Larne
Carrickfergus
Bangor
Newtownards
Lisburn
Lurgan
Portadown
Armagh
Newry
Downpatrick
Newcastle
Ballycastle
Ballymoney
Antrim
Holywood
Comber
Banbridge
Dundalk
TO STRANRAER
TO LIVERPOOL
TO DOUGLAS
CAR FERRY

Glossary

ambulatory an enclosed space for walking

apse a semi-circular or polygonal recess, with an arched or domed roof

bailey the open space or court of a castle, also known as a *ward*. See *motte and bailey*

baluster one of the posts or pillars supporting a rail and thus forming a balustrade

balustrade *see baluster*

barbican the outer defence of a castle that protects the entrance; often a double tower over a gate or bridge

Baroque architecture of the seventeenth and early eighteenth century characterized by exuberant decoration, curvaceous forms and large-scale compositions

bressummer a horizontal timber supporting a wall above it, such as the lintel of a fireplace. Also the principal horizontal beam in a timber-framed building

buttress masonry or brickwork projecting from or built against a wall to give additional strength

cap house the superstructure roofing a tower or stair-well

capital the head or crowning feature of a column

classical forms in architecture or decoration based on those developed in ancient Rome or Greece

collar-beam a horizontal timber that lies across the pitch of the roof above the point where roof and walls meet (*see tie-beam*)

corbel a projecting block or bracket, usually of stone, built into a wall to support a vault or beam

corbelling brick or masonry courses, each built out beyond the one below like a series of *corbels* to support, for example, a projecting window

cornice any projecting ornamental moulding on the top of a building, or wall of a room. Also the top projecting part of an *entablature* in classical architecture

cottage ornée an intentionally rustic building that was a product of the picturesque cult of the late eighteenth and early nineteenth century

cove a curved, concave junction of wall and ceiling

cruck a simple but massive construction used in some forms of *half-timbering*. Two curved timbers form an inverted V and support the roof, and in some cases the walls also

cupola a dome, especially a small dome crowning a roof or turret

curtain wall the outer wall encircling a castle, usually punctuated with towers

dado in *classical* architecture the cubic block forming the body of a pedestal; also a skirting along the lower part of the walls of a room

Decorated the middle phase of *Gothic* architecture in England, *c*.1290–1370, characterized by *ogee* arches and abundant carvings

doocot Scots form of English 'dovecote'

Doric denoting one of the Greek orders of architecture, distinguished by simplicity of design

enceinte in military architecture, the main enclosure of a fortress, surrounded by a wall or ditch

entablature the structure supported by the column of *classical* architecture. It consists of an architrave, *frieze* and *cornice*

escutcheon a shield on which a coat of arms is represented

foil a lobe or leaf-shaped curve formed by the cusping of a circle or an arch. A prefix indicates the number of foils, e.g. trefoil, quatrefoil

frieze a decorated band along the upper part of an internal wall, immediately below the *cornice*. In *classical* architecture, the middle division of an entablature

gable the triangular upper part of a wall at the end of a pitched roof, corresponding to a *pediment* in *classical* architecture

Gothic architecture of the medieval period featuring the pointed arch, stone vaults and huge traceried windows

Gothick the conscious use in the eighteenth and early nineteenth century of what was thought to be medieval Gothic style

Gothic Revival the nineteenth-century interpretation of Gothic architecture which developed from *Gothick*

ha-ha a sunken ditch, intended to be invisible from the house, which kept park animals away from the lawn but allowed an uninterrupted view into the park

half-timbering (*timber-framing*) a method of construction in which walls are built of interlocking vertical and horizontal timbers. The spaces are infilled with *wattle and daub*, lath and plaster or brick

hammer beam horizontal brackets of timber projecting at the level of the base of the rafts in a roof. The inner ends support hammer-posts and braces to a *collar beam*

hammer-pond an artificial pond providing water for a mill

hill-fort a prehistoric stronghold on a hill

hypocaust a space under a floor for heating by hot air or furnace gases, as characteristic of ancient Roman villas

inglenook a recess for a bench or seat built beside a fireplace

Ionic a style of Greek architecture characterized by *capitals* decorated with spiral scrolls

keep the principal central tower of a castle

king-post a vertical timber standing centrally on a *tie-* or *collar-beam* and rising to the apex of the roof where it supports a ridge

knot garden a garden of beds forming elaborate designs, planted with foliage and flowers in patterns. The beds are hedged in box or some other dwarf plant. The knot garden was at its height in the late sixteenth and early seventeenth centuries

linenfold Tudor panelling ornamented with a conventional representation of a piece of linen laid in vertical folds

loggia a gallery open on one or more sides, sometimes pillared; it may also be a separate structure, usually in a garden

loop a small, narrow and often unglazed window opening

louvre a series of overlapping boards or strips of glass (in a window) that can be opened or closed

machicolation a gallery or parapet built on the outside of castle towers or walls, with apertures through which missiles could be thrown

motte a steep mound, the main feature of many eleventh- and twelfth-century castles

motte and bailey a post-Roman and Norman defence system consisting of an earthen mound topped with a wooden tower, placed within a *bailey* encircled by a ditch and palisade

mullion a vertical post or other upright dividing a window or other opening

neo-classical the architectural style which developed after 1750 based upon the direct study of the buildings of ancient Greece and Rome

newel stair a spiral staircase with a continuous post supporting the narrow inner ends of the treads

ogee arch an arch formed of shallow S-shaped curves meeting in a point

oriel a bay window on an upper storey or storeys

Palladianism the architectural style influenced by the designs and buildings of Andrea Palladio, the sixteenth-century Italian architect, and introduced to England by Inigo Jones in the early seventeenth century. Palladio believed that architecture could be governed by certain universal rules reflected in the buildings of ancient Rome, notably symmetrical planning and the use of harmonic proportions. Palladianism was revived in England in the early eighteenth century

pargetting the exterior plastering of half-timbered buildings, usually decorated

parterre the elaborate, formal gardens, planted in intricate patterns and often to flowing designs, which developed from *knot gardens*

pediment in *classical* architecture, a low-pitched gable above a *portico*

pele tower a small or moderate-sized, easily defended tower or keep, usually built between the thirteenth and fifteenth centuries. Pele towers are peculiar to houses and castles on both sides of the Scottish border

piano nobile the main floor of a house, containing the reception rooms

pilaster a shallow rectangular column projecting slightly from a wall

portico a roofed space, open or partly enclosed, often forming the entrance and centre piece of the façade of a temple or house

potence in a dovecote, a vertical beam in the centre of the building to which several horizontal beams are attached at varying heights. The vertical beam pivots so that all nesting boxes can be reached from ladders fixed to the end of each horizontal beam

quatrefoil *see foil*

quoins the dressed stones at the corners of buildings, usually laid so that the exposed faces are alternately long and short (known as long-and-short work)

rococo the light-hearted sequel to *Baroque*. Formulated in France, it reached England after 1730 and remained for thirty years. The decoration is characterized by rocaille (shell-like and coral-like forms), C and S curves, and naturalistic scenes

rotunda a circular room or building, usually domed

screens passage the space or corridor at the service end of a medieval hall, dividing it from the buttery, pantry and kitchen

solar the living room in an upper storey of a medieval house or castle

studs (studding) in half-timbered buildings, the secondary vertical timbers in the walls

tie-beam the horizontal transverse roof beam connecting the base of the rafters

timber-framing *see half-timbering*

tower-house a medieval type of fortified house exclusive to Scotland. The main hall is raised above the ground and has one or more storeys above

transept the part of a building at right-angles to the main body, usually that part of a church at right-angles to the nave

transom a horizontal bar of stone or wood across the opening of a window, or across a panel

trefoil *see foil*

trompe l'oeil in painting, the representation of an object with such exactitude as to deceive the eye into believing the object real

truss a number of timbers framed together to bridge a space or form a bracket

vallum a rampart, usually formed of material from the associated ditch

vault an arched ceiling or roof of stone or brick. The simplest form is a tunnel vault or barrel vault, consisting of a continuous vault of semi-circular or pointed sections

ward the court of a castle

wattle and daub a method of simple wall construction in which branches or thin wooden laths (wattle) are roughly plastered over with mud or clay (daub) used as a filling between the uprights of a half-timbered house

---

Architects and Craftsmen

In the entries below, some examples of National Trust properties (where the architects etc worked) are mentioned in *italics*. These, for reasons of space, by no means comprise a complete list, nor are the architects, craftsmen and landscape gardeners necessarily always mentioned in the brief descriptions of the properties in the main text of this *Atlas*. The Trusts' guidebooks to individual properties will give the interested visitor full details.

Robert Adam (1728–92) Architect. A Scot by birth, working within a family firm, the Adam Brothers, he devised a neo-classical style lighter and more elegant than the prevailing Palladian. He enlivened the rather monumental Palladian style with ornament and decoration while retaining Palladian balance and proportion. Equally distinguished as an interior decorator; noted for his elegant fireplaces and furniture. *(Charlotte Square, Culzean Castle, Hatchlands, Nostell Priory, Osterley, Saltram)*

Thomas Archer (1668–1743) Successful English practitioner of the florid Baroque architecture of southern Europe.

Sir Herbert Baker (1862–1946) Worked with Lutyens in New Delhi. In general his style was a somewhat heavy imperial classicism. *(Owletts)*

Sir Charles Barry (1795–1860) Versatile early Victorian architect. His early work is neo-Gothic, but later he gracefully adapted Greek and Italian classical ideas, as in the rebuilding of *Cliveden*.

G. F. Bodley (1827–1907) Of Scottish descent, first pupil of George Gilbert Scott, he mainly worked on churches, always in the Gothic style. An early patron of William Morris. *(Clumber Chapel)*

Charles Bridgeman (d. 1738) Landscape gardener, credited with introducing the ha-ha into England from France (at Stowe in 1719). Little of his original work remains. *(Wimpole Hall)*

Lancelot ('Capability') Brown (1716–83) Most famous figure in English eighteenth-century landscape gardening. 'Improved' nature through informal, though carefully planned, parks, typically including wide sweeps of grass, clumped trees and serpentine lakes. *(Berrington Hall, Charlecote Park, Claremont Landscape Garden, Petworth Park, Wimpole Hall)*

William Burges (1827–81) Eclectic Victorian Gothic Revivalist. Created sumptuous interiors using a wide range of media from stained glass to fabrics, all of which he designed. Interesting and original architect. *(Knightshayes)*

William Burn (1789–1870) Initiator of 'Scottish Baronial' style for country houses *c.*1830. Richard Norman Shaw was a pupil. *(Brodie Castle, House of The Binns)*

Colen Campbell (1676–1729) One of the chief perpetrators of the large English Palladian country house. *(Stourhead)*

John Carr (1723–1807) Late exponent of Palladianism, working mainly in Yorkshire. Associated with Robert Adam in building Harewood House (begun 1759), and afterwards was responsible for many large country houses. *(Basildon Park)*

Sir William Chambers (1723–96) The leading official architect of his day in England, his reputation with public buildings (Somerset House, for instance) brought commissions for country houses – all in the Palladian style.

Thomas Chippendale (1718–79) Furniture maker, whose reputation was founded on his *Gentleman and Cabinet-Maker's Director* (in the 1750s), a catalogue of his firm's designs. Since others worked from Chippendale's designs, much that is called 'Chippendale' is in fact Chippendale-style, and not made by his firm. He worked in different styles, Chinese Chippendale being one of the most famous. *(Nostell Priory, Osterley)*

Thomas Cubitt (1788–1855) Speculative builder, who with his more architecturally gifted brother Lewis was largely responsible for Bloomsbury, Belgravia (not Belgrave Square) and Pimlico. *(Polesden Lacey)*

Henry Flitcroft (1697–1769) Protégé of Lord Burlington, and succeeded William Kent as Master Mason and Deputy Surveyor in the Office of Works. His work was in the Palladian style. *(Stourhead temples, Wimpole Hall)*

Grinling Gibbons (1648–1720) Of Dutch origin, he was the most gifted woodcarver to work in Britain. Using softwoods (pear, lime etc.) he created life-size and life-like festoons of flowers, fruits etc. *(Petworth House)*

James Gibbs (1682–1754) Influential early eighteenth-century London church architect. Influenced by Sir Christopher Wren and the Baroque, and also incorporating Palladian features in his work. St Martin-in-the-Fields in Trafalgar Square is his best-known work. *(Wimpole Hall)*

Henry Holland (1745–1806) Architect, once assistant to 'Capability' Brown, with a style owing something both to Chambers and Adam, his interior decoration approached French neo-classicism in elegance. *(Berrington Hall)*

Inigo Jones (1573–1652) Initially famous as a stage designer, he was the first to introduce classical Palladian architecture to England. (He encountered the designs of Andrea Palladio while journeying in Italy in 1613.) The Queen's House, Greenwich, was the first strictly classical building in England.

William Kent (1685–1748) Painter, furniture designer, landscape gardener and architect, starting life as a barely literate coach-painter. Protégé of Lord Burlington, he became Master Mason and Deputy Surveyor in the Office of Works in 1735. Major commissions were designed along Palladian lines. His interior decoration is rich with sumptuous carving and gilt. Historically most important as a landscape gardener – one of the first to revolt against the formal seventeenth-century garden and to harmonize landscape and country house. *(Claremont Landscape Garden)*

Giacomo Leoni (*c.*1686–1746) Born in Venice, he settled in England before 1715. An architect in the Palladian style. *(Clandon Park, Lyme Park)*

Sir Edwin Lutyens (1869–1944) Architect of some of the last spectacular English country houses, including *Castle Drogo* and *Lindisfarne*. Also responsible for a number of fine country houses in the Arts and Crafts style. The chief designer of New Delhi.

Sanderson Miller (1717–80) Gothic Revivalist and noted builder of sham castles in the 1740s. *(Lacock Abbey hall, Wimpole Hall Gothic tower)*

William Morris (1834–96) Vigorous opponent of Victorian industrialization and champion of traditional crafts. Designer of wallpapers, stained glass, fabrics, and carpets for the firm of Morris & Co. A profound influence on the arts and crafts of the time. *(Cragside, Standen, Wallington, Wightwick Manor)*

John Nash (1752–1835) Prolific architect in many styles, including the Picturesque. Greatest achievement was the layout of Regent's Park and its terraces and Regent Street. *(Attingham Park, Blaise Hamlet village)*

James Paine (1717–89) Architect in the Palladian tradition, working largely in the north of England. His interiors are noted for especially fine rococo ceilings. *(Felbrigg Hall, Nostell Priory, Wallington bridge)*

J. B. Papworth (1775–1847) Designed several country houses; also a landscape gardener. Much of his work was in Cheltenham. *(Claremont Landscape Garden)*

Augustus Welby Pugin (1812–52) A principal architect of the Victorian Gothic Revival and responsible for the decorative detail in Barry's Houses of Parliament. His work was chiefly ecclesiastical.

Humphry Repton (1752–1818) Leading landscape gardener of the generation after Brown. He introduced formal gardens with parterres and terraces close to the houses, contrasting with the landscaped parks beyond. *(Attingham Park, Tatton Park)*

Anthony Salvin (1799–1881) Medieval architecture expert and a central figure in the Victorian Gothic Revival, though using a wide range of styles. A pupil of Nash and an authority on the restoration and improvement of castles. *(Dunster Castle, Petworth House south front)*

Richard Norman Shaw (1831–1912) Influential domestic architect of the late Victorian era. His early work was Gothic in style but later he turned to the so-called 'Queen Anne style', influenced by Dutch examples and the architecture of the William and Mary period. *(Cragside)*

Sir Robert Smirke (1780–1867) The leading Greek Revival architect in England and designer of the British Museum.

Robert Smythson (*c.*1536–1614) Elizabethan architect, builder of spectacular houses for the magnates of the time. *(Gawthorpe Hall, Hardwick Hall)*

Sir John Soane (1753–1837) Notably individual architect and designer influenced by and of the generation after Robert Adam. *(Wimpole Hall)*

James 'Athenian' Stuart (1713–88) Important in the history of neo-Greek architecture for his temple at Hagley (1758). His best surviving works are his Doric Temple etc in the park at *Shugborough*.

William Talman (1650–1719) Leading country house architect until eclipsed by Vanbrugh. His large, lavish houses are Baroque in character. *(Dyrham Park)*

John Webb (1611–72) Pupil of Inigo Jones, with whom he worked closely. Little of his independent work survives. *(The Vyne portico)*

Philip Speakman Webb (1831–1915) With Norman Shaw, one of the most influential domestic architects of the late Victorian period. Designed furniture for William Morris's firm. *(Standen)*

William Winde (d. 1722) Starting in middle age, he became a leader of the Anglo-Dutch school of architects. None of his buildings definitely survive, though he may have been the architect of *Ashdown House*.

James Wyatt (1747–1813) Most successful architect of his day, willing to give his clients what they wanted. His classical houses include *Castle Coole* in Northern Ireland. He also designed neo-Gothic extravaganzas.

Sir Jeffry Wyatville (1766–1840) Nephew of James Wyatt, competent classical architect, but specialized in neo-Gothic and Tudor collegiate mansions. Knighted for his work on Windsor Castle. *(Philipps House)*

Index to text

Page numbers in italics denote illustrations of the properties concerned.

County index to properties

WALES

SCOTLAND

Great Britain map index

ABBREVIATIONS

Beds. – Bedfordshire
Berks. – Berkshire
Bucks. – Buckinghamshire
Cambs. – Cambridgeshire
Cas. – Castle
Ches. – Cheshire
Co. – County
Com. – Common
Corn. – Cornwall
Cumb. – Cumbria
Derby. – Derbyshire
Dumf. & Gall. – Dumfries & Galloway
Dur. – Durham
E. – East
E. Sussex – East Sussex
Glos. – Gloucestershire
Gt. – Great
Grn. – Green
Hants. – Hampshire
Heref. & Worcs. – Hereford & Worcester
Hth. – Heath
Herts. – Hertfordshire
Ho. – House
Humber. – Humberside
I.o.M. – Isle of Man
I.o.W. – Isle of Wight
Junc. – Junction
Lancs. – Lancashire
Leics. – Leicestershire
Lincs. – Lincolnshire
Lo. – Lodge
London – Greater London
Manchester – Greater Manchester
Mid Glam. – Mid Glamorgan
Norf. – Norfolk
N. – North
N. Yorks. – North Yorkshire
Northants. – Northamptonshire
Northumb. – Northumberland
Notts. – Nottinghamshire
Oxon. – Oxfordshire
Salop. – Shropshire
Som. – Somerset
S. – South
S. Glam. – South Glamorgan
S. Yorks. – South Yorkshire
Staffs. – Staffordshire
Sta. – Station
Suff. – Suffolk
War. – Warwickshire
W. – West
W. Glam. – West Glamorgan
W. Mid. – West Midlands
W. Sussex – West Sussex
W. Yorks. – West Yorkshire
W. Isles – Western Isles
Wilts. – Wiltshire

AB

96 Ab Kettleby H 4
39 Abbas Combe D 10
88 Abberley E 1
87 Abberton, Essex B 10
88 Abberton, Heref. & Worcs G 3
133 Abberwick B 9
86 Abbess Roding C 6
38 Abbey E 5
57 Abbey Dore A 7
38 Abbey Hill D 6
95 Abbey Hulton E 7
137 Abbey St. Bathans C 10
96 Abbey Town F 12
110 Abbey Village E 5
58 Abbeycwmhir E 6
114 Abbeylands, I.o.M. G 2
133 Abbeylands, Northumb. B 10
110 Abbeystead B 4
36 Abbots Bickington E 3
95 Abbots Bromley H 9
85 Abbots Langley D 11
57 Abbots Leigh G 8
88 Abbot's Morton G 4
91 Abbots Ripton G 3
88 Abbot's Salford G 4
39 Abbotsbury H 9
36 Abbotsham C 3
37 Abbotskerswell J 7
91 Abbotsley K 3
40 Abbotswood D 5
40 Abbots Ann B 5
59 Abcott E 9
59 Abdon D 11
55 Aber, Dyfed B 8
60 Aber, Gwynedd C 6
55 Aberarth A 8
58 Aber Gwydol B 3
60 Aber-Gwynant H 6
56 Aber Village B 4
55 Aberaeron A 8
56 Aberaman D 3
58 Aberangell A 4
145 Aberarder, Highland G 2
143 Aberarder, Highland L 8
140 Aberargie F 6
55 Aberavon H 11
55 Aber-banc C 7
56 Aberbeeg D 5
56 Aberbran A 3
56 Abercanaid D 4
56 Abercarn E 5
54 Abercastle D 2
58 Abercegir B 4
143 Aberchalder J 7
146 Aberchirder B 4
55 Abercraf F 11
56 Abercrave C 2
56 Abercregan E 2
56 Abercwmboi D 3
54 Abercych C 6
56 Abercynafon C 4
56 Abercynon E 4
56 Aberdare D 3
60 Aberdaron H 1
147 Aberdeen G 7
60 Aberdesach E 4
136 Aberdour A 5
58 Aberdovey C 2
55 Aberdulais G 11
58 Aberedw H 6
54 Abereiddy D 2
60 Abererch G 3
56 Aberfan D 4
140 Aberfeldy B 3
60 Aberffraw C 3
58 Aberffrwd E 2
112 Aberford C 2
139 Aberfoyle G 12
55 Abergarwed G 11
56 Abergavenny C 6
61 Abergele B 9
55 Abergiar C 8
55 Abergorlech D 9
58 Abergwesyn G 4
55 Abergwili E 8
56 Abergwynfi E 2
58 Abergynolwyn B 2
58 Aberhosan C 4
56 Aberkenfig F 2
137 Aberlady A 7
141 Aberlemno B 10
58 Aberllefenni A 3
58 Abermeurig G 1
59 Abermule C 7
55 Abernant, Dyfed E 7
56 Aber-nant, Mid Glam. D 3
141 Abernethy E 7
141 Abernyte D 7
54 Aberporth B 6
60 Abersoch G 3
56 Abersychan D 6
56 Aberthin G 3
56 Abertillery D 5
56 Abertridwr, Mid Glam. E 4
61 Abertridwr, Powys H 9
56 Abertysswg D 5
140 Aberuthven F 5
56 Aberyscir A 3
58 Aberystwyth D 2
84 Abingdon D 6
41 Abinger Common B 12
41 Abinger Hammer A 12
136 Abington G 2
91 Abington Pigotts L 4
84 Ablington, Glos. C 2
40 Ablington, Wilts. A 3
95 Abney B 10
147 Aboyne H 3
110 Abram G 5
144 Abriachan F 1
86 Abridge D 5
57 Abson G 10
89 Abthorpe G 10
97 Aby B 11
59 Acaster Malbis C 4
112 Acaster Selby C 3
36 Accott C 5
110 Accrington D 6
150 Achachork D 4
138 Achadun D 5
138 Achafolla F 5
149 Achagary B 7
134 Achahoish B 3
139 Achallader C 10
134 Achamore Farm E 1
142 Achanalt D 6
134 Achanamara A 3
144 Achandunie C 2
148 Achany F 6
143 Achaphubuil M 5
138 Acharacle A 4
138 Acharn, Highland C 4
140 Acharn, Tayside C 2
149 Acharole C 11
134 Acharosson B 4
138 Achateny A 3
146 Achath F 5
149 Achavanich C 11
144 Achavraat E 5
148 Achavraie F 2
55 Achddu G 8
149 Achentoul D 8
148 Achfary C 4
148 Achfrish F 6
148 Achgarve G 1
148 Achiemore, Kyle of Durness, Highland A 4
149 Achiemore, Highland B 9
150 A'Chill H 2
148 Achiltibuie F 2
149 Achina B 7
139 Achindarroch B 7
143 Achintee, Highland M 5
142 Achintee, Highland F 3
142 Achintraid F 2
143 Achlain H 6
145 Achlean K 4
138 Achleck C 1
134 A'Chleit E 2
139 Achlian E 8
143 Achluachrach L 7
148 Achlyness B 4
148 Achmelvich E 2
140 Achmore, Central D 1
142 Achmore, Highland F 2
151 Achmore, W. Isles D 4
139 Achnaba, Strathclyde D 7
134 Achnaba, Strathclyde A 4
145 Achnabat G 2
148 Achnacarnin D 2
143 Achnacarry L 5
150 Achnacloich G 5
139 Achnacon B 8
138 Achnacraig C 2
138 Achnacroish C 6
138 Achnadrish B 2
139 Achnafalnich E 9
143 Achnafraschoille L 6
144 Achnaggaron C 2
138 Achnaha A 2
148 Achnahanat G 6
138 Achnalea A 6
149 Achnaluachrach F 7
143 Achnanellan L 5
148 Achnanerain F 6
143 Achnangart H 3
143 Achnasaul K 5
142 Achnasheen D 5
142 Achnashellach E 4
144 Achnastank F 8
138 Achosnich A 2
138 Achranich C 4
149 Achreamie A 9
139 Achriabhach A 8
148 Achriesgill B 4
149 Achrimsdale F 9
149 Achtoty B 7
91 Achurch G 1
148 Achuvoldrach B 6
149 Achvaich G 7
145 Achvraid, Highland G 2
144 Achvraid, Highland F 2
149 Ackergill B 12
116 Acklam, Cleveland C 5
112 Acklam, N. Yorks. A 5
88 Ackleton B 1
133 Acklington C 10
112 Ackton E 2
112 Ackworth Moor Top F 2
92 Acle D 7
88 Acock's Green D 5
43 Acol A 11
133 Acomb, Northumb. F 7
112 Acomb, N. Yorks. B 4
57 Aconbury A 8
110 Acre E 6
41 Acre Street F 9
61 Acrefair F 12
94 Acton, Cheshire E 5
40 Acton, Dorset H 1
86 Acton, London F 2
59 Acton, Salop D 8
93 Acton, Suffolk L 2
94 Acton Bridge C 4
59 Acton Beauchamp G 12
59 Acton Burnell B 10
59 Acton Green G 12
94 Acton Park E 2
59 Acton Pigott B 11
59 Acton Round C 11
59 Acton Scott C 10
95 Acton Trussell H 8
57 Acton Turville F 11
94 Adbaston G 6
39 Adber D 9
94 Adderley F 5
133 Adderstone C 12
136 Addiewell C 3
111 Addingham B 9
85 Addington, Bucks. A 8
42 Addington, Kent B 5
86 Addington, London G 4
137 Addinston D 8
85 Addlestone H 11
97 Addlethorpe C 12
112 Adel C 1
94 Adeney H 5
58 Adfa B 6
59 Adforton E 9
43 Adisham C 11
84 Adlestrop A 3
112 Adlingfleet E 6
95 Adlington, Ches. B 7
110 Adlington, Lancs. F 5
59 Admaston, Salop. A 11
95 Admaston, Staffs. H 9
88 Admington G 5
85 Adstock A 8
89 Adstone G 9
41 Adversane D 12
144 Advie F
112 Adwick le Street F
112 Adwick upon Dearne G
36 Adworthy D
146 Adziel B
131 Ae Bridgend C 1
131 Ae Village C 1
36 Affeton Barton E
146 Affleck, Grampian D
146 Affleck, Grampian E
39 Affpuddle G 1
143 Affric Lodge G
61 Afonwen C 1
37 Afton, Devon J
40 Afton, I.o.W. G
135 Afton Bridgend H 1
116 Agglethorpe F
114 Agneash G
151 Aignish D
113 Aike C
152 Aikerness A
152 Aikers E
131 Aiket E 1
115 Aiketgate A
132 Aikton H
59 Ailey G
90 Ailsworth F
116 Ainderby Steeple F
87 Aingers Green B 1
110 Ainsdale F
115 Ainstable A
110 Ainsworth F
117 Ainthorpe D
110 Aintree G
130 Aird, Dumf & Gall. F
138 Aird, Strathclyde G
151 Aird, W. Isles C
150 Aird of Sleat H
151 Aird of Tunga C
151 Aird Uig C
148 Airdachuilinn C
135 Airdrie C 1
135 Airdsgreen F 1
149 Airdtorrisdale B
142 Airigh-drishaig F
112 Airmyn E
140 Airntully D
143 Airor J
140 Airth H
111 Airton A
130 Airyhassen G

7 Aisby, Lincs. F 7
6 Aisby, Lincs. A 6
5 Aisgill E 10
7 Aish K 6
8 Aisholt C 5
6 Aiskew F 3
6 Aislaby, N. Yorks. D 4
7 Aislaby, N. Yorls. G 8
7 Aislaby, N. Yorks. D 8
6 Aisthorpe B 6
2 Aith, Orkney Is. C 4
2 Aith, Shetland Is. D 7
2 Aith Hestwall C 1
0 Aitkenhead A 4
4 Aitnoch F 5
7 Akeld F 12
7 Akeld Steads F 12
9 Akeley H 10
3 Akenham K 5
5 Albaston C 11
9 Alberbury A 9
4 Albert Town E 3
2 Albourn F 1
38 Albrighton, Salop, B 2
4 Albrighton, Salop. H 4
3 Alburgh G 6
3 Alburgh Street G 5
36 Albury, Herts. B 4
1 Albury, Surrey A 12
2 Alby Hill B 5
4 Alcaig D 1
38 Alcester F 4
2 Alciston G 4
38 Alcombe, Som. B 3
7 Alcombe, Wilts. G 11
91 Alconbury H 3
91 Alconbury Hill G 3
91 Alconbury Weston H 3
35 Aldandulish M 5
92 Aldborough, Norf. B 5
6 Aldborough, N. Yorks. H 4
84 Aldbourne G 4
13 Aldbrough, C 10
16 Aldbrough St. John D 2
35 Aldbury C 10
40 Aldcharmaig A 3
10 Aldcliffe A 3
40 Aldclune A 4
93 Aldeburgh J 8
92 Aldeby F 7
86 Aldenham D 1
40 Alderbury C 3
92 Alderford D 4
57 Alderley E 11
95 Alderley Edge B 7
35 Aldermaston H 7
35 Aldermaston Wharf G 7
88 Alderminster G 6
59 Alder's End H 11
40 Alderholt E 3
41 Aldershot A 10
84 Alderton, Glos. A 1
89 Alderton, Northants G 10
94 Alderton, Salop H 4
93 Alderton, Suffolk L 6
57 Alderton, Wilts F 11
95 Alderwasley E 11
16 Aldfield H 3
94 Aldford D 3
87 Aldham, Essex A 9
93 Aldham, Suffolk L 3
93 Aldham Street L 3
44 Aldie B 3
41 Aldingbourne F 10
14 Aldingham H 5
88 Aldington H 4
43 Aldington Corner D 9
39 Aldochlay H 10
31 Aldoth G 12
91 Aldreth H 5
88 Aldridge B 4
93 Aldringham J 7
84 Aldsworth C 3
46 Aldunie E i
95 Aldwark, Derby D 10
12 Aldwark, N. Yorks. A 2
41 Aldwick F 10
91 Aldwincle G 1
84 Aldworth F 6
35 Alexandria A 9
38 Aley B 5
36 Alfardisworthy E 2
38 Alfington F 5
41 Alfold C 11
41 Alfold Crossways C 11
46 Alford, Grampian F 3
97 Alford, Lincs. C 11
39 Alfold, Somerset C 9
96 Alfreton E 1
88 Alfrick G 1
42 Alfriston H 4
90 Algarkirk B 4
39 Alhampton C 9
151 Aline Lodge F 3
143 Alisary L 1
112 Alkborough E 6
89 Alkerton H 7
43 Alkham D 11
94 Alkington F 4
95 Alkmonton F 10
84 All Cannings H 2
93 All Saints, South Elmham G 6
59 All Stretton C 10
148 Alladale Lodge G 5
37 Allaleigh K 7
145 Allanaquoich K 7
144 Allanfearn E 3
144 Allangrange Mains E 2
137 Allanton D 11
40 Allbrook D 6
133 Allendale Town G 7
115 Allenheads A 10
86 Allen's Green B 4
133 Allensford H 9
57 Allensmore A 8
95 Allenton G 12
136 Allenton D 1
39 Aller C 7
131 Allerby H 11
133 Allerdene C 8
38 Allerford B 3
117 Allerston G 9
112 Allerthorpe B 5
94 Allerton, Merseyside B 3
111 Allerton, W. Yorks. D 10
112 Allerton Bywater D 2
112 Allerton Mauleverer A 2
133 Allerwash F 7
88 Allesley D 6
95 Allestree F 11
89 Allexton B 11
95 Allgreave D 8
87 Allhallows F 8
142 Alligin Shuas D 2
95 Allimore Green H 7
96 Allington, Lincs. F 6
40 Allington, Wilts. B 4
84 Allington, Wilts. H 2
114 Allithwaite G 6
140 Alloa H 4
131 Allonby G 11
135 Alloway H 8
39 Allowenshay E 7
55 Allt G 9
143 Alltbeithe, Highland G 4
143 Alltneithe, Highland J 4
139 Alltchaorunn B 9
58 Alltmawr H 6
148 Alltnacaillich C 5
145 Allt-na-giubhsaich L 8
148 Allt na h'Airbhe G 3
143 Alltsigh H 8
55 Alltwalis D 8
55 Alltwen G 10
55 Alltyblacca B 8
39 Allweston E 10
96 Alma Park Estate F 6
59 Almeley G 9
59 Almeley Wooton G 9
39 Almer F 12
112 Almholme F 4
94 Almington G 5
36 Alminstone Cross D 2
140 Almondbank E 5
57 Almondbury F 10
57 Almondsbury F 9
133 Alndyke B 10
112 Alne A 3
144 Alness C 2
133 Alnham B 8
133 Alnmouth B 10
133 Alnwick B 10
93 Alphamstone M 2
93 Alpheton K 2
37 Alphington G 8
95 Alport D 10
94 Alpraham D 4
87 Alresford B 10
88 Alrewas A 5
94 Alsager E 6
94 Alsagers Bank E 6
95 Alsop en le Dale E 10
132 Alston, Cumb. H 5
38 Alston, Devon F 6
84 Alstone, Glos. A 1
38 Alstone, Som. B 6
95 Alstonefield E 9
36 Alswear D 6
148 Altandhu E 2
149 Altanduin E 8
35 Altarnun B 9
148 Altass G 6
134 Altgaltraig B 5
110 Altham D 6
87 Althorne D 9
112 Althorpe F 6
130 Alticry G 4
149 Altnabea E 10
149 Altnabreac Stn. C 9
144 Altnacardich E 1
148 Altnacealgach Hot. F 4
138 Altnacraig E 6
139 Altnafeadh B 9
148 Altnaharra D 6
111 Altofts E 12
96 Alton, Derby D 1
41 Alton, Hants. B 8
95 Alton, Staffs. F 9
84 Alton Barnes H 2
39 Alton Pancras F 10
84 Alton Priors H 2
135 Altonhill E 9
94 Altrincham A 6
143 Altrua K 6
139 Altskeith G 11
140 Alva G 4
94 Alvanley C 4
95 Alvaston G 12
88 Alvechurch E 4
88 Alvecote B 6
40 Alvediston D 1
88 Alveley D 1
36 Alverdiscott C 4
41 Alverstoke F 7
96 Alverton F 5
84 Alvescot D 4
57 Alveston, Avon E 9
88 Alveston, War. F 6
41 Alverstone G 7
145 Alvie J 4
97 Alvingham A 10
57 Alvington D 9
90 Alwalton F 2
133 Alwinton B 7
111 Alwoodley C 11
141 Alyth B 7
148 Amatnatua G 5
97 Amber Hill E 9
57 Amberley, Glos. D 11
41 Amberley, W. Sussex E 11
95 Ambersgate E 11
133 Amble C 11
88 Amblecote D 2
111 Ambler Thorn D 9
114 Ambleside E 6
54 Ambleston D 3
85 Ambrosden B 7
112 Amcotts F 6
141 Americanmuir D 8
85 Amersham D 10
85 Amersham Com. D 10
133 Amersidelaw C 12
40 Amesbury B 3
151 Amhuinnsuidhe F 2
88 Amington B 6
131 Amisfield Town C 11
60 Amlwch A 4
60 Amlwch Port A 4
55 Ammanford F 9
117 Amotherby H 7
40 Ampfield D 5
136 Ampherlaw D 3
116 Ampleforth G 6
116 Ampleforth Coll. G 6
84 Ampney Crucis D 2
84 Ampney St. Mary D 2
84 Ampney St. Peter D 2
40 Amport B 4
91 Ampthill L 1
93 Ampton H 2
54 Amroth F 5
140 Amulree C 4
150 An Caol C 5
150 An Coroghon H 2
138 Anaheilt A 5
142 Anancaun C 4
97 Ancaster F 7
59 Anchor D 7
137 Ancroft E 12
137 Ancroft Northmoor E 12
137 Ancrum G 9
97 Anderby C 12
39 Anderson F 12
94 Anderton C 5
40 Andover B 5
40 Andover Down B 5
84 Andoversford B 1
114 Andreas F 2
140 Angansk F 6
34 Angarrak F 3
132 Angerton G 1
54 Angle G 2
114 Anglers' Hotel D 3
60 Anglesey C 4
41 Angmering F 12
41 Angmering-on-Sea F 12
115 Angram, N. Yorks. E 11
112 Angram, N. Yorks. B 3
140 Anie F 1
144 Ankerville B 4
113 Anlaby D 8
90 Anmer C 8
40 Anna Valley B 5
131 Annan E 12
142 Annat, Highland D 3
139 Annat, Strathclyde E 7
135 Annathill B 12
135 Annbank G 9
135 Annbank Station G 9
96 Annesley Woodhouse E 2
146 Annfield F 3
133 Annfield Plain H 10
133 Annitsford F 11
59 Annscroft B 10
133 Annstead D 12
39 Ansford C 10
88 Ansley C 6
95 Anslow H 10
95 Anslow Gate H 10
41 Anstey, Hants. B 8
91 Anstey, Herts. M 5
89 Anstey, Leics. A 9
141 Anstruther Easter G 10
141 Anstruther Wester G 10
89 Ansty, War. D 7
42 Ansty, W. Sussex F 2
40 Ansty, Wilts. C 1
41 Anthill Common E 8
131 Anthorn F 12
92 Antingham B 6
35 Antony D 11
36 Anvil Corner E 2
97 Anwick E 8
130 Anwoth F 6
90 Apes Hall F 6
90 Apethorpe F 1
97 Apley C 8
96 Apperknowle B 1
57 Apperley B 11
115 Appersett F 10
138 Appin House C 6
115 Appleby, Cumbria C 9
113 Appleby, Humber. F 7
88 Appleby Magna A 6
88 Appleby Parva A 6
142 Applecross E 1
142 Applecross House E 1
36 Appledore, Devon C 3
38 Appledore, Devon E 4
43 Appledore, Kent E 8
43 Appledore Heath E 8
84 Appleford E 6
40 Appleshaw A 4
114 Applethwaite C 5
116 Appleton, N. Yorks. E 4
84 Appleton, Oxon. D 5
112 Appleton Roebuck C 3
94 Appleton Thorn B 5
117 Appleton-le-Moors F 7
117 Appleton-le-Street H 7
137 Appletreehall H 8
111 Appletreewick A 9
38 Appley D 4
110 Appley Bridge F 4
41 Apse Heath H 7
86 Apsley End A 1
41 Apuldram F 9
146 Aquhythie F 5
142 Araid D 2
142 Aranarff F 3
147 Arbeadie H 4
144 Arabella B 4
141 Arbirlot C 10
85 Arborfield G 8
85 Arborfield Cross G 8
130 Arbrack H 5
141 Arbroath C 11
147 Arbuthnott K 5
144 Archiestown E 8
94 Arclid Green D 6
134 Ardachearanbeg A 5
138 Ardachoil D 4
134 Ardachuple A 5
143 Ardachvie K 5
139 Ardanaiseig E 8
142 Ardaneaskan F 2
138 Ardanstur F 5
142 Ardarroch F 2
134 Ardbeg C 6
148 Ardcharnich G 3
138 Ardchiavaig F 1
139 Ardchonnell F 7
138 Ardchrishnish E 2
140 Ardchullarie More F 1
139 Ardchyle E 12
141 Ardcross G 10
139 Arddarroch H 9
59 Arddleen A 8
138 Ardelanish F 1
86 Ardeley A 3
143 Ardelve G 2
135 Arden A 8
116 Arden Hall F 5
138 Ardencaple Ho. F 5
88 Ardens Grafton G 5
138 Ardentallan Ho. E 5
134 Ardentraive B 5
140 Ardeonaig D 2
138 Ardery A 5
139 Ardess H 10
148 Ardessie G 2
138 Ardfern G 5
139 Ardgartan G 10
148 Ardgay G 6
151 Ardhasig G 2
142 Ardheslaig D 2
138 Ardinamar F 5
148 Ardindrean G 3
42 Ardingly E 2
84 Ardington E 5
143 Ardintoul G 2
146 Ardlair E 3
134 Ardlamont House C 5
138 Ardlarach F 5
93 Ardleigh M 3
141 Ardler C 7
84 Ardley A 6
139 Ardlui F 10
134 Ardlussa A 2
139 Ardmaddy D 8
148 Ardmair G 3
134 Ardmaleish C 6
139 Ardmay G 10
134 Ardminish E 2
143 Ardmolich M 1
149 Ardmore, Highland H 7
138 Ardmore, Strathclyde E 5
135 Ardmore, Strathclyde B 8
138 Ardnacross C 3
135 Ardnadam A 7
144 Ardnagrask E 1
143 Ardnamurach K 2
138 Ardnastang A 5
135 Ardneil D 7
139 Ardno G 8
146 Ardo House E 7
140 Ardoch C 6
135 Ardochrig E 11
149 Ardochu F 7
143 Ardochy House J 6
138 Ardow B 2
146 Ardoyne E 4
134 Ardpatrick C 3
134 Ardpatrick House C 3
135 Ardpeaton A 7
134 Ardrishaig A 3
151 Ardroil D 1
144 Ardross Castle B 2
135 Ardrossan E 7
138 Ardshealach A 4
111 Ardsley G 12
111 Ardsley East E 11
138 Ardslignish A 3
140 Ardtalnaig C 2
134 Ardtaraig A 5
138 Ardtoe A 4
140 Ardtrostan E 2
138 Arduaine F 5
144 Ardullie C 1
138 Ardura E 4
150 Ardvasar H 5
138 Ardvergnish E 3
145 Ardverikie L 1
151 Ardvey, Loch Finsbay H 2
151 Ardvey, Loch Stockinish H 2
139 Ardvorlich, Strathclyde F 10
140 Ardvorlich, Tayside E 1
151 Ardvourlie Castle F 3
140 Ardwell, Dumf. & Gall. G 2
130 Ardwell, Strathclyde B 3
88 Areley Kings E 2
41 Arford B 9
140 Argaty G 2
56 Argoed D 5
58 Argoed Mill F 5
139 Arichastlich D 10
138 Aridhglas F 1
142 Arinacrinachd D 1
138 Ariogan E 6
143 Arisaig L 1
143 Arisaig House L 1
138 Ariundle A 5
112 Arkendale A 2
91 Arkesden M 6
115 Arkholme H 8
115 Arkle Town E 12
131 Arkleby H 12
132 Arkleton D 2
86 Arkley D 2
112 Arksey F 4
96 Arkwright Town C 2
57 Arle B 12
114 Arlecdon C 3
91 Arlesey L 3
59 Arleston A 12
94 Arley, Cheshire B 5
88 Arley, War. C 6
57 Arlingham C 10
36 Arlington, Devon B 5
42 Arlington, E. Sussex G 4
84 Arlington, Glos. C 2
36 Arlington Beccott B 5
149 Armadale, Highland B 8
136 Armadale, Lothian C 2
150 Armadale Castle H 6
115 Armathwaite A 7
92 Arminghall E 5
88 Armitage A 4
111 Armley D 11
88 Armscote H 6
91 Armston G 2
112 Armthorpe G 4
115 Arncliffe H 11
115 Arncliffe Cote H 11
141 Arncroach G 10
40 Arne G 1
89 Arnesby C 9
134 Arnicle F 2
143 Arnisdale H 2
150 Arnish C 5
136 Arniston Engine C 6
151 Arnol B 4
113 Arnold, Humber. C 9
96 Arnold, Notts. F 3
140 Arnprior H 1
115 Arnside G 7
138 Aros Mains C 3
114 Arrad Foot G 5
113 Arram C 8
116 Arrathorne F 2
41 Arreton G 7
91 Arrington K 4
139 Arrivain D 10
139 Arrochar G 10
88 Arrow F 4
144 Artafallie E 2
111 Arthington C 11
89 Arthingworth D 11
58 Arthog A 2
146 Arthrath D 7
41 Arundel E 11
139 Aryhoulan A 7
114 Asby C 3
113 Asby cum Fenby G 10
134 Ascog C 6
85 Ascot G 10
84 Ascott-under-Wychwood B 4
116 Asenby H 4
96 Asfordby H 4
96 Asfordby Hill H 4
97 Asgarby, Lincs. D 10
90 Asgarby, Lincs. A 2
43 Ash, Kent B 11
42 Ash, Kent B 5
39 Ash, Somerset D 8
41 Ash, Surrey A 10
36 Ash Bullayne E 6
89 Ash Green D 7
94 Ash Magna F 4
36 Ash Hill D 6
38 Ash Priors C 5
38 Ash Thomas E 3
41 Ash Vale A 10
84 Ashampstead F 6
93 Ashbacking K 5
95 Ashbourne F 10
38 Ashbrittle D 4
37 Ashburton J 6
36 Ashbury, Devon F 4
84 Ashbury, Oxon. F 4
113 Ashby F 7
97 Ashby by Partney D 11
97 Ashby de la Launde E 7
95 Ashby de la Zouch H 12

92 Ashby Dell ....E 8
89 Ashby Folville ......A 10
89 Ashby Magna ....C 9
89 Ashby Parva ....C 8
97 Ashby Puerorum ....C 10
89 Ashby St. Ledgers ....E 9
92 Ashby St. Mary ......E 6
57 Ashchurch ....A 12
56 Ashcombe, Avon ....H 6
38 Ashcombe, Devon ...H 3
39 Ashcott ....C 8
85 Ashcroft ....F 8
91 Ashdon ....L 7
41 Ashe ....A 7
87 Asheldham ....D 9
91 Ashen ....L 8
85 Ashendon ....C 8
140 Ashfield, Central ....G 3
55 Ashfield, Dyfed .....D 10
93 Ashfield, Suffolk .....J 5
93 Ashfield Green ......H 6
36 Ashford, Devon .....C 4
40 Ashford, Hants. ......E 3
43 Ashford, Kent ....D 9
85 Ashford, Surrey ....G 11
59 Ashford Bowdler ....E 10
59 Ashford Carbonel ...E 10
84 Ashford Hill ....H 6
95 Ashford-in-the-
Water ....C 10
135 Ashgill ....D 12
115 Ashgillside ....A 10
38 Ashill, Devon ....E 4
92 Ashill, Norfolk ......E 2
38 Ashill, Somerset .....D 6
87 Ashington, Essex .....E 8
133 Ashington,
Northumb. ....D 10
39 Ashington, Som. .....D 9
41 Ashington, W. Sussex E 12
137 Ashkirk ....G 7
40 Ashlett ....F 6
57 Ashleworth ....B 11
91 Ashley, Cambs. ......J 8
94 Ashley, Cheshire .....B 6
36 Ashley, Devon ....E 5
57 Ashley, Glos. ....E 12
40 Ashley, Hants ....C 5
40 Ashley, Hants ....G 4
43 Ashley, Kent ....C 11
89 Ashley, Northants. ..C 11
94 Ashley, Staffs. ....F 6
85 Ashley Green ......D 10
40 Ashley Heath ....F 3
84 Ashmansworth ......H 5
36 Ashmansworthy .....D 2
39 Ashmore ....D 12
84 Ashmore Green ......G 6
88 Ashorne ....F 6
96 Ashover ....D 1
88 Ashow ....E 6
59 Ashperton ....H 11
37 Ashprington ....K 7
36 Ashreigney ....E 5
42 Ashtead ....B 1
94 Ashton, Cheshire ....C 4
34 Ashton, Cornwall ....G 3
59 Ashton,
Heref. & Worcs. ..F 10
89 Ashton, Northants. .G 11
91 Ashton, Northants. ..G 2
57 Ashton Common ...H 12
84 Ashton Keynes ....E 2
110 Ashton-in-Makerfield G 5
88 Ashton under Hill ...H 3
111 Ashton under Lyne ..G 8
110 Ashton-upon- Mersey H 6
57 Ashton Watering ....G 8
40 Ashurst, Hants. ....E 5
42 Ashurst, Kent ....D 4
42 Ashurst, W. Sussex ...F 1
42 Ashurstwood ....D 3
36 Ashwater ....F 3
91 Ashwell, Herts. ......L 4
89 Ashwell, Leics. ......A 12
92 Ashwellthorpe ....F 4
39 Ashwick ....A 9
90 Ashwicken ....D 8
137 Ashybank ....H 8
114 Askam in Furness ....G 4
112 Askern ....F 3
39 Askerswell ....G 9
115 Askham ....C 7
112 Askham Bryan ....B 3
112 Askham Richard .....B 3
138 Asknish ....H 6
115 Askrigg ....F 11
111 Askwith ....B 10
90 Aslackby ....C 2
92 Aslacton ....F 4
96 Aslockton ....F 5
146 Asloun ....F 3
131 Aspatria ....G 12
86 Aspenden ....A 4
89 Aspley Guise ....H 12
85 Aspley Heath ....A 10
110 Aspull ....F 5
112 Asselby ....D 5
97 Asserby ....B 12
93 Assington ....L 2
144 Assynt House ....C 2
95 Astbury ....D 7
89 Astcote ....G 10
59 Asterley ....B 9
59 Asterton ....C 9
84 Asthall ....C 4
84 Asthall Leigh ....C 4
88 Astley,
Heref. & Worcs. ...E 1
94 Astley, Salop. ....H 4
88 Astley, War. ....C 6
59 Astley Abbots ......C 12
110 Astley Bridge ....F 6
88 Astley Cross ....E 2
110 Astley Green ....G 6
85 Aston, Berks. ....F 9
94 Aston, Cheshire ......E 5
94 Aston, Cheshire ......B 4
61 Aston, Clwyd ......C 12
95 Aston, Derby ....B 10
59 Aston,
Heref. & Worcs. ..E 10
59 Aston,
Heref. & Worcs. ..F 10
86 Aston, Herts. ....B 3
84 Aston, Oxon. ....D 4
94 Aston, Salop. ....G 4
59 Aston, Salop ....A 11
96 Aston, S. Yorks. .....B 2
94 Aston, Staffs. ....F 6
95 Aston, Staffs. ....G 7
88 Aston, W. Midlands ..C 4
85 Aston Abbotts ....B 9
59 Aston Botterell .....D 11
88 Aston Cantlow ....F 5
85 Aston Clinton ....C 9
57 Aston Crews ....B 10
57 Aston Cross ....A 12
86 Aston End ....B 3
59 Aston Eyre ....C 12
88 Aston Fields ....E 3
89 Aston Flamville ......C 8
57 Aston Ingham ......B 10
94 Aston juxta Mondrum D 5
89 Aston le Walls ....G 8
84 Aston Magna ....A 3
59 Aston on Clun ....D 9
95 Aston on Trent .....G 12
59 Aston Pigott ....B 9
59 Aston Rogers ....B 9
85 Aston Rowant ....D 8
85 Aston Sandford ......C 8
88 Aston Somerville ....H 4
88 Aston Subedge ......H 5
84 Aston Tirrold ....F 6
84 Aston Upthorpe ......E 6
91 Astwick ....L 3
91 Astwood ....K 1
88 Astwood Bank ....F 4
90 Aswarby ....B 2
97 Aswardby ....C 10
59 Atcham ....B 11
93 Athelington ....H 5
39 Athelney ....C 7
137 Athelstaneford ......B 8
36 Atherington, Devon ..D 5
41 Atherington,
W. Sussex ....F 11
88 Atherstone B6
88 Atherstone on Stour ..G 5
110 Atherton ....G 5
143 Athnamulloch ....G 5
116 Atley Hill ....E 3
95 Atlow ....E 10
142 Attadale ....F 3
92 Attleborough, Norfolk F 3
89 Attleborough, War. ..C 7
92 Attlebridge ....D 4
147 Atton ....K 1
137 Attonburn ....G 10
113 Atwick ....B 9
57 Atworth ....H 11
96 Aubourn ....D 6
139 Auchachenna ....E 7
134 Auchagallon ....F 4
145 Auchallater ....K 7
130 Auchalton ....A 4
145 Auchavan ....M 7
134 Auchbroad ....A 3
146 Aucheldy ....D 6
131 Auchenbainzie ....B 9
147 Auchenblae ....J 5
131 Auchenbrack ....B 8
134 Auchenbreck ....A 5
131 Auchencairn,
Dumf. & Gall. ....C 10
131 Auchencairn,
Dumf. & Gall. .....F 9
135 Auchencarroch ......A 9
130 Auchencrosh ....D 2
137 Auchencrow ....C 11
136 Auchendinny ....C 5
131 Auchengibbert ......D 9
136 Auchengray ....D 3
131 Auchengruith ....A 9
146 Auchenhairig ....B 1
136 Auchenheath ....E 1
130 Auchenmalg ....F 3
130 Auchensoul ....B 3
130 Auchentibbert ....G 2
135 Auchentiber ....E 8
135 Auchenvennel ....A 8
131 Auchenvey ....D 8
145 Auchernack ....G 6
145 Auchgourish ....H 5
134 Auchinadrian ....D 2
146 Auchinderran ....B 2
139 Auchindrain ....G 6
142 Auchindrean ....B 6
146 Auchinhove ....B 2
146 Auchininna ....C 4
135 Auchinleck ....G 10
135 Auchinloch ....B 11
140 Auchinner ....F 2
146 Auchintender ....D 4
147 Auchintoul, Grampian G 4
146 Auchintoul, Grampian F 3
146 Auchiries ....D 8
146 Auchleven ....E 4
136 Auchlochan ....F 1
147 Auchlossan ....G 3
148 Auchlunachan ......H 3
147 Auchlunies ....G 6
139 Auchlyne ....E 12
146 Auchmacoy ....D 7
130 Auchmantle ....E 2
135 Auchmillan ....F 10
141 Auchmithie ....C 11
141 Auchmuirbridge .....G 7
147 Auchmull ....K 3
139 Auchnacloich Pier ...D 7
138 Auchnacraig ....D 4
147 Auchnacree ....L 2
143 Auchnadaull ....L 5
140 Auchnafree ....D 3
144 Auchnagallin ....F 6
146 Auchnagatt ....C 7
134 Auchnaha ....A 4
145 Auchnahannet ....G 5
144 Auchnahillin ....F 3
130 Auchnotteroch ....F 1
147 Aucholzie ....H 1
139 Auchrioch ....E 10
145 Auchroisk ....G 6
147 Auchronie ....J 2
140 Auchterarder ....F 4
143 Auchteraw ....J 7
141 Auchterderran ......H 7
141 Auchterhouse ....C 8
141 Auchtermuchty ......F 7
142 Auchterneed ....D 8
145 Auchterteang ....G 5
141 Auchtertool ....H 7
139 Auchtertyre, Central .E 10
144 Auchtertyre, Grampian D 7
143 Auchtertyre, Highland G 2
140 Auchtoo ....E 1
149 Auckingill ....B 12
112 Auckley ....G 4
146 Auckmair ....E 1
111 Audenshaw ....G 8
94 Audlem ....F 5
94 Audley ....E 6
91 Audley End ....L 6
146 Auds ....A 4
112 Aughton, Humber. ...C 5
110 Aughton, Lancs. .....G 3
115 Aughton, Lancs. .....H 8
96 Aughton, S. Yorks. ...B 2
84 Aughton, Wilts. .....H 3
141 Auldallan ....A 8
144 Auldearn ....D 5
59 Aulden ....G 10
131 Auldgirth ....C 10
137 Auldhame ....A 8
135 Auldhouse ....D 11
146 Auldtown ....B 3
146 Auldtown of
Carnousie ....C 4
140 Aulich ....A 1
96 Ault Hucknall ....D 2
143 Ault-a-chruinn ....H 3
148 Aultanrynie ....D 4
148 Aultbea ....G 1
142 Aultdearg ....C 7
144 Aultfearn ....E 1
142 Aultgowrie ....E 8
142 Aultgrishan ....A 1
142 Aultguish Inn ....C 7
146 Aulthash ....B 1
149 Aultiphurst ....A 8
146 Aultmore ....B 1
145 Aultnagoire ....G 1
144 Aultnamain Inn ......B 2
145 Aultnancaber ....H 5
143 Aultnaslat ....J 5
146 Aulton ....E 3
147 Aultonrea ....H 1
145 Aundorach ....H 5
38 Aunk ....F 4
90 Aunsby ....B 1
57 Aust ....E 9
85 Austenwood ....E 10
112 Austerfield ....H 4
88 Austrey ....B 6
115 Austwick ....H 10
97 Authorpe ....B 11
97 Authorpe Row .....C 12
84 Avebury ....G 2
86 Aveley ....F 6
57 Avening ....E 12
96 Averham ....E 5
37 Aveton Gifford ......L 6
145 Avielochan ....H 5
145 Aviemore ....H 4
134 Avinagillan ....C 3
84 Avington, Berks. .....G 5
41 Avington, Hants. ....C 7
144 Avoch ....D 3
84 Avon ....F 1
57 Avon, Co. ....F 9
89 Avon Dassett ....G 7
136 Avonbridge ....B 2
57 Avonmouth ....F 8
37 Avonwick ....K 6
40 Awbridge ....D 5
130 Awhirk ....F 2
57 Awkley ....F 9
38 Awliscombe ....F 5
57 Awre ....D 10
96 Awsworth ....F 2
39 Axbridge ....A 8
41 Axford, Hants. ....B 7
84 Axford, Wilts. ....G 3
38 Axminster ....F 6
38 Axmouth ....G 6
116 Aycliffe ....C 3
133 Aydon ....F 8
57 Aylburton ....D 9
132 Ayle ....H 5
38 Aylesbeare ....G 4
85 Aylesbury ....C 9
113 Aylesby ....F 9
36 Aylescott ....D 5
42 Aylesford ....B 6
43 Aylsham ....C 11
89 Aylestone ....B 9
92 Aylmerton ....B 5
92 Aylsham ....C 5
57 Aylton ....A 9
59 Aymestrey ....F 9
84 Aynho ....A 6
86 Ayot St. Lawrence ...B 2
86 Ayot St. Peter ....B 2
135 Ayr ....G 8
115 Aysgarth ....F 12
38 Ayshford ....E 4
114 Ayside ....G 6
89 Ayston ....B 12
86 Aythorpe Roding ....B 6
137 Ayton ....C 11
116 Azerley ....H 3
37 Babbacombe ....J 8
94 Babbinswood ....G 2
39 Babcary C9
55 Bw ....C 11
61 Babell ....C 11
39 Babington ....A 10
91 Babraham ....K 6
96 Babworth ....B 4
60 Bachau ....B 4
151 Back ....C 6
143 Back of Keppcoh .....L 1
152 Backaland ....B 3
152 Backaskaill ....A 3
114 Backbarrow ....G 6
146 Blackburn ....D 3
54 Backe ....E 6
146 Backfolds ....B 8
94 Backford ....C 3
94 Backford Cross ......C 3
146 Backhill, Grampian ..D 5
146 Backhill, Grampian ...F 5
146 Backhill, Grampian ..D 7
146 Backhill of Clackriach C 7
146 Backhill of Fortree ...D 7
147 Backhill of Trustach ..H 4
149 Backies ....F 8
141 Backmuir of
New Gilston ....F 9
57 Backwell ....G 8
133 Backworth ....F 11
86 Bacon End ....B 6
92 Baconsthorpe ....B 4
57 Bacton,
Heref. & Worcs. ...A 7
92 Bacton, Norfolk .....B 6
93 Bacton, Suffolk ......J 3
111 Bacup ....E 7
142 Badachro ....B 2
149 Badanloch Lodge ....D 8
142 Badavanich ....D 5
84 Badbury ....F 3
89 Badby ....F 9
148 Badcall, Highland ....G 2
148 Badcall, Loch Inchard,
Highland ....B 4
88 Baddersley Clinton ...E 5
95 Baddeley Green .....E 8
88 Baddesley Ensor .....B 6
148 Baddidarach ....E 2
57 Baddington ....B 12
144 Baddock ....D 4
146 Badenyon ....F 1
39 Badford Peverell ....G 10
88 Badger ....B 1
42 Badger's Mount .....B 4
57 Badgeworth ....B 12
39 Badgworth ....A 7
143 Badicaul ....G 1
93 Badingham ....H 6
148 Badintagairt ....F 5
43 Badlesmere ....C 9
148 Badluarach ....G 2
148 Badnabay ....C 3
148 Badnagyle ....F 2
145 Badnambiast ....M 3
144 Badnonan ....F 5
148 Badrallach ....G 2
88 Badsey ....H 4
41 Badshot Lea ....A 10
112 Badsworth ....F 2
93 Badwell Ash ....H 3
97 Bag Enderby ....C 10
39 Bagber ....E 11
116 Bagby ....G 5
84 Bagendon ....C 1
61 Bagillt ....C 11
89 Baginton ....E 7
55 Baglan ....H 10
94 Bagley ....G 3
95 Bagnal ....E 8
84 Bagnor ....G 5
85 Bagshot, Surrey ....H 10
84 Bagshot, Wilts. ......H 4
57 Bagstone ....F 10
92 Bagthorpe, Norf. .....B 1
96 Bagthorpe, Notts. ....E 2
89 Bagworth ....A 8
57 Bagwy Llydiart ......B 8
111 Baildon ....C 10
134 Baile Boidheach ......B 2
138 Baile Mor ....F 1
145 Bailebeag ....H 1
132 Baileyhead ....E 3
132 Bailiehill ....D 1
135 Baillieston ....C 11
146 Bailliesward ....D 2
115 Bainbridge ....F 11
146 Bainshole ....D 4
90 Bainton, Cambs. .....E 2
113 Bainton, Humberside .B 7
132 Bairnkine ....B 5
86 Baker Street ....F 6
86 Baker's End ....B 4
132 Bakethin ....D 4
95 Bakewell ....C 10
61 Bala ....G 8
140 Balado ....G 6
151 Balallan ....E 4
138 Balarumindubh .....H 1
145 Balavil ....J 3
145 Balbeg ....G 1
140 Balbeggie ....D 6
146 Balbithan ....F 5
144 Balblair, Highland ...E 1
144 Balblair, Highland ...C 3
131 Balcary ....G 9
59 Balchedre ....C 8
146 Belchers ....B 4
148 Balchladich ....D
144 Balchraggan ....F
148 Balchrick ....B
42 Balcombe ....E
141 Balcurvie ....G
115 Balder Head C
116 Baldersby ....G
116 Baldersby St. James ..G
110 Balderstone ....D
94 Balderton ....D
141 Baldinnie ....F
91 Baldock ....M
141 Baldovie ....D
114 Baldrine ....G
43 Baldslow ....G
114 Baldwin ....G
132 Baldwinholme ......H
94 Baldwins Gate ....F
92 Bale ....B
146 Balearn ....B
136 Balerno C
147 Balfeith ....K
147 Balfield ....K
152 Balfour C
135 Balfron ....A
146 Balgaveny ....D
131 Balgerran ....E
140 Balgonar ....H
146 Balgove ....D
145 Balgowan ....K
150 Balgown ....A
141 Balgray C
131 Balgrayhill C
135 Balgrochan ....B
142 Balgy ....D
140 Balhaldie ....G
146 Balhalgardy ....E
86 Balham ....G
141 Balharry C
152 Baliasta ....A
149 Baligill ....A
144 Balintore, Highland ..B
141 Balintore, Tayside ....A
144 Balintraid C
145 Balintuim ....K
140 Balintyre ....B
116 Balk ....E
141 Balkeerie C
112 Balkholme ....D
130 Balkissock C
94 Ball ....G
84 Ball Hill ....H
114 Ballabeg ....H
114 Ballacannell ....G
114 Ballacarnane Beg ....G
145 Ballachlaggan ....K
147 Ballachrosk ....H
114 Ballacraine ....G
114 Ballacuberagh ....G
131 Ballaggan ....B
114 Ballajora ....G
114 Ballakaigan ....H
114 Ballaleigh ....G
130 Ballantrae C
151 Ballantrushal ....B
87 Ballards Gore ....E
114 Ballasalla, I.o.M. ......F
114 Ballasalla, I.o.M. .....H
147 Ballater ....H
114 Ballaugh ....G
145 Ballcorah ....G
137 Ballencrieff ....B
134 Ballianlay C
138 Balliemore ....E
114 Ballig ....G
140 Balikinrain Castle ....H
139 Ballimeanoch ....F
139 Ballimore ....F
144 Ballindalloch ....F
141 Ballindean ....D
93 Ballingdon L
85 Ballinger Com. .....D
57 Ballingham ....A
140 Ballingry ....G
145 Ballinluig, Highland ..G
140 Ballinluig, Tayside ...B
145 Ballintean ....J
140 Ballintuim ....B
130 Ballminnoch ....E
144 Balloan ....E
144 Balloch, Highland ....E
135 Balloch, Strathclyde ..A
147 Ballochan ....H
130 Ballochbroe ....A
130 Ballochdoan ....D
130 Ballochdowan ....D
146 Ballochford ....D
134 Ballochgoy C
130 Ballochmorrie C
134 Ballochroy ....D

7 Ballogie H 3
1 Balls Cross D 11
2 Ball's Green D 4
8 Ballygown C 2
8 Ballymeanoch H 5
3 Balmacara G 2
1 Balmaclellan D 7
0 Balmacneil B 5
1 Balmacolm F 8
0 Balmacquien A 4
1 Balmae G 7
9 Balmaha H 11
8 Balmaneach D 2
1 Balmeanach G 7
6 Balmedie F 7
1 Balmerino E 8
0 Balmerlawn F 5
2 Balmore, Highland F 7
0 Balmore, Skye, Highland D 2
5 Balmore, Strathclyde B 11
0 Balmore, Tayside A 4
4 Balmuchy B 4
1 Balmule H 7
1 Balmullo E 9
4 Balmungie D 3
7 Balnaboth K 1
4 Balnabruaich C 3
4 Balnabual E 3
9 Balnacoil F 8
2 Balnacra E 3
4 Balnacraig F 1
4 Balnafoich F 2
4 Balnagall B 4
4 Balnageith D 6
7 Balnagowan G 2
0 Balnaguard B 4
4 Balnaguisich C 2
3 Balnain G 8
8 Balnakeil A 5
0 Balnaknock B 3
4 Balnapaling C 4
7 Balquharn L 2
9 Balquhidder E 12
8 Balsall E 6
8 Balsall Common D 6
9 Balscote H 7
1 Balsham K 7
2 Baltasound A 8
4 Balterley E 6
0 Baltersan E 5
6 Balterton E 5
6 Balthangie C 6
9 Baltonsborough C 8
8 Balure C 6
6 Balvack F 4
6 Balvaird D 1
6 Balvenie C 1
8 Balvicar F 5
43 Balvraid, Highland H 2
44 Balvraid, Highland F 4
10 Bamber Bridge E 4
36 Bamber's Green B 6
33 Bamburgh D 12
41 Bamff B7
36 Bamflatt F 3
95 Bamford B 10
15 Bampton, Cumbria C 7
38 Bampton, Devon D 3
84 Bampton, Oxon. D 4
15 Bampton Grange C 7
43 Banavie M 5
89 Banbury H 8
55 Bancffosfelen F 8
47 Banchory, Grampian G 7
47 Banchory, Grampian H 4
55 Bancycapel E 7
54 Bancyfelin E 6
55 Banc-y-ffordd C 7
41 Bandirran House D 7
46 Banff A 4
60 Bangor C 5
94 Bangor-Is-coed F 3
93 Banham G 4
40 Bank, Hants. E 4
59 Bank, Powys A 8
11 Bank Newton B 8
59 Bank Street F 11
31 Bankend, Dumf. & Gall. E 11
36 Bankend, Strathclyde F 1
35 Bankfoot, Strathclyde B 7
40 Bankfoot, Tayside D 5
35 Bankglen H 11
46 Bankhead, Grampian F 6
47 Bankhead, Grampian G 4
33 Bankhead, Northumb. B 8
35 Bankhead, Strathclyde D 8
36 Bankhead, Strathclyde E 3
35 Banknock B 12
132 Banks, Cumb. F 4
110 Banks, Lancs. E 3
131 Bankshill C 12
92 Banningham C 5
87 Bannister Green B 7
140 Bannockburn H 3
42 Banstead B 1
37 Bantham L 5
135 Banton B 12
57 Banwell H 7
43 Bapchild B 8
138 Barachandroman E 4
135 Barassie F 8
138 Baravullin D 6
144 Barbaraville C 3
95 Barber Booth B 9
135 Barbieston H 9
115 Barbon G 8
138 Barbreck House G 5
36 Barbrook A 6
89 Barby E 9
139 Barcaldine C 7
131 Barcaple F 7
88 Barchesten H 6
135 Barclaugh G 9
131 Barclosh E 9
42 Barcombe G 3
42 Barcombe Cross F 3
116 Barden F 2
111 Barden Scale A 9
130 Bardennoch B 6
152 Bardister C 7
149 Bardnabeinne G 7
97 Bardney C 8
89 Bardon A 8
132 Bardon Mill G 6
135 Bardowie B 10
135 Bardrainney B 8
114 Bardsea H 5
111 Bardsey C 12
93 Bardwell H 2
137 Barelees F 11
59 Barewood G 9
134 Barfad B 4
92 Barford, Norfolk E 4
88 Barford, War. F 6
84 Barford St. John A 5
40 Barford St. Martin C 2
84 Barford St. Michael A 5
43 Barfreston C 11
130 Bargaly E 5
56 Bargoed D 5
130 Bargrennan D 4
139 Barguillean Farm E 7
91 Barham, Cambs. H 2
43 Barham, Kent C 10
93 Barham, Suffolk K 4
131 Barharrow F 7
90 Barholm D 2
132 Barhough H 5
89 Barkby A 9
89 Barkby Thorpe A 9
96 Barkestone le Vale G 5
85 Barkham G 9
86 Barking, London E 5
93 Barking, Suffolk K 4
93 Barking Tye K 4
111 Barkisland E 9
96 Barkston, Lincs. F 6
112 Barkston, N. Yorks. D 3
91 Barkway M 5
95 Barlaston F 7
131 Barlay D 7
96 Barlborough C 2
112 Barlby D 4
89 Barlestone B 8
91 Barley, Herts. L 5
111 Barley, Lancs. C 7
133 Barley Mow H 11
133 Barleyhill H 8
89 Barleythorpe A 11
87 Barling E 9
96 Barlow, Derby C 1
112 Barlow, N. Yorks. D 4
133 Barlow, Tyne & Wear G 9
112 Barmby Moor B 5
112 Barmby on the Marsh D 5
92 Barmer B 1
137 Barmoor Castle E 12
137 Barmoor Ridge E 12
58 Barmouth A 2
116 Barmpton C 3
113 Barmston A 9
131 Barmurrie D 7
139 Barnacarry H 7
90 Barnack E 2
89 Barnacle D 7
139 Barnaline F 7
115 Barnard Castle C 12
91 Barnardiston K 8
131 Barnbarroch F 9
112 Barnburgh G 3
92 Barnby F 8
112 Barnby Dun F 4
96 Barnby in the Willows E 6
96 Barnby Moor B 4
130 Barncorkrie H 2
86 Barnes F 2
42 Barness Street C 5
86 Barnet D 3
113 Barnetby le Wold F 8
92 Barney B 3
93 Barnham, Suffolk G 2
41 Barnham, W. Sussex F 11
92 Barnham Broom E 4
147 Barnhead L 4
144 Barnhill D 7
130 Barnhills D 1
116 Barningham, Dur. D 1
93 Barningham, Suff. H 3
113 Barnoldby le Beck G 10
111 Barnoldswick C 7
41 Barns Green C 12
84 Barnsley, Glos. D 2
111 Barnsley, S. Yorks. F 12
36 Barnstaple C 4
86 Barnston, Essex B 6
94 Barnston, Merseyside B 1
96 Barnstone G 4
88 Barnt Green E 4
94 Barnton C 5
91 Barnwell All Saints G 2
91 Barnwell St. Andrew G 2
57 Barnwood C 11
59 Barons' Cross G 10
135 Barr, Dumf. & Gall. H 12
131 Barr, Dumf. & Gall. B 9
130 Barr, Strathclyde B 4
146 Barra Castle E 5
130 Barrachan G 4
138 Barrachrail E 5
151 Barraglom D 3
133 Barrasford F 7
138 Barravullin G 5
114 Barregaroow G 2
135 Barrhead D 10
130 Barrhill C 3
91 Barrington, Cambs. K 5
39 Barrington, Som. D 7
34 Barripper F 3
143 Barrisdale J 3
135 Barrmill D 8
149 Barrock A 11
110 Barrow, Lancs. C 6
89 Barrow, Leics. A 12
59 Barrow, Salop. B 12
39 Barrow, Som. C 10
93 Barrow, Suffolk J 1
57 Barrow Gurney G 8
113 Barrow Haven E 8
96 Barrow Hill C 1
96 Barrow-in-Furness H 5
110 Barrow Nook G 3
39 Barrow Street C 11
113 Barrow-upon-Humber E 8
96 Barrow-upon-Soar H 3
95 Barrow-upon-Trent G 12
133 Barrowburn B 7
96 Barrowby G 6
117 Barrowcliff F 10
89 Barrowden B 12
111 Barrowford C 7
94 Barrows Green D 5
139 Barrs D 8
56 Barry, S. Glam. G 4
141 Barry, Tayside D 10
89 Barsby A 10
92 Barsham F 7
88 Barston D 5
59 Bartestree H 11
146 Barthol Chapel D 6
94 Barthomley E 6
137 Bartlehill E 10
40 Bartley E 4
91 Bartlow L 7
39 Barton, Avon A 7
91 Barton, Cambs. K 5
94 Barton, Cheshire E 3
115 Barton, Cumbria C 7
37 Barton, Devon J 8
84 Barton, Glos. B 2
110 Barton, Lancs. C 4
110 Barton, Lancs. F 2
116 Barton, N. Yorks. D 3
88 Barton, War. G 4
90 Barton Bendish E 8
92 Barton Common C 7
57 Barton End E 11
85 Barton Hartshorn A 7
96 Barton in Fabis G 2
89 Barton-in-the-Beans B 7
91 Barton-le-Clay M 2
91 Barton Mills H 8
40 Barton-on-Sea G 4
84 Barton-on-the-Heath A 4
39 Barton St. David C 8
89 Barton Seagrave D 12
40 Barton Stacey B 6
36 Barton Town B 5
117 Barton-le-Street H 7
112 Barton-le-Willows A 5
95 Barton-under-Needwood H 10
113 Barton-upon-Humber E 8
111 Barugh F 11
151 Barvas B 5
91 Barway H 6
89 Barwell B 8
39 Barwick E 9
112 Barwick in Elmet C 2
94 Baschurch H 3
89 Basecote F 7
95 Basford Green E 8
110 Bashall Eaves C 6
40 Bashley F 4
85 Basildon, Berks F 7
87 Basildon, Essex E 7
41 Basing A 8
41 Basingstoke A 7
95 Baslow C 11
39 Bason Bridge B 7
56 Bassaleg F 6
137 Bassendean E 9
114 Bassenthwaite B 5
114 Bassenthwaite Lake Station B 4
36 Basset's Cross F 4
40 Bassett D 5
88 Bassett's Pole B 5
91 Bassingbourn L 4
96 Bassingfield F 3
96 Bassingham D 6
97 Bassingthorpe G 7
152 Basta B 7
90 Baston D 2
92 Bastwick D 7
86 Batchworth Heath E 1
39 Batcombe, Dorset F 9
39 Batcombe, Som. B 10
94 Bate Heath B 5
57 Bath H 10
57 Bathampton H 11
57 Bathealton D 4
57 Batheaston G 11
57 Bathford H 11
136 Bathgate B 3
96 Bathley D 5
35 Bathpool, Corn. B 10
38 Bathpool, Som. D 6
39 Bathway A 9
111 Batley E 11
84 Batsford A 3
116 Battersby D 6
86 Battersea F 3
93 Battisford K 4
93 Battisford Tye K 3
42 Battle, E. Sussex F 6
56 Battle, Powys A 3
39 Battleborough A 7
59 Battlefield A 10
87 Battlesbridge D 8
85 Battlesden A 10
38 Battleton C 3
40 Battramsley F 5
41 Batt's Corner B 9
146 Bauds of Cullen A 2
88 Baughton H 2
85 Baughurst H 7
147 Baulds H 4
84 Baulking E 4
97 Baumber C 9
84 Baunton D 1
40 Baverstock C 2
92 Bawburgh E 5
92 Bawdeswell C 3
39 Bawdrip B 7
93 Bawdsey L 6
96 Bawtry A 4
110 Baxenden E 6
88 Baxterley B 6
41 Baybridge D 7
114 Baycliff H 5
84 Baydon F 4
86 Bayford, Herts. C 3
39 Bayford, Som. C 10
115 Bayles A 9
93 Baylham K 4
84 Baynards' Green A 6
59 Bayston Hill B 10
59 Bayton E 12
57 Beach, Avon G 10
138 Beach, Highland B 5
89 Beachampton H 11
90 Beachamwell E 8
57 Beachley E 9
87 Beacon End A 9
40 Beacon Hill, Dor. G 1
41 Beacon Hill, Surrey B 10
85 Beacon's Bottom E 9
85 Beaconsfield E 10
151 Beacravik H 2
116 Beadlam G 6
133 Beadnell D 12
36 Beaford D 4
133 Beal, Northumb. B 12
112 Beal, N. Yorks. E 3
143 Bealachasan H 3
39 Beaminster F 8
133 Beamish H 10
111 Beamsley B 9
42 Bean A 5
57 Beanacre H 12
133 Beanley A 9
36 Beara Moor D 4
132 Bearbridge G 6
38 Beare F 3
42 Beare Green D 1
133 Bearl G 9
88 Bearley F 5
138 Bearnus C 1
116 Bearpark A 3
135 Bearsden B 10
43 Bearsted C 7
40 Bearwood F 2
38 Beasley B 3
131 Beattock A 11
86 Beauchamp Roding C 6
96 Beauchief B 1
56 Beaufort C 5
40 Beaulieu F 5
144 Beauly E 1
60 Beaumaris C 5
132 Beaumont, Cumb. G 2
87 Beaumont, Essex A 11
116 Beaumont Hill C 3
88 Beausale E 6
41 Beauworth C 7
36 Beaworthy F 3
87 Beazley End A 7
94 Bebington B 2
133 Bebside E 11
92 Beccles F 7
110 Becconsall E 3
115 Beck Foot F 8
117 Beck Hole E 8
91 Beck Row H 8
114 Beck Side G 5
88 Beckbury B 1
86 Beckenham G 4
114 Beckermet D 3
131 Beckfoot G 11
84 Beckford A 1
84 Beckhampton G 2
96 Beckingham, Lincs. E 6
96 Beckingham, Notts. A 5
39 Beckington A 11
40 Beckley, Hants. F 4
84 Beckley, Oxon. C 6
43 Beckley, E. Sussex F 7
111 Beckwithshaw B 11
86 Becontree E 5
116 Bedale F 3
116 Bedburn B 1
39 Bedchester D 12
56 Beddau F 4
60 Beddgelert E 5
42 Beddingham G 3
86 Beddington G 3
93 Bedfield J 5
91 Bedford K 2
91 Bedfordshire, Co. K 2
41 Bedhampton E 8
93 Bedingfield H 5
111 Bedlam A 11
133 Bedlington E 10
56 Bedlinog D 4
57 Bedminster G 9
85 Bedmond D 11
95 Bednall H 8
137 Bedrule H 8
137 Bedshiel D 9
59 Bedstone E 9
56 Bedwas E 5
56 Bedwellty D 5
89 Bedworth C 7
89 Beeby A 10
41 Beech, Hants. B 8
95 Beech, Staffs. F 7
85 Beech Hill, Berks. H 8
115 Beech Hill, Cumb. E 7
110 Beech Hill, Manchester F 4
84 Beechingstoke H 2
84 Beedon F 6
84 Beedon Hill F 6
113 Beeford B 9
95 Beeley C 11
113 Beelsby G 9
85 Beenham G 7
34 Beeny B 1
38 Beer, Devon G 6
39 Beer, Somerset C 7
39 Beer Hackett E 9
39 Beercrocombe D 7
37 Beesands M 7
97 Beesby B 11
37 Beeson L 7
91 Beeston, Beds. K 3
94 Beeston, Cheshire D 4
92 Beeston, Norfolk D 2
96 Beeston, Notts. G 3
111 Beeston, W. Yorks. D 11
92 Beeston Regis A 5
131 Beeswing E 10
115 Beetham G 7
92 Beetley D 3
56 Began F 5
84 Begbroke C 5
90 Begdale E 6
54 Begelly F 5
59 Beggar's Bush F 8
59 Beguildy D 7
92 Beighton, Norf. E 7
96 Beighton, S. Yorks. B 2
135 Beith D 8
43 Bekesbourne C 10
92 Belaugh D 6
88 Belbroughton D 3
93 Belchamp Otten L 1
93 Belchamp St. Paul L 1
93 Belchamp Walter L 1
146 Belcherrie D 1
97 Belchford C 10
133 Belford C 12
133 Belford Mains C 12
146 Belhelvie F 7
146 Belhinnie E 2
86 Bell Bar C 3
111 Bell Busk B 7
88 Bell Heath D 3
146 Bellabeg F 1
138 Bellanoch H 5
112 Bellasize D 6
111 Belle Vue E 12
97 Belleau B 11
144 Bellehiglash F 7
116 Bellerby F 1
37 Bellever H 5
137 Bellhaven B 9
85 Bellingdon D 10
133 Bellingham E 7
134 Belloch F 2
134 Bellochantuy F 2
42 Bells Yew Green D 5
130 Bellsbank A 5
133 Bellshill, Northumb. C 12
135 Bellshill, Strathclyde C 12
136 Bellspool F 4
136 Bellsquarry C 3
130 Bellymore C 3
144 Belmaduthy D 2
90 Belmesthorpe D 1
110 Belmont, Lancs. F 5
135 Belmont, Strathclyde G 8
152 Belmont, Shetland Is. B 8
135 Belmore A 7
146 Belnacraig F 1
35 Belowda D 7
95 Belper E 11
95 Belper Lane End E 11
133 Belsay E 9
93 Belstead L 4
135 Belston G 9
36 Belstone F 5
36 Belstone Corner F 5
110 Belthorn E 6
43 Beltinge A 10
132 Beltingham G 6
96 Belton, Leics. H 2
89 Belton, Leics. B 11
112 Belton, Humber. F 6
96 Belton, Lincs. F 6
92 Belton, Norfolk E 8
96 Belvoir G 5
41 Bembridge G 8
137 Bemersyde F 8
40 Bemerton C 3
117 Bempton H 12
149 Ben Armine Lodge E 7
151 Ben Casgro D 5
93 Benacre G 8

10 Charnock Richard....F 4
93 Charsfield..........J 5
43 Chart Sutton.........C 7
85 Charter Alley.......H 7
37 Charterhouse, Borders F 9
39 Charterhouse, Som. ..A 8
84 Charterville Allotments........C 4
43 Chartham..........C 9
43 Chartham Hatch.....B 9
40 Charton...........A 5
85 Chartridge........D 10
85 Charvil............G 8
89 Charwelton.........G 8
88 Chase Terrace.......A 4
88 Chasetown.........A 4
84 Chastleton..........A 3
36 Chasty............F 2
10 Chatburn...........C 6
94 Chatcull............G 6
42 Chatham...........B 6
33 Chathill...........E 12
42 Chattenden.........A 6
91 Chatteris..........G 5
93 Chattisham.........L 4
32 Chatto.............A 6
33 Chatton...........C 12
85 Chaul End.........B 11
36 Chawleigh..........E 6
91 Chawston..........K 3
41 Chawton...........B 8
95 Cheadle, Manchester .A 7
95 Cheadle, Staffs. ......F 8
95 Cheadle Hulme......B 7
86 Cheam.............G 2
85 Cheapside.........G 10
85 Chearsley...........C 8
95 Chebsey............G 7
85 Checkendon..........F 7
94 Checkley, Cheshire ...F 6
59 Checkley, Heref. & Worc. ..H 11
95 Checkley, Staffs. .....F 9
93 Chedburgh..........J 1
39 Cheddar............A 8
85 Cheddington.......B 10
95 Cheddleton.........E 8
38 Cheddon Fitzpaine ...C 6
92 Chedgrave..........E 7
39 Chedington.........F 8
93 Chediston..........G 7
84 Chedworth.........C 2
39 Chedzoy............B 7
137 Cheeklaw.........D 10
111 Cheetham Hill.....G 7
36 Cheglinch...........B 4
36 Cheldon............E 6
95 Chelford...........C 7
95 Chellaston.........G 12
91 Chellington.........K 1
88 Chelmarsh..........C 1
93 Chelmondiston......L 5
95 Chelmorton.........C 9
87 Chelmsford.........C 7
86 Chelsea............F 3
86 Chelsfield Village....G 5
93 Chelsworth.........K 3
57 Cheltenham, Glos. ..B 12
56 Cheltenham, Gwent ..C 5
91 Chelveston.........H 1
57 Chelvey............G 8
57 Chelwood...........H 9
42 Chelwood Com. .....E 3
42 Chelwood Gate......E 3
59 Cheney Longville....D 9
85 Chenies...........D 11
57 Chepstow...........E 8
84 Cherhill............G 1
57 Cherington, Glos.... D 12
88 Cherington, War. ....H 6
41 Cheriton, Hants......C 7
43 Cheriton, Kent .....D 11
36 Cheriton, Som. ......A 6
55 Cheriton, W. Glam. ..H 8
36 Cheriton Bishop.....F 6
37 Cheriton Cross......G 6
38 Cheriton Fitzpaine ...F 2
54 Cheriton or Stackpole Elidor ...G 3
94 Cherrington........H 5
113 Cherry Burton.......C 7
91 Cherry Hinton.......K 6
88 Cherry Orchard.....G 2
140 Cherrybank.........E 6
137 Cherrytrees........F 10
85 Chertsey..........G 11
39 Cheselbourne.......F 11
85 Chesham..........D 10
85 Chesham Bois......D 10
94 Cheshire, Co. ....D 5
86 Cheshunt...........D 4
88 Cheslyn Hay........A 3
86 Chessington........H 2
94 Chester............D 3
133 Chester Moor......H 1
39 Chesterblade.......B 10
96 Chesterfield.........C 1
88 Chesterfield.........B 4
136 Chesterhall..........F 2
136 Chesterhill..........C 6
133 Chester-le-Street....H 11
132 Chesters, Borders ....B 5
137 Chesters, Borders ....G 8
90 Chesterton, Cambs. ..F 2
84 Chesterton, Oxon ....B 6
95 Chesterton, Staffs.....E 7
132 Chesterwood........F 6
43 Chestfield.........B 10
94 Cheswardine........G 6
133 Cheswick..........A 11
133 Cheswick Bldgs......A 11
39 Chetnole...........E 9
38 Chettiscombe........E 3
91 Chettisham.........G 6
40 Chettle............E 1
59 Chetton...........C 12
94 Chetwynd Aston....H 6
94 Chetwynd Park......H 6
91 Cheveley...........J 8
42 Chevening..........B 4
93 Chevington..........J 1
133 Chevington Drift ...C 11
38 Chevithorne.........E 3
57 Chew Magna.......H 9
57 Chew Stoke.........H 9
57 Chewton Keynsham..H 9
39 Chewton Mendip....A 9
89 Chicheley.........G 12
41 Chichester.........F 10
39 Chickerell..........H 9
39 Chicklade..........C 12
59 Chickward.........G 8
41 Chidden............D 8
41 Chiddingfold.......C 11
42 Chiddingly.........G 4
42 Chiddingstone......D 4
42 Chiddingstone Causeway.........C 4
42 Chiddingstone Hoath D 4
39 Chideock...........G 7
38 Chidgley...........C 4
41 Chidham...........F 9
84 Chieveley...........G 5
86 Chignall St. James ...C 6
86 Chignall Smealy.....C 6
86 Chigwell............E 4
86 Chigwell Row.......E 5
40 Chilbolton..........B 5
40 Chilcomb...........C 6
39 Chilcombe..........G 9
39 Chilcompton........A 9
88 Chilcote............A 6
39 Child Okeford......E 11
84 Childrey............E 5
94 Child's Ercall.......H 5
88 Childswickham .....H 4
94 Childwall...........A 3
86 Childwick Green.....C 1
39 Chilfrome...........F 9
41 Chilgrove...........E 9
43 Chilham............C 9
40 Chilhampton........C 3
36 Chilla..............F 3
37 Chillaton...........H 3
43 Chillenden.........C 11
40 Chillerton..........H 6
93 Chillesford..........K 7
133 Chillingham.......C 12
37 Chillington, Devon ...L 7
39 Chillington, Somerset .E 7
40 Chilmark...........C 1
84 Chilson............B 4
35 Chilsworthy, Corn. .B 11
36 Chilsworthy, Devon ..E 2
39 Chilthorne Domer ...D 8
85 Chilton, Bucks. ......C 8
36 Chilton, Devon ......E 7
84 Chilton, Oxon.......F 6
116 Chilton, Durham ....B 3
41 Chilton Candover....B 7
39 Chilton Cantelo.....D 9
84 Chilton Foliat.......G 4
116 Chilton Lane........B 3
39 Chilton Polden......B 7
93 Chilton Street.......K 1
38 Chilton Trinity......B 6
96 Chilwell............G 2
40 Chilworth, Hants. ...D 5
41 Chilworth, Surrey ...A 11
84 Chimney...........D 4
41 Chineham..........A 8
86 Chingford..........E 4
95 Chinley.............B 9
95 Chinley Head.......B 9
85 Chinnor............D 8
94 Chipnall............G 6
91 Chippenham, Cambs. H 8
57 Chippenham, Wilts. .G 12
85 Chipperfield.......D 11
91 Chipping, Herts. ....M 5
110 Chipping, Lancs......C 5
88 Chipping Campden ..H 5
84 Chipping Norton ....B 4
57 Chipping Sodbury...F 10
89 Chipping Warden....G 8
38 Chipstable..........D 4
42 Chipstead, Kent .....B 4
42 Chipstead, Surrey ....B 2
59 Chirbury...........C 8
61 Chirk.............F 12
61 Chirk Green........F 12
130 Chirmorie..........D 3
137 Chirnside..........D 11
137 Chirnsidebridge ....D 11
84 Chirton............H 2
84 Chisbury...........G 4
39 Chiselborough.......E 8
84 Chiseldon...........F 3
111 Chiserley...........D 9
85 Chislehampton......D 7
86 Chislehurst.........G 4
43 Chislet............B 11
111 Chiserley...........D 9
86 Chiswell Green......C 1
86 Chiswick...........F 2
111 Chisworth..........H 8
43 Chitcombe..........F 7
41 Chithurst..........D 9
91 Chittering..........H 6
40 Chitterne...........B 2
36 Chittlehamholt......D 5
36 Chittlehampton.....C 5
57 Chittoe...........H 12
37 Chivelstone........M 6
85 Chobham.........H 10
137 Choicelee..........D 10
40 Cholderton.........B 4
85 Cholesbury........C 10
133 Chollerford..........F 7
133 Chollerton..........F 7
85 Cholsey............E 7
59 Cholstrey..........F 10
116 Chop Gate..........E 6
133 Choppington.......E 10
133 Chopwell...........G 9
94 Chorley, Cheshire ....E 4
110 Chorley, Lancs. ......E 5
59 Chorley, Salop......D 12
88 Chorley, Staffs.......A 4
85 Chorleywood.......E 11
94 Chorlton...........E 6
111 Chorlton cum Hardy .H 7
94 Chorlton Lane.......E 3
91 Chrishall...........L 5
90 Christchurch, Cambs. .F 6
40 Christchurch, Dorset .G 3
57 Christchurch, Gwent .E 7
84 Christian Malford....F 1
94 Christleton.........D 3
85 Christmas Com. .....E 8
39 Christon............A 7
133 Christon Bank......A 10
37 Christow...........G 7
41 Christ's Hospital ...C 12
135 Chryston..........B 11
37 Chudleigh..........H 7
37 Chudleigh Knighton .H 7
36 Chulmleigh.........E 6
111 Chunal............H 9
110 Church.............D 6
94 Church Aston.......H 6
89 Church Brampton ...E 10
95 Church Broughton ..G 10
41 Church Crookham....A 9
95 Church Eaton.......H 7
91 Church End, Beds. ...L 3
87 Church End, Essex ...A 7
91 Church End, Essex ...L 7
85 Church End, Hants. ..H 7
85 Church End, Hertfordshire.....C 12
113 Church End, Lincs. .G 12
86 Church End, London .E 3
90 Church End, Norf. ...E 5
88 Church End, War. ....C 6
84 Church End, Wilts. ...F 1
84 Church Enstone.....B 5
112 Church Fenton......C 3
38 Church Green.......G 5
95 Church Gresley ....H 11
84 Church Hanborough .C 5
94 Church Hill.........D 5
117 Church House.......E 7
117 Church Houses......E 7
40 Church Knowle......H 1
96 Church Laneham....C 5
89 Church Langton....C 10
89 Church Lawford.....D 8
95 Church Lawton......E 7
95 Church Leigh.......G 9
88 Church Lench.......G 4
94 Church Minshull ....D 5
59 Church Preen......C 11
59 Church Pulverbatch ..B 9
59 Church Stoke.......C 8
89 Church Stowe.......F 9
42 Church Street, Kent ..A 6
93 Church Street, Suffolk G 8
59 Church Stretton ....C 10
56 Church Village.......F 4
96 Church Warsop.....C 3
57 Churcham.........B 11
57 Churchdown.......B 12
57 Churchend, Avon ....E 10
86 Churchend, Essex ...B 6
87 Churchend, Essex ...E 10
88 Churchfield.........C 4
57 Churchill, Avon......H 7
36 Churchill, Devon ....B 5
38 Churchill, Devon ....F 6
88 Churchill, Heref. & Worc.....G 3
84 Churchill, Oxon......B4
88 Churchill, Salop......D 2
38 Churchingford.......E 5
89 Churchover.........D 8
38 Churchstanton ......E 5
37 Churchstow.........L 6
114 Churchtown, Cumb. .A 6
36 Churchtown, Dev.....F 2
114 Churchtown, I.o.M...G 2
110 Churchtown, Lancs...C 4
110 Churchtown, Merseyside........E 3
132 Churnsike Lodge.....E 5
37 Churston Ferrers.....K 8
41 Churt.............B 10
94 Churton...........E 3
111 Churwell..........D 11
40 Chute Standen.......A 5
60 Chwilog............F 4
61 Cilcain............D 11
55 Cilcennin...........A 8
55 Cilfrew...........G 11
56 Cilfynydd...........E 4
54 Cilgerran...........C 5
54 Cilgwyn............C 4
55 Ciliau Aeron.......A 8
55 Cilmaengwyn......F 10
58 Cilmery............G 5
54 Cilrhedyn..........D 6
55 Cilsan.............E 9
61 Ciltalgarth..........F 8
54 Cilwendeg..........C 6
55 Cilybebyll..........F 10
55 Cilycwm...........C 11
57 Cinderford........C 10
54 Cippyn............B 5
84 Cirencester.........D 1
116 Citadilla...........E 2
60 City Dulas..........B 4
145 Clachaig, Highland ..H 6
134 Clachaig, Strathclyde .A 6
150 Clachan, Highland ...E 5
138 Clachan, Strathclyde .C 6
138 Clachan, Strathclyde ..F 5
139 Clachan, Strathclyde ..F 9
134 Clachan, Strathclyde .D 3
135 Clachan of Campsie .A 11
134 Clachan of Glendaruel A 5
138 Clachan-Seil.........F 5
134 Clachbreck.........B 3
147 Clachnabrain........L 1
148 Clachtoll...........D 2
140 Clackmannan.......H 4
144 Clackmarras........D 8
87 Clacton on Sea .....B 11
135 Cladance..........E 11
139 Cladich.............E 8
138 Claggan............C 4
150 Claigan............C 2
88 Claines............F 2
148 Clais Charnach......A 4
148 Claisfearn..........C 3
39 Clandown.........A 10
41 Clanfield, Hants. ....D 8
84 Clanfield, Oxon.....D 4
40 Clanville...........A 5
134 Claonaig...........D 4
111 Clap Gate.........B 12
43 Clap Hill..........D 9
40 Clapgate, Dorset .....F 2
55 Clapgate, Herts. .....A 4
91 Clapham, Beds.......K 1
38 Clapham, Devon .....H 2
86 Clapham, London ....F 3
115 Clapham, N. Yorks. .H 9
41 Clapham, W. Sussex .E 12
137 Clappers..........D 12
114 Clappersgate........E 6
39 Clapton, Somerset....F 7
39 Clapton, Som.......A 10
57 Clapton-in-Gordano .G 8
84 Clapton on the Hill...B 3
36 Clapworthy.........D 5
58 Clarach............D 2
54 Clarbeston..........E 4
54 Clarbeston Road.....E 4
96 Clarborough........B 4
93 Clare...............L 1
131 Clarebrand..........E 8
131 Clarencefield.......E 11
137 Clarilaw............G 8
137 Clarilawmoor.......F 8
41 Clarken Green.......A 7
135 Clarkston.........D 10
149 Clashbuie...........B 7
149 Clashcoig...........G 7
146 Clashindarroch......D 2
149 Clashmore..........G 7
148 Clashnessie........D 2
145 Clashnoir..........G 8
140 Clathy.............E 5
146 Clatt..............E 3
58 Clatter............C 5
40 Clatterford.........G 6
147 Clattering Bridge....J 4
130 Clatteringshawes ....D 6
38 Clatworthy.........C 4
110 Claughton, Lancs. ...A 4
110 Claughton, Lancs. ...C 4
94 Claughton, Merseyside A 2
38 Clavelshay.........C 6
88 Claverdon.........F 5
57 Claverham.........H 8
91 Clavering..........M 6
88 Claverley...........C 2
57 Claverton.........H 11
56 Clawdd-coch........F 4
61 Clawddnewydd.....E 10
115 Clawthorpe........G 8
36 Clawton............F 2
113 Claxby, Lincs........H 9
97 Claxby, Lincs.......C 11
92 Claxton, Norfolk ....E 6
112 Claxton, N. Yorks....A 5
89 Clay...............D 9
93 Clay Common......G 8
96 Clay Cross.........D 1
145 Claybokie..........K 6
89 Claybrooke Magna ..C 8
89 Claybrooke Parva....C 8
89 Claydon, Oxon......G 8
93 Claydon, Suffolk.....K 4
147 Clayfolds...........H 6
132 Claygate, Dumf. & Gall...............E 2
42 Claygate, Kent......D 6
85 Claygate, Surrey ....H 12
38 Clayhanger, Devon ..D 4
88 Clayhanger, W. Midlands ......B 4
38 Clayhidon..........E 5
43 Clayhill, E. Sussex ....F 7
40 Clayhill, Hants.......E 5
146 Claymires..........E 7
96 Claypole...........E 6
95 Clayton, Staffs.......F 7
112 Clayton, S. Yorks.....F 2
42 Clayton, W. Sussex ..G 2
111 Clayton, W. Yorks. .D 10
110 Clayton Green.......E 5
111 Clayton West.......F 11
110 Clayton-le-Moors....D 6
110 Clayton-le-Woods ...E 4
96 Clayworth..........A 4
133 Cleadon...........G 12
37 Clearbrook..........J 4
57 Clearwell..........D 9
116 Cleasby............D 3
152 Cleat..............E 2
116 Cleatlam...........C 1
114 Cleator............D 3
114 Cleator Moor.......D 3
111 Cleckheaton.......E 10
59 Clee St. Margaret ...D 11
59 Cleedownton......D 11
59 Cleehill...........E 11
59 Cleestanton........D 11
113 Cleethorpes........F 10
59 Cleeton St. Mary....E 11
57 Cleeve, Avon........H 8
85 Cleeve, Oxon........F 7
84 Cleeve Hill..........A 1
88 Cleeve Prior.........G 4
57 Clehonger..........A 8
138 Cleigh.............E 6
140 Cleish.............G 6
136 Cleland............D 1
138 Clenamacrie.........E 6
84 Clench Common ....H 3
90 Clenchwarton......C 7
133 Clennell............B 7
88 Clent..............D 3
59 Cleobury Mortimer ..E 12
59 Cleobury North ....D 11
144 Clephanton.........E 4
135 Clerkland..........E 9
137 Clerklands..........G 7
152 Clestran............D 1
132 Cleuch Head........B 4
131 Cleuchbrae........D 11
132 Cleuchfoot..........E 2
131 Cleuchhead.........B 9
131 Cleuchheads.......C 12
131 Cleuchside.........D 12
84 Clevancy...........G 2
57 Clevedon...........G 7
116 Cleveland, Co. ......C 5
116 Cleveland Tontine Inn E 5
110 Cleveleys...........C 2
84 Cleverton...........F 1
56 Clevis..............G 2
39 Clewer.............A 8
92 Cley-next-the-Sea ....A 3
151 Cliasamol...........F 2
115 Cliburn............C 8
41 Cliddesden..........A 7
138 Cliff...............A 4
43 Cliff End...........G 7
42 Cliff Woods.........A 6
141 Cliffburn..........C 11
87 Cliffe, Kent..........F 7
112 Cliffe, N. Yorks......D 4
116 Cliffe, N. Yorks......D 2
36 Clifford, Devon .....D 2
59 Clifford, Heref. & Worc.....H 8
112 Clifford, W. Yorks. ..C 2
88 Clifford Chambers ...G 5
57 Clifford's Mesne ....B 10
43 Cliffsend..........B 12
57 Clifton, Avon.......G 9
91 Clifton, Beds.........L 3
139 Clifton, Central ....D 10
115 Clifton, Cumbria ....C 8
95 Clifton, Derby......F 10
88 Clifton, Heref. & Worc.....G 2
110 Clifton, Lancs. ......D 4
136 Clifton, Lothian .....B 4
111 Cliton, N. Yorks ....B 10
112 Clifton, N. Yorks.....B 4
133 Clifton, Northumb. .E 10
96 Clifton, Notts. ......G 3
84 Clifton, Oxon.......A 6
112 Clifton, S. Yorks. ....G 3
88 Clifton Campville....A 6
84 Clifton Hampden ....E 6
89 Clifton Reynes .....G 12
89 Clifton upon Dunsmore........D 8
59 Clifton upon Teme ..F 12
43 Cliftonville........A 12
41 Climping..........F 11
136 Climpy............D 2
39 Clink.............A 11
111 Clint..............A 11
92 Clint Green.........D 3
137 Clintmains..........F 8
92 Clippesby..........D 7
90 Clipsham...........D 1
36 Clipston, Devon .....F 5
89 Clipston, Northants .D 10
96 Clipston, Notts. .....G 4
96 Clipstone...........D 3
110 Clitheroe...........C 6
94 Clive..............H 4
152 Clivocast...........B 8
113 Clixby.............G 8
61 Clocaenog.........E 10
146 Clochan............B 1
55 Clochyrie...........F 8
94 Clock Face.........A 4
137 Clockmill.........D 10
56 Clodock............B 6
39 Cloford...........B 10
55 Cloigyn............F 8
146 Clola..............C 7
91 Clophill............L 2

113 Cottingham, Humberside D 8
89 Cottingham, Northants. C 11
111 Cottingley C 9
85 Cottisford A 7
95 Cotton, Staffs. F 9
93 Cotton, Suffolk J 4
91 Cotton End L 2
146 Cot-town, Grampian E 2
146 Cot-town, Grampian D 6
95 Cotwalton G 8
146 Cotwells B 5
35 Couchsmill D 8
57 Coughton, Heref. & Worc. B 9
88 Coughton, War. F 4
134 Coulaghailtro C 2
142 Coulags E 3
142 Couldoran E 2
142 Coulin Lodge D 4
147 Coull G 3
135 Coulport A 7
86 Coulsdon H 3
40 Coulston A 1
136 Coulter F 3
116 Coulton H 6
59 Cound B 11
116 Coundon, Durham B 3
88 Coundon, W. Midlands D 6
116 Coundon Grange B 2
115 Countersett F 11
89 Countesthorpe C 9
40 Countess B 3
38 Countess Wear G 3
36 Countisbury A 6
141 Coupar Angus C 7
137 Coupland F 12
38 Couple Cross B 3
134 Cour E 3
131 Courance C 11
85 Court Corner H 7
55 Court Henry E 9
143 Courteachan K 1
89 Courteenhall G 11
87 Courtsend E 10
38 Courtway C 5
136 Cousland C 6
42 Cousleywood E 5
134 Coustonn B 6
38 Cove, Devon D 3
41 Cove, Hampshire A 10
142 Cove, Highland A 2
135 Cove, Strathclyde A 7
147 Cove Bay G 7
93 Covehithe G 8
88 Coven A 3
91 Coveney G 6
113 Covenham St. Bartholomew H 11
113 Covenham St. Mary H 11
89 Coventry D 7
34 Coverack H 5
116 Coverham F 1
91 Covington H 2
88 Cow Honeybourne H 5
115 Cowan Bridge G 8
42 Cowbeech G 5
90 Cowbit D 4
56 Cowbridge, S. Glam. G 3
38 Cowbridge, Som. B 3
42 Cowden, Kent D 3
133 Cowden, Northumb. E 7
140 Cowdenbeath H 6
136 Cowdenburn D 5
40 Cowes F 6
116 Cowesby F 5
42 Cowfold F 1
140 Cowie, Central H 3
147 Cowie, Grampian J 6
133 Cowpen E 11
116 Cowpen Bewley C 5
95 Cowers Lane E 11
38 Cowley, Devon G 3
57 Cowley, Glos. C 12
86 Cowley, London F 1
84 Cowley, Oxon D 6
116 Cowling. N. Yorks. F 3
111 Cowling, N. Yorks. C 8
91 Cowlinge K 8
41 Cowplain E 8
115 Cowshill A 10
140 Cowstrandburn H 5
112 Cowthorpe B 2
85 Cox Green F 9
94 Coxbank F 5
95 Coxbench F 12
42 Coxheath C 6
43 Coxhill C 11
116 Coxhoe B 3
39 Coxley B 8
86 Coxtie Green D 5
116 Coxwold G 5
56 Coychurch F 3
135 Coylton G 9
145 Coylumbridge H 5
147 Coynach G 2
146 Coynachie D 2
56 Coytrahen F 2
142 Cozae Lodge F 6
88 Crabbs Cross F 4
42 Crabtree F 1
149 Crackaig F 9
115 Crackenthorpe C 9
34 Crackington B 2
34 Crackington Haven B 2
88 Crackley E 6
88 Crackley Bank A 1
115 Crackpot E 12
111 Cracoe A 8
38 Craddock E 4
88 Cradley G 1
88 Cradley Heath D 3
56 Cradoc A 3
35 Crafthole D 10
133 Cragend C 9
111 Cragg E 8
145 Craggan, Highland G 6
148 Craggan, Highland G 4
139 Craggan, Strathclyde H 10
144 Craggiemore F 3
133 Craghead H 10
146 Craibstone, Grampian F 6
146 Craibstone, Grampian B 2
141 Craichie B 10
131 Craig, Dumf. & Gall. D 7
131 Craig, Dumf. & Gall. E 8
142 Craig, Highland E 4
130 Craig, Strathcylde A 5
134 Craig Lodge B 5
56 Craig Penllyn F 3
55 Craig Trebanos G 10
140 Craiganour Lodge A 1
143 Craigard J 7
143 Craigbeg L 8
130 Craigcaffie E 2
55 Craig-cefn-parc G 10
146 Craigdam E 6
131 Craigdarrcoh, Dumf. & Gall. C 8
131 Craigdarroch, Strathclyde A 7
130 Craigdews D 6
142 Craigdhu F 8
146 Craigearn F 5
144 Craigellachie E 8
130 Craigencallie D 6
130 Craigencross E 1
136 Craigend, Strathclyde F 1
140 Craigend, Tayside E 6
135 Craigendoran A 8
130 Craigengillan A 5
130 Craigenrae C 4
135 Craigens G 10
147 Craiggiecat H 6
144 Craighead, Grampian F 8
136 Craighead, Strathclyde G 2
146 Craigie, Grampian F 6
135 Craigie, Strathclyde F 9
140 Craigie, Tayside C 6
131 Craigieburn A 11
136 Craiglockhart B 5
130 Craimalloch B 5
146 Craigmaud B 6
134 Craigmore C 6
147 Craigmoston K 4
94 Craignant G 1
130 Craigneil C 2
131 Craigneston C 8
135 Craigneuk D 12
138 Craignure D 4
147 Craigo L 4
140 Craigow F 6
141 Craigrothie F 8
141 Craigs G 7
147 Craigton, Grampian G 6
142 Craigton, Highland F 3
144 Craigton, Highland E 2
135 Craigton, Strathclyde D 10
141 Craigton, Tayside C 10
141 Craigton, Tayside B 8
149 Craigtown B 9
55 Craig-y-Duke G 10
56 Craig-y-nos C 2
132 Craik B 2
141 Crail F 11
137 Crailing G 9
137 Crailinghall G 9
112 Craiselound G 5
136 Cramalt G 5
112 Crambe A 5
133 Cramlington E 11
136 Cramond B 5
136 Cramond Bridge B 4
143 Cranachan L 7
94 Cranage C 6
95 Cranberry G 7
146 Cranbog F 7
40 Cranborne E 2
85 Cranbourne G 10
42 Cranbrook D 6
42 Cranbrook Com. D 6
111 Crane Moor G 11
91 Cranfield L 1
86 Cranford F 1
89 Cranford St. Andrew D 12
89 Cranford St. John D 12
57 Cranham, Glos. C 12
86 Cranham, London E 6
110 Crank G 4
41 Cranleigh B 12
40 Cranmore G 5
146 Cranna B 4
146 Crannach B 2
138 Crannich C 2
89 Cranoe C 11
93 Cransford J 6
137 Cranshaws C 9
114 Cranstal F 2
113 Cranswick B 8
34 Crantock D 5
97 Cranwell E 7
92 Cranwich F 1
92 Cranworth E 3
130 Cranyard H 2
37 Crapstone J 4
139 Crarae H 7
148 Crask Inn E 6
142 Crask of Aigas E 8
142 Craskie F 7
147 Craskins G 3
133 Craster A 10
93 Cratfield H 6
147 Crathes H 5
145 Crathie K 1
116 Crathorne D 5
59 Craven Arms D 10
133 Crawcrook G 9
136 Crawford G 2
136 Crawfordjohn G 2
131 Crawfordton B 9
135 Crawick H 12
40 Crawley, Hants. C 6
84 Crawley, Oxon C 4
42 Crawley, W. Sussex D 1
42 Crawley Down D 2
115 Crawleyside A 12
111 Crawshaw Booth E 7
147 Crawton J 6
115 Cray, N. Yorks. G 11
56 Cray, Powys B 2
86 Crayford F 5
116 Crayke H 6
87 Crays Hill E 7
85 Cray's Pond F 7
85 Crazies Hill F 9
138 Creach Bheinn Lodge E 4
36 Creacombe D 7
139 Creag a' Phuill G 8
139 Creagan C 7
134 Creagan Beag A 3
139 Creaguaineach Lo. A 10
89 Creaton E 10
132 Creca F 1
59 Credenhill H 10
36 Crediton F 7
130 Creebank D 4
130 Creebridge E 5
38 Creech Heathfield D 6
38 Creech St. Michael D 6
34 Creed E 6
86 Creekmouth F 5
130 Creeside C 4
93 Creeting St. Mary J 4
90 Creeton D 1
130 Creetown F 6
59 Cregerina G 7
139 Creggans G 8
114 Cregneish H 1
114 Creg-ny-Baa G 2
141 Creich E 8
56 Creigiau F 4
142 Crelevan F 7
35 Cremyll D 11
59 Cressage B 11
54 Cresselly F 4
85 Cressex E 9
87 Cressing B 8
54 Cresswell, Dyfed F 4
133 Cresswell, Northumb. D 11
95 Cresswell, Staffs. F 8
96 Creswell C 2
93 Cretingham J 5
134 Cretshengan C 2
59 Crew Green A 8
94 Crewe, Cheshire E 3
94 Crewe, Cheshire E 6
39 Crewkerne E 7
139 Crainlarich E 11
55 Cribyn B 8
60 Criccieth F 4
96 Crich E 12
136 Crichton C 6
57 Crick, Gwent E 8
89 Crick, Northants. E 9
58 Crickadarn H 6
39 Cricket Malherbie E 7
39 Cricket St. Thomas E 7
94 Crickheath H 2
56 Crickhowell B 5
84 Cricklade E 2
112 Cridling Stubbs E 3
140 Crieff E 3
59 Criggian A 8
111 Crigglestone E 11
146 Crimond B 8
146 Crimonmogate B 8
90 Crimplesham E 7
142 Crinaglack F 8
138 Crinan H 5
92 Cringleford E 3
54 Crinow F 5
40 Cripplestyle E 3
42 Cripp's Corner F 6
114 Croasdale C 3
39 Crock Street E 7
42 Crockenhill A 4
37 Crockernwell G 6
39 Crockerton B 11
131 Crocket or Ninemile Bar D 9
112 Crockey Hill B 4
42 Crockham Hill C 3
42 Crockhurst Street D 5
87 Crockleford Hth. A 10
56 Croes-Hywel C 6
56 Croeserw E 2
54 Croesgoch D 2
55 Croes-lan C 7
60 Croesor F 6
55 Croesyceiliog E 7
56 Croes-y-mwyalch E 6
54 Croft, Dyfed C 5
89 Croft, Leics. C 8
110 Croft, Merseyside H 5
97 Croft, Lincs. D 12
116 Croft, N. Yorks. D 3
135 Croftamie A 9
135 Crofthead E 12
140 Croftmill C 3
111 Crofton, W. Yorks. E 12
84 Crofton, Wilts. H 4
146 Crofts of Belnagoak C 6
146 Crofts of Haddo D 6
146 Crofts of Hillbrae C 3
146 Crofts of Meikle Ardo D 6
146 Crofts of Savoch B 8
146 Crofts of Shanquhar D 3
55 Crofty G 8
138 Croggan E 4
132 Croglin H 4
148 Croick G 5
151 Croir C 2
144 Cromarty C 3
142 Cromasiag D 4
146 Cromblet D 5
145 Cromdale G 6
60 Cromer, Herts. A 3
92 Cromer, Norfolk A 5
95 Cromford E 11
57 Cromhall E 10
57 Cromhall Com. E 10
151 Cromore E 5
145 Cromra K 1
96 Cromwell D 5
135 Cronberry G 11
41 Crondall A 9
114 Cronk-y-Voddy G 2
94 Cronton A 4
115 Crook, Cumbria F 7
116 Crook, Durham B 2
144 Crook of Alves D 7
140 Crook of Devon G 5
110 Crooke F 4
135 Crookedholm F 9
136 Crookedstane H 2
96 Crookes B 1
84 Crookham, Berks. H 6
137 Crookham, Northumb. F 11
41 Crookham Village A 9
137 Crookham Westfield F 11
136 Crookhaugh G 4
137 Crookhouse G 10
115 Crooklands G 8
135 Crookston C 10
137 Crookston North Mains D 7
88 Croome Court H 2
89 Cropredy G 8
89 Cropston A 9
88 Cropthorne H 3
117 Cropton F 8
96 Cropwell Bishop G 4
96 Cropwell Butler F 4
135 Crosbie D 7
131 Crosby, Cumb. H 11
114 Crosby, I.o.M. G 2
112 Crosby, Humber. F 6
110 Crosby, Merseyside G 2
116 Crosby Court F 4
115 Crosby Garrett D 9
115 Crosby Ravensworth D 8
131 Crosby Villa H 11
39 Croscombe B 9
39 Cross A 7
57 Cross Ash B 7
42 Cross-at-Hand C 6
58 Cross Foxes Hotel A 3
93 Cross Green, Suffolk K 2
93 Cross Green, Suffolk K 3
55 Cross Hands, Dyfed F 9
54 Cross Hands, Dyfed F 4
111 Cross Hills C 9
59 Cross Houses B 11
42 Cross in Hand F 4
55 Cross Inn, Dyfed A 7
55 Cross Inn, Dyfed A 9
55 Cross Inn, Dyfed D 11
56 Cross Inn, Mid Glam F 4
42 Cross Keys, Kent C 4
57 Cross Keys, Wilts. G 11
34 Cross Lanes, Corn. G 4
94 Cross Lanes, Clwyd F 2
39 Cross Lanes, Dorset F 11
112 Cross Lanes, N. Yorks. A 3
151 Cross North Dell A 6
56 Cross Oak B 4
146 Cross of Jackson D 5
95 Cross o'th Hands F 11
93 Cross Street H 5
134 Crossaig D 3
151 Crossbost D 5
131 Crosscanonby H 11
136 Crossleuch G 5
92 Crossdale Street B 5
110 Crossens E 3
136 Crossford, Fife A 3
136 Crossford, Strathclyde E 1
90 Crossgate C 3
136 Crossgatehall C 6
140 Crossgates, Fife H 6
116 Crossgates, N. Yorks. H 2
58 Crossgates, Powys F 6
115 Crossgill, Cumb. A 9
110 Crossgill, Lancs. A 4
37 Crossgreen, Devon G 3
59 Crossgreen, Salop A 10
137 Crosshall E 10
54 Crosshands, Dyfed E 5
135 Crosshands, Strathclyde F 9
140 Crosshill, Fife G 6
130 Crosshill, Strathcylde A 4
135 Crosshill, Strathclyde G 9
135 Crosshouse F 9
132 Crossings E 3
56 Crosskeys E 5
149 Crosskirk A 10
114 Crosslands F 6
94 Crosslanes H 2
136 Crosslee G 6
135 Crosslees D 10
136 Crossleuch G 5
131 Crossmichael E 8
110 Crossmoor C 3
42 Crosspost F 1
147 Crossroads, Grampian H 5
135 Crossroads, Strathclyde F 9
111 Crossroads, W. Yorks. C 9
152 Cross-voe-sand C 6
57 Crossway, Heref. & Worc. A 9
57 Crossway, Gwent B 8
58 Crossway, Powys G 6
88 Crossway Green E 2
39 Crossways, Dorset G 11
59 Crossways, Powys E 7
54 Crosswell C 5
58 Crosswood E 2
115 Crosthwaite F 7
110 Croston E 4
92 Crostwick D 6
42 Crouch C 5
39 Crouch Hill E 10
40 Croucheston D 2
84 Croughton A 6
146 Crovie A 5
40 Crow F 3
111 Crow Edge G 10
57 Crow Hill B 9
34 Crowan F 4
42 Crowborough E 4
38 Crowcombe C 5
111 Crowden G 9
85 Crowell D 8
89 Crowfield, Northants. H 9
93 Crowfield, Suffolk J 5
42 Crowhurst, E. Sussex G 6
42 Crowhurst, Surrey C 3
42 Crowhurst Lane End C 3
90 Crowland D 3
34 Crowlas F 2
88 Crowle, Heref. & Worc. G 3
112 Crowle, Humber. F 5
151 Crowlista D 1
85 Crowmarsh Gifford E 7
34 Crown Town G 3
37 Crownhill K 4
92 Crownthorpe E 4
130 Crows F 4
34 Crows-an-wra G 1
85 Crowthorne H 9
94 Crowton C 4
88 Croxall A 5
113 Croxby G 9
116 Croxdale B 3
95 Croxden F 9
85 Croxley Green E 11
91 Croxton, Cambs. J 3
113 Croxton, Humber. F 8
93 Croxton, Norfolk G 2
94 Croxton, Staffs. G 6
96 Croxton Kerrial G 5
144 Croy, Highland E 4
135 Croy, Strathclyde B 12
36 Croyde B 3
36 Croyde Bay B 3
91 Croydon, Cambs. K 4
86 Croydon, London G 3
145 Crubenmore Lo. K 2
59 Cruckmeole A 9
146 Cruden Bay D 8
94 Crudington H 5
84 Crudwell E 1
59 Crug E 1
34 Crugmeer B 6
55 Crugybar C 10
142 Cruive F 8
151 Crulivig D 3
56 Crumlin D 5
35 Crumplehorn E 9
54 Crundale, Dyfed E 3
43 Crundale, Kent C 9
132 Crurie D 1
38 Cruwys Morchard E 2
84 Crux Easton H 5
55 Crwbin F 8
85 Cryers Hill D 9
54 Crymych D 5
55 Crynant F 11
142 Cuaig D 1
89 Cubbington E 7
34 Cubert D 5
85 Cublington B 9
42 Cuckfield F 2
39 Cucklington D 10
96 Cuckney C 3
85 Cuddesdon D 7
85 Cuddington, Bucks. C 8
94 Cuddington, Ches. C 4
94 Cuddington Heath F 3
110 Cuddy Hill C 4
86 Cudham H 4
39 Cudworth, Som. E 7
112 Cudworth, S. Yorks. F 2
54 Cuffern E 2
86 Cuffley D 3
151 Cuiashader A 6
144 Culbo D 2
144 Culbokie D 2
144 Culburnie E 1
144 Culcabock E 2
144 Culcairn C 2
144 Culcharry E 4
110 Culcheth H 5

85 Fifield, Berks ..... F 10
84 Fifield, Glos. ..... B 3
40 Fifield, Wilts ..... A 3
40 Fifield Bavant ..... D 2
40 Figheldean ..... A 3
116 Fighting Cocks ..... D 4
92 Filby ..... D 8
117 Filey ..... G 11
89 Filgrave ..... G 12
84 Filkins ..... D 3
36 Filleigh, Devon ..... E 6
36 Filleigh, Devon ..... C 5
96 Fillingham ..... B 6
88 Fillongley ..... C 6
57 Filton ..... F 9
113 Fimber ..... A 7
147 Finavon ..... L 2
90 Fincham ..... E 8
85 Finchampstead ..... H 9
138 Fincharn ..... G 6
41 Finchdean ..... E 9
91 Finchingfield ..... M 8
86 Finchley ..... E 3
141 Fincraigs ..... E 8
95 Findern ..... G 11
144 Findhorn ..... C 6
145 Findhorn Bridge ..... G 4
146 Findochty ..... A 2
147 Findon, Grampian ..... H 7
41 Findon, W. Sussex ..... E 12
144 Findon Mains ..... D 2
147 Findrack House ..... G 3
89 Finedon ..... E 12
93 Fingal Street ..... H 5
146 Fingask, Grampian ..... E 5
140 Fingask, Tayside ..... E 6
88 Fingerpost ..... E 1
85 Fingest ..... E 8
116 Finghall ..... F 2
132 Fingland, Cumb ..... G 1
135 Fingland,
Dumf. & Gall. ..... H 12
43 Finglesham ..... C 12
87 Fingringhoe ..... B 10
143 Finiskaig ..... K 2
140 Finlarig ..... D 1
85 Finmere ..... A 7
139 Finnart ..... B 12
131 Finniegill ..... B 12
93 Finningham ..... H 3
112 Finningley ..... G 4
146 Finnygaud ..... B 3
151 Finsbay ..... H 2
86 Finsbury ..... F 3
88 Finstall ..... E 3
114 Finsthwaite ..... F 6
84 Finstock ..... C 4
152 Finstown ..... C 2
131 Fintloch ..... D 7
135 Fintry, Central ..... A 11
146 Fintry, Grampian ..... B 5
141 Fintry, Tayside ..... D 9
138 Fionnphort ..... F 1
116 Fir Tree ..... B 2
96 Firbeck ..... A 3
117 Firby, N. Yorks ..... H 7
116 Firby, N. Yorks ..... G 3
97 Firsby ..... D 11
148 First Coast ..... G 1
112 Fishlake ..... F 4
131 Fishbeck ..... C 11
41 Fishbourne, I.o.W. ..... G 7
41 Fishbourne,
W. Sussex ..... F 10
116 Fishburn ..... B 4
140 Fishcross ..... H 4
146 Fisherford ..... D 4
40 Fisher's Pond ..... D 6
41 Fisherstreet ..... C 11
144 Fisherton, Highland ..... E 3
135 Fisherton, Strathclyde H 7
40 Fisherton de la Mere ..... B 2
54 Fishguard ..... C 3
57 Fishponds ..... G 9
111 Fishpool, Manchester ..... F 7
96 Fishpool, Notts ..... E 3
90 Fishtoft ..... A 5
97 Fishtoft Drove ..... E 10
141 Fishtown of Usan ..... B 12
137 Fishwick ..... D 11
150 Fiskavaig ..... E 2
97 Fiskerton, Lincs ..... C 7
96 Fiskerton, Notts ..... E 4
113 Fitling ..... D 10
90 Fitten End ..... D 5
40 Fittleton ..... A 3
41 Fittleworth ..... D 11
94 Fitz ..... H 3
38 Fitzhead ..... C 5
112 Fitzwilliam ..... F 2
138 Fiunary ..... C 3
57 Five Acres ..... C 9
42 Five Ashes ..... F 4
110 Five Lane Ends ..... B 4
35 Five Lanes ..... B 9
42 Five Oak Green ..... D 5
41 Five Oaks ..... C 12
151 Five Penny Borve ..... A 5
151 Five Penny Ness ..... A 6
55 Five Roads ..... F 8
94 Fivecrosses ..... C 4
39 Fivehead ..... D 7
87 Flack's Green ..... B 7
85 Flackwell Heath ..... E 9
88 Fladbury ..... G 3
152 Fladdabister ..... E 7
95 Flagg ..... C 10
117 Flamborough ..... H 2
85 Flamstead ..... C 11
41 Flansham ..... F 11
111 Flappit Spring ..... C 9
150 Flashader ..... C 3
111 Flasby ..... B 8
95 Flash ..... C 8
85 Flaunden ..... D 11
96 Flawborough ..... F 5
112 Flawith ..... A 3
57 Flax Bourton ..... G 8
111 Flaxby ..... A 12
57 Flaxley ..... C 10
38 Flaxpool ..... C 5
112 Flaxton ..... A 4
89 Fleckney ..... C 10
89 Flecknoe ..... F 8
96 Fledborough ..... C 5
39 Fleet, Dorset ..... H 9
41 Fleet, Hants ..... A 9
41 Fleet, Hants ..... F 8
90 Fleet, Lincs ..... C 5
97 Fleet Hargate ..... H 11
133 Fleetham ..... E 12
110 Fleetwood ..... B 2
56 Flemingston ..... G 3
135 Flemington,
Strathclyde ..... C 11
135 Flemington,
Strathclyde ..... E 12
93 Flempton ..... H 1
114 Fletchertown ..... A 4
42 Fletching ..... F 3
132 Flex ..... B 3
36 Flexbury ..... E 1
41 Flexford ..... A 10
114 Flimby ..... B 3
42 Flimwell ..... E 6
61 Flint ..... C 11
61 Flint Mountain ..... C 11
96 Flintham ..... F 5
113 Flinton ..... D 10
90 Flitcham ..... C 8
91 Flitton ..... L 2
36 Flitton Barton ..... C 6
91 Flitwick ..... M 1
112 Flixborough ..... F 6
110 Flixton, Manchester ..... H 6
117 Flixton, N. Yorks ..... G 10
93 Flixton, Suffolk ..... G 6
111 Flockton ..... F 11
111 Flockton Green ..... F 11
137 Flodden ..... F 11
151 Flodabay ..... H 2
150 Flodigarry Hotel ..... A 4
90 Flood's Ferry ..... F 5
114 Flookburgh ..... H 6
92 Flordon ..... F 5
89 Flore ..... F 9
133 Flotterton ..... C 8
111 Flouch Inn ..... G 10
93 Flowton ..... K 4
34 Flushing, Cornwall ..... F 5
146 Flushing, Grampian ..... C 8
38 Fluxton ..... G 4
88 Flyford Flavell ..... G 3
87 Fobbing ..... E 7
146 Fochabers ..... B 1
56 Fochriw ..... D 4
112 Fockerby ..... E 6
145 Fodderletter ..... G 7
144 Fodderty ..... D 1
39 Foddington ..... C 9
58 Foel ..... A 5
55 Foelgastell ..... E 9
141 Foffarty ..... C 9
112 Foggathorpe ..... C 5
137 Fogo ..... D 10
137 Fogorig ..... E 10
148 Foindle ..... C 3
141 Folda ..... A 7
95 Fole ..... F 9
89 Foleshill ..... D 7
39 Folke ..... E 10
43 Folkestone ..... E 11
90 Folkingham ..... B 2
42 Folkington ..... H 4
90 Folksworth ..... F 2
117 Folkton ..... G 10
146 Folla Rule ..... D 5
111 Follifoot ..... B 12
36 Folly Gate ..... F 4
56 Fonmon ..... G 4
40 Fonthill Bishop ..... C 1
39 Fonthill Gifford ..... C 12
39 Fontmell Magna ..... E 12
41 Fontwell ..... E 10
95 Foolow ..... C 10
86 Foots Cray ..... G 5
146 Forbestown ..... F 1
38 Forches Corner ..... D 5
85 Ford, Bucks ..... C 8
37 Ford, Devon ..... L 7
36 Ford, Devon ..... D 3
84 Ford, Glos. ..... A 2
137 Ford, Northumb. ..... F 12
59 Ford, Salop ..... A 9
38 Ford, Somerset ..... C 4
95 Ford, Staffs ..... E 9
138 Ford, Strathclyde ..... G 6
41 Ford, W. Sussex ..... F 11
57 Ford, Wilts ..... G 11
38 Ford Barton ..... D 3
87 Ford End ..... B 7
38 Ford Street ..... D 5
42 Fordcombe ..... D 4
140 Fordel ..... F 6
140 Fordell ..... H 6
59 Forden ..... B 8
91 Fordham,
Cambridgeshire ..... H 7
87 Fordham, Essex ..... A 9
90 Fordham, Norfolk ..... E 7
88 Fordhouses ..... B 3
40 Fordingbridge ..... E 3
117 Fordon ..... H 10
147 Fordoun ..... K 5
87 Fordstreet ..... A 9
84 Fordwells ..... C 4
43 Fordwich ..... B 10
146 Fordyce ..... A 3
95 Forebridge ..... H 8
41 Forest Green ..... B 12
115 Forest Hall ..... E 8
132 Forest Head ..... G 4
85 Forest Hill ..... C 7
139 Forest Lo., Highland C 10
145 Forest Lo., Highland ..... H 6
140 Forest Lo., Tayside ..... A 4
140 Forest Mill ..... H 4
42 Forest Row ..... D 3
96 Forest Town ..... D 3
133 Forestburn Gate ..... C 9
144 Foresterseat ..... D 7
41 Forestside ..... E 9
141 Forfar ..... B 9
140 Forgandenny ..... E 6
56 Forge Hammer ..... E 6
56 Forge Side ..... D 6
146 Forgie ..... B 1
146 Forgieside ..... B 1
146 Forglen House ..... B 4
110 Formby ..... F 2
92 Forncett End ..... F 4
92 Forncett St. Mary ..... F 4
92 Forncett St. Peter ..... F 5
140 Forneth ..... C 6
93 Fornham All Saints ..... J 1
93 Fornham St. Martin ..... H 2
144 Forres ..... D 6
136 Forrestfield ..... C 1
95 Forsbrook ..... F 8
149 Forse ..... D 11
149 Forsinain Farm ..... C 9
149 Forsinard ..... C 9
149 Forsinard Station ..... C 8
39 Forston ..... G 10
143 Fort Augustus ..... J 7
144 Fort George ..... D 3
143 Fort William ..... M 5
135 Fortacres ..... F 9
140 Forteviot ..... E 5
136 Forth ..... D 2
57 Forthampton ..... A 11
140 Fortingall ..... B 2
40 Forton, Hants ..... B 6
110 Forton, Lancs ..... B 4
59 Forton, Salop ..... A 9
39 Forton, Somerset ..... E 7
94 Forton, Staffs ..... H 6
146 Fortrie ..... C 4
144 Fortrose ..... D 3
39 Fortuneswell ..... H 7
85 Forty Green ..... E 10
91 Forty Feet Bridge ..... G 4
93 Forward Green ..... J 4
84 Fosbury ..... H 4
84 Foscot ..... B 3
90 Fosdyke ..... B 4
90 Fosdyke Bridge ..... B 4
140 Foss ..... A 3
84 Fossebridge ..... C 2
86 Foster Street ..... C 5
112 Fosterhouses ..... F 4
95 Foston, Derby ..... G 10
96 Foston, Lincs ..... F 6
112 Foston, N. Yorks ..... A 5
113 Foston on the Wolds ..... B 8
97 Fotherby ..... A 10
90 Fotheringhay ..... F 2
152 Foubister ..... D 3
42 Foul Mile ..... F 5
137 Foulden, Borders ..... D 11
92 Foulden, Norfolk ..... E 1
144 Foulis Castle ..... C 1
111 Foulridge ..... C 7
92 Foulsham ..... C 3
146 Fountainbleau,
Grampian ..... D 8
146 Fountainbleau,
Grampian ..... E 7
137 Fountainhall ..... D 7
93 Four Ashes ..... H 3
61 Four Crosses, Powys H 12
58 Four Crosses, Powys ..... B 6
88 Four Crosses, Staffs. ..... A 3
42 Four Elms ..... C 3
38 Four Forks ..... C 6
110 Four Gates ..... F 5
90 Four Gates ..... D 5
94 Four Lane Ends, Ches. D 4
115 Four Lane Ends,
Cumbria ..... F 8
110 Four Lane Ends,
Lancashire ..... B 4
112 Four Lane Ends,
N. Yorks ..... B 4
34 Four Lanes ..... F 4
41 Four Marks ..... C 8
60 Four Mile Bridge ..... B 2
43 Four Oaks, E. Sussex ..... F 7
57 Four Oaks, Glos ..... B 10
88 Four Oaks,
W. Midlands ..... D 6
88 Four Oaks,
W. Midlands ..... B 4
55 Four Roads, Dyfed ..... F 8
114 Four Roads, I.o.M. ..... H 1
42 Four Throws ..... E 6
94 Fourlanes End ..... D 6
133 Fourlaws ..... E 7
133 Fourstones ..... F 7
40 Fovant ..... C 2
146 Foveran ..... E 7
35 Fowey ..... D 8
146 Fowlershill ..... F 7
141 Fowlis ..... D 8
140 Fowlis Wester ..... E 4
91 Fowlmere ..... L 5
57 Fownhope ..... A 9
41 Fox Corner ..... A 11
85 Fox Lane ..... H 9
39 Foxcote ..... A 10
114 Foxdale ..... H 1
93 Foxearth ..... L 1
114 Foxfield ..... G 5
84 Foxham ..... F 1
35 Foxhole ..... D 7
117 Foxholes ..... H 10
42 Foxhunt Green ..... F 4
92 Foxley, Norfolk ..... C 3
57 Foxley, Wilts ..... F 12
95 Foxt ..... E 9
91 Foxton, Cambs ..... K 5
116 Foxton, Durham ..... C 4
89 Foxton, Leics ..... C 10
115 Foxup ..... G 11
94 Foxwist Green ..... C 5
59 Foxwood ..... E 11
57 Foy ..... A 9
145 Foyers ..... G 1
39 Foys ..... E 9
34 Fraddam ..... F 3
34 Fraddon ..... D 6
88 Fradley ..... A 5
95 Fradswell ..... G 8
113 Fraisthorpe ..... A 9
42 Framfield ..... F 4
92 Framingham Earl ..... E 6
92 Framingham Pigot ..... E 6
93 Framlingham ..... J 6
39 Frampton, Dorset ..... G 9
90 Frampton, Lincs ..... B 4
57 Frampton Cotterell ..... F 9
57 Frampton Mansell ..... D 12
57 Frampton on Severn ..... D 10
90 Frampton West End ..... B 4
93 Framsden ..... J 5
116 Framwellgate Moor ..... A 3
88 Franche ..... D 2
94 Frandley ..... B 5
94 Frankby ..... B 1
88 Frankley ..... D 3
59 Frank's Bridge ..... G 7
89 Frankton ..... E 7
59 Frankwell, Salop ..... A 10
42 Frant ..... E 5
146 Fraserburgh ..... A 7
87 Frating ..... B 10
87 Frating Green ..... B 10
35 Freathy ..... D 11
96 Frecheville ..... B 1
91 Freckenham ..... H 8
110 Freckleton ..... D 3
96 Freeby ..... H 5
84 Freeland ..... C 5
92 Freethorpe ..... E 7
92 Freethorpe Com. ..... E 7
90 Freiston ..... A 5
36 Fremington, Devon ..... C 4
116 Fremington, N. Yorks E 1
57 Frenchay ..... F 9
37 Frenchbeer ..... G 5
139 Frenich, Central ..... G 11
140 Frenich, Tayside ..... A 3
41 Frensham ..... B 9
149 Fresgoe ..... A 9
110 Freshfield ..... F 2
40 Freshwater ..... G 5
54 Freshwater East ..... G 4
93 Fressingfield ..... H 5
149 Freswick ..... A 12
57 Fretherne ..... C 10
92 Frettenham ..... D 5
141 Freuchie ..... F 7
54 Freystrop Cross ..... F 3
39 Friar Waddon ..... H 10
140 Friarton ..... E 6
90 Friday Bridge ..... E 6
42 Friday Street ..... H 5
112 Fridaythorpe ..... A 6
86 Friern Barnet ..... E 3
97 Friesthorpe ..... B 8
96 Frieston ..... E 6
85 Frieth ..... E 9
84 Frilford ..... D 5
85 Frilsham ..... G 6
85 Frimley ..... H 9
85 Frimley Green ..... H 10
42 Frindsbury ..... A 6
90 Fring ..... B 8
85 Fringford ..... A 7
43 Frinsted ..... B 7
87 Frinton ..... B 12
141 Friockheim ..... B 10
58 Friog ..... A 2
96 Frisby on the Wreake ..... H 4
97 Friskney ..... E 11
42 Friston, E. Sussex ..... H 4
93 Friston, Suffolk ..... J 7
96 Fritchley ..... E 1
97 Frith Bank ..... E 10
59 Frith Common ..... E 12
40 Fritham ..... E 4
36 Frithelstock ..... D 3
36 Frithelstock Stone ..... D 3
85 Frithsden ..... C 11
97 Frithville ..... E 10
43 Frittenden ..... D 7
92 Fritton, Norfolk ..... F 5
92 Fritton, Norfolk ..... E 7
84 Fritwell ..... A 6
114 Frizington ..... D 3
57 Frocester ..... D 11
59 Frochas ..... B 7
59 Frodesley ..... B 10
113 Frodingham ..... F 7
94 Frodsham ..... B 4
137 Frogden ..... G 10
95 Froggatt ..... C 11
95 Froghall ..... E 9
57 Frogland Cross ..... F 9
37 Frogmore, Devon ..... L 6
85 Frogmore, Hants ..... H 9
89 Frolesworth ..... C 8
39 Frome ..... B 11
39 Frome St. Quintin ..... F 9
59 Fromes Hill ..... H 12
61 Fron, Clwyd ..... D 10
55 Fron, Dyfed ..... D 11
60 Fron, Gwynedd ..... E 4
60 Fron, Gwynedd ..... F 3
59 Fron, Powys ..... B 8
58 Fron, Powys ..... F
61 Fron Isaf ..... F 1
61 Froncysyllte ..... F 1
61 Fron-deg ..... E 1
61 Frongoch ..... F
60 Fron-oleu ..... G
115 Frosterley ..... A 1
152 Frotoft ..... B
84 Froxfield ..... G
41 Froxfield Green ..... D
41 Froyle ..... B
86 Fryerning ..... D
117 Fryton ..... H
96 Fulbeck ..... E
91 Fulbourn ..... K
84 Fulbrook C
112 Fulford, N. Yorks ..... B
38 Fulford, Somerset C
95 Fulford, Staffs ..... F
86 Fulham ..... F
42 Fulking ..... G
112 Full Sutton ..... B
36 Fullaford ..... B
135 Fullarton ..... F
87 Fuller Street ..... B
94 Fuller's Moor ..... E
40 Fullerton ..... B
97 Fulletby ..... C 1
135 Fullwood ..... D
85 Fulmer ..... F 1
92 Fulmodestone ..... B
97 Fulnetby ..... B
113 Fulstow ..... G 1
110 Fulwood, Lancs ..... D
38 Fulwood, Som ..... D
41 Funtington ..... E
41 Funtley ..... E
140 Funtullich ..... D
152 Funzie ..... B
38 Furley ..... F
142 Furnace, Highland C
139 Furnace, Strathclyde ..... G
88 Furnace End C
42 Furner's Green ..... E
112 Furness ..... E
95 Furness Vale ..... B
86 Furneux Pelham ..... A
85 Furze Platt ..... F
39 Furzebrook ..... H 1
36 Furzehill ..... B
38 Fyfett ..... E
86 Fyfield, Essex C
84 Fyfield, Glos. ..... D
40 Fyfield, Hants ..... A
84 Fyfield, Oxon ..... D
84 Fyfield, Wilts ..... G
117 Fylingthorpe ..... E
146 Fyvie ..... D
135 Gabroc Hill ..... D
89 Gaddesby ..... A 1
135 Gadgirth ..... G
56 Gaer ..... B
60 Gaerwen C
84 Gagingwell ..... B
145 Gaick Lodge L
135 Gailes ..... F
88 Gailey ..... A
116 Gainford C
96 Gainsborough, Lincs. ..... A
93 Gainsborough, Suff. L
91 Gainsford End L
131 Gairloch,
Dumf. & Gall. ..... D 1
147 Gairloch, Grampian ..... G
142 Gairloch, Highland ..... B
143 Gairlochy L
140 Gairney Bank ..... G
145 Gairnshiel Lodge ..... J
115 Gaisgill ..... E
132 Gaitsgill ..... H
137 Galashiels ..... F
89 Galby ..... B 1
130 Galdenoch ..... E
137 Galewood ..... F 1
110 Galgate ..... B
39 Galhampton C
131 Gallaberry ..... C 1
138 Gallanach ..... E
138 Gallanachmore ..... E
138 Gallchoille ..... H
88 Galley Common C
87 Galleyend ..... D
87 Galleywood ..... D
139 Gallin ..... C 1
141 Gallowfauld C
88 Gallows Green,
Heref. & Worc. ..... F
95 Gallows Green, Staffs. F
85 Gallowtree Common ..... F
143 Galltair ..... G 2

112 Goole Fields ....E 5
34 Goonbell ....E 4
34 Goonhavern ....D 5
42 Goose Green ....C 5
147 Goosecruives ....J 5
36 Gooseham ....D 1
37 Goosewell ....K 4
84 Goosey ....E 4
110 Goosnargh ....C 4
94 Goostrey ....C 6
88 Gorcott Hill ....E 4
60 Gorddinog ....C 6
137 Gordon ....E 9
149 Gordonbush ....F 8
146 Gordonstown,
Grampian ....D 5
146 Gordonstown,
Grampian ....B 3
136 Gorebridge ....C 6
90 Gorefield ....D 5
85 Goring ....F 7
41 Goring-by-Sea ......F 12
85 Goring Heath ....F 7
92 Gorleston-on-Sea ....E 8
88 Gornalwood ....C 3
35 Gorran Churchtown ..E 7
35 Gorran Haven ....E 7
132 Gorrenberry ....C 3
58 Gors ....E 2
84 Gorse Hill ....E 3
61 Gorsedd ....C 10
55 Gorseinon ....G 9
152 Gorseness ....C 2
95 Gorseybank ....E 11
55 Gorsgoch ....B 8
55 Gorslas ....F 9
57 Gorsley ....B 10
142 Gorstan ....D 7
143 Gorstanvorran ......M 2
94 Gorstella ....D 2
57 Gorsty Common .....A 8
111 Gorton ....G 7
93 Gosbeck ....K 5
90 Gosberton ....B 3
90 Gosberton Clough ...C 3
93 Gosfield ....M 1
59 Gosford ....F 10
137 Gosford House ......B 7
114 Gosforth, Cumb .....E 3
133 Gosforth,
Tyne & Wear .....F 10
86 Gosmore ....A 2
41 Gosport ....F 7
152 Gossabrough ....C 8
133 Goswick ....B 12
96 Gotham ....G 3
84 Gotherington ....A 1
42 Goudhurst ....D 6
97 Goulceby ....B 9
135 Gourock ....B 7
146 Gourdas ....C 5
147 Gourdon ....K 6
135 Govan ....C 10
96 Goverton ....E 4
37 Goveton ....L 6
131 Govig ....F 1
56 Govilon ....C 6
112 Gowdall ....E 4
55 Gowerton ....G 9
140 Gowkhall ....H 5
112 Gowthorpe ....B 5
113 Goxhill, Humber. ....E 9
113 Goxhill, Humber. ....C 9
113 Goxhill Haven ....E 9
55 Goytre ....H 11
131 Gracefield ....C 9
137 Graden ....F 10
41 Graffham ....D 10
91 Grafham, Cambs ....H 3
41 Grafham, Surrey ....B 11
57 Grafton,
Heref. & Worc ....A 8
59 Grafton,
Heref. & Worc....F 11
84 Grafton, Oxon ......D 4
94 Grafton, Salop ......H 3
112 Grafton, N. Yorks ...A 2
88 Grafton Flyford .....G 3
89 Grafton Regis ......G 11
89 Grafton Underwood D 12
43 Grafty Green ....C 7
61 Graianrhyd ....E 11
61 Graig ....C 7
61 Graig-fechan ....E 10
136 Graigmillar ....B 6
87 Grain ....F 9
113 Grainsby ....G 10
113 Grainthorpe ....G 11
34 Grampound ....E 6
34 Grampound Road ....E 6
85 Granborough ....B 8
96 Granby ....G 5
89 Grandborough ......E 8
140 Grandtully ....B 4
110 Grane ....E 6
114 Grange, Cumb. ......C 5
94 Grange, Merseyside ..B 1
116 Grange, N. Yorks.....F 6
135 Grange, Strathclyde ..F 9
141 Grange, Tayside .....E 7
146 Grange Crossroads ...B 2
144 Grange Hall ....D 6
111 Grange Moor ......E 11
141 Grange of Lindores ...E 7
133 Grange Villa ....H 10
136 Grangehall ....E 2
95 Grangemill ....D 11
136 Grangemouth ....A 2
114 Grange-over-Sands ...G 6
136 Grangepans ....A 3
116 Grangetown,
Cleveland ....C 6
56 Grangetown, S. Glam. G 5
113 Gransmoor ....A 9
54 Granston ....D 2
91 Grantchester ....K 5
96 Grantham ....G 6
146 Grantlodge ....F 5
136 Granton,
Dumf. & Gall......H 3
136 Granton, Lothian ....B 5
145 Granton-on-Spey ....G 6
59 Grantsfield ....F 10
137 Grantshouse ....C 10
94 Grappenhall ....B 5
113 Grasby ....G 8
114 Grasmere ....D 6
111 Grasscroft ....G 8
94 Grassendale ....B 3
115 Grassholme ....C 11
111 Grassington ....A 9
133 Grasslees ....C 8
96 Grassmoor ....D 1
96 Grassthorpe ....C 5
40 Grateley ....B 4
95 Gratwich ....G 9
91 Graveley, Cambs......J 4
86 Graveley, Herts. .....A 2
88 Gravelly Hill ....C 5
43 Graveney ....B 9
42 Gravesend ....A 5
151 Gravir ....E 5
113 Grayingham ....G 7
115 Grayrigg ....E 8
86 Grays ....F 6
41 Grayshott ....C 10
41 Grayswood ....C 10
116 Graythorp ....B 5
85 Grazeley ....G 8
112 Greasbrough ....H 2
94 Greasby ....B 1
96 Greasley ....E 2
91 Great Abington ......K 6
91 Great Addington ....H 1
88 Great Alne ....F 5
110 Great Altcar ....F 2
86 Great Amwell ....C 4
115 Great Asby ....D 9
93 Great Ashfield ......H 3
116 Great Ayton ....D 6
87 Great Baddow ....C 7
57 Great Badminton ...F 11
91 Great Bardfield .....M 8
91 Great Barford ....K 2
88 Great Barr ....C 4
84 Great Barrington ....C 3
94 Great Barrow ....C 3
93 Great Barton ....J 2
117 Great Barugh ....G 7
133 Great Bavington .....E 8
93 Great Bealings ......K 5
84 Great Bedwyn ....H 4
87 Great Bentley ......B 11
89 Great Billing ....F 11
92 Great Bircham ....B 1
93 Great Blakenham ....K 4
115 Great Blencow.......B 7
94 Great Bolas ....H 5
41 Great Bookham ....A 12
89 Great Bourton ......H 8
89 Great Bowden ......C 11
91 Great Bradley ....K 8
87 Great Braxted ....G 8
93 Great Bricett ....K 3
85 Great Brickhill .....A 10
95 Great Bridgeford ....G 7
89 Great Brington .....F 10
87 Great Bromley .....A 10
116 Great Broughton .....D 5
94 Great Budworth .....B 5
116 Great Burdon ....B 5
87 Great Burstead ......E 7
116 Great Busby ....E 5
86 Great Canfield ....B 6
97 Great Carlton ......B 11
90 Great Casterton ......E 1
57 Great Chalfield .....H 11
43 Great Chart ....D 8
88 Great Chatwell ......A 1
91 Great Chesterfield ....L 6
40 Great Cheverall ......A 1
91 Great Chishill ....L 5
87 Great Clacton ......B 11
114 Great Clifton ....B 3
113 Great Coate ....F 10
88 Great Comberton ....H 3
132 Great Corby ....H 3
93 Great Cornard ....L 2
113 Great Cowden .....C 10
84 Great Coxwell ....E 4
116 Great Crakehall ......F 3
89 Great Cransley .....D 11
92 Great Cressingham ...E 2
110 Great Crosby ....G 2
95 Great Cubley ....F 10
89 Great Dalby ....A 10
89 Gt. Doddington .....F 12
38 Great Dorweeke .....F 3
57 Great Doward ....C 9
92 Great Dunham ......D 2
86 Great Dunmow ......B 6
40 Great Durnford ......B 3
86 Great Easton, Essex ..A 6
89 Great Easton, Leics. .C 11
110 Great Eccleston ......C 3
117 Great Edstone ....G 7
92 Great Ellingham .....F 3
39 Great Elm ....A 10
91 Great Eversden ......K 5
116 Great Fencote ....F 3
93 Great Finborough ....J 3
92 Great Fransham .....D 2
85 Great Gaddesden ...C 11
91 Great Gidding ....G 2
112 Great Givendale .....B 6
93 Great Glenham.......J 6
89 Great Glen ....B 10
96 Great Gonerby ....F 6
57 Great Graig ....B 7
91 Great Gransden .....K 4
92 Great Green, Norf. ...F 6
93 Great Green, Suff. ...K 2
117 Great Habton ....G 8
90 Great Hale ....A 2
86 Great Hallingbury ...B 5
89 Great Harrowden ...E 12
110 Great Harwood .....D 6
85 Great Haseley ....D 7
113 Great Hatfield ....C 9
95 Great Haywood .....H 8
89 Great Heath ....D 7
112 Great Heck ....E 4
93 Great Henny ....L 2
57 Great Hinton ......H 12
92 Great Hockham ......F 2
87 Great Holland ......B 12
93 Great Horkesley ....M 3
91 Great Hormead .....M 5
111 Great Horton ......D 10
85 Great Horwood .....A 8
89 Great Houghton,
Northants ....F 11
112 Great Houghton,
S. Yorks. ....F 2
95 Great Hucklow ....B 10
113 Great Kelk ....A 8
85 Great Kimble ....D 9
85 Great Kingshill .....D 9
116 Great Langton ....F 3
87 Great Leighs ....B 7
113 Great Limber ....F 9
89 Great Linford ......H 12
93 Great Livermere .....H 2
95 Great Longstone ....C 10
133 Great Lumley ......H 11
88 Great Malvern ......G 2
93 Great Maplestead ...M 1
110 Great Marton ....D 2
92 Great Massingham ...C 1
92 Great Melton ....E 4
85 Great Milton ....D 7
85 Great Missenden ...D 10
110 Great Mitton ....C 6
43 Great Mongeham ...C 12
115 Great Musgrave ....D 10
94 Great Ness ....H 3
87 Great Oakley, Essex .A 11
89 Great Oakley,
Northants ....D 12
86 Great Offley ....A 1
115 Great Ormside ......C 9
132 Great Orton ....H 2
112 Great Ouseburn .....A 2
89 Great Oxendon ....D 10
86 Great Oxney Grn.....C 6
92 Great Palgrave ......D 1
86 Great Parndon ......C 4
91 Great Paxton ....J 3
110 Great Plumpton .....D 3
92 Great Plumstead .....D 6
96 Great Ponton ....G 6
112 Great Preston ....D 2
91 Great Raveley ....G 4
84 Great Rissington .....B 3
84 Great Rollright ......A 4
54 Great Rudbaxton ....E 3
92 Great Ryburgh ......C 3
133 Great Ryle ....B 8
87 Great Saling ....A 7
115 Great Salkeld ....B 8
91 Great Sampford ......L 7
94 Great Sankey ....A 4
93 Great Saxham ....J 1
84 Great Shefford ......G 5
91 Great Shelford ....K 6
116 Great Smeaton ....E 4
92 Great Snoring ....B 2
84 Great Somerford .....F 1
116 Great Stainton ....C 3
87 Great Stambridge ....E 9
91 Great Staughton .....J 2
97 Great Steeping .....D 11
43 Great Stonar ....B 12
115 Great Strickland .....C 8
91 Great Stukeley ......H 3
97 Great Sturton ....C 9
94 Gt. Sutton, Ches. .....C 2
59 Gt. Sutton, Salop....D 10
133 Great Swinburne .....E 7
87 Great Tarpots ....E 7
84 Great Tew ....A 5
87 Great Tey ....A 9
91 Great Thurlow ......K 8
36 Great Torrington ....D 4
133 Great Tosson ....C 8
87 Great Totham ....C 8
113 Great Tows ....H 10
114 Great Urswick ......H 5
87 Great Wakering......E 9
93 Great Waldingfield ...L 2
92 Great Walsingham ...B 2
87 Great Waltham ......C 7
86 Great Warley ....E 6
84 Great Washbourne ...A 1
93 Great Welnetham ....J 2
93 Great Wenham ......L 4
133 Great Whittington ...F 8
87 Great Whigborough ..B 9
91 Great Wilbraham ....J 6
40 Great Wishford ......C 2
57 Great Witcombe ....C 12
88 Great Witley ....E 1
84 Great Wolford ......A 3
89 Great Woolstone ...H 12
91 Great Wratting ......K 8
86 Great Wymondley ...A 2
88 Great Wyrley ....A 3
94 Great Wytheford ....H 4
92 Great Yarmouth .....E 8
93 Great Yeldham ......L 1
86 Greater London, Co. ..F 3
111 Greater Manchester,
Co. ....G 7
90 Greatford ....D 2
95 Greatgate ....F 9
116 Greatham, Cleveland .B 5
41 Greatham, Hants.....C 9
43 Greatham, W. Sussex E 11
43 Greatstone-on-Sea....F 9
89 Greatworth ....H 9
91 Green End ....K 2
112 Green Hammerton ...A 2
39 Green Ore ....A 9
42 Green Street Green ...A 5
87 Green Tye ....B 4
131 Greenbeck ....C 11
136 Greenburn ....C 2
114 Greendale ....E 4
39 Greendown ....A 9
133 Greendykes ....C 12
137 Greenend ....G 8
91 Greenfield, Beds. ....M 2
61 Greenfield, Clwyd ..B 11
143 Greenfield, Highland ..J 6
111 Greenfield,
Manchester ....G 8
85 Greenfield, Oxon. ....E 8
86 Greenford ....F 1
136 Greengairs ....B 1
110 Greenhalgh ....D 3
84 Greenham, Berks.....H 6
38 Greenham, Som......D 4
132 Greenhaugh ....D 6
131 Greenhead,
Dumf. & Gal. .....C 10
132 Greenhead, Northumb. F 5
135 Greenhead, Strathclyde E 9
136 Greenhill, Central ....B 1
43 Greenhill, Kent .....A 10
135 Greenhills ....D 8
42 Greenhithe ....A 5
135 Greenholm ....F 10
115 Greenholme ....E 8
137 Greenhouse ....G 8
111 Greenhow Hill ......A 9
137 Greenknowe ....E 9
149 Greenland ....A 11
85 Greenlands ....F 8
137 Greenlaw, Borders ...E 9
146 Greenlaw, Grampian .B 4
137 Greenlaw Walls .....E 12
131 Greenlea,
Dumf. & Gal. ....D 11
135 Greenlea,
Dumf. & Gal. .....A 7
140 Greenloaning ....F 3
135 Greenock ....B 8
114 Greenodd ....G 5
136 Greenrig ....E 1
131 Greenrow ....F 11
89 Greens Norton .....G 10
96 Greenscares ....F 3
136 Greenshields ....E 3
133 Greenside ....G 9
133 Greensidehill ....A 8
146 Greenskairs ....A 5
87 Greenstead Green ....A 8
86 Greensted Green .....D 5
152 Greenwall ....C 3
54 Greenway, Dyfed ....D 4
56 Greenway, S. Glam. ..G 4
86 Greenwich ....F 4
84 Greet ....A 1
59 Greete ....E 11
89 Greetham, Leics. ....A 12
97 Greetham, Lincs. ...C 10
111 Greetland ....E 9
39 Greinton ....C 7
89 Grendon, N'thants ..F 12
88 Grendon, War. ......B 6
88 Grendon Common ...B 6
59 Grendon Green .....G 11
85 Grendon Underwood .B 8
37 Grenofen ....J 4
111 Grenoside ....H 11
94 Gresford ....E 2
92 Gresham ....B 5
150 Greshornish ....C 3
151 Gress ....C 6
92 Gressenhall ....D 3
92 Gressenhall Grn. .....D 3
115 Gressingham ....H 8
116 Greta Bridge ....D 1
132 Gretna ....F 2
132 Gretna Green ....F 1
84 Gretton, Glos. ....A 1
89 Gretton, N'thants ...C 12
59 Gretton, Salop. .....C 10
116 Grewelthorpe ....G 2
146 Grey Stone ....E 6
116 Greygarth ....H 2
55 Greynor ....F 9
136 Greyrigg, Central ....B 2
131 Greyrigg,
Dumf. & Gall. ....C 11
114 Greysouthen ....B 3
115 Greystoke, Cumb.....B 7
141 Greystoke, Tayside ..C 10
131 Greystone ....D 10
41 Greywell ....A 8
36 Gribbleford Bridge ...F 4
112 Gribthorpe ....D 5
138 Gribun ....D 2
37 Gridley Corner ......G 2
89 Griff ....C 7
56 Griffithstown ....D 6
115 Grigghall ....F 7
152 Grimbister ....C 2
110 Grimeford Village ....F 5
112 Grimethorpe ....F 2
88 Grimley ....F 2
135 Grimmet ....H 8
97 Grimoldby ....A 11
110 Grimsargh ....D 5
113 Grimsby ....F 10
89 Grimscote ....G 10
36 Grimscott ....E 1
151 Grimshader ....D 5
90 Grimsthorpe ....C 2
113 Grimston, Humber. .D 10
96 Grimston, Leics. .....H
90 Grimston, Norfolk ...C
39 Grimstone ....G
37 Grinacombe Moor ...G
117 Grindale ....H 1
88 Grindle ....B
95 Grindleford ....B 1
110 Grindleton C
94 Grindley Brook ......F
95 Grindlow ....B 1
116 Grindon, Cleveland ..C
132 Grindon, Northumb. .F
137 Grindon, Northumb. E 1
95 Grindon, Staffs.......E
132 Grindon Hill ....F
137 Grindonrigg ....E 1
96 Gringley on the Hill ..A
132 Grinsdale ....G
94 Grinshill ....H
116 Grinton ....E
117 Gristhorpe ....G 1
92 Griston ....E
84 Grittenham ....F
57 Grittleton ....F 1
114 Grizebeck ....G
114 Grizedale ....F
152 Grobister C
89 Groby ....A
61 Groes, Clwyd ....D
55 Groes, W. Glam. ...H 1
56 Groesfaen ....F
60 Groesfford ....F
61 Groesffordd C
61 Groesffordd Marli ...C
59 Groesllwyd ....A
134 Grogport ....E
61 Gronant ....B 1
42 Groombridge ....D
151 Grosebay ....H
57 Grosmont, Gwent ....B
117 Grosmont, N. Yorks. .E
93 Groton L
39 Grove, Dorset ....H
84 Grove, Oxon. ....E
96 Grove, Notts. ....B
55 Grovesend ....G
142 Grudie ....D
148 Gruids ....F
148 Gruinard House .....G
138 Gruline House ......D
34 Grumbla ....G
93 Grundisburgh ......K
152 Grundsound ....E
152 Gruting ....D
152 Grutness ....F
60 Grwedog ....B
139 Gualachulain C
148 Gualin House ....B
141 Guard Bridge ....E
88 Guarlford ....H 2
140 Guay ....B
131 Gubhill ....B 1
43 Guestling Green .....G
43 Guestling Icklesham ..F
92 Guestwick ....C 3
110 Guide ....E
133 Guide Post ....E 1
91 Guilden Morden L
94 Guilden Sutton ......C 3
41 Guildford ....A 1
141 Guildtown ....D
89 Guilsborough ......E 1
59 Guilsfield ....A
43 Guilton ....B 1
135 Guiltreehill ....H
36 Guineaford ....B
143 Guisachan House ....G 7
116 Guisborough ....D
111 Guiseley ....C 1
92 Guist C
84 Guiting Power ......B 2
152 Gulberwick ....E 7
137 Gullane ....A 7
34 Gulval ....F 2
37 Gulworthy ....H 3
54 Gumfreston ....G
89 Gumley ....C 10
34 Gummow's Shop ....D 6
112 Gunby, Humber. ....D 5
96 Gunby, Lincs. ....H 6
41 Gundleton ....C 7
36 Gunn ....C 5
115 Gunnerside ....E 11
133 Gunnerton ....F 7
133 Gunnerton Fell ......E 7
112 Gunness ....F 6
35 Gunnislake ....C 11
152 Gunnista ....D 7
112 Gunthorpe, Humber. .G 6
92 Gunthorpe, Norf. ....B 3

96 Haughton, Notts. C 4
94 Haughton, Salop. A 11
59 Haughton, Salop. C 12
94 Haughton, Salop. G 2
95 Haughton, Staffs. H 7
133 Haughton Castle F 7
111 Haughton Green H 8
94 Haughton Moss E 4
88 Haunton A 6
133 Hauxley C 11
41 Havant F 8
59 Haven G 9
112 Havercroft F 2
54 Haverfordwest E 3
91 Haverhill L 8
114 Haverigg G 4
86 Havering E 5
86 Havering-atte-Bower E 5
89 Haversham H 11
114 Haverthwaite G 6
116 Haverton Hill C 5
61 Hawarden D 12
87 Hawbush Green B 8
55 Hawen B 7
115 Hawes F 11
88 Hawford F 2
132 Hawick B 3
95 Hawk Green B 8
39 Hawkchurch F 7
93 Hawkedon K 1
42 Hawkenbury D 5
39 Hawkeridge A 11
88 Hawkes End D 6
57 Hawkesbury F 10
57 Hawkesbury Upton F 11
133 Hawkhill B 10
42 Hawkhurst E 6
41 Hawkley C 8
38 Hawkridge C 2
110 Hawkshaw F 6
114 Hawkshead E 6
114 Hawkshead Hill E 6
136 Hawksland E 1
115 Hawkswick H 12
96 Hawksworth, Notts. E 5
111 Hawksworth, W. Yorks. C 10
86 Hawkwell E 8
42 Hawley A 4
85 Hawley H 9
84 Hawling B 2
116 Hawnby F 5
111 Haworth D 9
93 Hawstead J 1
116 Hawthorn, Dur. A 4
57 Hawthorn, Wilts. G 11
132 Hawthornside B 4
90 Hawthorpe C 2
96 Hawton E 5
112 Haxby A 4
112 Haxey G 5
42 Haxted D 3
59 Hay-on-Wye H 8
86 Hay Street A 4
54 Haycastle D 2
54 Haycastle Cross D 3
110 Haydock G 4
39 Haydon, Dorset E 10
133 Haydon, Northumb. F 7
133 Haydon Bridge G 7
84 Haydon Wick E 2
35 Haye C 10
86 Hayes, Kent G 4
86 Hayes, London F 1
95 Hayfield, Derby B 9
141 Hayfield, Fife H 7
135 Hayhill H 9
34 Hayle F 3
41 Hayling Island F 8
137 Haymount F 9
38 Hayne F 2
91 Haynes L 2
91 Haynes West End L 2
42 Haysden D 4
141 Hayshead C 11
131 Hayton, Cumb. G 11
132 Hayton, Cumb. G 3
147 Hayton, Grampian G 7
112 Hayton, Humber. C 6
96 Hayton, Notts. B 4
59 Hayton's Bent D 10
37 Haytor Vale H 6
42 Hayward's Heath F 2
96 Haywood Oaks E 3
95 Hazel Grove B 8
136 Hazelbank E 1
39 Hazelbury Bryan E 11
85 Hazeley H 8
88 Hazelslade A 4
141 Hazelton Walls E 8
95 Hazelwood F 11
85 Hazlemere E 10
133 Hazlerigg F 10
84 Hazleton B 2
133 Hazon C 10
90 Heacham B 8
40 Headbourne Worthy C 6
59 Headbrook G 8
43 Headcorn D 7
111 Headingley D 11
84 Headington C 6
116 Headlam C 2
88 Headless Cross F 4
41 Headley, Hants. C 9
84 Headley, Hants. H 6
42 Headley, Surrey C 1
41 Headley Down B 10
96 Headon C 5
135 Heads E 12
132 Heads Nook G 3
96 Heage E 1
115 Healaugh, N. Yorks. E 12
112 Healaugh, N. Yorks. B 3
36 Heale, Devon A 5
39 Heale, Somerset B 10
111 Healey, Lancs. E 7
133 Healey, Nothumb. G 8
116 Healey, N. Yorks. G 2
133 Healey Cote C 9
133 Healeyfield H 9
113 Healing F 10
34 Heamor G 2
96 Heanor F 2
36 Heanton Punchardon B 4
96 Heapham A 6
136 Hearthstane G 4
36 Heasley Mill C 6
150 Heast F 6
96 Heath C 2
85 Heath and Reach A 10
36 Heath Cross F 7
85 Heath End, Berks. H 7
41 Heath End, Surrey A 10
88 Heath End, W. Midlands B 4
88 Heath Hayes A 4
88 Heath Hill A 1
39 Heath House B 7
38 Heath Pault Cross C 3
88 Heath Town B 3
95 Heathcote D 10
89 Heather A 7
150 Heatherfield D 4
149 Heatherwood Park G 8
140 Heatheryhaugh B 6
131 Heathfield, Cumb. G 12
37 Heathfield, Devon H 7
42 Heathfield, East Sussex F 4
38 Heathfield, Som. D 5
135 Heathfield, Strathclyde C 8
131 Heathhall D 10
88 Heathton C 2
94 Heatley A 5
110 Heaton, Lancs. A 3
111 Heaton, Manchester H 7
95 Heaton, Staffs. D 8
111 Heaton, W. Yorks. D 10
110 Heaton's Bridge F 3
42 Heaverham B 4
38 Heavitree G 3
133 Hebburn G 11
111 Hebden A 9
111 Hebden Bridge D 8
94 Hebden Green D 5
54 Hebron, Dyfed D 5
133 Hebron, Northumb. D 10
131 Heck D 11
85 Heckfield H 8
93 Heckfield Green H 5
90 Heckington A 2
136 Hecklebirnie F 2
111 Heckmondwike E 10
84 Heddington G 1
84 Heddington Wick G 1
36 Heddon C 5
133 Heddon on the Wall F 9
92 Hedenham F 6
37 Hedge Cross G 4
40 Hedge End E 6
85 Hedgerley E 10
38 Hedging C 6
133 Hedley on the Hill G 9
88 Hednesford A 3
113 Hedon D 9
85 Hedsor E 10
59 Hedgon Hill G 11
133 Heiferlaw Bank A 10
116 Heighington, Dur. C 3
97 Heighington, Lincs. C 7
144 Heights of Brae D 1
142 Heights of Kinlochewe C 4
148 Heilam B 5
137 Heiton F 9
38 Hele, Devon F 3
36 Hele, Devon A 4
37 Hele, Devon G 2
38 Hele, Somerset D 5
135 Helensburgh A 8
135 Helentongate F 9
34 Helford G 5
34 Helford Passage G 5
92 Helhoughton C 2
91 Helions Bumpstead L 7
35 Helland C 8
35 Hellandbridge C 8
92 Hellesdon D 5
38 Hellidon F 8
111 Hellifield B 7
42 Helling G 4
92 Hellington E 6
133 Helm C 10
89 Helmdon H 9
93 Helmingham J 5
116 Helmington Row B 2
149 Helmsdale E 10
110 Helmshore E 6
116 Helmsley G 6
116 Helperby H 5
117 Helperthorpe H 9
90 Helpringham B 2
90 Helpston E 2
94 Helsby C 3
34 Helston G 4
35 Helstone B 8
115 Helton C 7
115 Helwith Bridge H 10
85 Hemel Hempstead D 11
112 Hemingbrough D 4
97 Hemingby C 9
112 Hemongfield G 2
91 Hemingford Abbots H 4
91 Hemingford Grey H 4
93 Hemingstone K 5
96 Hemington, Leics. G 2
91 Hemington, Northants. G 2
39 Hemington, Som. A 10
93 Hemley L 6
116 Hemlington D 5
88 Hempholme B 8
92 Hempnall F 5
92 Hempnall Green F 5
91 Hempstead, Essex L 7
42 Hempstead, Kent B 6
92 Hempstead, Norf. B 4
57 Hempsted C 11
92 Hempton, Norfolk C 2
84 Hempton, Oxon. A 5
92 Hemsby D 8
96 Hemswell A 6
112 Hemsworth F 2
38 Hemyock E 5
57 Henbury, Avon F 9
95 Henbury, Ches. C 7
36 Henderbarrow Corner F 3
86 Hendon, London E 2
133 Hendon, Tyne & Wear G 12
57 Hendre C 8
56 Hendreforgan E 3
54 Hendre-wen D 3
55 Hendy G 9
60 Heneglwys C 4
54 Hen-feddau D 6
57 Henfield, Avon F 10
42 Henfield, W. Sussex F 1
43 Hengherst D 8
56 Hengoed, Mid Glam. E 5
59 Hengoed, Powys G 8
94 Hengoed, Salop. G 2
93 Hengrave H 1
86 Henham A 5
133 Henhill E 12
59 Heniarth B 7
38 Henlade D 6
133 Henlaw C 11
39 Henley, Dorset F 10
59 Henley, Salop. D 10
39 Henley, Somerset C 8
93 Henley, Suffolk K 5
41 Henley, W. Sussex D 10
88 Henley-in-Arden E 5
85 Henley-on-Thames F 8
42 Henley Street A 5
61 Henllan, Clwyd C 9
55 Henllan, Dyfed C 7
54 Henllan Amgoed E 5
56 Henllys E 6
91 Henlow L 3
37 Hennock H 7
93 Henny Street L 2
61 Henryd C 7
54 Henry's Moat D 4
112 Hensall E 4
132 Henshaw G 6
114 Hensingham D 2
93 Henstead G 8
39 Henstridge D 10
39 Henstridge Ash D 10
39 Henstridge Bowden D 10
85 Henton, Oxon. D 8
39 Henton, Som. B 8
39 Henstridge Marsh D 11
88 Henwick G 2
35 Henwood B 9
152 Heogan D 7
56 Heol Senni B 3
55 Heol-las G 10
56 Heol-y-Cyw F 3
133 Hepburn A 9
133 Hepple C 8
133 Hepple Whitefield C 8
133 Hepscott E 10
111 Hepstonstall D 8
93 Hepworth, Suff. H 3
111 Hepworth, W. Yorks. F 10
54 Herbrandston F 2
59 Hereford H 10
88 Hereford & Worcester, Co. F 2
136 Heriot D 6
137 Hermiston G 8
84 Hermitage, Berks. G 6
132 Hermitage, Borders C 3
39 Hermitage, Dorset F 10
132 Hermitage, Dumf. & Gall. E 9
41 Hermitage, W. Sussex F 9
55 Hermon, Dyfed D 10
54 Hermon, Dyfed D 5
60 Hermon, Gwynedd C 3
43 Herne B 10
43 Herne Bay A 10
36 Herner C 5
43 Hernhill B 9
35 Herodsfoot D 9
43 Heronden C 11
86 Herongate E 6
130 Heronsford C 2
85 Heronsgate E 11
41 Herriard B 8
92 Herringfleet F 8
91 Herring's Green L 2
91 Herringswell H 8
133 Herrington H 11
43 Hersden B 10
85 Hersham H 12
42 Herstmonceux G 5
40 Herston, Dorset H 2
152 Herston, Orkney Is. E 2
86 Hertford C 3
86 Hertford Heath C 3
86 Hertfordshire, Co. B 2
86 Hertingfordbury C 3
114 Hesket Newmarket A 6
110 Hesketh Bank E 3
110 Hesketh Lane C 5
110 Heskin Green F 4
116 Hesleden A 4
132 Hesleyside E 6
112 Heslington B 4
112 Hessay B 3
35 Hessenford D 10
93 Hessett J 2
135 Hessilhead D 9
113 Hessle E 8
110 Hest Bank A 3
86 Heston F 1
94 Heswall B 1
85 Hethe A 7
92 Hethersett E 5
132 Hethersgill F 3
137 Hethpool G 11
116 Hett B 3
111 Hetton A 8
133 Hetton Downs H 11
133 Hetton Law C 11
133 Hetton Steads B 11
133 Hetton-le-Hole H 11
133 Heugh F 9
146 Heugh-head F 1
93 Heveningham H 6
42 Hever D 4
115 Heversham G 7
92 Hevingham C 5
57 Hewelsfield D 9
57 Hewish, Avon H 7
39 Hewish, Somerset E 7
112 Heworth B 4
133 Hexham G 7
137 Hexpath E 9
42 Hextable A 4
37 Hexworthy H 5
87 Heybridge, Essex C 8
86 Heybridge, Essex D 6
87 Heydridge Basin C 8
37 Heybrook Bay L 4
91 Heydon, Cambs. L 5
92 Heydon, Norfolk C 4
97 Heydour F 7
110 Heysham A 3
111 Heyshaw A 10
41 Heyshott D 10
40 Heytesbury B 1
84 Heythrop A 4
111 Heywood, Manchester F 7
39 Heywood, Wilts. A 12
113 Hibaldstow G 7
112 Hickleton G 3
92 Hickling, Norfolk C 7
96 Hickling, Notts. G 4
92 Hickling Green C 7
88 Hidcote Bartrim H 5
112 High Ackworth E 2
133 High Angerton E 9
115 High Bankhill A 8
86 High Beach D 4
115 High Bentham H 9
36 High Bickington D 5
115 High Birkwith G 10
135 High Blantyre D 11
136 High Bonnybridge B 1
131 High Borgue F 7
111 High Bradley B 9
36 High Bray C 6
42 High Brooms D 5
36 High Bullen D 4
116 High Burton G 2
133 High Buston B 10
133 High Callerton F 10
112 High Catton B 5
133 High Church E 10
135 High Cleughearn E 11
84 High Cogges C 5
116 High Conniscliffe D 3
137 High Cross, Borders E 8
41 High Cross, Hants. C 8
86 High Cross, Herts. B 4
95 High Cross Bank H 11
135 High Duncryne A 9
86 High Easter B 6
116 High Ellington G 2
116 High Entercommon E 4
59 High Ercall A 11
116 High Etherley B 2
87 High Garrett A 7
116 High Grange B 2
88 High Green, Heref. & Worcs. H 2
92 High Green, Norf. E 4
111 High Green, S. Yorks. G 12
43 High Halden D 8
42 High Halstow A 6
39 High Ham C 8
114 High Harrington C 3
116 High Haswell A 4
94 High Hatton H 5
117 High Hawsker D 9
115 High Hesket A 7
116 High Hesleden A 5
111 High Hoyland F 11
113 High Hursley D 7
42 High Hurstwood E 4
117 High Hutton H 8
114 High Ireby B 5
116 High Kilburn G 5
95 High Lane, Manchester B 8
59 High Lane, Heref. & Worcs. F 12
86 High Laver C 5
94 High Legh B 5
116 High Leven D 5
57 High Littleton H 9
114 High Lorton C 4
117 High Marishes G 8
96 High Marnham C 5
112 High Melton G 3
133 High Mickley G 9
130 High Mindork F 4
117 High Mowthorpe H 9
114 High Newton G 6
133 High Newton by-the-Sea E 12
114 High Nibthwaite F 5
94 High Offley H 6
86 High Ongar D 5
88 High Onn A 2
130 High Pennyvenie A 6
86 High Roding B 6
114 High Row B
115 High Shaw F 1
116 High Skelding H
133 High Spen G
116 High Stoop A
35 High Street, Corn. D
93 High Street, Suff. K
93 High Street, Suff. K
93 High Street Green K
116 High Throston B
97 High Toynton C 1
133 High Trewhitt B
136 High Valleyfield A
133 High Warden F
114 High Wray E
86 High Wych C
85 High Wycombe E
96 Higham, Derby D
42 Higham, Kent A
111 Higham, Lancs. D
91 Higham, Suffolk J
93 Higham, Suffolk L
133 Higham Dykes E
91 Higham Ferrers H
91 Higham Gobion M
89 Higham on the Hill C
42 Higham Wood C
36 Highampton E
143 Highbridge, Highland L
38 Highbridge, Som. B
42 Highbrook E
111 Highburton F 1
39 Highbury A 1
132 Highchesters B
84 Highclere H
40 Highcliffe G
39 Higher Alham B 1
39 Higher Ansty F 1
38 Higher Ashton H
110 Higher Ballam D
34 Higher Boscaswell F
38 Higher Combe C
34 Higher Crackington B
110 Higher End G 4
94 Higher Heath G 4
61 Higher Kinnerton D 1
39 Higher Nyland D 1
110 Higher Penwortham D 4
95 Higher Poynton B
34 Higher Town C 2
94 Higher Walton, Ches. B 4
110 Higher Walton, Lancs. D 5
39 Higher Whatcombe F 1
94 Higher Whitley B 5
94 Higher Wych F 3
96 Highfield, S. Yorks. B
135 Highfield, Strathclyde D 8
133 Highfield, Tyne & Wear G 9
91 Highfields, Cambs. J 5
137 Highfields, Northumb. D 12
86 Highgate, London E 3
112 Highgate, N. Yorks. E 4
132 Highgreen Manor D 6
116 Highlands, Dur. C 2
146 Highlands, Grampian F 6
96 Highlane B 1
57 Highleadon B 11
41 Highleigh F 9
88 Highley D 1
85 Highmoor Cross F 8
57 Highmoor Hill E 8
57 Highnam Green B 11
36 Highridge D 6
43 Highsted B 8
93 Highstreet Green M 1
93 Hightae D 11
95 Hightown, Ches. D 7
131 Hightown, Dumf. & Gall. C 11
110 Hightown, Merseyside G 2
131 Hightown of Craigs D 11
34 Highway, Corn. E 4
84 Highway, Wilts. G 2
37 Highweek J 7
84 Highworth E 3
92 Hilborough E 1
96 Hilcote D 2
84 Hilcott H 2
42 Hilden Park C 4
42 Hildenborough C 4
91 Hildersham K 6
95 Hilderstone G 8
113 Hilderthorpe A 9
39 Hilfield F 9
90 Hilgay F 7
57 Hill, Avon E 9
36 Hill, Devon E 9
88 Hill, W. Midlands B 5

41 Hill Brow D 9
17 Hill Cottages E 7
10 Hill Dale F 4
97 Hill Dyke E 10
15 Hill End, Dur. B 12
40 Hill End, Fife H 5
57 Hill Gate B 8
41 Hill Head, Hants. F 7
33 Hill Head, Northumb. F 7
54 Hill Mountain F 3
40 Hill of Beath H 6
44 Hill of Fearn B 4
46 Hill of Maud Crofts B 2
95 Hill Ridware H 9
91 Hill Row H 5
40 Hill Top, Hants F 5
11 Hill Top, W. Yorks. F 12
40 Hill View F 1
12 Hillam D 3
15 Hillbeck D 10
14 Hillberry G 2
43 Hillborough A 10
40 Hillbourne G 2
46 Hillbrae E 5
40 Hillbutts F 1
41 Hillcairnie E 8
38 Hillcommon D 5
36 Hillend, Fife A 4
36 Hillend, Strathclyde E 3
57 Hillersland C 9
85 Hillesden A 8
57 Hillesley E 11
38 Hillfarance D 5
37 Hillhead, Devon K 8
46 Hillhead, Grampian E 5
33 Hillhead, Northumb. B 9
35 Hillhead, Strathclyde F 10
35 Hillhead, Strathclyde G 9
36 Hillhead, Strathclyde E 3
46 Hillhead of Auchentumb B 7
46 Hillhead of Cocklaw C 8
37 Hillhouse D 7
88 Hilliard's Cross A 5
86 Hillingdon F 1
90 Hillington C 8
89 Hillmorton E 8
47 Hillockhead, Grampian G 1
46 Hillockhead, Grampian F 2
41 Hillpound D 7
31 Hillside, Dumf. & Gall. C 12
47 Hillside, Grampian H 7
52 Hillside, Shetlands C 7
47 Hillside, Tayside L 4
40 Hillstreet D 5
52 Hillswick C 6
41 Hillway G 8
52 Hillwell F 7
84 Hilmarton G 1
57 Hilperton H 12
57 Hilperton Marsh H 11
41 Hilsea F 8
13 Hilston D 10
91 Hilton J 4
37 Hilton, Borders D 11
16 Hilton, Cleveland D 5
15 Hilton, Cumbria C 9
95 Hilton, Derby G 11
39 Hilton, Dorset F 11
16 Hilton, Durham C 2
46 Hilton, Grampian D 7
88 Hilton, Salop C 1
44 Hilton of Cadboll B 4
88 Himbleton F 3
88 Himley C 2
15 Hincaster G 7
84 Hinchwick A 2
89 Hinckley C 7
93 Hinderclay H 3
17 Hinderwell D 8
94 Hindford G 2
41 Hindhead C 10
10 Hindley, Manchester G 5
33 Hindley, Northumb. G 8
10 Hindley Green G 5
88 Hindlip F 2
92 Hindolveston C 3
39 Hindon C 12
92 Hindringham B 3
92 Hingham E 3
94 Hinstock H 5
93 Hintlesham L 4
57 Hinton, Avon G 10
40 Hinton, Hants. G 4
59 Hinton, Heref. & Worcs. H 9
89 Hinton, Northants. G 8
59 Hinton, Salop. B 9
41 Hinton Ampner C 7
39 Hinton Blewett A 9
57 Hinton Charterhouse H 11
88 Hinton Green H 4
89 Hinton-in-the-Hedge H 9
41 Hinton Marsh C 7
40 Hinton Martell E 2
88 Hinton on the Green H 4
84 Hinton Parva F 3
39 Hinton St. George E 7
39 Hinton St. Mary E 11
84 Hinton Waldrist D 5
59 Hints, Salop. E 11
88 Hints, Staffs. B 5
89 Hinwick F 12
43 Hinxhill D 9
91 Hinxton L 6
91 Hinxworth L 3
111 Hipperholme E 10
116 Hipswell E 2
54 Hiraeth E 5
147 Hirn G 5
61 Hirnant, Powys H 10
58 Hirnant, Powys E 4
133 Hirst D 11
112 Hirst Courtney E 4
61 Hirwaen D 10
56 Hirwaun D 3
36 Hiscott C 4
91 Histon J 5
93 Hitcham K 3
131 Hitchill E 12
86 Hitchin A 2
86 Hither Green F 4
36 Hittisleigh Cross F 6
112 Hive D 6
95 Hixon H 8
43 Hoaden B 11
57 Hoaldalbert B 7
95 Hoar Cross H 10
57 Hoarwithy A 8
43 Hoath B 10
59 Hobarris E 8
152 Hobbister D 2
86 Hobbs Cross D 5
132 Hobkirk B 4
133 Hobson G 10
96 Hoby H 4
92 Hockering D 4
96 Hockerton E 4
87 Hockley E 8
88 Hockley Heath E 5
85 Hockliffe A 10
91 Hockwold cum Wilton G 8
38 Hockworthy D 4
86 Hoddesdon C 4
110 Hoddlesden E 6
131 Hoddomcross D 12
54 Hodgeston G 4
94 Hodnet G 5
42 Hodsoll Street B 5
84 Hodson F 3
96 Hodthorpe C 3
41 Hoe, Hampshire D 7
92 Hoe, Norfolk D 3
41 Hoe Gate E 8
115 Hoff C 9
41 Hog Patch A 9
85 Hoggeston B 9
110 Hoghton E 5
95 Hognaston E 11
97 Hogsthorpe C 12
90 Holbeach C 5
90 Holbeach Bank C 5
90 Holbeach Clough C 4
90 Holbeach Drove D 4
90 Holbeach Hurn C 5
90 Holbeach St. Johns D 4
90 Holbeach St. Marks C 5
90 Holbeach St. Matthew B 5
96 Holbeck, Notts. C 3
111 Holbeck, W. Yorks. D 11
88 Holberrow Green F 4
37 Holbeton L 5
95 Holbrook, Derby F 12
93 Holbrook, Suffolk L 5
40 Holbury F 6
133 Holburn B 11
37 Holcombe, Devon H 8
110 Holcombe, Manchester E 6
39 Holcombe, Som. A 10
110 Holcombe Brook F 6
38 Holcombe Rogus D 4
89 Holcot E 11
110 Holden B 6
89 Holdenby E 10
40 Holdenhurst G 3
59 Holdgate C 11
97 Holdingham E 7
39 Holditch F 7
137 Holefield F 10
135 Holehouse D 8
57 Hole-in-the-Wall A 9
131 Holestane B 9
38 Holford B 5
114 Holker G 6
92 Holkham A 2
36 Hollacombe F 2
152 Holland, Papa Westray, Orkney Is. A 3
152 Holland, Stronsay, Orkney Is. C 4
97 Holland Fen E 9
87 Holland-on-Sea B 11
152 Hollandstoun A 4
132 Hollee F 1
93 Hollesley L 6
110 Hollingfare H 6
43 Hollingbourne C 7
42 Hollingrove F 6
95 Hollington, Derby F 10
42 Hollington, E. Sussex G 6
95 Hollington, Staffs. F 9
111 Hollingworth G 8
110 Hollins Lane B 4
95 Hollinsclough D 9
36 Hollocombe E 5
88 Hollow Court F 3
95 Hollow Meadows A 11
95 Holloway E 11
89 Hollowell E 10
132 Hollows E 2
94 Holly Bush F 3
90 Holly End E 6
88 Holly Green H 2
57 Hollybush, Heref. & Worcs. A 10
135 Hollybush, Strathclyde H 9
113 Hollym E 11
88 Hollywood D 4
132 Holm, Dumf. & Gall. C 1
151 Holm, W. Isles D 5
36 Holmacott C 4
111 Holmbridge F 10
41 Holmbury St. Mary B 12
35 Holmbush D 7
95 Holmcroft H 8
91 Holme, Cambs. G 3
115 Holme, Cumbria G 7
113 Holme, Humber. F 7
116 Holme, N. Yorks. G 4
96 Holme, Notts. D 5
111 Holme, W. Yorks. F 9
111 Holme Chapel D 7
92 Holme Hale E 2
57 Holme Lacy A 9
59 Holme Marsh G 9
90 Holme next the Sea A 8
113 Holme-on-the-Wolds C 7
96 Holme Pierrepont F 3
114 Holme St. Cuthbert A 3
112 Holme-on-Spalding Moor C 6
59 Holmer H 10
85 Holmer Green D 10
94 Holmes Chapel C 6
95 Holmesfield B 11
110 Holmeswood E 3
96 Holmewood D 2
111 Holmfirth F 10
131 Holmfoot B 9
135 Holmhead G 10
150 Holmisdal C 1
113 Holmpton E 11
114 Holmrook E 3
133 Holmside H 10
132 Holmwrangle H 4
37 Holne J 6
36 Holsworthy F 2
36 Holsworthy Beacon E 2
94 Holt, Clwyd E 3
40 Holt, Dorset F 2
88 Holt, Heref. & Worcs. F 2
92 Holt, Norfolk B 4
57 Holt, Wilts. H 11
41 Holt End, Hants. B 8
88 Holt End, Heref. & Worcs. E 4
88 Holt Heath F 2
40 Holt Wood E 2
112 Holtby B 4
97 Holton, Lincs. B 8
85 Holton, Oxon. G 7
39 Holton, Som. D 10
93 Holton, Suffolk H 7
40 Holton Heath G 1
113 Holton le Clay G 10
113 Holton le Moor G 8
93 Holton St. Mary L 4
42 Holtye D 3
39 Holwell, Dorset E 10
86 Holwell, Herts. A 2
96 Holwell, Leics. H 5
84 Holwell, Oxon. C 3
61 Holwick C 11
39 Holworth H 11
88 Holy Cross D 3
133 Holy Island B 12
41 Holybourne B 9
60 Holyhead B 2
95 Holymoorside C 11
85 Holyport F 10
133 Holystone C 8
135 Holytown C 12
91 Holywell, Cambs. H 4
61 Holywell, Clwyd C 11
34 Holywell, Corn. D 5
132 Holywell, Cumb. E 3
39 Holywell, Dorset F 9
133 Holywell, Northumb. F 11
111 Holywell Green E 9
38 Holywell Lake D 5
91 Holywell Row H 8
131 Holywood C 10
57 Hom Green B 9
137 Homebank E 10
137 Homebyres E 9
59 Homer B 11
93 Homersfield G 6
40 Homington D 3
43 Honey Hill B 10
84 Honey Street H 2
93 Honey Tye L 2
94 Honeyborough F 2
88 Honeybourne H 5
36 Honeychurch F 5
88 Honiley E 6
92 Honing C 6
92 Honingham D 4
96 Honington, Lincs. F 6
93 Honington, Suff. H 2
88 Honington, War. H 6
38 Honiton F 5
111 Honley F 10
42 Hoo A 6
88 Hoobrook E 2
111 Hood Green G 11
37 Hooe, Devon K 4
42 Hooe, E. Sussex G 6
42 Hooe Common G 6
54 Hook, Dyfed F 3
41 Hook, Hants. A 8
112 Hook, Humber. E 5
86 Hook, London G 2
84 Hook, Wilts. F 2
42 Hook Green, Kent A 5
42 Hook Green, Kent D 5
84 Hook Norton A 4
39 Hooke F 9
94 Hookgate G 6
36 Hookway F 7
42 Hookwood D 2
94 Hoole C 3
42 Hooley B 2
94 Hooton B 2
96 Hooton Levitt A 2
112 Hooton Pagnell F 3
112 Hooton Roberts G 3
152 Hoove D 7
90 Hop Pole D 3
95 Hope, Derby B 10
37 Hope, Devon M 5
61 Hope, Clwyd D 12
148 Hope, Highland B 5
59 Hope, Powys B 8
59 Hope, Salop. B 9
59 Hope Bagot E 11
59 Hope Bowdler C 10
57 Hope Mansell B 9
59 Hope under Dinmore G 10
144 Hopeman C 7
59 Hopesay D 9
112 Hopperton B 2
95 Hopton, Derby E 11
94 Hopton, Salop. G 4
95 Hopton, Staffs. H 8
92 Hopton, Suffolk E 8
93 Hopton, Suffolk G 3
59 Hopton Cangeford D 11
59 Hopton Castle E 9
59 Hopton Wafers E 11
59 Hoptonheath E 9
88 Hopwas B 5
88 Hopwood E 4
42 Horam F 4
90 Horbling B 2
111 Horbury E 11
116 Horden A 5
59 Horderley D 9
40 Hordle F 4
94 Hordley G 2
55 Horeb, Dyfed C 7
55 Horeb, Dyfed D 8
57 Horfield F 9
151 Horgabost G 1
93 Horham H 5
87 Horkesley Heath A 9
113 Horkstow E 7
89 Horley, Oxon. H 7
42 Horley, Surrey D 2
39 Hornblotton Grn. C 9
115 Hornby, Lancs. H 8
116 Hornby, N. Yorks. F 2
116 Hornby, N. Yorks. E 4
97 Horncastle C 9
86 Hornchurch E 5
137 Horncliffe D 11
137 Horndean, Borders D 11
41 Horndean, Hants. E 8
37 Horndon H 4
86 Horndon-on-the-Hill F 6
42 Horne D 2
38 Horner B 3
92 Horning D 6
89 Horninghold B 11
95 Horninglow H 10
91 Horningsea J 6
39 Horningsham B 11
92 Horningtoft C 2
35 Horningtops D 9
36 Horns Cross, Devon D 3
43 Horns Cross, E. Sussex F 7
132 Hornsby H 3
113 Hornsea B 9
113 Hornsea Burton B 9
86 Hornsey E 3
89 Hornton H 7
37 Horrabridge J 4
93 Horringer J 1
41 Horringford H 7
136 Horsburgh E 6
95 Horse Bridge E 8
40 Horsebridge C 5
88 Horsebrook A 2
57 Horsecastle H 7
59 Horsehay B 12
91 Horseheath K 7
115 Horsehouse G 12
85 Horsell H 10
94 Horseman's Grn. F 3
85 Horsenden D 9
92 Horsey C 8
92 Horsford D 5
111 Horsforth C 11
88 Horsham, Heref. & Worcs. F 1
42 Horsham, W. Sussex E 1
92 Horsham St. Faith D 5
97 Horsington, Lincs. C 9
39 Horsington, Som. D 10
96 Horsley, Derby F 1
57 Horsley, Glos. E 11
133 Horsley, Northumb. C 7
133 Horsley, Northumb. F 9
87 Horsley Cross A 11
96 Horsley Woodhouse F 1
87 Horsleycross St. A 11
137 Horsleyhill G 8
42 Horsmonden D 6
85 Horspath D 7
92 Horstead D 5
42 Horsted Keynes E 3
57 Horton, Avon F 10
85 Horton, Bucks. B 10
85 Horton, Bucks. F 11
40 Horton, Dorset E 2
111 Horton, Lancs. B 7
89 Horton, Northants. G 11
38 Horton, Somerset E 6
95 Horton, Staffs. D 8
84 Horton, Wilts. H 2
55 Horton, W. Glam. H 8
39 Horton Cross E 7
94 Horton Green E 3
40 Horton Heath D 6
115 Horton in Ribblesdale H 10
42 Horton Kirby A 4
110 Horwich F 5
95 Horwich End B 8
36 Horwood C 4
132 Hoscote B 2
96 Hose G 5
137 Hoselaw F 10
114 Hoses F 5
152 Hoswick E 7
113 Hotham D 7
43 Hothfield D 8
96 Hoton H 3
132 Hott D 6
152 Houbie B 8
94 Hough E 6
96 Hough-on-the-Hill F 6
96 Hougham F 6
91 Houghton, Cambs. H 4
132 Houghton, Cumb. G 2
54 Houghton, Dyfed F 3
40 Houghton, Hants. C 5
41 Houghton, W. Sussex E 11
91 Houghton Conquest L 2
94 Houghton Green A 5
85 Houghton Regis B 11
133 Houghton-le-Spring H 11
89 Houghton on the Hill B 10
117 Houlsyke D 7
40 Hound E 6
85 Hound Green H 8
137 Houndridge F 10
137 Houndslow E 9
38 Houndsmoor D 5
137 Houndwood C 11
40 Hounsdown E 5
86 Hounslow F 2
152 Housay C 8
147 House of Glenmuick H 1
146 Housieside E 6
135 Houston C 9
149 Houstry D 10
42 Hove H 2
96 Hoveringham E 4
92 Hoveton D 6
117 Hovingham H 7
132 How G 3
84 How Caple A 9
42 How Green C 4
114 How Head E 6
111 Howbrook G 11
137 Howburn F 10
137 Howden, Borders G 9
112 Howden, Humber. D 5
111 Howden Clough D 11
116 Howden-le-Wear B 2
115 Howe, Cumbria F 7
149 Howe, Highland B 12
92 Howe, Norfolk E 6
87 Howe Green D 7
146 Howe of Teucher C 5
87 Howe Street, Essex B 7
91 Howe Street, Essex M 8
97 Howell F 8
131 Howes E 12
58 Howey F 6
136 Howford F 6
136 Howgate, Lothian D 5
136 Howgate, Strathclyde F 2
133 Howick A 10
94 Howle H 5
57 Howle Hill B 9
91 Howlett End M 7
38 Howley E 6
137 Howliston D 7
137 Hownam G 10
137 Hownam Mains G 10
132 Howpasley B 2
113 Howsham, Humber. G 8
112 Howsham, N. Yorks. A 5
137 Howtel F 11
152 Howth D 2
57 Howton A 7
115 Howtown C 7
135 Howwood C 9
152 Hoxa E 2
93 Hoxne G 5
94 Hoylake A 1
111 Hoylake Nether G 12
111 Hoylake Swaine G 11
54 Hubberston F 2
90 Hubbert's Bridge A 4
112 Huby, N. Yorks. A 3
111 Huby, N. Yorks. B 11
57 Hucclecote C 12
43 Hucking B 7
96 Hucknall E 3
111 Huddersfield E 10
88 Huddington F 3
116 Hudswell E 2
112 Huggate B 6
34 Hugh Town D 2
85 Hughenden Valley D 9
59 Hughley C 11
36 Huish, Devon E 4
84 Huish, Wilts. H 2
38 Huish Barton B 4
38 Huish Champflower C 4
39 Huish Episcopi D 8
85 Hulcott B 9
95 Hulland F 11

88 Long Marston, Warwick G 5
115 Long Marton C 9
93 Long Melford K 2
57 Long Newnton E 12
116 Long Newton D 4
111 Long Preston A 7
113 Long Riston C 9
112 Long Sandall F 4
91 Long Stanton All Saints J 5
91 Long Stanton St. Michael J 5
92 Long Stratton F 5
89 Long Street G 11
41 Long Sutton, Hants. A 9
90 Long Sutton, Lincs. C 5
39 Long Sutton, Som. D 8
59 Long Waste A 11
96 Long Whatton H 2
84 Long Wittenham E 6
135 Longbar D 8
133 Longbenton F 11
84 Longborough A 3
88 Longbridge, War. F 6
88 Longbridge, W. Midlands D 3
39 Longbridge Deverill B 11
142 Longbridgemuir E 11
39 Longburton E 10
132 Longbyre F 5
130 Longcastle G 5
95 Longcliffe E 10
84 Longcot E 4
137 Longcroft, Borders D 8
136 Longcroft, Central A 1
85 Longcross H 10
59 Longden B 10
88 Longdon A 4
88 Longdon Green A 4
59 Longdon upon Tern A 11
38 Longdown G 2
34 Longdowns F 4
133 Longdyke B 10
42 Longfield A 5
42 Longfield Hill A 5
95 Longford, Derby F 10
57 Longford, Glos. B 11
86 Longford, London F 1
94 Longford, Salop G 5
89 Longford, W. Midlands D 7
141 Longforgan D 8
137 Longformacus D 9
133 Longframlington C 9
40 Longham, Dorset F 2
92 Longham, Norf. D 2
146 Longhill B 7
133 Longhirst D 10
57 Longhope B 10
133 Longhorsley D 9
133 Longhoughton B 10
114 Longlands B 5
84 Longlane, Berks. G 6
95 Longlane, Derby F 11
57 Longlevens B 11
88 Longley Green G 1
146 Longmanhill A 5
41 Longmoor Camp C 9
144 Longmorn D 8
137 Longnewton G 8
57 Longney C 11
137 Longniddry B 7
95 Longnor D 9
59 Longnot B 10
40 Longparish B 6
110 Longridge, Lancs. D 5
136 Longridge, Lothian C 2
136 Longriggend B 1
95 Longsdon E 8
146 Longside C 8
94 Longslow G 5
40 Longstock B 5
35 Longstone B 7
91 Longstowe K 4
90 Longthorpe F 3
110 Longton, Lancs. E 4
95 Longton, Staffs F 7
132 Longtown, Cumb. F 2
56 Longtown, Heref. & Worc. A 6
59 Longville in the Dale C 11
57 Longwell Green G 10
85 Longwick D 8
133 Longwitton D 9
59 Longwood B 11
84 Longworth D 5
137 Longyester C 8
150 Lonmore D 2
42 Loose C 6
85 Loosley Row D 9
146 Lootcherbrae B 3
40 Lopcombe Corner C 4
39 Lopen E 8
94 Loppington G 3
133 Lorbottle B 8
133 Lorbottle Hall B 8
41 Lordington E 9
132 Lordsgate F 3
131 Lorg B 7
96 Loscoe E 2
144 Lossiemouth C 8
94 Lostock Gralam C 5
94 Lostock Green C 5
110 Lostock Junction F 5
35 Lostwithiel D 8
149 Lothbeg F 9
111 Lothersdale C 8
149 Lothmore F 9
39 Lottisham C 9
85 Loadwater E 10
96 Loughborough H 3
55 Loughor G 9
89 Loughton, Bucks. H 11
86 Loughton, Essex D 4
59 Loughton, Salop D 11
90 Lound, Lincs. D 2
96 Lound, Notts. B 4
92 Lound, Suffolk E 8
95 Lount H 12
97 Louth B 10
111 Love Clough D 7
41 Lovedean E 8
40 Lover D 4
112 Loversall G 4
86 Loves Green C 6
116 Lovesome Hill E 4
54 Loveston F 4
39 Lovington C 9
130 Low Ardwell G 2
115 Low Bentham H 9
111 Low Bradfield H 11
111 Low Bradley B 9
114 Low Braithwaite A 6
133 Low Brunton F 7
112 Low Burnham G 5
116 Low Burton G 3
133 Low Buston B 10
112 Low Catton B 5
116 Low Coniscliffe D 3
130 Low Craighead A 3
132 Low Cranecleugh D 5
132 Low Crosby G 3
117 Low Dalby F 8
116 Low Dinsdale D 4
112 Low Eggborough E 3
116 Low Ellington G 2
116 Low Etherley B 2
132 Low Geltbridge G 4
135 Low Grange H 8
88 Low Habberley D 2
39 Low Ham C 8
133 Low Hedgeley A 9
115 Low Hesket A 7
133 Low Hesleyhurst C 9
117 Low Hutton H 8
130 Low Knockbrex E 5
95 Low Leighton B 8
114 Low Lorton C 4
130 Low Malzie F 4
117 Low Marishes G 8
96 Low Marnham C 5
117 Low Mill F 7
133 Low Morsley H 11
133 Low Newton-by-the-Sea A 10
132 Low Row, Cumb. G 4
114 Low Row, Cumb. B 6
115 Low Row, N. Yorks. E 12
130 Low Salchrie E 1
113 Low Santon F 7
135 Low Shawsburn D 12
92 Low Street C 6
92 Low Thurlton E 7
136 Low Torry A 3
133 Low Town C 9
116 Low Worsall D 4
114 Low Wray E 6
114 Lowca C 2
96 Lowdham F 4
94 Lowe G 4
38 Lower Aisholt C 5
39 Lower Ansty F 11
38 Lower Ashton H 2
85 Lower Assendon F 8
151 Lower Bayble D 6
42 Lower Beeding E 1
90 Lower Benefield F 1
39 Lower Bockhampton G 10
89 Lower Boddington G 8
34 Lower Boscaswell F 1
41 Lower Bourne B 10
88 Lower Brailes H 6
150 Lower Breakish F 6
88 Lower Broadheath F 2
57 Lower Bullingham A 8
91 Lower Caldecote K 3
57 Lower Cam D 10
56 Lower Chapel A 4
40 Lower Chicksgrove C 1
40 Lower Chute A 4
42 Lower Cokeham H 1
95 Lower Crossings B 9
111 Lower Cumberworth F 11
110 Lower Darwen E 6
91 Lower Dean H 2
142 Lower Diabaig D 2
42 Lower Dicker G 4
59 Lower Dinchope D 10
149 Lower Dounreay A 9
59 Lower Down D 9
34 Lower Drift G 2
112 Lower Dunsforth A 2
40 Lower Everleigh A 3
57 Lower Failand G 8
41 Lower Farringdon C 8
114 Lower Foxdale G 1
54 Lower Freystrop F 3
41 Lower Froyle B 9
148 Lower Gledfield G 6
42 Lower Green, Kent D 5
92 Lower Green, Norf. B 3
93 Lower Hacheston J 6
150 Lower Halistra B 2
43 Lower Halstow A 7
43 Lower Hardres C 10
144 Lower Hempriggs C 7
59 Lower Hergest G 8
84 Lower Heyford B 6
42 Lower Higham A 6
94 Lower Hordley G 3
42 Lower Horsebridge G 4
139 Lower Kinchrackine E 8
39 Lower Kingcombe F 9
42 Lower Kingswoood C 1
94 Lower Kinnerton D 2
57 Lower Langford H 8
141 Lower Largo G 9
95 Lower Leigh G 8
145 Lower Lenie G 1
58 Lower Llanfadog F 5
36 Lower Loxhore B 5
57 Lower Lydbrook C 9
59 Lower Lye F 9
56 Lower Machen E 5
57 Lower Maes-coed A 7
87 Lower Mayland D 9
150 Lower Milovaig C 1
88 Lower Moor G 3
86 Lower Nazeing C 4
140 Lower Oakfield H 6
150 Lower Ollach D 4
56 Lower Penarth G 5
88 Lower Penn C 2
40 Lower Pennington G 5
94 Lower Peover C 6
111 Lower Place F 8
88 Lower Quinton G 5
59 Lower Rochford F 11
84 Lower Seagry F 1
151 Lower Shader A 5
91 Lower Shelton L 1
85 Lower Shiplake F 8
89 Lower Shuckburgh F 8
84 Lower Slaughter B 3
57 Lower Stanton St. Quintin F 12
43 Lower Stoke A 7
92 Lower Street B 6
88 Lower Strensham H 3
85 Lower Sundon A 11
40 Lower Swanwick E 6
84 Lower Swell B 3
150 Lower Tote B 4
54 Lower Town C 3
89 Lower Tysoe H 7
41 Lower Upham D 7
38 Lower Vexford C 5
110 Lower Walton H 5
39 Lower Waterston G 10
39 Lower Weare A 7
59 Lower Welson G 8
94 Lower Whitley B 5
41 Lower Wield B 8
85 Lower Winchendon C 8
85 Lower Woodend E 9
40 Lower Woodford C 3
88 Lower Wyche H 1
89 Lowesby A 10
92 Lowestoft F 8
92 Lowestoft End F 8
114 Loweswater C 4
42 Lowfield Heath D 2
110 Lowgill, Lancs. A 5
115 Lowgill, Cumbria E 8
91 Lowick, Northants. G 1
133 Lowick, Northumb. B 11
114 Lowick Green G 5
56 Lowlands E 6
88 Lowsonford E 5
115 Lowther C 8
113 Lowthorpe A 8
110 Lowton, Manchester G 5
38 Lowton, Som. D 5
110 Lowton Common G 5
38 Loxbeare E 3
41 Loxhill B 11
36 Loxhore B 5
88 Loxley G 6
39 Loxton A 7
41 Loxwood C 11
148 Lubachoinnich G 5
148 Lubcroy F 4
89 Lubenham C 10
139 Lubnaclach A 11
142 Lubriach B 7
38 Luccombe B 3
41 Luccombe Village H 7
133 Lucker D 11
35 Luckett B 11
57 Luckington F 11
141 Lucklawhill E 9
38 Luckwell Bridge B 2
59 Lucton F 10
113 Ludborough H 10
54 Ludchurch F 5
111 Luddenden E 9
111 Luddenden Foot E 9
42 Luddesdown B 5
112 Luddington, Humberside E 6
88 Luddington, War. G 5
91 Luddington in the Brook G 2
59 Ludford E 10
97 Ludford A 9
85 Ludgershall B 7
40 Ludgershall A 4
34 Ludgvan F 2
92 Ludham D 7
59 Ludlow E 10
113 Ludney G 11
39 Ludwell D 12
116 Ludworth A 4
36 Luffincott F 2
135 Lugar G 10
137 Lugate E 7
137 Luggate Burn B 8
135 Luggiebank B 12
135 Lugton D 9
59 Lugwardine H 11
150 Luib E 5
139 Luib Hotel E 12
139 Luibeilt A 9
59 Lulham H 9
88 Lullington, Derby A 6
39 Lullington, Som. A 11
88 Lulsey G 1
57 Lulsgate Bottom H 8
111 Lumb E 9
111 Lumbutts E 8
112 Lumby D 3
135 Lumloch B 11
147 Lumphanan G 3
140 Lumphinnans H 6
137 Lumsdaine B 11
146 Lumsden E 2
141 Lunan B 11
141 Lunanhead B 9
140 Luncarty D 6
113 Lund, Humberside B 7
112 Lund, N. Yorks. D 4
139 Lundavra A 8
146 Lunderton C 8
143 Lundie, Highland H 5
141 Lundie, Tayside D 8
141 Lundin Links G 9
138 Lungar (Hotel) G 5
152 Lunna C 7
152 Lunning C 7
55 Lunnon H 9
42 Lunsford B 6
42 Lunsford's Cross G 6
110 Lunt G 2
59 Luntley G 9
38 Luppitt F 5
111 Lupsett E 11
115 Lupton G 8
41 Lurgashall C 10
144 Lurgmore F 1
97 Lusby C 10
139 Luss H 10
150 Lusta C 2
37 Lustleigh H 6
59 Luston F 10
147 Luthermuir K 4
141 Luthrie E 8
85 Luton, Beds. B 12
37 Luton, Devon H 8
42 Luton, Kent A 6
89 Lutterworth D 9
37 Lutton, Devon K 5
90 Lutton, Lincs. C 5
91 Lutton, Northants. G 2
38 Luxborough B 3
35 Luxulyan D 7
149 Lybster D 11
59 Lydbury North D 9
43 Lydd F 9
43 Lydd-on-Sea F 9
43 Lydden D 11
89 Lyddington B 12
85 Lyde Green H 8
38 Lydeard St. Lawrence C 4
37 Lydford G 4
111 Lydgate E 8
59 Lydham C 9
84 Lydiard Millicent F 2
110 Lydiate G 2
39 Lydlinch E 10
57 Lydney D 9
54 Lydstep G 4
88 Lye D 3
57 Lye Cross H 8
85 Lye Green, Bucks. D 10
42 Lye Green, E. Sussex E 4
84 Lyford E 5
135 Lylestone, Strathclyde E 8
137 Lylestone, Borders D 8
43 Lymbridge Green D 10
39 Lyme Regis G 7
43 Lyminge D 10
40 Lymington F 4
41 Lyminster F 11
94 Lymm B 5
40 Lymore G 4
43 Lympne E 10
38 Lympsham A 6
38 Lympstone H 3
145 Lynaberack K 3
145 Lynachlaggan J 4
38 Lynch B 3
92 Lynch Green E 4
145 Lynchat J 3
40 Lyndhurst E 4
89 Lyndon B 12
136 Lyne, Borders E 5
85 Lyne, Surrey G 11
57 Lyne Down A 9
145 Lyne of Gorthleck H 1
146 Lyne of Skene F 5
94 Lyneal G 3
150 Lynedale House C 3
84 Lyneham, Oxon B 4
84 Lyneham, Wilts. F 1
132 Lyneholm D 1
132 Lyneholmeford F 4
145 Lynmore G 6
133 Lynemouth D 11
152 Lyness E 1
92 Lyng, Norfolk D 4
39 Lyng, Somerset C 7
36 Lynmouth A 6
43 Lynsted B 8
36 Lynton A 6
39 Lyon's Gate F 10
59 Lyonshall G 9
40 Lytchett Matravers G 1
40 Lytchett Minster G 1
149 Lyth B 11
110 Lytham D 3
110 Lytham St Anne's D 2
117 Lythe D 8
152 Lythes E 3
151 Maaruig F 3
34 Mabe Burnthouse F 5
131 Mabie D 10
97 Mablethorpe B 12
136 Macbiehill D 4
95 Macclesfield C 7
95 Macclesfield For. C 8
146 Macduff A 4
56 Machen E 5
134 Machrihanish G 1
138 Machrins H 1
58 Machynlleth B 3
95 Mackworth F 11
137 Macmerry B 7
140 Madderty E 4
136 Maddiston B 2
41 Madehurst E 11
94 Madeley, Staffs. F 6
94 Madeley Heath F 6
91 Madingley J 5
59 Madley H 9
88 Madresfield G 2
34 Madron F 2
60 Maenaddwyn B 4
54 Maenclochog D 4
56 Maendy G 3
60 Maentwrog F 6
55 Maen-y-groes A 7
94 Maer F 6
61 Maerdy, Clwyd F 9
55 Maerdy, Dyfed D 10
57 Maerdy, Gwent B 7
56 Maerdy, Mid Glam. D 3
94 Maesbrook Green H 2
94 Maesbury H 2
94 Maesbury Marsh H 2
54 Maesgwynne E 5
61 Maeshafn D 11
55 Maesllyn C 7
58 Maesmynis H 6
56 Maesteg E 2
55 Maestir B 9
55 Maestwynog C 10
55 Maesybont E 9
55 Maesycrugiau C 8
56 Maes-y-cwmmer E 5
55 Maesymeillion B 7
86 Magdalen Laver C 5
146 Maggieknockater C 1
42 Magham Down G 5
110 Maghull G 3
57 Magor F 7
39 Maiden Bradley B 11
133 Maiden Law H 10
39 Maiden Newton F 9
54 Maiden Wells G 3
37 Maidencombe J 8
136 Maidencotes G 2
85 Maidenhead F 10
115 Maidenhill B 7
130 Maidens A 3
85 Maiden's Green G 9
97 Maidenwell B 10
89 Maidford G 9
85 Maid's Moreton A 8
42 Maidstone C 6
89 Maidwell D 10
152 Mail E 7
56 Maindee E 6
149 Mains, Highland F 8
135 Mains, Strathclyde D 11
140 Mains, Tayside B 6
135 Mains of Airies E 1
147 Mainsof Allardice K 6
147 Mains of Altries H 6
146 Mains of Annochie C 7
141 Mains of Ardestie D 10
146 Mains of Arnage D 7
146 Mains of Auchindachy C 2
146 Mains of Auchmedden A 6
141 Mains of Balgavies B 10
141 Mains of Ballindarg B 9
147 Mains of Balnakettle K 4
146 Mains of Birness D 7
144 Mains of Bunachton F 2
146 Mains of Cairnborrow D 2
146 Mains of Cardno A 7
146 Mains of Crichie C 7
144 Mains of Dalvey F 7
147 Mains of Drum G 5
146 Mains of Drummuir C 2
144 Mains of Drynie E 2
146 Mains of Edingight B 3
146 Mains of Esslemont E 7
147 Mains of Glenfarquhar J 5
147 Mains of Haulkerton K 5
146 Mains of Inkhorn D 7
146 Mains of Keithfield D 6
146 Mains of Kirkhall F 6
146 Mains of Logie B 8
147 Mains of Melgund L 3
144 Mains of Newhall C 3
147 Mains of Thornton K 4
140 Mains of Throsk H 3
144 Mains of Tore D 2
146 Mains of Towie C 5
149 Mains of Ulbster C 12
141 Mains of Usan B 12
116 Mainsforth B 3
131 Mainsriddle F 10
59 Mainstone D 8
57 Maisemore B 11
37 Malborough M 6
86 Malden Rushett H 2
87 Maldon C 8
111 Malham A 8
143 Mallaig K 1

143 Mallaigvaig K 1
136 Malleny Mills C 4
140 Malling G 1
60 Malltraeth C 3
58 Mallwyd A 4
57 Malmesbury F 12
36 Malmsmead A 7
94 Malpas, Cheshire E 3
34 Malpas, Corn. E 5
56 Malpas, Gwent E 6
139 Malt Land F 8
116 Maltby, Cleveland D 5
96 Maltby, S. Yorks. A 3
97 Maltby le Marsh B 11
43 Maltman's Hill D 8
117 Malton H 8
88 Malvern Link G 1
88 Malvern Wells H 1
59 Mamble E 12
56 Mamhilad D 6
34 Manaccan G 5
59 Manafon B 7
37 Manaton H 6
97 Manby B 11
88 Mancetter C 6
111 Manchester G 7
61 Mancot D 12
143 Mandally J 7
90 Manea F 6
130 Maneight A 6
116 Manfield D 2
152 Mangaster C 7
151 Mangersta D 1
132 Mangertton D 3
57 Mangotsfield G 10
54 Manian Fawr B 5
151 Manish H 2
94 Manley C 4
56 Manmoel D 5
84 Manningford Bohune H 2
84 Manningford Bruce H 2
111 Manningham D 10
42 Mannings Heath E 1
40 Mannington F 2
93 Manningtree M 4
147 Mannofield G 6
54 Manorbier G 4
54 Manorbier Newton G 4
137 Manorhill F 9
54 Manorowen C 3
131 Mansfield B 9
55 Manselfield H 9
59 Mansell Gamage H 9
59 Mansell Lacy H 9
115 Mansergh G 8
135 Mansfield, Strathclyde H 11
96 Mansfield, Notts. D 3
96 Mansfield Woodhouse D 3
114 Mansriggs G 5
39 Manston, Dorset E 11
43 Manston, Kent B 12
40 Manswood E 2
90 Manthorpe, Lincs. D 2
96 Manthorpe, Lincs. F 6
113 Manton, Humber. G 7
89 Manton, Leics. B 12
84 Manton, Wilts. G 3
113 Manton Warren F 7
86 Manuden A 5
138 Maolachy F 6
39 Maperton D 10
85 Maple Cross E 11
96 Maplebeck D 4
85 Mapledurham F 7
41 Mapledurwell A 8
42 Maplehurst F 1
42 Maplescombe B 4
95 Mapleton E 10
96 Mapperley F 2
96 Mapperley Park F 3
39 Mapperton, Dorset F 12
39 Mapperton, Dorset F 8
88 Mappleborough Green E 4
113 Mappleton C 10
111 Mapplewell F 12
39 Mappowder F 10
145 Mar Lodge K 7
34 Marazion G 2
94 Marbury F 4
90 March, Cambs. F 5
136 March, Strathclyde H 3
84 Marcham D 5
94 Marchamley G 4
131 Marchbankwood B 11
135 Marchburn H 11
95 Marchington G 9
95 Marchington Woodlands G 9
94 Marchwiel E 2
40 Marchwood E 5
60 Marchros H 3
56 Marcross G 3
59 Marden, Heref. & Worc. H 10
42 Marden, Kent D 6
84 Marden, Wilts. H 2
86 Marden Ash D 5
42 Marden Beech D 6
42 Marden Thorn D 6
56 Mardy C 6
39 Mare Green D 7
85 Marefield, Bucks. E 9
89 Marefield, Leics. A 11
97 Mareham le Fen D 10
97 Mareham on the Hill C 10
96 Marehey E 1
42 Maresfield F 3
113 Marfleet D 9
94 Marford E 2
55 Margam H 11
39 Margaret Marsh D 11
86 Margaret Roding C 6
86 Margaretting D 6
43 Margate A 12
134 Margnaheglish F 5
90 Marham D 8
36 Marhamchurch F 1
90 Marholm E 2
60 Mariandyrys B 5
60 Marianglas B 4
36 Mariansleigh D 6
147 Marionburgh G 5
150 Marishader B 4
151 Mariveg E 5
131 Marjoriebanks C 11
131 Mark, Dumf. & Gall. F 7
130 Mark, Strathclyde D 2
39 Mark, Somerset A 7
39 Mark Causeway B 7
42 Mark Cross E 5
42 Markbeech D 4
97 Markby B 12
95 Markeaton F 11
89 Market Bosworth B 7
90 Market Deeping E 2
94 Market Drayton G 5
89 Market Harborough C 10
40 Market Lavington A 2
89 Market Overton A 12
97 Market Rasen A 8
97 Market Stainton B 9
92 Market Street C 6
112 Market Weighton C 6
93 Market Weston G 3
89 Markfield A 8
56 Markham D 5
96 Markham Moor C 4
141 Markinch G 8
111 Markington A 10
137 Markle B 8
87 Marks Tey B 9
57 Marksbury H 10
85 Markyate C 11
136 Marlage D 1
84 Marlborough G 3
59 Marlbrook, Heref. & Worc. G 10
88 Marlbrook, Heref. & Worc. E 3
88 Marlcliff G 4
37 Marldon J 7
93 Marlesford J 6
94 Marley Green F 4
133 Marley Hill G 10
40 Marley Mount F 4
137 Marleyknowe F 12
92 Marlingford E 4
54 Marloes F 1
85 Marlow, Bucks. E 9
59 Marlow, Heref. & Worc. E 9
85 Marlow Bottom E 9
42 Marlpit Hill C 3
96 Marlpool F 2
39 Marnhull D 11
146 Marnoch C 3
95 Marple A 8
112 Marr G 3
149 Marrel E 9
116 Marrick E 1
54 Marros F 5
133 Marsden, Tyne & Wear G 12
111 Marsden, W. Yorks. F 9
115 Marsett F 11
38 Marsh, Devon E 6
38 Marsh, Somerset C 4
84 Marsh Baldon D 6
84 Marsh Benham G 5
85 Marsh Gibbon B 7
38 Marsh Green, Devon G 4
42 Marsh Green, Kent D 3
59 Marsh Green, Shropshire A 11
38 Marsh Street B 3
86 Marshall's Heath B 2
92 Marsham C 5
110 Marshaw B 5
43 Marshborough B 11
59 Marshbrook C 10
113 Marshchapel G 11
57 Marshfield, Avon G 11
56 Marshfield, Gwent F 6
34 Marshgate B 2
96 Marshland B 1
110 Marshside E 2
39 Marshwood F 7
116 Marske E 1
116 Marske-by-the-Sea C 6
94 Marston, Ches. C 5
59 Marston, Heref. & Worc. G 9
96 Marston, Lincs. F 6
84 Marston, Oxon C 6
88 Marston, Staffs. A 2
95 Marston, Staffs. G 8
84 Marston, Wilts. H 1
88 Marston Green D 5
39 Marston Magna D 9
84 Marston Meysey D 2
95 Marston Montgomery F 10
91 Marston Moretaine L 1
95 Marston on Dove G 11
89 Marston St. Lawrence H 8
59 Marston Stannett G 11
89 Marston Trussell D 10
57 Marstow B 9
85 Marsworth C 10
84 Marten H 4
94 Marthall C 6
92 Martham D 8
40 Martin, Hants. D 2
43 Martin, Kent C 12
97 Martin, Lincs. D 8
40 Martin Drove End D 2
88 Martin Hussingtree F 2
36 Martinhoe A 5
36 Martinhoe Cross A 6
94 Martinscroft A 5
132 Martinshouse B 3
39 Martinstown G 10
93 Martlesham K 6
54 Martletwy F 4
88 Martley F 1
39 Martock D 8
95 Marton, Ches. C 7
116 Marton, Cleveland D 5
113 Marton, Humber. C 9
96 Marton, Lincs. B 5
117 Marton, N. Yorks. G 7
112 Marton, N. Yorks. A 2
59 Marton, Salop B 8
89 Marton, War. E 7
116 Marton le Moor H 4
116 Marton-in-the- Forest H 6
40 Martyr Worthy C 6
85 Martyr's Green H 11
131 Marwhirn B 8
152 Marwick C 1
36 Marwood Middle B 4
37 Mary Tavy H 4
142 Marybank D 8
144 Maryburgh D 1
147 Maryculter G 6
137 Marygold C 10
146 Maryhill, Grampian C 6
135 Maryhill, Strathclyde B 10
147 Marykirk L 4
144 Marypark F 7
114 Maryport, Cumb. B 3
130 Maryport, Dumf. & Gall. H 2
141 Maryton, Tayside B 8
141 Maryton, Tayside B 11
147 Marywell, Grampian H 3
147 Marywell, Grampian G 7
141 Marywell, Tayside C 11
116 Masham G 2
133 Mason F 10
96 Mastin Moor C 2
147 Mastrick G 6
86 Matching C 5
86 Matching Green C 5
86 Matching Tye C 5
133 Matfen F 8
42 Matfield D 5
57 Mathern E 8
88 Mathon H 1
54 Mathry D 2
92 Matlaske B 5
95 Matlock D 11
95 Matlock Bath D 11
57 Matson C 11
114 Matterdale End C 6
96 Mattersey A 4
96 Mattersey Thorpe A 4
85 Mattingley H 8
92 Mattishall D 4
92 Mattishall Burgh D 4
141 Mattocks C 9
135 Mauchline G 10
146 Maud C 7
55 Maudsland D 7
84 Maugersbury B 3
114 Maughold G 3
142 Mauld F 8
91 Maulden L 2
115 Maulds Meaburn D 8
116 Maunby F 4
59 Maund Bryan G 11
38 Maundown C 4
92 Mautby D 8
88 Mavesyn Ridware A 4
97 Mavis Enderby D 10
88 Maw Green B 4
131 Mawbray G 11
140 Mawcarse G 6
110 Mawdesley F 4
56 Mawdlam F 1
34 Mawgan G 4
34 Mawlaurgh D 4
90 Maxey E 2
88 Maxstroke C 6
137 Maxton, Borders F 8
43 Maxton, Kent D 11
137 Maxwellheugh F 10
130 Maxwellston B 4
131 Maxwellstown D 10
37 Maxworthy G 1
95 May Bank E 7
55 Mayals H 9
135 Maybole H 8
85 Maybury H 11
42 Mayfield, E. Sussex E 5
136 Mayfield, Lothian C 6
95 Mayfield, Staffs. F 10
85 Mayford H 10
87 Mayland D 9
42 Maynard's Green F 5
57 Maypole, Gwent C 8
34 Maypole, Is. of Scilly D 2
92 Maypole Green F 7
152 Maywick E 7
36 Mead D 1
57 Meadgate H 10
85 Meadle D 9
135 Meadowfoot E 11
59 Meadowtown B 8
115 Meal Bank F 8
113 Meals G 11
114 Mealsgate A 4
59 Meare B 8
38 Meare Green D 6
135 Mearns D 10
89 Mears Ashby E 11
89 Measham A 7
42 Meath Green D 2
115 Meathop G 7
151 Meavag G 3
37 Meavy J 4
89 Medbourne C 11
133 Medburn F 9
36 Meddon D 2
96 Meden Valley C 3
85 Medmenham F 9
133 Medomsley H 9
41 Medstead B 8
88 Meer End E 6
95 Meerbrook D 8
97 Meers Bridge B 12
91 Meesden M 5
36 Meeth E 4
132 Megdale C 1
136 Meggethead G 4
54 Meidrim E 6
59 Meifod A 7
141 Meigle C 7
131 Meikle Barncleugh D 10
131 Meikle Beoch D 9
135 Meikle Carco H 12
135 Meikle Earnock D 12
147 Meikle Fiddes J 5
140 Meikle Forter A 6
134 Meikle Grenach C 6
135 Meikle Hareshaw E 11
135 Meikle Ittington E 7
144 Meikle Kildrummie D 4
137 Meikle Pinkerton B 9
147 Meikle Strath K 4
146 Meikle Tarty E 7
146 Meikle Wartle D 5
131 Meikleholm C 11
135 Meiklelaught E 7
140 Meikleour C 6
146 Meikleton C 3
60 Meillteyrn G 2
131 Meinbank D 12
55 Meinciau F 8
95 Meir Heath F 8
151 Melbost D 6
151 Melbost Borve A 5
91 Melbourn L 5
95 Melbourne, Derby H 12
112 Melbourne, Humberside C 5
136 Melbourne, Strathclyde E 4
39 Melbury Abbas D 12
39 Melbury Bubb F 9
39 Melbury Osmond E 9
39 Melbury Sampford F 9
152 Melby D 6
91 Melchbourne J 1
39 Melcombe Regis H 10
37 Meldon, Devon G 4
133 Meldon, N'thumb. E 9
91 Meldreth L 5
146 Meldrum House E 6
138 Melfort F 5
143 Melgarve K 8
61 Meliden B 10
56 Melin Court D 2
58 Melin-byrhedin C 4
61 Melin-y-coed D 7
58 Melin-y-grug B 6
61 Melin-y-wig E 9
115 Melkinthorpe C 8
132 Melkridge G 5
57 Melksham H 12
142 Mellanguan A 2
134 Melldalloch B 4
115 Melling, Lancs. H 8
110 Melling, Merseyside G 3
110 Melling Mount G 3
93 Mellis H 4
148 Mellon Charles G 1
148 Mellon Udrigle G 1
95 Mellor, Manchester A 8
110 Mellor, Lancs. D 5
110 Mellor Brook D 5
39 Mells A 10
115 Melmerby, Cumb. B 8
116 Melmerby, N. Yorks. G 4
116 Melmerby, N. Yorks. G 1
39 Melplash F 8
137 Melrose F 8
152 Melsetter E 1
116 Melsonby D 2
111 Meltham F 9
111 Meltham Mills F 10
113 Melton, Humber. D 7
93 Melton, Suffolk K 6
92 Melton Constable B 3
96 Melton Mowbray H 5
113 Melton Ross F 8
112 Meltonby B 6
142 Melvaig A 1
59 Melverley A 9
149 Melvich B 8
38 Membury F 6
146 Memsie A 7
147 Memus L 2
35 Menabilly E 8
60 Menai Bridge C 5
93 Mendham G 6
93 Mendlesham J 4
93 Mendlesham Green J 4
35 Menheniot C 10
131 Mennock A 9
111 Menston C 10
140 Menstrie G 3
112 Menthorpe D 5
85 Mentmore B 10
143 Meoble L 2
59 Meole Brace A 10
41 Meonstoke D 7
42 Meopham B 5
42 Meopham Green B 5
42 Meopham Station A 5
91 Mepal G 5
91 Meppershall L 2
59 Merbach H 8
94 Mere, Cheshire B 6
39 Mere, Wilts. C 11
110 Mere Brow E 3
111 Mereclough D 7
43 Meresborough B 7
110 Mereside D 2
94 Meretown H 6
42 Mereworth C 5
147 Mergie H 5
88 Meriden D 6
150 Merkadale E 3
131 Merkland D 8
148 Merkland Lodge D 5
54 Merlin's Bridge F 3
94 Merrington H 3
54 Merrion G 3
39 Merriot E 8
37 Merrivale H 4
41 Merrow A 11
132 Merrylaw C 2
35 Merrymeet C 10
110 Merseyside, Co. H 3
43 Mersham D 9
42 Merstham C 2
41 Merston F 10
40 Merstone H 6
34 Merther E 6
55 Merthyr E 7
56 Merthyr Cynog A 3
56 Merthyr Mawr F 2
56 Merthyr Tydfil D 4
56 Merthyr Vale D 4
36 Merton, Devon E 4
86 Merton, London G 3
92 Merton, Norfolk F 2
85 Merton, Oxon B 7
132 Mervinslaw B 5
36 Meshaw D 6
87 Messing B 9
113 Messingham G 7
93 Metfield G 6
97 Metheringham D 8
141 Methil G 8
60 Methlem G 1
111 Methley D 12
146 Methlick D 6
140 Methven E 5
90 Methwold F 8
90 Methwold Hythe F 8
92 Mettingham F 6
92 Metton B 5
35 Mevagissey E 7
112 Mexborough G 3
149 Mey A 12
84 Meysey Hampton D 2
151 Miavaig C 2
146 Michael Muir D 6
57 Michaelchurch B 8
56 Michaelchurch Escley A 6
59 Michaelchurch-on-Arrow G 8
56 Michaelston-le-Pit G 5
56 Michaelston-super-Ely G 4
56 Michaelstone-y-Fedw F 6
35 Michaelstow B 8
40 Michelmersh C 5
93 Mickfield J 4
94 Mickle Trafford C 3
112 Micklebring H 3
117 Mickleby D 8
42 Mickleham C 1
95 Mickleover G 11
132 Micklethwaite H 1
115 Mickleton, Dur. C 12
88 Mickleton, Glos. H 5
111 Mickletown D 12
116 Mickley G 3
133 Mickley Square G 9
146 Mid Ardlaw A 7
147 Mid Beltie G 4
147 Mid Cairncross J 2
136 Mid Calder C 3
149 Mid Clyth D 11
144 Mid Coul E 3
146 Mid Cowbog B 6
142 Mid Crochail F 7
135 Mid Drumloch D 11
56 Mid Glamorgan, Co. E 4
136 Mid Hartwood C 3
131 Mid Laggan D 8
41 Mid Lavant E 10
142 Mid Mains F 8
134 Mid Sannox E 5
142 Mid Strom F 2
134 Mid Thundergay E 4
152 Mid Walls D 6
152 Mid Yell B 7
152 Midbea A 2
85 Middle Assendon F 8
84 Middle Aston A 6
84 Middle Barton B 5
39 Middle Chinnock E 8
147 Middle Drums L 3
146 Middle Essie B 8
96 Middle Handley B 1
85 Middle Claydon B 8

88 Middle Littleton G 4
54 Middle Mill D 2
137 Middle Ord D 12
97 Middle Rasen A 8
140 Middle Rigg F 5
57 Middle Street D 11
89 Middle Tysoe H 7
40 Middle Wallop B 4
40 Middle Winterslow C 4
40 Middle Woodford C 3
131 Middlebie D 12
145 Middlebridge M 4
137 Middlefield D 10
131 Middlegill A 11
116 Middleham F 2
59 Middlehope D 10
39 Middlemarsh E 10
146 Middlemuir House E 7
116 Middlesbrough C 5
115 Middleshaw, Cumb. F 8
131 Middleshaw, Dumf. & Gall. D 12
132 Middlesknowes B 6
116 Middlesmoor H 1
116 Middlestone B 3
116 Middlestone Moor B 3
111 Middlestown E 11
137 Middlethird E 9
95 Middleton, Derby E 11
95 Middleton, Derby D 10
93 Middleton, Essex L 2
146 Middleton, Grampian E 6
111 Middleton, Manchester F 7
40 Middleton, Hants. B 6
59 Middleton, Heref. & Worc. E 11
110 Middleton, Lancs. A 3
136 Middleton, Lothian D 6
90 Middleton, Norf. D 8
117 Middleton, N. Yorks. G 8
111 Middleton, N. Yorks. B 10
91 Middleton, Northants. C 11
133 Middleton, Northumberland E 9
133 Middleton, Northumb. B 12
59 Middleton, Salop E 11
94 Middleton, Salop G 2
135 Middleton, Strathclyde E 8
93 Middleton, Suffolk H 7
140 Middleton, Tayside F 6
140 Middleton, Tayside B 6
88 Middleton, War. B 5
55 Middleton, W. Glam. H 7
111 Middleton, W. Yorks. D 11
89 Middleton Cheney H 8
95 Middleton Green G 8
137 Middleton Hall G 12
116 Middleton-in- Leven D 5
115 Middleton-in-Teesdale C 11
146 Middleton of Rora C 8
41 Middleton-on-Sea F 11
59 Middleton on the Hill F 11
113 Middleton-on-the Wolds B 7
116 Middleton One Row D 4
59 Middleton Priors C 11
116 Middleton Quernhow G 3
116 Middleton St. George D 4
59 Middleton Scriven D 12
84 Middleton Stoney B 6
116 Middleton Tyas E 3
59 Middletown A 8
94 Middlewich D 6
93 Middlewood Green J 4
135 Middleyard F 10
39 Middlezoy C 7
116 Middridge C 3
57 Midford H 10
110 Midge Hall E 4
132 Midgeholme G 5
111 Midgeley F 11
84 Midgham G 6
111 Midgley D 9
111 Midhopestones G 11
41 Midhurst D 10
137 Midlem G 8
136 Midlock G 2
39 Midssomer Norton A 10
148 Midtown B 6
142 Midtown Brae A 2
146 Midtown of Buchromb C 1
97 Midville E 11
131 Miefield F 7
149 Migdale G 7
147 Migvie G 2
39 Milborne Port D 10
39 Milborne St. Andrew F 11
39 Milborne Wick D 10
133 Milbourne E 9
138 Milbuie H 1
115 Milburn B 9
57 Milbury Heath E 10
116 Milby H 4
84 Milcombe A 5
93 Milden K 3
91 Mildenhall, Suff. H 8
84 Mildenhall, Wilts. G 3
84 Mile Elm G 1
87 Mile End, Essex A 9
92 Mile End, Suffolk F 6
59 Milebrook E 8
92 Mileham D 2
57 Miles End C 9
94 Miles Green E 6
59 Miles Hope F 11
140 Milesmark H 5
137 Milfield F 12
95 Milford, Derby F 12
36 Milford, Devon D 1
95 Milford, Staffs. H 8
41 Milford, Surrey B 11
40 Milford, Wilts. C 3
54 Milford Haven F 4
40 Milford on Sea G 4
135 Milhall D 10
57 Milkwall C 9
40 Milkwell D 1
111 Mill Bank E 9
95 Mill Brow A 8
93 Mill Common G 7
85 Mill End, Bucks. F 9
91 Mill End, Cambs. G 4
85 Mill End, Herts. E 11
91 Mill End, Herts. M 4
86 Mill Green, Essex D 6
93 Mill Green, Suffolk L 3
86 Mill Hill E 2
115 Mill Houses H 8
41 Mill Lane A 9
146 Mill of Ardo, Grampian E 7
146 Mill of Ardo, Grampian D 6
146 Mill of Carden E 4
146 Mill of Culfork F 2
147 Mill of Gellan G 3
135 Mill of Haldane A 9
147 Mill of Monquich H 6
146 Mill of Muiresk C 4
146 Mill of Pot C 5
147 Mill of Uras J 6
92 Mill Street D 3
114 Millbeck C 5
152 Millbounds B 3
146 Millbreck C 7
146 Millbrex C 6
41 Millbridge B 10
91 Millbrook, Beds. L 1
35 Millbrook, Corn. D 11
36 Millbrook, Devon C 6
40 Millbrook, Hants. E 5
135 Millburn F 9
37 Millcombe L 7
43 Millcorner F 7
95 Milldale E 10
147 Millden Lodge J 3
141 Milldens B 10
136 Millerhill B 6
95 Miller's Dale C 10
95 Millers Green E 11
135 Millerston C 11
147 Millfield H 2
94 Millgreen G 5
59 Millhalf H 8
38 Millhayes E 5
137 Millheugh, Borders G 9
135 Millheugh, Strathclyde D 12
115 Millholme F 8
114 Millhouse, Cumb. B 6
134 Millhouse, Strathclyde B 4
111 Millhouse Green G 11
131 Millhousebridge C 11
96 Millhouses B 1
131 Milliganton C 10
135 Millikenpark C 9
112 Millington B 6
95 Millmeece G 7
114 Millom G 4
35 Millpool C 8
134 Millport D 6
131 Millquarter C 7
95 Millthorpe C 11
115 Millthrop F 9
147 Milltimber G 6
141 Millton C 8
145 Millton of Auchriachan H 7
146 Milltown, Grampian F 2
146 Milltown, Grampian F 7
147 Milltown, Grampian G 4
146 Milltown, Grampian C 3
96 Milltown, Derby D 1
36 Milltown, Devon B 4
147 Milltown, Tayside K 5
140 Milltown of Aberdalgie E 5
146 Milltown of Auchindoun D 1
147 Milltown of Campfield G 4
146 Milltown of Craigston B 5
144 Milltown of Edinvillie F 8
146 Milltown of Minnes E 7
146 Milltown of Towie F 2
135 Millwell D 11
141 Milnacraig B 7
140 Milnathort G 6
131 Milne B 12
135 Milngavie B 10
131 Milnmark C 7
111 Milnrow F 8
115 Milnthorpe G 7
59 Milson E 11
43 Milstead B 7
40 Milston B 3
56 Milton, Avon H 6
91 Milton, Cambs. J 6
139 Milton, Central G 12
132 Milton, Cumb. G 4
95 Milton, Derby G 11
131 Milton, Dumf. & Gall. C 9
131 Milton, Dumf. & Gall. D 9
130 Milton, Dumf. & Gall. F 3
54 Milton, Dyfed G 4
146 Milton, Grampian E 1
146 Milton, Grampian A 3
149 Milton, Highland C 12
145 Milton, Highland H 5
145 Milton, Highland G 1
144 Milton, Highland D 2
144 Milton, Highland E 1
144 Milton, Highland B 3
142 Milton, Highland E 1
84 Milton, Oxon E 6
84 Milton, Oxon A 5
39 Milton, Som. D 8
130 Milton, Strathclyde B 4
130 Milton, Strathclyde A 3
135 Milton, Strathclyde B 9
147 Milton, Tayside J 2
140 Milton, Tayside A 6
39 Milton Abbas F 11
37 Milton Abbot H 3
136 Milton Bridge C 5
91 Milton Bryna M 1
39 Milton Clevedon C 10
116 Milton Coldwells D 7
36 Milton Damerel E 3
84 Milton End D 2
91 Milton Ernest K 1
94 Milton Green D 3
84 Milton Hill E 6
89 Milton Keynes H 12
84 Milton Lilbourne H 3
89 Milton Malsor G 10
140 Milton Morenish D 1
146 Milton of Ardlethen D 6
147 Milton of Auchinhove G 3
145 Milton of Auchriaclan H 7
141 Milton of Balgonie G 8
135 Milton of Campsie B 11
146 Milton of Cushnie F 3
147 Milton of Dillavaird J 5
144 Milton of Farr F 2
146 Milton of Fishrie B 5
146 Milton of Lesmore E 2
147 Milton of Logie G 2
147 Milton of Murtle G 6
146 Milton of Noth E 2
134 Milton of Smerby G 2
147 Milton of Tullich H 1
39 Milton on Stour C 11
43 Milton Regis B 7
84 Milton under Wychwood B 4
37 Miltoncombe J 4
144 Miltonduff D 7
130 Miltonise D 3
38 Milverton D 4
95 Milwich G 8
139 Minard H 7
57 Minchinhampton D 12
137 Mindrum F 11
137 Mindrummill F 11
38 Minehead B 3
61 Minera E 12
84 Minety E 1
60 Minffordd F 5
138 Mingarrypark A 4
97 Miningsby D 10
35 Minions C 9
135 Minishant H 8
130 Minnigaff E 5
146 Minnonie B 5
114 Minorca G 2
132 Minsca E 1
112 Minskip A 2
40 Minstead E 4
43 Minster, Kent B 11
43 Minster, Kent A 8
84 Minster Lovell C 4
133 Minsteracres G 8
59 Minsterley B 9
57 Minsterworth C 11
39 Minterne Magna F 10
97 Minting C 9
146 Mintlaw C 7
137 Minto G 8
59 Minton C 9
54 Minwear F 4
88 Minworth C 5
152 Mirbister C 1
114 Mirehouse D 2
149 Mireland B 12
111 Mirfield E 10
57 Miserden C 12
56 Miskin, Mid Glam. F 4
56 Miskin, Mid Glam. D 4
112 Misson H 5
112 Misterton, Notts. H 5
39 Misterton, Som. E 8
89 Misterton, War. D 9
93 Mistley M 4
86 Mitcham G 3
57 Mitcheldean B 9
40 Mitcheldever B 6
57 Mitchel Troy C 8
34 Mitchell D 6
57 Mitcheltroy Com. C 8
133 Mitford D 10
34 Mithian E 4
88 Mitton A 2
85 Mixbury A 7
95 Mixon D 9
141 Moanzie E 8
132 Moat F 3
94 Mobberley B 6
59 Moccas H 9
61 Mochdre, Clwyd B 7
58 Mochdre, Powys D 6
130 Mochrum G 4
42 Mockbeggar, Kent C 6
42 Mockbeggar, Kent A 6
114 Mockerkin C 3
37 Modbury K 5
95 Moddershall G 8
149 Modsarie B 7
61 Moelfre, Clwyd G 11
60 Moelfre, Gwynedd B 4
131 Moffat A 11
91 Moggerhanger K 2
148 Moin House B 6
88 Moira A 6
43 Molash C 9
150 Mol-chlach G 4
61 Mold D 11
111 Moldgreen F 10
86 Molehill Green A 5
113 Molescroft C 8
133 Molesden E 9
91 Molesworth H 2
36 Molland C 7
36 Molland Cross C 6
94 Mollington, Ches. C 2
89 Mollington, Oxon G 8
135 Mollinsburn B 12
87 Molting Green B 9
55 Monachty A 8
139 Monachylemore F 11
134 Monamore Bridge F 5
142 Monar Lo. F 6
59 Monaughty F 8
147 Monboddo House J 5
139 Monevechadan G 9
93 Moneyden J 5
140 Moneydie D 5
131 Moniaive C 8
141 Monifieth D 9
141 Monikie C 9
141 Monimail F 8
54 Monington C 5
111 Monk Bretton F 12
112 Monk Fryston D 3
85 Monk Sherborne H 7
93 Monk Soham J 5
133 Monk-Wearmouth G 12
59 Monkhide H 11
59 Monkhopton C 11
59 Monkland G 10
36 Monkleigh D 3
56 Monknash G 3
36 Monkokehampton E 5
133 Monkridge D 7
93 Monks Eleigh K 3
42 Monk's Gate E 1
95 Monks' Heath C 7
89 Monks Kirby D 8
85 Monks Risborough D 9
146 Monkshill D 5
38 Monksilver C 4
88 Monkspath Street D 5
57 Monkswood D 7
38 Monkton, Devon F 5
54 Monkton, Dyfed G 3
43 Monkton, Kent B 11
38 Monkton, Som. C 6
135 Monkton, Strathclyde G 8
57 Monkton Coombe H 11
39 Monkton Deverill B 11
57 Monkton Farleigh H 11
38 Monkton Heathfield D 6
40 Monkton Up Wimborne E 2
39 Monkton Wyld F 7
135 Monktonhill F 8
41 Monkwood C 8
57 Monmouth C 8
57 Monmouth Cap B 7
59 Monnington on Wye H 9
141 Monorgan D 8
130 Monreith G 4
130 Monreith Mains G 4
39 Montacute E 8
146 Montcoffer House B 4
59 Montford A 9
59 Montford Bridge A 9
146 Montgarrie F 3
59 Montgomery C 8
135 Montgreenan E 8
141 Montrave F 8
147 Montrose L 5
40 Monxton B 5
95 Monyash D 10
146 Monymusk F 4
140 Monzie, Tayside E 4
145 Monzie, Tayside M 5
135 Moodiesburn B 11
111 Moor Allerton C 11
40 Moor Crichel E 2
112 Moor Monkton B 3
144 Moor of Granary D 6
114 Moor Row D 3
43 Moor Street B 7
97 Moorby D 10
40 Moordown G 3
94 Moore B 4
57 Moorend D 10
84 Moorends F 5
40 Moorgreen E 6
95 Moorhall C 11
59 Moorhampton H 9
132 Moorhouse, Cumb. G 2
96 Moorhouse, Notts. D 5
39 Moorlinch C 7
117 Moorsholm D 7
37 Moorshop H 4
97 Moorside, Lincs. D 9
40 Moortown, Hants. F 3
40 Moortown, I.o.W. H 6
113 Moortown, Lincs. G 8
143 Morar K 1
90 Morborne F 2
36 Morchard Bishop E 6
89 Morcott B 12
94 Morda G 2
39 Morden, Dorest G 12
86 Morden, London G 2
57 Mordiford A 9
137 Mordington Mains D 12
116 Mordon C 3
59 More C 9
38 Morebath D 3
137 Morebattle G 10
110 Morecambe A 3
39 Morecombelake G 7
148 Morefield G 3
115 Moreland C 8
37 Moreleigh K 6
140 Morenish D 1
114 Moresby C 2
40 Morestead D 6
39 Moreton, Dorest G 11
86 Moreton, Essex C 5
94 Moreton, Merseyside A 1
85 Moreton, Oxon D 8
84 Moreton-in-Marsh A 3
59 Moreton Jeffries G 11
88 Moreton Morrell F 6
59 Moreton on Lugg H 10
89 Moreton Pinkney G 9
94 Moreton Say G 5
57 Moreton Valence C 11
37 Moretonhampstead G 6
55 Morfa F 9
60 Morfa'Bychan F 5
56 Morfa Glas D 2
60 Morfa-Nefyn F 2
40 Morgan's Vale D 4
96 Morley, Derby F 1
116 Morley, Dur. B 2
111 Morley, W. Yorks. D 11
95 Morley Green B 7
92 Morley St. Botolph E 4
92 Morning Thorpe F 5
136 Morningside, Lothian B 5
136 Morningside, Strathclyde D 1
133 Morpeth D 10
95 Morrey H 10
131 Morrington C 9
91 Morris Green M 8
130 Morriston, Strathclyde A 3
55 Morriston, W. Glam. G 10
92 Morston A 3
36 Mortehoe B 3
96 Morthen A 2
85 Mortimer H 7
85 Mortimer West End H 7
59 Mortimer's Cross F 9
86 Mortlake F 2
57 Morton, Avon E 9
132 Morton, Cumb. H 2
96 Morton, Derby D 1
90 Morton, Lincs. C 2
96 Morton, Lincs. A 5
92 Morton, Norf. D 4
96 Morton, Notts. E 4
94 Morton, Salop H 2
88 Morton Bagot F 4
116 Morton-on-Swale F 3
116 Morton Tinmouth C 2
34 Morvah F 1
35 Morval D 9
143 Morvich G 3
149 Morvich Lodge F 8
59 Morville C 12
36 Morwenstow D 1
96 Mosbrough B 2
132 Moscow, Cumb. F 4
135 Moscow, Strathclyde E 9
114 Mosedale B 6
111 Moselden Height F 9
88 Moseley, Heref. & Worc. F 2
88 Moseley, W. Midlands D 4
61 Moss, Clywd E 12
138 Moss, Highland A 4
112 Moss, S. Yorks. F 4
110 Moss Bank G 4
85 Moss End G 9
144 Moss of Barmuckity D 8
146 Mossat F 2
152 Mossbank C 7
132 Mossburnford A 5
131 Mossdale D 7
135 Mossend C 12
114 Mosser C 4
135 Mossgiel F 9
137 Mosshouses E 8
95 Mossley, Ches. D 7
111 Mossley, Manchester G 8
94 Mossley Hill B 3
132 Mosspeeble D 2
144 Moss-side D 4
146 Mosstodloch B 1
39 Mosterton F 8
61 Mostyn B 11
39 Motcombe D 11
37 Mothecombe L 5
135 Motherwell D 12
86 Mottingham G 4
40 Mottisfont C 5
40 Mottistone H 5
111 Mottram in Longdendale H 8
95 Mottram St. Andrew B 7
94 Mouldsworth C 4
140 Moulin A 4
140 Moulinearn B 4
85 Moulsford F 7
89 Moulsoe H 12
94 Moulton, Ches. C 5
90 Moulton, Lincs. C 4
92 Moulton, Norf. E 7
116 Moulton, N. Yorks. E 3

115 Newby, N. Yorks. ... H 9
114 Newby Bridge ... G 6
132 Newby East ... G 3
132 Newby West ... H 2
116 Newby Wiske ... F 4
57 Newcastle, Gwent ... C 7
59 Newcastle, Salop ... D 8
54 Newcastle Emlyn ... C 6
95 Newcastle-under-Lyme F 7
133 Newcastle upon Tyne F 10
132 Newcastleton ... D 3
54 Newchapel, Dyfed ... C 6
95 Newchapel, Staffs. ... E 7
42 Newchapel, Surrey ... D 2
55 Newchurch, Dyfed ... E 7
57 Newchurch, Gwent ... E 8
41 Newchurch, I.o.W. ... H 7
43 Newchurch, Kent ... E 9
111 Newchurch, Lancs. ... C 7
111 Newchurch, Lancs. ... E 7
59 Newchurch, Powys ... G 7
95 Newchurch, Staffs. ... H 10
38 Newcott ... E 6
42 Newdigate ... D 1
85 Newell Green ... G 9
43 Newenden ... E 7
57 Newent ... B 10
57 Newerne ... D 9
131 Newfield, Dumf. & Gall. ... E 12
131 Newfield, Dumf. & Gall. ... E 9
116 Newfield, Dur. ... B 2
133 Newfield, Dur. ... H 10
144 Newfield, Highland ... B 3
41 Newfound ... A 7
54 Newglae ... E 2
92 Newgate ... A 3
86 Newgate Street ... C 3
152 Newgord ... A 8
136 Newhall, Borders ... F 6
94 Newhall, Ches. ... F 5
95 Newhall, Derby ... H 11
144 Newhallpoint ... C 3
86 Newham, London ... F 4
133 Newham, Northumb. E 12
133 Newham Hall ... D 12
42 Newhaven ... H 3
95 Newhaven House ... D 10
117 Newholm ... D 8
136 Newhouse ... C 1
133 Newhouses ... E 8
42 Newick ... F 3
43 Newingreen ... D 10
43 Newington, Kent ... B 7
43 Newington, Kent ... D 10
96 Newington, Notts. ... A 4
85 Newington, Oxen ... D 7
59 Newington, Salop ... D 9
57 Newland, Glos. ... C 9
88 Newland, Heref. & Worc. ... G 2
113 Newland, Humber. ... D 8
112 Newland, N. Yorks. ... E 5
38 Newland, Som. ... B 2
141 Newlandhead ... C 9
132 Newlands, Borders ... D 3
131 Newlands, Dumf. & Gall. ... C 10
144 Newlands, Grampian ... E 8
133 Newlands, Northumb. G 9
149 Newlands of Geise ... A 10
34 Newlyn ... G 2
146 Newmachar ... F 6
136 Newmains ... D 1
91 Newmarket, Suff. ... J 7
151 Newmarket, W. Isles ... C 5
132 Newmill, Borders ... B 3
34 Newmill, Corn. ... F 2
146 Newmill, Grampian ... B 2
147 Newmill of Inshewan ... L 2
111 Newmillerdam ... F 12
136 Newmills, Fife ... A 3
57 Newmills, Gwent ... D 8
144 Newmills, Highland ... C 2
136 Newmills, Lothian ... C 4
146 Newmills of Boyne ... B 3
140 Newmiln ... D 6
135 Newmilns ... F 10
57 Newnham, Glos. ... C 10
41 Newnham, Hants. ... A 8
91 Newnham, Herts. ... L 3
43 Newnham, Kent ... B 8
89 Newnham, Northants ... F 9
59 Newnham Bridge ... E 11
141 Newpark ... F 9
36 Newport, Devon ... C 4
54 Newport, Dyfed ... C 4
91 Newport, Essex ... M 6
57 Newport, Glos. ... E 10
56 Newport, Gwent ... F 6
149 Newport, Highland ... E 10
112 Newport, Humber. ... D 6
40 Newport, I.o.W. ... G 6
92 Newport, Norfolk ... D 8
94 Newport, Salop ... H 6
141 Newport-on-Tay ... D 9
89 Newport Pagnell ... H 12
54 Newport Sands ... C 4
41 Newpound Com. ... C 11
34 Newquay ... D 5
140 Newrow ... H 4
146 Newseat ... D 4
110 Newsham, Lancs. ... D 4
116 Newsham, N. Yorks. ... D 1
116 Newsham, N. Yorks. ... G 4
112 Newsholme, Humberside ... D 5
111 Newsholme, Lancs. ... B 7
111 Newsholme, W. Yorks. ... C 9
137 Newstead, Borders ... F 8
133 Newstead, Northumb. ... E 12
96 Newstead, Notts. ... E 2
112 Newthorpe ... D 3
137 Newton, Borders ... G 8
91 Newton, Cambs. ... K 5
94 Newton, Ches. ... C 3
94 Newton, Ches. ... C 4
94 Newton, Ches. ... D 4
111 Newton, Ches. ... G 8
116 Newton, Cleveland ... D 6
114 Newton, Cumbria ... H 5
96 Newton, Derby ... D 2
39 Newton, Dorset ... E 11
131 Newton, Dumf. & Gall. ... B 12
146 Newton, Grampian ... C 8
144 Newton, Grampian ... C 7
57 Newton, Heref. & Worc. ... A 7
59 Newton, Heref. & Worc. ... G 10
149 Newton, Highland ... C 12
144 Newton, Highland ... E 3
144 Newton, Highland ... C 3
144 Newton, Highland ... E 1
148 Newton, Highland ... D 4
110 Newton, Lancs. ... D 2
110 Newton, Lancs. ... D 3
115 Newton, Lancs. ... H 8
110 Newton, Lancs. ... B 6
90 Newton, Lincs. ... B 1
136 Newton, Lothian ... B 4
56 Newton, Mid Glam. ... G 2
90 Newton, Norfolk ... D 5
92 Newton, Norfolk ... D 1
89 Newton, Northants. D 12
133 Newton, Northumb. ... B 8
133 Newton, Northumb. ... G 8
96 Newton, Notts. ... F 4
38 Newton, Som. ... B 5
95 Newton, Staffs. ... H 9
136 Newton, Strathclyde ... F 2
93 Newton, Suffolk ... L 2
140 Newton, Tayside ... D 4
89 Newton, War. ... D 8
55 Newton, W. Glam. ... H 9
112 Newton, W. Yorks. ... D 2
40 Newton, Wilts. ... D 4
37 Newton Abbot ... J 7
131 Newton Arlosh ... F 12
116 Newton Aycliffe ... C 3
116 Newton Bewley ... C 5
89 Newton Blossomville G 12
91 Newton Bromswold ... J 1
89 Newton Burgoland ... A 7
97 Newton by Toft ... B 7
37 Newton Ferrers ... L 4
92 Newton Flotman ... F 5
89 Newton Harcourt ... B 9
146 Newton House ... E 4
110 Newton-le-Willows, Lancashire ... H 4
116 Newton-le-Willows, N. Yorkshire ... F 2
112 Newton Kyme ... C 2
85 Newton Longville ... A 9
135 Newton Mearns ... D 10
116 Newton Morrell ... D 3
117 Newton Mulgrave ... D 8
54 Newton Mountain ... F 3
138 Newton of Ardtoe ... A 4
140 Newton of Balcanquhal F 6
141 Newton of Falkland ... F 7
146 Newton of Murcar ... F 7
148 Newton of Ochtow ... G 5
140 Newton of Pitcairns ... F 5
112 Newton-on-Ouse ... A 3
117 Newton-on-Rawcliffe ... F 8
133 Newton-on-the-Moor C 10
96 Newton on Trent ... C 5
38 Newton Poppleford ... G 4
85 Newton Purcell ... A 7
88 Newton Regis ... A 6
115 Newton Reigny ... B 7
137 Newton St. Boswells ... F 8
36 Newton St. Cyres ... F 7
92 Newton St. Faith ... D 5
57 Newton St. Loe ... H 10
36 Newton St. Petrock ... E 3
95 Newton Solney ... H 11
40 Newton Stacey ... B 6
130 Newton Stewart ... E 5
40 Newton Toney ... B 4
36 Newton Tracey ... C 4
135 Newton upon Ayr ... G 8
112 Newton upon Derwent B 5
41 Newton Valence ... C 8
131 Newtonairds ... D 9
146 Newtongarry Croft ... D 3
136 Newtongrange ... C 6
147 Newtonmill ... L 3
145 Newtonmore ... J 3
95 Newtown, Ches. ... B 8
94 Newtown, Ches. ... E 5
34 Newtown, Corn. ... G 4
132 Newtown, Cumb. ... G 2
132 Newtown, Cumb. ... G 3
115 Newtown, Cumbria ... C 7
36 Newtown, Devon ... C 6
40 Newtown, Dorset ... G 2
57 Newtown, Glos. ... A 12
57 Newtown, Glos. ... D 10
144 Newtown, Grampian ... C 7
40 Newtown, Hants. ... D 4
41 Newtown, Hants. ... D 7
40 Newtown, Hants. ... E 4
41 Newtown, Hants. ... E 7
84 Newtown, Hants. ... H 6
59 Newtown, Heref. & Worc. ... G 10
59 Newtown, Heref. & Worc. ... H 11
143 Newtown, Highland ... J 7
114 Newtown, I.o.M. ... H 2
40 Newtown, I.o.W. ... G 5
110 Newtown, Lancs. ... E 4
133 Newtown, Northumb. A 8
133 Newtown, Northumb. C 8
137 Newtown, Northumb. ... F 12
58 Newtown, Powys ... C 6
94 Newtown, Salop ... G 3
95 Newtown, Staffs. ... D 7
95 Newtown, Staffs. ... D 9
39 Newtown, Wilts. ... C 12
89 Newtown Linford ... A 8
136 Newtown of Covington ... E 3
146 Newtown of Melrose ... A 5
141 Newtyle ... C 8
54 Neyland ... F 3
57 Nibley ... F 10
152 Nibon ... C 6
38 Nicholashayne ... E 5
55 Nicholaston ... H 8
132 Nickie's Hill ... F 4
111 Nidd ... A 11
147 Nigg, Grampian ... G 7
144 Nigg, Highland ... C 4
144 Nigg Station ... B 4
38 Nightcott ... D 2
86 Nine Ashes ... D 6
136 Nine Mile Burn ... D 4
132 Ninebanks ... H 6
42 Ninfield ... G 6
40 Ningwood ... G 5
137 Nisbet ... G 9
131 Nithside ... D 10
40 Niton ... H 6
94 No Man's Heath, Cheshire ... E 4
88 No Man's Heath, Warwickshire ... A 6
34 No Man's Land, Cornwall ... C 6
36 No Man's Land, Devon E 7
86 Noak Hill ... E 5
136 Noblehouse ... D 5
59 Nobold ... A 10
89 Nobottle ... F 10
97 Nocton ... D 8
84 Noke ... C 6
54 Nolton ... E 2
54 Nolton Haven ... E 2
94 Noneley ... G 3
43 Nonington ... C 11
115 Nook ... G 8
94 Norbury, Ches. ... E 4
95 Norbury, Derby ... F 9
59 Norbury, Salop ... C 9
94 Norbury, Staffs. ... H 6
152 Norby ... D 6
90 Nordelph ... E 7
111 Norden ... F 7
40 Norden ... H 1
59 Nordley ... C 12
84 Nore Marsh ... F 2
92 Norfolk, Co. ... D 4
137 Norham ... E 11
94 Norley ... C 4
40 Norley Wood ... F 5
90 Norman Cross ... F 3
112 Normanby, Humber. ... E 6
117 Normanby, N. Yorks. G 7
97 Normanby-by- Spital ... A 7
113 Normanby le Wold ... H 9
41 Normandy ... A 10
42 Norman's Bay ... G 6
38 Norman's Green ... F 4
40 Normansland ... D 4
95 Normanton, Derbyshire ... G 11
96 Normanton, Leics. ... F 5
96 Normanton, Lincs. ... F 6
96 Normanton, Notts. ... E 4
112 Normanton, W. Yorks. ... E 2
89 Normanton le Heath ... A 7
96 Normanton on Soar ... H 2
96 Normanton on the Wolds ... G 3
96 Normanton on Trent ... C 5
110 Normoss ... C 2
41 Norney ... B 10
57 Norrington Com. ... H 12
95 Norris Hill ... H 11
96 North Anston ... B 2
84 North Aston ... A 6
146 North Atrochie ... D 7
40 North Baddesley ... D 5
139 North Ballachulish ... B 8
39 North Barrow ... C 9
92 North Barsham ... B 2
87 North Benfleet ... E 7
41 North Bersted ... F 10
137 North Berwick ... A 8
41 North Boarhunt ... E 7
37 North Bovey ... G 6
135 North Brackenridge ... E 12
39 North Bradley ... A 12
37 North Brentor ... H 4
39 North Brewham ... C 10
36 North Buckland ... B 4
92 North Burlingham ... D 7
39 North Cadbury ... D 9
96 North Carlton, Lincolnshire ... B 6
96 North Carlton, Notts. B 3
134 North Carrine ... H 2
112 North Cave ... D 6
84 North Cerney ... C 1
41 North Chapel ... C 11
40 North Charford ... D 3
133 North Charlton ... A 10
39 North Cheriton ... D 10
39 North Chideock ... G 8
112 North Cliffe ... C 6
96 North Clifton ... C 5
113 North Coates ... G 11
97 North Cockerington A 10
39 North Coker ... E 9
96 North Collingham ... D 5
42 North Common ... F 3
56 North Cornelly ... F 2
138 North Corry ... B 5
146 North Cottown ... F 5
92 North Cove ... F 8
131 North Cowshaw ... C 11
116 North Cowton ... E 3
89 North Crawley ... H 12
86 North Cray ... G 5
92 North Creake ... B 2
39 North Curry ... D 7
113 North Dalton ... B 7
35 North Darley ... B 10
111 North Deighton ... B 12
135 North Drumboy ... D 10
112 North Duffield ... C 5
97 North Elkington ... A 10
92 North Elmham ... C 3
112 North Elmsall ... F 3
57 North End, Avon ... G 11
57 North End, Avon ... H 7
85 North End, Bucks. ... A 9
85 North End, Bucks. ... E 8
39 North End, Dorset ... D 11
86 North End, Essex ... B 6
41 North End, Hants. ... F 8
84 North End, Hants. ... H 5
113 North End, Humberside ... D 10
90 North End, Lincs. ... B 3
133 North End, Northumb. C 9
38 North End, Som. ... D 6
41 North End, W. Sussex E 12
142 North Erradale ... B 1
38 North Esworthy ... D 2
87 North Fambridge ... D 8
150 North Fearns ... D 5
134 North Feorline ... F 4
113 North Ferriby ... E 7
113 North Frodingham ... B 8
151 North Galson ... A 5
152 North Gluss ... C 7
40 North Gorley ... E 3
146 North Gorrachie ... B 5
92 North Green ... F 5
132 North Greenhill ... F 4
117 North Grimston ... H 8
42 North Halling ... B 6
135 North Halls ... F 11
41 North Hayling ... F 9
133 North Hazelrigg ... C 12
41 North Heath ... D 12
35 North Hill ... B 9
84 North Hinksey ... D 6
42 North Holmwood ... C 1
135 North Hourat ... D 8
37 North Huish ... K 6
96 North Hykeham ... D 6
54 North Johnston ... F 3
113 North Kelsey ... G 8
144 North Kessock ... E 2
113 North Killingholme ... E 9
116 North Kilvington ... G 4
89 North Kilworth ... D 9
146 North Kinmundy ... F 6
146 North Kirkton ... C 8
97 North Kyme ... E 8
42 North Lancing ... G 1
85 North Lee ... C 9
116 North Lees ... H 3
89 North Luffenham ... B 12
84 North Leigh ... C 5
96 North Leverton with Habblesthorpe ... B 5
88 North Littleton ... G 4
93 North Lopham ... G 3
133 North Lyham ... C 12
41 North Marden ... D 9
85 North Marston ... B 8
136 North Middleton, Lothian ... C 6
137 North Middleton, Northumb. ... G 12
36 North Molton ... C 6
146 North Monkshill ... C 5
117 North Moor ... H 12
84 North Moreton ... E 6
41 North Mundham ... F 10
96 North Muskham ... D 5
113 North Newbald ... C 7
89 North Newington ... H 7
84 North Newnton ... H 2
38 North Newton ... C 6
57 North Nibley ... E 10
41 North Oakley ... A 7
86 North Ockendon ... E 6
116 North Ormesby ... C 5
97 North Ormsby ... A 10
116 North Otterington ... F 4
113 North Owersby ... H 8
39 North Perrott ... E 8
38 North Petherton ... C 6
35 North Petherwin ... A 10
92 North Pickenham ... E 1
88 North Piddle ... G 3
39 North Poorton ... F 8
38 North Quarme ... C 3
136 North Queensferry ... A 4
36 North Radworthy ... C 6
97 North Rauceby ... F 7
111 North Rigton ... B 11
95 North Rode ... D 7
152 North Roe ... B 7
90 North Runcton ... D 7
152 North Sandwick ... B 8
114 North Scale ... H 4
96 North Scarle ... D 6
133 N. Seaton Colliery ... D 11
151 North Shawbost ... B 4
138 North Shian ... C 6
133 North Shields ... F 11
87 North Shoebury ... E 9
110 North Shore ... D 2
136 North Shortcleugh ... H 2
114 North Side, Cumb. ... B 2
90 North Side, Cambs. ... E 4
117 North Skelton ... C 7
113 North Somercotes ... G 12
116 North Stainley ... G 3
115 North Stainmore ... D 10
57 North Stoke, Avon ... G 10
85 North Stoke, Oxon ... F 7
41 North Stoke, W. Sussex ... E 11
85 North Street, Berks. ... G 7
41 North Street, Hants. ... C 8
133 North Sunderland ... D 12
36 North Tamerton ... F 2
36 North Tawton ... F 5
113 North Thoresby ... G 10
40 North Tidworth ... A 4
133 North Togston ... C 10
151 North Tolsta ... B 6
92 North Tuddenham ... D 3
133 North Walbottle ... F 10
92 North Walsham ... C 6
41 North Waltham ... B 7
41 North Warnborough ... A 9
147 North Water Bri. ... L 4
149 North Watten ... B 11
86 North Weald Bassett ... D 5
96 North Wheatley ... B 5
57 North Wick ... H 9
37 North Whilborough ... J 7
97 North Willingham ... A 8
96 North Wingfield ... D 1
96 North Witham ... H 6
39 North Wootton, Dorset ... E 10
90 North Wootton, Norfolk ... C 7
39 North Wootton, Somerset ... B 9
57 North Wraxall ... G 11
84 North Wroughton ... F 3
133 North Yardhope ... C 7
116 North Yorkshire, Co. ... F 5
116 Northallerton ... F 4
36 Northam, Devon ... C 3
40 Northam, Hants. ... E 6
89 Northampton ... F 11
89 Northamptonshire, County ... E 11
86 Northaw ... D 3
90 Northborough Peakirk E 3
43 Northbourne ... C 12
40 Northbrook ... B 6
85 Northchurch ... C 10
37 Northcott ... G 2
89 Northend ... G 7
137 Northfield, Borders ... C 11
147 Northfield, Grampian G 6
88 Northfield, W. Midlands ... D 4
42 Northfleet ... A 5
43 Northiam ... F 7
91 Northill ... K 3
41 Northington ... B 7
97 Northlands ... E 10
84 Northleach ... C 2
38 Northleigh ... G 5
36 Northlew ... F 4
84 Northmoor ... D 5
38 Northmoor Green or Moorland ... C 6
141 Northmuir ... B 8
41 Northney ... F 9
86 Northolt ... E 1
61 Northop ... C 11
61 Northophall ... C 12
90 Northorpe, Lincs. ... B 3
90 Northorpe, Lincs. ... D 2
113 Northorpe, Lincs. ... G 7
39 Northover, Som. ... B 8
39 Northover, Som. ... D 8
111 Northowram ... D 10
40 Northport ... G 1
92 Northrepps ... B 5
151 Northton ... H 1
152 Northtown ... D 3
133 Northumberland, County ... D 8
57 Northway, Glos. ... A 12
38 Northway, Som. ... C 5
94 Northwich ... C 5
57 Northwick ... F 9
90 Northwold ... F 8
40 Northwood, I.o.W. ... G 6
86 Northwood, Lond. ... E 1
94 Northwood, Salop ... G 3
91 Northwood End ... L 2
57 Northwood Green ... C 10
94 Northwood, Ches. ... B 4
116 Norton, Cleveland ... C 5
57 Norton, Glos. ... B 11

146 Plaidy ..... B 5
54 Plain Dealings ..... E 4
136 Plains ..... C 1
38 Plainsfield ..... C 5
59 Plaish ..... C 10
41 Plaistow ..... C 11
42 Plaistow Street ..... D 3
40 Plaitford ..... D 4
61 Plas Newydd ..... F 11
132 Plashetts ..... D 5
84 Plastow Green ..... H 6
61 Plas-yn-Cefn ..... C 9
42 Platt ..... B 5
110 Platt Bridge ..... G 5
133 Plawsworth ..... H 11
42 Plaxtol ..... C 5
85 Play Hatch ..... F 8
43 Playden ..... F 8
93 Playford ..... K 5
34 Playing Place ..... E 5
57 Playley Green ..... A 10
59 Plealey ..... B 9
140 Plean ..... H 3
141 Pleasance ..... F 7
110 Pleasington ..... E 5
96 Pleasley ..... D 2
132 Plenmeller ..... G 5
86 Pleshey ..... B 6
142 Plockton ..... F 2
151 Plocrapool ..... G 3
59 Ploughfield ..... H 9
137 Ploughlands ..... E 10
59 Plowden ..... D 9
59 Ploxgreen ..... B 9
43 Pluckley ..... D 8
43 Pluckley Thorne ..... D 8
131 Plumbland ..... H 12
94 Plumley ..... C 6
42 Plumpton ..... G 2
115 Plumptonfoot ..... A 7
42 Plumpton Green ..... F 2
115 Plumpton Head ..... B 7
115 Plumpton ..... B 7
92 Plumstead ..... B 4
96 Plumtree ..... G 3
96 Plungar ..... B 5
39 Plush ..... F 10
55 Plwmp ..... B 7
37 Plymouth ..... K 4
37 Plympton ..... K 4
37 Plympton St. Maurice K 3
37 Plymstock ..... K 4
38 Plymtree ..... F 4
116 Pockley ..... G 6
112 Pocklington ..... B 6
90 Pode Hole ..... C 3
39 Podimore ..... D 9
89 Podington ..... F 12
94 Podmore ..... G 6
90 Pointon ..... B 2
40 Pokesdown ..... G 3
130 Polbae ..... D 4
148 Polbain ..... F 2
35 Polbathic ..... D 10
136 Polbeth ..... C 3
131 Poldean ..... B 11
146 Poldullie Bridge ..... F 1
111 Pole Moor ..... E 9
91 Polebrook ..... G 2
42 Polegate ..... G 5
94 Polelane Ends ..... B 5
88 Polesworth ..... B 6
148 Polglass ..... F 2
35 Polgooth ..... E 7
41 Poling ..... F 11
41 Poling Corner ..... E 11
35 Polkerris ..... D 8
148 Polla ..... B 5
112 Pollington ..... E 4
138 Polloch ..... A 5
135 Pollockshaws ..... C 10
135 Pollokshields ..... C 10
131 Polmaddie ..... C 7
142 Polmaily ..... F 8
35 Polmassick ..... E 7
135 Polmont ..... B 2
136 Polmoody ..... H 4
135 Polnessan ..... H 9
143 Polnish ..... L 1
41 Polperro ..... E 9
35 Polruan ..... E 8
39 Polsham ..... B 8
131 Polskeoch ..... A 8
93 Polstead ..... L 1
38 Poltimore ..... G 3
136 Polton ..... C 5
137 Polwarth ..... D 10
35 Polyphant ..... B 9
34 Polzeath ..... B 6
90 Pondersbridge ..... F 4
41 Pondtail ..... A 9
34 Ponsanooth ..... F 5
37 Ponsworthy ..... H 6
55 Pont-Antwn ..... F 8
61 Pont Cyfyngf ..... D 7
55 Pont Hentry ..... F 8
58 Pont-Llogel ..... A 6
60 Pont Pen-y-benglog ..D 6
60 Pont Rhyd-goch ..... D 6
58 Pont-Robert ..... A 6
55 Pont Yates ..... F 8
55 Pontamman ..... F 9
56 Pont ar Hydfer ..... B 2
55 Pontardawe ..... G 10
55 Pontardulais ..... G 9
55 Pontargothi ..... E 8
55 Pont-ar-llechau ..... E 10
55 Pontarsais ..... D 8
61 Pontblyddyn ..... D 12
56 Pontbren Llwyd ..... D 3
112 Pontefract ..... E 2
133 Ponteland ..... F 10
58 Ponterwyd ..... D 3
93 Pontesbury ..... B 9
59 Pontesford ..... B 9
61 Pontfadog ..... F 11
54 Pontfaen, Dyfed ..... D 4
56 Pont-faen, Powys ..... A 3
55 Pontgarreg ..... B 7
56 Ponthir ..... E 6
54 Ponthirwaun ..... B 6
56 Pont-llan-fraith ..... E 5
55 Pontlliw ..... G 9
55 Pontlottyn ..... D 4
60 Pontlyfni ..... E 4
56 Pontneddfechan ..... D 2
56 Pontnewydd ..... E 6
58 Pontrhydfendigaid ..F 3
55 Pontrhydyfen ..... G 11
58 Pontrhydygroes ..... E 3
56 Pontrhydyrun ..... E 6
57 Pontrilas ..... B 7
60 Pont-rug ..... D 4
42 Ponts Green ..... F 5
55 Pontshaen ..... B 8
57 Pontshill ..... B 9
56 Pontsticill ..... C 4
55 Pont-tywely ..... C 7
55 Pontyberem ..... F 8
61 Pont-y-bodkin ..... D 12
61 Pont y Clogwyn ..... E 8
56 Pontyclun ..... F 4
56 Pontycymer ..... E 2
54 Pontyglazier ..... C 5
56 Pont-y-gwaith ..... E 3
61 Ponty-y-pant ..... E 7
56 Pontypool ..... D 6
56 Pontypool Road ..... D 6
56 Pontypridd ..... E 4
54 Pont-yr-hafod ..... D 3
59 Pont-ysgawrhyd ..... A 7
56 Pontywaun ..... E 5
40 Pooksgreen ..... E 5
34 Pool, Cornwall ..... E 4
59 Pool Heref. & Worc. H 10
38 Pool, Som. ..... D 3
111 Pool, W. Yorks ..... C 11
110 Pool Hey ..... F 2
59 Pool Head ..... G 11
140 Pool of Muckhart ..... G 5
59 Pool Quay ..... A 8
93 Pool Street ..... L 1
40 Poole ..... G 2
94 Poole Green ..... E 5
84 Poole Keynes ..... E 1
95 Poolend ..... D 8
142 Poolewe ..... B 2
115 Pooley Bridge ..... C 7
57 Poolhill ..... A 10
96 Poolsbrook ..... C 2
114 Poortown ..... G 1
42 Pootings ..... C 3
85 Popeswood ..... G 9
41 Popham ..... B 7
86 Poplar ..... F 4
40 Porchfield ..... G 6
142 Porin ..... D 7
34 Porkellis ..... F 4
38 Porlock ..... B 2
38 Porlock Weir ..... B 2
141 Port Allen ..... E 7
138 Port Appin ..... C 6
134 Port Bannatyne ..... C 6
132 Port Carlisle ..... G 1
116 Port Clarence ..... C 5
60 Port Dinorwic ..... C 5
134 Port Driseach ..... B 5
146 Port Elphinstone ..... F 5
114 Port Erin ..... H 1
146 Port Erroll ..... D 8
55 Port Eynon ..... H 8
135 Port Glasgow ..... B 8
142 Port Henderson ..... B 1
35 Port Isaac ..... B 7
134 Port Lamont ..... B 6
130 Port Logan ..... H 2
117 Port Mulgrave ..... C 8
140 Port of Menteith ..... G 1
151 Port of Ness ..... A 6
35 Port Quin ..... B 7
138 Port Ramsay ..... C 6
114 Port St. Mary ..... H 1
139 Port Sonachan ..... E 7
94 Port Sunlight ..... B 2
55 Port Talbot ..... H 10
55 Port Tennant ..... H 10
130 Port William ..... G 4
134 Portachoillan ..... D 3
134 Port an Eilein ..... B 5
134 Portavadie ..... B 4
57 Portbury ..... G 8
41 Portchester ..... F 7
135 Portencross ..... D 7
39 Portesham ..... H 9
146 Portessie ..... A 2
114 Port e Vullen ..... G 3
54 Portfield Gate ..... E 3
37 Portgate ..... G 3
146 Portgordon ..... A 1
149 Portgower ..... E 9
56 Porth ..... E 4
34 Porth Mellin ..... H 4
34 Porth Navas ..... G 5
35 Porthallow, Corn. ..... D 9
34 Porthallow, Corn ..... G 5
56 Porthcawl ..... G 1
34 Porthcothan Bay ..... C 6
34 Porthcurno ..... G 1
60 Porthdafarch ..... B 2
54 Porthgain ..... D 2
34 Porthilly ..... B 6
56 Porthkerry ..... H 4
34 Porthleven ..... G 3
60 Porthmadog ..... F 5
34 Porthmeor ..... F 2
43 Portholland ..... F 7
34 Porthoustock ..... G 5
34 Porthowann ..... E 4
35 Porthpean ..... D 7
55 Porthyrhyd, Dyfed ..... E 8
55 Porthyrhyd, Dyfed ..C 10
139 Portincaple ..... H 9
112 Portington ..... D 6
139 Portinnisherrich ..... F 7
114 Portinscale ..... C 5
57 Portishead ..... G 8
146 Portknockie ..... A 2
147 Portlethen ..... H 7
34 Portloe ..... F 6
149 Portmahomack ..... H 9
60 Portmeirion ..... F 5
35 Portmellon ..... E 7
40 Portmore ..... F 5
150 Port na Long ..... E 3
151 Portnaguran ..... C 6
143 Portnaluchaig ..... K 1
148 Portnancon ..... B 5
139 Portnellan, Central ..E 11
139 Portnellan, Central ..F 11
138 Portnocroish ..... C 6
136 Portobello ..... B 6
40 Porton ..... B 3
130 Portpatrick ..... F 1
34 Portreath ..... E 4
150 Portree ..... D 4
135 Portrye ..... D 7
34 Portscatho ..... F 6
41 Portsea ..... F 8
149 Portskerra ..... A 8
57 Portskewett ..... E 8
42 Portslade, Surrey ..... G 1
42 Portslade, Surrey ..... G 2
130 Portslogan ..... F 1
41 Portsmouth, Hants ..... F 8
111 Portsmouth, W. Yorks E 7
146 Portsoy ..... A 3
40 Portswood ..... E 6
138 Portuairk ..... A 2
148 Portvasgo ..... A 6
151 Portvoller ..... C 6
151 Portway, Heref. & Worc. ..... A 8
88 Portway, War. ..... E 4
35 Portwrinkle ..... D 10
130 Portyerrock ..... H 5
34 Postbridge ..... H 5
85 Postcombe ..... D 8
43 Postling ..... D 10
92 Postwick ..... E 6
147 Potarch ..... H 3
135 Poteath ..... D 7
132 Potholm ..... D 2
85 Potsgrove ..... A 10
90 Pott Row ..... C 8
95 Pott Shrigley ..... B 8
85 Potten End ..... C 11
117 Potter Brompton ..... G 10
92 Potter Heigham ..... D 7
86 Potter Street ..... C 5
97 Potterhanworth ..... D 7
97 Potterhanworth Booths ..... C 8
84 Potterne ..... H 1
84 Potterne Wick ..... H 1
86 Potters Bar ..... D 3
88 Potters Cross ..... D 2
89 Potterspury ..... H 11
116 Potto ..... E 5
91 Potton ..... K 3
36 Poughill, Corn ..... E 1
36 Poughill, Devon ..... E 7
84 Poulshot ..... H 1
94 Poulton, Ches. ..... D 3
84 Poulton, Glos. ..... D 2
110 Poulton-Le-Fylde ..... C 2
56 Pound ..... F 1
88 Pound Bank ..... E 1
42 Pound Green, E. Sussex F 4
40 Pound Green, I.o.W. . G 5
42 Pound Hill ..... D 2
117 Poundland, Dumf. & Gall. ..... C 9
130 Poundland, Strathclyde ..... C 3
85 Poundon ..... B 7
42 Poundsbridge ..... D 4
37 Poundsgate ..... J 6
34 Poundstock ..... A 2
141 Pourie ..... D 9
133 Powburn ..... A 9
38 Powderham ..... H 3
39 Powerstock ..... G 8
131 Powfoot ..... E 12
141 Powgavie ..... E 7
88 Powick ..... G 2
36 Powler's Piece ..... D 2
140 Powmill ..... G 5
58 Powys, Co ..... E 6
39 Poxwell ..... H 11
85 Poyle ..... F 11
42 Poynings ..... G 1
39 Poyntington ..... D 10
95 Poynton ..... B 8
94 Poynton Green ..... H 4
93 Poys Street ..... H 6
54 Poyston Cross ..... E 3
93 Poystreet Green ..... J 3
34 Praa Sands ..... G 3
150 Prabost ..... C 3
86 Pratt's Bottom ..... H 5
43 Pratt'sHeath ..... H 7
34 Praze ..... F 3
34 Praze-an-Beeble ..... F 3
34 Predannack Wollas ..H 4
94 Prees ..... G 4
110 Preesall ..... B 2
110 Preesall Park ..... C 2
54 Prendergast ..... E 3
133 Prendwick ..... B 8
55 Pren-gwyn ..... C 7
60 Prenteg ..... F 5
94 Prenton ..... B 2
94 Prescot ..... A 3
94 Prescott ..... H 3
137 Pressen ..... F 11
94 Pressgreen ..... G 4
61 Prestatyn ..... B 10
95 Prestbury, Ches. ..... C 7
57 Prestbury, Glos. ..... B 12
59 Presteigne ..... F 8
59 Presthope ..... C 11
39 Prestleigh ..... B 9
137 Preston, Borders ..... D 10
37 Preston, Devon ..... H 7
39 Preston, Dorset ..... H 10
42 Preston, E. Sussex ..... G 2
93 Preston, Essex ..... K 2
57 Preston, Glos ..... A 10
84 Preston, Glos ..... D 2
86 Preston, Herts ..... A 2
113 Preston, Humber. ..... D 9
43 Preston, Kent ..... B 9
43 Preston, Kent ..... B 11
110 Preston, Lancs ..... D 4
133 Preston, Northumb. . E 12
136 Preston, Lothian ..... B 6
137 Preston, Lothian ..... B 8
84 Preston, Wilts ..... F 1
88 Preston Bagot ..... E 5
85 Preston Bissett ..... A 7
38 Preston Bowyer ..... D 5
94 Preston Brockhurst ..H 4
94 Preston Brook ..... B 4
41 Preston Candover ..... B 7
89 Preston Capes ..... G 9
85 Preston Crowmarsh ..E 7
35 Preston Gubbals ..... H 4
88 Preston on Stour ..... G 5
94 Preston on the Hill ..B 4
59 Preston on Wye ..... H 9
39 Preston Plucknett ..... E 8
59 Preston upon the Weald Moors ..... A 12
59 Preston Wynne ..... H 11
131 Prestonmill ..... F 10
136 Prestonpans ..... B 6
116 Preston-under-Scar ..F 1
111 Prestwich ..... G 7
135 Prestwick, Northumb. ..... F 10
135 Prestwick, Strathclyde G 8
85 Prestwood ..... D 9
56 Price Town ..... E 3
91 Prickwillow ..... G 7
39 Priddy ..... A 8
115 Priest Hulton ..... H 7
132 Priesthaugh ..... C 3
135 Priesthill ..... C 10
135 Priestland ..... F 10
59 Priestweston ..... C 8
89 Primethorpe ..... C 8
90 Primrose Hill, Cambs. F 5
96 Primrose Hill, Notts. . D 2
117 Primrose Valley ..... G 11
137 Primrosehill, Borders D 10
85 Primrosehill, Herts ..D 11
137 Primsidemill ..... G 10
54 Princes Gate ..... F 5
85 Princes Risborough ..D 9
89 Princethorpe ..... E 7
37 Princetown, Devon ..H 5
56 Princetown, Mid Glam. ..... C 4
137 Printonan ..... E 10
61 Prion ..... D 10
59 Priors Frame ..... H 11
89 Priors Hardwick ..... G 8
89 Priors Marston ..... F 8
59 Priorslee ..... A 12
59 Priory Wood ..... H 8
57 Priston ..... H 10
87 Prittlewell ..... E 8
41 Privett ..... C 8
36 Prixford ..... B 4
34 Probus ..... E 6
131 Prospect ..... G 12
146 Protstonhill ..... A 6
133 Prudhoe ..... G 9
139 Ptarmigan Lodge ..... G 10
139 Pubil ..... C 11
57 Publow ..... H 9
86 Puckeridge ..... B 4
39 Puckington ..... D 7
57 Pucklechurch ..... G 10
40 Pucknall ..... D 5
94 Puddington, Ches. ..... C 2
36 Puddington, Devon E7
92 Puddledock ..... F 4
39 Puddletown ..... G 10
59 Pudlestone ..... F 11
111 Pudsey ..... D 11
41 Pulborough ..... D 12
94 Puleston ..... H 6
94 Pulford ..... D 2
39 Pulham ..... E 10
93 Pulham Market ..... G 5
93 Pulham St. Margaret . G 5
91 Pulloxhill ..... M 2
136 Pumpherston ..... B 3
131 Pumplaburn ..... B 12
55 Pumpsaint ..... C 10
54 Puncheston ..... D 3
39 Puncknoll ..... G 9
87 Punnett's Town ..... F 5
41 Purbrook ..... E 8
132 Purdomstone ..... E 1
40 Purewell ..... G 3
86 Purfleet ..... F 5
39 Puriton ..... B 7
87 Purleigh ..... D 8
85 Purley, Berks ..... F 7
86 Purley, London ..... H 3
91 Purls Bridge ..... G 6
39 Purse Caundle ..... D 10
59 Purslow ..... D 9
112 Purston Jaglin ..... E 2
39 Purtington ..... E 7
57 Purton, Glos ..... D 10
84 Purton, Wilts ..... E 2
84 Purton Stoke ..... E 2
137 Purvishaugh ..... E 8
89 Pury End ..... H 1
84 Pusey ..... D 4
36 Putford ..... D 2
57 Putley ..... A 9
86 Putney ..... F 2
36 Putsborough ..... B 3
85 Puttenham, Bucks. ..... C 9
41 Puttenham, Surrey ..A 10
57 Puxton ..... H 7
55 Pwll ..... G 8
54 Pwllcrochan ..... G 3
60 Pwlldefaid ..... H 1
56 Pwllgloyw ..... A 3
60 Pwllheli ..... G 3
57 Pwllmeyric ..... E 8
54 Pwlltrap ..... E 6
55 Pwll-y-glaw ..... H 11
61 Pydew ..... B 7
96 Pye Bridge ..... E 2
57 Pye Corner, Gwent ..... F 7
86 Pye Corner, Herts ..... C 4
88 Pye Green ..... A 3
42 Pyecombe ..... G 2
40 Pyle, I.o.W. ..... H 6
56 Pyle, Mid Glam. ..... F 2
39 Pylle ..... B 9
91 Pymore ..... G 6
85 Pyrford ..... H 11
56 Pyrgad ..... C 4
85 Pyrton ..... E 8
89 Pytchley ..... E 12
36 Pyworthy ..... F 2
59 Quabbs ..... D 7
90 Quadring ..... B 3
85 Quainton ..... B 8
40 Quarley ..... B 4
95 Quarndon, Derby ..... F 11
89 Quarndon, Leics. ..... A 9
135 Quarrier's Homes ..... C 8
90 Quarrington ..... A 2
116 Quarrington Hill ..... A 4
88 Quarry Bank ..... C 3
94 Quarrybank ..... D 4
146 Quarryburn ..... A 6
144 Quarrywood ..... C 7
135 Quarter ..... D 12
88 Quat ..... C 1
88 Quatford ..... C 1
116 Quebec ..... A 2
57 Quedgeley ..... C 11
91 Queen Adelaide ..... G 7
57 Queen Charlton ..... H 9
36 Queen Dart ..... D 7
39 Queen Oak ..... C 11
42 Queen Street ..... D 6
43 Queenborough in Sheppey ..... A 8
39 Queens Camel ..... D 9
94 Queens Head ..... G 2
94 Queen's Park ..... E 2
111 Queensbury ..... D 9
61 Queensferry, Clwyd . C 12
136 Queensferry, Lothian . B 4
110 Queenstown ..... D 2
135 Queenzieburn ..... B 11
84 Quemerford ..... G 1
152 Quendale ..... F 7
91 Quendon ..... M 6
89 Queniborough ..... A 10
84 Quenington ..... D 2
110 Quernmore ..... A 4
35 Quethiock ..... C 10
93 Quidenham ..... G 3
40 Quidhampton, Hants. A 6
40 Quidhampton, Wilts. . C 3
146 Quilquox ..... D 6
114 Quine's Hill ..... H 2
138 Quinish House ..... B 2
89 Quinton ..... G 11
34 Quintrel Downs ..... D 5
137 Quixwood ..... C 10
36 Quoditch ..... F 3
140 Quoig ..... E 3
136 Quothquan ..... E 3
152 Quoys ..... D 7
150 Rassay House (Hotel) D 5
36 Rabscott ..... C 6
94 Raby ..... B 2
60 Rachub ..... C 5
60 Rackenford ..... C 5
36 Rackenford ..... D 7
41 Rackham ..... E 11
92 Rackheath Com. ..... D 6
131 Racks ..... D 11
152 Rackwick, Orkney ..... D 1
152 Rackwick, Orkney ..... A 2
95 Radbourne ..... G 11
110 Radcliffe, Manchester . F 6
133 Radcliffe, Northumb. C 11

96 Radcliffe on Soar G 2
96 Radcliffe on Trent F 4
85 Radclive A 7
84 Radcot D 4
144 Raddery D 3
89 Radford Semele F 7
39 Radpole H 10
86 Radlett D 2
84 Radley D 6
85 Radnage D 8
39 Radstock A 10
89 Radstone H 9
89 Radway G 7
94 Radway Green E 6
91 Radwell J 1
91 Radwinter L 7
56 Radyr F 5
136 Raecleugh H 3
151 Raerinish D 5
148 Raffin D 2
144 Rafford D 6
96 Ragdale H 4
141 Ragfield F 10
57 Raglan D 7
96 Ragnall C 5
110 Rainford G 4
86 Rainham, Essex F 5
43 Rainham, Kent B 7
94 Rainhill A 4
94 Rainhill Stoops A 4
95 Rainow C 8
116 Rainton H 4
96 Rainworth D 3
115 Raisbeck D 9
132 Raise H 5
112 Raisthorpe A 6
141 Rait D 7
144 Raitcastle D 5
97 Raithby, Lincs. C 10
97 Raithby, Lincs. B 10
41 Rake C 9
43 Ram Lane C 8
150 Ramasaig D 1
35 Rame, Corn. E 11
34 Rame, Corn. F 4
39 Rampisham F 9
110 Rampside A 1
91 Rampton, Cambs. H 5
96 Rampton, Notts. B 5
111 Ramsbottom E 7
84 Ramsbury G 4
149 Ramscraigs D 10
41 Ramsdean D 8
85 Ramsdell H 7
84 Ramsden C 4
87 Ramsden Bellhouse E 7
87 Ramsden Heath D 7
91 Ramsay, Cambs. G 4
93 Ramsey, Essex M 5
114 Ramsey, I.o.M. G 2
87 Ramsay Island C 9
91 Ramsay St. Mary's G 4
136 Ramseycleuch H 5
43 Ramsgate B 12
92 Ramsgate Street B 4
116 Ramsgill H 1
133 Ramshaw H 8
132 Ramshope C 6
95 Ramshorn F 9
37 Ramsley G 5
41 Ramsnest Com. C 11
96 Ranby B 4
97 Rand B 8
57 Randwick D 11
135 Ranfurly C 9
95 Rangemore H 10
57 Rangeworthy F 10
135 Rankinston H 9
41 Ranmore Com. A 12
110 Rann E 6
114 Rannerdale C 4
139 Rannoch Station B 11
143 Ranochan L 2
38 Ranscombe B 3
96 Ranskill A 4
95 Ranton H 7
92 Ranworth D 7
152 Rapness B 3
143 Rarsaidh H 2
131 Rascarre G 9
134 Rashfield A 6
146 Rashiereive E 7
116 Raskelf H 5
56 Rassau C 5
111 Rastrick E 10
143 Ratagan H 3
89 Ratby B 8
89 Ratcliffe Culey B 7
89 Ratcliffe on the Wreake A 9
146 Rathen B 7
141 Rathillet E 8
111 Rathmell A 7
136 Ratho B 4
136 Ratho Station B 4
146 Rathven A 2
89 Ratley G 7
59 Ratlinghope C 9
149 Rattar A 11
37 Rattery K 6
93 Rattlesden J 3
141 Rattray C 7
114 Raughton Head A 6
91 Raunds H 1
137 Ravelaw D 11
112 Ravenfield H 3
114 Ravenglass F 3
92 Raveningham F 7
117 Ravenscar E 10
135 Ravenscraig B 7
114 Ravensdale G 2
91 Ravensden K 2
96 Ravenshead E 3
94 Ravensmoor E 5
89 Ravensthorpe E 10
89 Ravenstone, Bucks. G 11
89 Ravenstone, Leics. A 7
115 Ravenstonedale E 9
136 Ravenstruther E 2
116 Ravensworth D 2
117 Raw E 9
137 Rawburn D 9
112 Rawcliffe, Humber. E 5
112 Rawcliffe, N. Yorks. B 4
112 Rawcliffe Bridge E 5
111 Rawdon C 11
112 Rawmarsh G 2
88 Rawnsley A4
87 Rawreth E 8
38 Rawridge F 5
135 Raws E 9
111 Rawtenstall E 7
135 Rawyards C 12
146 Raxton D 6
93 Raydon L 3
133 Raylees D 7
87 Rayleigh E 8
39 Raymond's Hill F 7
87 Rayne B 7
91 Reach J 7
110 Read D 6
85 Reading G 8
43 Reading Street E 8
115 Reagill C 8
149 Rearquhar G 7
89 Rearsby A 10
149 Reaster A 11
133 Reaveley A 8
152 Reawick D 6
149 Reay B 9
43 Reculver A 11
38 Red Ball E 4
132 Red Dial H 1
88 Red Hill G 2
37 Red Post J 7
110 Red Rock F 5
54 Red Roses F 5
133 Red Row C 10
95 Red Street E 7
60 Red Wharf B 5
54 Redberth G 4
85 Redbourn C 12
113 Redbourne G 7
86 Redbridge E 4
94 Redbrook, Clwyd F 4
57 Redbrook, Gwent C 8
43 Redbrook Street D 8
144 Redburn, Highland E 5
144 Redburn, Highland C 1
132 Redburn, Northumb. G 6
116 Redcar C 8
144 Redcastle, Highland E 1
141 Redcastle, Tayside B 11
57 Redcliffe Bay G 7
135 Redcraig G 9
137 Redden F 10
136 Redding B 2
136 Reddingmuirhead B 2
111 Reddish H 8
88 Redditch E 4
135 Reddochbraes F 12
93 Redenhall G 6
132 Redesdale Camp C 6
133 Redesmouth E 7
141 Redford, Tayside C 10
147 Redford, Tayside K 5
136 Redfordgreen H 6
93 Redgrave G 3
147 Redheugh L 2
57 Redhill, Avon H 8
146 Redhill, Grampian D 4
147 Redhill, Grampian G 5
42 Redhill, Surrey C 2
134 Redhouse C 3
93 Redisham G 7
57 Redland, Avon G 9
152 Redland, Orkney C 2
93 Redlingfield H 5
91 Redlodge Warren H 8
40 Redlynch, Dorset D 4
39 Redlynch, Som. C 10
115 Redmain B 4
57 Redmarley D'Abitot A 10
116 Redmarshall C 4
96 Redmile G 5
116 Redmire F 1
35 Redmoor D 8
147 Redmyre K 5
94 Rednal G 2
137 Redpath F 8
142 Redpoint C 1
34 Redruth E 4
136 Redscarhead E 5
57 Redwick, Avon F 8
57 Redwick, Gwent F 7
116 Redworth C 3
91 Reed L 5
92 Reedham E 7
112 Reedness E 6
137 Reedy Loch D 11
151 Reef C 2
97 Reepham, Lincs. C 7
92 Reepham, Norf. C 4
116 Reeth E 1
114 Regaby F 2
144 Rehaurie E 5
149 Reidhbreac G 7
148 Reiff E 2
42 Reigate C 1
117 Reighton H 11
117 Reighton Gap G 11
146 Reisque E 6
149 Reiss B 12
34 Rejerrah D 5
34 Releath F 4
131 Relief D 12
34 Relubbus F 3
144 Relugas E 5
85 Remenham F 8
85 Remenham Hill F 9
140 Remony C 3
96 Rempstone H 3
84 Rendcomb C 1
93 Rendham J 6
135 Renfrew C 10
91 Renhold K 2
96 Renishaw B 2
133 Rennington A 10
135 Renton B 9
115 Renwick A 8
92 Repps D 7
95 Repton G 11
143 Reraig G 2
141 Rescobie B 10
138 Resipole A 4
144 Resolis C 2
56 Resolven D 2
143 Resourie M 2
137 Reston C 11
34 Retew D 6
87 Rettendon D 7
87 Rettendon Place D 7
138 Reudle C 1
97 Revesby D 10
40 Rew Street G 6
38 Rewe F 3
93 Reydon G 8
92 Reymerston E 3
54 Reynalton F 4
55 Reynoldston H 8
35 Rezare B 10
57 Rhadyr D 7
55 Rhandirmwyn C 11
58 Rhayader F 5
148 Rhegreanoch E 3
144 Rheindown E 1
138 Rhemore C 3
150 Rhenetra C 3
61 Rhewl, Clwyd D 10
61 Rhewl, Clwyd F 11
148 Rhicarn E 2
148 Rhiconich B 4
144 Rhicullen C 3
148 Rhidorroch G 3
148 Rhidorroch Old Lodge G 4
60 Rhid-y-sarn F 6
149 Rhifail C 7
56 Rhigos D 3
148 Rhimichie B 4
144 Rhinduie E 1
148 Rhiroy G 3
60 Rhiwbryfdir F 6
56 Rhiwderyn F 6
61 Rhiwlas, Clwd G 11
60 Rhiwlas, Gwynedd D 5
61 Rhiwlas, Gwynedd F 8
38 Rhode C 6
43 Rhodes Minnis D 10
96 Rhodesia B 3
54 Rhodiad D 1
56 Rhoose H 4
55 Rhos, Dyfed C 7
55 Rhos, W. Glam. G 10
55 Rhosamman F 10
60 Rhoscolyn C 2
54 Rhoscrowther G 3
61 Rhosesmor C 11
54 Rhosfach D 5
60 Rhos-fawr B 4
60 Rhosgadfan D 4
60 Rhosgoch, Gwynedd A 3
59 Rhosgoch, Powys H 7
54 Rhos-hill C 5
60 Rhos-lan F 4
58 Rhoslefain B 1
61 Rhosllanerchrugog F 12
55 Rhosmaen E 9
60 Rhos-meirch B 4
60 Rhosneigr C 3
61 Rhos-on-Sea B 8
55 Rhossili H 7
54 Rhosson D 1
60 Rhostryfan D 4
94 Rhostyllen E 2
60 Rhosybol A 4
61 Rhos-y-gwaliau G 9
60 Rhos-y-llan F 2
134 Rhu, Strathclyde C 3
135 Rhu, Strathclyde A 7
142 Rhu Noa C 4
61 Rhualt C 10
134 Rhubodach B 5
94 Rhuddall Heath D 4
61 Rhuddlan B 9
36 Rhude Cross E 1
148 Rhue G 2
59 Rhulen G 7
134 Rhunahaorine E 2
60 Rhyd, Gwynedd F 6
58 Rhyd, Powys B 5
60 Rhyd-Ddu E 5
61 Rhyd-Lydan E 8
55 Rhydargaeau D 8
56 Rhydberry A 3
55 Rhydcymerau C 9
88 Rhydd H 2
55 Rhydding G 10
55 Rhyddlan C 8
61 Rhyd-leos G 11
55 Rhydlewis B 7
60 Rhydlios G 1
58 Rhydlydan C 6
55 Rhydlydan C 6
55 Rhydowen C 8
58 Rhydrosser F 1
59 Rhydspence H 8
61 Rhydtalog E 11
60 Rhydwyn A 3
61 Rhyd-y-croesau G 11
60 Rhydyeclafdy G 3
56 Rhydyfelin E 4
58 Rhydyfelin D 2
55 Rhydyfro F 10
59 Rhyd-y-groes B 8
61 Rhydymain H 7
56 Rhyd-y-meirch D 6
61 Rhydymwyn D 11
58 Rhyd-yr-onmen B 2
58 Rhyfud F 2
61 Rhyl B 9
56 Rhymney D 4
141 Rhynd, Fife E 9
140 Rhynd, Tayside E 6
146 Rhynie E 2
115 Ribblehead G 10
110 Ribbleton D 4
110 Ribby D 3
110 Ribchester D 5
148 Ribigill B 6
113 Riby F 9
113 Riby Cross Roads F 9
112 Riccall C 4
135 Riccarton F 9
59 Richards Castle E 10
85 Richings Park F 11
86 Richmond, London F 2
116 Richmond, N. Yorks. E 2
142 Rickarton H 5
93 Rickinghall Inferior H 3
93 Rickinghall Superior H 3
91 Rickling M 6
86 Rickling Green A 5
85 Rickmansworth E 11
132 Riddings, Cumb. E 3
96 Riddings, Derby E 2
36 Riddlecombe E 5
111 Riddlesden C 9
40 Ridge, Dorset G 1
40 Ridge, Hants. D 5
86 Ridge, Herts. D 2
40 Ridge, Wilts. C 1
42 Ridge Green C 2
88 Ridge Lane C 6
58 Ridgebourne F 6
57 Ridgehill H 8
96 Ridgeway C 2
59 Ridgeway Cross H 12
91 Ridgewell L 8
42 Ridgewood F 3
91 Ridgemont L 1
133 Riding Mill G 8
42 Ridley, Kent B 5
132 Ridley, Northumb. G 6
94 Ridley Green E 4
89 Ridlington, Leics. B 11
92 Ridlington, Norf. B 6
133 Ridsdale E 7
140 Riechip B 5
140 Riemore B 5
148 Rienachait D 2
116 Rievaulx G 6
143 Rifern K 2
135 Rigfoot D 9
132 Rigg F 1
135 Riggend B 12
135 Righead F 10
115 Rigmaden Park G 8
97 Rigsby C 11
136 Rigside F 2
111 Rigton Hill C 12
88 Rileyhill A 5
35 Rilla Mill B 10
117 Rillington H 8
111 Rimington C 7
39 Rimpton D 9
149 Rimsdale C 7
113 Rimswell D 10
54 Rinaston D 3
131 Ringford F 8
95 Ringinglow B 11
92 Ringland D 4
42 Ringles Cross F 3
42 Ringmer G 3
37 Ringmore, Devon J 8
37 Ringmore, Devon L 5
144 Ringorm E 8
90 Ring's End E 5
93 Ringsfield G 7
93 Ringsfield Corner G 7
85 Ringshall, Bucks. C 10
93 Ringshall, Suffolk K 3
93 Ringshall Stocks K 4
90 Ringstead, Norf. B 8
91 Ringstead, Northants. H 1
40 Ringwood F 3
43 Ringwould C 12
146 Ringmore F 2
152 Rinnigill E 2
34 Rinsey G 3
42 Ripe G 4
96 Ripley, Derby E 1
40 Ripley, Hants. F 3
111 Ripley, N. Yorks. A 11
85 Ripley, Surrey H 11
113 Riplingham D 7
116 Ripon H 3
90 Rippingale C 2
88 Ripple,
Heref. & Worcs. H 2
43 Ripple, Kent C 12
111 Ripponden E 9
59 Risbury G 11
113 Risby, Humberside F 7
93 Risby, Suffolk J 1
56 Risca E 6
113 Rise C 9
90 Risegate C 3
97 Riseholme C 7
91 Riseley, Beds. J 1
85 Riseley, Berks. H 8
93 Rishangles H 4
110 Rishton D 6
111 Rishworth E 10
96 Risley G 2
116 Risplith H 3
148 Rispond A 5
84 Rivar H 4
87 Rivenhall End B 8
91 River Bank H 6
42 Riverhead B 4
110 Rivington F 5
36 Roachill D 7
89 Roade G 11
132 Roadhead F 4
136 Roadmeetings D 1
149 Roadside, Highland B 11
135 Roadside,
Strathclyde H 10
147 Roadside of Catterline J 6
147 Roadside of Kinneff K 6
38 Roadwater B 4
150 Roag D 2
130 Roan of Craigoch A 4
132 Roansgreen E 3
56 Roath F 5
131 Roberthill D 12
132 Roberton, Borders B 3
136 Roberton, Strathclyde F 2
42 Robertsbridge F 6
111 Roberttown E 10
54 Robeston Cross F 2
54 Robeston Wathen E 4
111 Robin Hood D 11
95 Robin Hood Inn C 11
117 Robin Hood's Bay E 9
36 Roborough D 4
94 Roby A 3
110 Roby Mill F 4
95 Rocester F 9
54 Roch E 2
54 Roch Gate E 2
111 Rochdale F 7
35 Roche D 7
42 Rochester, Kent A 6
132 Rochester, Northumb. C 6
42 Rochford E 8
34 Rock, Cornwall B 6
133 Rock, Northumb. A 10
88 Rock,
Heref. & Worcs. E 1
41 Rock, W. Sussex E 12
94 Rock Ferry B 2
88 Rock Hill E 3
38 Rockbeare G 4
132 Rockcliffe, Cumb. G 2
131 Rockcliffe,
Dumf. & Gall. F 9
57 Rockfield, Gwent C 8
149 Rockfield, Highland H 9
40 Rockford E 3
57 Rockhampton E 9
92 Rockheath D 6
59 Rockhill D 8
89 Rockingham C 12
92 Rockland All Saints F 3
92 Rockland St. Mary E 6
92 Rockland St. Peter F 3
84 Rockley G 3
132 Rockliffe Cross G 2
85 Rockwell End E 9
38 Rockwell Green D 5
57 Rodborough D 11
84 Rodbourne, Wilts. F 2
57 Rodbourne, Wilts. F 12
84 Rodbourne Cheney E 2
59 Rodd F 8
137 Roddam G 12
137 Roddam Rigg G 12
39 Rodden H 9
39 Rode A 11
94 Rode Heath D 6
95 Rodeheath C 7
151 Rodel H 1
59 Roden A 11
38 Rodhuish B 4
59 Rodington A 11
57 Rodley C 10
57 Rodmarton D 12
42 Rodmell G 3
43 Rodmersham B 8
39 Rodney Stoke A 8
95 Rodsley F 10
38 Rodway B 6
39 Rodwell H 7
111 Roecliffe A 12
86 Roehampton G 2
152 Roesound C 7
42 Roffey E 1
149 Rogart F 7
41 Rogate D 9
56 Rogerstone E 6
135 Rogerton D 11
57 Rogiet E 8
92 Rollesby D 7
89 Rolleston, Leics. B 10
96 Rolleston, Notts. E 5
95 Rolleston, Staffs. G 10
113 Rolston C 10
43 Rolvenden E 7
43 Rolvenden Layne E 7
115 Romaldkirk C 12

92 Roman Hill F 8
116 Romanby F 4
136 Romannobridge E 4
36 Romansleigh D 6
150 Romesdal C 3
86 Romford E 5
95 Romiley A 8
40 Romsey D 5
88 Romsley, Salop. D 1
88 Romsley, Salop. D 3
114 Ronague H 1
117 Rookdale H 9
115 Rookhope A 11
40 Rookley H 6
39 Rooks Bridge A 7
38 Rook's Nest C 4
113 Roos D 10
136 Rootpark D 2
41 Ropley C 8
41 Ropley Dean C 7
97 Ropsley G 7
146 Rora C 8
146 Rorandle F 4
59 Rorrington B 8
34 Rose D 5
36 Rose Ash D 7
42 Rose Hill F 3
42 Roseacre, Kent C 6
110 Roseacre, Lancs. C 3
136 Rosebank D 1
133 Rosebrough C 12
54 Rosebush D 4
34 Rosecare B 2
117 Rosedale Abbey F 7
133 Roseden A 8
146 Rosehearty A 7
94 Rosehill G 5
144 Roseisle C 7
54 Rosemarket F 3
144 Rosemarkie D 3
38 Rosemary Lane E 5
141 Rosemount C 7
34 Rosenannon C 6
34 Rosewarne F 3
136 Rosewell C 5
116 Roseworth C 4
34 Roseworthy F 3
115 Rosgill D 8
143 Roshven L 1
150 Roskhill D 2
114 Rosley A 6
136 Roslin C 5
95 Rosliston H 11
135 Rosneath A 7
131 Ross, Dumf. & Gall. G 7
133 Ross, Northumb. B 12
57 Ross-on-Wye B 9
94 Rossett D 2
140 Rossie Ochill F 6
112 Rossington G 4
144 Rosskeen C 2
135 Rossland B 9
149 Roster C 11
94 Rostherne B 6
114 Rosthwaite D 5
95 Roston F 10
34 Rosudgeon G 3
136 Rosyth A 4
133 Rothbury C 9
89 Rotherby A 10
42 Rotherfield E 4
85 Rotherfield Greys F 8
85 Rotherfield Peppard F 8
96 Rotherham A 2
89 Rothersthorpe F 10
85 Rotherwick H 8
144 Rothes E 8
134 Rothesay C 6
146 Rothiebrisbane D 5
146 Rothienorman D 5
152 Rothiesholm C 4
133 Rothill B 9
89 Rothley A 9
146 Rothmaise D 4
113 Rothwell, Lincs. G 9
89 Rothwell, Northants. D 11
111 Rothwell, W. Yorks. D 12
113 Rotsea B 8
147 Rottal K 1
42 Rottingdean H 3
114 Rottington D 2
131 Roucan D 11
40 Roud H 6
95 Rough Close F 8
43 Rough Common B 10
95 Rough Hay H 10
92 Rougham C 1
93 Rougham Green J 2
143 Roughburn L 7
111 Roughlee C 7
88 Roughley B 5
132 Roughsike E 3
97 Roughton, Lincs. D 9
92 Roughton, Norf. B 5
88 Roughton, Salop. C 1
135 Roughwood D 8
85 Round Oak H 7
39 Roundham E 7
111 Roundhay C 12
131 Roundstonefoot A 12
41 Roundstreet Com. C 12
84 Roundway H 1
88 Rous Lench G 4
38 Rousdon G 6
84 Rousham B 6
135 Routdaneburn D 7
113 Routh C 8
149 Rovie Lodge F 7
35 Row, Cornwall B 8
115 Row, Cumbria F 7
132 Rowanburn E 2
139 Rowardennan Hotel H 10
95 Rowarth A 8
84 Rowde H 1
61 Ro-wen C 7
132 Rowfoot G 5
87 Rowhedge B 10
41 Rowhook C 12
88 Rowington E 5
95 Rowland C 10
41 Rowland's Castle E 9
133 Rowland's Gill G 10
41 Rowledge B 9
113 Rowley, Humber. D 7
59 Rowley, Salop. B 8
88 Rowley Regis C 3
57 Rowlstone B 7
41 Rowly B 11
88 Rowney Green E 4
40 Rownhams D 5
85 Rowsham B 9
95 Rowsley D 11
97 Rowston E 8
94 Rowton, Ches. D 3
94 Rowton, Salop. H 5
137 Roxburgh F 9
137 Roxburgh Newtown F 9
113 Roxby, Humber. E 7
117 Roxby, N. Yorks. D 7
91 Roxton K 3
86 Roxwell C 6
110 Royal Oak G 3
143 Roybridge L 6
86 Roydon, Essex C 4
93 Roydon, Norfolk G 4
90 Roydon, Norfolk C 8
91 Royston, Herts. L 5
111 Royston, S. Yorks. F 12
111 Royton F 8
61 Ruabon F 12
34 Ruan High Lanes F 6
34 Ruan Lanihorne E 6
34 Ruan Minor H 4
57 Ruardean C 9
57 Ruardean Woodside C 9
88 Ribery D 3
115 Ruckcroft A 8
59 Ruckhall Com. H 10
43 Ruckinge E 9
97 Ruckland B 10
59 Ruckley B 10
116 Rudby D 5
133 Rudchester F 9
96 Ruddington G 3
57 Rudford B 11
39 Rudge A 11
57 Rudgeway F 9
41 Rudgwick C 12
57 Rudhall B 9
56 Rudry F 5
117 Rudston H 11
95 Rudyard D 8
137 Ruecastle G 8
110 Rufford F 3
112 Rufforth B 3
133 Ruffside H 8
89 Rugby E 8
95 Rugeley H 9
144 Ruilick E 1
38 Ruishton D 6
86 Ruislip E 1
86 Ruislip Common E 1
132 Ruletownhead B 4
137 Rumbletonlaw E 9
140 Rumblingbridge G 5
93 Rumburgh G 6
34 Rumford C 6
56 Rumney F 5
140 Runacraig F 1
94 Runcorn B 4
41 Runcton F 10
90 Runcton Holme E 7
37 Rundlestone H 4
41 Runfold A 10
92 Runhall E 4
92 Runham D 7
38 Runnington D 5
87 Runsell Green C 8
117 Runswick D 8
145 Runtaleave M 8
87 Runwell D 7
85 Ruscombe F 9
144 Rosehaugh House D 2
87 Rush Green B 11
57 Rushall, Heref. & Worcs. A 9
93 Rushall, Norfolk G 5
88 Rushall, W. Midlands B 4
40 Rushall, Wilts. A 3
93 Rushbrooke J 2
59 Rushbury C 10
91 Rushden, Herts. M 4
91 Rushden, Northants. J 1
93 Rushford G 2
42 Rushlake Green F 5
93 Rushmere G 8
93 Rushmere St. Andrew. K 5
93 Rushmere Street K 5
41 Rushmoor, Surrey B 10
40 Rushmore, Wilts. D 1
88 Rushock E 2
111 Rusholme H 7
94 Rushton, Ches. D 4
89 Rushton, Northants. D 11
59 Rushton, Salop. B 11
95 Rushton Spencer D 8
88 Rushwick G 2
116 Rushyford B 3
140 Ruskie G 1
97 Ruskington E 8
131 Rusko F 7
114 Rusland F 6
42 Rusper D 1
57 Ruspidge C 9
42 Russell's Green G 6
85 Russell's Water E 8
41 Rustington F 11
117 Ruston G 9
113 Ruston Parva A 8
117 Ruswarp D 9
137 Rutherford F 9
135 Rutherglen C 11
35 Ruthernbridge C 7
61 Ruthin D 10
147 Ruthrieston G 7
137 Ruthven, Borders E 10
146 Ruthven, Grampian C 3
144 Ruthven, Highland F 4
145 Ruthven, Highland J 3
141 Ruthven, Tayside B 7
141 Ruthven House B 8
34 Ruthvoes D 6
131 Ruthwell E 11
57 Ruxton Green B 8
94 Ruyton Eleven Towns H 3
133 Ryal F 8
39 Ryall G 7
42 Ryarsh B 5
114 Rydal E 6
41 Ryde G 7
36 Rydon F 2
43 Rye F 8
43 Rye Foreign F 7
43 Rye Harbour F 8
131 Ryemuir D 11
90 Ryhall D 1
113 Ryhill, Humber. E 10
112 Ryhill, W. Yorks. F 2
133 Ryhope H 12
97 Ryland B 7
111 Rylstone A 8
39 Ryme Intrinseca E 9
137 Ryslaw E 10
112 Ryther C 3
57 Ryton, Glos. A 10
117 Ryton, N. Yorks. H 8
59 Ryton, Salop. B 10
88 Ryton, Salop. B 1
133 Ryton, Tyne & Wear G 9
89 Ryton-on-Dunsmore E 7
110 Sabden C 6
86 Sacombe B 3
133 Sacriston H 10
116 Sadberge C 4
134 Saddell F 3
89 Saddington C 10
90 Saddle Bow D 7
40 Saddle Heath E 3
115 Sadgill E 7
91 Saffron Walden L 6
54 Sageston G 4
92 Saham Hills E 2
92 Saham Toney E 2
94 Saighton D 3
138 Sailean C 6
137 St. Abbs C 11
34 St. Agnes, Corn. E 4
34 St. Agnes, Is. of Scilly D 2
86 St. Albans C 2
34 St. Allen E 5
141 St. Andrews E 10
56 St. Andrews Major G 5
110 St. Anne's D 2
131 St. Ann's B 11
35 St. Ann's Chapel, Cornwall C 11
37 St. Ann's Chapel, Devon L 5
34 St. Anthony G 5
42 St. Anthony's Hill H 5
57 St. Arvans E 8
61 St. Asaph C 9
56 St. Athan G 3
35 St. Austell D 7
39 St. Bartholomew's Hill D 12
114 St. Bees D 2
35 St. Blazey D 8
35 St. Blazey Gate D 7
137 St. Boswells F 8
35 St. Breock C 7
35 St. Breward B 8
57 St. Briavels D 9
54 St. Brides F 2
56 St. Brides Major G 2
57 St. Brides Netherwent E 7
56 St. Bride's-super- Ely G 4
56 St. Bride's Wentlooge F 6
37 St. Budeaux K 3
34 St. Buryan G 1
57 St. Catherine G 11
139 St. Catherines G 8
54 St. Clears E 6
35 St. Cleer C 9
34 St. Clement E 5
35 St. Clether A 9
134 St. Colmac C 5
34 St. Columb Major C 6
34 St. Columb Minor C 5
34 St. Columb Road D 6
146 St. Combs A 8
93 St. Cross South Elmham G 6
137 St. Cuthberts E 11
141 St. Cyrus A 12
54 St. David's, Dyfed D 1
140 St. David's, Tayside E 4
34 St. Day E 4
38 St. Decumans B 4
34 St. Dennis D 6
57 St. Devereux A 7
54 St. Dogmaels B 5
54 St. Dogwells D 3
35 St. Dominick C 11
56 St. Donats G 3
84 St. Edith's Marsh H 1
35 St. Endellion B 7
34 St. Enoder D 6
34 St. Erme E 5
35 St. Erney D 10
34 St. Erth F 3
34 St. Ervan C 6
35 St. Ewe E 7
56 St. Faggans F 4
146 St. Fergus B 8
140 St. Fillans E 2
54 St. Florence G 4
34 St. Gennys B 2
61 St. George C 9
57 St. George's, Avon H 7
56 St. George's, S. Glam. G 4
35 St. Germans D 10
36 St. Giles in the Wood D 4
37 St. Giles on the Heath G 2
58 St. Harmon E 5
116 St. Helen Auckland C 2
92 St. Helena D 5
41 St. Helens, I.o.W. G 7
110 St. Helens, Merseyside G 4
34 St. Hilary, Corn. F 3
56 St. Hilary, S. Glam. G 3
42 Saint Hill D 3
56 St. Illtyd D 5
35 St. Ishmael's F 2
34 St. Issey C 6
35 St. Ive C 10
35 St. Ive Cross C 10
91 St. Ives, Cambs. H 4
34 St. Ives, Corn. F 2
40 St. Ives, Dorset F 3
93 St. James South Elmham G 6
40 St. Joan á Gores Cross A 2
35 St. John D 11
88 St. John's, Heref. & Worcs. G 2
114 St. John's, I.o.M. G 1
36 St. John's Chapel, Devon C 4
115 St. John's Chapel, Durham A 11
90 St. John's Fen End D 6
90 St. John's Highway D 6
114 St. Judas F 2
34 St. Just G 1
34 St. Just Lane F 6
146 St. Katherines D 5
34 St. Keverne G 5
35 St. Kew B 7
35 St. Kew Highway B 7
35 St. Keyne D 9
35 St. Lawrence, Corn. C 7
87 St. Lawrence, Essex C 9
41 St. Lawrence, I.o.W. H 7
85 St. Leonards, Bucks. C 10
40 St. Leonards, Dorset F 3
43 St. Leonards, E. Sussex G 7
34 St. Levan G 1
56 St. Lythans G 4
35 St. Mabyn B 7
38 St. Margaret D 4
93 St. Margaret, South Elmham G 6
57 St. Margarets, Heref. & Worcs. A 7
86 St. Margarets, Hertfordshire C 4
43 St. Margaret's at Cliffe D 12
152 St. Margaret's Hope E 2
114 St. Mark's H 1
35 St. Martin D 9
140 St. Martins, Tayside D 6
94 St. Martin's, Salop G 2
34 St. Martin's Green G 4
40 St. Mary Bourne A 6
56 St. Mary Church G 3
86 St. Mary Cray G 5
43 St. Mary in the Marsh E 9
86 St. Marylebone F 3
152 St. Marys D 3
43 St. Mary's Bay E 9
57 St. Mary's Grove G 8
87 St. Mary's Hoo F 8
57 St. Maughans C 8
34 St. Mawes F 5
34 St. Mawgan C 6
35 St. Mellion C 11
56 St. Mellons F 6
34 St. Merryn B 6
35 St. Mewan E 7
35 St. Michael Caerhays E 7
34 St. Michael Penkevil E 6
93 St. Michael, South Elmham G 6
43 St. Michaels, Kent E 7
59 St. Michaels, Heref. & Worcs. F 11
110 St. Michaels on Wyre C 3
35 St. Minver B 7
141 St. Monans G 10
35 St. Neot C 9
91 St. Neots J 3
34 St. Newlyn East D 5
54 St. Nicholas, Dyfed C 2
56 St. Nicholas, S. Glam. G 4
43 St. Nicholas at Wade A 11
140 St. Ninians H 3
92 St. Olaves E 8
87 St. Osyth B 11
57 St. Owen's Cross B 8
86 St. Pancras F 3
86 St. Paul's Cray G 5
86 St. Paul's Walden B 2
43 St. Peters A 12
54 St. Petrox G 3
135 St. Quivox G 8
34 St. Stephen D 6
35 St. Stephens, Corn. A 10
35 St. Stephens, Corn. D 11
35 St. Teath B 7
35 St. Tudy B 8
54 St. Twynnells G 3
35 St. Veep D 8
141 St. Vigeans C 11
35 St. Wenn C 7
57 St. Weonards B 8
88 Saintbury H 5
139 Salachail B 8
37 Salcombe M 6
38 Salcombe Regis G 5
87 Salcott C 9
111 Sale H 7
88 Sale Green F 3
97 Saleby B 11
42 Salehurst F 6
58 Salem, Dyfed D 2
55 Salem, Dyfed D 9
60 Salem, Gwynedd E 5
138 Salen, Highland A 4
138 Salen, Mull, Strathclyde C 3
110 Salesbury D 5
89 Salford, Beds. H 12
111 Salford, Manchester G 7
84 Salford, Oxon. A 4
88 Salford Priors G 4
42 Salfords C 2
92 Salhouse D 6
140 Saline H 5
40 Salisbury C 3
92 Sall C 4
139 Sallachan A 7
143 Sallachy, Highland G 3
148 Sallachy, Highland F 6
97 Salmonby C 10
131 Salmond's Muir C 10
59 Salop, Co. B 10
84 Salperton B 2
91 Salph End K 2
136 Salsburgh C 1
95 Salt G 8
35 Saltash D 11
144 Saltburn C 3
117 Saltburn-by-the Sea C 7
96 Saltby H 6
135 Saltcoats E 7
111 Salterforth C 7
90 Salters Lode E 7
94 Satterswall D 5
97 Saltfleet A 11
97 Saltfleetby St. Clement A 11
97 Saltfleetby St. Peter A 11
97 Saltfleetby All Saints A 11
57 Saltford G 10
113 Salthaugh Grange E 10
92 Salthouse A 4
112 Saltmarshe E 6
94 Saltney D 3
117 Salton G 7
36 Saltren's D 3
133 Saltwick E 10
43 Saltwood D 10
41 Salvington F 12
88 Salwarpe F 2
39 Salway Ash F 8
88 Sambourne F 4
94 Sambrook H 6
110 Samlesbury D 5
110 Samlesbury Bottoms D 5
38 Sampford B 4
38 Sampford Arundel D 5
36 Sampford Courtenay F 5
38 Sampford Peverell E 4
37 Sampford Spinney H 4
87 Samuel's Corner E 9
137 Samuelston B 7
142 Sanachan F 2
139 Sanahole G 7
34 Sancreed G 1
113 Sancton C 7
152 Sand D 7
112 Sand Hutton A 5
114 Sand Side G 5
143 Sandaig, Highland J 1
143 Sandaig, Highland H 1
111 Sandal Magna E 12
114 Sandale A 5
94 Sandbach D 6
134 Sandbank A 6
40 Sandbanks G 2
146 Sandend A 3
86 Sanderstead H 3
57 Sandford, Avon H 7
115 Sandford, Cumbria D 9
36 Sandford, Devon F 7
40 Sandford, Dorset G 1
41 Sandford, I.o.W. H 7
94 Sandford, Salop H 2
135 Sandford, Strathclyde E 12
84 Sandford-on- Thames D 6
39 Sandford Orcas D 9
84 Sandford St. Martin B 5
146 Sandfordhill C 8
152 Sandgarth C 3
43 Sandgate E 10
146 Sandhaven A 7
130 Sandhead G 2
135 Sandhill H 9

86 South Ockendon . . . . . F 6
97 South Ormsby . . . . . . C 10
116 South Otterington . . . . F 4
97 South Owersby . . . . . . A 8
86 South Oxhey . . . . E 1
39 South Perrott . . . . F 8
39 South Petherton . . . . . D 8
35 South Petherwin . . . . B 10
92 South Pickenham . . . . E 1
37 South Pool . . . . M 6
36 South Radworthy . . . . C 6
97 South Rauceby . . . . F 7
92 South Raynham . . . . . C 2
97 South Reston . . . . B 11
90 South Runcton . . . . . . E 7
96 South Scarle . . . . D 6
151 South Shawbost . . . . . B 3
133 South Shields . . . . F 12
110 South Shore . . . . D 2
113 South Skirlaugh . . . . . C 9
97 South Somercotes . . . A 11
111 South Stainley . . . . A 1
86 South Stifford . . . . F 6
57 South Stoke, Avon . . H 10
85 South Stoke, Oxon. . . . F 7
41 South Stoke,
W. Sussex . . . . E 11
43 South Street, Kent . . . . B 9
86 South Street, London . H 4
42 South Street E. Sussex . F 3
36 South Tawton . . . . F 5
97 South Thoresby . . . . C 11
40 South Tidworth . . . . . A 4
41 South Town . . . . B 8
92 South Walsham . . . . . D 7
41 S. Warnborough . . . . . A 8
86 South Weald E6
85 South Weston . . . . D 8
37 South Wheatley, Corn. G 1
96 South Wheatley, Notts. B 5
39 South Widcombe A9
89 South Wigston . . . . B 9
97 South Willingham . . . . B 9
96 South Wingfield . . . . . E 1
96 South Witham . . . . . . H 6
40 South Wonston . . . . . . B 6
87 South Woodham
Ferrers . . . . D 6
90 South Wootton . . . . . . C 7
57 South Wraxall . . . . . H 11
112 South Yorkshire, Co. . G 2
36 South Zeal . . . . F 5
86 Southall F1
84 Southam, Glos B1
89 Southam, War . . . . F 7
40 Southampton . . . . E 5
42 Southborough . . . . E 5
40 Southbourne, Dorset . G 3
41 Southbourne,
W. Sussex . . . . E 9
92 Southburgh . . . . E 3
113 Southburn . . . . B 7
87 Southchurch . . . . E 9
36 Southcott, Devon . . . . D 3
84 Southcott, Wilts . . . . . H 3
132 Southdean . . . . B 5
42 Southease . . . . G 5
134 Southend, Strathclyde H 2
84 Southend, Wilts . . . . . G 3
87 Southend-on-Sea . . . . . E 8
56 Southerndown . . . . . . G 2
131 Southerness . . . . F 10
137 Southernknowe . . . . G 11
90 Southery . . . . F 7
117 Southfield . . . . G 7
42 Southfleet . . . . A 5
86 Southgate, London . . . E 3
90 Southgate, Norfolk . . . B 8
92 Southgate, Norfolk . . . C 4
55 Southgate, W. Glam . H 9
91 Southill . . . . L 3
38 Southleigh . . . . G 5
87 Southminister . . . . D 9
133 Southmoor . . . . B 10
91 Southoe . . . . J 3
93 Southolt . . . . H 5
90 Southorpe . . . . E 2
111 Southowram . . . . E 10
110 Southport . . . . E 2
92 Southrepps . . . . B 6
97 Southrey D8
84 Southrop . . . . D 3
41 Southrope . . . . D 8
41 Southsea . . . . F 8
152 Southtown . . . . E 3
86 Southwark . . . . E 3
41 Southwater . . . . D 12
39 Southway . . . . B 8
39 Southwell, Dorset . . . . H 7
96 Southwell, Notts . . . . . E 4
133 Southwick,
Tyne & Wear . . . . G 12
41 Southwick, Hants . . . . E 8
90 Southwick, Northants F 1
42 Southwick, W. Sussex G 1
39 Southwick, Wilts . . . . A 11
93 Southwold . . . . H 8
92 Southwood, Norf . . . . E 7
39 Southwood, Som. . . . . C 9
137 Soutra Mains . . . . C 7
151 Soval Lodge . . . . D 4
116 Sowerby, N. Yorks. . . G 4
111 Sowerby, W. Yorks. . . E 9
111 Sowerby Bridge . . . . . . E 9
114 Sowerby Row . . . . A 6
38 Sowton . . . . G 3
132 Spadeadam Farm . . . . . F 4
90 Spalding . . . . C 3
112 Spaldington . . . . D 5
91 Spaldwick . . . . H 2
141 Spalefield . . . . F 10
96 Spalford . . . . C 5
90 Spanby . . . . B 2
92 Sparham . . . . D 4
114 Spark Bridge . . . . G 5
39 Sparkford . . . . D 9
95 Sparklow . . . . D 9
37 Sparkwell . . . . K 4
95 Sparrowpit . . . . B 9
40 Sparsholt, Hants, ... C 6
84 Sparsholt, Oxon . . . . . E 4
133 Spartylea . . . . H 7
117 Spaunton . . . . F 7
38 Spaxton . . . . C 6
143 Spean Bridge . . . . L 6
40 Spearywell . . . . C 4
131 Speddoch . . . . C 9
84 Speen, Berks. . . . . G 5
85 Speen, Bucks. . . . . D 9
117 Speeton . . . . H 11
94 Speke . . . . B 3
42 Speldhurst . . . . D 4
86 Spellbrook . . . . B 5
84 Spelsbury . . . . B 4
56 Spelter . . . . E 2
85 Spencers Wood . . . . . . G 8
116 Spennithorne . . . . F 2
116 Spennymoor . . . . B 3
88 Spetchley . . . . G 2
39 Spetisbury . . . . F 12
93 Spexhall . . . . G 7
146 Spey Bay . . . . A 1
145 Spey Bridge . . . . J 4
145 Speybridge . . . . G 6
144 Speyview . . . . E 8
97 Spilsby . . . . D 11
133 Spindlestone . . . . D 11
96 Spinkhill . . . . B 2
89 Spinney Hills . . . . B 9
149 Spinningdale . . . . G 7
97 Spital in the Street . . . . A 7
133 Spitalford . . . . A 10
42 Spithursthurst . . . . F 3
137 Spittal, Dumf. & Gall. E 5
130 Spittal, Dumf. & Gall. F 4
54 Spittal, Dyfed . . . . E 3
149 Spittal, Highland . . . B 10
137 Spittal, Lothian . . . . . . B 7
137 Spittal, Northumb. . . D 12
112 Spittal, Humberside . . B 5
147 Spittal of Glenmuick . . J 1
145 Spittal of Glenshee . . . M 7
147 Spittalburn . . . . J 4
140 Spittalfield . . . . C 6
92 Spixworth . . . . D 5
35 Splatt . . . . A 9
42 Splayne's Green . . . . . . F 3
111 Spofforth . . . . B 12
61 Spon Green . . . . D 12
96 Spondon . . . . G 1
92 Spooner Row . . . . F 4
92 Sporle . . . . D 2
137 Spott . . . . B 9
137 Spottiswoode . . . . D 8
89 Spratton . . . . E 10
41 Spreakley . . . . B 9
36 Spreyton . . . . F 6
97 Spridlington . . . . B 7
114 Spring Valley . . . . H 2
135 Springburn . . . . C 10
151 Springcotrie . . . . D 3
132 Springfield,
Dumf. & Gall. . . . . . F 2
141 Springfield, Fife . . . . . . F 8
144 Springfield, Grampian D 6
88 Springfield,
W. Midlands . . . . . . D 4
88 Springhill . . . . B 3
131 Springholm . . . . E 9
132 Springkell . . . . E 1
135 Springside . . . . E 8
96 Springthorpe . . . . A 6
133 Springwell . . . . G 11
96 Springthorpe . . . . A 6
133 Springwell . . . . G 11
113 Sproatley . . . . D 9
94 Sproston Green . . . . . . C 6
112 Spotbrough . . . . G 3
93 Sproughton . . . . L 4
137 Sprouston . . . . F 10
92 Sprowston . . . . D 6
96 Sproxton, Leics. . . . . . H 6
116 Sproxton, N. Yorks . . G 6
94 Spurstow . . . . E 4
145 Sronlairig Lodge . . . . . . J 1
145 Sronpadruig . . . . L 3
111 Stackhouse . . . . A 7
54 Stackpole . . . . G 3
111 Stacksteads . . . . E 7
37 Staddiscombe . . . . K 4
112 Staddlethorpe . . . . E 6
85 Stadhampton . . . . D 7
115 Staffield . . . . A 8
150 Staffin . . . . A 4
95 Stafford . . . . H 8
95 Staffordshire, Co . . . . H 8
137 Stagehall . . . . E 7
90 Stag's Holt . . . . E 5
91 Stagsden . . . . K 1
91 Stagsden W. End . . . . . K 1
111 Stainburn . . . . B 11
96 Stainby . . . . H 6
111 Staincross . . . . F 12
85 Staines . . . . G 11
97 Stainfield, Lincs. . . . . . C 8
90 Stainfield, Lincs. . . . . . C 2
115 Stainforth, N. Yorks. H 10
112 Stainforth, S. Yorks. . . F 4
110 Staining . . . . D 2
111 Stainland . . . . E 9
117 Stainsacre . . . . D 9
116 Stainton, Cleveland . . D 5
115 Stainton, Cumb. . . . . . B 7
115 Stainton, Cumbria . . . G 7
116 Stainton, Dur . . . . C 1
116 Stainton, N. Yorks. . . . F 1
96 Stainton, S. Yorks. . . . A 3
97 Stainton by Langworth B 8
113 Stainton le Vale . . . . . H 9
114 Stainton with Adgarley H 5
117 Staintondale . . . . E 10
114 Stair, Cumb. . . . . C 5
135 Stair, Strathclyde . . . . G 9
117 Staithes . . . . C 8
110 Stake Pool . . . . B 3
133 Stakeford . . . . D 11
39 Stalbridge . . . . D 10
39 Stalbridge Weston . . . E 10
92 Stalham . . . . C 7
92 Stalham Green . . . . . . C 7
43 Stalisfield Green . . . . . C 8
115 Stalling Busk . . . . G 11
113 Stallingborough . . . . . . F 9
110 Stalmine . . . . C 3
111 Stalybridge . . . . G 8
91 Stambourne . . . . L 8
90 Stamford, Lincs . . . . . . E 1
133 Stamford,
Northumb. . . . . A 10
112 Stamford Bridge . . . . . B 5
133 Stamfordham . . . . F 9
114 Stanah . . . . C 6
86 Stanborough . . . . C 2
85 Stanbridge, Beds. . . . . B 10
40 Stanbridge, Dorset . . . F 2
111 Stanbury . . . . C 9
135 Stand . . . . C 12
136 Standburn . . . . B 2
88 Standeford . . . . A 3
43 Standen . . . . D 7
39 Standerwick . . . . A 11
41 Standford . . . . C 9
110 Standish . . . . F 4
84 Standlake . . . . D 5
40 Standon, Hants. . . . . . C 6
86 Standon, Herts . . . . B 4
94 Standon, Staffs. . . . . . . G 6
86 Standon Massey . . . . . D 6
93 Standwell Green . . . . . H 4
136 Stane . . . . C 2
92 Stanfield . . . . C 2
91 Stanford, Beds. . . . . . . L 3
43 Stanford, Kent . . . . . D 10
59 Stanford Bishop . . . . . G 12
88 Stanford Bridge . . . . . . F 1
84 Stanford Dingley . . . . G 6
87 Stanford le Hope . . . . . F 7
89 Stanford on Avon . . . . D 9
96 Stanford on Soar . . . . H 3
59 Stanford on Teme . . . F 12
86 Stanford Rivers . . . . . . D 5
84 Stanford the Vale . . . . E 4
42 Stanford's End . . . . . . D 3
90 Strangground . . . . F 3
92 Stanhoe . . . . B 1
115 Stanhope . . . . A 12
89 Stanion . . . . C 12
140 Stank . . . . F 1
96 Stanley, Derby . . . . F 1
133 Stanley, Dur. . . . . H 10
95 Stanley, Staffs. . . . . E 8
96 Stanley, Tayside . . . . . D 6
84 Stanley, Wilts . . . . G 1
111 Stanley, W. Yorks. . . E 12
96 Stanley Common . . . . . F 1
59 Stanley Hill . . . . H 12
42 Stanmer . . . . G 2
84 Stanmore, Berks. . . . . . F 6
40 Stanmore, Hants. . . . . C 6
86 Stanmore, London . . . E 2
132 Stannersburn . . . . D 5
133 Stannington,
Northumb. . . . . E 10
95 Stannington,
S. Yorks . . . . A 11
59 Stansbatch . . . . F 9
93 Stansfield . . . . K 1
95 Stanshope . . . . E 9
93 Stanstead . . . . K 1
86 Stanstead Abbots . . . . C 4
93 Stanstead Street . . . . . . K 1
42 Stansted . . . . B 5
86 Stansted Mountfitchet A 5
95 Stanton, Derby . . . . . H 11
84 Stanton, Glos . . . . A 2
56 Stanton, Gwent . . . . . . B 6
133 Stanton, Northumb. . . D 9
95 Stanton, Staffs. . . . . . . F 9
93 Stanton, Suffolk . . . . . H 3
95 Stanton by Bridge . . . G 12
57 Stanton by Dale . . . . . . F 2
57 Stanton Drew . . . . H 9
84 Stanton Fitzwarren . . . E 3
84 Stanton Harcourt . . . . D 5
96 Stanton Hill . . . . D 2
95 Stanton in Peak . . . . . D 11
59 Stanton Lacy . . . . E 10
59 Stanton Long . . . . . . C 11
96 Stanton on the Wolds . G 3
57 Stanton Prior . . . . . . H 10
84 Stanton St. Bernard . . H 2
85 Stanton St. John . . . . . C 7
57 Stanton St. Quintin . . F 12
93 Stanton Street . . . . J 3
89 Stanton under Bardon A 8
94 Stanton upon Hine
Heath . . . . H 4
57 Stanton Wick . . . . H 9
94 Stanwardine in the
Fields . . . . H 3
87 Stanway, Essex . . . . . . B 9
84 Stanway, Glos. . . . . . . A 2
85 Stanwell . . . . G 11
85 Stanwell Moor . . . . . . G 11
91 Stanwick . . . . H 1
117 Stape . . . . F 8
40 Stapehill . . . . F 2
94 Stapeley . . . . E 5
95 Stapenhill . . . . H 11
43 Staple, Kent . . . . B 11
38 Staple, Somerset . . . . . B 4
38 Staple Cross, Devon . . D 4
42 Staple Cross, E. Sussex F 6
38 Staple Fitzpaine . . . . . D 6
57 Staple Hill . . . . G 9
42 Staplefield . . . . E 2
91 Stapleford, Cambs. . . . K 6
86 Stapleford,
Heref. & Worc. B3
96 Stapleford, Leics. . . . H 5
96 Stapleford, Lincs . . . . D 6
96 Stapleford, Notts. . . . . F 2
40 Stapleford, Wilts. . . . B 2
86 Stapleford Abbotts . . . D 5
86 Stapleford Tawney . . . D 5
38 Staplegrove . . . . D 6
38 Staplehay . . . . D 6
42 Staplehurst . . . . D 6
40 Staplers . . . . G 6
132 Stapleton, Cumb. . . . . F 3
59 Stapleton,
Heref. & Worc. . . . . F 9
89 Stapleton, Leics. . . . . . B 8
116 Stapleton, N. Yorks. . D 3
59 Stapleton, Salop . . . . B 10
39 Stapleton, Som . . . . . . D 8
132 Stapleton Grange . . . . . F 1
38 Stapley . . . . E 5
91 Staploe . . . . J 2
54 Star, Dyfed . . . . C 6
141 Star, Fife . . . . G 8
57 Star, Somerset . . . . H 7
115 Starbottom . . . . H 11
38 Starcross . . . . H 3
152 Starkigarth . . . . E 7
91 Starlings Green . . . . . M 6
93 Starston . . . . G 5
115 Starforth . . . . D 12
57 Startley . . . . F 12
39 Stathe . . . . C 7
96 Stathern . . . . G 5
116 Station Town . . . . B 4
91 Staughton Green . . . . . J 2
91 Staughton Highway . . . J 2
57 Staunton, Glos. . . . . . . C 9
57 Staunton, Glos. . . . . . A 11
95 Staunton Harold Hall H 12
96 Staunton in the Vale . . F 5
59 Staunton on Arrow . . . F 9
59 Staunton on Wye . . . . H 9
114 Staveley, Cumbria . . . G 6
115 Staveley, Cumbria . . . . E 7
96 Stavely, Derby . . . . C 2
111 Staveley, N. Yorks. . A 12
37 Staverton, Devon . . . . . J 7
57 Staverton, Glos. . . . . B 12
89 Staverton, Northants. . F 9
57 Staverton, Wilts . . . H 11
57 Staverton Bridge . . . . B 12
39 Stawell . . . . B 7
37 Stawford . . . . G 3
38 Stawley . . . . D 4
149 Staxigoe . . . . B 12
117 Staxton . . . . G 10
58 Staylittle . . . . C 4
110 Staynall . . . . C 2
96 Staythorpe . . . . E 5
116 Stean . . . . H 1
116 Stearsby . . . . H 6
38 Steart . . . . B 6
86 Stebbing . . . . B 6
152 Stebbligrind . . . . D 7
41 Stedham . . . . D 10
133 Steel Rigg . . . . E 8
132 Steele Road . . . . D 4
59 Steen's Bridge . . . . . . G 11
41 Steep . . . . D 9
39 Steeple, Dorset . . . . . H 12
87 Steeple, Essex . . . . D 9
39 Steeple Ashton . . . . . A 12
84 Steeple Aston . . . . B 6
84 Steeple Barton . . . . B 5
91 Steeple Bumpstead . . . L 8
85 Steeple Claydon . . . . . A 8
91 Steeple Gidding . . . . . . G 2
40 Steeple Langford . . . . . B 2
91 Steeple Morden . . . . . . L 4
111 Steeton . . . . C 9
150 Stein . . . . C 2
146 Steinmanhill . . . . C 5
133 Stelling Hall . . . . F 8
43 Stelling Minnis . . . . . C 10
35 Stenalees . . . . D 7
136 Stenhousemuir . . . . . . A 2
152 Stenness . . . . C 6
150 Stenscholl . . . . A 4
95 Stenson . . . . G 11
152 Stenswall . . . . D 7
137 Stenton . . . . B 9
54 Stepaside . . . . F 5
131 Stepends . . . . C 9
86 Stepney . . . . F 4
91 Steppingley . . . . M 1
135 Stepps . . . . C 11
93 Sternfield . . . . J 7
84 Stert . . . . H 1
91 Stetchworth . . . . J 7
86 Stevenage . . . . B 2
135 Stevenston . . . . E 7
41 Steventon, Hants. . . . . A 7
84 Steventon, Oxon. . . . . E 5
91 Stevington . . . . K 1
91 Stewarby . . . . L 1
134 Stewarton, Strathclyde G 2
135 Stewarton, Strathclyde E 9
85 Stewkley . . . . B 9
97 Stewton . . . . B 10
54 Steynton . . . . F 4
36 Stibb . . . . E 1
36 Stibb Cross . . . . D 3
84 Stibb Green . . . . H 3
92 Stibbard . . . . C 3
90 Stibbington . . . . F 2
137 Stichill . . . . F 9
35 Sticker . . . . E 7
97 Stickford . . . . D 10
36 Sticklepath, Devon . . . F 5
38 Sticklepath, Som. . . . . E 6
97 Stickney . . . . D 10
92 Stiffkey . . . . A 3
86 Stifford . . . . F 6
88 Stifford's Bridge . . . . . G 1
42 Stile Bridge . . . . C 6
112 Stillingfleet . . . . C 4
116 Stillington, Cleveland . C 4
116 Stillington, N. Yorks. H 6
90 Stilton . . . . F 3
57 Stinchcombe . . . . D 10
39 Stinsford . . . . G 10
59 Stirchley . . . . B 12
149 Stirkoke House . . . . . C 12
140 Stirling, Central . . . . . H 3
114 Stirling, Grampian . . . C 8
87 Stisted . . . . A 8
84 Stitchcombe . . . . G 3
34 Stithians . . . . F 4
144 Stittenham . . . . B 2
89 Stivichall . . . . D 7
97 Stixwould . . . . D 9
136 Stobo . . . . F 4
39 Stoborough . . . . H 12
39 Stoborough Grn. . . . H 12
132 Stobs Castle B3
137 Stobswood, Borders . . D 9
133 Stobswood,
Northumb. . . . . D 10
136 Stobwood . . . . D 2
87 Stock . . . . D 7
88 Stock Wood . . . . F 3
146 Stockbridge,
Grampian . . . . C 8
40 Stockbridge, Hants. . . C 5
131 Stockbridgehill . . . . . D 12
135 Stockbriggs . . . . F 12
43 Stockbury . . . . B 7
84 Stockcross . . . . G 5
114 Stockdale Wath . . . . . . A 6
89 Stockerston . . . . B 11
41 Stockholm . . . . B 11
135 Stockiemuir . . . . A 10
86 Stocking Pelham . . . . . A 4
89 Stockingford . . . . C 7
38 Stockland . . . . F 6
38 Stockland Bristol . . . . . B 6
36 Stockleigh English . . . . E 7
36 Stockleigh Pomeroy . . F 7
84 Stockley . . . . G 1
39 Stocklinch . . . . E 7
95 Stockport . . . . A 7
111 Stocksbridge . . . . G 11
133 Stocksfield . . . . G 9
59 Stockton,
Heref. & Worcs. . . F 10
92 Stockton, Norfolk . . . . F 7
59 Stockton, Salop . . . . . . B 8
88 Stockton, Salop . . . . . . B 1
89 Stockton, War. . . . . . . F 8
40 Stockton, Wilts. . . . . . B 1
94 Stockton Heath . . . . . . B 5
116 Stocktonon-Tees . . . . C 4
88 Stockton on Teme . . . . E 1
112 Stockton-on-the-
Forest . . . . B 4
43 Stodmarsh . . . . B 11
92 Stody . . . . B 4
148 Stoer . . . . D 2
39 Stoford, Som. . . . . E 9
40 Stoford, Wilts. . . . . C 2
38 Stogumber . . . . C 4
38 Stogursey . . . . B 5
36 Stoke, Devon . . . . D 1
40 Stoke, Hants. . . . . A 5
41 Stoke, Hants . . . . F 8
43 Stoke, Kent . . . . A 7
93 Stoke, Suffolk . . . . L 5
39 Stoke Abbott . . . . F 8
89 Stoke Albany . . . . C 11
93 Stoke Ash . . . . H 4
96 Stoke Bardolph . . . . . . F 4
59 Stoke Bliss . . . . F 12
89 Stoke Bruerne . . . . . . G 10
91 Stoke-by-Clare . . . . . . L 8
93 Stoke-by-Nayland . . . . L 3
38 Stoke Canon . . . . F 3
40 Stoke Charity . . . . B 6
40 Stoke Climsland . . . . B 10
59 Stoke Cross . . . . G 11
85 Stoke D'Abernon . . . H 12
91 Stoke Doyle . . . . G 1
89 Stoke Dry . . . . B 12
59 Stoke Edith . . . . H 11
40 Stoke Farthing . . . . . . D 2
90 Stoke Ferry . . . . E 8
37 Stoke Fleming . . . . L 7
37 Stoke Gabriel . . . . K 7
57 Stoke Gifford . . . . F 9
89 Stoke Golding . . . . B 7
89 Stoke Goldington . . . G 11
85 Stoke Green . . . . F 10
85 Stoke Hammond . . . . . A 9

86 Takeley Street B 5
56 Talachddu A 4
61 Talacre B 10
38 Talaton F 4
54 Talbenny F 2
56 Talbot Green F 4
40 Talbot Village G 2
58 Talerddig B 5
55 Talgarreg B 7
56 Talgarth A 5
58 Taliesin C 2
150 Talisker E 3
95 Talke E 7
132 Talkin G 4
136 Talla Linnfoots G 4
142 Talladale C 3
114 Tallantire B 3
61 Tallard G 8
94 Tallarn Green F 3
55 Talley D 9
90 Tallington E 2
148 Talmine B 6
55 Talog D 7
58 Talsarn, Dyfed G 1
56 Talsarn, Dyfed B1
60 Talsarnau G 5
34 Talskiddy C 6
60 Talwrn, Gwynedd C 4
61 Talwrn, Clwyd E 12
58 Talybont, Dyfed C 2
60 Tal-y-bont, Gwynedd H 5
60 Tal-y-bont,Gwynedd C 5
61 Tal-y-bont, Gwynedd C 7
56 Talybont, Powys B 4
61 Tal-y-cafn C 7
57 Tal-y-coed C 7
56 Tal-y-garn F 4
58 Tal-y-sn, Gwynedd A 3
56 Tal-y-llyn, Powys B 4
86 Tal-y-sarn E 4
56 Talywain D 6
58 Tal-y-wern B 4
116 Tame D 5
37 Tamerton Foliot K 3
110 Tameside G 8
88 Tamworth B 5
115 Tan Hill E 11
54 Tancredston D 2
43 Tanden D 8
135 Tandlemuir C 8
42 Tandridge C 3
133 Tanfield G 10
133 Tanfield Lea H 10
40 Tangley A 5
41 Tangmere E 10
152 Tankerness D 3
111 Tankersley G 12
60 Tan-lan F 5
149 Tannach C 12
147 Tannachie J 5
147 Tannadice L 2
93 Tannington H 5
95 Tansley D 11
95 Tansley Knoll D 11
90 Tansor F 2
133 Tantobie H 10
116 Tanton D 5
116 Tanworth in Arden E 5
60 Tan-y-bwlch F 6
61 Tan-y-fron D 9
58 Tan-y-graig, Dyfed E 3
60 Tan-y-graig, Gwynedd F 3
60 Tan-y-grisiau F 6
55 Tan-y-groes B 6
61 Tan-y-pistyll G 10
85 Taplow F 10
134 Tarbert, Strathclyde A 1
134 Tarbert, Strathclyde C 4
151 Tarbert, W. Isles G 2
143 Tarbet, Highland K 2
148 Tarbet, Highland C 3
139 Tarbet, Strathclyde G 10
135 Tarbolton G 9
135 Tarbrax D 3
94 Tarbuck Green A 3
132 Tarcoon E 2
88 Tardebigge E 3
147 Tarfside J 2
147 Tarland G 2
110 Tarleton E 3
110 Tarlscough F 3
57 Tarlton D 12
110 Tarnbrook B 5
94 Tarporley D 4
38 Tarr C 4
40 Tarrant Crawford F 1
40 Tarrant Gunville E 1
40 Tarrant Hinton E 1
40 Tarrant Keyneston F 1
40 Tarrant Launceston E 1
40 Tarrant Monkton E 1
40 Tarrant Rawston E 1
40 Tarrant Rushton E 1
149 Tarrel H 9
42 Tarring Neville H 3
59 Tarrington H 11
150 Tarskavaig G 5
146 Tarves D 6
142 Tarvie D 8
94 Tarvin D 4
92 Tasburgh F 5
59 Tasley C 12
84 Taston B 5
95 Tatenhill H 10
131 Tath Hill B 11
115 Tatham H 8
97 Tathwell B 10
85 Tatling End E 11
42 Tatsfield B 3
94 Tattenhall D 3
92 Tatterford C 2
92 Tattersett C 1
97 Tattershall D 9
97 Tattershall Bridge E 9
97 Tattershall Thorpe D 9
93 Tattingstone L 4
93 Tattingstone Whitehorse L 4
38 Tatworth F 6
146 Tauchers C 1
38 Taunton D 6
92 Taverham D 5
54 Tavernspite F 5
37 Tavistock H 3
36 Taw Green, Devon E 5
36 Taw Green, Devon F 5
36 Tawstock C 4
95 Taxal B 8
135 Tayburn E 10
139 Taychreggan E 7
134 Tayinloan E 2
140 Taymouth Castle C 3
139 Taynafead F 8
57 Taynton, Glos. B 10
84 Taynton, Oxon C 3
139 Taynuilt D 7
141 Tayport D 9
134 Tayvallich A 2
97 Tealby A 8
150 Teangue G 6
115 Tebay E 8
85 Tebworth A 10
36 Tedburn St. Mary F 7
84 Teddington, Glos. A 1
86 Teddington, London G 2
59 Tedstone Delamere F 12
59 Tedstone Wafre F 12
89 Teeton E 10
40 Teffont Evias C 1
40 Teffont Magna C 2
54 Tegryn D 6
89 Teigh A 12
37 Teigngrace H 7
37 Teignmouth H 8
144 Teindland D 8
132 Teindside B 3
59 Telford B 12
42 Telham G 6
39 Tellisford A 11
42 Telscombe H 3
131 Templand C 11
35 Temple, Cornwall B 8
55 Temple Bar, Dyfed B 8
55 Temple Bar, Dyfed E 9
136 Temple, Lothian D 6
88 Temple Ballsall E 5
39 Temple Cloud A 9
43 Temple Ewell D 11
88 Temple Grafton G 5
84 Temple Guiting A 2
112 Temple Hirst E 4
96 Temple Normanton C 1
115 Temple Sowerby C 8
39 Templecombe D 10
141 Templehall H 7
38 Templeton, Devon E 2
54 Templeton, Dyfed F 4
36 Tempelton Bridge E 7
91 Tempsford K 3
90 Ten Mile Bank F 7
59 Tenbury Wells F 11
54 Tenby G 5
87 Tendring B 11
87 Tendring Green A 11
152 Tenston C 1
43 Tenterden E 7
130 Terally G 2
87 Terling B 7
94 Ternhill G 5
34 Terras D 6
131 Terregles D 10
85 Terrick C 9
117 Terrington H 7
90 Terrington St. Clement D 6
90 Terrington St. John D 6
42 Teston C 6
40 Testwood E 5
57 Tetbury E 12
57 Tetbury Upton E 12
94 Tetchill G 3
36 Tetcott F 2
97 Tetford C 10
113 Tetney G 10
113 Tetney Lock G 11
85 Tetsworth D 8
88 Tettenhall B 2
146 Teuchan D 8
146 Teuchar C 5
141 Teuchatcroft B 9
96 Teversal D 2
91 Teversham J 6
132 Teviothead C 2
147 Tewel J 6
86 Tewin B 3
57 Tewkesbury A 12
43 Teynham B 8
43 Teynham Street B 8
111 Thackley C 10
114 Thackthwaite, Cumb. C 4
114 Thackthwaite, Cumb. C 6
41 Thakeham D 12
85 Thame D 8
85 Thames Ditton G 12
43 Thanington B 10
136 Thankerton F 2
92 Tharston F 5
84 Thatcham G 6
110 Thatto Heath H 4
91 Thaxted M 7
150 The Aird C 3
59 The Bage H 8
131 The Barony, Dumf. & Gall. C 11
152 The Barony, Orkney B 1
95 The Blythe G 9
150 The Braes E 4
59 The Broad F 10
56 The Bryn D 6
57 The Camp C 12
85 The City D 8
57 The Cleaver A 8
40 The Common C 4
59 The Corner D 10
148 The Craigs G 5
114 The Cronk F 2
135 The Den D 8
90 The Engine E 4
132 The Fauld F 2
132 The Flatt E 4
43 The Forstal C 7
114 The Green, Cumbria G 4
39 The Green, Wilts C 12
131 The Grove D 10
137 The Hardens D 10
41 The Haven C 12
93 The Heath L 2
42 The Hermitage C 1
134 The Highland Hotel A 5
114 The Hill G 4
114 The Howe H 1
87 The Hythe B 10
131 The Lake G 7
43 The Leacon E 8
85 The Lee D 10
114 The Lhen F 2
59 The Marsh C 8
133 The Middles H 10
42 The Moor E 6
149 The Mound G 8
135 The Murray D 11
152 The Ness A 8
147 The Neuk H 5
57 The Oval H 10
57 The Pill F 8
146 The Pole of Itlaw B 4
59 The Pound E 7
57 The Quarry D 10
54 The Rhos F 4
41 The Sands B 10
132 The Scare F 3
84 The Slade G 6
43 The Stocks E 8
87 The Stone C 9
85 The Throat G 9
34 The Towans F 3
59 The Vauld G 10
88 The Wyke B 1
116 Theakston G 3
113 Thealby E 7
85 Theale, Berks. G 7
39 Theale, Somerset B 8
85 Theale Green G 7
113 Thearne C 8
93 Theberton J 7
89 Theddingworth D 10
97 Theddlethorpe All Saints A 11
97 Theddlethorpe St. Helen A 11
36 Thelbridge Cross E 7
93 Thelnetham G 3
94 Thelwall B 5
92 Themelthorpe C 4
89 Thenford H 8
91 Therfield L 4
93 Thetford G 2
86 Theydon Bois D 4
57 Thickwood G 11
97 Thimbleby, Lincs. C 9
116 Thimbleby, N. Yorks. F 5
61 Thingwall B 11
116 Thirkleby G 5
116 Thirlby G 5
137 Thirlestane E 8
114 Thirlspot C 5
116 Thirn G 2
116 Thirsk G 4
113 Thirtleby D 9
114 Thistlebottom A 5
110 Thistleton, Lancs. C 3
96 Thistleton,Leics. H 6
91 Thistley Green H 8
112 Thixendale A 6
133 Thockrington E 8
90 Tholomas Drove E 5
116 Tholthorpe H 5
54 Thomas Chapel F 4
115 Thomas Close A 7
146 Thomastown D 3
92 Thompson F 2
144 Thomshill D 8
42 Thong A 5
115 Thoralby F 12
96 Thoresby C 4
113 Thoresway G 9
113 Thorganby, Lincs. G 9
112 Thorganby, N. Yorks. C 5
117 Thorgill E 7
93 Thorington H 7
93 Thorington Street L 3
111 Thorlby B 8
86 Thorley, Herts. B 5
40 Thorley, I.o.W. G 5
86 Thorley Street, Herts. B 5
40 Thorley Street, I.o.W. G 5
116 Thormanby H 5
43 Thorn F 7
116 Thornaby-on-Tees C 5
92 Thornage B 4
85 Thornborough, Bucks. A 8
116 Thornborough, N. Yorks. G 3
57 Thornbury, Avon E 9
36 Thornbury, Devon E 3
59 Thornbury, Heref. & Worc. F 11
89 Thornby E 10
95 Thorncliff D 8
39 Thorncombe F 7
41 Thorncombe Street B 11
91 Thorncote Green K 3
40 Thorncross H 6
93 Thorndon H 4
36 Thorndon Cross F 4
38 Thorne, Somerset D 4
112 Thorne, S. Yorks. F 5
111 Thorner C 12
90 Thorney, Cambs. E 4
96 Thorney, Notts. C 6
39 Thorney, Somerset D 7
113 Thorney Crofts E 9
40 Thorney Hill F 4
146 Thorneybank D 4
38 Thornfalcon D 6
39 Thornford E 9
132 Thorngrafton F 6
39 Thorngrove C 7
113 Thorngumbald D 9
90 Thornham A 8
93 Thornham Magna H 4
93 Thornham Parva H 4
90 Thornhaugh E 2
140 Thornhill, Central G 2
114 Thornhill, Cumb. D 3
95 Thornhill, Dumf. & Gall. B 9
40 Thornhill, Hants. E 6
56 Thornhill, Mid Glam. F 5
111 Thornhill, W. Yorks. E 11
113 Thornholme A 9
137 Thornielaw F 8
137 Thornington F 11
116 Thornley, Dur. A 4
116 Thornley, Dur. B 1
135 Thornliebank D 10
91 Thorns K 8
111 Thornseat H 11
95 Thornsett B 8
114 Thornthwaite, Cumb. C 5
111 Thornthwaite, N. Yorks. A 10
85 Thornton, Bucks. A 8
116 Thornton, Cleveland D 5
54 Thornton, Dyfed F 2
141 Thornton, Fife G 7
112 Thornton, Humber. C 5
110 Thornton, Lancs. C 2
89 Thornton, Leics. A 8
97 Thornton, Lincs. C 9
110 Thornton, Merseyside G 2
137 Thornton, Northumb. E 12
141 Thornton, Tayside C 9
111 Thornton, W. Yorks. D 9
113 Thornton Curtis E 8
86 Thornton Heath G 3
94 Thornton Hough B 2
111 Thornton in Craven B 8
115 Thornton in Lonsdale H 9
116 Thornton-le-Beans F 4
112 Thornton-le-Clay A 5
117 Thornton-le-Dale G 8
113 Thornton le Moor, Lincolnshire G 8
116 Thornton-le-Moor, N. Yorks. F 4
94 Thornton-le-Moors C 3
116 Thornton-le-Street G 4
135 Thornton Mains E 12
112 Thornton Moor A 4
115 Thornton Rust F 12
116 Thornton Steward F 2
116 Thornton Watlass G 3
135 Thorntonhall D 10
137 Thorntonloch B 10
137 Thorntonpark E 12
86 Thornwood Com C 5
137 Thorndykes E 9
114 Thornythwaite C 6
96 Thoroton F 5
112 Thorp Arch C 2
93 Thorp Green K 2
95 Thorpe, Derby E 10
113 Thorpe, Humberside B 7
97 Thorpe, Lincs B 12
92 Thorpe, Norf. F 7
111 Thorpe, N. Yorks. A 9
96 Thorpe, Notts. E 5
85 Thorpe, Surrey G 11
93 Thorpe Abbotts G 5
96 Thorpe Acre H 2
112 Thorpe Arch B 2
96 Thorpe Arnold H 5
112 Thorpe Audlin F 3
117 Thorpe Bassett H 8
87 Thorpe Bay E 9
89 Thorpe by Water C 12
88 Thorpe Constantine A 6
92 Thorpe End Garden Village D 6
111 Thorpe Hesley G 12
112 Thorpe in Balne F 4
96 Thorpe in the Fallows B 6
89 Thorpe Langton C 10
116 Thorpe Larches C 4
87 Thorpe-le-Soken B 11
112 Thorpe le Street C 6
89 Thorpe Malsor D 11
89 Thorpe Mandeville H 9
92 Thorpe Market B 5
93 Thorpe Morieux K 2
96 Thorpe on the Hill D 6
92 Thorpe St. Andrew D 6
97 Thorpe St. Peter D 11
96 Thorpe Salvin B 2
89 Thorpe Satchville A 10
116 Thorpe Thewles C 4
112 Thorpe Underwood A 3
91 Thorpe Waterville G 1
92 Thorpe Willoughby D 3
93 Thorpeness J 8
87 Thorrington B 10
39 Thorverton F 3
93 Thrandeston H 4
91 Thrapston G 1
114 Threapland A 4
94 Threapwood F 3
130 Threave A 4
42 Three Bridges D 2
34 Three Burrows E 4
43 Three Chimneys D 7
56 Three Cocks A 5
55 Three Crosses H 9
42 Three Cups Corner, F 5
116 Three Gates, Cleveland B 5
39 Three Gates, Dorset E 9
90 Three Holes E 6
40 Three Legged Cross E 3
43 Three Oaks G 7
137 Threeburnford D 7
90 Threekingham B 2
42 Threelag Cross E 6
95 Threelows E 9
85 Threemile Cross G 8
34 Threemilestone E 5
137 Threepwood E 8
114 Threlkeld C 6
111 Threshfield A 8
92 Thrigby D 7
115 Thringarth C 11
96 Thringstone H 2
116 Thrintoft F 3
91 Thriplow K 5
90 Throckenholt E 5
91 Throcking M 4
133 Throckley F 9
88 Throckmorton G 3
133 Throphill D 9
133 Thropton C 8
131 Throughgate C 9
37 Throwleigh G 5
43 Throwley C 8
43 Throwley Forstal C 8
96 Thrumpton G 2
149 Thrumster C 12
113 Thrunscoe F 10
133 Thrunton B 9
39 Thrupe B 9
57 Thrupp, Glos. D 11
84 Thrupp, Oxon C 6
37 Thrushelton G 3
86 Thrushesbush C 5
89 Tsington A 10
40 Thruxton, Hants. B 4
57 Thruxton, Heref. & Worc. A 7
112 Thrybergh H 3
89 Thurcaston A 9
96 Thurcroft A 2
36 Thurdon E 2
92 Thurgarton, Norf. B 5
96 Thurgarton, Notts. E 4
111 Thurgoland G 11
89 Thurlaston, Leics. B 8
89 Thurlaston, War. E 8
38 Thurlbear D 6
90 Thurlby, Lincs. D 2
96 Thurlby, Lincs. D 6
91 Thurleigh J 2
37 Thurlestone L 5
38 Thurloxton C 6
96 Thurlston G 1
111 Thurlstone G 11
92 Thurlton F 7
89 Thurmaston A 9
89 Thurnby B 10
92 Thurne D 7
43 Thurnham, Kent B 7
110 Thurnham, Lancs. B 3
92 Thurning, Norf. C 4
91 Thurning, Northants. G 2
112 Thurnscoe G 2
132 Thursby H 2
92 Thursford Green B 3
41 Thursley B 10
149 Thurso A 10
149 Thurso East A 10
94 Thurstaston B 1
93 Thurston J 2
132 Thurstonfield G 2
111 Thurstonland F 10
92 Thurton E 6
95 Thurvaston F 11
92 Thuxton E 3
93 Thwaite, Suffolk H 4
115 Thwaite, N. Yorks. E 11
92 Thwaite St. Mary F 6
117 Thwing H 10
140 Tibbermore E 5
131 Tibbers B 9
57 Tibberton, Glos. B 10
88 Tibberton, Heref. & Worc. F 3
94 Tibberton, Salop H 5
92 Tibenham F 4
96 Tibshelf D 2
113 Tibthorpe B 7
42 Ticehurst E 6

41 Tichborne C 7
41 Tichfield F 7
90 Tickencote E 1
57 Tickenham G 8
96 Tickhill A 3
59 Ticklerton C 10
95 Ticknall H 12
113 Tickton C 8
88 Tidbury Green E 4
84 Tidcombe H 4
85 Tiddington, Oxon D 7
88 Tidington, War. F 6
42 Tidebrook E 5
35 Tideford D 10
35 Tideford Cross D 10
57 Tidenham E 9
95 Tideswell C 10
85 Tidmarsh G 7
88 Tidmington H 6
40 Tidpit D 2
54 Tiers Cross F 3
89 Tiffield G 10
146 Tifty D 5
147 Tigerton L 3
142 Tighchuig F 8
140 Tighnablair E 3
134 Tighnabruaich B 5
139 Tigh-na-criche G 8
148 Tighnafiline G 1
37 Tigley K 6
91 Tilbrook H 2
86 Tilbury F 6
85 Tilehurst G 7
41 Tilford B 10
42 Tilgale E 2
146 Tillathrowie D 2
94 Tilley G 4
140 Tillicoultry G 4
87 Tillingham D 10
59 Tillington, Heref. & Worc. H 10
41 Tillington, W. Sussex D 11
59 Tillington Com H 10
147 Tillyarblet L 3
147 Tillybardine K 2
146 Tillycorthie E 7
147 Tillydrine House H 4
146 Tillyfar E 7
146 Tillyfourie F 4
146 Tillygreig E 6
146 Tillyminnate D 2
43 Tilmanstone C 11
96 Tiln B 4
90 Tilney All Saints D 7
90 Tilney High End D 7
90 Tilney St. Lawrence D 7
40 Tilshead A 2
94 Tilstock F 4
94 Tilston E 3
94 Tilstone Fearnall D 4
85 Tilsworth B 10
89 Tilton on the Hill B 10
57 Tiltups End E 11
97 Timberland D 8
95 Timbersbrook D 7
38 Timberscombe B 3
111 Timble B 10
137 Timpendean G 9
94 Timperley A 6
57 Timsbury, Avon H 10
40 Timsbury, Hants. D 5
151 Timsgarry D 2
93 Timworth Green H 2
39 Tincleton G 11
132 Tindale G 4
85 Tingewick A 7
111 Tingley D 11
91 Tingrith M 1
37 Tinhay G 3
136 Tinnis F 6
111 Tinshill C 11
35 Tintagel A 7
57 Tintern Parva D 8
39 Tintinhull D 8
111 Tintwistle G 9
131 Tinwald C 11
90 Tinwell E 1
36 Tippacott A 6
146 Tipperty, Grampian E 7
146 Tipperty, Grampian B 4
90 Tipp's End F 6
40 Tiptoe F 4
88 Tipton C 3
38 Tipton St. John G 4
87 Tiptree B 9
58 Tarabad H 4
138 Tirghoil E 1
57 Tirley A 11
56 Tirphil D 4
115 Tirril C 7
148 Tirryside F 6
40 Tisbury C 1
41 Tisman's Com C 12
95 Tissington E 10
36 Titchberry C 1
91 Titchmarsh G 1
92 Titchwell A 1
96 Tithby F 4
133 Titlington B 9
59 Titley F 9
42 Titsey C 3
95 Tittensor F 7
92 Tittleshall C 2
57 Tittups End E 11
94 Tiverton, Ches. D 4
38 Tiverton, Devon E 3
38 Tiverton Junction E 4
93 Tivetshall St. Margaret G 4
93 Tivetshall St. Mary G 4
88 Tividale C 3
38 Tivington B 3
88 Tixall H 8
90 Tixover E 1
152 Toab D 3
95 Toadmoor E 12
138 Tobermory B 2
138 Toberonochy G 5
151 Tobson C 2
146 Tocher D 4
84 Tockenham F 2
84 Tockenham Wick F 1
110 Tockholes E 5
57 Tockington F 9
112 Tockwith B 3
39 Todber D 11
85 Toddington, Beds. A 11
84 Toddington, Glos. A 1
88 Todenham H 6
141 Todhall E 8
132 Todhills G 2
111 Todmorden E 8
137 Todrig G 7
96 Todwick B 2
89 Toft, Cambs. K 5
90 Toft, Lincs. D 2
116 Toft Hill B 2
92 Toft Monks F 7
97 Toft Next Newton A 7
137 Toftbarns G 8
92 Toftrees C 2
149 Tofts A 12
92 Toftwood Com D 3
133 Togston C 10
143 Toigal K 1
150 Tokavaig G 5
85 Tokers Green F 8
112 Toll Bar F 3
88 Toll End C 3
146 Toll of Birness D 7
38 Tolland C 4
40 Tollard Royal D 1
39 Toller Fratrum F 9
39 Toller Porcorum F 9
96 Tollerton, Notts. G 3
112 Tollerton, N. Yorks. A 3
87 Tollesbury C 9
87 Tolleshunt D'Arcy C 9
87 Tolleshunt Major C 9
144 Tollie D 1
151 Tolmachan F 2
39 Tolpuddle G 11
151 Tolstachaolais C 3
145 Tolvah J 4
42 Tolworth B 1
145 Tomatin G 4
145 Tombain J 4
144 Tombreck F 2
143 Tomchrasky H 6
143 Tomdoun J 5
144 Tomich, Highland E 1
143 Tomich, Highland G 7
144 Tomich, Highland C 3
148 Tomich, Highland F 6
145 Tomintoul, Grampian K 7
145 Tomintoul, Grampian H 7
145 Tomintoul, Highland G 2
146 Tomnaven D 2
145 Tomnavoulin G 8
140 Tomphibil B 3
132 Tomshielburn E 2
56 Ton D 6
56 Ton-Pentre E 3
42 Tonbridge C 5
56 Tondu F 2
58 Ton-fanau B 1
151 Tong, W. Isles C 5
88 Tong, Salop A 2
111 Tong, W. Yorks. D 10
111 Tong Street D 10
96 Tonge H 2
41 Tongham A 10
131 Tongland F 8
148 Tongue B 6
148 Tongue House B 6
56 Tongwynlais F 5
55 Tonna G 11
56 Ton-teg F 4
86 Tonwell B 3
56 Tonypandy E 3
56 Tonyrefail E 3
84 Toot Baldon D 6
86 Toothill D 5
111 Top of Hebers F 7
116 Topcliffe H 4
92 Topcroft F 6
92 Topcroft Street F 5
91 Toppesfield L 8
110 Toppings F 6
38 Topsham G 3
145 Torbain H 7
134 Torbeg, Arran I. F 4
147 Torbeg, Grampian G 1
149 Torboll G 7
144 Torbreck F 3
37 Torbryan J 7
143 Torcastle L 5
37 Torcross L 7
145 Torcroy J 3
143 Torcuileainn J 2
144 Tore D 2
143 Torgyle Bridge H 7
134 Torinturk C 3
96 Torksey B 5
143 Torlundy M 5
57 Tormarton F 11
130 Tormitchell B 3
134 Tormore F 4
144 Tornagrain E 3
145 Tornahaish J 8
147 Tornaveen G 4
145 Torness G 1
116 Toronto B 2
114 Torpenhow A 4
136 Torphichen B 2
147 Torphins G 4
35 Torpoint D 11
37 Torquay J 8
137 Torquhan E 7
150 Torran C 5
135 Torrance B 11
138 Torraneidhinn B 3
138 Torrans E 2
135 Torranyard E 8
37 Torre, Devon J 8
38 Torre, Somerset B 4
142 Torridon D 3
142 Torridon House D 2
150 Torrin F 5
149 Torrisdale B 7
110 Torrisholme A 3
143 Torrlaoighseach H 3
148 Torrobole F 6
146 Torry, Grampian D 2
147 Torry, Grampian G 7
136 Torryburn A 3
146 Torterston C 8
131 Torthorwald D 11
41 Tortington F 11
150 Torvaig D 4
114 Torver F 5
136 Torwood A 1
96 Torworth B 4
36 Tosberry D 1
142 Toscaig F 1
91 Toseland J 3
110 Tosside B 6
138 Tostarie C 1
93 Tostock J 3
150 Totaig, Highland C 1
143 Totaig, Highland G 2
150 Totardor D 3
150 Tote C 3
149 Totegan A 8
40 Totland G 5
95 Totley B 11
39 Totnell E 9
37 Totnes K 7
150 Totscore B 3
86 Tottenham E 3
90 Tottenhill D 7
86 Totteridge E 2
85 Totternhoe B 10
110 Tottington F 6
40 Totton E 5
85 Touchen-end F 9
38 Toulton C 5
144 Toulvaddie B 4
142 Tournaig B 2
146 Toux C 7
116 Tow Law A 1
134 Toward C 6
134 Toward Quay C 6
89 Towcester G 10
34 Towednack F 2
86 Tower Hamlets F 4
42 Tower Hill E 1
85 Towersey D 8
146 Towie F 2
146 Towiemore C 1
115 Town End G 7
110 Town Green G 3
42 Town Row E 4
93 Town Street G 1
137 Town Yetholm G 10
131 Townfoot B 10
131 Townhead, Dumf. & Gall. C 10
131 Townhead, Dumf. & Gall. G 8
147 Townhead, Grampian K 5
133 Townhead, Northumb. F 7
130 Townhead, Strathclyde A 3
135 Townhead of Aber A 9
135 Townhead of Gree E 9
131 Town head of Greenlaw E 8
140 Townhill H 6
84 Townsend, Oxon E 5
39 Townsend, Som. A 8
34 Townshend F 3
112 Towthorpe A 4
112 Towton C 3
61 Towyn B 9
97 Toynton All Saints D 11
97 Toynton Fen Side D 11
97 Toynton St. Peter D 11
42 Toy's Hill C 3
135 Trabboch G 9
135 Trabboch Mains G 9
135 Trabbochburn G 9
34 Traboe G 4
144 Tradespark D 4
111 Trafford Park H 7
143 Traigh House K 1
56 Trallong A 3
137 Tranent B 7
94 Tranmere A 2
149 Trantlebeg C 8
149 Trantlemore B 8
133 Tranwell E 10
55 Trapp E 10
137 Traprain B 8
136 Traquair F 6
85 Traveller's Rest B 10
111 Trawden C 8
56 Trawscoed A 4
60 Trawsfynydd G 6
55 Tre-Herbert B 9
56 Trelaw E 3
110 Treales D 3
60 Trearddur Bay B 2
150 Treaslane C 3
56 Trebanog E 3
55 Trebanos G 10
35 Trebartha B 9
35 Trebarwith A 7
34 Trebetheric B 6
38 Treborough C 3
34 Trebudannon D 6
35 Trebullett B 10
35 Treburley B 10
35 Trebyan C 8
56 Trecastle A 2
56 Trecenydd F 5
54 Trecwn D 3
56 Trecynon D 3
94 Tredaule B 9
54 Tre-ddiog D 2
56 Tredegar C 5
88 Tredington H 6
34 Tredizzick B 6
56 Tredomen A 4
54 Tredrissi C 4
56 Tredustan A 5
34 Treen G 1
96 Treeton A 2
54 Trefasser C 2
60 Trefdraeth C 3
56 Trefecca A 5
58 Trefeglwys C 5
58 Trefenter E 2
54 Treffgarne E 3
54 Treffgarne Owen D 2
54 Treffynnon, Dyfed D 2
56 Trefil C 4
58 Trefilan G 1
61 Trefnant C 10
94 Trefonen G 1
60 Trefor B 3
56 Treforest Industrial Estate F 4
61 Trefriw D 7
61 Tref-y-nant F 12
35 Tregadillet A 10
60 Tregaian B 4
57 Tregare C 7
58 Tregaron F 2
60 Tregarth C 5
35 Tregeare A 9
61 Tregeiriog G 11
60 Tregele A 3
34 Tregeseal F 1
34 Treglemais D 2
34 Tregonetha C 6
34 Tregony E 6
35 Tregoss D 7
34 Tregowris G 5
56 Tregoyd A 5
55 Tre-groes C 7
34 Tregurrian C 5
58 Tregynon C 6
56 Trehafod E 4
35 Treharris E 4
56 Treherbert D 3
35 Trekenner B 10
35 Treknow A 7
35 Trelash A 9
34 Trelassick D 6
61 Trelawnyd B 10
54 Trelach D 6
54 Tre-lech-a'r-Betws D 6
54 Treleddyd fawr D 1
56 Trelewis E 4
35 Treligga A 7
35 Trelights B 7
35 Trelill B 7
34 Trelissick F 5
57 Trelleck D 8
57 Trelleck Grange D 8
61 Trelogan B 10
60 Tremadog F 5
35 Tremail A 8
54 Tremain B 6
35 Tremaine A 9
35 Tremar C 9
35 Trematon D 11
61 Tremeirchion C 10
35 Tremore C 7
34 Trenance, Corn. C 5
34 Trenance, Corn. C 6
34 Trenance, Corn. H 4
35 Trenarren E 7
59 Trench A 12
34 Trenear F 4
35 Treneglos A 9
35 Trenewan D 9
34 Trengune B 2
39 Trent Nether Compton D 2
95 Trentham F 7
36 Trentishoe A 5
56 Treoes F 3
56 Treorchy E 3
56 Trequite B 7
58 Tre'r-ddol C 2
35 Trerule Foot D 10
54 Tresaith B 6
35 Tresayes D 7
88 Trescott B 2
34 Trescowe G 3
57 Tresham E 11
34 Tresillian E 6
54 Tresinwen C 2
34 Treskinnick Cross A 2
35 Tresmeer A 9
34 Tresparrett B 2
34 Tresparrett Posts B 2
140 Tressait A 3
152 Tresta, Zetland B 8
152 Tresta, Zetland D 7
96 Treswell B 5
34 Trethosa D 6
35 Trethurgy D 7
54 Tretio D 1
57 Tretire B 8
56 Tretower B 5
61 Treuddyn D 11
35 Trevadlock B 9
35 Trevalga A 8
94 Trevalyn D 3
35 Trevanson B 7
34 Trevarren D 6
34 Trevarrian C 5
35 Trevarrick E 7
54 Trevaughan, Dyfed E 5
55 Trevaughan, Dyfed E 7
34 Trevellas D 4
35 Trevelmond C 9
34 Treverva F 5
56 Trevethin D 6
35 Trevigro C 10
54 Trevine D 2
35 Trevivian A 9
34 Trevone B 6
60 Trevor F 3
34 Trevose B 6
35 Trewarmett A 8
35 Trewassa A 8
34 Trewellard F 1
35 Trewen A 9
34 Trewennack G 4
59 Trewern A 8
35 Trewethern B 7
35 Trewetha B 7
35 Trewidland D 9
54 Trewilym C 5
34 Trewint B 2
34 Trewithian F 6
35 Trewoon D 7
34 Treyarnon Bay B 6
41 Treyford D 9
111 Triangle E 9
40 Trickett's Cross F 3
132 Triermain F 4
116 Trimdon B 4
116 Trimdon Colliery B 4
116 Trimdon Grange B 4
92 Trimingham B 6
93 Trimley St. Mary L 6
93 Trimley St. Martin L 6
88 Trimpley D 1
55 Trimsaran F 8
56 Trinant D 5
85 Tring C 10
85 Tring Wharf C 10
38 Trinity, Devon F 3
147 Trinity, Tayside L 4
38 Triscombe C 5
143 Trislaig M 5
34 Trispen E 5
133 Tritlington D 10
140 Trochry C 5
56 Troedrhiw D 4
55 Troedyraur B 7
55 Troed-y-rhiw B 8
135 Troon, Strathclyde F 8
34 Troon, Cornwall F 4
131 Troqueer D 10
139 Trossachs Hotel G 12
93 Trostan H 2
42 Trottiscliffe B 5
41 Trotton D 9
133 Troughend D 7
114 Troutbeck, Cumbria C 6
114 Troutbeck, Cumbria E 6
114 Troutbeck Bridge E 6
57 Trow Green D 9
96 Troway B 1
57 Trowbridge H 11
96 Trowell F 2
57 Trowle Common H 11
85 Trowley Botton C 11
137 Trows F 9
92 Trowse Newton E 5
39 Trudoxhill B 10
38 Trull D 6
150 Trumpan B 2
59 Trumpet H 12
91 Trumpington K 6
38 Trumps E 4
92 Trunch B 6
34 Truro E 5
35 Truscott A 10
38 Trusham H 2
95 Trusley G 11
97 Trusthorpe B 12
88 Trysull C 2
84 Tubney D 5
37 Tuckenhay K 7
34 Tuckingmill F 4
91 Tuddenham, Suff. H 8
93 Tuddenham, Suff. K 5
42 Tudeley D 5
116 Tudhoe B 3
57 Tudorville B 9
60 Tudweiliog G 2
41 Tuesley B 11
57 Tuffley C 11
54 Tufton D 4
89 Tugby B 11
59 Tugford D 11
133 Tughall E 12
145 Tulchan M 7
140 Tullibardine F 4
140 Tullibody H 3
139 Tullich, Central D 12
145 Tullich, Highland G 2
142 Tullich, Highland E 3
139 Tullich, Strathclyde F 8

40 Walkford G 4
37 Walkhampton J 4
113 Walkington C 8
96 Walkley A 1
133 Wall, Northumb. F 7
88 Wall, Staffs. B 4
132 Wall Bowers G 4
59 Wall under Heywood C 10
131 Wallaceton C 9
130 Wallacetown A 4
94 Wallasey A 2
114 Wallend, Cumbria G 5
87 Wallend, Kent F 8
85 Wallingford E 7
41 Wallington, Hants. E 7
91 Wallington, Herts M 4
86 Wallington, London H 3
41 Walliswood B 12
152 Walls D 6
133 Wallsend F 11
114 Wallthwaite C 6
136 Wallyford B 6
43 Walmer C 12
110 Walmer Bridge E 3
111 Walmersley F 7
88 Walmley C 5
93 Walpole H 7
90 Walpole Crosskeys D 6
90 Walpole Highway D 6
90 Walpole Island D 6
90 Walpole St. Andrew D 6
90 Walpole St. Peter D 6
88 Walsall B 4
88 Wallsall Wood B 4
111 Walsden E 8
89 Walsgrave on Sowe D 7
93 Walsham le Willows H 3
110 Walshaw F 6
111 Walshford B 12
90 Walsoken D 6
136 Walston E 3
86 Walsworth A 2
85 Walter's Ash D 9
56 Walterston G 4
57 Walterstone B 7
43 Waltham, Kent C 9
113 Waltham, Humber. G 10
86 Waltham Abbey D 4
41 Waltham Chase E 7
86 Waltham Cross D 4
86 Waltham Forest E 4
96 Waltham on the Wolds H 2
85 Waltham St. Lawrence F 9
86 Walthamstow E 3
89 Walton, Bucks. H 12
90 Walton, Cambs E 3
132 Walton, Cumb. G 3
96 Walton, Derby C 1
89 Walton, Leics C 9
59 Walton, Powys F 8
94 Walton, Salop H 4
39 Walton, Som. C 8
93 Walton, Suffolk L 6
88 Walton, War. G 6
112 Walton, W. Yorks. B 2
111 Walton, W. Yorks. E 12
57 Walton Cardiff A 12
39 Walton Elm D 11
54 Walton East E 4
57 Walton-in-Gordano G 7
110 Walton-Le-Dale D 4
85 Walton-on-Thames G 12
110 Walton on the Hill, Merseyside H 3
95 Walton-on-the-Hill, Staffordshire H 8
42 Walton on the Hill, Surrey C 1
87 Walton on the Naze B 12
96 Walton on the Wolds H 3
57 Walton Park G 7
95 Walton upon Trent H 10
54 Walton West F 2
61 Walwen C 11
133 Walwick F 7
133 Walwick Grange F 7
116 Walworth C 3
54 Walwyn's Castle F 2
38 Wambrook E 6
131 Wamphraygate B 12
132 Wampool H 1
41 Wanborough, Surrey A 10
84 Wanborough, Wilts F 3
136 Wandel G 2
133 Wandon C 11
86 Wandsworth F 3
133 Wandylaw A 9
93 Wangford G 8
89 Wanlip A 9
136 Wanlockhead H 2
42 Wannock H 4
90 Wansford, Cambs. F 2
113 Wansford, Humber. B 8
86 Wanstead E 4
39 Wanstrow B 10
57 Wanswell D 10
84 Wantage E 5
57 Wapley F 10
89 Wappenbury E 7
89 Wappenham H 9
112 Warcop D 9
42 Warbleton F 5
41 Warblington E 8
85 Warborough E 7
91 Warboys G 4
110 Warbreck C 2
34 Warbstow B 2
94 Warburton A 5
93 Ward Green J 4
43 Warden A 9
89 Wardington G 8
136 Wardlaw, Borders H 5
135 Wardlaw, Strathclyde E 8
94 Wardle, Ches. E 5
111 Wardle, Lancs. E 8
89 Wardley B 11
95 Wardlow C 10
133 Wardon F 7
91 Wardy Hill G 6
86 Ware, Herts. C 4
43 Ware, Kent B 11
40 Wareham G 1
43 Warehorne E 8
133 Waren Mill C 12
133 Warenford C 12
133 Warenton C 12
86 Wareside B 4
91 Waresley, Cambs. K 3
88 Waresley, Heref. & Worc. E 2
85 Warfield G 9
37 Warfleet L 7
90 Wargate C 3
85 Wargrave F 9
92 Warham All Saints A 3
92 Warham St. Mary A 2
133 Wark, Northumb E 7
137 Wark, Northumb. E 11
36 Warkleigh D 5
89 Warkton D 12
89 Warkwork H 8
133 Warkworth B 10
116 Warlaby F 4
111 Warland E 8
35 Warleggan C 8
88 Warley C 3
42 Warlingham B 2
111 Warmfield E 12
94 Warmingham D 5
41 Warminghurst D 12
90 Warmington, Cambs. F 2
89 Warmington, War. G 7
39 Warminster B 11
43 Warmlake C 7
57 Warmley G 10
57 Warmley Tower G 10
112 Warmsworth G 3
39 Warmwell H 11
88 Warndon F 2
41 Warnford D 8
42 Warnham E 1
41 Warningcamp E 11
42 Warninglid E 1
95 Warren, Ches. C 7
54 Warren, Dyfed G 3
37 Warren House Inn H 5
85 Warren Row F 9
43 Warren Street C 8
89 Warrington, Bucks. G 12
94 Warrington, Ches. A 5
40 Warsash E 6
95 Warslow D 9
96 Warsop C 3
96 Warsop Vale C 3
112 Warter B 6
116 Warthermarske G 2
112 Warthill B 4
42 Wartling G 5
96 Wartnaby H 4
110 Warton, Lancs. D 3
115 Warton, Lancs. H 7
133 Warton, Northumb. C 8
88 Warton, War. B 6
132 Warwick, Cumb. G 3
88 Warwick, War. F 6
132 Warwick Bridge G 3
88 Warwickshire, Co. F 6
132 Warwicksland E 3
152 Wasbister B 2
114 Wasdale Head D 4
84 Wash Common H 5
35 Washaway C 7
37 Washbourne K 7
95 Washerwall E 8
38 Washfield E 3
116 Washfold E 1
38 Washford B 4
36 Washford Pyne E 7
97 Washingborough C 7
133 Washington, Tyne & Wear G 11
41 Washington, W. Sussex E 12
85 Wasing H 7
116 Waskerley A 1
88 Wasperton F 6
116 Wass G 6
38 Watchet B 4
84 Watchfield, Oxon E 3
39 Watchfield, Som. B 7
115 Watchgate E 8
131 Watchhill G 12
114 Watendlath D 5
37 Water, Devon H 6
111 Water, Lancs. E 7
86 Water End, Herts. C 2
112 Water End, Humber. C 6
90 Water Newton F 2
88 Water Orton C 5
85 Water Stratford A 7
56 Water Street F 1
114 Water Yeat F 5
91 Waterbeach J 6
132 Waterbeck E 1
92 Waterden B 2
85 Waterend C 11
95 Waterfall E 9
111 Waterfoot, Lancs. E 7
135 Waterfoot, Strathclyde D 10
40 Waterford, Hants. G 5
86 Waterford, Herts. B 3
114 Waterhead, Cumb. E 6
131 Waterhead, Dumf. & Gall. B 12
131 Waterhead, Dumf. & Gall. C 8
135 Waterford, Strathclyde H 10
147 Waterhead, Tayside K 2
136 Waterheads D 5
116 Waterhouses, Dur A 5
95 Waterhouses, Staffs. E 9
97 Watering Dyke Houses B 7
42 Wateringbury C 6
152 Wateringhouse E 2
57 Waterlane D 12
96 Waterloo, Derby D 1
40 Waterloo, Dorset G 2
54 Waterloo, Dyfed G 3
110 Waterloo, Merseyside G 2
92 Waterloo, Norf. D 5
150 Waterloo, Skye F 6
136 Waterloo, Strathclyde D 1
140 Waterloo, Tayside C 5
38 Waterloo Cross E 4
41 Waterlooville E 8
136 Watermeetings H 2
85 Waterperry C 7
38 Waterrow D 4
94 Waters Upton H 5
41 Watersfield E 11
132 Waterside, Cumb. H 1
146 Waterside Grampian E 7
130 Waterside, Strathclyde A 5
135 Waterside Strathclyde E 9
135 Waterside, Strathclyde B 11
85 Waterstock D 7
54 Waterston F 3
86 Watford, Herts. D 1
89 Watford, Northants. E 9
116 Wath, N. Yorks. G 3
116 Wath, N. Yorks. H 2
114 Wath Brow D 3
112 Wath upon Dearne G 2
57 Watley's End F 9
90 Watlington, Norf. D 7
85 Watlington, Oxon E 8
96 Watnall Chaworth F 2
149 Watten B 11
93 Wattisfield H 3
93 Wattisham K 3
59 Wattlesborough Heath A 9
113 Watton, Humberside B 8
92 Watton, Norf. E 2
86 Watton-at-Stone B 3
135 Wattston B 12
56 Wattstown E 3
143 Wauchan L 3
58 Waun Fawr D 2
55 Waunarlwydd G 9
60 Waunfawr D 5
56 Waunlwyd D 5
89 Wavendon H 12
132 Waverbridge H 1
94 Waverton, Ches. D 3
132 Waverton, Cumb. H 1
113 Wawne C 8
92 Waxham C 7
113 Waxholme D 11
38 Way Village E 3
42 Wayfield B 6
39 Wayford F 7
39 Waytown F 8
38 Weacombe B 5
84 Weald D 4
86 Wealdstone E 2
111 Weardley C 11
39 Weare A 7
36 Weare Giffard D 3
115 Wearhead A 11
115 Weasdale E 9
92 Weasenham All Saints C 1
92 Weasenham St. Peter C 1
94 Weaverham C 5
117 Weaverthorpe H 9
88 Webheath E 4
57 Webton A 7
146 Wedderlairs D 6
137 Wedderlie D 9
89 Weddington C 7
84 Wedhampton H 2
39 Wedmore A 8
88 Wednesbury C 3
88 Wednesfield B 3
85 Weedon B 9
88 Weedon Bec F 9
89 Weedon Lois G 9
88 Weeford B 5
36 Week, Devon C 4
36 Week, Devon D 6
36 Week St. Mary F 1
40 Weeke C 6
89 Weekely D 12
113 Weel C 8
87 Weeley B 11
87 Weeley Heath B 11
140 Weem B 3
59 Weeping Cross, Shropshire A 10
95 Weeping Cross, Staffordshire H 8
93 Weeting G 1
110 Weeton, Lancs. D 3
111 Weeton, N. Yorks. B 11
137 Weetwoodhill F 12
111 Weir E 7
57 Weirend B 9
96 Welbeck Abbey C 3
92 Welborne E 4
97 Welbourn E 7
117 Welburn, N. Yorks. G 7
117 Welburn, N. Yorks H 7
116 Welbury E 4
97 Welby F 7
91 Welches Dam G 6
36 Welcombe D 1
89 Weldon C 12
84 Welford, Berks. G 5
89 Welford, Northants. D 9
88 Welford-on-Avon G 5
89 Welham C 11
86 Welham Green C 2
41 Well, Hants. A 9
97 Well, Lincs. C 11
116 Well, N. Yorks. G 3
39 Well Bottom E 12
85 Well End E 9
42 Well Hill B 4
38 Well Town E 3
88 Welland H 2
141 Wellbank C 9
131 Welldale E 12
88 Wellesbourne G 6
116 Wellfields A 4
147 Wellford L 2
86 Welling F 5
89 Wellingborough E 12
92 Wellingham C 2
97 Wellingore E 7
114 Wellington, Cumb. E 3
59 Wellington, Heref. & Worc. H 10
59 Wellington, Salop A 12
38 Wellington, Som. D 5
59 Wellington Heath H 12
59 Wellington Marsh H 10
57 Wellow, Avon H 10
40 Wellow, I.o.W. G 5
96 Wellow, Notts. D 4
39 Wells B 9
92 Wells-next-the-Sea A 2
146 Wells of Ytham D 4
89 Wellsborough B 7
37 Wellswood J 8
140 Wellwood H 6
90 Welney F 6
36 Welsford D 1
57 Welsh Bicknor C 9
94 Welsh Frankton G 2
54 Welsh Hook D 3
57 Welsh Newton B 8
56 Welsh St. Donats G 4
94 Welshampton G 3
59 Welshpool B 8
39 Welton, Avon A 10
114 Welton, VB. A 6
113 Welton, Humberside D 7
97 Welton, Lincs. B 7
89 Welton, Northants E 9
97 Welton le Marsh C 11
97 Welton le Wold B 10
113 Welwick E 11
86 Welwyn B 2
86 Welwyn Garden City C 2
94 Wem G 4
38 Wembdon C 6
86 Wembley E 2
37 Wembury L 4
36 Wembworthy E 5
135 Wemyss Bay B 7
91 Wendens Ambo L 6
84 Wendlebury B 6
92 Wendling D 2
85 Wendover C 9
34 Wendron G 4
91 Wendy K 4
93 Wenhaston H 7
91 Wennington, Cambs. G 3
115 Wennington, Lancs. H 8
86 Wennington, London F 5
95 Wensley, Derby. D 11
116 Wensley, N. Yorks. F 1
112 Wentbridge E 3
59 Wentor C 9
91 Wentworth, Cambs. G 6
111 Wentworth, S. Yorks G 12
56 Wenvoe G 4
59 Weobley G 9
59 Weobley Marsh G 9
90 Wareham E 8
88 Wergs B 2
56 Wern C 4
55 Wernffrwd H 8
57 Wernyrheolydd C 7
90 Werrington, Cambs. E 3
35 Werrington, Corn. A 10
95 Werrington, Suffolk E 8
94 Wervin C 3
110 Wesham D 3
96 Wessington D 1
145 West Aberchalder G 1
92 West Acre D 1
84 West Adderbury A 5
38 West Adsborough C 6
137 West Allerdean E 12
133 West Allotment F 11
37 West Alvington L 6
40 West Amesbury B 3
36 West Anstey C 7
36 West Ash D 2
97 West Ashby C 9
41 West Ashling E 9
39 West Ashton A 12
116 West Auckland C 2
117 West Ayton G 10
147 West Balhagarty K 5
38 West Bagborough C 5
97 West Barkwith B 8
117 West Barnby D 8
137 West Barns B 9
130 West Barr G 4
92 West Barsham B 2
39 West Bay G 8
92 West Beckham B 4
85 West Bedfont G 11
133 West Benridge D 10
87 West Bergholt A 9
39 West Bexington H 9
90 West Bilney D 8
137 West Blackadder D 11
42 West Blatchington G 2
136 West Bold F 6
133 West Boldon G 11
131 West Bowhill D 12
111 West Bowling D 10
92 West Bradenham E 2
110 West Bradford C 6
39 West Bradley C 9
111 West Bretton F 11
96 West Bridgford G 3
88 West Bromwich C 4
135 West Browncastle E 11
36 West Buckland, Devon C 5
38 West Buckland, Som. D 5
152 West Burrafirth D 6
41 West Burton, W. Sussex E 11
115 West Burton, N. Yorks F 12
116 West Butsfield A 1
112 West Butterwick G 6
85 West Byfleet H 11
137 West Byres C 7
92 West Caister D 8
136 West Calder C 3
39 West Camel D 9
146 West Cannahars E 7
112 West Carr F 5
135 West Cauldcoats E 11
39 West Chaldon H 11
84 West Challow E 4
39 West Chelborough F 9
133 West Chevington C 10
41 West Chiltington D 12
41 West Chiltington Common D 12
39 West Chinnock E 8
40 West Chisenbury A 3
41 West Clandon A 11
43 West Cliffe D 12
149 West Clyne F 9
149 West Clyth D 11
39 West Coker E 8
39 West Compton, Dorset G 9
39 West Compton, Som. B 9
112 West Cowick E 4
39 West Cranmore B 10
93 West Creeting Grn. J 4
145 West Croftmore H 5
55 West Cross H 9
147 West Cullerley G 5
132 West Curthwaite H 2
134 West Darlochan G 2
40 West Dean, Hants. C 4
41 West Dean, Sus. E 10
90 West Deeping. E 2
94 West Derby A 3
90 West Dereham E 7
133 West Ditchburn A 9
36 West Down B 4
86 West Drayton, London F 1
96 West Drayton, Notts. C 4
133 West Edington E 9
113 West Ella D 8
57 West End, Avon G 8
85 West End, Berks. G 9
60 West End, Gwynedd G 3
40 West End, Hants. E 6
86 West End, Herts C 3
113 West End, Humber. D 7
113 West End, Lincs. G 11
92 West End, Norf. D 8
136 West End, Strathclyde E 2
85 West End, Surrey H 10
40 West End, Wilts. D 1
133 West Fallodon A 10
42 West Farleigh C 6
94 West Felton H 2
42 West Firle G 3
84 West Ginge E 5
55 West Glamorgan, Co. G 10
85 West Grafton H 3
85 West Green H 8
40 West Grimstead D 4
42 West Grinstead F 1
112 West Haddlesey D 3
89 West Haddon E 9
84 West Hagbourne E 6
88 West Hagley D 3
132 West Hall F 4
96 West Hallam F 2
113 West Halton E 7
86 West Ham F 4
84 West Hanney E 5
87 West Hanningfield D 7
112 West Hardwick E 2
40 West Harnham C 3
39 West Harptree A 9
133 West Harrington H 11
116 West Hartlepool B 5
38 West Hatch D 6
57 West Hay H 8
90 West Head E 7
149 West Helmsdale E 9
84 West Hendred E 5
117 West Heslerton H 9
57 West Hill, Avon G 8
38 West Hill, Devon G 4

Northern Ireland map index

159 Acton G 8
158 Aghadowey B 7
159 Aghagallon E 8
159 Aghalee E 8
158 Aghyaran D 3
158 Agivey B 7
159 Ahoghill C 8
158 Annagary B 1
159 Annalong H 10
159 Antrim D 8
158 Ardara D 1
159 Ardglass G 11
158 Ardstraw D 4
159 Armagh F 7
159 Armoy A 8
158 Arney G 3
159 Articlave A 6
158 Artigarvan C 4
159 Artrea E 7
158 Aughagault C 3
158 Augher F 5
158 Aughnacloy F 6
159 Baileysmill F 9
158 Ballinafad H 1
158 Ballinagleragh H 2
158 Ballinamallard F 4
158 Ballinamore H 3
159 Ballinderry E 8
158 Ballindrait C 4
158 Ballintogher G 1
159 Ballintoy A 8
158 Ballybay H 6
158 Ballybofey D 3
158 Ballybogey A 7
159 Ballycarry D 10
159 Ballycastle A 8
159 Ballyclare D 9
158 Ballyfarnan H 1
158 Ballygawley F 6
158 Ballygowan E 10
158 Ballyhaise H 5
159 Ballyhalbert E 11
159 Ballykeel F 9
159 Ballykelly B 6
159 Ballyleny F 7
159 Ballymartin H 9
159 Ballymena C 8
158 Ballymoney B 7
158 Ballymore A 2
159 Ballynahinch F 10
158 Ballynamallaght C 5
159 Ballynure D 9
159 Ballyronan D 7
159 Ballyroney G 9
158 Ballyshannon E 1
159 Ballyskeagh E 9
159 Ballyvoy A 8
159 Ballywalter E 11
159 Ballyward G 9
159 Ballywoodan F 11
159 Banbridge F 8
159 Bangor D 10
159 Bannfoot E 7
158 Baronscourt D 4
158 Belcoo G 3
159 Belfast E 9
159 Bellaghy C 7
158 Bellanaleck G 3
158 Bellanode G 5
158 Bellarena A 6
159 Belleek, Armagh G 7
158 Belleek, Fermanagh F 2
159 Beltoy D 10
158 Belturbet H 4
158 Benburb F 6
158 Beragh E 5
159 Bessbrook G 8
158 Blacktown E 3
159 Blackwatertown F 7
158 Boho F 3
158 Braddock G 6
158 Breenagh C 2
159 Broadmills F 9
158 Brookeborough G 4
159 Broughshane C 8
159 Bryansford G 9
159 Buckna C 9
158 Bunbeg B 1
158 Buncrana A 4
158 Bundoran F 1
158 Burnfoot B 4
159 Burren H 8
158 Burtonport B 1
159 Bushmills A 7
158 Butler's Bridge H 4
158 Caledon F 6
159 Camlough G 8
159 Carlingford G 9
159 Carncastle C 9
158 Carndonagh A 5
159 Carnlough B 9
158 Carrickart A 3
159 Carrickfergus D 10
158 Carrickmore E 5
158 Carrigans C 4
159 Carrowdore E 11
158 Carrowkeel, Donegal A 5
158 Carrowkeel, Donegal A 3
159 Carryduff E 10
158 Caskeam A 5
159 Castleblayney H 7
158 Castlecaulfield E 6
159 Castledawson D 7
158 Castlederg D 3
158 Castlefin C 3
158 Castlerock A 6
159 Castlewellan G 9
159 Chapeltown G 11
159 Charlemont F 7
158 Church Hill, Donegal B 3
158 Church Hill, Fermanagh F 3
159 Churchtown, Down F 11
158 Churchtown, Londonderry D 6
158 Clady D 4
158 Clanabogan E 4
159 Clare F 8
158 Claudy C 5
158 Clements Town H 5
158 Clobby F 4
158 Cloghan C 2
158 Clogher F 5
159 Cloghy F 11
158 Clonelly E 3
158 Clones G 5
158 Clontibret G 6
159 Clough, Antrim B 8
159 Clough, Down G 10
159 Cloughmills B 8
159 Coagh D 7
159 Coalisland E 7
158 Cock Hill A 4
159 Coleraine A 7
159 Comber E 10
159 Conlig D 10
159 Connor C 8
158 Convoy C 3
158 Cookstown E 6
158 Coolmore E 1
159 Coolranny A 9
159 Cooneen F 4
158 Cootehill H 5
158 Corlough H 3
159 Craigavon F 8
159 Craigs C 8
159 Crawfordsburn D 10
158 Creagh F 4
158 Creeslough A 2
159 Creggan, Armagh H 7
158 Creggan, Tyrone D 6
158 Crindle B 6
158 Crolly B 1
158 Cross Roads D 3
158 Crossgar F 10
159 Crossmaglen H 7
158 Crossna H 1
159 Crumlin E 8
159 Cullybackey C 8
159 Cullyhanna H 7
158 Culmore B 5
158 Curran D 7
159 Cushendall B 9
159 Cushendun A 9
159 Darkley G 7
158 Derryboy F 10
158 Derrygonnelly F 3
159 Derrykeighan A 7
158 Derrylin G 4
159 Dervock A 7
159 Desertmartin D 7
159 Doagh, Antrim D 9
158 Doagh, Donegal A 3
159 Dollingstown F 8
158 Donagh G 4
159 Donaghadee D 11
159 Donaghcloney F 8
158 Donaghmore E 6
158 Donegal D 2
158 Doochary C 1
158 Douglas Bridge D 4
158 Downhill A 6
158 Downies A 3
159 Downpatrick F 10
158 Draperstown D 6
158 Dromahair G 1
159 Dromara F 9
159 Dromore, Down F 9
158 Dromore, Tyrone E 4
158 Drum H 5
158 Drumahoe B 5
159 Drumaness F 10
159 Drumbeg E 9
158 Drumbologe B 3
158 Drumcard G 3
158 Drumkeeran G 2
158 Drumnakilly E 5
158 Drumquin E 4
158 Drumshanbo H 2
158 Dundalk H 8
159 Dundonald E 10
158 Dundrod E 9
159 Dundrum G 10
158 Dunfanaghy A 2
158 Dungannon E 6
158 Dungiven C 6
158 Dunglow C 1
158 Dunkineely E 1
158 Dunlewy B 2
158 Dunloy B 8
159 Dunmurry E 9
158 Dunnamanagh C 5
158 Dyan F 6
159 Eden D 10
158 Ederny E 3
158 Eglinton B 5
158 Eglish F 6
158 Emyvale F 6
158 Enniskillen F 3
158 Fahan B 4
158 Falcurragh A 2
158 Feeny C 5
158 Fenagh H 3
158 Fintona E 4
158 Fintown C 2
158 Finvoy B 7
158 Fivemiletown F 5
159 Forkhill H 8
158 Fort Stewart B 3
158 Galbally E 6
159 Galgorm C 8
159 Garvagh B 7
158 Garvaghy E 5
158 Geevagh H 1
159 Gilford F 8
158 Glaslough G 6
158 Glenade F 1
159 Glenariff B 9
159 Glenarm B 9
159 Glenavy E 8
158 Gleneely A 5
158 Glenfarne G 2
159 Glengormn D 9
159 Glenoe C 10
158 Glenties D 1
158 Glentogher A 5
158 Glenvar A 4
159 Glynn C 10
158 Gortahork A 2
158 Gortin D 5
159 Grange E 7
159 Grange Corner D 8
158 Granville E 6
158 Greencastle, Donegal A6
159 Greencastle, Down H 9
159 Greenisland D 10
159 Greenore H 9
159 Greyabbey E 11
159 Groomsport D 10
158 Gweedore B 1
159 Hamilton's Bawn F 7
159 Hillsborough F 9
159 Hilltown G 9
159 Holywood D 10
159 Hyde Park D 9
158 Inch B 4
159 Inishrush C 7
158 Irvinestown F 3
159 Jonesborough H 8
159 Katesbridge G 9
159 Keady G 7
159 Kells C 8
158 Kesh E 3
158 Keshcarrigan H 2
159 Kilclief F 11
159 Kilkeel H 9
158 Kill H 5
158 Killarga G 1
158 Killashandra H 4
158 Killeevan G 5
158 Killegar H 3
158 Killeter D 3
159 Killough G 10
158 Killyclogher E 5
158 Killygordon D 3
158 Killylane B 5
158 Killylea F 6
159 Killyleagh F 10
158 Kilmacrenan B 3
159 Kilrea C 7
158 Kiltyclogher F 2
158 Kinawley G 3
158 Kinlough F 1
159 Kircubbin E 11
158 Knockmoyle D 5
158 Laragh H 6
158 Largydonnell F 1
159 Larne C 10
159 Laurel Vale F 8
159 Lawrencetown F 8
159 Legoniel E 9
158 Letterkenny C 3
158 Lettermacaward C 1
158 Lifford C 4
158 Limavady B 6
158 Lisbellaw G 4
159 Lisburn E 9
159 Lisnacree H 9
158 Lisnaskea G 4
158 Londonderry B 4
159 Longford Lodge E 8
159 Loughbrickland G 8
159 Loughgall F 7
159 Lurgan F 8
158 Maas C 1
158 Mackan G 3
159 Maghaberry E 9
159 Maghera, Down G 10
159 Maghera, Londonderry C 7
158 Magherabane A 4
159 Magherafelt D 7
159 Magheragall E 9
159 Magheralin F 8
158 Magheraveely G 5
158 Maguiresbridge G 4
158 Manorcunningham C 3
158 Manorhamilton G 2
159 Markethill G 7
159 Mayobridge G 8
159 Meigh H 8
158 Middletown, Armagh G 6
158 Middletown, Donegal B 1
159 Mill Town H 7
159 Millford, Armagh F 7
158 Millford, Donegal B 3
159 Millisle E 11
158 Milltown, Cavan H 4
159 Milltown, Down G 8
159 Minerstown G 10
159 Moira E 8
158 Monaghan G 6
158 Monea F 3
159 Moneyglass D 8
158 Moneyhaugly B 4
159 Moneymore D 7
159 Moneyneany C 6
159 Moneyreagh E 10
159 Monkstown D 9
159 Mossley D 9
159 Moss-side A 8
158 Mount Hamilton D 6
158 Mountcharles D 1
158 Mountfield D 5
158 Moville A 5
159 Moy F 7
158 Muff B 4
158 Mullagharry A 4
159 Mullaghboy C 10
159 Muckamore D 8
158 New Buildings C 4
158 Newbliss H 5
159 Newcastle G 10
158 Newmills, Donegal C 3
159 Newmills, Tyrone E 7
159 Newry G 8
159 Newtown Crommelin B 8
158 Newtown Cunningham B 4
158 Newtown Gore H 3
159 Newtownabbey D 9
159 Newtownards E 10
159 Newtownbreda E 10
158 Newtownbutler G 4
159 Newtownhamilton G 7
159 Nutt's Corner D 9
158 Old Town C 3
158 Omagh E 4
159 Omeath H 8
158 Oritor D 6
158 Park C 5
159 Parkgate D 9
159 Parkmore B
158 Pettigoe E
158 Plumbridge D
158 Pomeroy E
159 Portadown F
159 Portaferry F 1
159 Portavogie F 1
159 Portaballintrae A
159 Portglenone C
159 Portrush A
158 Portsalon A
158 Portstewart A
159 Poyntz Pass G
158 Rahony F
159 Randalstown D
158 Raphoe C
158 Rasharkin B
159 Rathfriland G
158 Rathmelton B
158 Rathmullan B
159 Rich Hill F
158 Ringsend B
158 Riverstown H
158 Rockcarry H
158 Rosapenna A
158 Rosnakill A
158 Rossinver F
158 Rosslea G
159 Rosstrevor H
158 Rousky D
158 St. Johnstown C
159 Saintfield F 1
158 Sandholes E
159 Saul F 1
159 Scarva F
158 Scotshouse H
158 Scotstown G
159 Seaforde G 1
159 Seapatrick F
158 Seskinore E
158 Shantonagh H
159 Shrigley F 1
158 Sixmilecross E
158 Smithborough G
159 Stewartstown E
159 Stonyford E
158 Strabane C
159 Straid Hill D
159 Strangford F 1
159 Stranocum B
158 Stranorlar C
158 Stroove A
158 Swanlinbar G
159 Swatragh C 7
159 Tanderagee F
158 Tawny A
158 Tedavnet G
159 Templepatrick D 9
158 Tempo F
158 Termon B
159 The Loup D 7
158 The Rock E
159 The Sheddings C 9
159 The Temple F 1
159 Tobermore C 7
159 Toome D 7
158 Trillick F 4
158 Tullaghan F
159 Tullaghoge E 7
158 Tynan F 6
159 Tyrella G 10
159 Upperlands C 7
159 Waringsford F 9
159 Waringstown F 8
159 Warrenpoint H 8
159 Whiteabbey D 9
159 Whitecross G 7
159 Whitehead D 10
159 Whitehouse D 9